AMERICAN CARNAGE

AMERICAN CARNAGE

Wounded Knee, 1890

JEROME A. GREENE

Foreword by Thomas Powers

University of Oklahoma Press : Norman

Also by Jerome A. Greene

Yellowstone Command: Colonel Nelson A. Miles and the Great Sioux War, 1876–1877
 (Lincoln, Neb., 1991; Norman, Okla., 2006)

(ed.) *Lakota and Cheyenne: Indian Views of the Great Sioux War, 1876–1877* (Norman,
 Okla., 1994)

Nez Perce Summer, 1877: The U.S. Army and the Nee-Me-Poo Crisis (Helena, Mont.,
 2000)

Morning Star Dawn: The Powder River Expedition and the Northern Cheyennes, 1876
 (Norman, Okla., 2003)

Washita: The U.S. Army and the Southern Cheyennes, 1867–1869 (Norman, Okla., 2004)

(ed.) *Indian War Veterans: Memories of Army Life and Campaigns in the West, 1864–1898*
 (New York, 2007)

Stricken Field: The Little Bighorn since 1876 (Norman, Okla., 2008)

Beyond Bear's Paw: The Nez Perce Indians in Canada (Norman, Okla., 2010)

Library of Congress Cataloging-in-Publication Data

Greene, Jerome A.
 American carnage : Wounded Knee, 1890 / Jerome A. Greene ; foreword by Thomas
Powers.
 pages cm
 Summary: "American Carnage—the first comprehensive account of Wounded Knee
to appear in more than fifty years—explores the complex events preceding the tragedy,
the killings, and their troubled legacy"—Provided by publisher.
 Includes bibliographical references and index.
 ISBN 978-0-8061-4448-1 (hardback)
1. Wounded Knee Massacre, S.D., 1890. I. Title.
 E83.89.G74 2014
 973.8'6—dc23
                          2013042680

The paper in this book meets the guidelines for permanence and durability of the
Committee on Production Guidelines for Book Longevity of the Council on Library
Resources, Inc. ∞

1 2 3 4 5 6 7 8 9 10

To all those lost for Wounded Knee

Contents

Contents

Illustrations

Figures

MAPS

Foreword

⁓

Thomas Powers

Wounded Knee, the place, is named for a winding creek lined with willows and cottonwoods in South Dakota. It is where the Teton Lakotas and every other Northern Plains tribe that had been paying attention learned that their old life was gone forever. The place is beautiful, but it is remembered for Wounded Knee, the event—a mass killing of men, women, and children on December 29, 1890, by white soldiers who thought they were suppressing an armed uprising. Explaining how this tragedy occurred is part of the unfinished business of America.

The Indian wars of the 1860s and 1870s, sometimes referred to as the "conquest" of the West, were notable for blood and bitterness, but Wounded Knee did not fit the usual pattern of conflict. It was not a "fight" and it did not begin as so many classic assaults and massacres: with a first-light attack on a sleeping village, often in winter, where confusion reigned as mounted soldiers raced among lodges shooting at fleeing figures wrapped in blankets. On that fatal day at Wounded Knee, a large body of troops was disarming a band of mainly Miniconjou Lakotas who had crossed nearly two hundred miles of frigid prairie to escape trouble in the north. Few, certainly, and perhaps none of the Lakotas wanted a fight, but the moment was tense and something happened—and I'll leave it to Jerry Greene to tell you what that was. In a moment, a storm of firing erupted, so heavy and confused that of the thirty or so soldiers killed outright or fatally wounded, some were likely shot by their own men.

But the thing that started the shooting was a small thing. Setting the stage for the small thing, however, was a big thing: a spontaneous religious movement that swept the Northern Plains in 1890—an outpouring of mingled fervor, hope, and despair that is one of the most extraordinary, and ultimately one of the most heartbreaking, events in American history.

Jerome A. Greene is an ideal candidate to write the definitive history of Wounded Knee. He is a longtime National Park Service historian, now retired, who is deeply schooled in the history of the West, of the frontier military, and of the Indian wars. He grew up in Watertown, New York, where he fell under the spell of George Armstrong Custer and the 1876 fight at the Little Bighorn, a common event in the lives of a notable group of Park Service historians who have been filling in the details of western history in a cascade of books over the last four or five decades. Greene has written a lot of these books, which include meticulous reconstructions of notable fights (*Morning Star Dawn* about the Dull Knife fight of November 1876, *Washita* about a classic dawn attack on Cheyennes by Custer in 1868) and collections of Cheyenne and Lakota accounts of these and other encounters, primary sources long neglected by white historians. Greene brings both a deep experience of the West and an immense quantity of new research to his history of Wounded Knee. Much of the new materials are the previously overlooked Lakota perspective and neglected documents—contemporary letters, obscure newspaper accounts, official reports, telegrams, and the like. But Greene also had the help of Michael Her Many Horses, an Oglala historian who opened doors on the Pine Ridge Reservation in South Dakota, where many descendants of victims and survivors now live.

There is an arc to Greene's life and to his interest in the Plains Indian wars—from the East he moved to the West, and from the frontier military he moved to include the other side, using their own term, "the people," to record their experience. This is not only a sad story of innocent people left dead in the snow, but also a story about something deep and mysterious that occurred during the months leading up to Wounded Knee. The buffalo had been nearly exterminated, the Lakotas had been confined to reservations, more land was being taken away, and government rations were cut, leaving the people to starve. At this moment of despair a messiah appeared in the West, a Paiute seer named Wovoka, who taught many of the people to pray, sing, and dance in a special way. If they did this, he said, the buffalo would return and the dead would be raised and the old life would be restored.

So they danced the Ghost Dance. Whites were frightened. The Army was called in. We know what is going to happen, but reading about it is painful anyway. Greene tells this powerful story with the care and richness it has always wanted.

Preface

The landscape at Wounded Knee is stark more than a century after the horrific killings that occurred there in late 1890. Winds blow almost incessantly over the ground where as many as 200 Lakota men, women, and altogether innocent children died, with many more desperately wounded, during an unseemly and unwarranted convulsion of violence perpetrated by U.S. Army troops. Often referenced as the last armed conflict between whites and Indians in the United States (which it was not), the event coincided with what historians and demographers have recognized as the closing of the American frontier. Perhaps not unfittingly, it has also come to symbolize the worst elements in America's long and tragic history of relations with its Native peoples.

For the Lakotas today, Wounded Knee is omnipresent. The site on South Dakota's Pine Ridge Reservation is revered by the people. Many frequent the mass grave on the brow of a low hill overlooking the place where the furor erupted and where 146 victims lie buried. Some of the survivors who lived for decades after Wounded Knee and who vainly sought amends from the government now rest nearby in separate plots. Each December, for more than twenty years since the centennial observance in 1990, Lakota people have made an annual pilgrimage of well over 200 miles on horseback as they trace the route that Chief Big Foot's band followed when its members traversed the Badlands bound for Pine Ridge Agency, before the army intercepted them and precipitated the wholesale deaths at Wounded Knee. The purpose of the yearly journey is to memorialize the tragedy and to honor the Lakota victims. Thus, in their latent grief and struggle to have what happened recognized, the people have never forgotten Wounded Knee. They have not forgotten the human trauma that the event caused or the federal government's failure to acknowledge the great wrong done there.

My personal interest in Wounded Knee was whetted in the summer of 1969 by a chance visit to the site. Over ensuing decades the story's allure not only lingered but increased, encouraged in part by the availability of many new and diverse sources, Lakota as well as white. This new information, I believed, warranted reconsideration and demanded a new and comprehensive effort to relate what happened before, during, and after the massacre of December 29, 1890. I hope that the present study will enhance the history of that winter's day long ago, when the Lakotas' world exploded and the survivors' lives changed radically forever. In its totality, Wounded Knee stands as a benchmark in Lakota and American history, and indeed in all of human history. It is a haunting narrative that continues to resonate.

I AM INDEBTED TO MANY individuals and institutions for their significant contributions to this study. But I owe particular thanks to longtime friends R. Eli Paul, manager of the Missouri Valley Special Collections, Kansas City Public Library, in Kansas City, Missouri; and John D. McDermott of Rapid City, South Dakota, formerly of the National Park Service and the President's Advisory Council on Historic Preservation. Both are widely acknowledged scholars who urged me to undertake an inclusive study of Wounded Knee and supported its completion by sharing with me the bounty of their collective knowledge and sleuthing on the subject over many years. I am eternally grateful for their help, trust, and generosity. Similarly, I thank my friend, colleague, and former National Park Service chief historian Robert M. Utley of Scottsdale, Arizona, for contributing many data that he collected years ago. Utley's classic *The Last Days of the Sioux Nation,* which first appeared in 1963 and continues to be in print, inspired my own interest in Wounded Knee as well as in many other aspects of the western Indian campaigns. On the Pine Ridge Reservation in South Dakota, Michael Her Many Horses, past executive director of the Oglala Sioux Tribe and a member of the Wounded Knee community, became a close associate and friend. He readily introduced me to the area, guided me to sites and knowledgeable people, provided access to his own rich repository of books and pertinent documents, and entrusted me with many materials for study and use. Paul Harbaugh of Cherry Hills Village, Colorado, who accompanied me on many of my Pine Ridge visits, helped promote useful contacts, provided photos and documents from his vast collection, and served as my unofficial expedition photographer. Marc Abrams of Brookyn, New York, generously offered his extensive newspaper files related to the events of 1890–91 for my use. I also appreciate the unfailing help and constant support of steadfast friends and facilitators Thomas R. Buecker of Lincoln, Nebraska, and Paul L. Hedren of Omaha, Nebraska, who gave advice, assistance, and encouragement throughout this lengthy and consuming venture.

I received additional assistance and support from many others throughout the course of this work, and I wish to recognize the following for their considerable help: John Doerner of Hardin, Montana, formerly of Little Bighorn Battlefield National Monument, Crow Agency, Montana; Eric Halverson of the Big Horn County Library, Hardin, Montana; L. Clifford Soubier of Charles Town, West Virginia; Douglas C. McChristian of Tucson, Arizona; Gail DeBuse Potter of the Museum of the Fur Trade, Chadron, Nebraska; Ken Stewart, Nancy Tystad Koupal, and Matthew T. Reitzel of the South Dakota State Historical Society, Pierre; James E. Potter of the Nebraska State Historical Society, Lincoln; David Hays of the Western History Collections, University of Colorado Libraries, Boulder; Randy Kane of Crawford, Nebraska; Lori Cox-Paul of the National Archives at Kansas City, Kansas City, Missouri; Jeff Broome of Littleton, Colorado; John H. Monnett of Lafayette, Colorado; Glenwood J. Swanson of Agua Dulce, California; Gregory F. Michno of Frederick, Colorado; Paul A. Hutton of Albuquerque, New Mexico; Douglas D. Scott of Grand Junction, Colorado; Robert G. Pilk of Lakewood, Colorado; Daniel Cullity of East Sandwich, Massachusetts; Chris and Inge Fox-Jones of Denver, Colorado; Dennis L. Gahagen of Boulder, Colorado; Gordon S. Chappell of Sacramento, California; Marvin Stoldt of Pine Ridge, South Dakota; Richard J. Sommers of the U.S. Army Military History Institute, Army War College, Carlisle, Pennsylvania; Peter Koch of Two Rivers, Wisconsin; the late Rocky Boyd of Spearfish, South Dakota; James ("Putt") Thompson of Crow Agency, Montana; Tony Wounded Head of Porcupine, South Dakota; John Siebert of Chicago, Illinois; Jennifer Capps of the Benjamin Harrison Presidential Site, Indianapolis, Indiana; Stephen C. Gregory of the Fort Huachuca Museum, Sierra Vista, Arizona; Dick Harmon of Lincoln, Nebraska; Bob Reece of Firestone, Colorado; Jeanne Goetzinger of Chadron, Nebraska; Merete Leonhardt-Lupa of Boulder, Colorado; Leona Broken Nose of Oglala, South Dakota; Tibbie Kocher of Rocky Ford, South Dakota; Hal

Carspecken of Centennial, Colorado; Robert Pille of Manderson, South Dakota; Merle Temple of Rocky Ford, South Dakota; Richard B. Williams of the American Indian College Fund, Denver, Colorado; James Donovan of Dallas, Texas; Violet Catches of the Pierre Indian Learning Center, Pierre, South Dakota; Roberta Sago of the Special Collections, Leland D. Case Library, Black Hills State University, Spearfish, South Dakota; Leonard Little Finger of Lakota Circle Village, Oglala, South Dakota; Linus Gray Eagle of Fort Yates, North Dakota; Doris Peterson of the Archives and Special Collections, I. D. Weeks Library, University of South Dakota, Vermillion, South Dakota; Donovin A. Sprague Hump of Black Hills State University, Spearfish, South Dakota; Douglas Sall of Yankton, South Dakota; Daniel Martinez of the USS *Arizona* Memorial, Honolulu, Hawaii; Barbara Dull Knife and the late Wilmar Young Man Afraid of His Horses of Drywood, South Dakota; William J. Hoskins and Lisa Studts of the Pettigrew Home and Museum, Sioux Falls, South Dakota; Richard W. Sellars of Santa Fe, New Mexico; Pinky Iron Plume of Manderson, South Dakota; Peter Strong and Miriam Norris of the Heritage Center, Red Cloud Indian School, Pine Ridge, South Dakota; Linn Cross Dog of the Red Cloud Indian School, Pine Ridge, South Dakota; Ephriam Dickson of the National Museum of the U.S. Army, Fort Belvoir, Virginia; Paul Sutter of the University of Colorado, Boulder; Michael O'Keefe of Placitas, New Mexico; John D. Mackintosh of Lexington, South Carolina; the late Donald J. Berthrong of Arlington, Virginia; the late Peter M. Wright of Oklahoma City, Oklahoma; Danelle Orange and Laurie Langland of the Special Collections, George and Eleanor McGovern Library, Dakota Wesleyan University, Mitchell, South Dakota; Herbert T. Hoover of Beresford, South Dakota; Edwin C. Bearss of Arlington, Virginia; Donald B. Connelly of the U.S. Army Command and General Staff College, Fort Leavenworth, Kansas; Steve Friesen of the Buffalo Bill Grave and Museum, Lookout Mountain, Colorado; Wayne Amiotte of Pine Ridge, South Dakota; Russ Taylor of the L. Tom Perry Special Collections, Brigham Young University Library, Provo, Utah; Kingsley M. Bray of Manchester, England; Richard Iron Cloud of Porcupine, South Dakota; James A. Hanson of Santa Fe, New Mexico; Vonnie Zullo of Arlington, Virginia; Steven Smith of Audubon, New Jersey; Harry Burk and Lula Red Cloud of Hermosa, South Dakota; D'Arcy Johnson of Spearfish, South Dakota; Jeffrey M. Greene of Erie, Colorado; Audrey M. Greene of Las Vegas, Nevada; Margot Liberty of Sheridan, Wyoming; Edward Jones of Albuquerque, New Mexico; Ellen Bishop of Rapid City, South Dakota;

Peter Cozzens of Rockville, Maryland; Carol Simpson of the National Park Service Library, Lakewood, Colorado; Thomas Powers of South Royalton, Vermont; Mary Casey of Denver, Colorado; Nan V. Rickey of Evergreen, Colorado; and John C. Paige of Broomfield, Colorado.

In addition, I must express gratitude to the staffs of the following institutions, who provided invaluable information throughout the course of research: the National Archives, Washington, D.C. (including the Cartographic and Architectural Section, College Park, Maryland); Manuscript Division, Library of Congress, Washington, D.C.; U.S. Army Military History Institute, Army War College, Carlisle, Pennsylvania; U.S. Military Academy Library, West Point, New York; Fort Robinson Museum, Fort Robinson State Park, Nebraska; Jefferson County Public Library, Colorado; Pritzker Military Library, Chicago, Illinois; Gilcrease Museum, Tulsa, Oklahoma; Western History Department, Denver Public Library, Denver, Colorado; Lilly Library at Indiana University, Bloomington, Indiana; Brigham Young University Library, Provo, Utah; Rare Books and Special Collections, Princeton University Library, Princeton, New Jersey; Special Collections Division, University of Washington Library, Seattle; Bureau of Indian Affairs, Branch of Realty, Pine Ridge, South Dakota; U.S. Army Command and General Staff College, Fort Leavenworth, Kansas; Robert and Shirley Small Special Collections Library, University of Virginia, Charlottesville; Parmly Billings Library, Billings, Montana; State Historical Society of North Dakota, Bismarck; University of Colorado Libraries, Boulder; Newberry Library, Chicago, Illinois; Ohio Historical Society, Columbus; Little Bighorn Battlefield National Monument, Crow Agency, Montana; Oglala Lakota College, Kyle, South Dakota; Colorado Historical Society, Denver; American Heritage Center, University of Wyoming, Laramie; Frederic Remington Art Museum, Ogdensburg, New York; Nebraska State Historical Society, Lincoln; Catholic Archives, Marquette University, Milwaukee, Wisconsin; Beinecke Rare Book and Manuscript Library, Yale University, New Haven, Connecticut; Sicangu Heritage Center Museum and Archives, Mission, South Dakota; Western History Collections, University of Oklahoma, Norman; the Historical Society of Pennsylvania, Philadelphia; Holy Rosary Mission and Red Cloud Indian School, Pine Ridge, South Dakota; the Huntington Library, San Marino, California; Jefferson National Expansion Memorial Archives, St. Louis, Missouri; and the Center for Western Studies, Augustana College, Sioux Falls, South Dakota.

I must acknowledge the unswerving efforts of special projects editor Alice Stanton and editor Emily Jerman of the University of Oklahoma Press, as well as other press employees whose talents and resourcefulness helped shape the final product. Finally, Editor-in-Chief and Associate Director Charles E. Rankin deserves my special thanks for his patience, guidance, and exceptional professional courtesies.

To all of these individuals and institutions, I extend heartfelt gratitude.

Jerome A. Greene
Arvada, Colorado

AMERICAN CARNAGE

Prologue

Early on Monday, March 7, 1938, a clear breezy day in Washington, D.C., with temperatures in the low 40s, three Sioux Indian men made their way beneath the east portico of the United States Capitol and entered the building. Sixty-year-old James Pipe on Head and seventy-six-year-old Dewey Beard were members of the Oglala and Miniconjou Lakota tribes of South Dakota. Charles White Wolf, their youthful interpreter, accompanied them. They had arrived by train in response to a request from Congress for Pipe on Head and Beard to testify before a House of Representatives Subcommittee on Indian Affairs on behalf of a measure introduced by Republican congressman Francis H. Case of South Dakota. Despite the country's ongoing economic doldrums in the closing years of the Great Depression, Case's bill was intended to indemnify Lakota victims and their descendants for human losses sustained in the so-called Battle of Wounded Knee. Also known as the Wounded Knee Massacre, the tragedy had occurred almost a half-century earlier on the Pine Ridge Reservation on December 29, 1890.

The two older men were survivors of Wounded Knee. James Pipe on Head was a grandson of Big Foot, the Miniconjou leader killed by U.S. troops at Wounded Knee with many of his followers. Pipe on Head had been twelve years old and was with his grandfather when he was killed. In more recent years he was chair of the Wounded Knee Survivors Association, headquartered on the Pine Ridge Reservation in South Dakota.

Dewey Beard, still tall and lean from a lifetime spent riding horseback, was a longtime rancher on the Pine Ridge Reservation. Well known and honored by his people, Beard was a veteran of the old buffalo days. He spoke no English but had converted to Catholicism and taken a Christian name, Dewey, along with a Sioux name, Hawk Beard, later shortened to Beard. Born in 1862, Dewey Beard had fought as a youth at the Little Bighorn in 1876 against George Armstrong Custer's soldiers. He and his people had followed Chief Sitting Bull into Canada, only to surrender later to reservation life in Dakota Territory. Beard, twenty-eight at the time of Wounded Knee, had received bullet wounds. Most of his family had not been so fortunate. His parents, two of his brothers and his sister, his wife, and his infant child had been killed.

Amid the edifices of power in the nation's capital, nearly fifty years after that action, the old warriors had garbed themselves in traditional clothing for their testimony on Case's legislation. Beard wore a buckskin war shirt decorated with beadwork and ermine tails, an ancient bear claw necklace, and a picturesque eagle-feather warbonnet imbued with the sacred power of that great bird. Pipe on Head donned a beaded floral-pattern vest and hair-pipe breastplate, and his colorful eagle headdress equaled Beard's. In such attire they had left South Dakota, signifying the seriousness of their mission to Capitol Hill. Joined in the building by Representative Case, Pipe on Head, Beard, and White Wolf passed resolutely along the marbled corridors and into the House of Representatives Indian Affairs Committee Room.[1]

At 10:30 that morning the hearing opened. Case's legislation, House Resolution 2535, was "a bill to liquidate the liability of the United States for the massacre of Sioux Indian men, women, and children at Wounded Knee on December 29, 1890." The measure provided for disbursement of $1,000 "for each Sioux Indian man, woman, or child who suffered death in the massacre of Sioux Indians at Wounded Knee Creek," to be allocated among the heirs, and the same amount for those survivors who had been wounded or otherwise bodily injured in the action or for their heirs as appropriate.[2] In addition to Case, his Lakota witnesses, and interpreter White Wolf, present for the proceedings were congressmen John R. Murdock, Democrat of Arizona, presiding as subcommittee chair; Bruce Barton, Republican of New York; and Anthony J. Dimond, Democrat of Alaska Territory, plus a congressional reporter who took down the entire session in shorthand for later transcription and printing. Another attendee was Ralph H. Case (unrelated to Congressman Case), a Washington attorney who often represented the Lakotas on legal matters. At the congressman's request, Ralph Case offered a synopsis of Sioux history and the tribe's historical relationship with the federal government.[3]

But it was the two warbonneted delegates from the Survivors Association who riveted the attention of all in the room. Pipe on Head spoke first, his words in Lakota translated by Charles White Wolf. "I do not come here to condemn anybody, but I come here for the good of my people." He described what happened that day and the events preceding the outbreak of shooting:

> The soldiers surrounded us with their guns all ready and I heard something just about that time, and somebody yelled out very loud. The minute that fellow hollered, . . . the rifles all fired at the same time. Immediately after the firing the smoke got very thick, and right behind me I could see the muzzle of a gun, and at the same time I saw Big Foot, my grandfather, the first man to be shot. Immediately after the firing I had some powder burns in my eyes, so I worked my way through the smoke, and right in front of me I saw an old woman who had already been killed; and as I passed that old woman I ran into a dead horse. . . . I ran across a woman who had a girl about 1 year old on her back. This little girl had her head all blown off. . . . She took the child off a little ways and laid it down on the prairie, and she went right on. . . . It was a case of slaughtering a bunch of defenseless mothers and some babies in the cradle; and one of the saddest parts was a little boy whose mother was killed and lying there, and the little boy didn't know that his mother was dead, and he was nursing on his mother's breast. That boy is now living . . . in Rapid City at the present time. . . . There were many cases. There was one case of a mother carrying her child on her back, and they put a bullet right through the both of them. That was the son of a man by the name of High Hawk.[4]

Pipe on Head spoke of other incidents connected with the engagement. He brought out two detailed paintings that he had created, depicting the scene along Wounded Knee Creek on December 29, 1890. One showed the landscape that morning before the shooting started, with soldier tents, tipi frames, and wagons along with troops and Indian people, with cannon on an adjoining hilltop trained on the scene below. The other showed the utter desolation of the same ground after the shooting stopped. "He wants to prove to you gentlemen that this is how the condition looked after they wiped us out," said White Wolf. When chairman Barton interrupted to ask if it were true that "about 90 men were killed and 200 women and children," Pipe on Head concurred.[5]

Dewey Beard, speaking calmly in his native tongue in a voice slightly high yet resonant, prefaced his testimony: "I would like to tell you gentlemen today that there was no reason at all that the United States troops massacred the Big Foot band. I want to bring out the fact that the United States has done what we call one of the biggest murders, as we call them, and that the United States must be ashamed of it, or something, because they have never even offered to reimburse us or settle in any way." In measured tones, he spoke of that day:

> At that time we stuck up our white flag, and they took our guns away from us. . . . The children did not know what was going on. . . . All at once they cut loose on us, and at that time I was shot in the leg. . . . At that time I had a baby of 22 days old, and right at the time when the firing started I missed my wife, and later I found out that she was shot through the breast. The little 22-day-old baby was nursing from the same side where the mother was wounded and the child choked with blood. A few days afterward the little boy died. . . . I was shot in the leg, and I fell down; they knew I was wounded and helpless, and they came and shot me all over again, in the breast. I was laying off there to one side, right by the camp site, and the soldiers were going through the field, and the men and women were wounded and could not help themselves, and the soldiers came over there and put the bullets through them again.

The Indians with Big Foot had been on their way to Pine Ridge Agency, affirmed Beard. "They were on peaceful business." In a supplementary written statement to his testimony, he pleaded: "All that I ask is that Congress pass this bill and pay those poor Indians back on the reservation the money which is provided in the bill and help us to forget the whole Wounded Knee affair."[6]

Army casualties were also briefly discussed, as well as the long-standing controversy about whether they had mostly been brought on by a reported faulty disposition of the troops that caused them to fire upon themselves as they leveled their weapons against the Indians. With that Congressman Case thanked the committee members and offered to insert additional historical data into the record of the proceeding, to verify "the account that has been given us here this morning." The subcommittee then adjourned.[7]

Pipe on Head, Beard, and White Wolf remained in Washington for several days. On one occasion the House Committee on Indian Affairs arranged "a kind of powwow" during which Dewey showed the members where he had been wounded in the leg and chest at Wounded Knee and told how he had somehow eluded death by remaining still and "playing 'possum" as the troops ranged the field, shooting the fallen people. On another occasion the men posed for photos with Representative Case and other subcommittee members. Still in traditional garb, Beard and Pipe on Head also paid a courtesy call on the commissioner of Indian Affairs, John Collier, at the Department of the Interior, where the three were photographed together. The Sioux delegates urged Collier to continue his support for Case's bill.[8]

The trio departed Union Station for home early on March 11. Case wrote Pipe on Head and the Survivors Association, reviewing the proceedings, offering thanks for their participation, and assuring them that the witnesses had "made a very fine showing." "After the sub-committee has further considered this evidence," he noted, "it indicated that it desired to call in witnesses from the War Department before making its report on the bill." Although encouraging, Case was realistic in his assessment. Explaining the procedure that the bill would have to go through for approval in the House before going to the Senate for referral to that body's own Indian Affairs Committee, Case advised the people not "to expect early passage . . . , because it has a long course to follow and is subject to trouble all along the line."[9]

Back in South Dakota, James Pipe on Head and Dewey Beard resumed their lives on the impoverished Pine Ridge Reservation. The survivors' association members continued to meet regularly, hoping to hear from Congressman Case of any progress on H.R. 2535. When the people learned of the U.S. Army's interest in appearing on the measure, they grew apprehensive. "We . . . want to know if some officer of the War Department has testified," Pipe on Head wrote to Case, "and if a delegation should be there to counteract any destructive statement made by such officer."[10] They had waited almost half a century for a semblance of redress for what had happened to them and their families on that bloody landscape along Wounded Knee Creek. Now, after decades of anguished patience, Case's bill held forth the promise of atonement. Their spirits buoyed, the people waited, cautiously optimistic.

ONE

Wild Indians

L ife in the Pine Ridge country had not always seemed so troubled, so
uncertain, but those times were mostly gone, lost in the shadows of
memory and the reality of Depression-era hardship. Long ago, it had been
different.

Over the course of their known history as a free-roaming people between
1750 and the 1870s, groups of Sioux Indians at various times had extended
their influence from the wooded tracts of what is now northwestern Wisconsin west through Minnesota and beyond to the vast plains enveloping
the Pine Ridge and the Black Hills and on to Montana and eastern Wyoming and from as far north as Canada south into Kansas and beyond. This
movement had ebbed and flowed as conditions changed for the people over
time. In the early years the number of Sioux in their linguistic divisions of
Dakota, Yankton-Yanktonai (also known as Nakota), and Lakota was estimated at 25,000 people. By the end of the period, after the United States
government had subdued them, concentrated them on reservations, and
counted them, the number stood at slightly more than 39,000 people.[1]

Together, these broad tribal entities were one of the largest indigenous
populations in the conterminous United States. While each Sioux group
had its own defined history, each also was inextricably bound to the others
biologically, culturally, and historically. As time passed, all were pressed by
expanding eastern white populations and by neighboring tribes that caused

them to edge farther west during the eighteenth century. The Dakota and Yankton-Yanktonai divisions came to occupy the prairies of Minnesota, northern Iowa, and present eastern North Dakota and South Dakota. The Dakotas, generally known as Santees, consisted of four tribes: the Wahpetons, Mdwakantons, Sissetons, and Wahpekutes. They were closely aligned with the Yanktons and Yanktonais who commonly occupied tracts adjoining them to the west. The Lakotas or Tetons, also known as Western Sioux, were the largest tribe of the linguistically affiliated bodies. By the mid-eighteenth century they consisted of seven subtribes: Hunkpapas (Campers at the Entrance of the Camp Circle), Oglalas (Those Who Scatter Their Own Grain), Sichangus (Burned Thighs People, commonly known as Brulés), Miniconjous (Planters by the Water), Itazipchos (Those without Bows, referred to as Sans Arcs), Sihasapas (Blackfeet Sioux or Wearers of Black Moccasins), and Oohenunpas (Two Kettles or Two Boilings People).[2]

In their movements west, all these groups transformed culturally to various degrees. Primarily horticultural during their time on the prairies of Wisconsin and eastern Minnesota, the people, especially the Lakotas, came to embrace hunting in their westward progression. The Lakotas extended their reach farthest west of all. Much in the manner of the Cheyennes and Arapahos, who preceded them west from the area of the Great Lakes, the Tetons had been gradually pushed by neighboring tribes as those peoples in turn contended with growing white populations farther east. The availability of horses among tribes to the west also drew the Lakotas onto the plains. In the course of their movement west and occupation of game territory, the Lakotas intermittently met, fought, reconciled, and fought again with Arikaras, Crows, Cheyennes, Arapahos, Pawnees, and other tribes that had preceded them there. By 1776 the Lakotas had established their presence west to the Black Hills, and from that time forward their history would be synonymous with that vast region.

Within decades of the Tetons' arrival on the northern Great Plains, the people became part of an evolving lifestyle and economy almost exclusively based on the ubiquitous buffalo, the most important food source and preeminent cultural fixture that centered many tribes in the region. As they followed the vast herds seasonally for sustenance, they competed with other tribes for game, horses, guns, and territory. Each tribe fought for its place. The Sioux notably collided with the Blackfeet, Shoshonis, and Crows during their migrations, especially the Crows. As the presence of white emigrants grew in the years preceding and following the Civil

War, intertribal conflict increased. Like virtually all other Indian tribes, the Lakotas through time had evolved their own deeply spiritual practices that infused their daily lifestyle and religion. Their cultural and political similarities with the Northern Cheyennes and Northern Arapahos flourished to include not only social and military alliances with those people but intermarriage and mutual participation in ceremonial activities.[3]

As the white population surged west during the nineteenth century, it was only a matter of time before contact increased between all the tribes of the Santees, Yankton-Yanktonais, and Lakotas, on the one hand, and settlers, traders, government officials, and the army, on the other. During the period of national expansion of the 1840s, 1850s, and 1860s, and as the presence of whites increased through overland migration and settlement, the United States government treated with the Santees to garner cessions in Iowa and Minnesota. At Fort Laramie in present Wyoming in 1851, government negotiators acknowledged the land base status quo for the Lakotas, Cheyennes, Crows, Arapahos, and other tribes in an effort to keep them distant from the corridors of emigrant traffic. In so doing, they acknowledged the regional supremacy of the Teton Sioux as well as the likelihood of inevitable conflict with them. The expanse of land recognized for the Lakotas extended from the Heart River in present North Dakota south (encompassing the entirety of the Black Hills) to modern Nebraska's North Platte River and west from the Missouri River in North and South Dakota to the western reaches of the Belle Fourche, Cheyenne, and North Platte Rivers in present Wyoming. This broad area of approximately 78,000 square miles was an empire larger than the state of Wisconsin. The government also conceded to the Lakotas hunting grounds below the North Platte.[4]

The greater Sioux tribes were an ascendant population, expanding in both numbers and power and on a collision course with a far more numerous and intrusive white population. Confrontations between the Sioux and whites started soon after the 1851 treaty in and around Fort Laramie. In August 1854 an issue between Sioux and emigrants near the post intensified into a deadly encounter in which Brulés wiped out an army detachment of thirty soldiers. Little more than a year later, troops from Fort Leavenworth under Brevet Brigadier General William S. Harney avenged the deed in an attack on a camp of Brulés under Chief Little Thunder in present western Nebraska that killed eighty-six people and effectively imposed a federal declaration of war against the Lakotas. It remained in place over the next quarter-century.[5]

Other Sioux tribes encountered similar difficulties with Euro-Americans. Within five years of Harney's retaliation, conditions among the Santees worsened as white settlement engulfed them in Minnesota. Confined solely to lands designated by the 1851 accord, the people were subjected to continued encroachment, along with ill treatment by officials, traders, and creditors, all of whom regularly cheated the Indians. During the summer of 1862, while the Civil War raged in other parts of the nation, warriors led by Little Crow broke from their reserve to strike civilian populations. In a week they killed eight hundred settlers and captured hundreds more before troops arrived. Colonel Henry H. Sibley succeeded in quelling the violence and subjugating the tribesmen at Wood Lake. Soon afterward Little Crow was killed, and as many as three hundred Santees were condemned to hang following the outbreak. President Abraham Lincoln commuted most of the sentences, but thirty-nine of the Indians died on the gallows.

In its aftermath, the warfare in Minnesota carried west into the newly designated Dakota Territory as the army conducted follow-up operations against Santees and Yankton-Yanktonais who had fled the tumult. Many of those people fled into Canada to find relief, and some of them stayed there. Others pressed westward, variously joining camps of Yankton-Yanktonais and Lakotas and other tribes, bringing word of what had happened to their people. Within a year the government relocated almost fifteen hundred Santees out of Minnesota to a tract along the Missouri River in Dakota Territory.

Although Sibley and Brigadier General Alfred Sully quelled the Indians in Minnesota and eastern Dakota, their campaigns of 1863 and 1864 produced a contagion of resistance that spread west via the Upper Missouri. In July 1864 one of Sully's expeditions struck a body of several thousand Sioux near the Killdeer Mountains in present western North Dakota that included not only Santees and Yanktonais but Hunkpapa, Miniconjou, Sans Arc, and Blackfeet Lakotas as well. While the attack killed a disputed number of Indians, it ominously threatened the future sanctity of the Tetons. Sully shortly pressed on to the Yellowstone River, where his troops and artillery produced even more casualties among the Lakotas as a harbinger of things to come.[6]

Within five months of Killdeer Mountains came the Sand Creek Massacre in Colorado Territory. There, as in other venues, migrants moving west to the Rocky Mountain goldfields in past years had destroyed or otherwise disrupted game resources while defoliating lands along the trails. Hoping to stem retaliatory raiding by the tribesmen, a mounted U.S. volunteer force charged down on a peaceful Southern Cheyenne and Arapaho village in the cold dawn of November 29, 1864, unmercifully killing many of its inhabitants. Although the attack had occurred far south of the area claimed by the western Sioux, its dastardly import swept far and wide and galvanized the Indians of the plains. The Cheyennes had friends and relatives in the North who were socially aligned with the Lakotas by intermarriages, especially with the Oglalas and Brulés. Sand Creek, coming soon after the Minnesota and Dakota events, added to Indian grievances and angered many tribesmen. Thereafter retaliating warriors posed substantial risks for emigrants and settlers on the plains.[7]

More than any other single incident, the Sand Creek Massacre set the tone for future relations between the U.S. government and the tribes of the plains. The tragedy, magnified in the public consciousness by one military and two congressional hearings, brought universal condemnation from many white Americans, though it was applauded in the West. From its epicenter, the horror resonated in all directions, prompting backlash among wide segments of the Indian population. It directly inspired the conflicts that arose with the Southern Cheyennes, Southern Arapahos, Kiowas, Comanches, and other tribes along the overland trails. Furthermore, to them it characterized the whites' brutality and injustice and influenced events respecting the Lakotas, Northern Cheyennes, and their allies north of the trails for the remainder of the nineteenth century.[8]

The Lakotas played a major role in the erupting fury after Sand Creek. Early in 1865, along with Cheyennes and Arapahos, their warriors laid siege to emigrant paths in Wyoming, Nebraska, and Kansas, destroying property while besieging mail routes and telegraph lines and attacking Julesburg along the South Platte River in Colorado Territory. Elsewhere, in gaining hegemony over enemy tribes, the Lakotas had gradually usurped much Crow territory in Wyoming and Montana. When white entrepreneurs blazed the Bozeman Trail across north-central Wyoming and southern Montana territories to reach new gold diggings farther north and west, the Sioux and their Cheyenne and Arapaho allies attacked them. The attacks brought repeated skirmishes with troops from Fort Laramie along the North Platte River near modern Casper, Wyoming. These exchanges brought on a punitive expedition composed of volunteer troops headed by

Brigadier General Patrick E. Connor that in the summer of 1865 ranged north from Fort Laramie to cooperate with two eastern columns in punishing the tribes. Connor's command found and destroyed an Arapaho village along Tongue River, but the cooperating columns faced debilitating weather and logistical problems combined with repeated attacks by Sioux and Cheyennes, which forced their withdrawal.

At treaty councils held in the fall of 1865 at Fort Sully along the Missouri River, most of the seven tribes of Lakotas agreed to retire from existing and future overland routes. As in other such accords, however, specifics were vague and often inscrutable to Indian leaders who lacked authority to speak for those not present or to enforce treaty provisions among their people. In the Powder River country, the Sioux paid scant attention to the Fort Sully pact and refused to withdraw from the lands adjoining the Bozeman Trail. Nor did they recognize Crow rights to their long-held hunting grounds in the Yellowstone drainage. Their attacks continued, and the army sent troops to occupy several posts built along the Bozeman Trail.[9]

All of this was a precursor for Red Cloud's War of 1866–68, a conflict that finally ruptured relations between the United States and the Teton Sioux. Following numerous small clashes, the warfare climaxed in December 1866 when a coalition of Sioux, Cheyenne, and Arapaho warriors under the Oglala leader Red Cloud and other chiefs ambushed a detachment of eighty men under Captain William J. Fetterman near Fort Phil Kearny, one of the new posts in present northern Wyoming. In destroying Fetterman's command, the Indians signaled their indignation over invasion of their domain and their determination to hold their hunting lands. The "Fetterman Massacre," as the incident became known, shocked the government, but the tribesmen continued their pressure on the forts astride the Bozeman Trail, delivering attacks on the garrisons of Fort Phil Kearny and Fort C. F. Smith, ninety miles to the north in Montana Territory, and threatening Fort Reno to the south.[10]

Faced with continuing loss and expense, government officials finally conceded to Red Cloud's demands in early 1868. At Fort Laramie in April, representatives of the Lakotas, Northern Cheyennes, and Northern Arapahos won their principal objective in the removal of the three posts, although Red Cloud personally did not sign the document until late 1868.[11] Of major significance, the Fort Laramie Treaty of 1868 created the Great Sioux Reservation. Encompassing the western half of present South Dakota from the Missouri River and including the Black Hills, the area embraced 41,000 square miles, the equivalent of Kentucky. The treaty also gave these tribes common title and extended hunting privileges to them over an area stretching west of the designated reserve to the crest of Wyoming's Big Horn range and south to the North Platte River in Nebraska. This so-called unceded Indian territory was only vaguely defined, particularly when acknowledging the Indians' "right to hunt on any lands north of [the] North Platte," which was sometimes construed as extending well into the Yellowstone country of Montana. Not all Lakota bands signed the treaty. In their view, they were therefore not bound by it. A treaty completed concurrently with the Crow tribe, which had resisted Lakota and Cheyenne encroachment, severely restricted the Crows' own land base in Wyoming and Montana.[12]

The Fort Laramie Treaty of 1868 held implications that would impact the destiny of the Lakota people for generations. The government promised to care for them by building an agency on the reservation with commensurate facilities and to provide food, clothing, and annuities at specified rates over thirty years. Hoping to acculturate the Lakotas into the dominant society, the treaty promised them education, land ownership and cultivation, and seeds and implements to get them started. "It is further stipulated," read the document, "that the United States will furnish and deliver to each lodge of Indians or family of persons legally incorporated with them, who shall remove to the reservation . . . and commence farming, one good American cow, and one good well-broken pair of American oxen within sixty days after such lodge or family shall have so settled upon said reservation."[13] The pact permitted the government to construct "railroads, wagon-roads, mail-stations, or other works of utility or necessity" on the reservation, with compensation for allowing such development. Article 12, a provision of profound significance as events later unfolded, stated: "No treaty for the cession of any portion or part of the reservation herein described which may be held in common shall be of any validity or force as against the said Indians, *unless executed and signed by at least three-fourths of all the adult male Indians, occupying or interested in the same.*"[14]

This article addressed the common ownership feature to ensure that each tribe or band on the reserve would be protected "from a combination of the others to part with any portion of the territory to the injury of any other band or tribe."[15] In other words, to be legally binding any change to the basic treaty was to be formally sanctioned by no less than three-quarters of the adult men residing on the reserve.

Although the Senate ratified the Fort Laramie Treaty early in 1869, Indian assignees started moving onto their designated tract in summer 1868. The unfolding reservation system in effect amounted to a continuance of the old removal policy reshaped to concentrate Indians on tracts away from the routes of westward expansion. Under the Ulysses S. Grant administration, a "Peace Policy" existed whereby the government turned control of the reservations over to members of Christian religious denominations. The plan was meant to halt further outbreaks and acculturate the Indians through food, education, and the precepts of agriculture. Conflicts arose between the army and the Bureau of Indian Affairs over validity of the Peace Policy and continued civilian direction of Indian affairs, which most army officers opposed. Meanwhile Episcopalians took over management of the several agencies on the Great Sioux Reservation. Whetstone Agency temporarily stood far to the east along the Missouri River, where steamboats could readily deliver promised annuities. Others were established farther north along the Missouri, and an agency named for Red Cloud was raised near Fort Laramie in 1871.

By the mid-1870s the principal offices on the Great Sioux Reservation were Red Cloud Agency, Spotted Tail Agency, Cheyenne River Agency, Standing Rock Agency, Lower Brulé Agency, and Crow Creek Agency. Red Cloud Agency, relocated along White River in western Nebraska near the modern town of Crawford, was established for Oglalas, Northern Cheyennes, and Northern Arapahos. Spotted Tail Agency, named for the prominent Brulé leader, served the Upper and Lower Brulés, Miniconjous, and other northern Sioux. It stood twenty miles northeast of Red Cloud, near present Chadron, Nebraska. Both the Red Cloud and Spotted Tail agencies were located south of the reservation boundary. Cheyenne River Agency (to serve Miniconjous, Two Kettles, Sans Arcs, and Blackfeet Sioux) and Standing Rock Agency (to serve Hunkpapas, Upper and Lower Yanktonais, and Blackfeet Sioux) were both on the Missouri River. The Lower Brulé Agency and Crow Creek Agency (established in 1862) were posted on the Missouri as well. Both served the Lower Brulés and Lower Yanktonais.[16]

Although there were eventually some twenty-five thousand Lakotas, Cheyennes, and Arapahos tenuously registered at the six Sioux agencies on the reservation, some became only part-time tenants. Each year when the weather improved, hundreds of the people who came to be called "summer roamers" slipped away from the reserve to hunt game and reside with their nontreaty relatives in the unceded tract. They would then return to the agencies for rations and annuities as winter approached. The several thousand Tetons who had refused to subscribe to the Fort Laramie Treaty continued to occupy the unceded hunting grounds of eastern Wyoming and the Powder River/Yellowstone country of Montana. These people, mostly Hunkpapas, Sans Arcs, Miniconjous, Two Kettles, and Blackfeet Sioux, represented the so-called Northern Sioux bands whose primary leadership lay with Sitting Bull, an impressive Hunkpapa healer, holy man, and leader who claimed broad influence over all the Western Sioux. Authorities contended most frequently with Sitting Bull and his followers, beginning in the 1870s as the federal government sought to promote economic development and settlement in the Yellowstone region.[17]

Two events aggravated relations with the nontreaty Tetons. In 1873 the Northern Pacific Railroad extended its surveying operations along a projected route into Montana. The survey party was accompanied by a military escort for protection. In August two spirited clashes took place between Hunkpapas and Oglalas under the nominal leadership of Sitting Bull and Crazy Horse and the Seventh Cavalry, commanded by Lieutenant Colonel George A. Custer. The clashes occurred along the lower Yellowstone River as angry warriors augmented by summer roamers from the reservation protested the intrusions into their country. The fighting set the tone for confrontation and signified the Indians' resolve to resist ever-growing white intrusion. More ominous aggravation occurred in 1874, when Custer, ostensibly seeking to locate a military post, led an expedition that penetrated the Black Hills to verify reports of gold there. Isolated in the western third of the Great Sioux Reservation, the pine-forested granite peaks and sedimentary spires of the Black Hills were spiritually revered by the Indians on and off the reserve. While the government rationalized the movement in terms of national interest, the invasion of the sacred part of their treaty lands alarmed the Indians, who condemned Custer's route as "the thieves' road." Commissioner of Indian Affairs Edward P. Smith feared that the resulting clamor regarding the gold country might bring abrogation of the Fort Laramie Treaty. "Scarcely a greater evil could come to the Sioux people," he warned, "than the disturbance and demoralization incident to an attempt to dispossess them of their country."[18]

Economic doldrums resulting from the Panic of 1873 ultimately forced the issue. Confirmation of gold in the Black Hills within a year touched off a hurried rush that impelled hundreds of citizens onto the reservation. While the army initially tried to counter interlopers who raised shanties and sluices wherever they pleased, troops sent into the region became overwhelmed by the rapid influx and eventually conceded their presence. Inflamed by the violation, the Indians struck back, killing miners and stealing livestock and other property. In September 1875 the government, which viewed protection of its citizens, though trespassers, as a major concern, sent commissioners to meet with the Indians near Red Cloud Agency. After tribal leaders including Red Cloud and Spotted Tail rejected their proposal to buy the Black Hills from the Sioux, officials adopted a policy of relentlessly pressing the Indians to relinquish the area. Simultaneously, soldiers undertook to force the nontreaty followers of Sitting Bull and Crazy Horse out of the unceded territory and onto the Great Sioux Reservation.[19]

The sporadic struggle between troops and Indians that ensued over twenty months of 1876–77 through vast expanses of southeastern Montana, eastern Wyoming, southwestern Dakota territories, and western Nebraska is known as the Great Sioux War. Campaigning proved to be lengthy and disastrous for the army and Indians alike. During the conflict, columns of troops operating with Indian auxiliaries from tribes hostile to the Sioux (including the Crows) fought them on numerous occasions. In March 1876 a contingent from Brigadier General George Crook's command struck a Northern Cheyenne village along Montana's Powder River, believing the occupants to be Tetons, and succeeded in further cementing the alliance between that tribe and the Sioux. In June the combined Indian force held Crook to a standstill at Rosebud Creek, Montana, in what was a prelude for their overwhelming victory days later against Custer's Seventh Cavalry at the Battle of the Little Bighorn River. In that engagement the soldiers attacked a village of about 5,000 people including perhaps 1,500 warriors, and Custer and more than 260 of his men perished. Many of the warriors who fought in that encounter had only recently joined Sitting Bull, Crazy Horse, Two Moons, Crow King, and other chiefs from the reservation in Dakota Territory.

Late that summer, after army reinforcements gained the field, Crook pursued the scattering tribesmen eastward into Dakota Territory. In early September a detachment from his command finally defeated one mixed camp of Sioux and Northern Cheyennes at Slim Buttes. In November a column of Crook's cavalry under Colonel Ranald S. Mackenzie surprised a Cheyenne village in Wyoming's snowy Big Horn range, killing many and driving its refugees north to join Crazy Horse's people south of the Yellowstone in Montana.

Meanwhile, on orders from the army hierarchy, Colonel Nelson A. Miles established a cantonment along the Yellowstone and campaigned relentlessly through the fall and winter with his Fifth Infantry regiment to find and destroy elements of the Indian coalition. In October Miles met Sitting Bull in council and then fought him at Cedar Creek, Montana. A detachment from his force struck the chief again in December. In January 1877 Miles's troops, garbed in heavy buffalo overcoats, registered significant success in the Wolf Mountains, south of the Yellowstone, where they fought and defeated a combined force of Lakotas and Northern Cheyennes under Crazy Horse and Two Moons. Except for small-scale campaigning thereafter that lasted into September, the Battle of Wolf Mountains largely ended the fighting. By then the people were starving and lacked the resources necessary to prevail. Many of the Tetons and Northern Cheyennes turned themselves in at the agencies, and in May 1877 Crazy Horse and his people surrendered at Camp Robinson, Nebraska. That event, symbolically coupled with the chief's killing four months later, marked the conclusion of the Great Sioux War.[20]

The warfare of 1876–77, of course, flew in the face of the government's touted Peace Policy. Even as the fighting continued, Congress laid plans to approach the reservation people again on the Black Hills matter. Later in summer 1876 as U.S. troops continued their pursuit of the warriors who had wiped out Custer's command, other soldiers seized the Sioux agencies and confiscated the horses and arms of returning warriors. The government simultaneously reopened negotiations respecting sale of the Black Hills. Impetus for the action had come on August 15, when Congress appropriated 1877 funds for feeding the Lakotas on the Great Sioux Reservation. Offended by the Indians' refusal to sell the mineral-rich tract and angered over the Little Bighorn and other army losses, Congress ruled that unless the Indians relinquished both the Black Hills ("so much of their . . . permanent reservation as lies west of the one hundred and third meridian of longitude": approximately 12,000 square miles) and the unceded territory specified in the Fort Laramie Treaty, as well as grant access through the reservation to the Black Hills, future food and provisions that had been guaranteed to them would not be forthcoming.[21]

When another delegation appeared at Red Cloud and Spotted Tail agencies, the Indians' suspicions ran high. Throughout September and October the commissioners visited the different agencies, where they lectured and browbeat the adult males among the signatory tribes and attempted to instill in them the gravity of Congress's wrath. In due course they coerced only lame consent for the plan, yet they enticed such prominent chiefs as Red Cloud, Spotted Tail, and John Grass to sign their marks to the document. In gaining the Indians' endorsement, however, the commissioners disregarded the provision of article 12 of the treaty, specifying that such change be ratified by three-fourths of the adult males occupying the reservation. The presence of the army at the agencies no doubt added an element of intimidation. The commission literally imposed its will on the people, squeezing them with the threat of starvation. Congress ratified the agreement on February 28, 1877.

Within weeks of this proceeding other Lakotas, weary of fighting yet refusing to surrender, fled to refuge beyond the international border in the British Possessions. Some crossed what the Indians call the Medicine Line into Canada late in 1876, but the pace quickened in March 1877. Sitting Bull appeared in May, and by late that month authorities estimated the number of Sioux arrivals at between four thousand and five thousand. Some were people from the reservation. Over time others from the agencies joined their kin in the North. On their arrival, most of the people camped near the border, where their proximity to the United States vexed American officials.

The Lakotas were not well received in Canada, either by government administrators or by the dominion's own Indian population, which resented the competition for game resources, especially the thinning herds of buffalo. Canada regarded the people as alien refugees and provided them neither sustenance nor other support, and the North-West Mounted Police monitored them closely. Despite efforts by Great Britain and Canada to encourage the Lakotas to leave, they remained in Canada for several years. During that time they occasionally hunted south of the boundary, where they often raided ranches for food and livestock. Beginning in 1880, as the buffalo herds continued their decline, bands of destitute Tetons under leaders like Big Road, Spotted Eagle, Gall, and Hump made their way south to surrender their arms and horses. In like manner, Sitting Bull and his immediate followers arrived at Fort Buford, Dakota Territory, in July 1881, marking the conclusion of more than two decades of intermittent conflict between the government and the Teton Sioux. Army records disclose that during the surrenders between February 1880 and July 1881 a total of 5,694 Lakota people turned themselves in to troops along the Yellowstone.[22] As things stood, most would end up on the now truncated Great Sioux Reservation, where some Sioux leaders would assume positions of consequence in the years to come.

TWO

New World

H owever different reservation life had been for the Lakotas, it was even more so after the government took the Black Hills. The modified broad tract that stretched west from the Missouri River to the 103rd meridian (minus the area lying between the forks of the Cheyenne River that was part of the Black Hills taking) consisted of 34,125 square miles.[1] Many of the Indians, especially those leaders who realized exactly what had transpired, were sick over the loss of their revered ground. Now it would be given over to miners who would tear the earth asunder in their quest for gold. Even those who went into Canada, including those who had never subscribed to the Fort Laramie Treaty, were saddened by the loss of what they considered their special land. "Once I was rich, plenty of money [wealth]," lamented Sitting Bull, "but the Americans stole it all in the Black Hills."[2]

Still, the modified tract left to the people was broad and expansive. Even without the Black Hills it reflected topographical diversity. Part of the Great Plains Province, it offered stunningly wide panoramas of grasslands, buttes, and valleys formed by eons of glacial action and wind erosion. The whole region is part of a giant plateau that slopes gently down toward the Missouri River, the demarcation between the plains and the eastern prairie country.

Within this majestic region, all of the Great Sioux Reservation lay astride the Missouri Plateau, an expansive area characterized by wide, level tablelands interspersed with deeply fissured canyons and buttes. Five principal streams knife across it, generally flowing west or southwest. From north to south, the Grand, Moreau, Cheyenne, Bad, and White Rivers and their respective tributaries find their way to the Missouri. Between the White and Cheyenne Rivers lie the Big Badlands, also known as the White River Badlands, stretching some one hundred miles from west to east and thirty miles north to south. They compose a brooding lunar-like enclave of fissured domes and pinnacles, buttes and gorges peppered by lofty tablelands colored and sculpted by time. The Badlands have a unique ecosystem of grass, forests, and a panoply of animal life. The one constant is the wind. It is an area widely known today for its Oligocene-epoch fossils and paleontological discoveries. Its core geologic area constitutes some 244,000 acres of today's Badlands National Park, originally established as a national monument in 1930.

South of the Badlands, below the Pine Ridge and near the Nebraska border, lies the Sand Hills country. Except for this area and parts of the Badlands, the soil of the lands then embraced by the Great Sioux Reservation is generally composed of dark and gray-brown loam, sandy loam, or sand. When wet the gray-brown loam yields a heavy, intractable gumbo. Groundcover on this rolling semiarid terrain consists largely of mixed-grass prairie (grama, buffalo, bluestem, and wheatgrass) with carpets of wildflowers in spring and summer. It is a beautiful, deceivingly gentle land that can be suddenly overtaken by stunningly volatile weather. High winds and precipitation can bombard the country with driving thunderstorms, hail the size of baseballs, and killing blizzards. Spring-fed tributaries are lined with ash, elm, and willow. Oak is common and cottonwood ubiquitous; ridges and draws sport clusters of pine, while seasonal shrubs offer currents, chokecherries, buffalo berries, and wild grapes. Rainfall averages about fifteen inches. Winters vary in snowfall and intensity, but temperatures can fluctuate widely, producing springlike conditions in deep winter or raging blizzards. The grasslands historically supported large herds of buffalo and pronghorn, but other wildlife was abundant, including deer, elk, bighorn sheep, bears, coyotes, foxes, wolves, rabbits, eagles, hawks, and wild turkeys. Some of these species were more common in areas closer to the Black Hills. The entirety of the reduced Great Sioux Reservation boasted a rich ecosystem, but for much of the nineteenth century it was considered part of the "Great American Desert," the mythical trans-Mississippi province believed to possess few redeeming qualities for white settlement.[3]

With the Black Hills taken from the Sioux and the returnees from Canada surrendering in large numbers in 1880–81, other changes were afoot in and around Sioux country. The people had resisted efforts to be removed to the dreaded Indian Territory (present Oklahoma), but both Red Cloud Agency and Spotted Tail Agency had been moved onto the Great Sioux Reservation in Dakota Territory. In late July 1878 the Brulés with Spotted Tail, who had variously relocated from sites in western Nebraska to distant places along the Missouri River, were permitted to go to a new location on Rosebud Creek. Henceforth this would be known as Rosebud Agency. Four months later the Oglalas, along with a contingent of Northern Cheyennes and Arapahos, moved from Red Cloud Agency to a site along Big White Clay Creek within the reservation that Red Cloud approved personally. Renamed for the adjacent conifer-topped escarpment to blunt Red Cloud's stature, Pine Ridge would thereafter be the administrative office of the Oglala Lakotas. In the years ahead Sioux activities centered on these two southern agencies.[4]

In the aftermath of the Great Sioux War, the army functioned more as a constabulary. Its primary purpose was to dissuade Indians from leaving the reservation or from joining with Sitting Bull's followers in the North. To this end the government maintained a wide perimeter of posts. Some of these were existing forts, and some represented troop detachments stationed at the Sioux agencies. On the south and west sides of the reservation they included Fort Robinson, Nebraska, raised as a camp in 1874 near present Crawford and given permanent status in 1878; Camp Sheridan, established in 1874 near present Chadron, Nebraska; Fort Niobrara, Nebraska, built in 1879 near modern Valentine; and Fort Meade, Dakota, established in 1878 at the eastern edge of the Black Hills near present-day Sturgis. On the north side of the reserve at Standing Rock Agency on the Missouri River stood Fort Yates, established in 1874 but renamed after one of Custer's fallen officers in 1878. Along the river bordering the eastern side of the reservation, north to south, were soldier garrisons at Grand River Agency; Fort Bennett, raised in 1870 at the Cheyenne River Agency; Fort Sully (the second post by that name), established in 1866; and Fort Randall, built on the river in 1856 near what became the reservation's extreme southeastern boundary.

Beyond this immediate perimeter, a secondary tier of posts guarded the hinterland. They included Sidney Barracks near modern Sidney, Nebraska, built in 1867 and redesignated Fort Sidney in 1879. Situated on the Union

Pacific Railroad, Fort Sidney linked to Fort Laramie, Wyoming Territory, the esteemed military bastion of the northern plains since the late 1840s. Other secondary posts included Fort Fetterman, established along the North Platte River in Wyoming Territory in 1867; Fort McKinney, built in 1876 near modern Buffalo, Wyoming; the Yellowstone country posts of Forts Custer and Keogh, Montana Territory (1877); Fort Buford, Dakota Territory (1866); and Fort Abraham Lincoln, near Bismarck, Dakota, established in 1872. More posts lay beyond this outlying zone; two new posts, Fort Assinniboine and Fort Maginnis in Montana Territory, in particular were poised to protect against Indian refugees returning from sanctuary in Canada.[5]

Those so-called wild Indians—people who had never known reservation life and had gone to Canada with Sitting Bull—came to realize the purpose of the troops surrounding them. In 1880–81 U.S. soldiers ultimately escorted them to the reservation agencies, where many of their relatives had lived since 1869 and 1870. Among the some 2,800 Lakota prisoners arriving at Standing Rock in July 1881 for delivery to their home agencies were Miniconjous under Hump and Fool Heart and Sans Arcs under Circle Bear and Spotted Eagle, all bound for the Cheyenne River. Others belonging to these bands arrived later, well into 1882, and many of these people congregated with Hump's followers near Cherry Creek, sixty miles west of the agency.[6] Sitting Bull posed a special problem. Because of his disruptive potential among the Hunkpapas, the army decided that he should not settle at Standing Rock, at least not immediately. Instead, within days of his arrival at Fort Yates, infantry soldiers wielding bayoneted rifles forced him and his followers onto a steamer bound for Fort Randall, the longtime bastion overlooking the Missouri River near the far eastern edge of the Great Sioux Reservation. From September 1881 on, Sitting Bull and his family, along with other chiefs and headmen and their families, occupied a guarded prison camp among the hills and bottoms just beyond the garrison. They were permitted occasional visits from their relatives at Standing Rock Agency, but they spent most of their days in boredom. Sitting Bull's lobbying for removal to Standing Rock eventually paid off, and in early May 1883 he and others arrived at Fort Yates by steamboat. Sitting Bull and his coterie quickly withdrew to Grand River, some forty miles south of the post and agency, comfortably removed from white influence.[7]

Other changes had occurred since 1869 as well. Army officers served as agents at an early stage. But when that practice was outlawed in 1871, prevailing national politics determined the assignments and became a source of contention in later years. Contention also arose with the arrival of the Canadian refugees, many of whom clung to the old ways and had always resisted going into the agencies. Schisms emerged between these people and those who had resided on the reservation for more than a decade and were somewhat acclimated to new lifeways. After the 1880–81 surrenders the Lakota social fabric began to mend, but subtle fissures remained. One source of these divisions was the old warrior status. While women's roles still focused on family, the role of the warrior and hunter was redirected on the reservation to political and religious matters. Others found fulfillment in service as army scouts and agency police. Those who acclimated to the new order, including past reservation dwellers, were termed "progressives." Opposed to them were people who did not adapt easily, if at all. They came to be known as "nonprogressives," "conservatives," and "traditionalists." Factions arose, and agents and their subordinates often encouraged and thus exacerbated the distinctions with their programs to acculturate the people. Units of Indian police, recruited at the Lakota agencies in the late 1870s, were a means to break down the authority of the old chiefs. This was not lost on the traditionalists, who viewed them as tools of the progressives.

In the early 1880s the Department of the Interior established Courts of Indian Offenses on the reservation. Tribal judges were empowered to work with the police to keep order and safeguard property. They also were supposed to promote acculturation and the progressive lifestyle. By the late 1880s, with furor growing over land, government negotiators regarded these nonprogressives as the "hostile" party. "They are in no way hostile now, in the true sense of the word," noted one commissioner, "but their feelings towards the white people and towards the Government are not so agreeable as the feelings of those who have never occupied a hostile attitude."[8]

The decline of wild game destroyed the traditional Sioux lifestyle. In the fifteen years after the Fort Laramie Treaty the buffalo and other large game all but vanished. In 1881 the Northern Pacific Railroad steamed across western Dakota into Montana, opening the former Sioux hunting lands to white settlement. Stock raising and agriculture followed the railroad, devastating wildlife habitat. Throughout the region, but especially in the Yellowstone country in Montana and between the Cannonball and Moreau Rivers north and west of the reservation, commercial hide hunters waged yearlong slaughter on the dwindling buffalo herds. Buffalo robes, horns, and skins were sent east by rail, with the skins used to operate machinery in eastern and European manufacturing hubs. With the decline of the herds, fewer and fewer of the beasts migrated onto reservation land. Traditionally the Sioux relied on buffalo and other wild game not only for food and shelter but for clothing, furniture, and other staple goods, even trade items. Absence of the buffalo forced them to depend on unreliable and often paltry government subsidies, including foodstuffs and dress, or on what agriculture might provide from unproductive land. The loss of the buffalo meant the end of tribal independence.[9]

In the new world order, the agency became the nucleus of Indian life. Headmen took charge of freighted annuities and food rations and parceled them out to the people. The influence of chiefs waned, because the agents, many of them political hacks, fostered competition within their ranks. Some agents purposely promoted discord, bypassed the chiefs, and disrupted the traditional tribal structure. Some of this interference was well intentioned. A mix of agency employees and others—schoolteachers, district farmers, blacksmiths, and missionaries—brought new concepts and ways of thinking. As the authority of the chiefs faded, the Sioux became decentralized, nonprogressive people moving to outlying areas to farm and raise cattle, as part of the process promoted for their acculturation. The social interconnectivity among Lakota extended families, what the Lakotas called *tiospaye*, grew strained. Without buffalo they had little need to move about to hunt them, so many of the tribesmen moved from the tipis of old into solid log or frame cabins and worked their land. Outside these homes stood one or more wagons for hauling people and goods. Inside the structures the people now slept in beds above the floor rather than on pads or mattresses. In addition to stock raising, the men labored as woodchoppers and freight haulers, mostly for government and contract suppliers. In some communities the mixed-blood population increased and prospered over the full-bloods, intensifying economic disparity and jealousy.

Agents gave heartening prospects for the future in their annual reports, but the remodeling of the Sioux into husbandmen was neither quick nor easy. The Indians planted the land and raised their cattle, but nature challenged them. Grasshopper and locust infestations came with discouraging frequency. Blistering hot winds brought drought conditions or made them worse. Game grew ever scarcer. Government provisions were generally insufficient and often of poor quality, and the people frequently had to butcher and eat their cattle to survive.

Education and religion were key elements of the acculturation plan. Day schools and boarding schools, both government-funded ones and those maintained by the Roman Catholic Church, were established and flourished. Industrial farm schools were also opened. Churches, mainly Catholic and Episcopalian, became mainstays for the people who converted to Christianity. It was through the churches and schools that much of the local transformation of the Sioux progressed. Indeed, through church and school influence, many of the Lakotas at last took Christian names.

Not all change occurred on the reservation. Off-reservation boarding schools, established for Indians from many tribes in Carlisle, Pennsylvania, and Hampton, Virginia, increasingly took Sioux students away for long periods. At these "away schools" Indian children learned assorted domestic, industrial, and social skills, but they also learned to read and write English. When they returned home, their newly acquired abilities were not always so useful, but their learning in English proved valuable in unexpected ways. Having attended school—either on the reservation or far away in Pennsylvania or Virginia—they had a better understanding of white ways, including how the government worked. They could also digest what was said in the newspapers, which they found in the traders' stores in towns such as Chamberlain and Pierre. They grasped how the government's actions affected their people and could explain these things to the chiefs. Because they could write in English and Lakota, they could send letters. Besides the mail, they learned to get information from the telegraph and telephone, which eventually came to the agencies. As transportation improved, it also became a means of communication. Over the decades myriad trails were forged among reservation communities and with the white towns along the Missouri. With permission, some of the people journeyed by wagon or train to other agencies and reservations to visit friends and relatives, which broadened networks of communication even more.

Despite these changes, the quality of Lakota life generally worsened. Supplies and beef issues stipulated in the 1868 treaty came late or not at all. Sometimes they were fraudulently reduced. The agents were the supreme authority. The role of the chiefs diminished, and tribal society weakened. Hoping to speed the process, the government banned the sacred Sun Dance, a profound cultural mainstay of the Sioux, and further proscribed or degraded other dances, traditional practices, and rituals. Subtle sharing of authority occasionally arose between an agent and his wards. In 1881, for example, the Brulé headman Crow Dog, chief of Indian police at the

Rosebud Agency, shot and killed Chief Spotted Tail following a local dispute. The incident reflected the growing dichotomy between the tenets of traditional Sioux leadership and power attained under reservation conditions. The Great Sioux Reservation was a difficult place, as one observer noted: "a forlorn, straggling concentration camp in the middle of the vast empty spaces of Dakota Territory."[10]

In these difficult times whites connived to gain more Teton land. As settlement and development surged in the Black Hills, officeholders coveted the remaining Lakota holdings. A single major wagon trail led from Fort Pierre on the Missouri to Deadwood in the Black Hills. As the mayor of Pierre concluded, "Our future depends upon the country west of us. It is not land we want—but communication with the Black Hills." Simply put, the presence of the reservation impeded progress. Improved access to that region demanded new roads across Sioux land between the Black Hills and the burgeoning farm communities east of the Missouri River. Those going to the Hills traveled west from Sioux City, Iowa, across Nebraska via the Fremont, Elkhorn & Missouri Valley Railroad, and then to the Black Hills from the south. By the early 1880s a coalition of economic interests, including freighters, railroad and business conglomerates, cattle owners, land boomers, and prospective immigrants, all encouraged by the territorial press, began calling for yet another cession of Sioux land. Two railways had completed preliminary surveys across Indian country and now idled on the east bank of the Missouri at Pierre and Chamberlain, awaiting only congressional approval to initiate construction toward the Black Hills. Because the Indians could no longer be removed from the path of civilization, non-Indians found new justifications, some grounded in tenets of European land-use philosophy. Their goal was to diminish the Indians' land base and open the excess for their own purposes.[11]

In 1882, only six years after the taking of the Black Hills, the House of Representatives Committee on Indian Affairs endorsed breaking up what remained of the Great Sioux Reservation. Observing that the Indian-held tract was larger than the states of Indiana, South Carolina, and West Virginia combined, the committee argued that the reservation isolated the Black Hills "from the civilized world." Only 24,000 Indians lived there, only 6,000 of them adult males. Conversely, east of the reserve, Dakota boasted occupancy by 150,000 white people "who have brought into cultivation nearly 2,000,000 acres of land, [besides] organized into districts, townships, and counties, liberally dotted with cities and villages, with 1,100 miles of railroads in active operation."[12] The secretary of the interior reported that "the quantity of land within the reservation is much greater than is needed for the Indians living thereupon" and recommended that the reservation be reduced, "and the Indians established on the reserved portion [be] best adapted to their wants."[13]

The resulting congressional act, shepherded by Dakota Territorial delegate Richard F. Pettigrew, created a commission to meet with the Sioux and gain release of 11,000,000 acres (approximately 17,000 square miles). This time the land to be taken ran generally in a swath between the Black Hills cession and the 102nd meridian of longitude, besides all of the tract running east to the Missouri between the Big Cheyenne River and White River. What remained of the Great Sioux Reservation was to be split into five reserves in respect to each of the five agencies—Standing Rock, Cheyenne River, Pine Ridge, Rosebud, and Lower Brulé (Crow Creek, on the east side of the Missouri, would be unaffected). Instead of money the Indians would receive 26,000 head of cattle for the tract, translated to about eight cents per acre. The Indians would also receive personnel to educate and train them for ten years, and each head of family might claim 320 acres of land, with 80 acres added for each child under eighteen.[14]

Headed by former Dakota Territory governor Newton Edmunds and including territorial officials Peter C. Shannon and James H. Teller of Yankton, all with vested interests in the outcome, the commission was to ascertain whether the Indians were open to conceding more land "and, if so, what portion." As in 1876, the commission ignored article 12 of the Fort Laramie Treaty calling for approval by three-fourths of the adult males on the reservation, claiming that the precedent had already been set. Honesty was not their chief concern. Joined by Episcopal missionary the Reverend Samuel P. Hinman, who interpreted the proceedings, Edmunds and his colleagues misrepresented, cajoled, and threatened the people with removal to the Indian Territory. Most Indians did not fully understand the agreement, and the commission was clearly dishonest in its representations. The people at Cheyenne River were especially opposed because so much of their land was targeted for white settlement. In the end those Indians who approved the agreement signed from fear, and the commission obtained only 384 signatures from Pine Ridge, Rosebud, Cheyenne River, and Standing Rock (besides 20 signatures acquired from the Santee Reservation). Those at Crow Creek had not been consulted (31 later signed), and those at Lower Brulé rejected the plan outright.[15]

Members of the Indian Rights Association (IRA), a Philadelphia-based activist group dedicated to Indian acculturation, challenged the Edmunds commission's procedures. So poorly had the commission done its work that the U.S. Senate appropriated $10,000 to consult with the Sioux again. Reappointed by the secretary of the interior, the Edmunds body's efforts were similarly fraudulent. As a later inquiry showed, they secured signatures from as many as 144 Indian boys aged three to sixteen. Their negotiations throughout lacked full disclosure of what would become of remaining Sioux lands after the five reservations were created. A subcommittee of its Indian Affairs Committee visited the Great Sioux Reservation to inquire into allegations of fraud, after which the Senate spurned the Edmunds accord altogether. Nothing was resolved, however; the Indians would have to give up their land eventually. Knowing this, Senate committee members proposed establishment of a permanent fund to benefit the Indians from sale of their surplus land once an agreement was reached.[16]

Occasional draft bills emerged in the interim, but Congress did not reopen the matter meaningfully for six years.[17] Meanwhile white settlement in eastern Dakota continued, and the Black Hills prospered. The national mood was not in the Indians' favor. Almost unanimously the American public embraced breaking up large Indian reservations and providing for allotment in severalty (individual land ownership) as a means to assimilate Indian peoples. It was a long-held concept championed in the 1880s by Republican senator Henry L. Dawes of Massachusetts and others. Antithetical to the communal view of land that the tribes still held, allotment drew broad political support from non-Indians, especially in its promotion of the supposedly civilizing influences inherent in private property ownership. Ownership of private property should stimulate Indians' work ethic and further erode the authority of the chiefs, which often blocked acculturation. Even humanists supported its precepts.[18]

In 1887 Congress passed the General Allotment Act—the so-called Dawes Act. Western politicians claimed to agree with its objectives, but they especially welcomed it as a means to divest the Indians of surplus acreage. Army captain Richard H. Pratt, director of the Indian boarding school in Pennsylvania, and others went even farther. Pratt believed that the Indians would soon fritter away their holdings and be forced into jobs. Thomas J. Morgan, commissioner of Indian Affairs, summed it up for everyone when he said the Dawes Act prefaced a "new era in the status of the Indians." The measure authorized the president to allot land to reservation occupants at his own discretion without their consent and with title to be held tax-free by the government for twenty-five years. At the conclusion of that period individuals would receive patents in fee for allotted lands and full citizenship. Each head of family would be given 160 acres, with smaller plots going to others and the surplus targeted for sale to white settlers under the Homestead Act. Significantly, a critical proviso permitted the government to opt for purchasing the surplus lands and opening them to white settlers even before Indian allotments were assigned. President Grover Cleveland signed the measure with misgivings, knowing, as did Dawes, that whites would exploit its provisions. Few of the Indians on any of the western reservations understood what the law required. Fewer still could conceive of what 160 acres even looked like. Notwithstanding its stated high purposes, allotment tragically accelerated Indian dispossession.[19]

Armed with the Dawes Act and a new Sioux bill, another commission sought to gain the same tract from the Sioux in 1888, specifically, to divide "a portion of the reservation of the Sioux Nation of Indians in Dakota into separate reservations and to secure the relinquishment of the Indian title to the remainder."[20] Its chairman was Captain Pratt. Pratt's associates were John V. Wright (former Confederate colonel, Democratic congressman, and judge of the Tennessee Supreme Court) and the Reverend William J. Cleveland (Episcopal minister to the Brulés at Rosebud). As before, the commission traveled to the different agencies and, except for the price, offered almost identical terms as in 1882. Unlike the 1882 commission, however, it would seek the required three-fourths approval. This time the acquired land would be sold to white settlers at fifty cents per acre (slightly higher for town site lots), with proceeds going into a trust fund for the Indians to facilitate allotment. The reservation would then be broken up into five entities, with the boundary of Crow Creek remaining unaffected.

Many white Dakotans who supported the proposal urged extra rations, wagons and buggies, and even teams of horses as gifts as well as other bribes to procure Indian signatures. One Sioux leader was told that "the Indian better take what he can get as the land would be taken in any event."[21] At the outset the National Indian Defence Association (NIDA), a rights group countering the IRA and headquartered in Washington, D.C., urged the Lakotas to stand fast against the measure. The NIDA's leader, Dr. Thomas Bland, believed that it was too disadvantageous to the Sioux.

Pratt's presence was also a problem. For many Sioux, he symbolized the separation of parents from their children, so they resented him. The tribesmen at Standing Rock duly resisted. The commissioners, having garnered only twenty-two adult male signatures in three weeks from the more than one thousand present, moved on to Cheyenne River. At Cheyenne River they encountered a mood just as unfriendly, so they continued down the Missouri to Crow Creek, where the largely non-Teton Sioux inhabitants appeared more approachable. Pratt's members netted ninety signatures at Crow Creek before crossing over to Lower Brulé. The commissioners were clearly discouraged, but then they received word from Washington to halt further visits pending a change of tactic. Instead of the commission going to individual agencies, delegates from all the reservation agencies, along with their respective agents, should meet at Lower Brulé in the autumn to hear the plan and approve it.

The council that opened on September 24 brought together many Lakota chiefs and headmen, including Miniconjous Bear Eagle, White Swan, and Charging Eagle; Sans Arcs Charger and Spotted Eagle; Two Kettles leader Swift Bird; Blackfeet Sioux leader Little No Heart; Brulés Two Strike and Swift Bear; Oglalas No Flesh, American Horse, and George Sword, who was chief of the agency police at Pine Ridge; and Hunkpapas Gall and John Grass from Standing Rock. Sitting Bull was also in attendance but played little role in the proceedings. Neither Chief Red Cloud nor Chief Young Man Afraid of His Horses, an instrumental Oglala progressive at Pine Ridge Agency, attended. Each was known to oppose the plan. Many of these leaders, as well as others, would become prominent voices on behalf of their people and would factor significantly in events over the months ahead.

At Lower Brulé, the delegates stood united in their resistance to any negotiation that would yield more land. Progressives among them argued that former Indian lands east of the Missouri were selling for $1.25 per acre. Lakotas, they said, should at least get the same. They repeatedly countered the commission's arguments, in one instance protesting a bid to extend the school program specified in the 1868 Fort Laramie pact by twenty years. The government had not yet fulfilled the original treaty, the Indians told Pratt and his cohorts. Schools had not been established on the reservation until five or ten years after 1868, and existing schools still had ample time to operate before the proposed extensions were required. Following interminable meetings with no promise of agreement, the council finally ended. The frustrated commissioners departed. A perturbed Captain Pratt proposed in his report that the agreement be finalized without the Indians' consent.[22]

The Indians at Lower Brulé left the door open for further discussions, however, even for potential agreement. They argued openly among themselves over various aspects and showed an amenable attitude toward terms more favorable to the government. They even indicated that a meeting in the national capital might yield results. Just such an assembly occurred the following month when the Indians met with secretary of the Interior William F. Vilas in Washington, D.C., on October 13. Among the sixty-one chiefs in attendance were Sitting Bull, Gall, and Gray Eagle from Standing Rock Agency; American Horse, George Sword, Little Wound, and the Northern Cheyenne Little Chief from Pine Ridge; and Spotted Eagle, Charger, and Big Foot from Cheyenne River. Both Red Cloud and Young Man Afraid of His Horses were opposed. Neither was invited to the proceedings.

At the Interior Department, the Indians criticized the government's broken promises from past treaties, particularly its noncompliance with provisions involving education and farming. They complained of the proposed payment of $0.50 per acre in the recent bill, asking for $1.25, and demanded to know which lands were to be ceded as surplus. Secretary Vilas initially balked at the price, terming it "nearly as much money as was paid to France for the entire territory of Louisiana." In response, the secretary offered an accommodation via a graduating scale that would permit the land to be sold for $1.00 per acre over the first three years. The price would fall to $0.75 for the next two years, then $0.50 for the next five. Thereafter the government would purchase all remaining unsold land for $0.50 an acre. Monies derived from the sale of Sioux land would go into a special Treasury Department account for the people for five years. After that receipts would go to the government. Amid much doubt, forty-seven of the chiefs acceded to the proposal and took the train back to Dakota Territory for what would prove to be the last days of the Great Sioux Reservation. The Pratt Commission expressed regret that its failure disappointed Dakotans and citizens across the nation.[23]

In December 1888 a number of chiefs convened at Pine Ridge to revisit their complaints in a missive to Secretary Vilas. The council included Red Cloud, Young Man Afraid of His Horses, and Little Wound. Expressing long-standing discontent, their report diplomatically concluded: "We want to know what it is that the Great Father has asked us to do that we did not do. We dress like white people and send our children to the schools. We think the Great Father's Indian children pay more attention to what he says than his white children do."[24] Their frustration mirrored concerns of Native peoples throughout the country, who dreaded the historical inevitability rooted in the ways of all colonial powers. What the Lakotas were enduring was the culmination of the long process of Indian removal that had begun generations earlier along the eastern seaboard—a continuum of displacement, decline, and loss.

THREE

Broken Faith

The Tetons had a long history and had weathered difficult periods before. They had survived wars with enemy tribes as well as with whites, crippling diseases, repeated dispossession from their traditional domain, and now sedentary reservation existence. But the two years from early 1889 through early 1891 were the most devastating of all. A convergence of misfortunes was to blame, including further manipulative land losses. Coupled with natural disasters, these caused unprecedented desperation and at last appalling human tragedy.

The Lakotas stood in the way of progress, defined largely as greed. Dividing Dakota Territory into two states had long been discussed. The idea took on increasing momentum in the late 1880s, especially when a Republican presidential victory in November 1888 raised hopes ever higher and with them pressure to negotiate the Sioux land issue anew. In February 1889 Congress passed an omnibus measure providing for admission of North Dakota and South Dakota later that year. Rapid dissolution of the previously reduced Great Sioux Reservation seemed more of a necessity than ever, and Congress responded with more inspired actions to achieve that end. Westerners applauded the prospect. The new tracts would provide land for an estimated 70,000 new settlers. Caught up in an increasing flurry of economic expansion, prospective political dominance, and the business opportunities presented by the accelerated dismantling of the reservation, Republican politicians were jubilant.

With the Indian Appropriation Act, signed by outgoing president Grover Cleveland on March 2, 1889, Congress authorized incoming president Benjamin Harrison to appoint yet another commission to deal with the Lakotas. Its purpose was to win "full and complete cession and relinquishment to the United States of a portion of their reservation." On the same day the Senate drafted a new Sioux bill that contained more generous concessions than the bill of the previous year. The new bill proposed dividing the reservation into the familiar five components, provided allotment privileges to individual Indians, with surplus property to be made available to settlers, and extended educational benefits under the 1868 treaty by twenty years. The Indians would receive their requested $1.25 per acre, but only for all land homesteaded in the first three years following the act's ratification. Over the ensuing two years they would receive $0.75 an acre, and $0.50 an acre thereafter. Furthermore, the secretary of the Interior would appropriate $3,000,000 from the treasury as a permanent fund for the Sioux, with yearly interest set at 5 percent. Proceeds from sales of Lakota land would reimburse the government for the fund. The government pledged to assume all expenses connected with surveying and opening the ceded property, something that it had refused to do in 1888 when it decreed that such costs should be deducted from the Indians' proceeds. Finally, Congress allocated $28,000 (forty dollars per head) to repay Chief Red Cloud's Oglalas for ponies confiscated by the army in 1876. All parts of the 1868 Fort Laramie Treaty not otherwise in conflict with the new bill would remain in effect. The Indians must ratify the proposal as specified in article 12, with majority approval of three-fourths of all adult males on the reservation over the age of eighteen.[1]

A commission appointed by President Harrison was to present the measure to the Indians. Only if the Sioux rejected it would the commissioners attempt a modified settlement. To ensure its success, Congress gave the commission incentive, earmarking $25,000 "for procuring the assent of the Sioux." Promised rewards gave Indian Department officials small comfort, however. They feared that the Sioux would yet hold out for a better price, despite reports from Dakota suggesting their willingness to sign. Even the conservative Red Cloud, who had resisted all previous measures, was said to support the new bill. But officials remained apprehensive lest a diplomatic setback induce an invasion of Sioux land by settlers who awaited word of success along the Missouri River.[2]

Such fears were justified. Boomers were already perched along the eastern fringe of the reservation. Their roughshod claim shanties dotted the treeless prairie. The towns of Pierre and Chamberlain reported large rushes of settlers early in May, and boomers were said already to have preempted land on a small strip of the reservation south of Rosebud and Pine Ridge. Such intrusions threatened to emulate recent land openings in Oklahoma and evoked stern warnings from the territorial press. A Yankton newspaper breathlessly admonished would-be adventurers that they faced "a tribe of vigorous, well-fed, stouthearted barbarians, armed to the teeth, superbly mounted and with their native love for atrocities hardly subdued." Newly appointed secretary of the Interior John W. Noble deplored settlers' impatience and suspended survey operations for fear of alarming the Sioux. Further encroachment might embarrass the commission and prevent success, so on May 14 orders to investigate the disturbances reached reservation agents.[3]

Dakota territorial officials, meanwhile, urged speedy selection of the commissioners. President Harrison announced three appointees on April 19. Former Ohio governor Charles Foster, a political crony destined to be secretary of the treasury, would be chairman. Responding to his appointment with the cynical viewpoint of many, he intoned: "The Indian is a queer character and pretty soon he will become extinct, so that if a man wants the experience of serving on an Indian Commission he has no time to lose." Harrison's second selection was equally fatuous. William Warner, one-time mayor of Kansas City, lately a Republican representative from Missouri, and newly elected commander-in-chief of the Grand Army of the Republic, otherwise possessed few credentials. The Cherokee Indians had once opposed Warner's appointment to a commission negotiating for their lands. Unlike Foster, however, he represented western interests and, as the *Yankton Daily Press* observed, was "not likely to be hampered in his dealing with the Sioux by any overstrained sentimentalism."[4]

Harrison's third choice actually augured well for success. Major General George Crook, commander of the Military Division of the Missouri, was familiar to the Tetons. They remembered his dogged campaigning in 1876, which had contributed to ending widespread conflict with them on the northern plains. Whether the presence of "Three Stars," as the Indians called Crook, reflected Harrison's hopes to intimidate the people militarily or whether his appointment reflected his well-known humanitarian philosophy toward them remains unclear. Many Sioux expressed utmost trust in the general, but his presence provoked bitter memories among others. Either way, Crook appeared to be the ideal man to persuade the Indians to accept the Sioux bill. The body was commonly called the Crook Commission among Indians and non-Indians alike. On at least one Lakota winter count calendar, 1889 would be portrayed as the year "'Three Stars' Came to Buy Land." Pleased with Crook's selection, Dakotans regretted the absence of representatives more responsive to local interests. "It cannot be written," declared the *Yankton Daily Press and Dakotaian*, "that any one of the three is the right man in the right place." Even so, attention to the commission's progress rivaled press coverage of statehood, a linkage by which the Lakotas in the end lost much of their remaining land.[5]

The Crook Commission assembled in Chicago for preliminary meetings in May. The number of adult Sioux males totaled 5,678, so the commissioners would need to win 4,259 to assure ratification. To eliminate jealousy that might arise among tribesmen should they choose a smaller station, Foster, Warner, and Crook strategized to start work at Rosebud, largest of the Sioux agencies. Moreover, because the Pratt Commission had quit before reaching Rosebud, it was believed that those Indians might be less entrenched against the measure. Nor was the Pratt Commission's fiasco at Standing Rock forgotten. Foster, Warner, and Crook would work Rosebud first. On May 29, 1889, the commissioners and their clerical staff departed by train for the reservation.[6]

Reaching Rosebud two days later, the commissioners were quickly disabused. Agent Libbeus F. Spencer had failed to assemble his charges, and several days elapsed as scattered bands of Brulé, Miniconjou, and Two Kettle Sioux slowly congregated at the agency. Hoping to instill a receptive mood among them, the commissioners staged lavish meals and even permitted dancing, forbidden since 1883. Of the three commissioners, only Crook commanded immediate respect. Foster and Warner "were strangers to the Indians' customs, and were looked upon with more suspicion." After one feast, however, the Indians adopted Chairman Foster, dubbing him "Young Man Proud of His Tail." Crook became principal speaker for the commission for the balance of the proceedings at Rosebud and elsewhere.[7]

Beyond such ceremony, no genuine amity existed among the Rosebud Sioux. On June 3 they gathered to listen as Foster introduced the bill through interpreters then adjourned to consider it in council. The next day Warner explained the allotment system, the educational benefits, and the $3,000,000 interest-bearing fund. The Brulés stalled, typifying fears shared by Indians across the reservation as they contemplated past government deception over the Black Hills. They saw no reason to sacrifice their present status for one that many could hardly comprehend. Some in fact believed that allotment was a contrived effort to force their imprisonment on fenced property. The traditional chiefs rightly suspected that approval meant tribal disintegration and further loss of their power among the people.[8]

The Rosebud Sioux particularly resented the government's dereliction in regard to the 1868 treaty. When they charged default on the educational clause, the commissioners explained that teachers often refused reservation employment because of the Indians' hostility during the 1870s. The Sioux also objected to including Santee Sioux and Poncas who had settled on the small Nebraska tract. Some had been party to the 1868 pact, however, and the commissioners firmly defended their rights, knowing that their signatures might be more easily obtained. Some of the Rosebud mixed-bloods understood and favored the new bill, but more populous full-bloods, who could not shake suspicions of deceit, were staunchly opposed. The schism between progressives and nonprogressives deepened as time passed at Rosebud, and even those who favored the agreement became reluctant to sign for fear of reprisal.[9]

The commissioners employed bold tactics to break the impasse. Crook worked on individual Indians behind the scenes. He talked, persuaded, intimidated, and played the factions against one another. Doubtless all three members utilized the expense fund to full advantage. At length the full-bloods began to waver. The old Brulé Swift Bear, a progressive, led the way after Crook promised that the agreement would not affect the quantity of rations supplied to the Sioux. When the commissioners reconvened with the Indians on June 7, Crook berated the holdouts: "This indolent life . . . has made squaws of you, and if you don't work and help yourselves you will get such a bad record that the Government will have to send out dolls and rattles to amuse you."[10] The tide turned after Standing Bear spoke for the bill, and Crook ordered the signing to begin. Many Indians and mixed-bloods rushed forward amid general excitement. But malcontents led by Hollow Horn Bear and High Hawk shouted the full-bloods away from the table, and they filed out of the council. About 300 mixed-bloods and progressive Brulés approved the bill. The next few days drew an even better response, as the full-bloods now feared exclusion from the benefits. When the commissioners left for Pine Ridge on June 13, success at Rosebud was assured; of 1,476 adult males registered there, 1,455 had signed.[11]

Chairman Foster credited the victory to Crook, and the territorial press echoed the praise: "General Crook stands solid with the scalp lifters of the Sioux domain." But success at Rosebud undermined the fragile Sioux unity. The factional divisions that Foster, Warner, and Crook had encountered soon ruptured completely. Nevertheless, Dakotans rejoiced at the news from Rosebud. They now foresaw success at all the agencies.[12]

The commission's visit to the next agency, Pine Ridge, shattered this optimism. Unlike the tribal mix encountered at Rosebud, Pine Ridge was the home of the Oglala Tetons, many of whose chiefs had been contemporaries of Crazy Horse. Most were followers of the aging and unreconstructed Red Cloud, who had led the war effort along the Bozeman Trail in the 1860s then gone to the Great Sioux Reservation and stayed there. Reflecting their leader, the Indians at Pine Ridge exhibited hostility from the outset and greeted the commissioners armed and decked out in war regalia. They dispersed only after Crook rebuked them. When they reassembled, Foster read them the bill, explained the commission's task, and told them, "You must know that you cannot now live as your fathers did."[13]

Reluctance remained manifest, however, due largely to the machinations of the National Indian Defence Association (NIDA), based in Washington, D.C. Headed by Dr. Thomas A. Bland, the association worked to capitalize on and consolidate Red Cloud's disdain for cession. Unlike the Indian Rights Association, which promoted the concept of allotment, the NIDA argued against rapid change and mustered its resources to oppose it. NIDA members believed that the Indians would request desired benefits from the government when they were ready. Even before the commission reached Pine Ridge, Bland's group distributed flyers printed in Lakota among Oglalas, urging total resistance to cession. Bland had even written personally to Red Cloud, advising him against discussing the matter with the commissioners. Most of the other Pine Ridge leaders, including progressive band leaders Little Wound, Young Man Afraid of His Horses, and Big Road, stood with Red Cloud, although American Horse and No Flesh remained uncommitted. Thus near-total disapproval lingered throughout the first meeting at Pine Ridge on June 15.[14]

After Foster and Warner finished explaining the bill's provisions, a large group of mounted Oglalas rushed the council and scattered the assembled tribesmen, forestalling a favorable response by progressives. So determined to resist any discussion were the Sioux that they threatened to dismantle their tipis and return to their homes. "Red Cloud's influence," observed the

New York Times, "for the time seems to prevail with apparent unanimity." When the council reconvened on June 17, Indian spokesmen denounced the bill and again charged the government with not having fulfilled pledges made in 1868. "You want to buy more land," Red Cloud told the commissioners, "and I looked around to see if I could see any boxes of money that you brought here to buy more land, and I could not see any, and now I think this is the talk of sugar again." The commission won one small victory. At the end of the meeting a number of Northern Cheyennes, sustained at Pine Ridge since their flight from the Indian Territory in 1878, marked the signature rolls. Crook had secretly promised to protect them from the Sioux and to inform the president of their wishes for removal to their tribe's reservation in Montana.[15]

Northern Cheyenne accession failed to inspire the Oglalas. Several mixed-bloods attached their names, but all the others refused. American Horse, who was "a better speaker than any of us," according to Crook, questioned the legality of the Nebraska borderline, which violated the reservation boundary stipulated in 1868. When he further demanded that plots of 80, 160, and 320 acres be staked out to give the Indians an idea of how much land they would actually receive, the commissioners obliged. They also assured the Lakotas that neither the money appropriated to compensate the loss of Red Cloud's ponies nor the commission's working expenses were to be deducted from the proceeds from Indian land sales.[16]

American Horse was in his late forties. He had been a leader since his days fighting alongside Crazy Horse in the Fetterman battle of 1866 before siding with Red Cloud on the reservation. He worried the commissioners, because their audiences diminished considerably when American Horse filibustered the sessions for several days. Crook worked to prevent total collapse of the negotiations by cajoling individuals and small groups behind the scenes, which infuriated Red Cloud. The old chief, now nearly blind, reacted angrily, fearing his people's susceptibility. On June 20 he ordered the commission off the reservation and paraded past its members with 400 protesting Oglalas. On the next day, however, American Horse, No Flesh, and other progressives privately coached by Crook came out for the bill. The general had convinced them that they would never receive a better offer; Congress would take the land with or without Sioux permission. One week later No Flesh, American Horse, and their bands signed the measure in full view of the dissenters, who, as Warner declared, would rather "slap the Great White Father in the face." By no means all progressives had signed, however, and those who did formed only a minority. The commission won less than 50 percent support at Pine Ridge. Of the more than 1,500 eligible voters, only 684 assented, mostly mixed-bloods and Cheyennes.[17]

The will of Red Cloud had clearly prevailed at Pine Ridge, and his uncompromising attitude irked Indian bureau officials even more after the commission's departure. The veteran Oglala, along with Little Wound and Young Man Afraid of His Horses, scorned bribes of $200 each to sign the bill. Agent Hugh D. Gallagher termed the chief's presence "the least promising element among the Indians of this agency." Two days after the commission's departure, the secretary of the Interior, John W. Noble, directed that Red Cloud be stripped of all authority and labeled an "obstructionist." Noble further directed that the progressive American Horse be identified as "Chief of the Sioux, or the one favored by the Government among them."[18]

Leaving Pine Ridge, Warner and Crook proceeded to Lower Brulé Agency on the west bank of the Missouri, while Chairman Foster visited the Santee tract in Nebraska and won nearly unanimous approval there. The Eastern Sioux already held lands in severalty and had showed marked progress over the Tetons. Foster rejoined the others at Lower Brulé, where opposition centered on the old chief Iron Nation, who had prevented many of his people from signing the 1888 measure. On July 3 the chairman called on the Indians to sign and "commence our Fourth of July here this afternoon." But to achieve the bargain it took a feast, a baseball game, and Crook's written promise to resettle the Indians at Rosebud if homesteaders overran their reservation. With success assured at Lower Brulé, the commissioners ferried the Missouri to Crow Creek Agency.[19]

There they encountered resistance. The Crow Creek Indians composed a conglomerate of various Sioux bands, including Brulés and Santees. The largest group were the Lower Yanktonais, who appeared evenly divided on the bill. Two chiefs, White Ghost and Drifting Goose, led the opposition. They objected primarily to past government negligence in removing whites already settled on their land. In 1885 President Chester A. Arthur had restored Crow Creek to the public domain. Grover Cleveland had soon revoked the order, but whites had occupied Crow Creek in the interim. Now they refused to leave, and the government had done little but issue warnings to the intruders. Foster acknowledged the grievance and declared the squatters' actions illegal but offered no solution. The Yanktonais also desired land proportions under allotment equitable with those assigned to other agencies in the bill or fair compensation. General Crook, regarded by White Ghost as the "Great Father's big whip," promised to recommend congressional action on the complaint. To facilitate approval the commissioners also agreed to let the chiefs sign in Washington, D.C., in return for delivering the immediate signatures of their men. The council adjourned on July 9 with fewer than half the total 305 possible votes in favor. With only two agencies remaining, and both reportedly opposed to the measure, hopes for victory dimmed. At Crow Creek, wrote Crook, "Foster got his fill of negotiations with the Indians."[20]

Cheyenne River Agency indeed proved difficult. By calculation the commission needed about 1,500 more adult male signatures to attain the three-fourths majority required for Sioux ratification. But most of the 749 Miniconjou, Sans Arc, Two Kettle, and Blackfeet Sioux men at Cheyenne River appeared committed to defeating the bill. Many of them had gone with Sitting Bull into Canada in 1876 and 1877 rather than face reservation confinement. "These Indians," reported the commissioners, "were practically as little civilized as when they first surrendered [in 1880–81], and [remained] opposed unalterably to progress of any kind." Furthermore, many of them occupied lands directly in the path of white settlement if the agreement was signed.[21]

Leading the resistance was Hump, the Miniconjou traditionalist, who posed a constant concern to agent Charles E. McChesney. McChesney hoped to present at least an appearance of control over his charges and for that reason had appointed Hump as chief of the agency police. The defiant old warrior now held sway over all the Indians at Cheyenne River. Crook knew this and ordered Major George M. Randall from nearby Fort Bennett to join the commission at the agency, as a safeguard against trouble. If kind words failed, psychological coercion might induce the signings. The Indians remained adamant. Many believed that the government would simply hold the land five years before disposing of it for fifty cents per acre rather than at the graduated prices stipulated in the bill. The Cheyenne River Sioux also disliked the proposed southern boundary of the reservation along Cheyenne River, which, if implemented, would prevent them from using fertile bottomlands along the south bank for farming. Existing agency buildings all stood south of the river as well.[22]

Notwithstanding all explanations, the Indians were steadfast in their unwillingness to sign. The commissioners began to suspect outside factors. At Cheyenne River, they reported, "the source of the adverse influence was found to be money." They discovered neither the amount of money given the Indians nor who was supplying it, but the NIDA likely entered their minds. Once more Crook undertook his personal means for gaining assent. Soon the mixed-bloods showed interest. Many of them lived near Bad River, south of and away from Hump's troublesome followers. Should the bill win approval, the Bad River mixed-bloods hoped that settlers might homestead between their land and the turbulent element at Cheyenne River.[23]

Almost inevitably, factional bickering erupted among the people as the councils proceeded. On July 18 tempers flared when the commissioners called for signatures. Two of Hump's warriors leaped into the council room, brandishing clubs to prevent tribesmen from marking the rolls. Lakota policemen hustled them away. A short time later further commotion broke out among the full-bloods. When Crook quieted them by threatening to bring troops from Fort Bennett, many of the Indians came forward to sign. Still, not enough signed. Crook, clearly in charge at Cheyenne River, sought to expedite matters with more promises. He pledged reimbursement for ponies taken from them in 1876, the same promise given to the Pine Ridge Sioux. He agreed to recommend higher salaries for tribal judges on the Court of Indian Offenses and later permitted dancing and distributed free beeves for feasting. Hump and his followers still refused to sign and tried to prevent others from doing so. On July 22 Hump's armed warriors again broke up the council. Angered by this "impolite old reprobate," Crook and the others decided to leave the task of collecting more votes to agent McChesney and Major Randall: the commissioners moved on to Standing Rock Agency.[24]

At Standing Rock the fate of the Sioux bill rested with 600 eligible voters among the 1,121 Hunkpapa, Yanktonai, and Blackfeet Sioux. Almost all these Indians belonged to bands under Sitting Bull, Gall, Mad Bear, and other leaders who had returned from Canada, a tough crowd. The commission's visit was bound to generate apprehension at Standing Rock, and the army command at nearby Fort Yates stood ready for action. Still, despite initial reports, chances for success were not without promise. Reaching no agreement would mean that these Indians could not share in the benefits with other Tetons when the bill passed, and an apparent schism between the Hunkpapa followers of Gall and Sitting Bull might allow persuasion of fence-sitters. Not all of the undecided were Indians. Agent James McLaughlin had passively opposed former proposals and was unenthusiastic about this one, until Morgan, as commissioner of Indian Affairs, explicitly instructed him to ensure success. The government also had armed the commission with more ammunition this time around. To dispel complaints of insufficient compensation, terms of the bill had been modified to correspond more closely with what the chiefs had demanded a year earlier. And the commission had hedged its bet by purposely scheduling its visit to Standing Rock last in hopes of building on success elsewhere.[25]

Foster opened the council on July 26. "My friends," he intoned, "there never was a time in the history of this country when the white man felt so kindly to the Indian as now." Foster and Warner flattered the Sioux for three-quarters of an hour but drew little response. A few days later John Grass, a tall, slender Blackfeet Sioux wearing moccasins, a black suit, and a white shirt with bow tie, began a dialogue in opposition, astounding the commissioners with "monuments of logic" as he raised pertinent questions regarding the treaty of 1868 and its relation to the present bill. John Grass, observed Foster, "struck me as an intellectual giant in comparison with other Indians." On the matter of allotment, the wary Grass told the commissioners:

> You may think it will be a great benefit for us to have our land cut up into small tracts, the same as they are among the white people, but we don't understand that, and we know that the Indians cannot get along and live the same as the white man with the land cut up. The ones that will be able to follow the way the Great Father wishes us to go . . . are those that are in the schools now, and have been brought up with education and can understand these things.[26]

The commissioners sat silent as Grass and others presented their arguments. Foremost, the Standing Rock men wanted permission to choose their own allotments and wanted guarantees of continued subsistence as specified in 1868. Among other things, they accused the government of bad faith. The commissioners agreed to these requests, but no Indians signed. Chagrined, Crook repeated his warning: "In case you do not accept this bill, . . . Congress may open it [the land] without asking your consent again."[27]

With no agreement imminent, McLaughlin and the commissioners turned their attention to individuals who might waver. They passed over Sitting Bull's Hunkpapas, already bolstered by Bland's disapproving NIDA. Besides, McLaughlin's attempt to prod the medicine man into submission with liquor had failed. Sitting Bull remained implacable. "There are things they tell us [that] sound good to hear," Sitting Bull warned his people, "but when they . . . accomplish their purpose, they will go home and will not try to fulfill our agreements with them." The commissioners turned to the Blackfeet Sioux. McLaughlin met secretly with John Grass one evening and promised certain rewards for his support. At length the Blackfeet leader acquiesced, and McLaughlin prepared a statement for him to deliver at the next council. The agent similarly won over Sitting Bull's archrival Gall and Chiefs Mad Bear and Big Head, even as Foster, Warner, and Crook made headway with other tribesmen whose Catholic missionaries supported ratification.[28]

When Chairman Foster reopened the discussion on August 3, John Grass, reading McLaughlin's speech, changed his position gracefully and advised his tribesmen to do likewise if they wished to receive any benefits. He then stepped forward and signed the bill, followed by Gall and others. As they marked the rolls, Sitting Bull and about twenty mounted Hunkpapas tried to break into the enclosure and stampede the assembly. But quick work by the Yanktonai police thwarted them. Sitting Bull, wrote Crook, "flattened out, his wind bag was punctured." Other signers included the chief's nephew, stepson, and son-in-law. When asked what effect opening the reservation would have on the Indians, Sitting Bull replied: "Don't talk to me about Indians; there are no Indians left except those in my band." Signing continued until August 6. The commissioners had more than 600 votes, so they announced their work completed. Foster cabled Secretary Noble: "We have won the fight."[29]

Dakotans cheered news of the success as territorial papers rejoiced for "the good sense of Grass prevailing over the barbarous stupidity of Sitting Bull." In weighing their achievement while en route to Chicago, however, Foster, Warner, and Crook discovered that they in fact lacked the absolute three-quarters of adult male votes required for ratification. Accordingly, they wired McLaughlin, who promptly forwarded more signatures. Standing Rock's final tally stood at 803 and brought the grand total from all Lakota agencies to 4,463 out of 5,678 eligible voters, thereby securing the objective with more than 78 percent. They praised McLaughlin's help as "invaluable."[30]

At Chicago the commissioners received Noble's congratulations. "You have done a great work for humanity," he said, "the Indians included." Within the week the members adjourned to prepare their final report and then meet again at Foster's direction. Their effort seemed a total success.

After passage the Sioux bill would pave the way for the settlement of Dakota even as it complied with federal policy regarding the Tetons. Its enactment, Secretary Noble happily declared, would mark "a long step toward the disintegration of their tribal life."[31]

It would do more. For four decades the Lakotas had endured a succession of treaties grounded in hollow promises of a better life that instead spurred their cultural deterioration and unending impoverishment. The people had gradually accustomed themselves to their dormant reservation status, an existence that guaranteed their security only through dependence. Convinced of the untrustworthy nature of most whites, the Sioux had successfully opposed further transactions until 1889. In that year General Crook, a familiar yet feared player in their history, cowed them into believing they had everything to gain and nothing to lose except more of their land. Ironically, Crook appears to have been willing to connive. His persuasive and somewhat excessive devices, coupled with those of agents like McLaughlin, helped instill in the people something long missing: hope for their future.

Less than three weeks after the commission departed from Standing Rock that hope took a mortal blow. The order came down late in August. Beef rations at Rosebud would be slashed by 2 million pounds, at Pine Ridge by 1 million, and at Standing Rock, Cheyenne River, Crow Creek, and Lower Brulé by proportional amounts. By the Indian Appropriation Act, an economy-minded Congress appropriated only $900,000 for the Sioux for fiscal year 1890—$100,000 less than in the two previous years and the smallest appropriation since 1877. Allowing for beef shrinkage between autumn purchase and springtime distribution, Commissioner Morgan estimated daily beef subsistence per individual at about 1.9 pounds versus the 3 pounds promised in 1877. The measure took the Lakotas by surprise and stunned the land commissioners, who had assured the Indians repeatedly that their accession to the bill would in no way affect their rations. "No action," they stated, "could possibly have been more ill timed." Bemoaned Crook: "It will be impossible to convince them that it is not one result of their signing." The commissioners appealed to Noble: "If there is any way that can be devised to remedy the (in our opinion) grave error . . . , we most earnestly urge such action as will result in its speedy correction." They added: "It is . . . an act of injustice closely approaching cruelty."[32]

Predictably, Washington officials did nothing to correct the deficiency. As Crook had feared, the Sioux reacted bitterly. At Pine Ridge agent Gallagher said that those Oglalas who signed the measure "were made the

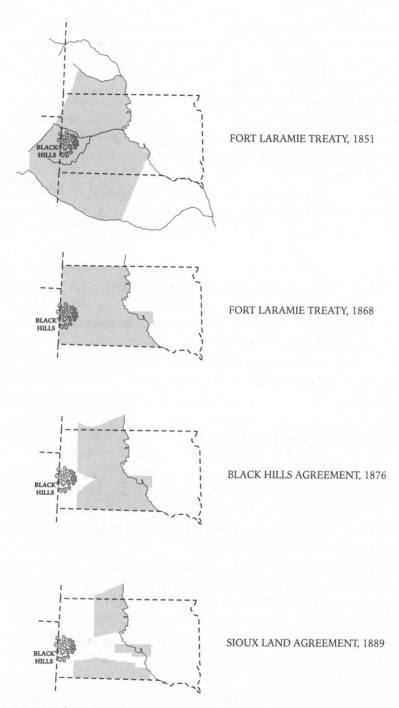

FORT LARAMIE TREATY, 1851

FORT LARAMIE TREATY, 1868

BLACK HILLS AGREEMENT, 1876

SIOUX LAND AGREEMENT, 1889

Map 1. Lakota Cumulative Land Losses, 1851–90. Map by Robert G. Pilk.

targets for derision by the non-signers, who called them fools and dupes."
Turbulence mounted throughout the reservation. In an attempt to allay
Sioux concerns, the commissioners arranged for a delegation of chiefs to
visit Washington in late autumn 1889. They hoped that in a forum setting
government leaders could perhaps explain the ration cut to the Indians'
satisfaction. Foster, Warner, and Crook hoped as well to dramatize Sioux
feelings on the matter while advancing promises made to the people not
specifically contained in the agreement.[33]

On November 2 North Dakota and South Dakota entered the Union
as the thirty-ninth and fortieth states. Six weeks later, on December 18, accompanied by Lakota leaders from the Teton agencies, the commissioners
met with Noble and congressional representatives at the Department of
the Interior. The meeting produced nothing. Bureaucratic dissembling out-
weighed real interest in the Indians' grievances. The next day the commissioners escorted the chiefs to the White House, where the Oglala American
Horse eloquently addressed President Harrison, asking for restoration of
"our rations that have been cut away from us." The president listened sym-
pathetically but made no commitment. Depressed and word weary, the delegation returned to South Dakota as empty handed as when it departed.[34]

On Christmas Eve the commission sent Secretary Noble its report along
with its recommendations. The members advocated appropriations to repay
Indians other than those at Pine Ridge for army seizures of ponies in 1876
and further urged an equitable monetary settlement with the Crow Creek
people whose land under the Sioux act was proportionately less than that
assigned to other bands. The commissioners urged that surveys be made on
the ceded tract before opening it to homesteaders, who might otherwise
jeopardize the peace. Finally, they asked for an immediate appropriation
to raise the beef ration to its former quantity. For the moment Congress
deferred action.[35]

In the meantime Dakota boomers congregated along the Missouri to
await formal opening by the president. To guard against premature invasion, Noble asked for soldiers to be posted at different points along the river.
Brigadier General Thomas H. Ruger, commander of the Department of
Dakota, led troops into the region to ward off intruders. But rumors of the
reservation's opening spread, and on February 7, 1890, a large rush ensued at
Chamberlain. Indian police, called in to assist authorities, "stood dazed and
helpless" as scores of boomers raced onto Sioux land. Three days later President Harrison proclaimed cession to the United States of 9,274,669 acres to

"be disposed of . . . under the provisions of the homestead law." Settlers immediately dashed across the frozen Missouri River to take possession of coveted claims. Galloping horses drew wagons loaded with lumber and other building materials across the ice. "A house on wheels was dragged across the river at Chamberlain," one observer reported, "and made the nucleus of a new town on the opposite bank." In a message to Congress the same day, Harrison urged consideration of promises that the commission had given the Sioux but declared that "the consent of the Indians to the act was not made dependent upon the adoption of any of these recommendations."[36]

The president had acted impulsively. No surveys had been conducted to determine the boundaries of the new reservations, and the land rush had begun before Indians could select promised allotments. Foster, Warner, and Crook would have failed without assuring the tribesmen extra concessions. In bribing, cajoling, and intimidating the Sioux into signing the bill, the commissioners had intensified divisions among the Indians. Too often they had threatened that Congress would take the land anyway. The commission had come to the reservation at a time when the people normally worked their fields. Crops had languished even as Foster, Warner, and Crook promised repeatedly that there would be no cut in rations. Worst of all, the commissioners raised hopes among many of the people for a better life. Now, with their rations cut and non-Indians overrunning their land, the Sioux were betrayed yet again.

Congress only made everything worse. In April the Senate passed the Sioux Land Act, but the House of Representatives rejected some of its provisions. Compounding the calamity, the House cut Sioux appropriations by $50,000 for fiscal year 1891 and delayed passage of the Indian Appropriation Act until August 1890, too late for the people to receive annuities before winter. The news devastated the Tetons. Oglalas at Pine Ridge considered themselves cheated all around: "There has been gradually growing among them a feeling of indifference as to the future," agent Gallagher reported, "which I attribute to an entire loss of faith in the promises of the Government." At Cheyenne River the Miniconjous required "constant and careful attention." Besides the beef reduction and prospects of facing a cold winter on scattered, imminently constricted reservations with inadequate supplies and the government's failure to begin reservation surveys and provide allotments, the Sioux resented federal sanctions on tribal practices. At some of the agencies, especially Standing Rock, diseases such as whooping cough and influenza wracked the people.[37]

Tragically, all this did not unite the people. It had just the opposite effect. Turning against each other, the Indians aligned more resolutely into divisive factions. At Cheyenne River a correspondent noted the sentiment of Chief Big Foot's people: "That they should be governed by the votes of their brethren in other parts of South Dakota seems to them unjust and cruel."[38] Most signers of the bill acknowledged their blunder. But the nonsigners, mostly traditionalists, taunted them unmercifully, further exacerbating intratribal schisms. Dissension appeared at agency day schools, where conflicts among children reflected the disaffections of their parents. The Lakota Sioux, physically vulnerable to illness and death and psychologically scarred by long internal strife, faced an ominous future—and crisis.

FOUR

Trauma

In March 1890 an old-time beef issue took place just east of the Pine Ridge Agency. Scores of visitors from the Nebraska communities showed up to watch the Oglalas go through what had become a traditional rite since establishment of the agencies on the Great Sioux Reservation two decades earlier. Some 275 head of cattle were held in a V-shaped corral. As the names of families were called out, the beasts were released from the enclosure, singly or in pairs or sometimes in threes, as each issue demanded. Out the animals would run "into a gauntlet" of up to two thousand Indians. Those for whom the particular quarry was intended would peel away to pursue it and eventually dispatch it with a rifle. The women of the family then descended with knives. "In an incredibly small space of time," commented a reporter for the *Chadron Democrat,* "nothing would be left to mark the spot of the butchery but the blood-stained sand. Hide, horns, hoofs and entrails all disappeared with the flesh." In this manner all of the animals were dispatched in forty-five minutes. "Imagine yourself looking over a vast plain covered with a mass of excited semi-barbarous beings and lamed and infuriated animals, some of them yet uncaptured, and their masters in full chase, a mile or two away; here and there a group of braves . . . and squaws skinning, cutting and stowing away the gory mass; near by a crippled and frantic beast being attacked by a retinue of earnest workers for the necessaries of life." For the Lakotas, it was the end of an era; what had carried over onto the reservation as a survival of their buffalo hunting days would soon be supplanted by the establishment of slaughterhouses and the procedural distribution of rations in what one newspaper termed "a more humane manner."[1]

The accounts of this issue of live cattle neglected to characterize the condition of the beef, but it was probably subpar. Cattle that reached Pine Ridge in summer 1889, according to local papers, were "better subjects for the taxidermist than the butcher." Driven up from the south, they were not acclimated to the northern plains and failed to attain measurable weight over winter. "They had not been fit for beef at all," observed a Chadron reporter. "Added to that the reduced allowance, it [is] no wonder the Indians have become restless and dissatisfied."[2]

Meat eaters throughout their history, the Lakotas regarded the beef distribution as essential. But they were also troubled by the partitioning and loss of their land and other unfulfilled commission promises. Much of what remained of the Great Sioux Reservation was opened to homesteaders early in 1890, but Congress delayed implementing the mandated surveys to set new reservation boundaries. The Indians had to await their allotments for almost another year. Meanwhile nothing was done to offset cutbacks in Indian rations.

Nor did the expected land boom materialize. The rush of settlers crossing the iced-over Missouri to claim cultivable parcels on the west bank and the close-in river bottoms had died out quickly. Severe drought conditions discouraged many, and the country farther west between the Cheyenne and White Rivers went largely unoccupied as before. Indeed those who swarmed onto reservation lands in March 1890 soon found that farming west of the Missouri was no better than east of it. The drought had worsened progressively in 1887, 1888, and 1889 and affected Indian farmers and white settlers alike. Not all white South Dakotans living east of the Missouri River faced destitution, but many did. Some wrote letters to eastern tabloids complaining of 5,000 people "in Dakota this winter that must have help or perish." Some had only potatoes, milk, and corn for food. Verging on starvation, they openly pleaded for clothing and bedding to be sent to help families through the winter. After touring affected areas of the territory, Governor Arthur C. Mellette appealed to citizens of eastern cities for donations. "The geographies we studied when boys," wrote one discouraged farmer, "were not so far out of the way when they spoke of the Great American Desert. Occasionally we have a good year—after heavy winter snows." While the national tabloid *Harper's Weekly* speculated that one day wheat and grain production there might be profitable, current conditions were dissuading any who might settle in the area. "The murmur of want in the Dakotas has already reached the ears of the men in Kansas, Missouri, and Kentucky who were thinking of seeking their fortunes in the newly opened lands," the paper said, "and grave doubts will arise as to the propriety of venturing in upon so uncertain a region."[3]

For more than a decade western Dakota had beckoned with greater certitude. Stock growers especially had made the best part of the country their province, especially between the Cheyenne and White Rivers. Both white and Indian ranchers worked the grazing trade, although white ranchers often grazed cattle on reservation land illegally. Indian families at all the agencies had received heifers and bulls in 1877, and the animals at Cheyenne River had proliferated best. In 1890 Indian ranchers there produced one-quarter of the cattle distributed for consumption on the reservation. Decline of the buffalo after 1877 and the Black Hills mining rush had drawn non-Indian cattle ranchers from Texas, Nebraska, and Wyoming to the vast grazing areas east of the Black Hills and between the confluence of the Cheyenne and Belle Fourche. Still, grazing was a dicey business, susceptible not only to weather but to competition from homesteading. Intent on farming, new settlers had come to that part of the territory as well, especially in the Fall River County west of Pine Ridge Reservation. Their numbers increased when the railroad provided ready access. In 1885–86 the Chicago and North Western line extended north from Chadron, Nebraska, to Rapid City, promoting towns like Oelrichs and Buffalo Gap. But additional homesteaders forced cattle ranchers to diminish their herds or leave altogether. The railroad also competed with stock raisers in the Black Hills freighting trade. More cattle ranchers, farmers, and sheepherders took up lands between the White and Cheyenne Rivers and in the Bad River Valley when surplus lands were opened under the 1889 Sioux Land Act. But the devastating winter of 1886–87 that killed cattle by the thousands had forced many of the ranching companies out of business. Grazers and homesteaders alike were abandoning their claims—or seriously thinking about it—under the pressure of unrelenting drought.[4]

Like their eastern South Dakota neighbors, the Lakotas had been especially hard hit by the incrementally punishing drought conditions of the late 1880s. About 20,000 Indian people were connected with the six different agencies by 1890 (Standing Rock held about 4,100; Cheyenne River, 2,800; the consolidated agencies of Crow Creek and Lower Brulé, about

2,100; Rosebud, some 5,300; and Pine Ridge, 5,700). All were almost entirely dependent on the federal government for food and material goods. The agents indexed how "civilization" was proceeding among them by tallying the numbers of those who wore "citizens' dress" wholly or in part. Rosebud had the fewest (1,705 out of 5,345), and McLaughlin's Standing Rock the most. Literacy was greatest at Pine Ridge and Cheyenne River (2,500 and 1,375 Sioux, respectively). Indians at Pine Ridge and Standing Rock could claim the largest numbers of log-framed "dwelling houses" (1,248 and 1,000, respectively). Pine Ridge and Cheyenne River had the largest number of missionaries (64 between them) and consequently the highest number of Christian weddings performed among the Sioux (248), with correspondingly fewer at the other agencies. Divorces were negligible. Through day schools and boarding schools, Catholic and Protestant churches labored to achieve religious conversions and provide education at each agency or reservation.[5]

Two decades into a tortuous transition from free-roaming buffalo hunters to farmers and stock raisers, these people took the brunt of the drought. The commission of 1889 had compounded the problem as a major distraction at a critical time. Several chiefs at Pine Ridge critiqued the timing of the meetings: "We all left our houses and gathered together at the Agency as we were told to do," explained one Indian leader, "and in doing so we lost all of our crops that we depended on for winter for the reason [that] there was no one at home to keep the cattle from destroying them, and our chickens and turkeys were killed by the wolves." As homesteaders in Dakota and Nebraska fled the drought in droves, the Indians stayed put. Not unlike homesteaders who did remain because they were too broke to move, the Indians had nowhere else to go. Caught in a political maelstrom yielding further land loss now compounded by natural disaster, they were obliged to try to ride it out.[6]

The drought was indeed staggering. Former governor Foster, who chaired the commission, complained publicly of Dakota temperatures reaching 110 degrees that "scorched everything and blasted the crops." Agent McLaughlin reported no rain at all at Standing Rock between August 1889 and June 1890 and hot winds in July that "stunted, blighted, or ruined all vegetation." "This is not a farming country," wrote agent McChesney from Cheyenne River, "and until some means is found to overcome the effects of the hot, drying winds it never will be." Time and money, he concluded, "are wasted in attempting to farm here." Other agents voiced similar opinions.

Gallagher said that dry weather had killed all of the corn at Pine Ridge. "This succeeding the drought of last year . . . will compel the Indians to depend for subsistence almost entirely upon what is issued to them by the Government." The new agent at Rosebud, J. George Wright, reported some improvement in farming operations there but conceded that "excessive heat . . . with lack of rain and [with] hot winds, which invariably prevail, has . . . very much injured and in some cases entirely destroyed the growing crops." One witness recalled the entire Sioux region as "a veritable dust bowl," adding that "the pitiful little gardens curled up and died in the persistent hot winds. Even young men displayed gaunt limbs and lack-luster faces. Old folks lost their hold on life, and heart-broken mothers mourned the last of a series of dead babes."[7]

As the drought conditions persisted into the summer of 1890, and with game scarce and beef rations dwindling, the Indians' diet suffered. Starvation loomed, and with starvation came disease. Waves of influenza, whooping cough, and measles swept through the agency populations, killing large numbers. Rosebud suffered most. Epidemics killed adults and children there in both 1889 and 1890. Pneumonia, consumption, and scrofula compounded the epidemics at Standing Rock and fatally infected undernourished children. Boarding school and day school students at Cheyenne River likewise succumbed: twenty-five to thirty children died from whooping cough alone in the spring of 1890.[8]

Reduction of beef rations had been part of an overall plan to encourage the Indians to become farmers and wean them away from government dependence. But the latest reductions came at a particularly bad time. In earlier years the Indians at Pine Ridge had tried to offset the gradual and illegal diminution of their rations by padding their census tallies, allegedly not reporting deaths and even presenting neighbors' children for the counts. The drought and ensuing starvation and disease epidemics certainly played into and magnified the central stinging issue regarding shortage of rations in the wake of the Sioux Land Commission's visit. Historically, part of the problem was systemic: government officials believed that by increasingly cutting back on rations the Indians would be further inclined to grow crops and thus become self-sustaining. During the early 1880s some Indians at Pine Ridge had padded their census numbers. That was more difficult now, and the U.S. House's delay in approving the Indian Appropriations Act until late summer ensured belated distribution of annuities. Not until late November 1890, as tensions mounted among the Sioux of western South

Dakota, did Robert V. Belt, acting commissioner of Indian Affairs, submit through the Interior Department a request to Congress for $100,000 to fulfill the deficiency and rectify what the Sioux Commission had promised for Rosebud and Pine Ridge for fiscal year 1889–90. In early December 1890 another request was forwarded to Congress, seeking $150,000 more to correct the same deficiency on all the Lakota reservations for fiscal year 1890–91.[9]

Thus delays compounded the impact of reduced rations. Shortages exacerbated the hunger of all, but especially those on the largest reservations: Standing Rock, Cheyenne River, Rosebud, and Pine Ridge—and most severely on Rosebud and Pine Ridge.[10] With remarkable restraint, American Horse and other Oglala chiefs wrote to Secretary Noble that the commissioners "had no sooner left than the Government took one million pounds of our [Pine Ridge] allowance of Beef away from us. . . . Both the President and yourself told us it would be given back to us. . . . We have been patiently waiting but have not got it yet. . . . We pray you to intercede for us and hurry up the case as we are in a starving condition." Groups of hungry Indians from Pine Ridge turned up at Fort Robinson, along White River forty miles southwest of the agency, to solicit rations from the post commissary officer. Similar feelings pervaded the Sioux leaders at Rosebud, where the cut of 2,000,000 pounds of beef was even more drastic. Desperate Brulé families showed up at Valentine and nearby Fort Niobrara to beg food. Even those people who attempted to grow their own beef on the Great Sioux Reservation faced tough going after the die-offs in the winter of 1886–87 and black leg disease that infected the herds in 1888.[11]

Indian trader Charles P. Jordan, an advocate of turning Indian agency administration over to the army, calculated that Indians at Rosebud had received almost 1.4 million fewer pounds of beef than they were due, not only from the reductions but from lost cattle weight over winter.[12] The Indians felt cheated, and others agreed. Disgusted Indian inspector Frank C. Armstrong told his superiors that the reductions hit hardest in winter because of poor communication. Speaking of Pine Ridge, he explained that in former years "this agency was allowed five million pounds of beef. This year [1890] it has been reduced to four million pounds." But he had been given no instructions that a million pounds of beef would be cut: "consequently, issues were made from the beginning of the fiscal year, July 1, 1889, until the date of the final delivery of beef, about October 15, 1889, on the basis of five million pounds for the year." Beef issues had to be reduced proportionately thereafter, he said, "to catch up with the [diminished] amount, and came just at the worst season of the year." Furthermore, Armstrong accused the government of intentional deception. The Sioux commissioners, he said, had assured the Indians that their rations would not be cut, yet "while this very talk was going on the Department in Washington was fixing to cut one-fifth of their meat supply, but did not let them know it, nor did the agent know it until they had signed the Sioux Bill." The Sioux "had a good start in cattle" but had "to kill over three times as many of their own [breeding] cattle, old and young, as they did the year before." With obvious disgust at the government's dishonesty, Armstrong declared that the Indians "have been deceived in doing what they did by the Government, and . . . they don't get as much now as they did before. . . . The government must keep faith as well as the Indians."[13]

As with all peoples, concern for the health and well-being of their children was paramount for the Lakotas. But the Indians perceived other reasons for their illness in addition to malnourishment. They especially resented the education system and particularly the off-reservation boarding schools that took their youth away for months or years. Many of those children became susceptible to pulmonary disorders, and a high percentage died while away or upon returning to their homes from eastern vocational schools at Carlisle, Pennsylvania, and Hampton, Virginia. "The breath of the earth rises up and poisons our children," expressed one Sioux leader during a meeting in Washington. Indian leaders urged that such schools be transferred back to the reservations, away from coastal climes. Also, unemployment often awaited students returning home. The curriculum negated their traditional lifeways, even turning children against their parents. Many believed that existing boarding schools at the agencies could do a better job than those located so far away.[14]

Reservation boundaries constituted another source of frustration—and even tension. Plans for creation of the new reservations called for pushing the west boundary of Rosebud fifteen miles east from Pass Creek to Black Pipe Creek, thus making the people who lived there part of a different reservation and answerable to a different agency. The Brulés who already occupied homes in the area opposed this change, because it placed them beyond the jurisdiction of Rosebud. Many demanded to be placed on the Pine Ridge rolls for rations and annuities. The matter rankled Sioux at both agencies, especially at Rosebud, where it added to the general discontent. Agent Wright also urged removing the Rosebud Agency offices closer to the

Missouri River, arguing that existing facilities had become "depopulated" as the people moved to more fertile areas on creek bottoms farther east to pursue farming. Believing that this notion was inspired by Dakota politicians on behalf of their constituents, both traders and Indians, especially the Brulés, opposed such a move.[15]

The long-time presence of Northern Cheyennes among the Oglalas near the Pine Ridge Agency was another source of tribal contention. The Northern Cheyennes had lived there since 1879, following their desperate run from the Indian Territory in the autumn of 1878. En route north, those following Morning Star (also known as Dull Knife) had been arrested and imprisoned at Fort Robinson pending their return south. Held in a freezing overcrowded barrack, Morning Star's people broke away in January 1879, fighting soldiers across a frozen landscape for two weeks and losing many dead and wounded. Once they were caught, troops escorted the survivors to Pine Ridge to reside with the Oglalas, with whom many had intermarried in years past. Those Cheyennes under Chief Little Wolf, who had in the meantime circumvented the Fort Robinson soldiers and made their way to Montana, eventually surrendered and remained at Fort Keogh as quasi–prisoners of war. In 1881 and 1883 other Cheyennes from the Indian Territory were permitted to join those at Pine Ridge. By 1890 the number of Northern Cheyennes there stood at 517.[16]

The Cheyennes were no longer happy at Pine Ridge, especially as times grew more difficult. Tensions were also mounting with the Sioux over food rationing and over the fact that many Northern Cheyennes had signed the Sioux land agreement. They had reason to fear conflict with the Oglalas. Through the years the Northern Cheyennes in Dakota and Montana had often exchanged visits. During the 1880s many of those at Pine Ridge began agitating to rejoin several hundred of their kin on the Fort Keogh Military Reservation and the Tongue River Indian Reservation in Montana. In spring 1890 a number of starving Northern Cheyennes under Tangle Hair left Pine Ridge for Montana, but troops from Fort Robinson stationed at Oelrichs, west of the agency, stopped them and forced them back. That fall, as the Lakotas grew restless themselves, plans were afoot to move the Cheyennes to Montana, to Fort Keogh, to Tongue River, or even to a vacant part of the Crow reservation. Whatever the plans for them were, their continued presence among the Oglalas was another irritation at Pine Ridge.[17]

Hopelessness gave way to senselessness in early spring 1890 when the popular schoolteacher Frank E. Lewis was shot and killed on April 4 near

No. 2 Day School, a few miles north of the Pine Ridge Agency. A young man from Washington, D.C., Lewis was the son of the former post chaplain at Fort Niobrara, Nebraska. Having taught at Rosebud Agency for several years, Lewis was considered a person of "exemplary habits" and was well liked. The fatal shot was fired by a thirty-year-old manic Oglala named Eagle Horse, who apparently did not know Lewis but was dying from tuberculosis and looking for a white man to kill. Hiding in some rose bushes, Eagle Horse waited until Lewis was within ten feet and ambushed the teacher as he rode horseback from the school to his home at the agency, killing him instantly. Telling his parents that he expected to die from the disease, Eagle Horse reportedly said: "I want a white man to go with me." After shooting Lewis, he ascended a nearby hilltop, motioned other Indians to stay clear, and then fatally shot himself. The tragedy was without reason, and yet it seemed symptomatic of what was happening to the Sioux. Many Indians had thought highly of Lewis, and the inexplicability of his death seemed to mirror the senseless desperation of life on the reservation.[18]

Only two weeks earlier a death farther away had reverberated through Lakota society as well. Late in March 1890 came word that General Crook had died in Chicago. Crook's firm promises, while sometimes insincere, had helped sustain the land commission among the Sioux the previous year, and many of the tribesmen who had signed the rolls at his urging felt his loss. "The cardinal principle of his Indian policy," editorialized *Harper's Weekly*, "was sincerity." Whatever disingenuousness Crook had used to secure Sioux approval of the land transaction, he had sought to rectify the beef ration crisis and had been a friend to the Indians. Because they respected him, his passing took on special meaning and certainly brought a heightened sense of uncertainty. The stalwart holdout Red Cloud, who had stubbornly refused to sign the land deal, purportedly said upon learning of Crook's death: "He, at least, had never lied to us. His words gave the people hope. He died. Their hope died again. Despair came again."[19]

Caught in a maelstrom of anxiety with no ready answers and with grinding hunger a daily presence, the Sioux lived a tortured existence in spring 1890. The future seemed to offer nothing but more apathy and dissonance and an acculturation process that was coming at them too quickly. Frustrated, Red Cloud addressed missives to the secretary of the Interior through a trader, seeking fulfillment of past promises. The Sioux pony issue grated on him, and he told Secretary Noble that his people at Pine Ridge were starving. They desperately needed the compensation that Crook and others had pledged for the ponies taken from them in 1876, which was supposed to have come when the Sioux agreement became law. "Now kind Friend," he told Noble firmly but with the greatest forbearance, "some one [*sic*] has made a mistake, or if the Great Father has sent some one here, he has got lost, for up to date no one has made his appearance." Red Cloud appealed to the secretary: "at least treat us in this matter as you would any other human being." As before, official Washington was implacable. Little was done to mediate any of the Sioux troubles, which was especially galling to men and women who had once prospered by following prereservation ways of life and hunted buffalo across the vast North American steppes without restraint. The newer generations would know of this life only in the telling.[20] To one degree or another, unrelenting despair affected everyone. Government indifference to the Indians' plight and to its own perfidy was dumbfounding and fostered an extreme hopelessness. The people were at a crossroads. Few knew which way to turn, but some began to look elsewhere for deliverance.

FIVE

Seeking to Endure

Out of desperation many of the Lakotas sought deliverance through religion. Precedent lay in history, wherein populations facing ominous circumstances beyond their means turned to deities as their ultimate last hope. It is a transcendent solution documented among diverse cultures that appear to have lost all faith in their earthly devices. Experts on this phenomenon note that a society that feels directly threatened or otherwise impacted by another to a point of calamity is inclined "to seek comfort in ritual designed to bend time backward" (searching for an ideal point to return to in its past) or to quicken its movement forward (striving for utopian resolution).[1]

Wherever Old World colonial powers ventured during the eighteenth and nineteenth centuries reactionary movements by the subjugated peoples in their way arose. Examples of this response can be found throughout North American history, after Spain, France, Great Britain, and the United States successively impacted Native societies. Often the term "messianic" is applied when a leader has arisen to deliver the people from persecution and deprivation (a resistance movement) or ethnic anguish and show the way to happiness of an uncorrupted past (a reform, regeneration, or restoration movement) through a millennium reached by supernatural intervention. Such individual facilitators or brokers—often teachers and messengers—have been referred to as prophets.[2]

What happened among the Lakotas in 1890 had precedents. Similar responses had occurred in the eighteenth century when a Delaware prophet, Neolin, sought to combat white corruption of his people with a reform message partly based in the Old Testament. This message reportedly influenced Chief Pontiac of the Ottawas in his struggle against the British. Similarly, a Seneca sachem named Handsome Lake articulated an adaptive theology grounded in indigenous beliefs and post–Revolutionary War tenets of the Quaker religion to rescue his people from the corrosive impacts of white society. His revelations helped all the Iroquois to revive traditional values and coexist with the intruders among them. Similar duress in the Old Northwest provoked the Shawnee leader Tecumseh and his mystical brother, Tenskwatawa. Following monumental land losses to the Americans, they urged reversion to traditional ways and promised their people that they would become impervious to American guns.[3]

As the westward advance of white Americans ensued, other prophets arose to ease the suffering of Indian populations. Perhaps most significant to western tribes was Smoholla, a Wanapam shaman whose Columbia River Valley homeland was beset by whites in the 1860s, who ravaged the earth in their quest for gold. Tribes of the Northwest—including Yakimas, Nez Perces, and Palouses—found solace in Smoholla's Catholic-inspired Dreamer ideology that embraced the resurrection of long-dead Indians, the renewal of game, and the obliteration of all whites, themes that became pervasive elsewhere.[4]

Some cases are closer geographically and chronologically to the Lakota crisis. The Comanches of the southern plains instituted a Sun Dance in the 1870s as part of a movement led by Isatai, an accomplished shaman. Among his claims were an ability to raise the dead and immunity to bullets fired by whites, qualities derived from his meeting in heaven with the Great Spirit that he vowed to impart to his people. Moved by reservation strife, Isatai sought to restore Comanche prosperity, including the return of the buffalo and the destruction of the intruders. Following the Indians' disastrous fight with buffalo hunters at Adobe Walls in the Texas panhandle and their failed efforts in the Red River War of 1874–75, Isatai fell from grace. In 1881 a Kiowa medicine man named Pautapety pledged to restore the buffalo through ritual, while six years later another Kiowa, P'oinkia, claimed abilities to make his people invulnerable to bullets. P'oinkia told the people to dispose of white-related contrivances, to discard white clothing, and to remove children from reservation schools.

In Montana in 1887 a Crow shaman named Sword Bearer (also known as Wraps Up His Tail) attempted a resurgence against growing white influence in the Yellowstone region but died in an engagement with soldiers sent to quell it.[5]

All these Indian responses had similarities, although some also included distinct elements. They all faced loss of lands, wanted to counter corruptive white influences (including liquor), and sought a return to traditional beliefs and values. Some responses envisioned peaceful coexistence with whites, while others (notably later) thought that God would make the whites disappear or go away. Some preached imperviousness to white bullets, yet all were messianic (a death followed by new life). Some sought resurrection of long-dead ancestors, and some of the more recent western-generated movements sought return of the buffalo. All conveyed notions of death and resurrection, loss and redemption, and especially hope.

The messianic movement that affected many Lakotas in 1890 held similar precepts. Pervasive rumors of a new messiah had appeared among the southern tribes, all of whom faced social distresses, though none as serious as those confronting the Sioux. Some genesis for the phenomenon lay in Wyoming, where in late 1889 a Northern Cheyenne man named Porcupine visiting the Arapaho and Shoshoni Agency learned of a visionary experience wherein a redeemer predicted restoration to a time before the coming of the white settlers. Seeking to verify the incident, Porcupine traveled to Walker Lake in western Nevada. An assembly of representatives of western tribes, including Lakotas, had also gathered there to comprehend the new messiah. As reported by Porcupine, "I had always thought the Great Father [Christ] was a white man, but this man looked like an Indian. . . . He rose and said he was very glad to see his children. . . . 'I am going to talk to you after awhile about your relatives who are dead and gone. . . . I will teach you, too, how to dance a dance.'" Porcupine studied the messiah. "I had heard that Christ had been crucified, and I looked to see, and I saw a scar on his wrist and one on his face, and he seemed to be the man." The messiah later told his audience that "all our dead were to be resurrected; that they were all to come back to earth. . . . He told us not to quarrel, or fight, nor strike each other, nor shoot one another; that the whites and Indians were to be all one people." On his return to the Northern Cheyennes, Porcupine spoke of his experience. "Ever since the Christ I speak of talked to me I have thought what he said was good. I see nothing bad in it. Through him you can go to heaven and meet your friends."[6]

Word of the Nevada messiah had reached the Lakota agencies about the summer of 1889 through letters sent from tribes in Utah, Oklahoma, Wyoming, Montana, and Dakota territories and interpreted for the people there.[7] It is likely, too, that word from the Shoshoni and Arapaho reservation in Wyoming and the Northern Cheyenne reservation in Montana had spread southeast to their relatives in the Indian Territory. Following Porcupine's odyssey, word reached Pine Ridge via the presence of the Northern Cheyennes there, who regularly traded visits with friends and relatives in Montana and the Indian Territory. Not surprisingly, in terms of its Nevada origins and proximity to adherent tribes directly north, this form of the religion likely drew its tenets from the Dreamer faith promoted by Smoholla among the Plateau tribes of the Northwest. The particular aspects that would powerfully impact many Lakotas, however, lay with the disciples of the prophet known as Wovoka (spoken of by Porcupine), living in the area of the Walker River Paiute Reservation.[8]

Like preceding Indian prophets, Wovoka (meaning "the cutter") rose from modest beginnings. Born in western Nevada about 1856, he was the Northern Paiute (Numu) son of Numutibo'o, a headman who was possibly a Dreamer, perhaps even a prophet and mystic among his people. Wovoka worked for a white rancher named David Wilson, learned English, and received from him the name Jack Wilson, by which he became known to whites. Apparently affected to some degree by his father's insights and of like contemplative mind, Wovoka gained knowledge of Christian (Presbyterian) theology from the Wilson family and other white ranchers. He married and continued working as before. Around the age of thirty he declared the revelation by which he afterward influenced so many tribes: "When the sun died [during an eclipse]," he reported, "I went up to heaven and saw God and all the people who had died a long time ago. God told me to come back and tell my people they must be good and love one another, and not fight, or steal, or lie. He gave me this dance to give to my people."[9]

In 1892, after the immediate Lakota crisis was over, Wovoka told anthropologist James Mooney of the Smithsonian Institution about his visit with God and of his instructions that "by performing this dance at intervals, for five consecutive days each time, they would secure this happiness to themselves and hasten the event [of reunification with spirits of friends and relatives who had died]." Wovoka "then returned to earth and began to preach as he was directed." Wovoka also claimed to have seen all the people who had died before. He said that God had given him the power to make it rain, snow, or turn dry and to keep people happy and forever youthful. In sum, he described his time with God as a revelation and his mission as one of brotherly love and universal peace: "he was to tell the Indians to love each other and . . . live peacefully with the whites. He did not profess to be the Son of God, but only a prophet who had experienced time with the Maker."[10]

Following the land agreement of 1889 the Sioux faced an extraordinary period of anguish, disease, land loss, starvation, and lost hope set against more gradual culturally impacting changes that they had experienced during the nineteenth century.[11] Some became curious about Wovoka's timely message of restoration as hinted at in gossip and rumors abounding at the agencies. In September 1889, for example, Lakotas at Pine Ridge told of Arapaho hunters who had seen an apparition of Jesus Christ that relieved their thirst. The reports prompted formal inquiry by Lakota leaders to determine its validity. At Pine Ridge a council convened with Chiefs Red Cloud, Young Man Afraid of His Horses, American Horse, and Little Wound in attendance. The Indians agreed to send a deputation west to learn about the messiah and his message. Those chosen were Good Thunder, Cloud Horse, and Yellow Knife from Pine Ridge and Short Bull, Flat Iron, Yellow Breast, and Broken Arm from Rosebud, while Kicking Bear, an Oglala from Cheyenne River, joined the party en route. Evidently no one attended directly from Standing Rock, Crow Creek, or Lower Brulé. The eight remained in the West through the winter, constituting the collateral Sioux presence that Porcupine mentioned as being at the Nevada convocation. The Lakotas evidently did not return to South Dakota until March 1890.[12]

For the Lakotas, the messiah was Wovoka. In essence, their report confirmed the widespread rumors: that the messiah was indeed the Son of God who had been killed by the whites and even bore scars from his crucifixion. Their interpretation (or at least the translated wording given by Mooney) does not resemble the peaceful and upbeat portrayal that the ethnologist later obtained from Wovoka after the Sioux crisis was over: they said that the messiah had come back to earth "to punish the whites for their wickedness, especially for their injustice toward the Indians." When spring 1891 arrived "he would wipe the whites from the face of the earth," bring back all dead Indians, restore the buffalo and other game animals, and in effect return the Indian people to ascendancy.[13] This change would be facilitated through practicing the special dance. Wovoka's instructions to the Sioux were essentially the same for the other tribes attending the assembly, although the language addressing rainfall needs was likely tailored to tribe-specific drought conditions:

> When you get home you must make a dance to continue five days. Dance four successive nights, and the last night keep up the dance until the morning of the fifth day, when all must bathe in the river and then disperse to their homes. You must all do in the same way. . . . When you get home I shall give you a good cloud [rainfall] which will make you feel good. . . . In the fall there will be such a rain as I have never given you before. . . . Do not tell the white people about this. Jesus is now upon the earth. He appears like a cloud. The dead are all alive again. I do not know when they will be here; maybe this fall or in the spring. When the time comes there will be no more sickness and everyone will be young again. Do not refuse to work for the whites and do not make any trouble with them until you leave them. When the earth shakes [at the coming of the new world] do not be afraid. It will not hurt you. I want you to dance every six weeks. Make a feast at the dance and have food that everybody may eat. Then bathe in the water. That is all.[14]

Accounts of the visit to Wovoka by the Sioux attendees differ in tone and content. It is difficult to be precise about their meaning and interpretation, as each attendee appears to have experienced an individual view of the proceedings. It seems as though the messiah can be seen as God, Jesus, or a prophet—or amorphously as all in one—perhaps as the result of meanings lost in translation. Elaine Goodale, articulate supervisor of education for the Lakotas, interviewed one of the Sioux delegates, Good Thunder, within weeks of his return. He told her:

> We traveled three years (months) to find the Christ. On a broad prairie covered with Indians I saw him at last—a man of surpassing beauty, with long yellow hair, clad in a blue robe. He did not look at us nor speak, but read our thoughts and answered them without words. I saw the prints of the nails in his hands and feet. He said that the crying of the Indians had sounded loud in his ears. He would come to them tomorrow—(meaning next summer). Then they would be with him in Elysium, living in skin tents and hunting the buffalo.[15]

Four of the Sioux men who traveled to Nevada related their experience to George Sword of the Pine Ridge Agency police, whose words were translated for publication. They told of a mystical visit wherein the messiah appeared from heaven and told them of a land where all the Indians were "coming home," although it was not yet time for that to occur. He gave Good Thunder certain paints (apparently red and white) and told the Indians to grow crops and send their children to school. He said that God had directed him to visit them and that the whites had killed him and were "not good." The Sioux reported seeing friends who had died: "Chasing Hawk, who died not long ago, was there, and we went to his tepee. He was living with his wife, who was killed in war long ago. . . . A son of Good Thunder, who died in war long ago, was one who also took us to his tepee, so his father saw him." Years later Short Bull affirmed the message of peace. "He taught us to dance, and he says this is the dance we must perform. He showed us his robe and told us that we should worship him by wearing robes like this. He told us that we must throw away the rifle and the war club. 'Live in peace,' he said, 'and let the white man live in peace with you.'"[16]

Practicing the so-called Ghost Dance (properly, *wanagi wacipi*, a spiritual union of a person with the spirit world through dance) would transmit the core of Wovoka's peaceful message to the Indians long after the delegates had left western Nevada and returned to their respective tribal homes. Moreover, its faithful performance would encourage the anticipated millennium and its promised rejection of white civilization. After the Sioux delegates arrived home, the word quickly spread. Most initial reaction was inquiring yet tentative, even cautious. "Suddenly everyone seemed unable to talk of anything but the 'new religion,'" recalled Goodale, then at Standing Rock. "Some were merely curious; others vaguely apprehensive of they knew not what. Only the more unsophisticated were ready to accept the notion of a miraculous intervention in their favor, at a moment when all hope failed and heaven itself seemed to have turned against them."[17]

Alarmed reservation personnel greeted the delegates from Pine Ridge upon their arrival back in Sioux country from Nevada. Postmaster William Selwyn, who had seen letters describing the messiah activity, reported the information to agent Hugh D. Gallagher, who quickly jailed Good Thunder and two of his colleagues for two days. None of the three would describe the essence of their journey. Then Kicking Bear, the Cheyenne River delegate, visited Pine Ridge en route home. He had diverted from the others and brought news that the Northern Arapahos in Wyoming had started the dance in accordance with Wovoka's instructions. Kicking Bear told of dancers collapsing and reviving to tell of seeing and talking with dead relatives. The word they brought was that the messiah's doctrine was true. Despite proscriptions from Gallagher, some of the Oglalas met away from the agency along White Clay Creek. Red Cloud (although he embraced Catholicism) and other leaders endorsed the proceedings, stating that the people should begin the dances as the Arapahos had done. In August agent Gallagher and the Pine Ridge Indian police broke up a meeting of two thousand Indians convened on White Clay Creek to discuss the messiah, many likely Red Cloud's followers and some reportedly armed. After a petty confrontation, the people scattered and simply reassembled elsewhere.[18]

Not all of the Lakota Sioux were affected the same by the arriving Ghost Dance, and some rejected it. Although its tenets found adoption and certain adaptations across the spectrum of reservation society, most who became its devotees hailed from the so-called nonprogressive or conservative camps, as Elaine Goodale suggested. They were mainly people (including the old chiefs who feared growing loss of their authority) who had been among the last to surrender their age-old freedom to the strictures of reservation life. Most of them were full-bloods who followed Sitting Bull and others of his ilk who steadfastly resisted being acculturated in the white image and most recently had resisted approval of the land bill. Many of the conservatives occupied communities away from the agencies of Standing Rock, Cheyenne River, Rosebud, and Pine Ridge. Their counterparts, the progressives, who had become inured to reservation existence after two decades, had largely adapted and were otherwise transitioning well, if not enthusiastically, to the alien culture. Most were mixed-bloods and religious converts. Many could read and speak English well and lived within or adjoining the agency communities where they farmed and raised cattle, hauled freight, or worked for the agency offices. By and large most progressives took no part in the arriving religion or its dance. (Almost all of the residents of the Crow Creek Reservation, and many of those at Lower Brulé, were progressives.) Whether progressive or nonprogressive, most of their school-aged children (except those sent to distant boarding schools) attended public or parochial schools on the reservation.[19]

Prominent old-time nonprogressive chiefs Red Cloud and Big Road at Pine Ridge philosophically countered American Horse, Young Man Afraid of His Horses, and Little Wound among the progressives; the principal nonprogressives at Rosebud were Two Strike and Crow Dog, while the progressive leadership remained unclear; Miniconjous Big Foot and Hump represented the nonprogressive element at Cheyenne River; and Sitting Bull stood as the traditionalist bulwark at Standing Rock, while Gall and John Grass represented the foremost progressive leaders. Although the followers of these chiefs and others generally mirrored their political leanings, this was not altogether true. Some probably stood independent from their tribal chiefs in respect to the Ghost Dance.[20]

Kicking Bear and Short Bull, both about forty-five years old, became the principal explainers and boosters of the budding dance among the Lakotas. The clear-eyed Oglala leader Kicking Bear had joined with his cousin Crazy Horse in fighting army troops in 1876 and had played an instrumental role at the Little Bighorn. After his return from Canada, Kicking Bear was assigned to Cheyenne River Agency yet maintained close ties with Oglalas at Pine Ridge and finally settled there following the troubles of 1890–91. Short Bull in the meantime had become an effective Christianized leader, preacher, and medicine man among Brulés at Rosebud Agency. Although the two men often worked independently, Short Bull and Kicking Bear together wielded clear influence among Teton believers after their visit to Wovoka: nonprogressive leaders and their followers, whose hopelessness made them ready candidates for mystical deliverance.[21]

It took several months for the Ghost Dance fully to germinate among the Sioux. Late in March Kicking Bear introduced it at Cheyenne River from fifty to ninety miles west of the agency so that there would be limited interference from tribal police. There the Miniconjou leaders Big Foot and Hump and several hundred followers began almost ceaseless dancing near the forks of the Belle Fourche and the Cheyenne and at Cherry Creek on the Cheyenne.[22] As early as June 20, 1890, a dance took place on White Clay Creek near Pine Ridge. Kicking Bear also presided over dances at Pine Ridge within three weeks of the meeting disrupted by Gallagher on August 24. Interest was widespread, and Father Aemilius Perrig noted that "all our Indians [at the Holy Rosary Mission] went to the Ghost dances except 6 families." From that point on, the dances appear to have happened more or less regularly. Perrig recorded his concern:

> It gets more and more the appearance of deviltry. The appearing of Ghosts are said to express dislike for baptized persons. The apparition of him, who pretends to be our Lord (with the five wounds), forbids

the Indians to call him Jesus, but wants only to be called Father. The entranced Indians pretend to have seen the happy hunting grounds. All the apparitions are inspiring the Indians with distrust, dislike, contempt or even hatred of the whites.[23]

One dance at Pine Ridge took place north of the agency at the head of Cheyenne Creek. A later one organized by Good Thunder occurred on Wounded Knee Creek some eighteen miles northeast of the agency near present Manderson, South Dakota.[24] Father Perrig seems to have sensed what was underway. While the fundamental peaceful objectives remained, Wovoka's word was becoming skewed: because of the gravity of the issues weighing on the Sioux, local passion occasionally instigated narrow divergences from the prophet's teachings. The dance was apparently protean, not fully standardized, as it evolved with the Lakotas.

The dances also occurred at Rosebud at about the same time as those at Pine Ridge, perhaps at the junction of Iron Creek and Little White River, eight miles west of Rosebud Agency. Short Bull sermonized followers on Pine Ridge Reservation in November, telling them that because whites appeared to be meddling, he, as an apostle to the messiah, would urge the advance of the time for deliverance "from what my Father above told me. The time will be shorter."

Whenever this thing occurs I will start the wind to blow. We are the ones who will then see our fathers, mothers and everybody. We, the tribe of Indians are the ones who are living the sacred life. God, our Father, himself has told [and] commanded and shown me to do these things. Our Father in Heaven has placed a mark at each point of the four winds[:] First, a clay pipe, which lies at the setting of the sun and represents the Sioux tribe. [Second,] there is a holy arrow lying at the north, which represents the Cheyenne tribe; third, at the rising of the sun there lies hail, representing the Arapahoe tribe; and fourth, there lies a pipe and nice feather at the south, which represents the Crow tribe. My father has shown me these things, therefore we must continue to dance. Soldiers may surround you, but pay no attention to them. Continue the dance. If the soldiers surround you four deep, three of you upon whom I put holy shirts will sing a song which I have taught you, and some of them will drop dead; then the rest will start to run, but their horses will sink into the earth and you can do what you desire with them.[25]

The last of the Lakotas to receive instructions about the messiah religion and the accompanying dance were conservatives at distant Standing Rock, who had so far evinced little interest in the coming millennium. In early October Kicking Bear, by invitation, arrived in Sitting Bull's camp at Grand River, about forty miles southwest of the agency at Fort Yates, to preach and instruct. Agent McLaughlin tried to stem the activity that his visit generated there but was too late. Within days the Ghost Dance was in full swing, anticipating the messiah's arrival in the spring. Day school attendance fell as parents took part in the dances. McLaughlin went to Grand River to stop the dances but without success. When the agent sent Indian police to remove Kicking Bear, the police backed down. McLaughlin had to send another party to conduct the apostle and his companions from the reservation. Disturbed over the entrée and angry about the dance, McLaughlin wrote Commissioner Morgan, terming it "absurd nonsense," but expressed fear that "a great many of the Indians of this agency actually believe it." "The infection," said the agent, was "so pernicious that it now includes some of the Indians who were formerly numbered with the progressive and more intelligent." He added: "Many of our best Indians appear dazed and undecided when talking of it, their inherent superstition having been thoroughly aroused."[26]

While the dance that Kicking Bear and Short Bull promoted stressed the Christianized elements espoused by Wovoka and embraced by many of its practitioners, it also reflected localized differences unique to Lakota lifeways and their present dilemma. The poignant dance of desperation was the primary means to the desired end—the millennium as foreseen by the messiah himself. Observers' accounts of the ritual details of its practice among the Sioux give an idea of its purpose over its few months of rigorous observance on the Lakota reservations. It appears that the Lakota form of the dance adapted familiar elements from the long-practiced Sun Dance (banned by the government since the early 1880s), including a cut-down tree as a sacred center pole, which was lacking altogether in Wovoka's dance. Each dance lasted at least two days but sometimes longer, thereby diverging from the version specified by Wovoka. As described by Kicking Bear, the primary proponent of the dance on the reservations, participating men, women, and children would go in advance "through a sweat lodge to cleanse the body, then at the outset raise hands in the direction of the northwest as entreaty to the messiah and start the dance with a song, 'Ate Nusun-Kala.'" Men and women then alternated in a broad circle, all holding hands. As the dance proceeded, the people started moving round and round in one direction until weariness took hold and they dropped onto the ground one by one, "as though dead, with foam in the mouth, all wet by perspiration." The others continued moving in the circle until they too fell from exhaustion.[27]

It was during the ensuing unconsciousness that the dancers made contact with the messiah as well as dead relatives and friends and would see their promised future. Throughout the proceeding the dancers, whose faces were painted red, wore special attire. As described by Kicking Bear, "they made holy shirts and dresses . . . with blue across the back, and alongside of this is a line of yellow paint. They also paint in the front part of the shirts and dresses. On the shoulders and on the sleeves, they tie eagles' feathers." Such feathers also graced their heads, and the dancers were not to wear any metal on their persons, although some inexplicably toted guns, possibly for protection against intruders.[28]

Black Elk, an Oglala, took part in the Ghost Dance at the age of twenty-six near Manderson and recalled his experience years later. "Kicking Bear and Good Thunder were on either side of me. . . . We began to pray: 'Father, behold me! The nation that you have and the nation that I have, they are in difficulty. The new earth you promised, I want my nation to behold it!' After the prayer we stood with outright hands raised to the west and we all began to weep." When the dance started, Black Elk fell into a swoon, during which he met the messiah and twelve men. "The man with outstretched arms looked at me and I didn't know whether he was a white or an Indian. He did not resemble Christ. He looked like an Indian, but I was not sure of it. He had long hair . . . hanging down loose. On the left side of his head was an eagle feather. His body was painted red. . . . [Then] his body changed into all colors and it was very beautiful. All around him there was light. Then he disappeared all at once. It seemed as though there were wounds in the palms of his hands." The twelve men spoke to Black Elk again and presented to him the future, "the greenward of the earth," meaning the plains. Twelve women appeared, telling him the same. Then the men showed Black Elk a vast expanse covered with buffalo and full drying racks—again the future—before a strong wind picked him up and carried him away. He looked down to see his people struggling. "They looked up to me and said: 'Help us!' . . . When I came down I came back to my body again." Black Elk told the people of his vision through song; he interpreted his prophecy as direction to work hard for his people during the harsh times. He interpreted the sacred pole as a "tree that never blooms" and hoped that his meeting with the messiah foretold a future when the tree would bloom again.[29]

Another Sioux who participated in a Ghost Dance had been a young student at the government school at Pine Ridge. Out of curiosity he and about fifty boys ran off to a dance on Porcupine Creek and took part in it. He remembered a man calling out, "'You runaway boys, come here.' They stripped our ugly clothes from us and sent us inside [a long sweat lodge]." Following purification, the boys donned sacred shirts. "Everyone [dancing] wore one magpie and one eagle feather in his hair, but in our case there was nothing to tie them to. The school had promptly ruined us by shaving off our long hair till our scalps showed lighter than our faces!" The people all formed in a ring, joined hands, and waited quietly and expectantly. "It was not a glad time, though," recalled the former student. "All walked cautiously and in awe, feeling their dead were close at hand." As the people danced to the drumbeat, moving "to the left in a sidewise step," they began to collapse and lie "dead." "Quickly those on each side . . . closed the gap and went right on." Those now "dead" were "seeing their dear ones. As each one came to, she, or he, slowly sat up and looked about, bewildered, and then began wailing inconsolably." When asked, a young girl mournfully told a medicine man what she had seen, and he announced it to the throng. "Then all wailed with her. It was very dismal."[30]

A youth named Robert Higheagle and several other boys were curious about a dance held near Sitting Bull's at Grand River on the Standing Rock Reservation in August 1890:

There were guards all around the camp. Anybody not wearing Indian clothes was not allowed in the camp. We took out our saddle blankets to wear, but they wouldn't let us in unless we also took off our store clothes. So we stayed back. They were dancing, holding hands. After a while one fell down and they all stopped to see what he would say. He would then tell his vision. Then they would continue dancing until some more fell down. . . . I had an uncle who was one of the main administrators of this ceremony. He came over and asked me if I wanted to join in. "Don't you want to be saved? All those who wear white men's clothes are going to die." He gave me a feather to wear and wouldn't let me in unless I would discard my civilian clothes.[31]

Accounts by whites who witnessed some of the dances revealed much similarity in their performances but also subtle differences. An unidentified schoolteacher at Pine Ridge Agency detailed an Oglala Ghost Dance on White Clay Creek:

As the crowd gathered about the [sacred] tree the "high priest," or master of ceremonies, began his address, giving them directions as to his chant and other matters. After he had spoken . . . they arose and formed in a circle. As nearly as I could count there were between three hundred and four hundred persons. One stood directly behind another, each with hands on his neighbor's shoulders. After walking about a few times, chanting, "Father, I come," they stopped marching, but remained in the circle, and set up the most fearful, heart-piercing wails I ever heard— crying, moaning, groaning, and shrieking out their grief, and naming over their departed friends and relatives, at the same time taking up handfuls of dust at their feet, washing their hands in it, and throwing it over their heads. Finally, they raised their eyes to heaven, their hands clasped high above their heads, and stood straight and perfectly still, invoking the power of the Great Spirit to allow them to see and talk with their people who had died. This ceremony lasted about fifteen minutes, when they all sat down. . . . When they arose again they enlarged the circle by facing toward the center, taking hold of hands, and moving around in the manner of school children in their play of "needle's eye." . . . They would go as fast as they could, their heads moving from side to side, their bodies swaying, their arms with hands gripped tightly in their neighbor's, swinging back and forth with all their might. If one, more weak and frail, came near falling, he would be jerked up and into position until tired nature gave way. The ground had been worked and worn by many feet, until the fine flour-like dust lay light and loose to the depth of 2 or 3 inches. The wind, which had increased, would some times take it up, enveloping the dancers and hiding them from view. In the ring were men, women, and children; the strong and robust, the weak, consumptive, and those near to death's door. . . . First one and then another would break from the ring and stagger away to fall down. One woman fell a few feet from me; she came toward us, her hair flying over her face, which was purple, looking as if the blood must burst through; her hands and arms moving wildly; every breath a pant and a groan; and she fell on her back and went down like a log. . . . She seemed perfectly unconscious. . . . No one ever disturbed those who fell or took any notice of them except to keep the crowd away. They kept up their dancing until fully 100 persons were lying unconscious. Then they stopped and seated themselves in a circle, and as each one recovered from his trance he was brought to the center of the ring to relate his experience. Each told his story to a medicine man, and he shouted it to the crowd.[32]

Accounts by other white observers were similar. One mentioned the "dirge-like chant of a graveyard significance" uttered by the worshippers, referencing the variety of incantations composed for the Ghost Dance. The stanzas, uttered either alternately or in unison by the men and women dancers as appropriate, translated into refrains, such as "Saith my mother" or "Saith my father," often in the form of a wail. These and specific longer songs were given in monotone and often were accented to an accompanying beat.[33]

The Congregationalist missionary Mary C. Collins watched a Ghost Dance at Sitting Bull's camp on the Standing Rock Reservation and also found similarities with the Sun Dance, including the presence of the sacred center pole. Moreover, "they all looked at the sun as they danced. They stopped going round now and then, and all faced the sun with uplifted faces and outstretched arms." When they collapsed into a trance state, "some of them wallowing and rolling on the ground and frothing at the mouth, others throwing their arms and running around and whooping like mad men, . . . [they were] still gazing sunward." (Ethnologist Raymond J. DeMallie has suggested that by adding the sacred pole the Lakotas adapted a familiar component to a new idea "to establish continuity with their past.")[34] In their spasmodic elements, too, the dances to a degree exuded physical aspects mirroring the religious revivalism of certain white Americans during the middle years of the nineteenth century.

As time wore on in the fall of 1890 and the Ghost Dances occurred more frequently at Pine Ridge, Rosebud, Cheyenne River, and Standing Rock, the fear often imparted to things unknown was conveyed to much of the regional white population. Apprehension over potential Indian hostility against settlers in areas all around the reservations began to take hold. Whites in the area who learned of the Ghost Dance had assorted reactions, many of which greatly distorted what was going on. Non-Indians knew little of the roots of the dance, and most could not surmise what it was about: an effort by some Lakotas to seek resolution for the predicament that affected virtually all aspects of their lives. As the dances proceeded, rumor, misunderstanding, and untruths abounded on and off the reservations. George H. Bartlett, a deputy U.S. marshal and entrepreneur who lived at Pine Ridge, wrote that "the women and girls who participate in the 'Ghost Dance' dance . . . fall senseless to the ground, throwing their clothing over their heads, and laying bare the most prominent part of their bodies, viz., '*their butts*' and '*things*.' The men go wild, run and jump into creeks, brush and over banks. In all it is raising quite a ques[tion], but as yet no one is greatly fearing an outbreak."[35]

Even far from the reservations at the Carlisle school efforts were made to communicate the news of the Ghost Dance in a manner best tailored for its students. Staff members told them through the school newspaper that "the Messiah craze . . . may have been [purposefully] sprung upon those poor ignorant people by white men who are after their lands. . . . What a shame and an outrage it is! What is the real reason for it all? Ignorance on the part of the Indians, nothing else." Carlisle faculty clearly downplayed the import yet alarmingly addressed the Lakotas in their charge: "Our boys and girls who have learned to read and reason, know better than to be led into trouble in that fashion. Thousands, perhaps, of your people will suffer and many be killed before they get their eyes open. Dear boys and girls, if you were there you could not help them. Be content that you are where you can get the education that will save you from such a fearful mistake in the future."[36]

In addition to its largely misunderstood character, the Lakota Ghost Dance introduced a potentially lethal trapping. Among the accessories of the dancers that came to the notice of whites were the unbleached cotton muslin shirts and dresses worn during the ritual. Black Elk recalled making such shirts to give to Oglala and Brulé dancers. Fashioned from flour sacks, the shirts and dresses were adorned with fringe, eagle feathers, and braided sweet grass and brightly decorated on front and back with paintings of the moon, sun, and stars and sometimes fish and birds, with painted V-shaped yokes. Such imagery was said to represent the visions of dance participants. The garments seemingly appeared on the scene within weeks and months after the dance took hold on the reservations. But perhaps only after troops arrived in late November 1890 did the attire take on a protective aspect, evidently promoted by Kicking Bear and Short Bull. Its most enduringly controversial and ultimately deadly quality was a purported power to stop bullets. The shoddy construction of their clothes possibly suggested this protective attribute and perhaps reflected the expected fulfillment of the dances' purpose just months away, in the spring of 1891.[37]

Thus, although the Ghost Dance was fundamentally a religious ceremony grounded in peaceful pursuits, most area whites gradually associated its practice with coming conflict. The introduction of the special garb with its notorious bullet-stopping aspect only added to the fears of whites. Through confusion, anticipation, and ignorance they gradually ascribed an unsettling war mentality to the Sioux. This was directly contrary to the adherents' own belief that their peaceful performance of the dance would hasten the removal of all whites and assuage their own earthly tribulations.

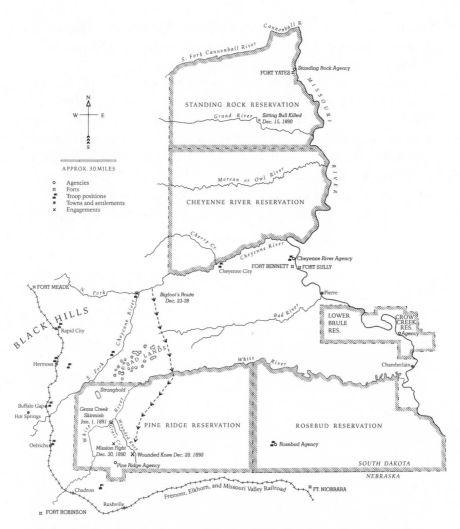

Map 2. Lakota Reservations and Vicinity, 1890–91. Map by Robert G. Pilk.

SIX

Perception

On July 4, 1890, American Independence Day was observed on the Pine Ridge Reservation at the tiny community of Wounded Knee near the creek of that name. The Indians passed the day with a mix of pony races, foot races, wrestling matches, a greased pig chase, and a trapeze performance, all capped off with a grand Omaha dance in the evening. Some not yet fully caught up in the Ghost Dance might also have visited Chadron or Rushville. As in the past, some Indians partook of white celebrations (including getting drunk) in the Nebraska panhandle settlements where Red Cloud occasionally addressed the crowds, while at nearby Fort Robinson erstwhile Sioux powwows pulled crowds from Crawford and Harrison. In July and August a paleontological expedition from Princeton University set up camp along the Cheyenne River near Oelrichs.[1]

Amid the burgeoning Ghost Dance phenomenon, many of its believers, as well as those not bound by its premise, continued their day-to-day lives on the reservations. As the dance brought hope for their future, many of the people strove to coexist with whites and others in their present world and initially did not altogether shut them out. Nor were the progressives and nonprogressives starkly divided at this juncture. Because of family allegiances, some Christian Indians coexisted with the Ghost Dancers, just as some nonprogressives did not altogether accept the dance. Only toward midsummer as the Ghost Dances became better organized, grew in number and attendance, and drew more notice from whites did they take on a new gravity that made the practitioners begin to pull back among themselves.

The newly configured Lakota reservations had similarities but also localized differences. The Oglalas were transferred in 1878 to Pine Ridge Agency, at the junction of Wolf Creek with White Clay Creek. It had become the paramount administrative base among agencies on the Great Sioux Reservation and retained that status as that once large reserve was dismantled and further reduced after the Sioux land agreement. In the evolving turbulence of 1889–90, owing to the large reservation population (5,531 people, including Oglalas, mixed-bloods, and nearly 600 Northern Cheyennes), its initial prominence in the emergent Ghost Dance movement, as well as its ready access to railroads in Nebraska, Pine Ridge Agency became the face of the coming discord to most white Americans as registered in news coverage across the nation. As the closest Sioux agency to the Black Hills, Pine Ridge had come to represent the ever-mounting efforts toward dispossession that the Lakotas had sustained repeatedly in the years after 1876. As turbulence among all the Sioux people increased during 1890, the agency became the primary locus of attention for the duration of the crisis.

Following reduction of the Great Sioux Reservation, Pine Ridge Agency sat near the southwestern corner of the newly designated Pine Ridge Reservation, a province that ran roughly 115 miles east to west and 60 miles north to south. Delineated largely by politically appointed borderlines, the reservation boundary also traced White River for part of its length on the north before adjoining the boundary of the Rosebud Reservation on the east. (Indians questioned the purpose of such political boundaries. At a council convened at Pine Ridge to discuss seemingly ever-encroaching whites, some asked: "Why does not the white man take boundaries made by God, like the rivers, mountain ranges, or buttes? He takes imaginary lines laid down on paper and these lines all the time keep moving toward the Indian.")[2] Pine Ridge Agency stood about twenty miles east of the western reservation boundary along the 103rd parallel and only two miles from the Nebraska state border on the south. In fact the reservation extended into Nebraska below the agency with inclusion of a five-by-ten mile Executive Addition in 1882 to buffer liquor merchants. Like the other tracts carved from the former Great Sioux Reservation, Pine Ridge Reservation shortly became subdivided into districts dedicated to monitoring the people with managers known as agency farmers, all overseen by a designated subagent appointed by the reservation agent at the agency headquarters.

Instilling the rudiments of husbandry among the Lakotas was a primary duty of the agent in promoting acculturation among his wards while distributing supplies and services and fostering education, as called for in the 1868 treaty. As noted, children who were not sent to boarding schools back east were instructed at agency day schools, at a government-run boarding school, or at a mission boarding school operated north of the agency by the Jesuits. The Indian agent, who reported directly to the commissioner of Indian Affairs in Washington, D.C., was responsible for all agency activities. After the establishment of the Pine Ridge Reservation, the agent came to exercise ultimate control over all of the land, tribal people, and activities within its boundaries.[3]

A swirling thundercloud of events settled over the Sioux reservations in the spring, summer, and fall of 1890. Pine Ridge Agency became successively occupied by government officials, whites, so-called half-breed (mixed-blood) French families left over from the fur trade, Indian, Mexican, and mixed-race workers, including freighters, visiting tribal leaders, an assemblage of press representatives, and eventually the army. The community included a small but growing complex of federal, church-related, and secular buildings, roads, fenced tracts, outlying Indian encampments, and related structures. Agency facilities stood less than a mile east of White Clay Creek, which trended north and northwest to join White River some fifteen miles away. Most government buildings enclosed part of a squared enclave housing the agent and his employees, the Pine Ridge Indian police station and jail, various storehouses and issue houses, a forage yard for hay and grain, and a wood yard, in addition to the requisite sawmill and lumber yard, carpenter, wagon, harness, and blacksmith shops, and stables.

Beyond the northeast corner of the enclave was a cattle yard. East and across the street from these fundamental amenities lay fenced tracts harboring a few trader stores (one combined with a post office), an eight-room hotel built in 1888, occasional tipis, and assorted log homes. Larger tribal encampments occupied tracts scattered on the outskirts of town. The community had three churches. The Presbyterian church was located on a dirt road entering the community from the east. An Episcopal church stood a short distance to the southwest, while a large Catholic church dominated a broad tract south of the core agency offices. Farther west and beyond the employee houses, approximately midway between the government area and White Clay Creek, stood the frame government boarding school raised in 1883–84, the largest building at Pine Ridge. The community also had eight separate day schools. Besides the road from the east, two other roads entered Pine Ridge Agency from the south: one from Rushville, Nebraska, along the railroad twenty-five miles southeast of the agency, and the other from Chadron, southwest of Rushville. Another artery stretched north four miles from the agency to the Jesuits' Holy Rosary Mission and boarding school, an imposing four-winged brick edifice erected through the labors of Catholic bishop Martin Marty as the gift of philanthropist Katherine Drexel of Philadelphia. One observer commented that Pine Ridge resembled "a well-kept country village" with "no fortifications of any kind, not even a stockade or strong house to retreat to in case of trouble. The most formidable barriers in the way of a hostile [Indian] are the picket fences and the wire screens over the windows."[4]

Despite the area's placid appearance, the tribal leaders at Pine Ridge Reservation reflected differences in thinking in the debate over the land bill. The outcome of the measure had divided the Oglalas. The staunchly conservative Red Cloud, in fact, had been joined in his resistance to the bill by Little Wound, Young Man Afraid of His Horses, and Big Road, while progressives American Horse and No Flesh urged their people to sign the measure, thereby splitting the moderate Indians. There the issue had been left to simmer, but schisms surfaced after the drastic cut in beef rations announced after Sioux ratification of the land agreement. As a further frustration, the Northern Cheyennes living at Pine Ridge who had signed the measure to give away more Sioux land now felt threatened and openly agitated to join their kinfolk in Montana. As the Ghost Dance gained popularity among the Sioux in 1890, American Horse and Young Man Afraid of His Horses openly opposed the movement, while Little Wound came to endorse it. Red Cloud remained skeptical, offered only passive acceptance, and generally stayed aloof on the subject. While the old chief continued to garner respect from the people, not all of them accepted his influence unquestioningly. Red Cloud had been somewhat marginalized by Washington. Many Oglalas had aligned themselves politically with American Horse, Little Wound, and other progressive chiefs. Sometimes the schisms ran deeper. Red Cloud's earlier killing of Little Wound's father doubtless complicated his relationship with that chieftain.[5]

Some outside observers with little sympathy for the chief believed that Red Cloud's influence had waned altogether by 1890. "There seems to be no break in the unanimity which declares him to have long outlived whatever usefulness he may ever have possessed," asserted one correspondent late that autumn. "Today he is the champion American beggar, ready to be placated at any time with a larger portion of rations and a greater degree of consideration." Yet much of rising tumult at Pine Ridge and the other Lakota agencies was based not only on the growing adoption of the Ghost Dance but on uncertain administration by politically appointed agents of the federal government. At Pine Ridge Agency, for example, the relationship between Red Cloud and the local administration thrived amid mutual toxicity going back a decade.[6]

The first agent at Pine Ridge was Dr. Valentine T. McGillycuddy, who had previously served as a contract surgeon with the army in 1876. A feisty, stern-eyed Republican, the goateed McGillycuddy was appointed to the relocated agency in 1879. He proved a strong if strict innovative administrator. Among his accomplishments was the institution of a fifty-man Indian police force to help govern and enforce the agent's decrees for acculturating the Oglalas. Under McGillycuddy and the efficient police captain George Sword, the cleavage between progressives and nonprogressives accelerated. Red Cloud came to resent his own diminishing influence and to disdain McGillycuddy. When the experienced yet oft-investigated agent exited as a victim of patronage politics in 1886 after the election of Democrat Grover Cleveland, Hugh D. Gallagher, a Catholic Civil War veteran who at the time occupied a home in Chadron, Nebraska, became his replacement as agent at Pine Ridge. The people soon recognized Gallagher's tact and honesty. In 1888 he endorsed establishment of the Holy Rosary Mission north of Pine Ridge, a gesture that pleased Red Cloud, who had been baptized in the church. But it was Gallagher who first addressed the rising messiah "craze" and tangled with Ghost Dancers at Pine Ridge in the summer of 1890. As the movement gained momentum throughout the Lakota reservations in the wake of the beef issue, Gallagher, who became targeted by the newly seated Harrison regime despite his success, prudently resigned.[7]

As events unfolded, McGillycuddy (who had remained in nearby Rapid City) became a gadfly on the subject of the deteriorating conditions among the Sioux. He grew particularly incensed upon learning of the appointment of Dr. Daniel F. Royer on August 14, 1890, to succeed Gallagher at Pine Ridge. Although experience was not mandated by spoils politics, Republican Royer was no match for either of his predecessors. Undersized and portly, the thirty-six-year-old Pennsylvanian had earned a medical degree in Philadelphia in 1875 before relocating to eastern Dakota Territory in 1883. Royer pursued a medical practice in the town of Alpena while serving in various municipal positions, including postmaster and county coroner. He owned a livery stable, a lumberyard, and a drugstore. Royer also held interests in the local bank and newspaper and served in the territorial legislature in 1888–89. After Harrison's election, South Dakota governor Arthur C. Mellette urged an Interior Department appointment for Royer. In the end Senator Pettigrew joined with Senator Gideon C. Moody and Representative Oscar S. Gifford to recommend Mellette for what then must have been viewed as a potentially volatile position at Pine Ridge.[8]

Royer did not assume his post until early October. In the meantime the dances intensified, mainly among the nonprogressive Indians, but the authorities showed no immediate concern. When army leaders in Washington, D.C., inquired about the initial dancing in June, Brigadier General John R. Brooke, who commanded the Department of the Platte from Omaha, responded that things were under control and that a military presence would only provoke matters. After Royer's arrival, dances at Pine Ridge occurred some ten miles north of the Holy Rosary Mission. The Jesuit superior Father John (Johann) Jutz (pronounced "Yootz") attended one and "tried to explain . . . that this dance was coming from the evil spirit and . . . they should give it up and go home." But the dancers were lost "in the darkness of heathenism" and could not be dissuaded. Jutz, who would play an influential role in coming events, believed that the Indians had been victimized by the government and mistreated "by whites in general." This view was echoed in the local press, which blamed the dancing on "bad faith on the part of the government, bad rations, and not enough of them." Father Perrig similarly believed that the ghosts that appeared during the dances "are inspiring the Indians with distrust, dislike, contempt or even hatred of the whites." A few weeks later the ceremonies took place in a hall only half a mile from the mission. By mid-late November they were occurring at No Water, twenty miles north of the agency, and at Medicine Rock, ten miles further north. Yet the reactions were mixed, for some whites who witnessed the dancing reported that the Indians were unarmed and that "there was nothing of a warlike nature in the appearance of the Indians or in any of their actions."[9]

Similar unrest occurred on the adjacent Rosebud Reservation, especially at Rosebud Agency amid watered and wooded sand hills ninety miles east of Pine Ridge Agency and a hundred miles west of the Missouri River. The dancing took hold through the summer and early fall and quickly caused open commotion. Rosebud Reservation harbored almost 5,400 Indians, mostly Brulés but with several hundred mixed-bloods, Two Kettles, and other Lakotas, some of whom held allotments under the 1868 treaty. Agency facilities mirrored those at Pine Ridge, and a "reliable and trustworthy" Indian police force had been organized. Most Indians lived in log buildings with dirt floors and roofs. St. Mary's Episcopal mission boarding school stood fifteen miles east of the agency, while St. Francis Catholic Mission boarding school was eight miles southwest. Only a single day school was located at the agency, but a dozen more were scattered through the countryside within sixty miles. Some thirty-five miles south of the reservation stood Valentine, Nebraska, along the Fremont, Elkhorn, and Missouri Valley Railroad, which transported goods and supplies bound for the agency. A few miles east of Valentine, troops of the Eighth Infantry at Fort Niobrara monitored conditions at the agency as the messiah movement took hold.[10]

At Rosebud the continuing hunger issue exacerbated the Ghost Dance situation. The Sioux remained agitated over the severity of their ration cuts. So hungry were the Brulés that and an officer at Fort Niobrara described their frequent visits to that post, pleading "for the refuse from the slaughter pen and from the company kitchens." In early November Chief Hollow Horn Bear wrote directly to President Harrison, asking him to "give us just so as you have promised." The chief further suggested that the reason the Ghost Dance appealed to so many was because "it is a *feast* to which the hungry and starving Indians are attracted and where they are fed, [and] would cease if the people received sufficient rations to live upon." Special agent E. B. Reynolds complained on November 2 that the Indians at Rosebud "kill [and eat] cows and oxen issued to them for breeding and working purposes, make no secret of doing so, and openly defy arrest." Reynolds added that two Indians recently had killed their stock "for a feast at the Ghost Dance." Tribal policemen sent to arrest these men confronted at least seventy-five armed Indians who refused to turn the men over. Reynolds concluded that "the religious excitement aggravated by almost starvation is bearing fruits in this state of insubordination; Indians say they had better die fighting than to die a slow death of starvation, and as the new religion promises their return to earth, . . . they have no fear of death." Further, said Reynolds, "these Indians have within the past three weeks traded horses and everything else they could trade for arms and ammunition, and all the cash they become possessed of was spent in the same way." As early as November 2, Reynolds urged that "a sufficient force of troops" be sent to Rosebud to forestall an outbreak.[11]

At Rosebud such incidents proliferated under agent J. George Wright, who had been in charge for nearly a year. Although Short Bull, resident medicine man and prophet/messiah, had halted the dancing at the agency following admonishment from Wright, it resumed at outlying camps among "the most nonprogressive and disturbing element of Indians, which attracted the attention and curiosity of nearly all on the reserve." Moreover, the high volumes of dust rising above them during the day readily identified all of the communities where dances were being held. Some progressive Indians moved their families west to Pine Ridge to avoid trouble.[12]

Among the major nonprogressive leaders at Rosebud were Two Strike, White Horse, Lance, and Crow Dog, assassin of the Brulé peace chief Spotted Tail in 1881. Leaders like Swift Bear, Hollow Horn Bear, and Standing Bear headed the progressives at Rosebud. When Wright again terminated the dances, the Indians in turn abandoned their livestock and farming activities and openly continued to pursue the ceremony. And when rumors flew of troops on the reservation, warriors rode out to meet them, brandishing guns and wearing war paint. Wright managed to counter the false alarm and convinced them to return home. In any case the dances grew in intensity. The Rosebud leaders were influenced by happenings at neighboring Pine Ridge Agency and encouraged by the temporary replacement of Wright by an army officer at Rosebud Agency, as well as Short Bull's prediction that other tribes (Cheyennes, Arapahos, and Crows) would be included and his unilateral advancement of the millennium to spring 1891 or sooner. The apostle called on his followers to abandon their homes and move to Pass Creek, the boundary between Rosebud and Pine Ridge reservations. They should assemble there to await the millennium near a tree that would shoot forth.[13]

Conditions at the more distant Lakota reservations were similar, if seemingly less turbulent than at Pine Ridge and Rosebud. As elsewhere, the people had striven to overcome pervasive drought and disappearing game. Some earned money hauling freight, while others worked maintenance jobs. At Cheyenne River Agency adjoining Fort Bennett, neither agent McChesney nor his recent successor Perrain P. Palmer had reported much disruption despite rampant interest in the messiah there. The Tetons living close to the Missouri River were largely progressives. But to preempt difficulties Palmer ordered the Indian police to arrest Kicking Bear, who lived on the reserve (he was soon freed by the Indian court at the agency). It was the more remote Miniconjous to the west near the forks of the Cheyenne River who had been influenced by Kicking Bear, triggering Ghost Dances under Big Foot there and under Hump, Low Dog, and other leaders downstream, near the confluence of Plum and Cherry Creeks. In early November Palmer reported 400 dancers at the confluence of the creeks. "The Ghost Dance [is] still in progress and increasing rather than diminishing," he wrote. "When told that the Department is displeased with their actions, these dancers sullenly answer [that] the Indian is displeased with the Department." As November wore on, others along the Cheyenne River took up the dance, which soon affected at least a third of the reservation people. Palmer, who revisited the camps late that month, grew concerned. The dancers refused to permit whites to approach their meetings, and the Indian police held little authority over them. Nonetheless, as reports circulated that the Indians at Cheyenne River had "abandoned" their dancing in favor of retrieving their rations, the day school at Cherry Creek closed. Students excited by the dances became unruly amid rumors that Sitting Bull's followers were readying a breakout from Standing Rock. As elsewhere, the Cheyenne River people were allegedly using their money to purchase weaponry.[14]

Standing Rock, straddling the boundary between North Dakota and South Dakota, had been the last of the Lakota reservation bastions to embrace the Ghost Dance. The dance had gained momentum there in the late summer and fall as conservative Sioux adopted its practice in the vicinity of Sitting Bull's camp along Grand River, forty miles southwest of Standing Rock Agency, adjoining Fort Yates on the Missouri. In regard to the four thousand or more reservation occupants, an officer at the post noted that "the Indian situation here is not serious. Everything is quiet, the Indians taking it easy, so to speak." The progressives under chiefs Gall, John Grass, and Mad Bear maintained control near agency headquarters, and the dance had not spread elsewhere on the reservation. As at the other agencies, an Indian police force responded to situations across the reserve, backed by a functioning court with Indian judges. As a visiting correspondent observed, "The Indians [near the agency] are loyal to the government and as much afraid of the Messiah Indians as [are] the white people."[15]

As at the other reservations, virtually all of the people lived in rough-cut log homes that cost the government $10 each to build. Most of the progressive population at Standing Rock vainly tried planting corn, oats, and wheat; stock raising was little more successful, and some of the men took to freighting as a livelihood or cut wood for sale to the government. Children at Standing Rock attended seven day schools dispersed through the reservation. An agricultural school, as well as an industrial school, taught enrollees the tenets of farming, harness making, blacksmithing, and carpentry. The area had five churches of the Catholic, Episcopalian, and Congregational denominations. The agency also boasted a hospital, a "neat little building" with two wards that might accommodate twelve patients, twenty by crowding. At Standing Rock the police force numbered thirty permanent policemen—two officers and twenty-eight privates. The Indian court consisted of judges (including John Grass) appointed by the agent, who could overrule decisions if he pleased. Judicial sessions took place biweekly, each lasting two days, and meted out punishment of hard labor or solitary confinement as required.[16]

Concern at Standing Rock centered almost exclusively on the person and presence of the Hunkpapa leader Sitting Bull. Like Red Cloud, Sitting Bull evinced a certain cynicism over the hybrid dance and its promised result and was not personally involved in it. Yet missionaries protested against the dance, so the old medicine man presided over and encouraged the dance under apostles like Circling Bear. Sitting Bull believed that promoting its promise as prospective relief for the troubled Sioux and resisting officials and missionaries trying to prevent it enhanced his own influence.

Agent James McLaughlin was in charge at Standing Rock. The slightly built, goateed, and flinty-eyed McLaughlin—a tough, no-nonsense bureaucrat whose long record had solidified his successive reappointments there despite the patronage system—predicted that the dancing would die out as cold weather approached. But he denounced Sitting Bull to Commissioner Morgan as an obstructionist embodying the worst attributes of the nonprogressive Sioux who had become the resident antagonist on the reservation by defending the Ghost Dance. "He is a chief mischief-maker at this agency, and if he were not here, this craze so great among the Sioux would never have gotten a foothold at this agency." McLaughlin urged removal of the chief and others of his kind. Washington responded passively, however, and did not immediately call for Sitting Bull's arrest. Late in October Sitting Bull visited the agency to retrieve rations but ignored a message from McLaughlin to visit his office before returning to his home on Grand River. As weeks went by, the issues at play between these two prevailing personalities on Standing Rock would dramatically affect circumstances throughout the disparate components of the former Great Sioux Reservation.[17]

In the meantime the growing number of Ghost Dances among the Sioux through the summer and early fall created excessive anxieties for white populations near the reservations. Oft-magnified coverage by competing newspaper and wire service correspondents generated much rising concern. As the dances proceeded through November into December, a media pool took shape at Pine Ridge Agency. Some newsmen were "space writers," paid on the basis of volume production, who tended toward sheer fabrication in their output. Indeed one local paper in early December announced that "the Indian excitement is accountable for . . . having produced a crop of . . . sensational mongers [sic] and liars of the first water." Another reported that "stories of the most alarming character are told about once an hour and contradicted in less time." But some major city reporters colored their copy too. As events progressed, about two dozen reporters convened at Pine Ridge, churning out good and bad human interest copy for consumption by American readers, with only an iota of truth if not total disregard for it. Rumors and published stories generated by reporters at Pine Ridge using official intelligence as well as potentially dubious sources among white and Indian agency workers, cowboys, and scouts contributed to the rousing gossip that affected citizens in the vicinity of the reservations. Columnists hung around the trader stores, often converting blather caused by boredom into formal coverage, which they dutifully forwarded to Rushville for telegraphic dispatch to their papers.[18]

Following the arrival of soldiers in November, notices of spurious troop movements abounded. One paper's article headlined "Rumors of a Battle" contained allegations by unchecked sources suggesting an engagement wherein "sixty soldiers and Indians have been killed." Another ludicrously proclaimed that "the Indians under Red Cloud declare they will meet the troops in battle tomorrow." Yet another spoke of "the Messiah, who is coming tomorrow in the form of a buffalo" to begin "the conflict . . . to annihilate the white race." By late December local editors called such accounts a "farce" and a "fiasco," effectively blaming them for creating frenzy and driving away settlers and prospective business through a trumped-up "phony" Indian war with headlines that influenced public perception. The *Hot Springs Daily Star*'s editor denounced the "sanguine hued reports of . . . irresponsible correspondents describing an imaginary Indian outbreak in South Dakota." Specifically calling out the "*Omaha Bee* and its ilk," the *Star* denied the existence of internecine war. While admitting that Ghost Dances and local disturbances had occurred, the newspaper reported that Indians "did not wantonly destroy any buildings or property, and the wild rumors printed day after day by the eastern papers, for the sake of a few nickels to be gained by selling extras, have proved disastrous to our country." Nonetheless, the news stories were chock full of important details otherwise lost to history, and the reporters proved valuable recorders in spite of themselves.[19]

As misinformation flew, whites could not comprehend the rationale of dancers attempting to improve their lot in this manner. But for many in the white population, Indian dances so rigorously pursued meant but one thing: "Outbreak!"—an ethnocentrically loaded term casually repeated by whites in coming days to forecast Indian menace and violence. As Ghost Dance participants sought spiritual reunion with departed relatives, white settlers believed that adherents expected to die while "caught up in a frenzy of reckless fatalism," rather than await the messiah who would restore the old days and remove the whites. Most whites never knew, for example, that items produced by white people (particularly firearms with their metal components) were expressly forbidden in the dances.[20]

Concerns mounted among settlers, traders, farmers, and stock raisers near the reservations in the manner of past Indian wars throughout the West, though with a greater concentration of well-settled citizens. As the dancing persisted, whites largely watched from afar, most of them assuming the worst. Explanations for what the Indians were doing were confusing, conflicting, inadequate, erroneous, and most of all simply misunderstood, and they all evolved into fear. Away from the reservations, few people distinguished between progressive (including Christian) and nonprogressive Sioux. Most assumed that all of the Indians embraced the dancing.

Although Indians had not as yet physically harmed any whites, by November settlers west of Pine Ridge in the communities in Custer, Fall River, and Pennington Counties all the way down to the Nebraska border streamed into the Black Hills communities for protection. Impelled by concern if not outright fear, many others left their homes from September into late November and relocated to Rapid City. A settler in Moulton, South Dakota, wrote his father about the Indian scare: "When it first began two weeks ago every family on this creek below us . . . moved to Rapid City." Those on the western extremities of the Cheyenne River headed for Piedmont, Belle Fourche, and Sturgis. Others sent dependents east to Sioux Falls and Minneapolis and beyond and held public meetings to organize home guard units to protect their property. Occasionally a lone soul stayed on the prairie to guard property. Rumors from Pine Ridge and elsewhere abounded, only adding to the uncertainty of the moment.[21]

Fearing trouble from the Ghost Dances, some communities petitioned state and national governments for protection. Governor Mellette acknowledged requests for arms and ammunition from Rapid City, Hermosa, and Buffalo Gap adjacent to Pine Ridge; from Bowdle, Eureka, and Gettysburg near Standing Rock and the Cheyenne River; and even from Highmoore, north of Crow Creek Reservation (a dance had been disrupted by Indian police at Lower Brule on November 27). The *Black Hills Daily Times* at Rapid City called for federal intervention to stem an uprising. As usual individuals saw potential sales to the military in any such offing.[22]

In Nebraska the situation was much the same. In November settlers south of the Rosebud Reservation began leaving their homes to congregate in Valentine. Others stuffed bedding into wagons and flocked to Harrison, near the Wyoming line, filling homes, hotels, and even the courthouse on rumors that sixteen families had already been wiped out. Some flew in panic to Crawford and nearby Fort Robinson for protection. "Believing the Indians were dealing death and destruction," reported the *Sioux County Herald,* "people with few exceptions have loaded their families into wagons and gone to the towns." Near the Montrose community northeast of Harrison locals raised an earthen bulwark around a hilltop with an underground chamber fitted out with stores, water, and ammunition, while others at nearby Bodarc fashioned a log shelter. At Appleton they fortified a root cellar with heavy planks while reconnoitering parties roamed through the countryside on horseback, watching for Indians. Entrepreneur David Moffatt built a huge sod buttress around the two-story schoolhouse at Gordon, east of Rushville. Several families in Sheridan County hitched their horses to wagons to converge on a homestead boasting a thick-walled sod house atop high ground. Elsewhere citizens formed "rifle" clubs then solicited Governor John M. Thayer for guns to protect families and livestock. Anxious townspeople in Chadron prepared resolutions calling on Washington, D.C., for protection, while orders from the state capital alerted national guard units across the state.[23]

The impulse carried into North Dakota, too, where frantic settlers in river communities north of Fort Yates headed for Mandan and Bismarck and readied local militias, raised sod fort defenses, and filed dispatches to state and federal authorities for protection. A concerned woman in Mandan wired McLaughlin at Standing Rock: "If there is any sign of danger please tell my daughter Delia Carey to close school [and] come home." Such trepidation proved unnecessary. "Mandan people and a few others deserve a roasting for their worked-up wild scare," commented a scribe at Fort Yates. Back in South Dakota, some Indians who could read visited Pierre and Chamberlain to buy newspapers; they learned of the ongoing alarm among the whites over the dancing and reportedly took delight in sharing the stories. But some believed that jingoist defiance among correspondents who were loose with the truth unduly created apprehension.[24]

When Daniel Royer took over at Pine Ridge in early October, rumors abounded and excitement reigned. The neophyte agent could barely keep up with swirling events. On October 12, mortified by the conditions that he found, Royer notified the commissioner's office that "I . . . have an elephant on my hands." Because of its location and large population relative to the other reservations and its readier access to the outside world, Pine Ridge quickly became the epicenter of the Ghost Dance manifestation. Although the other agencies faced disorder with the dances, most reported significant unrest only after the dances assumed more frequency and intensity in the fall as the dancers' day of reckoning drew nearer and the dances became "a serious element of disturbance." The affected agents received instructions from the commissioner "to exercise great caution in the management of the Indians, with a view to avoiding an outbreak, and, if necessary, to call upon this office to secure military aid to prevent disturbances." Furthermore, the commissioner of Indian Affairs asked the War Department to initiate the arrest of certain Ghost Dance exponents: Sitting Bull, Circling Hawk, Circling Bear, and Black Bird, all Hunkpapas at Standing Rock. The agent at Cheyenne River urged the same treatment for Hump and presumably for Big Foot on that reservation.[25]

Within weeks of his arrival, Royer was stretching his capabilities to assess and respond to what was going on. He quickly became an alarmist. As Short Bull's Brulés gravitated toward Pass Creek, Royer became excited and anxious: it quickly became clear that he wanted troops at his station. Colonel Joseph G. Tilford, commanding officer at Fort Robinson, learning of "a dance of some magnitude" at Pine Ridge, advised the agent to leave the Indians alone to avoid trouble but to alert him if troops were needed. In the meantime Royer pulled his outlying staff and their families into the agency. In a statement to Morgan he identified four major Ghost Dance groups on his reservation. One was located along White Clay Creek, twenty miles north of the agency, and numbered 600 members under Torn Belly, His Fight, Bear Bone, and Jack Red Cloud, the old chief's son. Another at Wounded Knee Creek, eighteen miles northeast, had about 250 people under Big Road, Shell Boy, and Good Thunder. Another at Porcupine Creek, a few miles further east, consisted of 150 followers of Knife Chief, Iron Bird, and Whetstone. The last group, at Medicine Root Creek, perhaps forty miles away, contained about 500 adherents under the formerly progressive-minded Little Wound. Royer called him "the most stubborn, headstrong, self-willed, and unruly Indian on the reservation." It did not take long for observers to take the new agent's measure. The Chadron paper called him out for blaming his predecessor for everything that had gone wrong: "The only good reason that can be assigned . . . is that his own rule has been notoriously weak and incompetent, and by alleging mismanagement to others he hopes to cover up his own shortcoming." Before long Royer's charges referred to him as "Young-Man-Afraid-of-Indians."[26]

On occasions when Royer directed his Indian police to shut down Ghost Dances, they had no apparent effect on the large crowd in attendance. The police leader informed the agent that he should simply let the dances play out and the Indians would tire of them. Others told Royer the same thing. Episcopal bishop William H. Hare, who toured the agencies in October–November, believed that the Ghost Dance was declining: "The promised crisis will not come, and meanwhile the Indians will have danced themselves out." Cold weather was also thought to be an imminent destroyer of the movement. Yet Royer quickly lost all semblances of respect and authority. Scarcely a month into the job he complained that the Ghost Dancers regularly defied the law, made threats, and pulled their children from school. Furthermore, "when an Indian violates any law the first thing they do is join the ghost dance, and then they feel safe to defy the police, the law, and the agent." "The only remedy," he concluded, ". . . is the use of military, and until this is done, you need not expect any progress from these people." "I have used every means at my command to persuade the chiefs to give this ghost dance up, but all in vain," he told Morgan, before urging that troops be sent "to arrest the leaders and place them in prison under guard, and then disarm the balance of the Indians." As conditions worsened, more incidents occurred. When Major General Nelson A. Miles appeared at Pine Ridge Agency on October 27 to consult with the Cheyennes on their request for removal to Montana, he spoke with Royer and agreed to provide soldiers if needed. Miles believed that the Ghost Dance was a fleeting aberration that would pass on its own.[27]

As the pace quickened around him, Royer experienced an incident with the Ghost Dancers on ration day (Monday, November 10) that prompted him into what he believed was permissible action. He directed the arrest of an Oglala man named Little charged with killing a beef in violation of policy. When the police sought to comply, an unruly crowd surrounded them.

American Horse intervened, but Jack Red Cloud, asserting a leadership role among the dancers, challenged him. He flourished a pistol in American Horse's face while berating him for having signed the land agreement. Eventually the disturbance subsided, but it had clearly distressed Royer. Late that night he convened a meeting in his office to gauge opinion on his course. Present were the Reverend Charles Smith Cook, a mixed-blood Yankton Sioux and prelate at the Holy Cross Episcopal church; the agency physician, Dr. Charles A. Eastman, a Santee Sioux recent graduate of Boston University Medical School; Royer's chief clerk, Bishop J. Gleason; and a visiting inspector. Royer solicited their views on calling in troops. Cook and Eastman believed that such a plan was inadvisable, while Royer and the others supported it. Royer thereupon approved the decision. At the agent's request, Captain George Sword, his lieutenant, Thunder Bear, and Chief American Horse appeared and concurred with the ruling.

On November 11 Royer formalized his judgment by wiring Commissioner Morgan, seeking consent to visit Washington and address the situation with him personally: "Please grant authority for me to come at once as the circumstances justify it":

> As reported in former communications the ghost dance at this agency has assumed such large proportions that it has become a serious matter, and if some action is not taken soon the worst results may be expected. To-day I ordered the second lieutenant of police force to arrest an Indian that had violated the law in several instances, one of the charges being that he has been killing cattle promiscuously over the reservation. On being informed by the police that I wished him brought to the office, he drew his knife and positively refused to be arrested, and a mob of the ghost dancers rushed in and relieved their fellow dancer from the hands of the police, taking him away to their camps, and boasting of their power and making all kinds of fun over the attempted arrest and the inefficiency of the police force, etc. . . . It is useless for me to try and make anything out of these people against such opposition, and it should be stopped at once.[28]

Thus began a barrage of crucial appeals from Royer. The next day he sent a terse message telling Morgan that "[I] can not explain matters satisfactorily by telegraph or letter," adding that "you will agree with me when I see you personally that it is important for me to come." Morgan was out of town, but acting commissioner Robert V. Belt denied the request. Acting Interior secretary George Chandler concurred with Belt that Royer "should remain at his post and do his duty." Later that day Royer dispatched the following telegram, recounting the incident with Little while expanding on his lament:

The condition of affairs at this Agency when I took charge, whether intention[al] or not, were to render my administration a failure. Orders of Constituted [*sic*] authority are daily violated and defied and I am powerless to enforce them. The condition of affairs is growing from bad to worse. Yesterday in attempting to arrest an Indian for violation of regulations the offender drew a butcher knife on the police and in less than two minutes he was reinforced by two hundred ghost dancers all armed and ready to fight. Consequently the arrest was not made. To-day I received communication from the offender stating that the policemen who attempted to enforce any orders must be discharged or I could expect trouble and I was given four weeks to do it. The Police force are over-powered and disheartened. We have no protection and are at the mercy of these crazy dancers. The situation is serious and I urgently request that I be permitted to proceed to Washington at once and confer with you personally as a correct idea of the situation cannot be conveyed otherwise. The Indians have received their beef and rations and are going home and there is no immediate danger until next big issue. I can leave now without the service being injured and I do hope you will grant my request or let the blame rest where it belongs. Have no other object in view save the best interests of the service.[29]

Belt responded directly: "The interests of the service require that you remain at agency at this time." The exchange continued, with Royer next day resubmitting his lengthy missive of November 12, finally eliciting the following from acting commissioner Belt to the secretary of the Interior:

I deem the situation at said agency arising from the ghost dance as very critical and believe that an outbreak may occur at any time, and it does not seem to be safe to longer withhold troops from the agency. I therefore respectfully recommend that the matter be submitted to the honorable Secretary of War, with the request that such instructions as may be necessary be given to the proper military authorities to take such prompt action as the emergency may be found by them to demand, to the end that any outbreak on the part of the Indians may be averted and the Indians be shown that the authority of this Department and its agent must be respected and obeyed by them.[30]

Two days later, November 15, while communications passed between the Interior Department and War Department, agent Royer sounded a final anxious plea:

Indians are dancing in the snow and are wild and crazy. I have fully informed you that employees and government property at this Agency have no protection and are at the mercy of these dancers. Why delay by further investigation? We need protection and we need it now. . . . Nothing short of one thousand soldiers will settle this dancing. The leaders should be arrested and confined in some military post until the matter is quieted, and this should be done at once.

Acting commissioner Belt forwarded Royer's message with his own recommendation that "the War Department . . . take whatever steps are necessary for the protection of life and property at this agency."[31]

Following his exchange with Belt, Royer made a hurried visit to Fort Robinson to encourage the assignment of troops to Pine Ridge. He later met with officials tasked to help with his situation. Special U.S. Indian agent James A. Cooper arrived from Kansas and over ensuing days joined the agent in council with Red Cloud, Little Wound, Big Road, and other chiefs. Little Wound, speaking evasively, explained the dancing as a means by which the Indians vented discontent over their well-known grievances, an assuredly credible assertion. Cooper also worked with Royer to enlarge the agency police force to 100 men.

In the meantime, in order to complete a correct tally of the Lakota people, the administration had earlier sent special Indian agent A. T. Lea with instructions to count them and determine their true ration needs in regard to the beef apportionment issue. Lea had observed many of the people far afield as well as those around the agency, and his conclusions were inflammatory. Regarding the Oglalas, he stated that "the hostile portion of the tribe had their young men, painted and decorated in war costume, riding all over the country notifying those who desire to go to war to meet on White River, at [the] mouth of White Clay Creek. . . . The war party disclaimed any intention to make an attack, but proposed to continue to dance in defiance of all authority." Lea's observations not only interpreted the events as a manifestation of a war passion but further clouded the picture at Pine Ridge. He concluded that the Indians were in fact overfed and possessed more food than they needed: "in my judgment hunger has nothing to do with the present trouble upon Pine Ridge Reservation." He denied that the people were desperately slaughtering and consuming their breeding stock. Yet some in the know rejected Lea's conclusions as being politically charged to favor an administration view. Furthermore, in his visits to Indian homes, Lea kept tab on the number of firearms he saw, later telling authorities that "they are the best armed people that I ever saw. . . . I find from one to three repeating rifles in nearly every house, with an abundance of fixed ammunition, besides many revolvers. . . . [I am] satisfied they are fully prepared for a fight and will fight, if crowded."[32]

At Pine Ridge, the eye of the potential storm, Deputy Marshal Bartlett acknowledged the rising tension: "Considerable excitement exists here now, although things are seemingly quiet." "Several of the whites have removed their families from the Reservation. Watches are continuously kept on duty, day and night," he wrote. Bartlett elaborated on what presumably were commonly shared views: "The Ghost dance is in full bloom. Indians are truly in an excited condition, but I do not fear an outbreak, but any sudden impulse might cause one." As a long-time resident of the area, he supported a hard line on the matter. "The Ghost dance should be broken up. It has a very demorilizing [sic] influence." Bartlett supported Royer's solution. "I think it will take an action on the part of the Military to overcome it. I tell you all this confidentially."[33] On the verge of army intervention, conditions at Pine Ridge and Rosebud reservations had become dangerously unstable during the Ghost Dance autumn of 1890. They threatened to spill over onto Cheyenne River and Standing Rock, where the simmering grudge between McLaughlin and Sitting Bull was escalating to a point of explosion.

For many Tetons, dancing in all quarters undoubtedly expressed hope in regard to the status of their families and future, but huge misapprehensions existed in the regional white communities. In their fears, few non-Indians understood what was happening. They found it hard to recognize that the Ghost Dance was merely symptomatic of what ailed the Sioux or that through the dance the people hoped to rid themselves of whites and all the detrimental qualities that they embodied. Non-Indians understood even less that the messiah—not the Lakotas themselves—would bring it all to fruition by spring 1891: to ascribe to the Indians a general uprising (as special agent Lea's comments suggested) was altogether mistaken. Any warlike tendencies on the part of Ghost Dancers manifested themselves late in the fall as authorities tried to stifle their religious expression and curb the dance, surely a prime reason why the ghost shirts that the people had fashioned began to assume their protective dimension.

Compounding all this, the arrival of such a feckless bureaucrat as Royer epitomized the worst extremes of patronage politics. A correspondent who studied Royer called him "a spineless agent" who had lost the respect of his Indians and who was attempting to promote their "warlike demonstration" to justify his fretful dispatches and retain his job.[34] Furthermore, much of the government reaction to that point as well as most of the public response was driven by rumors, fears, exaggerations, and unsubstantiated reports from media falling back on shoddy reports bordering on xenophobia, alarming settlers and townspeople around the Lakota reservations while erroneously finding warlike intent in the Indians' behavior. The Indians also had access to newspaper intelligence, so it is plausible that such reports alarmed and confused them too, distorting many of their own views of what was occurring and fixing their responses to the misinformation flying about. A self-perpetuating whirl of propaganda was confounding almost every observer. Under a government founded on precepts of religious tolerance, that very notion had been denied to its Native people. With Royer's anxious entreaties followed by imminent commitment of military resources, events had rushed beyond conciliation to confrontation, perhaps past the point of return.

1. Major General Philip H. Sheridan and his generals, 1865

Sheridan's subordinate generals later made names in the West during the period of the Indian campaigns. *From the left:* Wesley Merritt, Sheridan, George Crook, James W. Forsyth, and George A. Custer. Forsyth, shown here as a brigadier general, would command the Seventh Cavalry at Wounded Knee as a Regular Army colonel in 1890. Photo by Alexander Gardner. Author's collection.

2. The Sioux Land Commissioners, 1889

Major General George Crook, former Ohio governor Charles W. Foster, and former Kansas City mayor William Warner served on the government commission that orchestrated the Sioux Land Agreement of 1889. Here the members meet at Standing Rock Agency in July. The transaction capped the inexorable dispossession of the Lakotas from their historically occupied lands and helped frame the issues and events culminating in the massacre at Wounded Knee on December 29, 1890. Photo by David F. Barry. Courtesy of the Denver Public Library and Paul Harbaugh.

3. Kicking Bear and Short Bull, 1891

Kicking Bear and Short Bull played instrumental roles in the evolving Ghost Dance on the Sioux reservations in 1889–90. Kicking Bear, at left, an Oglala resident at Cheyenne River, notably propounded the movement among the Lakotas, including Sitting Bull's people at Standing Rock. Brulé medicine man Short Bull became an apostle of Wovoka, the Paiute manifestation of God among the Indians, but gradually assumed the role of messiah among the Sioux, a representation that he later denied. Photo by George F. Spencer. Courtesy of Paul Harbaugh.

4. Ghost Dance in progress, 1890

This view of an ongoing Sioux Ghost Dance was reportedly taken near Sitting Bull's home along Grand River on the Standing Rock Reservation. It is said to have been snapped by a news correspondent using a small box camera hidden beneath his coat. Eighth Cavalry Sergeant George DuBois quipped: "The Indians did not know that they were being taken in with a Kodac [*sic*]." Photo by George W. Scott. Courtesy of Minnesota Historical Society.

5. Red Cloud

Chief Red Cloud opposed allotment and denounced the 1889 Sioux Land Act. An avowed Catholic, he personally rejected the Ghost Dance but endorsed its practice among Oglalas on the Pine Ridge Reservation. By 1890 the venerated chief, whose influence was waning, sought to reconcile divergent views among progressives and traditionalists and cautiously sided with the government in its handling of the Sioux crisis. Red Cloud lived another nineteen years after Wounded Knee, dying at age eighty-seven in 1909. Photo by Clarence G. Moreledge. Courtesy of Paul Harbaugh.

6. Pine Ridge Agency, 1890–91

Pine Ridge Agency was the epicenter of the army occupation in 1890–91. This broad view from the north shows the government Indian school at the far right, the agent's office and employee residences beyond the hay ricks and water tower at the right center, a sawmill and wood yard at the approximate center, and the large government store house and issue house to their immediate left. Farther to the left is a complex of traders' stores and homes, a hotel, and a residence for Presbyterian pastors. In the left distance rises the steeple of the Episcopal church used as a hospital to treat those injured Lakotas brought in from Wounded Knee. An Oglala encampment occupies the foreground. Courtesy of the Denver Public Library.

7. Agent Daniel F. Royer

A spoils system appointee without previous experience in Indian affairs, agent Daniel F. Royer reached Pine Ridge in October 1890 amid the growing Ghost Dance fervor. His overreaction to the Sioux unrest promoted the military takeover, providing the combustible elements leading to Wounded Knee. Courtesy of the South Dakota State Historical Society.

8. George Sword and Indian police

George Sword (also known as Hunts the Enemy), at left, served as captain of the Indian police at Pine Ridge Agency. Originally fifty men strong, the force was enlarged to one hundred in 1890 and helped maintain order throughout the reservation over the following months, including dealing with disruptions from outlying Ghost Dances. Sword's police stabilized the agency in the immediate aftermath of Wounded Knee, when distant warriors fired on government buildings there. Courtesy of the Denver Public Library.

9. President Benjamin Harrison

As myriad problems confronted the Sioux in 1889–90, Republican president Benjamin Harrison ordered the occupation of Pine Ridge and Rosebud, hoping to assure peace and stem an outbreak throughout the Lakota reservations. He supported General Miles's efforts to avoid bloodshed but ultimately aligned with the army hierarchy in opposing the investigation of Colonel Forsyth's operations at Wounded Knee and the subsequent Mission Fight. Courtesy of the Benjamin Harrison Presidential Site.

10. Commanding General John M. Schofield

Major General John Schofield commanded the U.S. Army from headquarters in Washington, D.C. It was under his purview that General Miles directed efforts against the Sioux in 1890–91. While Schofield and secretary of war Redfield Proctor supported Miles's operations, they bridled at his perceived excesses. In 1895, on the basis of seniority, Miles succeeded the retiring Schofield as commanding general. Photo by Charles M. Bell. Courtesy of the U.S. Army Military History Institute.

11. Major General Nelson A. Miles

Major General Nelson Miles oversaw initial army operations on the Sioux reservations from his Chicago headquarters. After Sitting Bull's death Miles moved his command post to Rapid City and assumed direct charge at Pine Ridge Agency after Wounded Knee. He had hoped to avoid bloodshed and held Colonel Forsyth accountable for what had happened, a view at odds with the Washington hierarchy. In retirement Miles became an advocate on behalf of the Lakotas in their efforts to seek restitution. Courtesy of the Denver Public Library and Paul Harbaugh.

12. Brigadier General John R. Brooke and staff, Department of the Platte, 1891

General John Brooke was a competent if single-minded officer who oversaw the military occupation of Pine Ridge Agency in 1890. His planned assault on the Indians' Badlands position was superseded by events following the killing of Sitting Bull. Brooke grew frustrated over Miles's imposed strictures as well as the army imbroglio surrounding Wounded Knee and the Mission Fight. After the massacre Miles supplanted Brooke, who finished the campaign in the field. Here he poses with his staff in Omaha in 1891. *Left to right, seated:* Lieutenant Colonel Thaddeus H. Stanton, deputy paymaster general; Lieutenant Colonel William B. Hughes, chief quartermaster; General Brooke, commanding the department; Major Michael V. Sheridan, assistant adjutant general; Lieutenant Colonel/surgeon Dallas Bache, medical director; Major Daniel W. Benham, Seventh Infantry, inspector of small arms practice. *Back rows, left to right:* Major John M. Bacon, Seventh Cavalry, acting inspector-general; Captain Charles Bird, assistant quartermaster; Major/surgeon Albert Hartsuff; Captain John Simpson, Omaha Quartermaster Depot; Captain Enoch Crowder, Eighth Cavalry, acting judge advocate general (who participated in the aftermath of the Sitting Bull Fight); First Lieutenant Charles M. Truitt, aide-de-camp to General Brooke; Captain Charles A. Worden, Seventh Infantry, acting engineer officer; Major Edmond Butler, Second Infantry; and Captain James C. Ayres, chief ordnance officer (commanding the Omaha Ordnance Depot). Courtesy of John Siebert.

13. Soldiers in camp

This view depicts infantry soldiers enduring the burdens of everyday camp life at Pine Ridge Agency during the routine occupation preceding and following Wounded Knee. Posed before Sibley tents, the men variously sport fatigue blouses and overcoats along with muskrat caps and campaign hats as they gather wood to cook a meal. Judging from the hands and coats of several, they have been mixing flour, likely for making biscuits. Courtesy of the Denver Public Library.

14. Ninth Cavalry bivouac at Pine Ridge

Ninth Cavalry troopers played an important role during the occupation of Pine Ridge Agency. In this candid view some of the Buffalo Soldiers appear in their camp area with their white officers. The hay was strewn over the ground for the horses after the recent snowfall. Courtesy of Paul Harbaugh.

15. Dr. Charles A. Eastman

Dr. Charles Eastman (1858–1939), also known as Ohiyesa, of mixed Dakota and white ancestry, served as agency physician at Pine Ridge at the time of Wounded Knee. One of the first to visit the massacre site, he helped rescue Lakota survivors on the field and treated the wounded in the improvised Episcopal church hospital. Eastman married educator Elaine Goodale and later became a noted author and lecturer on American Indian topics. Courtesy of the South Dakota State Historical Society.

16. Elaine Goodale

Elaine Goodale (1863–1953), supervisor of Indian education in the Dakotas, was at Pine Ridge during the Ghost Dance fervor and subsequent events in 1890–91 and helped treat Indian casualties after Wounded Knee. She provided important perspectives on events at that time in her subsequent writings. In later years Goodale supported Lakota survivors' claims for compensation for what had happened to them and their families. Courtesy of the South Dakota State Historical Society.

17. Sitting Bull

Hunkpapa Lakota leader Sitting Bull, who found refuge in Canada following Custer's defeat, surrendered to reservation life in 1881 and became a staunch traditionalist on the Standing Rock Reservation. His embrace of the right of his people to practice the Ghost Dance, which he personally eschewed, helped bring on his death at the hands of Indian policemen and spurred fleeing Hunkpapas to join with Big Foot's people in the days preceding Wounded Knee. Photo by George W. Scott. Courtesy of Paul Harbaugh.

18. Agent James McLaughlin

Standing Rock Reservation agent James McLaughlin resented interference in attempting to meet and possibly remove Sitting Bull; he scuttled Buffalo Bill's effort and directed the arrest himself, an effort resulting in the medicine man's death. A hard but fair administrator, McLaughlin conceptually rejected compensation for Big Foot's people after Wounded Knee yet later endorsed it and recorded some of their human and material losses in the massacre. Courtesy of the Denver Public Library.

19. Lieutenant Bull Head

First Lieutenant Henry Tatankapah (Bull Head) of the Standing Rock Agency Police worked with agent McLaughlin to neutralize Sitting Bull, an effort that culminated in the medicine man's death near Grand River on December 15, 1890. At Grand River bullets fired by Bull Head helped kill the chief, although he was himself badly wounded and died within days. Here Bull Head wears traditional dress in posing for photographer David F. Barry. Courtesy of Paul Harbaugh.

20. Sergeant Red Tomahawk

Sergeant Marcellus Red Tomahawk proved a steadfast component of agent James McLaughlin's police cadre at Standing Rock Agency. He carried out the agent's order to arrest Sitting Bull but in the resulting affray fired one of the shots that killed the medicine man. In after years Red Tomahawk became known as the slayer of Sitting Bull. Courtesy of Paul Harbaugh and the Denver Public Library.

21. Sitting Bull's cabin

Sitting Bull's cabin at Grand River on the Standing Rock Reservation near the spot where he was killed on December 15, 1890. The holy man's family members appear near the doorway. The cabin was subsequently dismantled and shipped for exhibition at the World's Columbian Exposition in Chicago in 1893. Courtesy of the Denver Public Library.

22. Chief Big Foot, ca. 1889–90

This faded picture by an unknown photographer shows Miniconjou Chief Big Foot, fourth from the left, together with Chief Horned Cloud, at the far left. A traditionalist leader whose followers embraced the Ghost Dance, Big Foot nonetheless promoted peace and sought to get along with army leaders. Apparently fearing attack by troops, he started for Pine Ridge Agency to meet with Red Cloud. Big Foot's subsequent capture and detainment at Wounded Knee set the stage for the disaster that followed. This image is said to have been found in the destroyed Sioux camp. Courtesy of Michael Her Many Horses.

23. Lieutenant Colonel Edwin V. Sumner

Lieutenant Colonel Edwin Sumner commanded Eighth Cavalry troops along the Cheyenne River. His negligence in permitting Big Foot and his people to flee south toward the Rosebud and Pine Ridge reservations incensed General Miles, changed the focus of the army's campaign, and promoted the historic encounter at Wounded Knee. Photo by LeRue Lemer. Courtesy of the Missouri History Museum, St. Louis.

SEVEN

Deployment

The advent of Major General Nelson Appleton Miles into the surging Lakota crisis was fortuitous, for he shared a long and discordant history with those people. He had spent considerable time in Montana and knew them and many of their leaders well since rigorously campaigning against them in 1876–77 after Custer's defeat. Miles, fifty-one, had been accorded large credit for concluding the Great Sioux War. Much of his résumé was well known in 1890. Born and raised in Massachusetts, and with scant formal military training, he joined the state volunteer force in 1861 as a lieutenant and rose quickly in rank for stellar performances on the Virginia battlefields of Seven Pines "Fair Oaks" (where he was wounded), Antietam, Fredericksburg (where he received another wound), and Chancellorsville (where he was wounded yet again), for which service he would receive the Medal of Honor. Miles also fought in the battles of the Wilderness, Spottsylvania, Reams's Station, and Petersburg (where he received still another wound). By the spring of 1864 he was a brigadier general of volunteers. The following year, at the age of twenty-six, he was appointed major general of volunteers and given command of the Army of the Potomac's Second Corps.

After the war Miles served as custodian of the imprisoned Confederate president Jefferson Davis. Mustered out of the volunteers, Miles was appointed colonel of the Fortieth Infantry. In the reorganization of the army in 1869 he received the colonelcy of the Fifth Infantry Regiment. Miles, who lacked the West Point credentials typically ensuring such advancement, overcame this perceived deficiency through his accomplishments. He also married well, taking as his bride in 1868 Mary Hoyt Sherman, a niece of Senator John Sherman of Ohio and General William T. Sherman, who would become commanding general of the army. The ambitious Miles exploited this political relationship to full advantage for much of his career. On the Great Plains with the Fifth Infantry, Miles quickly emerged as one of the top army field commanders, leading troops against Kiowas, Comanches, and Southern Cheyennes during the Red River War in 1874–75 and against the Lakota and Northern Cheyenne coalition on the Montana plains after Little Bighorn.

Known as "Bear's Coat" among the Indians for his winter campaign garb, Miles proved an effective officer on whom his superiors could depend, a plugger who unflaggingly pursued his foe on diverse fields in all seasons and under the most extreme conditions. In the decade after 1876 Miles's record as an Indian fighter exceeded those of his contemporaries George A. Custer, George Crook, Ranald S. Mackenzie, Oliver O. Howard, Eugene A. Carr, and Wesley Merritt. He campaigned against the Nez Perces in 1877, the Bannocks in 1878, and the Chiricahua Apaches in 1886 and won advancement to brigadier general in the regular army hierarchy. Miles successively commanded the departments of the Colombia in Portland, Arizona in Tucson, and the Missouri in St. Louis. After Crook's death in March 1890 Miles's record and reputation helped assure his promotion to the Division of the Missouri headquarters.

While always the brave soldier, Miles possessed an outsized ego that often affected his image as well as his acceptance by others. As an ardent self-promoter, his marriage to Sherman's niece contributed an air of presumptuousness and pomposity that no doubt flawed his personality. He had an unforgiving disposition; among the officer cadre of the army he, like others, was frequently contemptuous of colleagues and held grudges. Miles and Crook—his chief rival for promotion—disliked each other intensely due to long-term personal jealousy and the Geronimo Campaign, wherein Miles had supplanted Crook and succeeded in winning the Chiricahuas' surrender. Improbably, it was Crook whom Miles had replaced in Chicago. Hence many associates, in addition to President Harrison, a Republican, perceived Miles, a likely Democrat, as problematic. Only after the officer conversed at length with the commander-in-chief was the promotion to Chicago tendered. A conspicuously attractive man as he entered middle age, the articulate and spirited Miles stood five feet seven inches tall, carried himself with military bearing, and cut a strong positive image in uniform. His steel-gray hair and mustache reflected an agreeable mellowing of his temperament and to some degree his vanity by 1890, by which time he had become a familiar national figure with a solid record of achievement.

Miles's intuitive grasp of the circumstances facing the Teton Sioux reflected his many years in the West dealing with Indian people. Importantly, he commiserated with what had happened to the Lakotas over the thirteen years since the conclusion of the Great Sioux War and particularly over the course of the past sixteen months. Both Miles and Commanding General John M. Schofield informed the president that a meaningful solution to the crisis would not be achieved until Congress addressed the Indians' grievances. Miles empathized with the Sioux. Using contemporary expressions for Indian people, he noted that "the causes of the difficulty are easy of location—insufficient food supplies, religious delusions, and the innate disposition of the savage to go to war. These hostiles have been starved into fighting, and they will prefer to die fighting rather than to starve peaceably."[1]

In 1890 the U.S. Army was an institution whose leaders (perhaps excluding Miles) incessantly anticipated more conventional conflicts with the powers of Europe in spite of recurrent campaigns against the western tribes since the close of the Civil War. Since 1886 and the end of operations against the Apaches, federal soldiers, beyond manning coastal fortifications, had occasionally served as strikebreakers in labor disputes in midwestern and eastern cities or in a police capacity on posts near the western Indian reservations. As of 1890 the Regular Army totaled approximately 22,000 officers and men. Most, beyond staff personnel, were assigned to twenty-five regiments of infantry, ten of cavalry, and five of artillery, each numerically designated within its branch and variously stationed at several hundred garrisons spanning the nation, with most of the artillery units located along the coasts. Two of the infantry regiments and two of the cavalry regiments were segregated black units officered by whites and known to Indians as "Buffalo Soldiers" because of the supposed similarity of their hair to the fur of the shaggy beasts.

Troops stationed on the northern plains at posts like Fort Robinson were administered from the War Department in Washington, D.C., through subordinate geographical division and department headquarters in cities like Chicago (Military Division of the Missouri), Omaha (Department of the Platte), and St. Paul (Department of Dakota). These troops served mostly in cavalry, infantry, and, occasionally, artillery regiments—the primary fighting forces. Each regiment contained several hundred enlisted men under the command of officers commissioned by the government. Fulfilling the supporting staff functions, the quartermaster, subsistence, medical, ordnance, and engineer departments supplied the troops with necessary food, supplies, weaponry, and all other services.

Miles would draw from this broad collective to initiate operations in South Dakota. He feared that a large part of the force had grown lethargic and inefficient on the plains since the 1870s. Ever melodramatic, the general penned an admonition to army headquarters: "It would not be strange if the Indians, who have contended for every foot of ground from the Atlantic to the Pacific in more than two hundred years of warfare, should make one final desperate effort in the death struggle of their race."[2]

As of late November 1890, while Miles prepared to send troops to the Lakota reservations to curb the Ghost Dance, prevent an outbreak, and insure order, the major military posts situated around the concerned reservations consisted of Forts Niobrara, Robinson, Meade, Yates, Bennett, Sully, and Randall, incorporating in all some fourteen cavalry troops and twenty-five infantry companies, all below optimum designated strength.[3]

By 1890 the army's mission in regard to Indians had changed, as most observers understood. It had become clear over the past decade that the forced removal of tribes to reservations had moderated the military function from the punitive campaigning of old to constabulary oversight of the internees inhabiting those tracts. Although some officers still argued stridently for the return of Indian administration to army control (the army had not overseen Indian affairs since 1849), the decades-long debate had worn thin. With few supporters to champion such change, transfer was a dead issue. Even so, while the intensifying Ghost Dances played out across the Sioux reservations through much of November, quiet measures had been underway to determine the extent of Indian disaffection and whether it would indeed require significant military involvement.

Following President Harrison's order to assess the Sioux predicament, General Miles had delegated Brigadier General Thomas H. Ruger, commander of the Department of Dakota with headquarters at St. Paul, Minnesota, to tour the area of the reservations under his purview, investigate conditions, and, if required, determine appropriate measures to quell

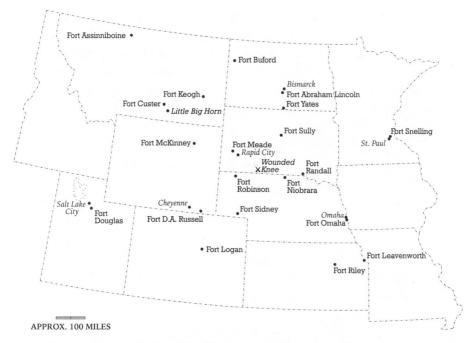

Map 3. Regional Military Establishment, Northern Great Plains, 1890–91.
Map by Robert G. Pilk.

potential trouble. Ruger visited Standing Rock, Cheyenne River, Lower Brulé, and forts in the vicinity of these reservations along the Missouri River. He shifted troops accordingly among these posts to meet perceived needs, outwardly quieting the concerns of settlers in those areas. At Cheyenne River Ruger noted agent Palmer's fading authority but reported decreasing ardor for the dancing. He concluded that no outbreak would occur and that the onset of cold weather would indeed finish the movement. Ruger stated further that the "opinion of the best and most intelligent ['progressive'] Indians was . . . that those concerned in *originating* the excitement should be arrested." Ruger did not visit Pine Ridge or Rosebud, where the Ghost Dance was reaching the most people and having the most profound impact, no doubt partly owing to Short Bull's influence there. But he urged that a force be sent to intimidate the Pine Ridge Indians. In fact troop detachments from Forts Meade and Robinson already monitored the scene from points off the western boundaries of the Pine Ridge and Cheyenne River reservations.[4]

Besides directing the War Department investigation, the president expressed concern after reading correspondence between the Indian Bureau and its agents at Pine Ridge, Rosebud, and Cheyenne River regarding their difficulties in maintaining authority and their recent requests for troops. On November 13, two days after reading Royer's last frantic message, he concluded that the situation was serious: "the authority and discipline of the agents must be maintained, and adequate and early steps taken to prevent any outbreak [that] may put in peril the lives and homes of the settlers in the adjacent States." The president directed the secretary of war to prepare sufficient forces to take the field, as required, and further instructed Secretary Noble to counsel agents to segregate progressive from nonprogressive Indians and try to avoid an eruption pending the War Department's readiness. By this action, the president not only began a constitutionally authorized civil function to use the army to protect a state (South Dakota) against domestic violence, but simultaneously empowered the War Department to manage the Lakotas on their reservations, following initiation by the Bureau of Indian Affairs.[5]

Harrison's directive set in motion the military occupation of the Sioux reservations. On Friday, November 14, three days after Royer's first angst-ridden telegram (and a day before his "wild and crazy" communiqué), Major General Schofield forwarded Harrison's order to General Miles at the Chicago headquarters of the Division of the Missouri. This administrative domain embraced much of the Great Plains, including the states of Nebraska, North Dakota, and South Dakota, and thus the entirety of the troubled reservations.[6] Schofield, an 1853 West Point graduate and Medal of Honor recipient (Wilson's Creek, Missouri, 1861), possessed vast and diverse command experience through and beyond the Civil War, including a stint as secretary of war, and was steeped in administrative knowledge. While soliciting Miles's views on the Sioux matter, Schofield reiterated the purpose for the action in his own accompanying directive: "First to prevent an outbreak on the part of the Indians which shall endanger the lives and property of the people in the neighboring country, and second to bring to bear upon the disaffected Indians such military force as will compel prompt submission to the authority of the Government." Significantly, the order to Miles formalized the action, specifying "the arrest of such of the leaders as may be necessary to insure peaceful conduct of the tribes."[7]

Miles did not respond immediately. While well versed on the Sioux situation through the media and his army dispatches, besides his accrued knowledge of the people, he took a temperate view of the matter. On November 15 he proceeded to St. Louis, ostensibly to complete an inspection of Jefferson Barracks in that city. There he spoke with secretary of war Redfield Proctor about the Sioux situation, returning to Chicago on the evening of November 16. The next day he wired Schofield, telling him that he had directed troops into Pine Ridge and Rosebud, a decision with which Schofield concurred. They were soldiers from Forts Omaha, Niobrara, and Robinson, Nebraska, which were more immediately accessible to those agencies. The anticipated movement of Brigadier General John R. Brooke's troops from the Department of the Platte into Ruger's Department of Dakota would constitute, at the least, something of an administrative irregularity that was tacitly approved by Miles and the army hierarchy for convenience of military action.[8]

The commanding general endorsed Miles's decision to protect those agencies and to restrain "the turbulent Indians, to avoid, if possible, an outbreak or any active hostilities . . . until the advancing season and further preparations shall make the operation of the troops more surely effective, with less danger to surrounding settlements." (Short Bull's address of mid-November has sometimes been referenced as the motive driving the troop deployment. While media notice of the speech helped define the mounting disturbance, its significance as the catalyst for military involvement has most likely been overdrawn.) Schofield told Miles that cavalry and artillery troops at Fort Riley, Kansas, would be made available for his command, and "all other available troops will be placed under your orders" should the emergency dictate. Within days he gave his division commander his own broad views on how best to implement operations: "In my judgment the ghost dancers should not be disturbed for the present, nor anything be done to precipitate a conflict. When all your troops are concentrated and ready for action we can judge better of the measures that may be necessary and advisable. The troops should all be prepared for a winter campaign and encamped at convenient points near the scene of action, where they will best serve to deter the disaffected Indians from commencing hostilities." He instructed Miles to have his staff requisition "by contract or otherwise" equipment sufficient for his force. Through the press Schofield assured the public that the army posts surrounding the Sioux reservations already provided enough soldiers to meet any emergency. On Miles's behest, Governor Thayer of Nebraska issued a proclamation forbidding the supply of arms and ammunition to Indians.[9]

Thus in relatively short time Agent Royer's persistent dispatches to Washington had set in motion a military response to quell the Lakota Ghost Dance and avert trouble at both the Pine Ridge and Rosebud reservations. By November 19 the agent and his family had relocated to a hotel in Rushville. Still fearing the Indians in his charge, he claimed: "I have come into town at night to send my telegrams to the commanding officer of the department [of the Platte in Omaha] to keep them [the Indians] from knowing anything of the approach of troops, and [I] have slept in town a large portion of the time." Royer was also there to meet General Brooke. He told a reporter that on that morning an Indian at the railroad depot in Rushville had raised a knife to strike him but did not carry through. The man had not been arrested.[10]

Brooke reached Rushville as sensational reports of battles swept the region, precipitating the scramble of more settlers for safety. He had left Omaha at midnight, preceded by four companies of the Second Infantry and their wagons, which entrained from Fort Omaha for Rushville the evening of November 18. The *Omaha World-Herald* reported that as they departed "some of the younger men playfully cut off a lock of their hair and gave [it] to comrades or the girls they left behind them, . . . as they said the Sioux should not get all their hair."[11] Three troops of the Ninth Cavalry Buffalo Soldiers and one company of the Eighth Infantry (as acting artillerymen) joined next day from Fort Robinson fitted out with horses, mules, wagons, supplies, and campaign gear. Fearful of the Indians' awareness of what was happening, Miles had asked newspapers not to publish information about troop movements, although word quickly spread when the cavalry units gained Rushville. As notice went out to army posts as far away as Texas and Arizona to prepare commands for deployment to South Dakota as required, even more infantrymen at Fort Omaha readied themselves to start west over the Fremont, Elkhorn, and Missouri Valley line.

Late on the afternoon of November 19 Brooke and the men of the Second, nearly 500 strong with two light artillery pieces and with Royer in tow, took the road for Pine Ridge, twenty-six miles away. It was a chilly night, and most of the men lacked overcoats. Smoking or talking above a whisper was not allowed. In the course of the march over hilly terrain several wagons overturned. In one mishap a teamster suffered a broken hip. The soldiers stopped briefly for coffee and hardtack then resumed, reaching the agency at 7 A.M. on Thursday amid a raging sandstorm as news of the military presence circulated. There they began laying out their camp, unpacking baggage, and digging latrines in accordance with army protocol. In concert with Brooke's advance, at 3 A.M. on November 21 Lieutenant Colonel Alfred T. Smith, from Fort Niobrara with two troops of the Ninth Cavalry and three companies of the Eighth Infantry as well as Hotchkiss and Gatling guns, reached Rosebud Agency, ninety miles east of Pine Ridge Agency. They set up camp and began raising earthworks atop the surrounding hills. A dispatch from Rosebud predicted that "when the Indians on this and the Pine Ridge Agency wake up . . . they will find themselves surrounded by the strongest body of United States troops which has been mustered in the West since the defeat of Geronimo."[12]

The entry of occupation forces at Pine Ridge and Rosebud for the first time since creation of the Great Sioux Reservation in 1868 caused instant consternation. Many of the people felt that they were about to be attacked, a reaction that troop commanders had hoped to avoid. Oglala schoolchildren at Pine Ridge Agency pointed to the rising dust in the distance and told their teacher that "soldiers are coming."[13] At Rosebud the troops aroused fear in older Brulés who had lived through the sudden army attack on their camps at Blue Water Creek, Nebraska, in 1855. From Rosebud, a mass of panicked tribesmen under Short Bull and Two Strike (perhaps as many as 600 warriors besides their families) fled west toward Pine Ridge, destroying much property in their flight, including livestock.

When the tribesmen gained the Pine Ridge boundary and realized that soldiers were ahead there too, they deviated north, fearing confiscation of their arms and horses. They rode away from the agency, down Pass Creek toward White River and the edge of the Badlands. En route the Brulés killed and butchered cattle, wrecked cabins, and destroyed property of Indians, mixed-bloods, and whites, nearly all of whom had deserted the locality. Short Bull's followers halted near the confluence of Wounded Knee Creek with White River, thirty miles north of Pine Ridge Agency, where the dancing resumed. "They are very defiant," reported Brooke.[14]

Other Brulé and Oglala progressives who had not yet subscribed to the Ghost Dance but feared mistaken attack by the troops fled in the opposite direction to gain refuge at their respective agencies. Red Cloud, who had anticipated troops at Pine Ridge and was now clearly concerned over where the Ghost Dances were leading, wrote the editor of the *Chadron Democrat* on the eve of the soldiers' arrival at Pine Ridge, reminding him that "I have been a friend to the whites that are living near the reserve, and I want to have peace. . . . I do not want to have trouble with the soldiers and other good white people that are near me. I want you to publish my letter so the people of Chadron may know that I am a friend to them."[15]

The soldiers who arrived on November 20 and 21 were not the only troops bound for Pine Ridge and Rosebud or the other agencies. General Miles had clearly availed himself of the carte blanche offered by his superiors to go beyond the geographical limits of his division in assembling his field command.[16] Owing to an increase in connecting railroads in the 1880s that permitted rapid transport of troops and animals almost anywhere across the West, Troop D of the Ninth Cavalry, as well as the regimental pack train, would reach Pine Ridge via Rushville from Wyoming on November 24, under Major Guy V. Henry, legendary Indian fighter and squadron commander of the Ninth. Companies G and K of the Second Infantry likewise arrived from Fort Omaha on the November 25. Late in the month four companies of the Twenty-First Infantry from Fort Sidney, Nebraska, under Lieutenant Colonel John S. Poland joined at Rosebud to augment that force.

Within days additional troops followed. Of special note is the arrival at Pine Ridge on Thanksgiving Day of the headquarters and two squadrons (eight troops) of the Seventh Cavalry of Little Bighorn fame, stationed at Fort Riley, Kansas, under command of Colonel James W. Forsyth, along with Light Battery E of the First Artillery. An infantryman mused to his sweetheart back at Fort Robinson: "I think after all them troops get here, it will about scare the Indians and they will all surrender."[17]

Over the following weeks more reinforcements arrived in the principal zone of operations, some from far afield. In early December nine troops of the Sixth Cavalry, numbering nearly 500 soldiers as well as the same number of horses and the unit's equipment, joined from stations in New Mexico and Colorado, arriving in Rapid City on December 9 and 10 for service along the Cheyenne River. The unit's grizzled commander, Colonel Eugene A. Carr, had campaigned through western Dakota fourteen years earlier in pursuit of many of these same Lakotas. A veteran of numerous clashes with Indians since the 1860s, Carr now reckoned how best to acclimate his men to wintry climes. (Among the officers of the Sixth under Carr's command was Second Lieutenant John J. Pershing, who would rise to become general and commander of the American Expeditionary Forces [AEF] in World War I.)[18]

Later that month seven companies of the Seventeenth Infantry under Lieutenant Colonel Robert H. Offley reached the Cheyenne River from Fort D. A. Russell, Wyoming. Other units arriving as events dictated included two companies of the Third Infantry, also posted near the Cheyenne, five of the Seventh Infantry riding Pullman cars from Denver to Pierre to bolster the garrison of Fort Sully (where a sixth joined from Fort Leavenworth), four more of the Twenty-First Infantry summoned from Utah to garrison Fort Robinson, and four of the Sixteenth Infantry from Utah, as well as a platoon of the Fourth Artillery dispatched from Kansas to Fort Meade.

Units quartered in the region included the Eighth Cavalry, with five troops located at Fort Meade near Sturgis, north of Rapid City, and two at Fort Yates at Standing Rock, which would factor materially in activities evolving out of these posts. Twelfth Infantrymen garrisoned Fort Bennett at Cheyenne River Agency and Fort Sully downstream on the Missouri, while soldiers of the Fifteenth Infantry occupied Fort Randall, below Sully. Through December and beyond, troops of the First, Second, Fifth, and Ninth Cavalry regiments from Fort Leavenworth, as well as the First Infantry Regiment from Angel Island, California, would establish guard posts in the vicinity of the Pine Ridge and Rosebud agencies. Farther west, commands in General Ruger's department would advance from Montana to be nearer the Sioux reservations as operations played out. Even General Miles's old Fifth Infantry regiment and the Third Cavalry assumed readiness status, awaiting word from Washington. Neither was called up.[19]

Each of these troop components contained enlisted soldiers, the backbone of the American army. Often foreign-born, undereducated, and unemployed, these men had signed up, sometimes repeatedly, for five-year hitches at a base rate of thirteen dollars per month to do the government's bidding and to lay their lives on the line if necessary in the performance of that duty. Those assigned on and around the Sioux reservations in 1890 represented the mix of backgrounds, preparedness, and efficiency that often marked soldiers through all periods of history. Their commissioned leaders represented another varied lot. Many were educated and capable; others were not. With diverse backgrounds, some had risen from the ranks, while others had been seasoned with decades of experience in the lower grades of lieutenant and captain. As with the enlisted men, many were immigrants, often veterans of army service in their native lands.

The schism between officers and enlisted men was ever present. As rumors coursed through the ranks at the outset of every campaign, senior leaders imparted little pertinent information. Many officers as well as enlisted men took to heavy drinking, and alcohol was a constant bane throughout the frontier military establishment. On the eve of starting from

Fort Robinson, Private August Hettinger of the Eighth Infantry recalled a "jollification" at the post canteen, wherein the troops stole liquor stored by the officers for their private use. The regimental quartermaster told the enterprising Hettinger to care for a single filled gallon jug: "I managed to get [it] . . . to the Rosebud Agency by putting it in a nosebag and filling it to the top with oats." As for the Indians' situation, many of the soldiers believed that the ruckus with the Sioux in 1890 was caused by dilatory agents whose actions brought on starvation of the people and that the Indians knew they had been cheated.[20]

Besides the introduction of regular troops to the scene at the Pine Ridge and Rosebud agencies and all around the other reservations, the army resolved to raise as many as 500 Indian scouts to augment these forces and serve as added insurance for success. On November 22 General Miles received authority for such recruitment, with the admonition that "great care should be taken in selecting the Indians; only those known to be loyal and friendly should be enlisted." Three days later a body of applicants, including forty-four Northern Cheyennes but also Oglalas living at the agency, "a bright, intelligent looking lot of young braves," was selected by First Lieutenant Charles W. Taylor, an experienced officer of the Ninth Cavalry. About 110 of the chosen recruits accompanied Taylor to Fort Robinson for enlistment. They furnished their own mounts and at the post received uniforms, weapons and other equipment, and training before returning to Pine Ridge as Company A, Indian Scouts. "This action and the willingness of the Cheyennes to enlist as scouts [against the Sioux]," noted one correspondent, "engendered a bitter feeling between the two tribes." "The alliance of the Cheyennes with the military . . . is likely to make the Sioux even more bitter toward the soldiers than they have been."[21]

The presence of the troops transformed things. Almost immediately the road from Rushville became an alternating dusty and muddy umbilical for government and contract wagons, many driven by Indian freighters hauling commissary and quartermaster goods from the railroad. Visitors to Pine Ridge in late November described and photographed the hundreds of Sioux tipis belonging to progressive Lakotas (now called "friendlies") stretched out in the vicinity of White Clay Creek west and south of the agency along both sides of the road from Chadron. Nearer the community stood the white conical Sibley tents of the cavalry and infantry, where the soldiers "piled in, nine to eleven to each tent," as one doughboy recalled.

"Two or three would pool their blankets, place their feet towards the stove and try to keep warm." The horsemen also camped west of the creek, on a plateau a mile above the agency, where they assumed a routine of daily drill. All troop encampments were under command of Major Edmond Butler, veteran officer of the Second Infantry.[22]

One who was present on November 26 portrayed the agency with its streets packed with Sioux babies and children while soldiers laundered their clothing and hung it to dry. "Smoke of a thousand teepees rose in the still, hazy air," as grazing ponies crowded the hills. "There was peace at Pine Ridge, whatever might be at the homes of frightened settlers and in the great newspaper offices. The impression was general at the agency that the Indians would be disarmed and that there would not be serious trouble."[23]

Upon his arrival on November 20 General Brooke immediately became the man on the ground. The fifty-two-year-old Pennsylvanian brought uncertain experience to his role in what became known as the Pine Ridge Campaign. A captain of volunteers at the outbreak of the Civil War, Brooke rose to colonel of the Fifty-Third Pennsylvania Infantry six months later. As a regimental and brigade commander, he had served with distinction, receiving wounds at Seven Pines "Fair Oaks," Gettysburg, and Cold Harbor. He commanded the First Division of the Second Corps of the Army of the Potomac during "Pickett's Charge" at Gettysburg, emerging from the war a brigadier general of volunteers with brevet promotions, including major general, for gallantry and meritorious service.

In the reorganized postwar Regular Army Brooke served with infantry units in the South and West and in 1879 became colonel of the Third Regiment, where he remained until his appointment in 1888 as brigadier general commanding the Department of the Platte. Known as a pleasant man of good judgment, he proved a competent commander, acknowledged for his background in conventional warfare and administration. Despite tenures in New Mexico, Kansas, Colorado, the Indian Territory, and Montana, however, the tall and hefty Brooke had few striking credentials regarding Indian service. As a non–West Pointer, Brooke's advancement to brigadier over those claiming more pertinent credentials kindled complaints within the officer corps. Notwithstanding his relative seniority within the army by 1890, Brooke was little known to the general public compared with officers of similar background and station.[24]

At Pine Ridge, while the soldiers bivouacked on November 20, Brooke took over Royer's quarters and began a time-consuming correspondence with his department offices in Omaha via telephone and telegraph at the Rushville station (the broken telegraph line from Pine Ridge would be reinstalled two days later). His pressing objective was to ensure protection of lives and property at the agency. In fact the soldiers' arrival spooked the Indian children in the government school, many of whom tried to run away. All white people employed at the agency assembled at the agent's office and received instructions to arm themselves.

While reporters nearby predicted an immediate advance to disrupt and disarm the dancers, Brooke cautiously awaited direction from Washington and Chicago. He postponed interfering at tribal communities along Wounded Knee, Medicine Root, and Porcupine Creeks, northeast of the agency, where inflated reports told of dancers with rifles "strapped on their backs" making threats against the soldiers. Other information indicated that as yet no blatant hostility toward whites had appeared. Some had continued to witness the dances without resistance. Yet Royer fretted that among the dancers were as many as 600 Winchester-toting warriors, each carrying 200–300 rounds, who would not hesitate to fight the soldiers. He speculated that if they bypassed the agency to the south they might breach its telephone communication. On November 21 some 200 Pine Ridge Northern Cheyennes charged yelling into an ongoing dance near White Clay Creek. It was a moment of audacity, a sham, and the Lakotas quickly extended their hands in friendship as the dance proceeded.[25]

On Thursday and Friday Brooke consulted with Royer and special agent Cooper, who counseled patience until the removal of identified ringleaders might be finessed by higher authority. Only on November 24 had the general received orders telling him that "the ghost dances should not be disturbed for the present nor anything be done to precipitate a conflict, and that when the troops are all concentrated ready for action it can be better judged of the measures that may be necessary and advisable." Until then Brooke and his constituents planned to lie low and study the situation. The presence of several thousand purportedly friendly Indians at the agency nonetheless caused considerable unrest among the troops. As one correspondent noted, "it is well kept in mind that blood is thicker than water." The prevailing view among the soldiers was that they would shortly be required to put down the dancing. Within a day of the arrival of the command, the children and wives of all whites working at Pine Ridge Agency started for Rushville and Chadron. On learning of developments with Brooke, General Miles expressed satisfaction that his presence at Pine Ridge "will have the effect of sustaining the authority of the government and give protection to the loyal element among the Indians."[26]

The troops remained on alert through subsequent nights. Brooke directed the picket line advanced well beyond the bivouac area and to incorporate the Indian police force, at last one hundred men strong. By coincidence, forty-two Oglala members of William F. ("Buffalo Bill") Cody's Wild West Show, "loaded with good clothes, flashy jewelry, and gaudy neckties," had reached Rushville, having finished their European tour. Now back at Pine Ridge Agency and mostly oblivious or skeptical of the Ghost Dance, many of them cut their long hair, donned uniforms, and signed up as Indian police. Additionally, a group of scouts headed by Frank Grouard, who had worked for the army during the Great Sioux War and had arrived from Fort McKinney, patrolled the agency grounds and country beyond. Soldiers slept on their arms. The camp guard was doubled, ready for any contingency, while white workers arranged a point at which to meet in an emergency.[27]

On Friday, on orders from Miles, Brooke undertook to separate progressives from nonprogressives, a problematical task at best because of the difficulty in differentiating among the Indians. At Brooke's direction, Royer sent police and scouts far afield to summon friendly tribesmen to the agency as well as to notify settlers of potential disturbances. (A man named William Courier, married to a schoolteacher, told Royer that while approaching the agency by wagon he had crossed a trail of Indians headed for White River and that he discovered hundreds of empty cardboard boxes for Winchester ammunition, suggesting that the warriors had filled their cartridge belts from them.)

By the time Brooke's task was completed, anticipated reinforcements would be at hand and serious consultation with the belligerent males might begin, to include arrests of those who refused to stop dancing. When news of the stampede of Brulés from Rosebud reached Pine Ridge, it brought great distress. Some of those people had desired to attach themselves to Pine Ridge in accordance with a tentative agreement regarding the reservation boundaries. Brooke wanted to authorize the transfer, believing that it would further "weaken and disintegrate the hostile element." But after the

Rosebud people warily redirected their path north toward White River, some of the Oglalas furtively took flight and joined them near the mouth of Wounded Knee Creek.[28]

In the meantime the venerable Chief Red Cloud, who had previously straddled the issue of the dances and whose son Jack had become a proponent of them, on Friday made a vigorous statement coming out squarely against the movement, no doubt in the hope of stemming confusion over where he stood on the matter and maintaining peace at Pine Ridge:

> We are all friends of the agent and we are friendly with the soldiers. . . . I don't want to fight and I don't want my people to fight. . . . We have lots of old women and lots of old men. We've got no guns and we can't fight, for we have nothing to eat, and are too poor to do anything. . . . I haven't been to see the dancing. My eyes are sore and I can't see very well, but when they get well I will go to see it. I will try to stop it. Those Indians are fools. The winter weather will stop it, I think. Anyway, it will be all over by spring. I don't think there will be any trouble. They say that I have been in the dance. That is not right. I have never seen it. When we made our treaty it was promised there should be no troops on the reservation unless it was at the order of the Great Father. They are here, though, and I suppose it is all right.[29]

The next day Royer received a letter from Little Wound, at odds with Red Cloud and fulminating against the presence of the soldiers. "Our dance is a religious one, and we are going to dance until spring. If we find then that the new Christ does not appear we will stop dancing, but in the meantime troops or no troops we are going to start our dance." Royer interpreted the message as meaning that the warriors intended to fight. On November 23 throngs of the summoned tribesmen began arriving from more than thirty miles away, as hundreds of families with teams and wagons raised volumes of dust on the roads north and east. Estimates placed the number at 3,500 to 4,000 people. Many raised lodges near Red Cloud's house west of White Clay Creek. On this day Jack Red Cloud told reporters that the people down White Clay Creek had discontinued the dancing and were coming to the agency. He saw no harm in the dancing, as it was a religious matter similar to those of the white people. He denied reports of guns being brandished in the dances, insisting that all forms of metal were proscribed.

In the confusion of the moment, gossip flew among press representatives that the Rosebud Indians were en route to kill Brooke, which would signal a general attack on all the soldiers at Pine Ridge. Other reports forecast the imminent arrival of progressive leaders He Dog and Big Road, now also cast among the dancers.[30]

The real reason for the influx was that ration day was at hand. Brooke grew alarmed as the agency swarmed with friendlies and nonfriendlies, as his force was too small to risk arresting leaders for fear of reprisal. Miles had telegraphed confidential instructions to him: "One thing should be impressed upon all officers, never to allow their command to be mixed up with the Indians or taken at a disadvantage." On November 23 he repeated this maxim: "Do not allow your command to become mixed up with Indians, friendly or otherwise. Hold them all at a safe distance from your command. Guard against surprise or treachery." In response Brooke prohibited tribesmen from coming within the perimeter of the army camp. He and other officers spent the balance of the day peering at the Sioux through binoculars. Distant signal fires among the Indians after dark prompted worry, as the troops envisioned the Pine Ridge Sioux plotting to join the ranks of the Ghost Dancers. Conversely, in the morning a scout reported that it had been rumored among the friendlies that a detachment of troops "had been sent to Wounded Knee and were shooting the Indians down as though they were animals."[31]

One of Brooke's charges from Miles had been to investigate Sioux treaty violations respecting rations, including the beef issue matter. The general met with Royer and his chief clerk on November 24. Both confirmed that the people could not successfully raise produce at Pine Ridge, but neither could they live on the scant government rations accorded them. The alarming deficiency, including the now-paltry beef allotment, stunned the officer. "My eyes have been opened very wide since coming here," said Brooke. "Too little, too little, entirely too little. . . . I don't care whether they are Indians or what they are. People can't be satisfied, contented or anything else if they don't have enough to eat, and the government should be finding it out pretty soon." Royer concurred in the assessment, and the reporter who recorded the dialogue surmised that it was small wonder that the people, "poor as crows," had embraced the messiah movement and its accompanying Ghost Dance as a last hope.[32] "In addition to disarming the Indians," Brooke told Miles, "I would recommend that the broken or deferred promises be made good, [and] that the food [rations] of those living in regions where the white man's crops have failed . . . be increased, that this may in time render the Indians 'law abiding and peaceable' and ultimately, I hope, 'contented and prosperous.'"[33]

As rations were doled out that day, Little Wound and No Water appeared and in a turnabout announced their peoples' cessation of the dancing for good on the basis of the Great Father's demanding it, a pronouncement that Brooke doubted. Two days later, however, Big Road arrived, stating that he too was abandoning the dances and that the presence of the soldiers had settled the matter for him. The first reinforcements also appeared on November 24: the two anticipated infantry companies from Omaha and the cavalry troop under Major Henry from Wyoming, who brought word of the Seventh Cavalry's approach. Three days later the arrival of Custer's old regiment, with Light Battery E, First Artillery, required realigning of the soldier camp, now to be commanded by Colonel Forsyth by virtue of rank. The troops pitched their tents a mile south of the agency, with the horsemen on either side of White Clay Creek. The press correspondents made much of the Seventh Cavalry troops' appearance in the land of their former victors. Some suggested that their motive was vengeance, though few of the officers and men had been at the Little Bighorn in 1876.[34] The additions brought the total force at the agency to twelve troops of cavalry, six companies of infantry, and a battery of light artillery with four rifled Hotchkiss cannon and one Gatling gun.

The quickly expanding army camp imparted a threatening aura for many of the Sioux. When one of the chiefs complained of Brooke's howitzers being trained on his people, the general refused to redirect them. Brooke authorized the government-friendly Chief Young Man Afraid of His Horses and several other progressives, accompanied by Indian police, to leave Pine Ridge for a hunting trip into Wyoming's distant Powder River country, a decision that he would later regret. He notified Wyoming authorities as well as staff at Fort McKinney that the Indians would be passing through. Thus the initial occupation proceeded. As Elaine Goodale recalled:

We were now practically under martial law. . . . The infantry set up tents on the common, by degrees protecting them with trenches and crude breastworks. The streets were patrolled, and a buffalo-coated sentinel stood guard night and day around the Oglala boarding-school, whose doors were kept locked upon hundreds of children from all parts of the reservation, partly, no doubt, as hostages for the good behavior of their parents. . . . Old, sick and little ones were suffering from exposure in thin cotton tents; the grazing was soon gone and the ponies were starving. Worse still, police, mixed-bloods and even church members were threatened with reprisals from the excited ghost-dancers.[35]

On Wednesday Brooke issued an order directing all nonregistered visitors except members of the press off the reservation. Under this edict the traders Edward and Thomas Asay were told to depart from the agency for speaking critically of the troops. News of the imminent presence of the Seventh Cavalry had caused Brooke to delay the beef distribution until Thursday, November 27, so that he might keep all the Indians within sight while having more troops at hand if needed. Despite professions of peace by certain of the Ghost Dance chiefs, the messages were mixed. The general concluded that to thwart an outbreak would require the disarmament of all the Indians and the removal of as many as seventy leaders from Pine Ridge, a perspective that he shared with Miles. On Thanksgiving Day the beef distribution took place east of the agency, where some 2,600 people turned out to receive and witness the slaughter of ninety cattle—"as woebegone and gaunt as the wretches that were to eat them," said a witness. The next day agent Royer learned of an assemblage of dancers along Wounded Knee Creek, still "swearing vengeance against the whites" for scheming to stop them.[36]

Two days later Brooke met in conference with Little Wound and his headmen, Royer, Cooper, and former Pine Ridge agent McGillycuddy, who was present at the behest of Governor Mellette (and apparently expecting to replace Royer, who was undoubtedly chastened by his attendance). They heard again that the starving Indians did not want war and that the Ghost Dances were but a means to express their grievances. From his former charges McGillycuddy had gathered that the Indians were not planning an attack. Big Road, the prominent Oglala chief, told him that they would fight only if the troops halted their dancing. But when McGillycuddy proposed to visit the Ghost Dancers down White Clay Creek Brooke would not allow it.

Throughout all of these discussions, perhaps the most dreaded threat for the chiefs lay in the loss of individual freedom should the army decide to seize their guns and ponies—the dreaded disarm and dismount routine that they had all experienced in the past. By Sunday, November 30, many of the Pine Ridge progressives had made up their minds to join the dancers. When Brooke and Royer awoke on that windy Sabbath they discovered that perhaps 2,000 of the people—fully two-thirds of the Pine Ridge Oglalas—had vacated the agency and headed north, ostensibly to join Short Bull's followers away from the martial presence. Referencing the dances ongoing there, yet with unconscious foresight, a Pine Ridge newsman declared: "The scene of difficulty, if there is any, will be at Wounded Knee Creek, about twenty miles distant."[37]

Meanwhile at Rosebud Agency the ration issue took place without disturbance, with the soldiers under Colonel Smith overseeing the distribution. Any trouble from the remaining Brulés, noted a correspondent, "seems out of the question, as they have no rations on hand and no place to leave their wives and children." Amid the quietude at Rosebud, however, some of the Ghost Dancers stealthily attended ration distribution as well as the beef installment. Intelligence of Short Bull's location following the flight on November 20–21 placed him and several hundred warriors and their families along White River, thirty miles north of the agency at the edge of the Badlands. With him were Crow Dog and Two Strike, who along with other leaders had been looting, raiding livestock, and burning property, while constantly seeking recruits from Pine Ridge and the other agencies. As the days passed Short Bull's assemblage, containing perhaps 700 warriors, gained the north side of White River north of and across from the mouth of Wounded Knee Creek. Back at Rosebud Agency, troop reinforcements arrived under Colonel Poland, who took charge.[38]

When General Brooke wrote his wife on November 29 that "there is no more danger [here at Pine Ridge] now than there is in Omaha," he was reassuring her, for uncertainty indeed existed. The government response to the Ghost Dance was enacted through the military deployment. A semblance of federal authority was initiated for the relief of apprehensive citizens in the area of the reservations. The occupation of the Pine Ridge and Rosebud agencies, where respective forces of 1,200 and 370 men had settled in under Brooke's overall command, had been accomplished by the first week of December. By the end of the first week, however, many of the Indians belonging to either agency (progressives as well as nonprogressives)—driven by anxiety created by the military presence—vacated their homes for destinations near the Badlands, leaving Brooke and his officers momentarily perplexed over what to anticipate. With the unabated buildup, the targeted reservations containing approximately 20,000 Sioux people were seized and surrounded. By the time the enterprise was complete, it would constitute the biggest troop deployment west of the Mississippi River since the Great Sioux War of 1876–77. It occupied nearly a quarter of the fighting strength of the U.S. Army—well over 5,000 officers and men—and thus represented the nation's largest military mobilization between the close of the Civil War in 1865 and the outbreak of the Spanish-American War in 1898.[39]

EIGHT

Stronghold

In the early days of December temperatures at Pine Ridge fell to zero and a driving sleet pounded the agency. "The troops are hugging their camp fires," wrote a correspondent for the *Omaha Bee,* "while the Indians are freezing in their gauze-like [canvas] tipis just outside the agency precincts." On December 3 agent Royer offered a special meal to the Indians who had remained within his jurisdiction. Elsewhere troop encirclement of the reservations to protect the settlements proceeded smoothly. Within this perimeter large cavalry and infantry contingents minded the hot spots at the Pine Ridge and Rosebud agencies. Two troops of cavalry remained at Oelrichs west of the Pine Ridge Reservation as seven companies of infantry formed at Hermosa, south of Rapid City.[1]

A battery of artillery augmented the soldiers garrisoning Fort Meade, and more men arriving or en route bolstered the garrisons at Forts Yates, Bennett, Sully, Niobrara, and Robinson. By the end of the month the enveloping command would incorporate even more infantry between Rosebud and Pine Ridge as well as troops and Indian scouts along both forks of the Cheyenne River, with additional outlying detachments near Dickinson, North Dakota, and at Slim Buttes and at Camp Crook along the Little Missouri River in northwestern South Dakota. Farther afield, the army increased existing garrisons at Fort Abraham Lincoln, near Bismarck, North Dakota, and at Fort Keogh, on the Yellowstone River in Montana. Indian scouts and cavalry received directions to cover trails east from Keogh to the Little Missouri and routes running north and west from Standing Rock.[2]

This vast concentration of force in accordance with presidential decree was intended to protect citizens and intimidate the Lakotas, in theory preempting regional eruptions such as had occurred in Minnesota in 1862.

Notwithstanding this intensifying military presence, non-Indian inhabitants still feared for their safety. Many settlers fortified their shacks and dugouts as others withdrew from their holdings into Pine Ridge and Rapid City, having received warnings to drive their cattle away from the Badlands. Frightened ranchers clamored for arms and ammunition, some of which the governor provided. Inflated reports of Winchester-wielding Indians massing along White River inflamed apprehension, as did false reports of fighting between troops and warriors. This in turn raised alarm among settlers, who might kill Indians and touch off a wave of violence. Armed citizens patrolled at night in towns like Hot Springs, Rushville, and Gordon. Rumors of imminent Indian raids were common at Rushville and Chadron.

Late in November Governor Mellette notified General Miles that two reliable cattlemen, James ("Scotty") Philip and Charles Waldron, who ranched up Bad River between the White and the Cheyenne, had experienced verbal contacts with Sioux who appeared "surly and defiant" and were killing ranch cattle. In determining defensive needs for his state, Mellette called on Secretary Proctor to establish posts at the Missouri River towns of Chamberlain and Forest City. Mellette approved distributing guns to a home guard unit in Rapid City even as Congress authorized the War Department to ship surplus Civil War guns and ammunition to the settlements.[3]

As newspapers east of the Missouri River agitated editorially, farther downstream at Fort Randall fearful settlers gathered on learning of Lakota Sioux in the area. The Indians themselves feared growing trouble and camped nearby until they felt safe to return to Lower Brulé. Back at Pine Ridge, Lawrence County judge John H. Burns from Deadwood, a would-be peacemaker known to the Rosebud Indians as "Chief of the Black Hills," reported to General Brooke that he had visited Two Strike's Ghost Dance camp and seen preparations for war. Burns, who also reported for the *Deadwood Pioneer* and was a stringer for the *Chicago Times*, brought three chiefs to confer with Brooke and told how the White River Indians practiced the new dances interspersed with traditional war dances. Excitement, he said, was largely confined to the young men. Authoritative reports also detailed how Short Bull's followers had gleaned at least several hundred head of stock from the government beef herds.

As matters unfolded in the South Dakota region, attempts were made in Washington, D.C., to formalize absolute army control. On November 29 General Miles arrived in the nation's capital to consult with Proctor and Schofield, who renewed approval for the course that he had outlined. Proctor told Miles that the president concurred with all plans executed thus far and that the division commander had full discretion to do everything necessary to avert an outbreak. The next evening Proctor and Miles visited the White House to confer with President Harrison over the crisis. In endorsing the army mission, the president asked what role he himself might play to facilitate matters. Miles took the opportunity to impress upon Harrison (and through him Congress) the critical need for feeding the people without delay in accordance with existing agreements. They discussed the arrest of Ghost Dance leaders, particularly Sitting Bull, and the need to prepare for preventing an outbreak before making any arrests. On Monday, December 1, Proctor delivered to Miles a letter recapping the points of the White House meeting:

> [The president] looks to you to take every possible precaution to prevent an Indian outbreak and to suppress it promptly if it comes. He depends upon you for this; and everything in the way of men and material that in the opinion of the Major-General Commanding can be spared from other points will be supplied. He recognizes your success in the past in your dealings with the Indians, and has full confidence that the responsibility is placed in good hands.[4]

In conference with Secretary Noble the same day Miles learned that Sioux agents had at last received orders to increase rations for the people, as he had long urged. He wired the news to Brooke. Equally imperative, the president granted full authority for handling the crisis to the War Department (and thus to Miles), formalized in the following directive from Noble to Morgan, the commissioner of Indian Affairs:

> Sir: You will convey to the several agents on duty among the Sioux the following order, which is hereby made: During the present Indian troubles you are instructed that while you shall continue all the business, and carry into effect the educational and other purposes of your agency, you will, as to all operations intended to suppress any outbreak by force, cooperate with and obey the orders of the military officer commanding on the reservation in your charge.[5]

Before he departed Washington, Miles convinced Schofield to requisition additional horses and mules and to authorize Miles to hire one thousand progressive Sioux, together with their mounts, to work as teamsters and packers on the rolls of the Quartermaster Department. Doubtless out of self-interest, and somewhat excessively, the general told reporters of his concern that the Ghost Dance movement might spread to other tribes throughout the Northwest if not properly contained at the Lakota front. "It is a more comprehensive plot than anything ever inspired by the prophet Tecumseh, or even Pontiac," he intoned. "I hope the problem may be solved without bloodshed, but such a happy ending to the trouble seems improbable." Once back in Chicago, however, Miles received a report of precisely the opposite nature. Colonel Edward M. Heyl, inspector-general of the Division of the Missouri, who was just back from Sioux country, reported "no imminent danger of any serious trouble." He agreed with Miles on the causes of the strife but said that the Ghost Dancing at Pine Ridge was slackening and that the Indians "were quiet and peacefully disposed." Like others, Heyl believed that snowstorms and blizzards would "cool the ardor of the young bucks." Miles announced that he would soon be off to the field to assess matters and oversee the placement of troops at practicable locations.[6] Such were the changing interpretations of affairs in the bureaucracy early in December.

The general's strategic plan at last began to take shape. As Miles later emphasized, "it was the design of the division commander *to anticipate the movements of the hostile Indians and arrest or overpower them in detail before they had time to concentrate in one large body*, and it was deemed advisable to secure, if possible, the principal leaders and organizers, namely Sitting Bull, and others, and remove them for a time from that country." The general intended to preempt large-scale Indian movements by the swift deployment of troops, vehicles, and supplies via rail lines at the onset of winter. Miles also hoped to forestall violence and shield the settlements and their populations from danger by completing the encirclement of the Lakota reservations as quickly as possible, using existing forts and outposts and their garrisons. This surrounding net would be firmly in place when the time came to arrest influential Ghost Dance leaders and physically remove them from their points of influence. Such an overwhelming army presence also would permit Miles to modify and refine troop placement almost at will as the changing situation might demand.[7]

The arrest and imprisonment of principal leaders in the Ghost Dance movement held the greatest risk for violence. In repeatedly advocating arrests in telegrams of mid- and late November, agent Royer also called for disarming the dancers. Special agent Cooper endorsed Royer's plan, calling the objectives "the best course" and urging that action "be taken at once." Acting commissioner Belt agreed. When Belt asked for the names of "fomenters of disturbances" to be targeted, Royer furnished a list of sixty-five individuals, including Kicking Bear. The list was then forwarded to the War Department. The special agent in charge at Rosebud submitted a much smaller list containing twenty-one names, including Short Bull and Two Strike. Agent Palmer at Cheyenne River named only four individuals, notably Hump and Big Foot.[8]

As the grand strategy took shape and the deployment proceeded, the soldiers already posted at Rosebud and Pine Ridge as well as those farther afield at stations like Oelrichs and the forks of the Cheyenne settled into camp pending developments and tried to stay warm. Many of the units to converge on the reservations that November and December brought what gear and supplies they had with them, including clothing, arms, wagons, tentage, stoves, desks, tables, chairs, tools, wood, hay and horse gear, and all related field matériel. But much more was needed and had to be requisitioned or rented through offices of the army Quartermaster Department. Field rations had to be supplied through the Subsistence Department, with much initially coming from storehouses at Forts Niobrara and Robinson. With the constant arrival of supplies, wrote a newsman, "the yard about the supply shed [at Pine Ridge Agency] resembles one huge city warehouse. Under shed and upon the outside platform are piled bags of flour, beans, etc., fully thirty feet high, covered with large pieces of canvas, while in the yard are mountains of hay, baled and unbaled, and oats and such other provender."[9]

In the field the men consumed a monotonous diet of coffee, hardtack (crackers), and salt pork. Much of the food issued was substandard. Years later one cavalryman complained of having been issued hardtack packed during the Civil War. "The labels and date of packing were still on the boxes. The hardtack had a green mold on it, but we just wiped it off and they were all right." Canned baked beans and tomatoes were also staples for the troops.[10]

Most of the enlisted men wore heavy dark blue wool shirts and blouses with lighter blue wool trousers, together with underwear, stockings, and field shoes for daily wear. Over these garments they donned heavy blue wool caped overcoats or weightier tanned buffalo skin or blanket-lined canvas coats. They wore muskrat fur gauntlets as well as caps with ear flaps that tied under the chin to help combat the cold, although on warmer days they might wear wide-brimmed campaign hats. To keep their feet warm and dry they wore heavy felt boots inside tweed and rubber overshoes called "arctics."

The Ordnance Department provided weaponry. Arms consisted of standard-issue breech-loading single-shot .45-caliber Springfield rifles for infantry and carbines for cavalry, the same basic weapons that the army had used since the 1870s. Cavalrymen were additionally armed with six-shot .45-caliber revolvers for close combat on horseback. Sabers had been dispensed with for the horse soldiers as well as bayonets for the foot soldiers. All the men carried haversacks, canteens, tin cups, blankets, and rubber ponchos. Infantry soldiers also wore backpacks. Officers wore comparable field clothing, occasionally civilian jackets, and carried similar weaponry and accouterments, all of which they acquired by private purchase.

Often the supplies arrived late, and the men suffered from the cold. A soldier with Carr's Sixth Cavalry from New Mexico recalled arriving with the regiment and 500 horses at Rapid City late in the afternoon of December 9: they "found a lot of snow and mercury near zero. Next morning we went on the march. We did not get overcoats and [over]shoes for nearly two weeks." The major field transportation facility, the Army Pack Train Service under thirty-year veteran chief packer "Colonel" Thomas Moore, was headquartered at Camp Carlin, outside Cheyenne, Wyoming. On telegraphic directive from Brooke, Moore soon departed for Pine Ridge with two trains.[11]

Besides the constant need for food and supply, the possibility of combat required more than simply the small arms and ammunition issued to the soldiers. The Gatling gun (an early machine gun) and the four light Hotchkiss cannon (mule-transported breech-loading single-shot weapons, each of 1.65-inch caliber, capable of delivering two-pound exploding projectiles as well as canister from a compressed steel barrel) had been time-tested armaments in Indian warfare since the 1870s. The soldiers of Battery E, First Artillery, under Captain Allyn Capron, who had accompanied the Seventh Cavalry to Pine Ridge, had become proficient in their use. On December 4 Brooke's office in Omaha notified Capron that, in addition to whatever ammunition stock had arrived with the ordnance, they had "five hundred shells with hotchkiss [sic] percussion fuzes for Capron's guns, and one Thousand friction primers go to Rushville tonight." Brooke further learned that four more Howitzers and 1,000 additional rounds were en route from arsenals in California and Illinois. In due course Miles would order two steel mortars capable of firing 20-pound shells delivered to Pine Ridge Agency.[12] All of these weapons would assuredly provide adequate firepower for army needs through the balance of the occupation.

While the army command prepared for a lengthy stay among the Lakotas, the Indians prepared to seek a safe haven. Sioux who had distanced themselves from the agencies at Pine Ridge and Rosebud were joined by others from Cheyenne River and Standing Rock. These were tumultuous times, and the Ghost Dances that proceeded night and day were accompanied by accidents. Curious dancers sometimes tested their supposedly impenetrable ghost shirts. One man so arrayed challenged his peers to fire at him and fell, fatally wounded, when they did so. (When Brooke heard of this, he is said to have quipped dryly: "Probably the shirt was not long enough.") As talk and the written word (in regard to Little Wound) had indicated, many of the people were anxious and openly rebellious at the massing presence of troops and cannon. The soldiers might seek to take away their horses and arms or even to exterminate them. Worst of all, they feared that the army would somehow keep the prophecies of the messiah from coming to pass.[13]

Fearful of the soldiers yet confident that good weather would providentially continue, Short Bull and his ghost-shirted followers removed themselves beyond threat by heading north and west of White River into the unforgiving fastness of the Badlands. They traveled slowly, grazing their stock as they went. Many of their ponies were in bad condition, and arriving Oglalas donated a large number of horses obtained from a white man on Wounded Knee Creek. The movement of the 300 lodges (approximately 2,000 people) began on November 29. Some of the Oglalas leaving Pine Ridge Agency twenty-five miles away soon joined them. Besides the leaders Short Bull and Kicking Bear, other chiefs present included Eagle Pipe, High Hawk, Lance, Turning Bear, No Flesh, Crow Dog, Pine Bird, Two Strike, and White Horse. Others would join with their families from the remaining Lakota reservations.

Disagreements flared within this congregation of Lakota people. Some Brulés disposed to leave were kept from returning to the agency. Word was that if the army approached them they would fight, a prospect frightening to Brulés inclined to turn back but prevented from doing so. Within a short time all were hidden among the tortuous defiles north of the White River, a coarsely etched region considered by some "worse than the [northern California] lava beds in which the Modocs took shelter" in 1872–73. Through his scouts and other informers, General Brooke learned of the development and apprised his superior officers. "There are several roads across the Bad Lands between the White and Cheyenne Rivers, and the distance is not great across," he advised them. "These Bad Lands end on the east about the mouth of Pumpkin Creek, I am told, so that they are not extensive."[14] The White River Badlands extend over a broad area covering roughly 3,000 square miles in southwestern South Dakota, a dreaded and yet majestically scarred terrain. This eons-old eroded declivity was difficult for white people to access and almost impossible to inhabit in the later decades of the nineteenth century. Isolated and remote, it promised the Lakotas a measure of security from the soldiers.

At the margins of the region stood broad and ascending grass-covered tablelands that whites did occupy, harboring timber and water sources. As they withdrew from White River in early December, Short Bull, Two Strike, and the other chiefs looked to these highlands for sanctuary and protection. When a party of Sioux made a side trip to the Cheyenne River seeking sugar and other needed items while en route, white ranchers fired on them, killing Circle Elk, a nephew of Short Bull who had attended the Carlisle school in Pennsylvania. The incident made plain the degree of growing tensions. After crossing the White River, the main body of Lakotas and others with them headed toward a broad, flat-topped escarpment rising 300 feet above the surrounding floor. It was known to them as Top of the Badlands and is today called Cuny Table after a historic local family. The people camped south of the table and ascended the west side the next day. Families in broken-down carts and ox-drawn wagons with their dunnage, dogs, and ponies followed trails up the steep and fissured precipice to gain the height. They rested that night near springs in cedar-lined canyons.

As sentries watched in all directions from points on the southern perimeter, the people resumed their trek north the following morning. Soon they passed over a narrow, appendix-shaped isthmus leading onto a another elevation that they called High Pocket's Place, Place of Shelter, and, most significantly, Maka Nawchizin, meaning "Ground that Defends Us." Smaller than Cuny Table, it became known to the army as the Stronghold. The grassy tract ran little more than a mile from north to south and less than half a mile from east to west. Cedar and juniper copses dotting the fringe of the ground afforded firewood. Within two days of crossing White River, the women had set up tipis facing east in the traditional circular arrangement as men and women together began erecting ditch and breastwork defenses across the neck of land connecting the plateaus. Perhaps as many as 3,000 people camped there, probably the largest gathering of the people since they had come together at the Little Bighorn fourteen years earlier in 1876. The height and precipitous slopes on all sides made the Stronghold formidable. Only the narrow passage from Cuny Table and a few animal trails provided restricted access. A military assault would be costly. The young men had guns and ammunition and grass for their ponies, and the families were well stocked with water and food. As word got around, other Sioux joined them. Amid subzero temperatures and fierce winds, the dancing resumed. Forty miles northwest of Pine Ridge Agency the people were restless yet secure. From their lofty fortification at the Stronghold, foraging parties ranged over the countryside to augment food and supplies, killing cattle and capturing horses pastured by the government and local ranchers.[15]

Brooke's scouts kept him informed of the Indians' movements. Hoping to contact and negotiate with them, the general wanted those willing to come into the agency to do so. But the scouts and Indian police were not acceptable emissaries, and Brooke could not send soldiers, whose appearance would likely provoke shooting. Privately he told his wife:, "I am getting the one chance of my life, maybe, and I shall stay here and work it out if it takes all winter." He was abetted by Austrian-born Father John J. Jutz, S.J., of the Holy Rosary Mission, a few miles below Pine Ridge Agency. The fifty-two-year-old Jutz had previously worked among tribes in Wyoming and helped establish St. Francis Mission on the Rosebud Reservation. He knew many of the people, held their trust, and believed that "they would surely take a word of friendly advice." On Tuesday, December 2, Jutz met with Brooke, telling him: "I am willing to go to the Hostiles tomorrow, and I will bring back to you accurate information concerning their sentiments." When Brooke hesitated but agreed, the priest approached Red Cloud and asked him to accompany him north. The chief declined, citing age, failing eyesight, and the freezing conditions. The old chief said that his son Jack, lately removed from the dances, should go in his stead to help give credibility to the undertaking.[16]

The next morning the priest and the chief's son, accompanied by an elderly man named Frank Martinez who knew the route and could interpret, departed the mission by buggy down White Clay Creek. They traveled perhaps twenty-five miles. After they crossed the White River it grew dark and began to snow. The three spent an unpleasant night on the periphery of the Badlands with neither fire nor food. Early the next morning warriors armed with Winchesters found them and in due course ushered them afoot to the Stronghold camp, where they met with Two Strike. The Indians reiterated their grievances of short rations, inability to settle at Pine Ridge as had been promised them, and concern over punishment for their recent pillaging. Father Jutz recalled:

I told the Indians that I had come to rescue them from their sorry plight, for they could not stay where they were. Besides their food supply would soon run out, and they were not allowed to kill cattle which did not belong to them. I also told them that the soldiers had not come to wage war against them, and that the General was a very kind gentleman, who would give them meat and everything else they needed. All they had to do was to come to the Agency, and from there they could quietly go back to their camp at Rosebud. They listened to me with great attention, and then one of them stood up and said: "Father, if what you say is true, lift up your right hand and swear to the Great Spirit that it is true." I stood up and lifted up my right hand. All the Indians arose and lifted up their hands as a token that they believed me. After this most solemn protestation, I said: "Very well, if you believe my word, I will take you to the General, and you will see that I have spoken the truth. Do you want to come with me at once, or when will you come?" The spokesman replied: "Father, we cannot go with you now; it is very cold, and we have many old people and children with us, but we men, we will go tomorrow." "Very well," said I, "you men come to the Mission tomorrow; you can stay over night there, and the next morning I will escort you to the General." All consented to this arrangement, and so the purpose of my mission had been attained.[17]

Jutz, with Jack Red Cloud and Martinez, left immediately to retrace their way back to Holy Rosary. The next morning, December 5, Jutz reported to Brooke. Late that afternoon about forty nervous Brulés, including chiefs Two Strike, Big Turkey, Turning Bear, High Pine, Bull Dog, Red Willow, and Big Bad Horse, appeared at the mission. After breakfast the next day (a Saturday) the chiefs and headmen, armed with Winchesters, Springfields, and belts of ammunition, and carrying a flag of truce made from a sheet, entered Pine Ridge Agency cautiously on horseback. Jutz and Two Strike accompanied them in the buggy. Philip Wells joined the group as interpreter, and the Indians hesitatingly left their guns outside Brooke's office door. As Jutz related:

The General was very friendly towards the Indians, told them they had nothing to fear, that the soldiers were good friends of theirs, and had only come to tell them that they should return to their camp in the Rosebud Agency, where he would furnish them with supplies, and give them everything they needed, and then they could return quietly to their homes. The Indians were pleased, and after one of their number had made a few remarks expressive of their satisfaction, and a promise to come to the Agency in a body, the meeting was dissolved. The Indians took their rifles again, paid a visit to Chief Redcloud [sic] and other acquaintances and appeared at night at the Mission where they were cared for. . . . The following morning the Indians returned to their camp [at the Stronghold] with the best of intentions of coming to the Agency with all their families, [to] procure the necessary supplies, and then to go back to Rosebud. The precarious situation seemed to be cleared up in a most satisfactory way without the shedding of one drop of blood.[18]

Jutz later told Brooke that more than one thousand armed braves defended the Indian encampment, that he saw enormous quantities of dried beef on hand, that pickets surrounded the place, and that it was unapproachable by troops. Nonetheless, Brooke brimmed with optimism and reported to his superiors that the Indians would come in. "I will furnish them food and give as many employment and rations as I can. . . . The prospect is that trouble with these Indians is in a fair way to speedy settlement."[19]

Upon the return of Two Strike and the others to the Stronghold, however, a schism arose with Short Bull and his followers, who sought to estrange the tribesmen who had met with Brooke and to keep any of the young people from going to Pine Ridge Agency. When Brooke learned of the stalemate, he attempted to forward an Indian delegation to the Stronghold but was unsuccessful. Jutz again offered his services, but his offer was not accepted. Instead, on December 8, scouts Louis Shangrau, Baptiste ("Little Bat") Garnier, and other mixed-bloods at Brooke's request traveled to the Stronghold and for several days met with the friendly Indians present as well as with Short Bull, Two Strike, and their followers. When No Neck, who had accompanied Shangrau, called on the Indians to return to the agency, Short Bull rejoined: "It is better to die here as brave men . . . than to live like cowards at the agency on scanty rations, disarmed, without horses or guns. . . . We will not return." As Ghost Dancing proceeded, the two sides erupted in fractious dispute largely instigated by some of the young men who, anxious to distinguish themselves further as warriors, had committed most of the area raids and opposed going to the agency.[20]

On December 12 Two Strike and Crow Dog declared their resolve to return with 145 lodges of people, whereupon Short Bull's impassioned followers leveled guns at them. A brief scuffle and some shooting ensued before order prevailed. The friendlies departed with Shangrau and the scouts for Pine Ridge Agency. Before long a much smaller assemblage including Short Bull, Kicking Bear, and the remaining people packed up and followed with their own tipis, only to turn back after trailing a few miles, miffed and fearful of going near the soldiers. As they headed back to the Stronghold that night these people camped on Willow Creek. It was perhaps then that Short Bull addressed the following missive to Shangrau:

To Chief of Indian Scouts
From Short Bull & Kicking Bear
We don't want to fight. You told us to quit the ghost dance and we will quit my friend. I understand that you said in that case all the Soldiers would go home. I am very anxious that that should be done—in that case my movements will be slow & careful in settling down again at the Agency and, after we have settled down on White Clay Creek I do not want any more Soldiers to come back again my Friend. I shake hands with you with a good heart
I am Short Bull

Two Strike's convoy, which included chiefs Turning Bear, High Hawk, and Iron Foot, gained Red Cloud's camp near the agency at noon on Monday, December 15, hopeful that trouble had subsided. At Pine Ridge Agency, in the meantime, Royer had finessed a supplemental allowance of 1 million pounds of beef and began dispensing it. Although Brooke would later send wagons loaded with supplies along with American Horse and a body of Oglala men several hundred strong to coax in Short Bull's people, the matter of the remaining Stronghold Indians went unresolved, dominated by surrounding events.[21]

The trouble was not over. Occupation of the Stronghold during early December soon produced the first of several armed confrontations. The initial movements of the Brulés and Oglalas after the arrival of the soldiers at Rosebud and Pine Ridge in November frightened settlers in the upper White and Cheyenne River areas. While many closest to the reservations departed for Rapid City and Black Hills communities, other settlers remained at their homesteads and boarded up their windows. Some of the ensuing scares had more validity than others. The first incident occurred on December 7 when a foraging group of young warriors from the Ghost Dance camp on White River exchanged gunfire with ranchers near Buffalo Gap, along the Cheyenne River west of Pine Ridge Reservation. As a Ninth Cavalry officer reported: "The Indians withdrew when [ranchers Ned] Warren & [Henry] Brewer got onto a hill and returned their fire; about 15 shots being exchanged." Settlers in the region north to Hermosa reported similar encounters with tribesmen who stole horses and supplies and looted sugar and other commodities from abandoned homes. While cavalry from the Oelrichs camp investigated these incidents, many of the settlers gathered at a few ranches. As one observer described it, "considerable excitement prevails among them & fear among the women." No residents were injured in the raids, but the warriors hit other homes in the area, notably along Spring, Battle, and French Creeks, beyond the reservation boundary. From these areas they took cattle, horses, tack, clothing, blankets, and household goods. They also destroyed furniture and other property and often set fire to grass and haystacks and occasionally to buildings. Although no one was harmed physically, numbers of settlers congregated for defense at rancher John B. McCloud's place.[22]

Thus in the first two weeks of December occasional and largely bloodless clashes—mostly long-range skirmishing—occurred between warriors from the Stronghold and ranchers along the upper Cheyenne River and its tributaries. That changed on the afternoon of December 12, however, when a body of home guardsmen under Mellette appointee Colonel Merrit H. Day, recently mustered to patrol the reservation boundary and scout for stolen livestock, encountered thirty Sioux. The Indians were targeting John Daily and Nelse Torkelson's ranch just above the mouth of Battle Creek on the west bank of the Cheyenne. Indians had previously stolen money from Daily and plundered the ranch. But when the warriors returned and leveled gunfire into the buildings the next morning, the cowboys fired back. One of them, Fred Thompson, killed a single brave whose body was retrieved by his companions. After a protracted exchange the cowboys drove the remaining warriors across the river without further casualty. A detachment of cavalry soon reached the scene from French Creek.

Within days another engagement followed at Cole's ranch between Rapid and Spring Creeks on the Cheyenne. A warrior wearing a ghost shirt and armed with a repeating rifle, a revolver, and a belt of ammunition was killed. The Daily-Torkelson ranch thereafter became a standard outpost for troops patrolling the region. In December a troop of the Fifth Cavalry joined the Eighth Cavalrymen already at Oelrichs and moved north a short distance to Buffalo Gap, along the railroad leading to and from Rapid City. Colonel Day distributed the relatively few arms and little ammunition available among home guardsmen in several communities surrounding Rapid City, mostly in the area of the Cheyenne River. At General Miles's insistence, however, the local militia distanced itself from the Pine Ridge reservation and maintained its patrols west of the Cheyenne.[23]

As events with the home guards and cowboys proceeded west of Pine Ridge Reservation and along the upper Cheyenne River, Colonel Carr arrived with the Sixth Cavalry on December 9–10. In keeping with Miles's plan to encompass the reservations, those troops prepared to start east of Rapid City toward the junction of the Cheyenne with the Belle Fourche River.[24] There they were to coordinate with troops already stationed along the south boundary of the Cheyenne River Reservation. At Rapid City Carr's troopers received supplies of rations, tentage, and heavy winter clothing shipped from Fort Meade, all of which was soon piled about the cavalry camp at the town outskirts. Knowing that his men would extend the cordon that began with the cavalry under Lieutenant Colonel George B. Sanford at Oelrichs, Carr hurried to prepare his regiment for field service on a fifty-mile front along the Cheyenne between Battle and Box Elder Creeks. From Oelrichs Captain Almond B. Wells's two troops of Eighth Cavalry oversaw the country between Buffalo Gap and Battle Creek, while Lieutenant Colonel Edwin V. Sumner, Jr., occupied a point near the Belle Fourche with troops of the Eighth and companies of the Third Infantry. From there they would monitor the Cheyenne River Reservation and keep the Indians from leaving. Beyond observing conditions around them, the troops ranged over their appointed grounds and reported to senior commanders (ultimately Brooke, Ruger, and Miles).

As unsubstantiated word spread of a bloody affray at Pine Ridge, on December 10 two troops of Carr's cavalry began a ten-day scout along the upper Cheyenne. They were accompanied by three Hotchkiss cannon for possible use in dislodging the Indians from the Stronghold. By noon on December 15 Carr himself had reached the mouth of Rapid Creek on the Cheyenne, forty miles beyond Rapid City. With 400 soldiers he established Camp Carr and contemplated approaching the Stronghold area, only ten miles away. He might advance via Battle Creek Draw in coordination with troops from Pine Ridge Agency. More cavalry and artillery, along with wagons, mules, and a loaded pack train were en route to him, while 200 soldiers of the Seventeenth Infantry would help patrol the country between Oelrichs and Rapid City while guarding settlers along the upper

Cheyenne. Forty-five of the Cheyenne scouts that Lieutenant Taylor had enlisted at Pine Ridge Agency, sent by train to Rapid City, would also patrol the stream. Carr dispersed his troops along the river until orders from Brooke warning of a possible attack directed him to reassemble his men. Carr's soldiers, neither equipped nor acclimated to the freezing high winds, suffered exceedingly.[25]

Farther east along the Cheyenne troops from Forts Meade, Bennett, and Sully reported conditions in these areas. Eighth Cavalrymen from Fort Meade, posted at Camp Cheyenne at the forks of that stream, had been monitoring the Miniconjous at the Cheyenne River Reservation since April. Troops of the Seventh Infantry, en route by train from Colorado, would reach Fort Bennett on the Missouri on December 17 before starting for the mouth of Cherry Creek, sixty miles up the Cheyenne.

As attention focused on the Pine Ridge and Rosebud people, another incident at the Lower Brulé Reservation early in December suggested growing interest in the messiah movement among the Indians there. Agent Andrew P. Dixon reported that on December 5 Indian policemen at Lower Brulé had arrested seventeen Lakotas for "participating in the 'Ghost Dance' and for endeavoring to induce others to engage therein, with object of inaugurating the 'Messiah Craze' . . . [and] for disturbing the peace and mental quietude of the Indians of that reserve." Two days later an escort of soldiers from Fort Randall started with them for Fort Snelling, Minnesota, where they would be incarcerated for an unspecified period. The arrest displeased not only the Indians at Lower Brulé but whites across the Missouri at Chamberlain too. Both thought "it mighty peculiar," reported the *Chicago Tribune*, "that these comparatively harmless Indians are promptly ordered taken to Fort Snelling, while at the same time the order has been issued not to molest Sitting Bull and hosts of other Indians who are really dangerous and are tireless peace disturbers." The Indians at Lower Brulé, the *Tribune* reported, "insist that it is unjust discrimination, as they are and have been friendly to the Government, and signed the Sioux treaty [1889]."[26]

While such episodes prevailed on the periphery, and as Carr's troops and others took position along the Cheyenne in accordance with Miles's grand strategy, the soldiers at Pine Ridge and Rosebud watched and waited as matters played out with the Lakotas at the Stronghold. The weather fluctuated between cold and mild but was mostly fair, and the men scarcely needed their greatcoats through the days. Major Samuel M. Whitside of the Seventh Cavalry took advantage of the weather to obtain lumber with which to floor, frame, and add a door to his tent. "I am well prepared for a change in the temperature," he wrote. A reporter at Pine Ridge Agency noted that the constant traffic of soldiers, wagons, visitors, and Indians covered everything with a deep layer of dust. "The least breeze raises a cloud, while anything like a wind shuts everything out of sight at times like a London fog." Almost everyone, he wrote, had a cold or sore throat, with many complaining of irritated eyes. Brooke, meanwhile, prepared for campaign contingencies. "I am having the tents doubled so that the wind will not penetrate them," he wrote his wife. "This with our stoves and plenty of bedding will keep us from any suffering if we should take the field in earnest."[27]

The men were paid on December 10, but the customary revelry apparently did not ensue; liquor was legally prohibited on the reservation. Thus the days passed tediously for the soldiers. Variously they stood formation, practiced drill, patrolled the agency and camps, ate their meals, idled, and welcomed new recruits to their bivouac. Major Henry's Ninth Cavalrymen practiced a distinctive whistle-implemented drill exercise to combat the high incidence of deafening winds. "Drills were always in overcoats and full armament," commented a Ninth officer. A junior officer of the Signal Corps added something of a novelty when he used a heliograph device in training exercises. Recalled a lieutenant of the Second Infantry, "Most of our time was given to taking long tramps and rides over the adjoining country." Occasionally officers and enlisted men attended standard dances in the camps of the friendly Sioux. At one of these affairs a soldier tried eating dog meat "and found it pretty good." The Seventh Cavalry received sixty-five new men, most untested, and officers pressed them into skirmish exercises to ready them for field service. Two of them quickly deserted. Far to the east, similar activities took place at Rosebud Agency, where campaign preparations ensued. Remembered an Eighth Infantryman: "Everybody was busy drilling, [conducting] target practice for the recruits, breaking in a string of sixty pack mules, drilling a detachment of Indian scouts, organizing the remaining 500 or 600 Indians [who had not fled the place], and issuing rations." In the evening, as tented soldiers read letters from home by candlelight, officers assembled to swap tales and discuss the upcoming campaign.[28]

By mid-December that "campaign" was an impending movement against the remaining people in the Stronghold. A few hundred followers of Short Bull and the chiefs who had refused to come in and submit to Brooke's command at Pine Ridge Agency remained there, except for wide-ranging and unchecked foraging activities that confounded civil and military authorities throughout southwestern South Dakota. Reports from army scouts already indicated that the Indians were tiring of their circumstances. Tribesmen were cutting loose their captured livestock, suggesting their willingness to submit, and Brooke, who had met with other Sioux leaders, believed that no war was forthcoming. Although his men were restless, Brooke himself remained patient and mostly silent. "General Brooke keeps his own counsel, and is very shy when newspaper men are about," wrote one reporter. Added an officer: "I begin to think that General Brooke does not know anything more regarding the situation than I do." Brooke himself admitted as much. "The fact is there is but little to do now but to wait for a few days to see how this Sioux cat is going to jump."[29]

Still, Brooke firmed up his plan to drive the Ghost Dancers from the Stronghold if necessary. With Carr's regiment in place along the Cheyenne, and with concurrence from Miles, the department commander steeled his resolve. Short Bull and Kicking Bear and their constituents might flee north, and there were reports of renewed attacks on citizens from Stronghold warriors. "I felt that the time had arrived when the Indians now camped in the 'Bad Lands' should be surrounded and brought in by the troops," Brooke later reflected. "I believed that this should be done at the earliest possible moment, and thus prevent these Indians leaving the reservation and endangering the border settlements." Burning haystacks illuminating the night sky several miles north of Pine Ridge Agency seemed to the scouts to signify the "hostiles'" intent to flee. Through couriers and telegraph, Brooke coordinated preparations with Forsyth, Carr, and the other field commands and finally set the time for a unified advance to begin on Wednesday, December 17.[30]

Under the plan Forsyth would move toward the Badlands with twelve troops of the Seventh and Ninth Cavalry and Taylor's Indian scout company, altogether about 800 men, besides three Hotchkiss cannon and a 3.2-inch gun of Battery E, First Artillery. Brooke directed Forsyth first to communicate with the Sioux, "giving them when found first an opportunity to surrender without conditions, and if they refuse attack and if possible destroy them." Carr would proceed east-southeast from positions along the Cheyenne River while Forsyth closed from the south and Colonel Sanford's Leavenworth cavalry came on from the west. Colonel Sumner with troops of the Eighth Cavalry would guard the line farther north. On

December 15 Brooke notified Carr of the Indians' precise location at the Stronghold: "a high table which has a spur towards the Cheyenne above the mouth of Battle Creek." He wished to have that point occupied "in good force. Troops under Forsyth will move in from White river . . . , covering all points and may drive them out on the ridge towards Battle Creek or down the trail on Badwater. . . . The force of the Indians is variously estimated and is, I think, not over two hundred and fifty [warriors], more likely not over two hundred." On December 16 the general conveyed to his men Miles's directive relating the "vital importance that the troops win the first engagement. . . . The different columns will be expected to be constantly on the offensive, and pursue the Indians with the utmost energy." At long last Brooke was assured in his course. With a sense of conclusiveness regarding the holdouts under Short Bull and Kicking Bear, he announced resolutely to Miles: "Against these . . . I will send a sufficient force to capture or fight them. All has been done that can be done. . . . I hope to be able to end the matter now."[31]

Miles was mostly pleased with the course of the campaign thus far. He approved the restraint that his subordinates, led by Brooke, showed in the field. Intent on preventing undue bloodshed, Brooke himself had contemplated evolving circumstances while marshaling vast resources to intimidate the Sioux before instituting direct operations against them. For his part, Miles sympathized with the Ghost Dancers' plight and had made known those feelings to the army and civilian hierarchies as well as to his field commanders. He welcomed the chance to use his knowledge and Indian experience to achieve a passive solution to the crisis and promote his own aspirations as well.[32] For the Lakotas still at the Stronghold, the tentacles of closing military dominance in the winter of 1890 signified their imminent last stand against forces that would outwardly deny their quest for a better existence but also indicated their willingness to risk their own destruction, pending a failure of anticipated divine intercession. They faced not only overwhelming military force but the interminable smothering impact of American society upon all Native peoples and the inevitability of what was happening to them.

NINE

Grand River

As the cordon of soldiers tightened on the Stronghold, the second component in the army's twofold strategy for ending the crisis played out. The army's goal was to remove designated Indian leaders that the federal government believed were instrumental in promoting the messiah movement. These were the supposed troublemakers who threatened disruption on all the Lakota reservations. Brooke himself quietly focused his efforts toward that end. His limited success culminated in the surrender of several of the Brulé and Oglala Ghost Dance chiefs and hundreds of their followers led by Two Strike, clearly now a wavering disciple of Short Bull and Kicking Bear, among those who refused to submit to the government. With the surrender of Two Strike, Brooke directed his troops against the holdouts. He wanted to make an example of them to other wayward tribesmen.[1]

Among the other Sioux leaders that the army hierarchy sought to neutralize were Hump and Big Foot of the Cheyenne River Miniconjous and Sitting Bull of the Standing Rock Hunkpapas. Late in October agent Perrain Palmer at Cheyenne River summoned Hump and Big Foot to his office. Big Foot spoke to the agent in friendly fashion, expressing his concern over the reservation boundary that was not where the 1889 commissioners had agreed it would be. He said that his interest in the Ghost Dance was only as an investigator and advisor to his people. Hump spoke little. He had been a member of Big Foot's band who had put his "X" on the land measure and in doing so offended many of Big Foot's followers. But when agent McChesney appointed Hump a district farmer, Palmer maintained that Hump tried to regain his former stature by urging the people to disobey agency rules and flaunt authority. Soon thereafter Hump quit his appointment and became a leader among the Ghost Dancers at Cheyenne River. Palmer maintained that Hump emerged there as "the most dangerous character on this agency." The best way to prevent "an outbreak among the Indians," Palmer insisted, "would be to take these leaders entirely out of the reach of their followers. With their influence gone the Christian and well-disposed Indians would not be intimidated."[2]

Palmer reported other difficulties controlling the people. For one thing Indian police had little success in keeping the Ghost Dances from proceeding. On November 5 Palmer wired Commissioner Morgan: "Temper of Indians unchanged; hope to be able to manage them if no new apostles come." But five days later he noted that the dancing was still underway "and increasing rather than diminishing. Indians come from other agencies at will and go from this to other agencies. The police have no longer any control of these dancers. . . . About 400 people were dancing at the camp on Cherry Creek [Hump's camp] on November 7, and would not allow any of the police to go near them." In later communications Palmer claimed that both Big Foot and Hump, along with Low Dog and others, were overseeing the dancing at Cherry Creek, that at one dance on November 25 Big Foot directed the people to secure arms and ammunition, and that progressive Indians on the reserve expected trouble to result. None of those leaders would speak with Big Foot. Furthermore, the dancers at Cherry Creek had intimidated white residents into leaving tiny Cheyenne City, on the ceded tract across the river.[3]

The Big Foot people were also suspected of trying to recruit followers from among the band of "partly civilized" Two Kettle Lakotas, located up Bad River west of Pierre and between the Cheyenne and the White River. So far those people had rejected the overtures. Officers at Fort Bennett believed that the Miniconjous of Hump and Big Foot were exchanging information with the Rosebud and Pine Ridge people, hoping they would join them for grand Ghost Dances. Many believed, however, that no outbreak would occur unless those two bodies of Lakotas joined forces. Troops stationed at the forks of the Cheyenne and Belle Fourche Rivers watched for movements that might indicate such a union. They had been instructed to remain in position until the spring to help forestall any such link-up. Agent Palmer visited the Ghost Dance camp late in November with an officer from Fort Bennett and reported that cold weather had stopped the dances. Almost simultaneously, however, Indians from the Cherry Creek camp had captured from the nearby subagency the herd designated for the Miniconjous' beef ration and driven the beasts to the Ghost Dance camp to feed the dancers. The venture might also attract potential converts.[4]

Hump (High Back Bone) was better known to army personnel than Big Foot. During the closing days of the Great Sioux War in early 1877, Hump, who had fought beside his people at the Little Bighorn, was one of the Indian leaders who answered to then colonel Miles's request for a conference at the Tongue River Cantonment on the Yellowstone River in Montana. Soon afterward Hump and others capitulated and became scouts for the army against those Sioux and Cheyennes who had not yet surrendered, which brought him long-standing resentment from his people. The young Miniconjou quickly became a favorite of Miles and played important roles in the army's closing operations against the Lakota and Northern Cheyenne coalition. Hump also served with Miles against the Nez Perces in fall 1877 and was wounded in the shoulder at the Bear's Paw Mountains. As a scout for the Fifth Infantry, Hump later served for several years under Captain Ezra P. Ewers, who became a good friend. But in 1890 Hump had quit his position as chief of police at Cheyenne River Agency to assume a leadership role in the Ghost Dances. Palmer viewed him as particularly influential and thus dangerous.[5]

Recalling the friendship between Ewers and Hump, Miles solicited the help of Captain Ewers in November. Ewers was still with the Fifth Infantry but now stationed in Texas. Miles hoped that he could nullify Hump's influence with the Miniconjou Ghost Dancers and perhaps remove him from the scene. Arriving at Pierre, Ewers proceeded to Fort Bennett the next day and then rode out for Cherry Creek, more than fifty miles away, accompanied only by Second Lieutenant Harry C. Hale of the Twelfth Infantry. Ewers's orders were to convince Hump and his followers to go to Fort Bennett and not join the Indians in the Badlands.

Approaching Cherry Creek on December 6, Captain Ewers dispatched a runner to Hump to announce his arrival. When the chief appeared, he and Ewers greeted each other as friends, entered the camp, and sat and talked. The captain reminded Hump of their work at Fort Keogh and told him of Miles's request that he and his followers divorce themselves from the dances and go to Fort Bennett. Ewers convinced the chief and all of his supporters ("except thirty," said Miles's report) to do just that. Likely mindful of protecting his people based on the word of Ewers, Hump once more yielded and swore fidelity to the government. Ewers tried unsuccessfully to contact Big Foot through Hump. On Ewers's suggestion Hump and chiefs Iron Shield and Spotted Eagle applied for enlistment as scouts. Soon after Hump's acquiescence, the Miniconjou chief White Swan turned up in Pierre offering to assist in disarming Big Foot's people. "He wants the Messiah notion dispelled," recorded a correspondent, "stating that many ghost dancers are suffering and even dying now from a form of grippe induced by dancing outdoors during the cold weather." The malady was supposedly spreading quickly for want of medical attention.[6]

With Hump neutralized and Big Foot engaged with the dancers at Cheyenne River and thus remote, Miles turned to the last member of the triumvirate designated for arrest. Agent James McLaughlin at Standing Rock had called for the removal of Sitting Bull as early as June. Since early October and Kicking Bear's instructional appearance on Standing Rock Reservation, McLaughlin's relationship with Sitting Bull had deteriorated. It was more than a mutual dislike. The Hunkpapa leader's unceasing traditionalist stance had challenged the changes that the government had worked to instill among the Sioux. When Sitting Bull persisted in his defiance of McLaughlin's authority, the agent urged his transport to a distant military prison. An eastern newspaper commentator probably crystallized the agent's disdain for the Sioux leader best: "He is the exponent of all that is opposed to the progress and elevation of his people—the Jefferson Davis of the Sioux." Sitting Bull's unrelenting support of the Ghost Dances following Kicking Bear's visit infuriated McLaughlin, and his repeated refusal to listen to the progressive leaders that the agent sent to him or to the Congregationalist missionary Mary C. Collins (who also sought to dissuade him) heightened the frustration of all.[7]

Sitting Bull may have seen the dance as a way to reassert the influence that he had enjoyed before surrendering in 1881. Even an immediate benefactor, Catherine Weldon, a reformer of Dr. Bland's National Indian Defence Association who had logged weeks in the chief's secluded community along the Grand River, could not turn him. She had befriended Sitting Bull while teaching domestic arts to his people but was steadfastly opposed to the dancing.

When Weldon departed Standing Rock, discouraged by her failure, rumors of the chief's impending arrest flew through the agency. Thereafter, Sitting Bull avoided Fort Yates, tethering himself to the security of his settlement on the north bank of Grand River. Despite his past influence among the Tetons, his immediate following had dwindled during the years of enforced acculturation. Still, he was highly regarded among elements at the other reserves, especially Cheyenne River, Rosebud, and Pine Ridge. Despite his ongoing dispute with agent McLaughlin, Sitting Bull remained respected in his community. In his remoteness, isolated from the agency with his Ghost Dancer followership, he had done relatively well. He owned about sixty head of cattle and a goodly number of horses, maintained a tilled field, kept chickens, and occupied two small houses on his tract.[8]

Soon after Kicking Bear's departure, McLaughlin penned a strident critique of Sitting Bull to Commissioner Morgan, forcefully calling for his removal from the reservation. He blamed Sitting Bull for the current "excitement" and "disaffection" at Standing Rock, caused largely by "the Sitting Bull faction over the expected 'Indian Millennium.'" McLaughlin roundly denounced Sitting Bull throughout a thirteen-page missive, concluding that

> since this new doctrine has been engrafted here from the more southern Sioux agencies the infection has been wonderful, and so pernicious that it now includes some of the Indians who were formerly numbered with the progressive and more intelligent. . . . "Sitting Bull" is high priest and leading apostle of this latest Indian absurdity; in a word he is the chief mischief maker at this agency, and if he were not here this craze so general among the Sioux would never have gotten a foothold at this agency.[9]

McLaughlin made it personal. Sitting Bull was a coward, "a man of low cunning, devoid of a single manly principle in his nature, or an honorable trait of character, but on the contrary is capable of instigating and inciting others . . . to do any amount of mischief." Besides embracing the messiah movement, he had opposed the imminent surveys of the reservation "and is continually agitating and fostering opposition to such surveys among his followers who are the more worthless, ignorant, obstinate and non-progressive of the Sioux." McLaughlin urged the chief's elimination from the reservation (along with cohorts Circling Bear, Blackbird [Black Bird], and Circling Hawk) and incarceration "in some military prison some distance from the Sioux country. . . . With these individuals removed the advancement of the Sioux will be more rapid and the interests of the Government greatly subserved thereby."[10]

When McLaughlin arrived at Sitting Bull's settlement along Grand River on November 18 and witnessed a Ghost Dance involving some 300 people, including onlookers, he reproached the chief for promoting the activities. Sitting Bull, McLaughlin declared, knew better and was aware that he was hurting his people by such efforts. In response the chief proposed that they together visit the places farther west where the messiah had appeared and then determine if the message was true. If so, the Indians should be permitted to continue their dances. McLaughlin countered by offering to show Sitting Bull the irrationality of the creed. Sitting Bull did not appear on the appointed day, however, citing an ill child. Instead he sent a letter in which he stated that he had curtailed the dances. He probably had learned by then that military forces had entered the agencies at Rosebud and Pine Ridge far to the south. Still resolved on the Hunkpapa leader's removal, however, McLaughlin strategized having the Standing Rock Indian police execute an arrest after the onset of cold weather minimized resistance at Grand River. On November 21 he wired Morgan:

> Sitting Bull, Circling bear [*sic*], Black Bird, Circling Hawk, Iron White Man and Male Bear, being leaders of Excitement [*sic*] and fomenters of disaffection should be removed before next spring. But every thing being quiet here at present with no snow and the weather summer like, do not think it prudent to make arrests now.[11]

The agency's progressive faction, led by Gall, John Grass, Mad Bear (all of whom had supported the 1889 land bill), and others, reportedly spurned the dissenters at Grand River, saying that they would present Sitting Bull in chains forthwith if the agent sanctioned it. Gall, in fact, held a council to dissuade the dancers not far from Grand River. A company of the Twenty-Second Infantry from Fort Totten arrived at adjacent Fort Yates to bolster the Twelfth Infantry and Eighth Cavalry soldiers garrisoned there. More troops were en route from Forts Keogh and Custer in Montana, all as part of the initial military buildup. Over the next week Sitting Bull resisted the entreaties of progressive relatives and friends, including the Indian policemen that McLaughlin sent to try to reason with him. Rations were distributed on the appointed day, but fewer recipients showed up. The Ghost Dancers kept aware of happenings at Pine Ridge, Rosebud, and Cheyenne River while McLaughlin waited for the weather to change so that his policemen might enforce the chief's departure from Standing Rock. Lieutenant

Colonel William F. Drum, commandant at Fort Yates, and General Ruger, commander of the military department, aligned with the agent. Even before his meeting at the White House on November 29, however, General Miles had been formulating yet another plan. Consulting no authority beyond his own, he had in fact already begun to implement it.[12]

Little more than two weeks earlier fifty Oglala Sioux members of Buffalo Bill's "Wild West" troupe had debarked from the steamer *Belgendland* at Philadelphia. They had been touring Europe since spring 1889. Within days, escorted by Cody's business manager "Major" John M. Burke, the Indians boarded a train for Pine Ridge. Accompanied by Burke, they proceeded to the agency, where some enlisted as agency policemen. Burke would remain at Pine Ridge through the crisis to support Buffalo Bill's Indians and help ease their transition at the agency.

As efforts to arrest Sitting Bull's intensified, Miles wired Cody, just back in New York City, to request his assistance. The redoubtable showman knew the Hunkpapa leader and had employed him as an attraction in his Wild West show in 1884–85. Moreover, Cody, a former army scout and known publicity seeker, was also a brigadier general in the Nebraska National Guard, which gave him credence in Miles's eyes. On November 23 Cody told a reporter that "Sitting Bull will always be found with the disturbing element. If there is no disturbing element he will foment one." Cody met Miles at the general's Chicago headquarters and departed on November 25 in conformance with Miles's request to go to Standing Rock and meet with Sitting Bull. He appeared at Bismarck with three friends and a reporter two days later and reached Fort Yates by wagon on November 28. McLaughlin and Colonel Drum were aware of Cody's impending arrival, but the showman's appearance with authority from Miles in the form of a confidential directive on Division of the Missouri stationery caught them off guard. On the reverse of Miles's calling card the general had penciled: "Com'dg officers will please give Col. Cody transportation for himself and party and any protection he may need for a small party. Nelson A. Miles[,] Major General[,] Comd. Division[.]"[13]

Neither McLaughlin nor Drum was happy with this outside interference. As Cody recalled, the agent "informed me that he thought my mission extraordinary and unwise. . . . Both requested me to remain at the Agency, and not to attempt to arrest Sitting Bull. McLaughlin . . . unhesitatingly denounced the undertaking saying that if Sitting Bull's arrest was *necessary*, he could accomplish it inside of two weeks." The agent refused Cody's request for a second wagon, although Drum provided an interpreter. The next morning, November 29, Cody's party struck southwest along a road tracing the open grasslands in a wagon loaded with goods purchased from the post trader. As Buffalo Bill departed, Drum prepared his cavalry for field duty if required. "We had gone as I judged about 25 miles," Cody related,

> when I met, coming from Bull's camp, a half-breed named Louis Primeau, whom I know to be Major McLaughlin's chief interpreter. He informed me that to his personal knowledge Bull had started for the Agency on the previous afternoon, and had camped the night before on Oak Creek. He further asserted that Bull must have reached the Agency already. . . . He said that Bull generally traveled to the Agency on a road about 3 miles to the north of the one we were on.[14]

Cody sent one of his colleagues back to Fort Yates to learn if Sitting Bull had indeed arrived there and then started back to the agency himself. While en route, however, he received word from Drum via the courier, Marcellus Red Tomahawk, that his mission had been canceled. On reaching Fort Yates on November 30, Cody asked to see the order turning him back. "His reply," Cody said of Drum, was "'I haven't it with me, but that the order to arrest Sitting Bull had been suspended and it could not be done.'" Cody reportedly penciled and signed a note: "The President's orders have been received and will be obeyed." Rather than use the fort's telegraph to contact Miles, Cody set out for Mandan. Failing to communicate with the general from there, he took the cars east to La Crosse, Wisconsin, wiring Miles of his intention to remain there "as I do not want to show up among the Chicago reporters until after I hear from you." From there he headed to his Nebraska home.[15]

In reality McLaughlin had wired Commissioner Morgan requesting immediate repeal of Miles's order to Cody. "I have matters well in hand," he wrote. "When proper time arrives [I] can arrest Sitting Bull by Indian police without bloodshed." Acting commissioner Belt responded: "Have handed your telegram concerning Cody's mission to Secretary [Noble] who will see President and Secretary of War immediately on subject." Late that evening Secretary Proctor wired Miles: "The President thinks any arrest of Sitting Bull or other Indian leaders should be deferred." Late the next day Miles telegraphed Colonel Drum: "Cody's orders were to quietly carry out the letter of his instructions. If he or you secure the person of S.B. hold him. This will comply with the Secretary's wishes, and he authorizes this construction."[16]

Miles then headed for Washington and conferred with Proctor and President Harrison at the White House the next evening about the arrest strategy, among other things. As Proctor reiterated to Miles on December 1, "When in your opinion adequate preparations are complete and you think arrests should be made, he [the president] will not interfere, feeling that your judgment of these matters would be better than his." Miles later reported his belief that Cody "had perhaps as much influence over him [Sitting Bull] as any living man" and could thereby induce him "to come in with him . . . and if unsuccessful in this, . . . arrest him quietly and . . . remove him quickly from his camp to the nearest military station."[17]

Bizarre from its inception, the Buffalo Bill affair quickly drew press criticism. A visit between Cody and Sitting Bull might have yielded a conference with Miles that could have removed the Hunkpapa leader from the reservation, but chances for success were probably remote. Truncated preliminaries largely precluded it. In any event a political ruckus soon flared, reflecting newspaper partisanship. Some deemed the exercise a calculated provocation toward an outbreak that "a discreet and sagacious commander" would have avoided at all costs. The *Army and Navy Journal* asserted that General Ruger, in whose department the event occurred, was said to have "felt some resentment in that General Miles had given Cody an important military commission and had ignored him (Ruger) completely. There can be no doubt that General Ruger and Agent McLaughlin . . . convinced the Secretary of War and the Secretary of the Interior that the time to arrest Sitting Bull had not arrived." The *Brooklyn Daily Eagle* protested: "a more reckless and injudicious mission . . . could hardly be conceived." "General Miles," the paper complained, "is acting as if it were his desire to bring on an Indian war." There had been "so far no justification of the plan of interfering with the Indians in their ceremonies in honor of the alleged Messiah." The *Eagle* went on to critique Miles harshly, in the end calling for his relief and retirement.[18]

The whole episode incensed and discomfited Miles. On December 6 he cabled Schofield confidentially: "I am satisfied from reports received that the interference of Agent McLaughlin . . . prevented the arrest of Sitting Bull last Monday as I had intended and desired. . . . If there is now no objection, I will endeavor to secure the person of that Indian, but it will be more difficult now than before." Accordingly Ruger received a telegram on December 10 from Major Henry C. Corbin, Miles's assistant adjutant general in Chicago:

> The Division Commander is not entirely satisfied with the action of the military at Fort Yates, when authority was recently given to a party at these headquarters to secure the person of Sitting Bull and turn him over to the commanding officer, or the action of the agent in interfering in the matter, also in giving publicity to his plans and programs. To accomplish the same object you will now direct the commanding officer Fort Yates to consider it his especial duty to secure the person of Sitting Bull, using any practical means. The agent at that post is under his direction and orders for any purpose of this kind affecting the police control and government of these Indians.[19]

In the wake of Cody's visit, the pace of events quickened toward the means of arrest that McLaughlin did favor, using Indian policemen (known to the Sioux as "metal-breasts" because of their badges) at a time that the agent deemed most appropriate. Beyond Sitting Bull's unbridled promotion of the Ghost Dances in the camps along Grand River, McLaughlin told the press that he was also displeased with the medicine man's failure to deliver his children for schooling and had policemen stationed about and ready to seize him should he appear within agency limits. "His influence is strongly and constantly for evil," McLaughlin griped, "and while he does not participate in the ghost dance to the extent of jumping and yelling he keeps the frenzy at the highest pitch." The December 1 decree requiring army sanction for "all operations intended to suppress any outbreak by force" would handily facilitate McLaughlin's purpose. Believing that conditions would be right, he set the date of the arrest for the night of December 6, ration day. But the hoped-for approval did not arrive. The agent had to postpone. In Bismarck on December 11 McLaughlin told reporters that no outbreak was imminent and that the Ghost Dancing was subsiding because of colder weather. Authority finally came on December 12 in a communication from General Miles to Colonel Drum directing Drum to collaborate with McLaughlin "to secure the person of Sitting Bull." Drum ordered a command readied. With his concurrence McLaughlin deferred the arrest to Saturday morning, December 20, the next ration day, when he expected most of the Hunkpapa leader's followers at Grand River to have gone to the agency to receive provisions. During the interim the agent's police continued their careful surveillance of Sitting Bull's home and activities.[20]

Concern that Sitting Bull and his followers might strike south toward the Stronghold and the southernmost agencies and thereby incite a general outbreak was long-standing. To McLaughlin's police, who kept watch under the pretense of cutting trees for construction purposes, such a movement appeared to be in the works. Sitting Bull had requested formal permission to go off reservation, and the agent denied it. To thwart his departure further, McLaughlin ordered First Lieutenant Henry Bull Head, his informer at Grand River and leader of the augmented police detachment there, to carefully monitor developments. He should await further orders unless it appeared that Sitting Bull was close to leaving the reservation. Bull Head, an intelligent and devoted officer and a progressive loyal to the government, had clashed with Sitting Bull and his followers in the recent past. He could be counted on. To get word to Bull Head, McLaughlin used agency employee John Carignan, teacher at the Grand River School just a mile and a half below Sitting Bull's home.

On December 14 McLaughlin received a message from Bull Head, written by Carignan, informing him that Sitting Bull was indeed preparing to leave the reservation. Bull Head said that the Hunkpapa leader was fitting out his horses for a journey and urged that the police seize him at once. Colonel Drum agreed. The arrest should be made immediately. The officer and the agent planned for it to take place early the next morning, December 15. It should be executed by the police, McLaughlin said, because of "the salutary effect that it would have upon the Indians." Cavalry from Fort Yates, operating at an appropriate distance, would be on hand to receive the prisoner from the police and take him to Fort Yates. Above all, said the agent, "I desired to have the arrest made without bloodshed, which I believed the police would be able to effect." McLaughlin prepared two letters ordering the arrest—one in English and the other in Lakota—addressed to both First Lieutenant Bull Head and First Sergeant Shave Head. He added: "P.S. You must not let him escape under any circumstances." The agent explained to Second Sergeant Marcellus Red Tomahawk, a Yanktonai-Hunkpapa, how the capture was to occur. He impressed upon the sergeant, as he had upon Lieutenant Bull Head, "the importance of having a light wagon with them when they went to make the arrest, so that they could put Sitting Bull into it as soon as they had made him prisoner, and to drive out of the village as rapidly as possible [before] . . . a disturbance might be created." Red Tomahawk then set out with the messages with orders to pick up additional police while en route to Bull Head.[21]

At midnight, on Drum's direction, Captain Edmond G. Fechet departed Fort Yates in support of the police with a squadron of two troops totaling ninety-nine men of the Eighth Cavalry, as well as assistant surgeon Alonzo R. Chapin, a Hotchkiss gun and a Gatling gun, a spring wagon, an ambulance with hospital steward, one guide, and two Indian scouts. "Our destination was not announced," recalled former trooper James Connelly, "but we knew where we were going."[22] Attired in heavy greatcoats with muskrat caps and gauntlets to ward off the bitter cold and equipped with Springfield carbines and Colt's revolvers, the command, dubbed the "Flying Squadron," moved quickly through a night of freezing rain. They took what was called "Sitting Bull's Road" to Oak Creek then continued toward the settlement on Grand River. Near daylight the soldiers approached from the northeast toward a point on the hills overlooking the Grand, about three miles from the river. There they halted to await the prearranged arrival of the police with their prisoner.

Sitting Bull occupied a tract along the north side of Grand River. Two log cabins stood on the site. Sitting Bull, his two wives, and his sons lived in the westernmost cabin, whose entrance was on the east face. The smaller cabin stood perhaps thirty feet farther east. To the north, across the road that led ultimately to Standing Rock Agency, stood Sitting Bull's stable and chicken coop and beyond that his corral and sheds, all a few dozen paces east of a large tented Ghost Dance site. Some distance north stood a large cluster of tipis. All the Indians now lived in log cabins, but many maintained tipis for attendance at dances and for the journey to and from the agency for rations. South of Sitting Bull's home site, in the timber along Grand River, stood more Sioux tipis, while directly east of the log buildings were several more Indian cabin homes. A mile and a half downriver was the Grand River Day School, where John Carignan taught.

Five miles northwest of Sitting Bull's community and forty-three miles southwest of the agency stood the log home of Lieutenant Henry Bull Head. Red Tomahawk carried McLaughlin's letter there through the freezing rain on the night of December 14. At Bull Head's direction, most of the other police had congregated at his cabin to plan, pray, and converse excitedly over their pending arrest of the Hunkpapa holy man. The teacher Carignan was also there but would start for the agency when the arrest team left in the early morning darkness. Police Private John Lone Man, a Hunk-papa, recalled a sense of gravity about the mission. "We were called to take a final action to suppress this ghost dance," he said, "which was becoming a menace to the Tribe."[23]

Long before sunrise on Monday, December 15, the assembled party of blue-clad police and special police, mounted on ponies and arranged by twos, trotted over the icy road leading southeast through the darkness on their way to Sitting Bull's. More special police joined them as they went, and they stopped en route to pick up a volunteer and to ford the Grand. They then headed east through the frozen river bottom dense with willows, cottonwoods, and box elders toward Sitting Bull's settlement, whose inhabitants were sound asleep after a lengthy Ghost Dance the previous night. Together the police party totaled forty-three: one officer (Bull Head), four sergeants, fourteen privates, twenty special police without uniforms but with white neckerchiefs to distinguish them, and four volunteers, most of them Hunkpapas and Yanktonais.[24] In their anticipation, they had left behind the wagon for conveying their prisoner to Fort Yates.

The following account is composite, reconstructed from official documents and the recollections of participants and eyewitnesses. At 5:30 A.M., a mile from their objective and approaching from the west, the policemen broke into a gallop, racing to a point between Sitting Bull's cabins. They dismounted and surrounded the structures while their officers first banged on the doors then pushed them open and burst inside: eight men into one cabin, ten into the other. "It was still dark and everybody was asleep," said Lone Man. "Only dogs which were quite numerous greeted us . . . and no doubt by their greetings had aroused and awaken[ed] the ghost dancers." There in the larger hand-hewn chinked log building, facing east but a short distance from the riverbank, the police lit matches and found a responsive Sitting Bull naked in his blankets on a floor mattress with one of his wives and one of his children. A cast-iron stove stood in the center of the room, and kerosene lamps hung on the walls. Followed inside by Shave Head, Red Tomahawk, and several others who seized his firearms, Bull Head told Sitting Bull that he was under arrest.[25] Elsewhere in the room were two older men, visitors who had stayed overnight after the Ghost Dance, in addition to Sitting Bull's fourteen-year-old boy, Crow Foot, and the wife of his nephew One Bull, named Red Whirlwind. All were awakened by the ensuing tumult. Sitting Bull sat upright and said in effect: "This is a great

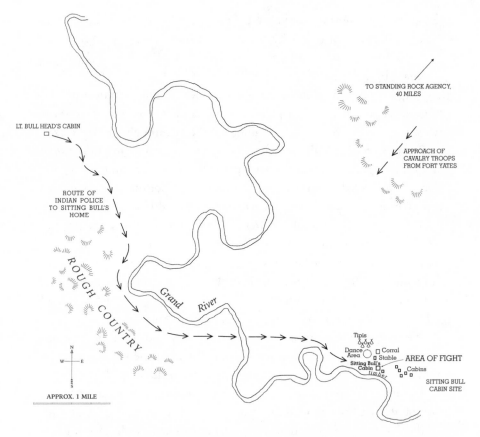

Map 4. Area of the Sitting Bull Fight, December 15, 1890.
Map by Robert G. Pilk.

way to do things. All right. I will go with you. I will put on my clothes." He dispatched one of his wives to the smaller cabin, occupied by his other wife and children, to find them. He asked that a preferred horse—a gray circus mount given him by Buffalo Bill in St. Louis—be saddled and brought over from the stable, and the policemen quickly obliged.[26]

Sitting Bull slowly pulled on his breechclout, leggings, and moccasins and began to berate the police for the disturbance. The two older men and One Bull's wife exited the cabin, while Sitting Bull's wife began wailing loudly. The commotion inside, and the barking of frenzied dogs outside, quickly drew the attention of the neighboring Sioux in the dawn. By the time the police began ushering Sitting Bull out the door as he fussed with his shirt, the medicine man's followers, particularly those charged with guarding him, were all about and pressing closer, calling out against the police. Bull Head and the others tried to reassure them and to ease them back so that Sitting Bull might get to his horse. When they were only a few dozen feet from the house Crow Foot suddenly appeared from the cabin and began chiding his father for permitting himself to be taken away in such manner, calling him a "fool" and "crazy." Sitting Bull, taunted by his son and encouraged by the presence of his followers, became agitated, responding, "Then I will not go." He called on the assembly to attack the police and save him. Bull Head told him not to listen to anyone and asked the chief's adopted brother, Little Assiniboine, who had just arrived, to help persuade him. Lone Man spoke too, telling the Hunkpapa leader that he would not be harmed. When Sitting Bull began to resist more actively, Bull Head, Shave Head, and Red Tomahawk all took hold of him.[27]

At this moment Lieutenant Bull Head stood to Sitting Bull's right as they faced the crowd, grasping his right arm and waist, while Sergeant Shave Head took his left arm and Sergeant Red Tomahawk moved directly behind him with his revolver pointed at the chief's head, together forcing him out the door. "By this time," said Lone Man, "the whole camp was in commotion—women and children crying while the men gathered all round us." Several of Sitting Bull's leading supporters—Catch the Bear, Strike the Kettle, and two others—abruptly appeared, pushing through the crowd to confront the party. Catch the Bear yelled out to let Sitting Bull go and without another word tossed his blanket aside and fired his Winchester, striking Bull Head in his right side. The lieutenant, still holding Sitting Bull's arm, wheeled and discharged a round from his rifle that ripped open the medicine man's chest. Almost simultaneously Red Tomahawk fired a bullet that struck Sitting Bull in the head. Another shot hit him in the right cheek. Strike the Kettle fired too, hitting Shave Head in the abdomen. The exploding gunfire collapsed all three men into a pile. Sergeant Little Eagle likewise fell dead from a bullet near the stable as he started away from the turmoil. Lone Man now scuffled with Catch the Bear and shot him. As Catch the Bear fell mortally wounded, the furor crescendoed into a fierce hand-to-hand melee amid a flurry of shooting that killed five more of Sitting Bull's followers, including Little Assiniboine, and wounded three others. Bull Head, on the ground, took three more rounds. Another policeman, Hawk Man No. 2, fell dead in the struggle outside the cabin.[28]

After almost half an hour the remaining policemen, now under Sergeant Red Tomahawk's command and sheltered behind small sheds and the walls of the log stable northwest of the house, gradually managed to repel the throng, estimated at perhaps 160 strong. Some they drove from a distant stable back several hundred yards into the timber along the river. At Red Tomahawk's direction, another policeman, Hawk Man No. 1, managed to mount Sitting Bull's horse and break away to the north, from which direction Fechet's troops were expected to come. Red Tomahawk and the others quickly took refuge inside the cabin. They remained there for two hours as the firing gradually waned. Securing the dwindling ammunition and preventing the loss of horses from the corral, the policemen presently recovered their casualties, brought them into the shelter of the cabin, and began treating the wounded. Soon after withdrawing inside they discovered Crow Foot hiding behind sheeting covering the walls. Lone Man recalled: "As soon as he was exposed to view, he cried out, 'My uncles, do not kill me. I do not wish to die.' The police asked the officers what to do. Lieut. Bull Head, seeing what was up, said, 'Do what you like with him. He is one of them that has caused this trouble.' I do not remember who really fired the shot that killed Crow Foot—several fired at once." Lone Man and One Feather were later identified as the killers. For now, they hurled Crow Foot's body out the door.[29]

In the meantime the cavalry rode to the crest of the heights a few miles north of the river, with shooting continuing in the distance. There the troops encountered Hawk Man No. 1, who had braved the gunfire around the cabin and ridden through to find Fechet. Excitedly he had explained the policemen's predicament. Fechet understood him to say that all of the policemen had been killed. Dispatching Hawk Man No. 1 to carry the news back to Colonel Drum at Fort Yates, Fechet directed his men to advance in two columns down the slopes, with the artillery in between and skirmishers in front. As the gloomy first light revealed the scene before them, the soldiers removed their overcoats and gauntlets for the advance. At the crest of the hill several troopers unlimbered the Hotchkiss gun to send exploding rounds toward the Indians in the distant timber.

At an agreed-upon signal, the police, running short of ammunition, showed a white flag from the corral to indicate their presence. But the artillery nonetheless lobbed two Hotchkiss rounds directly at them before Red Tomahawk personally advanced on horseback, waving the flag to gain the soldiers' attention. From his vantage point Private William G. Wilkinson recalled: "We had dismounted and were lying on the brow of the hill firing at them with our carbines. Then G Troop was ordered to follow them up the valley, while Capt. Fechet took F Troop down into the village." Soon afterward the troops, now dismounted as skirmishers, reached the scene. It was about 8:30 A.M. as troops positioned the Gatling gun and opened on the warriors in the brush. Wilkinson explained: "As G Troop went up the valley we noticed that some of the Indians had gone up the bluffs on the other side of the river. Lt. Crowder then ordered four of us to go down into the valley and up on to a high knowl [*sic*] and keep firing at the ones that had gone up the other side, to keep them back so they could not snipe at the troop down in the village."[30]

A brief confrontation followed between Fechet's cavalrymen and a single ghost-shirted warrior who repeatedly passed in and out of the willow thickets, drawing their fire. The individual, later reported to have been testing the validity of his ghost shirt, eluded many shots before fading off to the west. As Wilkinson recalled the incident:

Suddenly we heard a shout and as we looked up, there directly in front of us, about 100 yards away, sat a naked painted Indian on a white horse with the sun just rising, shining directly on him. He made quite a picture. We all immediately jumped for our guns. . . . The Indian . . . turned his horse and disappeared in the thicket out of which he had appeared. We all began shooting into the thicket. We made no attempt to follow him, as our horses were tired after an all night run and his was fresh. The Indian emerged from the thicket about one-quarter of a mile away and disappeared over the hill. There must have been over 100 bullets fired at him in that thicket. Of course we could not see him, but it was little short of a miracle that one of those bullets did not hit him.[31]

The impetuous warrior captivated the attention of all, but the soldiers did not pursue him or other Indians withdrawing up the Grand for fear of unduly frightening so-called loyal tribesmen. Most who fled were younger men; women, children, and the elderly for the most part stayed behind. As the warriors passed by Bull Head's home en route west, they shot bullets into it. Fechet stationed pickets at the advance points then pulled his men back to the cabins, where several women continued wailing loudly. "In the vicinity of the house, within a radius of 50 yards," he reported, "there were found the dead bodies of eight hostiles, including Sitting Bull. Two horses were also killed. Within the house were found 4 dead and 3 wounded policemen. Surgeon Chapin administered to Bull Head, Shave Head, and [Alexander] Middle." Fechet learned through an interpreter that Sitting Bull's followers had carried away one of their dead and five or six of their wounded, "making an approximate total of 15 casualties in Sitting Bull's band." Lone Man recalled that Fechet "proceeded to where Sitting Bull's corpse was and with a (branch/brush) took the third coup and said: 'Sitting Bull—big chief, you brought this disaster upon yourself and your people.' Louis Primeau was interpreting." As the frustrated police viewed the body of Sitting Bull, some fired bullets into him and mutilated his body. According to Shoots Walking, when the half-brother of Little Eagle saw the policeman dead, "he seized a club and beat the head of Sitting Bull into a shapeless mass." (Others claimed that a relative of another dead policeman later wielded an ox yoke against Sitting Bull's head.) Fechet placed a guard over the chief's body and then had his men lay all of the dead in a straight row on the ground.[32]

After breakfast the troops fed their horses. Some scavenged the scene of the fight for souvenirs, and F Troop members reportedly made off with Sitting Bull's ghost shirt. The captain took time to dispatch a message to those who had fled, telling them that they would not be harmed if they returned peaceably to their homes. The bodies of Sitting Bull and the dead policemen were placed in the wagon. The wounded police were secured in the ambulance for direct transport to the agency and arrived there that night. Sitting Bull's two wives, along with two youths found in the second cabin (Sitting Bull's deaf stepson and a nephew) accompanied the troops for delivery to agent McLaughlin. Sitting Bull's dead followers were placed in one of the community's houses. Red Tomahawk then dismissed the police, praising them for their brave service and requesting their appearance at the funeral for their companions.

Fechet led his command over the road back to Oak Creek, eighteen miles northeast, with a sizable number of area Lakota residents who desired protective escort to the agency. About six o'clock that evening the command halted at Oak Creek, where a courier from Drum brought word that the colonel had started from Fort Yates with sixty-seven infantrymen and wagons with provisions for ten days. Colonel Drum's force reached Oak Creek after midnight with rations, forage, tents, bedding rolls, and buffalo overcoats. There the united command camped before returning to the post the next day.[33]

When word of the action at Grand River reached McLaughlin at the agency, the agent wired the following message to the commissioner's office:

> Fort Yates, N. Dak., December 15, 1890
>
> Commissioner Indian Affairs, Washington, D.C.:
>
> Indian police arrested Sitting Bull at his camp 40 miles southwest of agency this morning at daylight. His followers attempted his rescue and fighting commenced. Four policemen killed and three wounded. Eight Indians killed, including Sitting Bull and his son Crow Foot, and several others wounded. Police were surrounded for some time but maintained their ground until relieved by United States troops, who now have possession of Sitting Bull's camp and all women, children, and property. Sitting Bull's followers, probably 100 men, deserted their families and fled west up Grand River. Police behaved nobly, and great credit is due them. Particulars by mail.
>
> McLaughlin, Agent.[34]

Drum wired his superiors as well. The news went first to Ruger's headquarters in St. Paul and then to Miles's headquarters in Chicago. Miles was already en route to Rapid City, however, so the news had to be telegraphed to him in transit from Chicago. Drum's message also went to the adjutant general in Washington. The colonel briefly described the fight at Sitting Bull's house together with Fechet's rescue of the Indian police. "The courier who brought the word," Drum said, "saw Sitting Bull on the ground, and is sure he is dead." McLaughlin filed a longer report on December 16 that included documentation for his decision to make the arrest, an updated list of casualties, and a sketch of the engagement site. He informed the commissioner's office that he had sent runners to overtake those tribesmen who fled the scene to tell them to return to the agency, for "if found outside the reservation they must suffer the consequences." In fact some 160 fleeing Indians returned within a few days and 88 more came back within two weeks. Others yielded to soldiers of the Twelfth Infantry near the mouth of Cherry Creek on the Cheyenne River.[35]

As McLaughlin enumerated them, the losses in what came to be known as the Sitting Bull Fight (known among the Lakotas as the Battle in the Dark) were as follows:

Casualties in the police force:

First Lieutenant of Police Henry Tatankapah (Bull Head) in command. Dangerously wounded, four wounds. Died 82 hours after the fight.

First Sergeant of Police Charles Kashlah (Shave Head). Mortally wounded. Died 25 hours after the fight.

Fourth Sergeant of Police James Wambdichigalah (Little Eagle). Killed.

Private of Police Alexander Hochokah (Middle). Painfully wounded, but recovered.

Private of Police Paul Akichitah (Afraid of Soldier). Killed.

Special Policeman John Armstrong. Killed.

Special Police David Hawk Man (No. 2). Killed.

Indians killed outright:

Sitting Bull, age 59 [*sic*]

Black Bird, age 43

Catch the Bear, age 44

Little Assiniboine, age 44

Crow Foot (Sitting Bull's son, 14 years old)

Spotted Horn Bull, age 56

Brave Thunder (No. 1), age 46

Chase Wounded, age 24

Indians wounded:

Bull Ghost, recovered.

Brave Thunder (No. 2), recovered.

Strike the Kettle, recovered.[36]

On Wednesday afternoon, December 17, two days after the Sitting Bull Fight, joint Protestant and Catholic services for four of the five dead police took place at the Congregational mission. A ceremony in both English and Lakota followed in the nearby Catholic cemetery along with interment with full military honors. The entire Fort Yates garrison turned out, and a company of the Twenty-Second Infantry only recently arrived from Montana fired a three-volley salute. Lakota friends and relatives and other residents of the Standing Rock Reservation community stood by, mourning openly. One of the slain, Little Eagle, who was Protestant, was removed for burial along Grand River at the community later named for him. Fatalities from the struggle increased late the following afternoon, when Lieutenant Bull Head expired from his wounds in the Fort Yates hospital, bringing the total of dead police to six. He was buried with his fellows in the Catholic cemetery on December 19. Alexander Middle, another wounded policeman, underwent amputation of a foot and lived. From the time of its arrival at Fort Yates on the afternoon of December 16, the body of Sitting Bull remained under guard in the post dead house behind the hospital. No postmortem examination of his remains took place, although acting assistant surgeon Horace M. Deeble removed his bloodstained leggings and cut the plaited scalp lock from his head. Sitting Bull was buried in the northwest corner of the military cemetery at Fort Yates, a few hundred yards south of where the police were interred. McLaughlin, the medicine man's old nemesis, stood by with two army surgeons and the Fort Yates post quartermaster as four prisoners from the guardhouse excavated the grave. No service was held. They watched as Sitting Bull's mortal remains, bound in canvas and consigned to a rough-cut pine coffin fashioned by the agency carpenter, were lowered into the grave.[37]

Official Washington generally welcomed the news of Sitting Bull's demise. The army leadership through General Schofield applauded the effort, making clear that it was the Interior Department that had undertaken the arrest. With Sitting Bull gone, President Harrison said that he hoped the Sioux difficulties might be settled without further bloodshed. Miles was doubtless relieved that no whites had been directly involved. From his headquarters in Rapid City, he issued an order on December 27 commending the policemen and troops who participated in the arrest and death of Sitting Bull. McLaughlin and others justified the killing because it effectively ended the Ghost Dancing so far as Standing Rock was concerned, but the Bureau of Indian Affairs hierarchy immediately sought to attribute the affair to the army. Concerned with the residual impact of Sitting Bull's death not only on the Indians but within the Indian rights organizations as well, Secretary Noble preferred that McLaughlin's order for the arrest be presented in context with the agent's report of the event itself. He wired McLaughlin: "Send me report immediately stating exactly order given for Indian police to go to Sitting Bull's camp to arrest him, from whom received, and when and all tending to show origin of order, its nature, the superintendence of its execution, the taking of the body of Sitting Bull and what disposition was made of it." To Morgan he proclaimed: "Agent McLaughlin is so proud of his exploit, that he rather suppresses the source of his action. But it is necessary that it be shown and understood that this was the act of the *Military, without qualification.*" The agent presented his case, concluding that he was operating under Colonel Drum's "direct verbal orders" and that his police were "in this case what may be termed concomitants of the military."[38]

In the aftermath, the loss of the policemen was of special consequence to their relatives as well as to McLaughlin. Early in 1891 he applied for relief for the families of the killed and wounded victims. He also applied for bronze medals for the police participants who survived and reimbursement for ponies lost to Sitting Bull's followers in the fighting. Not until 1908, however, did Congress pass fitting legislation enabling the pensions and medals.[39]

News of the death of Sitting Bull spread quickly across the county, and reactions were mixed. It was the first significant bloodletting since the Ghost Dance crisis began. Many believed that, while the Hunkpapa leader was now a "good Indian," the incident could provoke the feared general outbreak. Fear also spread through areas bordering Sioux country that Sitting Bull's followers would react by attacking settlers. Curiously, the event caused little excitement at Pine Ridge, where a major response might have been expected. Views differed. *Harper's Weekly* in the East editorialized: "If the death of Sitting Bull should prevent an Indian war it would have a most happy effect." But in Aberdeen, South Dakota, well east of the Missouri, L. Frank Baum, editor of the *Aberdeen Saturday Pioneer* (and future author of *The Wonderful Wizard of Oz*), irreverently opined that with Sitting Bull's death "the nobility of the Redskin is extinguished, and what few are left are a pack of whining curs who lick the hand that smites them." In the spirit of the moment, and perhaps satirically, Baum rationalized: "Whites, by law of conquest, by justice of civilization, are masters of the American continent, and the best safety of the frontier settlers will be secured by the total annihilation of the few remaining Indians."[40]

Some wondered, in fact, if Sitting Bull had been killed intentionally. Buffalo Bill—stung from his embarrassment in attempting to arrest the Lakota, and likely with theatrical hyperbole—told the press in Chicago that the killing "was a cold blooded murder," although its "effect was good." Cody said that the Indian police shot the Hunkpapa leader as they presented him the warrant for his arrest, adding ruefully that a sister to the Hunkpapa leader had told him Sitting Bull had been "anxious" to see the showman and looked forward to their "friendly pow-wow."[41]

Despite Cody's dramatics, the Wild West manager might have been closer to the truth than he imagined. The *Chicago Tribune* ran a sinister dispatch from Standing Rock that carried disturbing implications:

> It is said that there was a quiet understanding between the officers of the Indian and military departments that it would be impossible to bring Sitting Bull to Standing Rock alive, and that if brought in, nobody would know precisely what to do with him. Though under arrest he still would be a source of great annoyance, and his followers would continue their dances and threats against the neighboring white settlers. There was, therefore, a complete understanding from the commanding officer and the Indian Police that the slightest attempt to rescue the old medicine man should be a signal to send Sitting Bull to the happy hunting ground.[42]

Reacting to criticism that it thought besmirched the national honor, the House of Representatives through its Military Affairs Committee requested an investigation of pertinent documents to determine whether the Indian police "did, in arresting the late Sitting Bull, . . . unjustifiably kill the said Sitting Bull, and afterwards barbarously mutilate his remains."[43] Beyond assembling various materials, however, little came of the effort. The charge of conspiracy alone is not incriminating, but it resonates. Plans for arrest of the Ghost Dance leaders had called for their incarceration at prisons far distant from the reservations, yet no records of such a plan for Sitting Bull ever existed, beyond jailing him at Fort Yates. It is highly unlikely that Sitting Bull would have remained long in the Fort Yates guardhouse, and the notion of his remaining in local custody more than temporarily runs counter to the plans for distant confinement. Transporting Sitting Bull to the railroad at Mandan en route, say, to Fort Snelling, Minnesota, would have taken only a day. No evidence in the correspondence and transcripts examined even suggests that such particulars were contemplated, much less recommended, by McLaughlin, his superiors, Drum, or those in higher authority at the army's department or division levels. (By contrast, the military's relocation plan for Miniconjou chief Big Foot is well documented.)

In the end Sitting Bull's death, whether coldly engineered or the result of a plan gone horribly wrong, ended the Ghost Dancing on the Standing Rock Reservation for all practical purposes. The violence drove away most if not all of its adherents there, and some of them would never return.

Although he had not participated personally, the medicine man as advocate had symbolized to his followers the tenaciousness of purpose that the dance expressed among its nonprogressive believers. Sitting Bull was a symbol of the old days, and the Ghost Dance represented hope for what faith might restore. When he learned the specifics of Sitting Bull's demise, General Miles thought it fitting that the Hunkpapa leader had been kept from joining the dancers to the south. In reality, however, certain of his followers were already headed that way. The bloody violence that erupted in the dark that morning along Grand River was but a prelude to something altogether worse.

TEN

Pursuit

The killing of Sitting Bull changed the calculus of the army campaign because it heightened the likelihood of a general outbreak. As word of Sitting Bull's death circulated, troops of the Sixth and Eighth Cavalry, poised along the Cheyenne River ready to join General Brooke's massing offensive against the Stronghold, abruptly redirected their attention from an attack on the Stronghold to Sitting Bull's people in the North. It was feared that they had fled from the Grand River settlement and were now headed for refuge in the Badlands. By Monday night, December 15, Brooke's force of the Seventh and Ninth Cavalry regiments, the First Artillery battery, and an infantry component were prepared to advance the next morning against the holdouts under Short Bull and Kicking Bear. Then came word of Sitting Bull's death, followed by a telegram from General Miles suspending any advance on the Stronghold until matters at Standing Rock were clarified. Brooke and his force held their breath, still hoping to move against the Stronghold. "So sure were the officers . . . of going this morning," a *Bee* correspondent wrote, "that last night they had their tent stoves taken down and stored away in the commissary department. Today [Tuesday] they are freezing in cold tents or catching a warming here and there in agency offices." But it was not to be.[1]

On December 16 Miles finally shut the operation down. En route west from Chicago, he wired Brooke of his hope to prevent the Indians from leaving the reservations. Ruger, he said, was concentrating a reserve force along the line of the Northern Pacific Railroad in North Dakota. "I realize and appreciate your desire to attack those in the Bad Lands," he told Brooke, "but I have considered it of vital importance to confine them to the reservation or near it and delay decisive action until cold weather and deep snow." Miles said that he preferred keeping the Stronghold Indians surrounded with cavalry on three sides. Should the Indians move out, "either column could strike an effective blow or pursue and overtake them by forced marches." Besides, he added, "I believe Infantry would be more effective for fighting in the Bad Lands." Later that day Miles further advised Brooke that it was more important to hold the Stronghold Indians where they were. "I fear if you attack them you may drive them off the reservation, and the President's orders are to prevent an Indian war." He urged Brooke to "send word to those in [the] Bad Lands with orders for them to come in." He mollified his subordinate, saying that all Brooke had accomplished "could not have been better." But he doubted that the Stronghold Indians had not given themselves a retreat option—"it would be the first in the history of Indian warfare."[2]

Brooke's troops were not losing anything; nor were the hostiles in the Bad Lands gaining anything by staying where they were. "You have succeeded in drawing out and restraining the great majority of the disaffected, and the number of hostiles [is] greatly reduced," Miles said. "If it was not for the danger of driving them out into the settlements, I would say attack them at once." When Brooke persisted in urging an attack, Miles answered firmly: "There must be no move on these Indians unless to prevent their immediate escape . . . and the order given by myself." The main objective of Colonel Sumner and Carr's commands, he said, should be to prevent Sitting Bull's followers from joining those in the Bad Lands.[3]

Miles's reaction seemed measured, but Brooke was crushed. To Ruger he grumbled that the attack "would have been successful and would have been over in three or four days." To his wife he complained, "Everything was ready to finish business here when 'Sitting Bull' and a few others had to get [themselves] killed," adding that "my movement . . . would have closed out all the trouble here by Thursday evening." He thought Miles conniving. "There is something in the wind," he said. "I have never seen anyone who changes his mind so often." On December 17 Brooke penned his wife: "It seems the President wants a war to be avoided. Well, had I not been stopped I believe there would have been no war in this section after tonight."[4]

Even as Brooke and Miles exchanged views, Red Cloud, Little Wound, and other leaders at Pine Ridge councilled on how they thought Brooke should deal with the Stronghold Indians. Having split from Short Bull and departed the Stronghold on December 12, Two Strike and 184 lodges of his people continued their approach and reached the agency on December 16. For the most part the Pine Ridge people were restrained in their reaction to Sitting Bull's loss. Still, Brooke urged the reporters not to question the people on the topic (Sitting Bull's death "does not cause any excitement among these Indians," he wrote to his wife). By December 18 Brooke's planned attack on the Stronghold was termed "impracticable" in the press. In its stead the general assented to yet other attempts by the Pine Ridge tribal leaders to induce the Stronghold occupants to come in and thus, as he termed it, "disintegrate the camp." The Oglala chief Plenty Buffalo Chips headed one failed effort. Another attempt, a bi-tribal venture led by the Brulé chief High Hawk and including such Oglala leaders as American Horse and Big Road, totaled more than 140 participants. Hopeful of success, this mission departed Pine Ridge en route to the Stronghold on December 21. Mindful of potential disruptions to this delicate effort, Miles again directed Colonel Day and his cowboy militia, which had been lingering about the Stronghold, to "confine itself to protecting the settlements off the Indian reservation." Let the regular troops attend to the Indians on the reservation, Miles advised. "It is . . . very important that none of your men cross the Cheyenne River or go on the reservation."[5]

General Miles arrived in Rapid City on Wednesday morning, December 17, and quickly established his headquarters at the Hotel Harney, a three-story brick edifice. From there he would oversee operations. Miles had closed down Brooke's Stronghold attack while traveling. In passing through Rushville en route, he had telegraphed Brooke to reposition various troops to facilitate potentially capturing the Stronghold tribesmen. He had also seen dispatches from Ruger telling of Sitting Bull's followers fleeing with as many as 100 "fighting men" up Grand River. When Miles told Ruger to intercept these people, Ruger replied that he had directed his troops to patrol the Grand River country below Dickinson, North Dakota, to find the fleeing Hunkpapas and "head them off and capture them." Miles further alerted Ruger to guard against an Indian break for Canada or elsewhere north and west and that officer activated his outer perimeter along the general line of the Northern Pacific Railroad. Orders also sent First Cavalry troops and Cheyenne scouts out of Fort Keogh to cover passes along the Little Missouri River. At one point rumor held that five hundred warriors had cornered troops of Captain Samuel W. Fountain's command of Fort Keogh infantrymen near the Cave Hills in northwestern South Dakota. A First Cavalry unit augmented by infantry marched there through snow squalls and subzero temperatures but found neither Indians nor soldiers. Troops also patrolled the upper Grand, Moreau, and Cannonball Rivers. Captain Fechet, fresh from the Sitting Bull Fight, established a field station with his command at Slim Buttes, complete with heliographic equipment.[6]

Upon his arrival Miles granted several media interviews in which he pointedly noted the government's repeated failure to deliver on its promises to the Indians. He also wrote to General Schofield that to address the problem of the Sioux Congress should fulfill its treaty obligations "which the Indians were entreated and coerced into signing." The Indians, he continued, "signed away a valuable portion of their reservation, and it is now occupied by white people, for which they have received nothing." Congress "could in a single hour confirm the treaties and appropriate the necessary funds for the fulfillment," he suggested. "I hope that you will ask the Secretary of War and the Chief Executive to bring this matter directly to the attention of Congress." Schofield forwarded Miles's comments to Secretary Proctor with a request they be conveyed to President Harrison for action. Clearly Congress was doing nothing. To his wife, Miles deplored the incompetence in Washington: "The administration and the Republican Party are making a fatal mistake in not at once confirming the treaty their commissioners made with the Sioux."[7]

Miles was nothing if not forceful, and his personality could be grating. He had enviable achievements to his credit and held a lofty position in the army. Now he was making politically charged and to some unpopular public statements. It is little wonder that he became a target of jealousy and criticism. He had incurred the exasperation of Brooke, and an unknown accuser (later identified as Colonel Chauncey McKeever) had disparaged him in the pages of the *Washington Evening Star*. Even more recently Brigadier General Wesley Merritt, commander of the Department of the Missouri, from whose province came the Seventh Cavalry and artillery components to supplement Miles's forces on the reservations, directed more criticism. Merritt had considered Miles a rival for promotion since the close of the Civil War. Earlier he had groused about moving the Seventh to Pine Ridge, and in December he strongly criticized what he construed as headline grabbing by the man who beat him in attaining the rank of major general. Merritt was a West Pointer, whereas Miles was not, yet Merritt's frontier career paled by comparison to that of Miles, who was also younger. Nevertheless, in a news interview, Merritt minced few words. "Much more has been made of this threatened outbreak than the situation warranted," Merritt declared. "A man like Gen. Crook would not have called all the troops from the South in an emergency of this kind, and he would have been pretty apt to have been master of the situation." When pressed on his comment, Merritt said, "It is pretty well understood in Army circles that private ambitions have had more or less to do with the present Indian situation." Some officers, he asserted, had questioned the deployment of troops to the northern plains from New Mexico, California, and Texas, rather than from a neighboring division—"men not acclimated, and therefore ill prepared for the rigors of an Indian campaign in winter." Disingenuously, he added: "Remember that I do not join in this criticism."[8]

Whether appropriate or not, the distraction was momentary. After settling into his hotel offices in Rapid City, Miles would monitor and direct what became the army's main focus: tracking down and capturing or destroying the Sitting Bull refugees before they reached the Stronghold, 160 miles southwest. After Sitting Bull's violent death, these people (many of them afoot) likely moved in at least two groups up the Grand River before turning south along its tributaries toward the Cheyenne, watchful for soldiers all the way. On December 17 they camped at the mouth of Thunder Butte Creek on the Moreau River. Along the way 166 men, women, and children with wagons and horses stopped at Cherry Creek on the Cheyenne River Reservation above the stream's confluence with the Cheyenne and the abandoned community of Cheyenne City, whose citizens had fled to Fort Bennett in panic. Some 80 miles south of Grand River, they camped with friends and counseled with the Cherry Creek Indians still remaining in the area. The community had thinned noticeably when several hundred Cherry Creek Miniconjous departed with Narcesse Narcelle, a local mixed-blood farmer. That group reached the Cheyenne River Agency on December 21.

Help for the Hunkpapas at Cherry Creek came in an unexpected form. On December 18 Captain Joseph H. Hurst, commanding officer at Fort Bennett, had dispatched Lieutenant Harry Hale west to determine if the Ghost Dancers truly represented a situation of "alarming character." Hump, whom Hale had brought in earlier, now joined him, as did a local settler, Henry Angell. As they wended their way toward Cherry Creek, the three alerted Indians along the Cheyenne River to expect Seventh Infantry soldiers in the area. Fifty-two miles west of Fort Bennett they encountered the Hunkpapas. Angell could barely communicate in Lakota but through signs and with some help from Angell, Hale told the people that he would leave Hump with them and return to Bennett for help, which he did. Returning on December 21, Hale, now accompanied by Captain Hurst, Sergeant Philip Gallagher, and two Indian scouts as interpreters, brought teams and wagons to help transport the women and children. Late that evening, after a meeting that included food, smoking, and presents, Hurst convinced the Hunkpapas to give up their arms and go with him to Fort Bennett. If they chose to join Big Foot, Hurst told them, "the result would be certain destruction." When Hurst said he had nothing more to say, the Indians conferred among themselves and then agreed to turn over their arms and go with the soldiers. With sixty-five Miniconjous, who wanted to camp near the post for security on the advice of their mixed-blood neighbors, the Sitting Bull runaways made their way east. Altogether, 221 people arrived at Fort Bennett in late afternoon on Christmas Eve.[9]

Of the some 500 people who had scattered in the wake of Sitting Bull's death, almost 250 had returned to Standing Rock or would do so in coming weeks. With the surrenders to Hurst and Hale, fewer than 90 of Sitting Bull's followers remained unaccounted for. Of those, at least 38, plus some 30 of Hump's band, had joined Chief Big Foot and his Miniconjou followers at a Ghost Dance camp ten miles west of Cherry Creek. Big Foot's village itself stood along Deep Creek, near its junction with the south bank of the upper Cheyenne, perhaps ten miles east of its confluence with the Belle Fourche. The Ghost Dance had come late to these Miniconjous, largely as a replacement for other dances permitted them, including the grass dance. Big Foot was not well known among outsiders, but he had drawn attention lately because many of his followers, now augmented by Indians from Standing Rock, participated in what many whites regarded as an alarming dance.

A tall, heavy man, Big Foot (Sitanka) was an elder, probably about sixty-five. Born about 1825 and orphaned in his youth, he was the adopted son of One Horn (or Lone Horn), himself the adoptive brother of a youth who also went by the name One Horn. In earlier days Big Foot had been known as Spotted Elk, and he sometimes still went by that name. If he was present at the Battle of the Little Bighorn, Lakota sources indicate that he did not take a prominent role in the action. In the months after Custer's defeat, Spotted Elk had aligned with Sitting Bull and was a headman in the councils. He was involved in the clash with then colonel Nelson Miles at Cedar Creek, Montana, in October 1876 and had acted as a headman in preliminary councils there. Rather than go with Sitting Bull to Canada, however, Spotted Elk chose instead to return to Cheyenne River, where he advocated peace with the whites, stressed the importance of retaining Lakota traditions, and, somewhat incongruously, promoted education on the reservation. With other Lakotas, he had gone to Washington, D.C., in 1888 concerning the Sioux land measure, which did not pass. He neither approved nor signed the land agreement of 1889 that downsized the Great Sioux Reservation.[10]

The chain of circumstances that led Big Foot and his band to Wounded Knee had begun on December 15. On that day the chief and several of his headmen had ridden west to Camp Cheyenne to inform Lieutenant Colonel Edwin Sumner of their intention to go with their 335 people to the Cheyenne River Agency adjoining Fort Bennett to receive annuities. No stranger at Sumner's camp, Big Foot had earlier professed his intent to cooperate with the military there. The chief assured the colonel that he had no plans to unite with the "hostiles" at Pine Ridge.[11] On December 17, as they moved down the Cheyenne toward Bennett, two Hunkpapas, one of them wounded, approached Big Foot with disconcerting word of the fight at Grand River and the killing of Sitting Bull two days earlier. The news frightened the people, who feared that they might be targeted next. In response Big Foot sent a delegation of young men to invite the Hunkpapa refugees to his camp, and a number returned with them. Sumner learned of the Hunkpapas' presence with Big Foot on December 19. Ruger had directed him to intercept the chief. Sumner was intentionally delaying until the people had reached the agency, when their arrest would be easier. Now it was reported that the Standing Rock Indians might influence Big Foot's band to run for Pine Ridge or to the Stronghold to join the holdouts under Short Bull and Kicking Bear. Miles ordered more cavalry and infantry into the area and instructed Sumner to report all "important information" directly to him. He told Sumner and Colonel Henry C. Merriam, who was stationed with his Seventh infantrymen nearer Fort Bennett on the Cheyenne, to cooperate with each other, but their ability to do that would be limited. Sumner caught up with the chief on December 21 at the deserted village of Touch the Cloud, near the mouth of Tick Timber Creek some twenty miles below Big Foot's village. Big Foot agreed to let the troops escort his people west to

Camp Cheyenne, at the forks. When Sumner asked the chief why he had accepted the Standing Rock people, the chief's reply

was certainly human[e], if not a sufficient excuse, and was to the effect that they were brothers and relations; that they had come to him and his people almost naked, were hungry, footsore, and weary; that he had taken them in, had fed them and no one with any heart could do any less. The Standing Rock Indians with Big Foot, that is, those whom I saw, answered his description perfectly, and were, in fact, so pitiable a sight that I at once dropped all thought of their being hostile or even worthy of capture. Still my instructions were to take them, and I intended on doing so.[12]

As the troops and Indians with their wagons en route to Camp Cheyenne approached Big Foot's village on December 22, a number of warriors, animated by the soldiers' movements, bolted and stormed ahead past the accompanying troops. As they did, the remaining Indians fell out of column and rushed for their cabins. Surprised by the incident yet desirous of preventing trouble by acceding to Big Foot's request to shelter his people from dropping temperatures, Sumner reassured them and permitted them to remain (he reported that the Indians had not yet surrendered to him). He moved his command seventeen miles upstream to Camp Cheyenne after eliciting a promise from Big Foot that he would report the next morning and that his people would thereupon proceed to Fort Bennett. (Sumner at first insisted that the Indian men should go with him but later relented.) Sumner, a highly regarded officer, son of a general with the same name, and with his own brevet of brigadier general earned during the Civil War, later explained: "I confess that my ambition was very great, but it was not sufficient to justify me in making an unprovoked attack on those Indians at that time." Despite orders received, he said that he was "desirous only of accomplishing what I understood to be the wishes of my superiors, especially those of the division commander, believing that his plans were to settle matters, if possible, without bloodshed."[13]

Indian accounts differ from Sumner's description of events. Andrew Good Thunder, a Miniconjou, stated that when the soldiers overtook them along the Cheyenne River, Sumner ("Three Fingers") upbraided Big Foot for not sending his young men to the agency to obtain provisions. Sumner told him that he had "enough provisions at my camp to provide for you."

Good Thunder said that the tumult on the march back to Big Foot's village happened when two of the Indians' wagons collided: one fell over a bank and broke its tongue. The wagon owner was a woman named Good Enemy, who belonged to Big Foot's band. The event caused a considerable stir, including collecting and repacking her items. "Three Fingers was impatient," Good Thunder recalled, and "rode up & used profane language."

> He whipped up the horse as the woman was in act of mounting. The horse started up & threw [the] woman off & she started crying. . . . The incident now threw the whole band into excitement. They began to throw away tent poles & to lighten up loads & then broke & ran [through] the timber toward [their] own village at mouth of Deep Creek. A scout now came to us & said . . . that we should be sure to run to timber if shooting started. Once in the village, Big Foot directed that beeves be killed for sharing with the Hunkpapas and the Miniconjous who had joined them from downstream.[14]

Miles added a favorable nuance to what Sumner had reported. He sent forth word that Big Foot had surrendered on December 21 and that he was confident that all of Sitting Bull's people at last had been captured. "Had the connection been effected," he told press representatives with gross overstatement, "these Indians in the absence of military protection could have massacred as many settlers as the Sioux did in the Minnesota trouble of 1862."[15]

Sumner's delay in closely following up with Big Foot opened an opportunity for Big Foot, who took it, fearful of army intentions. Sumner did not start back to Big Foot's village immediately on December 23; nor did Big Foot arrive as promised. Sumner sent a messenger telling the chief to start his people for Fort Bennett. He notified Miles: "Did not succeed in getting the Indians to come into my camp on account of want of shelter for women and children. Did not feel authorized to compel them by force to leave their reservation." Sumner lamely explained that, if the chief did not respond, "I would like to go down and capture his village. He has heavy log buildings admirably situated for defense, and I would like a couple of guns sent out from Meade for this purpose." Incensed, Miles fired back: "You have two Hotchkiss guns and over 200 men, which certainly ought to be enough to handle 100 warriors in any place."[16]

The colonel started his column east and received word from a citizen late in the day that Big Foot had been ill but would start for Bennett in the morning. That evening Sumner camped about five miles from Big Foot's village. During the night word came that the Indians had packed up their few belongings and slipped away south in the gathering darkness. The next morning a scout brought word from Big Foot that his people feared "a trap" at Fort Bennett and that "he was compelled to go to Pine Ridge." Sumner told Colonel Merriam that the tribesmen had been alerted by a local settler named John Dunn that Sumner's command was returning to "attack and kill them all." On December 24 Sumner sent a courier to Colonel Carr, sixty miles southwest at the mouth of Rapid Creek on the Cheyenne, to urge that Carr's troops somehow block Big Foot's flight south. Sumner's seeming appeasement and consequent blunder exasperated Miles. Believing Big Foot dangerous, he ordered Merriam to assume command and go in immediate pursuit: "The division commander is much embarrassed that Big Foot [was] allowed to escape and directs you to use the force under your command to recapture him." Miles wired Brooke of the development and set a new course for him:

I regret exceedingly to say that Big Foot has eluded Sumner & is now going south in Light order on ponies[.] Will probably join those in the Bad Lands[.] Carr has been notified to endeavor to intercept them. If a command were to move quickly from Pine Ridge a little northeast and thence down Porcupine or in that vicinity it might possibly intercept them. They need not disturb any [Indians] that may be coming from the Bad Lands. We must now close up all possible avenues of escape, shorten the line & enclose them. Big Foot has 100 men.[17]

When Sumner apologized for Big Foot's escape, Miles curtly reprimanded him: "Your orders were positive, and you have missed your opportunity. . . . Endeavor to be more successful next time." He ordered Sumner to "use your scouts to ascertain the whereabouts of Big Foot's band." Using scouts and cavalry, Sumner soon verified Big Foot's course from the Cheyenne River to the Badlands. Agitated by the failure, Miles alerted Schofield: "This was most unfortunate just at this time, and may turn all the scale against the efforts that have been made to avoid an Indian war. Up to this time the prospects looked favorable."[18]

Why did Big Foot leave? Colonel Sumner came to believe that the chief and his people headed south because of "a desire on the part of all to seek the crowd at Pine Ridge Agency, and being there to get better terms than at Bennett. My opinion is that the advance of Col. Merriam up Cheyenne River and the report that the Standing Rock Indians at Bennett had been disarmed caused a sudden change of plan in Big Foot's village, and that the young men, on account of the situation, were able to overcome all objections to going south." The Miniconjou Joseph Horn Cloud recalled that Red Cloud and other leaders repeatedly had asked Big Foot, a peace advocate, to come to Pine Ridge to help alleviate potential trouble with the troops there. They even had offered Big Foot an incentive of 100 horses to do so. Long Bull, another Miniconjou, stated: "We did not like the way we were treated at Cheyenne river [sic]. Our rations were poor and many hearts were bad. Red Cloud had sent to us to say that if we were not well treated we might come to Pine Ridge and live." And Hump said: "I think Big Foot was coming to Pine Ridge to get better than he was getting at Cheyenne River, or to fight." Others maintained that the Indians were frightened into leaving. According to Andrew Good Thunder, near evening on December 23 three men on horseback visited the Indian village. "The three riders were a scout, an interpreter & a white man called Red Whiskers [John Dunn]." Dunn told Big Foot that he should leave that night: "Col. Sumner intends to surround your camp before daybreak & fire a cannon over [the] camp & if your warriors answer it the soldiers will start firing into village. . . . Spotted Elk [Big Foot] now sent an old man to tell the people to prepare to leave that night for Pine Ridge, some with wagons & some with packs." Thus although Big Foot apparently had been inclined to go to Pine Ridge Agency, rapidly changing circumstances now impelled him to go in that direction.[19]

The penalty for Sumner's casual response ultimately would be profound. On December 26 Miles telegraphed Brooke more information about the size and disposition of Big Foot's convoy: "About one hundred and thirty men, three hundred and thirty Indians in all. . . . I hope you will round up the whole body of them, disarm them and keep them all under close guard." He added: "Big Foot is cunning and his Indians are very bad." To expedite communication with the field, Miles installed a heliograph system between his headquarters and Carr's and outfitted some of his moving command with the units, much as he had done in Arizona during his pursuit of the Apaches. On receiving notification of Big Foot's departure by Sumner's courier on Wednesday, December 24, Colonel Carr prepared to head immediately into the Badlands. He ordered "Boots and Saddles" sounded, recalled an officer, "and in half an hour was forcing a crossing of the Cheyenne through floating ice with four troops of cavalry and two Hotchkiss guns." Two more troops caught up with the command that night. Carr worked his way into the Badlands and examined two roads without success but placed pickets at both. The troops had left hurriedly with scarcely any provisions. "We spent Christmas eve standing, sitting and lying around the fires," wrote Carr, "sleeping from time to time till wakened by the cold." The next day the command divided. The units together covered seventy-five miles before regrouping along Bull Creek without any success in locating the Indians. "No Big Foot," Carr reported. "He had gone forty miles east, clear around my other Battalion [technically termed a 'squadron' for cavalry as of 1889]." On December 28 Carr received orders to leave two troops to continue the search in the Badlands and to move with the balance of his command to White River.[20]

Carr later reflected on his search for Big Foot, the many dispatches he received, and how his troops scouted daily up and down the Cheyenne River. But Carr's Sixth cavalrymen never located Big Foot. They soon returned to the mouth of Rapid Creek on the Cheyenne.[21]

In the meantime at Pine Ridge Agency Brooke prepared to respond with alacrity and purpose. He had observed the proceedings to his north. Ever mindful of the tribesmen still positioned within the Stronghold north of White River, he was concerned that Big Foot's followers retreating from the Cheyenne might seek refuge with them. "The Indians in the Bad Lands [now] disclaim any intention to fight and are only preparing for defense," he informed Miles. "If Big Foot gets there this purpose may change."[22]

Four days before Christmas an individual garbed in a white blanket and claiming to be the long-anticipated messiah arrived in Red Cloud's camp. He said that he had come because the Sioux had confused his message. The Indian police quickly took the man into custody. He was Albert C. Hopkins from Nashua, Iowa, described as "a medium sized, well dressed, quite good looking man about forty years old, with evidently considerable education. . . . He is dead broke and possibly a little daft." While some of the Indians grew incensed over Hopkins's arrest, others found amusement in the comic relief that he afforded until he was taken off to Chadron. Red Cloud simply told him to go home: "You are no son of God." Wags in Chadron suggested that he might be crucified regardless. Although there was a swell of interest in Hopkins as news of his appearance spread, the diversion was momentary.[23]

Following repeated meetings with parties from the Stronghold, Brooke strove to induce the remaining Indians to come in. The party of High Hawk, American Horse, and Big Road that had left the agency on December 21 was still out. Brief clashes between Cheyenne scouts and warriors from the Stronghold took place at the mouth of Battle Creek along Cheyenne River on December 21 and early the next morning. Freezing temperatures and profound discomfort were changing some minds at the Stronghold. High-velocity winds compounded their agonies on the exposed plateau. On Christmas Day news finally arrived that the recent mission to Short Bull and Kicking Bear had succeeded. The holdouts were at last on their way in. By the next day several small groups were reported as having already started. Larger numbers were to follow. Within two days most had camped along White River in preparation for moving to Pine Ridge. Word spread through the wire that "the Indian troubles are about to be brought to a close without the sacrifice of any more lives." Miles sent orders to Colonel Carr and other officers with troops on the Cheyenne to search carefully for stragglers and cached arms in the Badlands as they closed toward Pine Ridge Agency. "Now," said Miles, "I want to know where Big Foot is."[24]

Following the curtailment of Brooke's planned movement against the Stronghold after Sitting Bull's death, the troops had lapsed back into the torpor of recent weeks. But now a sense of urgency gripped the soldiers at Pine Ridge. With the news of Big Foot's break from Colonel Sumner, going afield seemed likely again. Yet on Christmas Eve (coincidentally ration day at the agency) and Christmas Day evergreen garlands festooned the tents. While the Indians downed their sparse fare, the soldiers ate heartily of turkey, goose, pig and pastries made by the company bakers. Second Lieutenant Herbert G. Squiers provided the men of Troop K, Seventh Cavalry, with "a big blowout," and all devoured a large cake shipped in by his wife. One trooper recalled that the officers established "a kind of saloon by combining some tents in a row, in the middle of which was a long table, groaning under its abundant spread of both substantial and delicious foods, flanked by bottles and decanters of all calibers and colors." He said that the feast was accompanied by speeches, toasts, and songs, which made the time pass unnoticeably. "There were also Christmas gifts from near and far, but funniest were those which one gave to one another." All through the camp "one heard choir after choir, innocent laughter, and merry talk that interrupted the usual deserted emptiness of the nights." Elsewhere among the troops, eggnog and holiday punch proliferated. One infantry company paid a Nebraska family to prepare a chicken dinner complete with cakes and pies. "What a strange Christmas day!" wrote the *Illustrated American* correspondent. "Indians and soldiers, Mexicans and half breeds [*sic*], squaw men and cowboys all mingled in the crowded spaces about Pine Ridge. Tents and avenues alike full!"[25]

On other days during the enforced lull, officers and men took occasion to compose letters to loved ones and friends. One officer took the time to raise donations for a Christmas tree and presents for the Sioux children. Even with relaxation evident, Elaine Goodale remembered the season in the Pine Ridge community as "a time of grim suspense. We seemed to be waiting—helplessly waiting—as if in some horrid nightmare, for the inevitable catastrophe."[26]

The military activity prompted by Big Foot's disappearance no doubt encouraged the Stronghold people to give up their plateau fortress and head to the agency. On receipt of Miles's December 24 telegram urging him to send Henry's command, Brooke ordered the Ninth Cavalry Buffalo Soldiers afield, thereby ending their involvement in the revelry at the agency. He also notified the Indian peace messengers of the movement so as not to alarm the Stronghold occupants. At 2:30 P.M., outfitted in heavy fur overcoats against the prevailing cold, the four troops (D, F, I, and K: approximately 230 men) departed. Preceded by assorted scouts and all rationed for five days, they spurred their animals past cheering comrades northeast down the Wounded Knee Road toward White River in search of the elusive Miniconjous with the Sitting Bull people. Major Guy V. Henry was one of the premier cavalry leaders in the army. His combat record boasted of many Civil War and Indian engagements, including the desperate Rosebud Creek battle in Montana in 1876, in which a warrior's bullet had smashed into his face, damaging his optic nerve and rendering him blind in the left eye. With escorted pack mules plus two Hotchkiss guns and crews trailing at a distance—and a wagon train made ready to follow that night—the column advanced alternately at a trot and a walk. Skirting well east of the Stronghold, it wound northeast along the White River for forty miles well into the frigid night before ascending Cottonwood Creek north of the river and camping at 4 A.M. at its springs.

On Christmas Day Henry's command continued north a dozen miles to Harney Springs and there ate breakfast. Through field glasses from lofty points on December 26, officers searched the countryside, observing all the north-south trails. They discerned the Indians at the Stronghold dismantling tipis in preparation for going to Pine Ridge Agency. Over the next two days the troopers canvassed the surrounding landscape, facing freezing, gale-force winds. Troop I scouted to Sheep Mountain and back and Troop K patrolled the lower parts of Wounded Knee and Porcupine Creeks and monitored fords along the White, but they saw no sign of Big Foot. On December 28 they returned to White River. "It was so cold," remembered one of Henry's soldiers, "the [tobacco] spit froze when it left your mouth." Pending word from Short Bull and Kicking Bear that they would not come into the agency (news of their capitulation did not reach Brooke until December 25), Henry's men would potentially add an eastern dimension to the encircling force of Carr, Sanford, and Offley on the west and Sumner and Merriam on the north. Colonel Forsyth's Seventh Cavalry was set to advance from the south should circumstances dictate. Brooke soon received Henry's reports that the Stronghold had been vacated, the Indians having moved down to White River. On December 29, at Brooke's direction, Troop F from Henry's command explored the abandoned highlands site while the balance of his Buffalo Soldiers proceeded to the White seeking Big Foot. Although Brooke proposed the immediate occupation of the Stronghold, this was not accomplished.[27]

As with Carr, Henry's scouting for the Indians was in vain. Like Carr, his men had focused too narrowly to the west and would not intercept Big Foot. After departing their village along the Cheyenne on Tuesday evening, December 23, Big Foot's more than three hundred Miniconjous with the thirty-eight Hunkpapas in tow, accompanied by wagons of necessaries, ponies, and a profusion of dogs, passed along Deep Creek for more than twenty miles almost due south. Crossing the Pierre Road near the head of Bad River, they continued to the high ridges composing the storied wall with its abrupt 200- to 300-foot drop into the Badlands. The Indians labored greatly to descend the wall then moved on to a point known as the Gate. They trended farther southeast to Cottonwood Creek then south, threading the drainage of present Big Foot Creek to White River, where they forded and at last camped late on December 24. On the next day the chief's illness worsened. Having entered Pine Ridge Reservation, the people passed Potato Creek and camped six miles south of the White at Cedar Spring, known later as Big Foot Spring. On December 26 they passed southwest to Redwater Creek, where they paused in camp more than a day because of Big Foot's deteriorating condition. On December 27 they gained Medicine Root Creek (near the present town of Kyle). After another five miles they reached American Horse Creek, where they spent the night.[28]

Alice Ghost Horse, who was thirteen years old when she accompanied Big Foot south, years later recalled the departure from Cheyenne River:

First wagon to leave was Chief Big Foot's, with all his relatives following behind, some on horseback, some were walking alongside for the time being. We crossed the river and headed up the hill towards the Southeast direction. I looked back and saw more wagons joining in and so the caravan moved at a faster pace as the horses broke into a trot. It was exciting for me, as we were running from the military. We ran like this all morning without stopping. Late afternoon, we stopped in a draw to eat what little we had, but we were not to start a fire, lest we would be seen from a distance. When we are on the move usually some riders will fall back to check everyone at the request of the chief. After a brief rest we were on our way again, keeping to the draws, and sometimes the going was hard on the wagons, because we were running along the creek beds. Going in a southerly direction, again we trotted most of the time, keeping to the low land, valleys and washouts.[29]

In an abbreviated summary of the travel from the Cheyenne River, Andrew Good Thunder said:

We traveled that night [December 23–24] & got to White River & Spotted Elk [Big Foot] said we will travel at night. [South of White River] we crossed Potato Creek & went to Medicine Root [Creek] & camped at foot of Medicine Root & sent out three scouts, two of whom returned to this camp. All the time traveling thro [to] Pine Ridge [from Cheyenne River] we did not meet a single Ind[ian]. Two of our scouts returned with a Pine Ridge Ind[ian]. Spotted Elk asked the Pine Ridge man where are all the people[?] We find their houses locked up & no footprints. Where have the people gone to? He replied that on east side of reservation some Rosebud Inds had come there & raised a disturbance. Since this there have factions arisen. One faction gone to badlands & faction gone to agency for protection. The head men of these have negotiated a peace treaty & a pipe of peace has been taken into the badlands band & everything is now settled & quiet. Big Foot now told the Pine Ridge man "I have come to this reservation to avoid trouble and I will take the main road to the agency & join the peaceable people there," & the Oglallalla [*sic*] man said he thought it would be a satisfactory movement.[30]

Still perturbed over Sumner's failure with Big Foot, Miles implored Brooke: "Make no mistake about his capture this time." With the knowledge that the Stronghold Indians were at last on their way to the agency, General Brooke ordered the first squadron of the Seventh Cavalry (Troops A, B, I, and K) out on Henry's heels to help seek and intercept Big Foot's Ghost Dancers. It was December 26, a cold and overcast Friday with spitting snow and wind driven sand. Theoretically the Indians were en route to the Stronghold or to the agency and were believed to be inveterately hostile.[31]

New reports put Big Foot at White River and heading up Porcupine Creek. Brooke notified Miles of his intent "to head him off and capture him if possible." The general added: "I am pretty well satisfied Big Foot is on his way here, travelling by night and laying by during the day." Nonetheless, he alerted Lieutenant Colonel Poland at Rosebud Agency to watch for the Miniconjous and Hunkpapas possibly coming there. Accompanying the troops departing Pine Ridge Agency was part of Light Battery E of the First Artillery, consisting of two portable mule-mounted Hotchkiss guns and their ten operational personnel garbed in overcoats with redlined capes, commanded by Second Lieutenant Harry L. Hawthorne, attached from the Second Artillery. Squadron commander Major Samuel M. Whitside was to coordinate his march with Henry's command and, if required, connect with the Buffalo Soldiers. (Colonel Forsyth, who ordered Whitside out at Brooke's order, wrote: "I asked and urged Gen'l Brooke to let me go out with Major Whitside's command, but he would not agree to it—said 'No!'")[32]

Brooke directed Whitside to proceed east along the Rosebud Road and turn northeast to the Wounded Knee Post Office near the bridge crossing of Wounded Knee Creek, some eighteen miles from the agency. Whitside was to scout the area and, if possible, intercept and capture the Miniconjou chief and his followers. A sizable component of white and Oglala Indian scouts was sent with the major to help assure that objective. The blustery weather had intensified by the time the cavalry squadron and its artillery component prepared to leave the agency, before 1:30 P.M. "It grew to a hurricane . . . ," remembered one trooper. "The air filled with smoke and dust so that one could hardly see; tents collapsed or were wrenched from the hands of those who tried to fold them up, and people ran into one another or tumbled headlong on the ground." Yet the column of 10 officers and 225 enlisted men with civilian guides and several correspondents pulled out along the road running northeast to Wounded Knee Creek, along with a train of slow-moving pack animals escorted by cavalrymen marching afoot, with Indian scouts leading the way.[33]

Whitside's Seventh Cavalry squadron had arrived four weeks earlier. Its departure to the field now marked the beginning of the regiment's active involvement in the Pine Ridge Campaign. All told, the eight troops of the Seventh at Pine Ridge included 25 officers and some 470 enlisted men present for duty. Constituted in 1866, the regiment evolved its reputation as a stellar fighting unit with participation in Major General Winfield S. Hancock's offensive against the tribes of the south-central plains in 1867 that led eventually to Custer's controversial attack on the Cheyennes at the Washita River in the Indian Territory late in 1868. Dispersed over parts of the South during the postwar Reconstruction period, the regiment reassembled in Dakota Territory beginning in 1873 and played a central role in advancing the route of the Northern Pacific Railroad into Montana Territory, where its soldiers initially clashed with the Lakotas. The troops marched into the Black Hills with Custer the following year, a movement that in due course generated the army campaign to force the nontreaty Indians onto their appointed reservation. This led directly to the Seventh Cavalry's defeat and partial destruction by those people at the Battle of the Little Bighorn in 1876, when 268 of the regiment's soldiers died.

This event, along with the controversial Custer persona, would dominate all discussion about the unit through the intervening years. In 1887–88 most of the Seventh transferred to Fort Riley, Kansas. Those officers and men who had fought at the Little Bighorn were mostly gone from the regiment by 1890 when Whitside's squadron took the field on December 26. Nonetheless, the Indian-fighting history of the Seventh Cavalry distinguished it as the most renowned unit in contemporary service and one seemingly marked by destiny.

Whitside, a gray-haired, fifty-one-year-old career officer born in Canada, had enlisted in the U.S. Army before the Civil War. Commissioned in the Sixth Cavalry in 1861, he served under Major General George B. McClellan in the Army of the Potomac, took part in numerous engagements, and was wounded near Culpeper Court House, Virginia. Whitside became assistant aide-de-camp for Major General Nathaniel Banks during the operations at Port Hudson, Louisiana, and by war's end had emerged a captain with brevets for faithful and meritorious service. Thereafter he served with the Sixth Cavalry in Texas and Arizona Territory before joining the Seventh as a major in 1885.

As he left Pine Ridge Agency on the afternoon of December 26, 1890, Whitside rode ahead with a certain anticipation after the weeks of tepid doings since the regiment's arrival. The men with him likewise welcomed the opportunity for action. They rode along the Wounded Knee road for several hours, whipped by the constant sandstorm, with their wagons slowed by muddy hollows brought on by rapidly warming temperatures. Nearing the crossing at dusk the scouts in advance reported contact with four Indians who said that they were Sitting Bull's people. Troop A under Captain Myles Moylan gave chase, but the Indians quickly faded in the closing darkness. Whitside sent word of the contact to Brooke then made camp after 5 P.M., although some troopers with the train did not get in until near midnight. They camped along rising ground amid the undulating terrain southwest of the bridge spanning Wounded Knee Creek and that evening sent fifteen Oglala scouts east toward Porcupine Creek to learn something of the Indians' presence there. The next morning cavalry troopers ranged northwest and south from Camp Whitside, skirting the bottoms and ridges along Wounded Knee as they searched for recent trails. Those moving north kept alert for Henry's command too, but nothing turned up. Early that day the major received repeated and anxious orders from Brooke reflecting late reports that Big Foot was somewhere in Whitside's front. Brooke directed him: "Find his trail and follow, or find his hiding place and capture him." He added: "If he fights, destroy him."[34]

On December 28, a clear and warm yet blustery day, Whitside offered a $25 bounty to any scout who could find Big Foot and lead him to the chief. Among others he sent out French-Oglala mixed-blood Baptiste Garnier, who was post guide and interpreter from Fort Robinson. Together with scouts John Shangrau and Yankton Charley and two other Indians, Garnier traced along the high ground near Porcupine Creek several miles below the army camp. They discovered a column of Indians moving on horseback with travois and wagons, approaching from the east. "Little Bat," as Garnier was known, quickly mounted and raced the distance to Whitside's outpost to report that he had sighted Big Foot's people advancing toward Wounded Knee from Porcupine. In the meantime other scouts had brought in two of Big Foot's people, who refused to speak to the commander, although one later acknowledged the Miniconjous' movement to Pine Ridge Agency because Red Cloud had sent for them. Ordering "Boots and Saddles," Whitside mounted most of his command and at noon trotted away to head off the Indians with Garnier and the scouts in the lead. Roughly nine miles from their camp and perhaps two miles east of an imposing pine-forested knoll called Porcupine Butte, the command spotted Big Foot's column. It had halted on high ground in the distance ahead. Just east of Pine Creek and within 800 yards of the people, as Whitside reported, "I formed my command in double column of fours, dismounted and formed line to the front, placing the Hotchkiss guns in the centre." The soldiers, without greatcoats in the clement air, lay silently on the ground, concealed behind the top of a ridge, with carbines at the ready. The Hotchkiss pieces were loaded and ready for action.[35]

With the troops thus poised, the major and squadron adjutant First Lieutenant William J. Nicholson, John Shangrau, and Garnier advanced on horseback toward an estimated 120 armed warriors. Half the warriors were mounted, and half were afoot. Together they moved in line up a rise in the soldiers' direction, chanting and waving branches, recalled an observer. "Some had half of their faces painted black and the other half streaked with red and yellow," stated another. When some of the horsemen sought to flank the troops' left, Whitside commanded them to desist. They pulled back. The late appearance of the pack train perhaps signified to them the arrival of more troops.[36]

Whitside sent word that the chief should come forward. Instead, three Indians appeared, and one spoke as the chief's representative. Whitside demanded that Big Foot approach. The Miniconjou leader, by now extremely sick and hemorrhaging yet professing friendship, was brought forward in a wagon. Whitside demanded his immediate submission, to which the chief assented. The two men shook hands. With his own concurrence, Big Foot was lifted from his wagon and placed in an army ambulance. One trooper recalled that Whitside gave orders to

"halt" and "dismount," and deployed the squadron forward right and left. Our small mountain gun also came up in a flying hurry and was placed in front of the centre, loaded with case shot. There we stood now, "order carbines," and the Indians murmured, with their magazines full of cartridges, 30 metres ahead of us. Finally a white flag became visible, and a cart drawn by a team of mustangs came slowly through the Indian ranks. Silence spread everywhere, and Major Whitside made for the vehicle that was occupied by Big Foot himself and his squaw. . . . The negotiations seemed to go well and after a lot of handshaking, it was announced that the band was willing to surrender and follow as prisoners. The redskins came forward with outstretched hands and many tokens of friendship; they even was [sic] permitted to look at the cannon. "Heap good, heap big gun," they mumbled while they came forward to tap it. . . . Big Foot was placed in an army ambulance and with the Indians in front of us we started towards Wounded Knee.[37]

In a short time the soldiers surrounded the band, counted them, and started back to the cavalry camp on Wounded Knee Creek with the Indians, their pony herd, and the wagons. The flanks were guarded to prevent escape, with two troops in front and two others plus the artillery behind. They reached their goal by 3 P.M. A sentimental Lieutenant Hawthorne, with the artillery, articulated the moment:

There before us, trailing along, is the wild man of America; his fierceness expending itself in a savage song of peace; his picturesque figure swaying gracefully in the saddle; his feathered head nodding with the motion of his pony. Over his saddle's pommel rests his Winchester, while at his naked thigh gleams his cruel knife. Today the game is not his—he understands the language of force, and now, carelessly riding, he smokes his cigarette and smiles upon his captors. Seemingly there is no guile in his heart—indeed, he appears thankful that he is captured.[38]

Swedish-born First Sergeant Theodore Ragnar, watching the unfolding drama, observed: "They were tall, scowling figures with fiendish tattooings, ornamental embellishments, and with menacing gestures. . . . Even our commander seemed nervous for the moment, although the advantage was now with him." An Omaha paper reported that Whitside approached Big Foot on foot. "Big Foot extended his hand in token of peace. 'I am sick,' he said. 'My people here want peace and—' Major Whiteside [sic] cut him short with: 'I won't [talk] nor will I have any parleying at all. It is either unconditional surrender or fight. What is your answer, sir!' 'We surrender,' said the chief. 'We would have done so before, but we could not find you and could not find any soldiers to surrender to.' Then . . . his warriors raised a white flag."[39]

Upon capturing the Indians, Whitside sent men versed in use of the heliograph to the rocky top of Porcupine Butte to signal the news to Brooke at Pine Ridge. He also sent Lieutenant Nicholson as courier to the agency with a penciled note:

> I have just arrested Big Foot & 120 Indians [warriors] all well armed & plenty of ammunition in their belts, [and] about 250 women and children, in the party. Entire outfit are now enroute to Wounded Knee P.O. [Post Office] guarded by my battalion. Big Foot is sick and is riding in my ambulance. I have not disarmed the Bucks & do not think it prudent to do so until after they reach camp this Evening. I respectfully request that the 2nd battalion of the 7th Cavalry be send [sic] to report to me by day light [sic] tomorrow morning, which will Enable me to have sufficient force to disarm the Indians without accident.

He requested rations for 300 prisoners.[40]

Tribal accounts of the arrest of Big Foot's followers add significant details to the event and those directly preceding it. Good Thunder told how he and two other men patrolling ahead of the column suddenly encountered three army Indian scouts near Porcupine Creek. As the scouts started to flee, "One of us yelled to them & they came back. We sat beside them and smoked with them. We asked them about the situation on Pine Ridge, etc., & they said the hostiles who had gone to the badlands [Stronghold] would return today or tomorrow in peace, but we think you are the people we are ordered to look for." The scouts told them of the troops approaching some distance behind them. Big Foot's column caught up and halted to eat near the crossing of Porcupine Creek, then three young men advanced to talk with the soldiers. After dinner, as Good Thunder related, the men mounted and "marched toward the soldiers, leaving the women & wagons at the crossing. After going about 1/3 mile we passed over the hill & a little way beyond there were lots of soldiers. There were two scouts & on each road was a cannon ready for battle & between the two cannon there was an officer. We agreed not to fight but to get in line & go toward them abreast." "If the soldiers began firing," he said, "we would chase & wipe them out. We started down hill on a . . . trot & the soldiers got off horses & were leaning on guns. When they saw we were not prepared to fight, they bunched up around the cannons . . . & an officer began greeting us with both hands & saying How, How etc. & he asked us where was Spotted Elk [Big Foot]. We told him S. Elk was sick. He had a pain in his breast & could hardly breathe & he was in a wagon in rear of the train coming very slowly." When Spotted Elk's wagon arrived, Good Thunder said, "four hospital soldiers carefully transferred S.E. from his own wagon to an ambulance. An interpreter now told the people that the soldiers & Inds [Indians] would have a peaceable meeting." The tribesmen still feared that Colonel Sumner's soldiers might find and attack them and wanted Whitside's assurances to protect their women and children. "We requested that soldiers guard front & rear & Inds in middle—he [Whitside] consented & that is the way we marched."[41]

Twenty-seven-year-old Iron Hail recalled the event vividly. As the people stopped for dinner that day, he said, they encountered the Indian scouts:

We called for them to come to us but they ran away. . . . After noon we hitched up and started towards Porcupine Butte, and when . . . northeast of the butte, we saw soldiers. . . . The soldiers formed in a line and set a cannon pointing at us. Then Big Foot said he would go ahead and meet the soldiers and tell them we only wanted to go to Red Cloud's camp at the agency. Big Foot was so sick that he could not ride on a horse and he had been lying in a wagon. . . . He had the wagon driven towards the soldiers, and the officer came to meet the wagon. . . . The soldiers brought a sick wagon (ambulance), and four soldiers put Big Foot on two gray blankets like the soldiers have and they carried him and put him in the sick wagon. I was then afraid for Big Foot, for the officers laughed when they put Big Foot in the wagon. Then the soldiers moved back towards Wounded Knee Creek with a guard around Big Foot and all the Indians followed.[42]

Iron Hail's brother, Joseph Horn Cloud, related much the same. He said that the meeting with the scouts took place on the divide as they moved southwest between American Horse and Porcupine Creeks. The people ate after reaching the Porcupine then met the soldiers at Dry Creek east of Porcupine Butte. "We came up facing the guns and most of the soldiers went a little way back of the guns. . . . Colonel Whiteside [sic] came to Big Foot and asked him where he was going. Big Foot replied, 'I am going to Pine Ridge agency, where my people are.'" They discussed his illness at length.

Whitside offered him use of an ambulance, to which the chief agreed. They all then moved to Wounded Knee, reaching there "about 4 o'clock or about sundown," said Horn Cloud.[43]

Following their arrival, the major directed the bedraggled Indians with their animals, farm wagons, and buggies to camp on level ground about 300 yards south-southwest down the gentle slope from the soldiers' bivouac along a wide and deep ravine. Running west-to-east toward the creek, the ravine coursed along the eastern perimeter approximately the same distance from the two parties' encampment areas. Locating the camp near the ravine would allow privacy for the women. The people raised only few tipis and instead threw together wickiups, small temporary shelters made of limbs and brush and covered with blankets or canvas. They then built fires in the enveloping darkness. One officer remembered that "several large [army] tents" were "put up for them between their village and the camp, as they were seen to be short of tepees." But the Indians "were suspicious and would not use them." Whitside issued coffee, sugar, bacon, and hardtack to Big Foot's people, and their ponies were allowed to graze. He placed Big Foot and his wife in a separate, guarded wall tent, complete with stove, near the south side of the army bivouac area. There assistant surgeon James D. Glennan treated the Miniconjou leader for pneumonia as he lay on a buffalo coat. Around the Indian camp, the major established a strong chain of sentinel guards from Troops A and I. The two remaining troops slept in their tents up the rise, fully clothed and armed. Whitside located Lieutenant Hawthorne's Hotchkiss guns slightly below the southeast crest of a gentle hill rising about 250 yards northwest of the center of Big Foot's camp.[44]

On receiving news of Big Foot's arrest, Brooke at Pine Ridge telegraphed word to Miles, who responded, "All right. Use force enough. Congratulations." Brooke sent a courier to Major Henry, directing him to move up Wounded Knee Creek on December 30, watching the lands to the west to keep any agency Indians from heading north but also to intercept any of Whitside's prisoners who might break away. In the meantime scouts brought news to Whitside that Short Bull's people, at last verging on capitulation, were now approaching the Catholic mission four miles below the agency. At Wounded Knee troops and Indians alike prepared for a discomfiting and apprehensive night. But from all appearances General Miles's vision of a bloodless resolution was indeed at hand.[45]

ELEVEN

Bloodbath

The news from Whitside brought an animated response. Within moments "Boots and Saddles" pierced the air. Minutes later troops with an ammunition pack train pulled up before Brooke's office. At 4:40 P.M. on December 28 Colonel Forsyth started from Pine Ridge Agency with the second squadron of the Seventh Cavalry (Troops C, D, E, and G), the remaining section of two Hotchkiss Mountain Guns, plus forty-eight Cheyenne and Oglala Indian scouts. They were accompanied by assistant surgeon (Captain) John Van R. Hoff with a detachment of five Hospital Corpsmen. Off-duty assistant surgeon Charles B. Ewing and Second Infantry regimental adjutant First Lieutenant John Kinzie accompanied the command, as did the teenaged son of First Lieutenant William W. Robinson, Jr., the squadron adjutant. The teenager's presence seemed to indicate that little trouble should be expected in disarming Big Foot's people.[1]

Leaving behind a camp guard of forty men under regimental quartermaster First Lieutenant Ezra B. Fuller, Forsyth's contingent traveled with few provisions and no tents or baggage. General Brooke's verbal orders to Forsyth had been "to take every precaution to prevent the escape of any of Big Foot's band, and to be particularly careful in disarming them." After disarming Big Foot's people, Forsyth was to leave Whitside in command and return to the agency. As a hedge against violence, General Brooke had also seen to it that thirty-eight-year-old Father Francis M. Craft also rode with Forsyth. Craft was a well-traveled and politically active itinerant

Catholic priest. Of Welsh and Mohawk ancestry, he had experience at the Pine Ridge, Rosebud, and Standing Rock agencies and spoke Lakota. Craft, whose Sioux name was Hovering Eagle, had recently met with secretaries Proctor and Noble in Washington, D.C., where he agreed to visit Holy Rosary Mission and the Catholic schools at Pine Ridge as a representative of the Bureau of Catholic Indian Missions. It was believed that he might help mitigate the Ghost Dance unrest. Now Brooke hoped that he might help negotiate with Big Foot as well.[2]

As they moved northeast along the road to Wounded Knee, the prospect of field service rejuvenated Forsyth and his men. During his thirty-four-year army career, the Ohio-born Forsyth, fifty-six, had amassed an enviable military record. After graduation from West Point in 1856, he had served in the Pacific Northwest until the Civil War took him east. During the conflict he rose swiftly from captain of infantry through successive staff positions to the rank of brigadier general of volunteers in May 1865. In 1864 Phil Sheridan appointed him chief of staff of the Cavalry Corps. "He saw everything and forgot nothing," reported a contemporary of Forsyth. He was cited repeatedly with regular and volunteer army brevets for gallantry at Chickamauga, Cedar Creek, Five Forks, Opequan, Fisher's Hill, and Middletown. In the postwar Regular Army from 1869 to 1876, "Tony" Forsyth became Sheridan's aide-de-camp and military secretary, accompanying the general in the field during the campaign against the Southern Cheyennes and Arapahos that resulted in Custer's Washita victory. Forsyth traveled with Sheridan to Europe as an observer during the Franco-Prussian War. Thereafter he served as lieutenant colonel with the First Cavalry, including his oversight of field operations against the Bannock Indians in the summer of 1878. Promoted colonel of the Seventh Cavalry in 1886, Forsyth commanded the regiment in Dakota and Kansas. On December 28, 1890, as his squadron rode rapidly through the closing twilight toward Wounded Knee, the white-haired and goateed colonel perhaps reflected on his long career and past service. Certainly he could not have fathomed what loomed ahead.[3]

On learning from General Brooke of Whitside's success in capturing Big Foot and his people, General Miles sent word to colonels Merriam, Carr, and Sumner and notified the Adjutant General's Office in Washington. Plans called for removing these Indians from the reservation. Miles had told Brooke on December 26 that, after capturing the Indians, "it would be well to march [them] straight to the railroad and put them on the cars." Miles approved Brooke's plan to send the people to Omaha but cautioned that loose talk could frighten away those Indians coming in from the Stronghold; it was imperative that both groups be secured. Furthermore, if Brooke required more troops, Miles said that they could be readily advanced from the Cheyenne River line to White River and also moved in from Oelrichs and Rosebud Agency. Early on December 29 Brooke dispatched couriers to Whitside at Wounded Knee, offering Miles's congratulations and directing him to escort his prisoners to the railroad at Gordon, Nebraska, to be turned over to Colonel Frank Wheaton next day for delivery to Fort Omaha. "The ponies and wagons will not accompany the Indians," Brooke directed. He ordered Wheaton from Pine Ridge with four companies of the Second Infantry to Gordon, where they were to "receive from Major Whitside 7th Cav. about 370 Indians of Big Foot's band." He added: "It is desirable that you take special care that none of the Indians escape en route, and also that they are reasonably comfortable. If it should be found [on arrival at Fort Omaha] that the shelter they have is not adequate you will put them in conical wall tents which will be furnished you by the chief Q.M. of the Department."[4]

Colonel Forsyth and his soldiers reached Wounded Knee shortly after 8:30 P.M. They approached the rear flank of Whitside's camp via a circuitous detour, arriving on a hilltop behind Hawthorne's artillery so as not to alarm the Indians in the camp below. The troops unsaddled and bivouacked without shelter beyond the rise west of the first squadron and artillery battery camp. Some of the men slept on the ground in buffalo overcoats while others walked about to stay warm. Forsyth assumed command from Whitside, who had just paid a visit to the Indian camp. He made no changes in Whitside's troop dispositions and sent a courier back to Brooke to announce his arrival. He told Brooke that all was in perfect condition and that he would disarm Big Foot's people in the morning. He would leave Whitside to escort the Indians to the railroad at Gordon, where the government train ordered for their removal would be waiting for them. Forsyth would then report back to Brooke with the squadron to help deal with those tribesmen arriving from the Stronghold. He learned that Whitside had fed the Miniconjous and Hunkpapas from troop rations and asked that additional rations for 400 Indians be sent out early the next day with a scheduled forage train.

Through the night approximately 100 men of Troops A and I, inter-spersed among campfires, maintained their guard in alternating shifts around the Indian camp. They only permitted the Lakota women to go down into the ravine to collect firewood and as required for personal rea-sons. "The night was cold," recalled Lieutenant John C. Gresham, officer of the guard. It invited, he said, "rapid motion of sentinels on their beats, and made sleep impossible even for the reserve." Troopers relieved of guard duty were to remain near at hand and in the open to ensure that the Indians did not try to flee as they had done with Colonel Sumner. Doctors Hoff and Glennan treated the ailing Big Foot, while atop the hill Captain Capron as-sembled his Hotchkiss guns to the right of and slightly above Hawthorne's pair. He completed the task by midnight. Although their friction primers had been removed, all four guns were ominously trained directly on the Indian camp below. First Lieutenant Ernest A. Garlington, a former arctic explorer, along with Second Lieutenant John C. Waterman, oversaw the guard detail throughout the night. Beyond occasional wailing and sing-ing among the Indians, children crying, and the neighing and stamping of nearby horses, nothing unusual occurred. All remained generally quiet after Forsyth's arrival. Yet, as one private recalled, "we spent a sleepless night."[5]

Following Forsyth's trail under a clear moonlit sky, a party of civilian news correspondents and others soon reached the army camp by horseback and buggy. Besides William F. Kelley, who represented the *State Journal* of Lincoln and had arrived with Whitside's squadron on December 26, other reporters now present were Charles W. Allen of the *Chadron Demo-crat,* Charles H. Cressey of the *Omaha Bee,* and Thomas H. Tibbles of the *Omaha World-Herald.* Tibbles would leave early in the morning to return to Pine Ridge Agency. On arrival the reporters found their way to a large tent at the southwest edge of the first squadron bivouac, where Captain George D. Wallace of Whitside's squadron was recounting for Forsyth and others the events of the capture of Big Foot on December 28. Wrote Allen: "Captain Wallace's broad bed was spread on the ground in the middle of the tent, and on a nice new gray army blanket he was building with matches and explaining a diagram showing the position of various parts of the run-away band and the troops at the time of their meeting." Richard C. Stirk, another of the civilians at Wounded Knee that night, recalled that trader James Asay had brought a barrel of whiskey from Pine Ridge and that it flowed freely among the officers as they celebrated Big Foot's capture. Stirk did not recall the enlisted men getting any of the liquor and said that the officers who partook did not appear intoxicated in the morning.[6]

Later, after the assembly broke up, Charles Allen found himself alone with Colonel Forsyth. "The bright moonlight and balmy breeze caused him to become reminiscent," Allen said, "and as we paced back and forth on the grassy walk I was unforgettably entertained with a graphic account of many incidents in his European tour with General Phil Sheridan while still on his staff after the Civil War. We finally withdrew sometime after midnight." Each of them wrapped "the drapery of his couch about him" and "lay down to 'pleasant dreams.'"[7]

The area encompassed by the Indians and their soldier custodians on December 28 incorporated a rolling topography from the low rise 600 yards west of Wounded Knee Creek where the four Hotchkiss guns stood, sloping gently east-southeast toward the stream to form a fairly level tract upon which the first squadron shelter tents had been set up. At the south edge stood the wall tent raised for Big Foot. A picket line for mules had been established in the area between the troop bivouac and Big Foot's tent. Just east of the soldiers' shelter tents stood a line of supply, transport, and kitchen wagons. During the night several Sibley wall tents were raised in a line west of the Miniconjou chief's tent to accommodate the Indian scouts. By dawn several army wagons fronted this line. From that point the ground was mostly flat to the ravine, which itself was about 150 feet across and up to twenty-five feet deep. The Lakota camp occupied this area, with its shelters arrayed in a loose crescent over about two acres of ground (perhaps 200 yards from east to west and 75 yards deep). The eastern part of the encampment was closer to the large dry ravine than the west part, which angled to the northwest. A white flag had been raised on a stick above the shelters at the center of camp. Most of the Indian ponies grazed just west of the camp, apparently monitored by troops through the night.

Between the area of the army bivouac (which included Big Foot's adjacent tent) and the main Indian camp lay an expanse of open level ground some 170 yards square, north to south and east to west. During the night of December 28–29 troops and Indians together occupied an approximately square area of 600 yards on a side or about 74 acres. The broad ravine itself, which would figure in events ahead, angled east about two miles from the divide country separating the drainages of White Clay and Wounded Knee Creeks. Narrower west of the camp, the densely thicketed ravine would afford natural twists, turns, and cavities that would also prove significant for hiding and escape. Wounded Knee Creek itself was lined with ash, plum, and twisted brush. East of it stretched a close-in range of low, sparsely wooded hills of pine and cedar.

Formerly known as Red Dog Camp, the area was part of the lightly settled Wounded Knee community of reservation people. The name Wounded Knee reflected an old Lakota story wherein an elderly man in the vicinity was accidentally struck by an arrow in his knee, breaking his kneecap. The name Cankpe Opi (shot in the knee) was later translated as "Wounded Knee." Most of the community's inhabitants had left to escape the Ghost Dance agitation and especially the arrival of Whitside's troops. Several roads intersected the landscape. Whitside's force had arrived on December 26 via the Wounded Knee Road, which skirted the west side of Wounded Knee Creek. It led south and west toward Pine Ridge Agency and north-northwest along the meandering stream toward White River. Beyond the bridge crossing of Wounded Knee Creek, roads led north and east to Porcupine and Medicine Root Creeks and to the Rosebud Reservation. Just west of the creek and north of the bridge stood the vacated Wounded Knee Post Office and store that had been operated by mixed-blood Louis Mousseau, while farther northwest and downstream stood a small church. Several well-kept yet deserted log homes as well as a day school lay scattered through the countryside, along with a number of older abandoned cabins. One of these cabins stood on the far end of the hill on which the artillery pieces rested. Other routes crisscrossed the ground occupied by the soldiers and the Indians. One, called Fast Horse Road, led from Wounded Knee Road above the ravine to pass northwest through the western part of the Indian camp as it ascended the hill. It would prove of critical import as the day progressed. Barbed wire fences enclosed a few dormant land parcels. Farther north along the east side of Wounded Knee Creek stood a large dance site called the Omaha.[8]

Through the night the chain of sentinels from Troops A and I, overseen by Captain Myles Moylan of Troop A at the posts along the line, had remained stationary around the Indian camp. These dismounted soldiers had been arranged some ten feet apart, with their line transecting the ravine at two points and extending along its south edge. Pickets had kept watch along the north side of the first squadron bivouac. Four dozen more troopers were brought up to strengthen the south and west lines in the morning.

Reveille came at 5:15 A.M. on Monday, December 29, sunrise at 7:22. At 8 A.M. Forsyth made preparations for disarming the Indians by bolstering the chain guard. He sent the troops who had arrived with him (C, D, E, and G) to assume mounted positions all around the east and west sides of the camp, to the south across the ravine, and at some distance back from the perimeter of existing sentinels, all in sheltered areas if possible. The troops rode quickly to their designated stations, in a display of overwhelming strength to impress the Lakotas and emphasize how senseless any resistance would be. Troop G took position east of the sentinels and beyond the agency road, perhaps 150 yards from Big Foot's tent. To the south and across the ravine, behind the sentinels, stood Lieutenant Taylor and his mounted Troop A, Indian Scouts. Some fifty yards to the rear of the scouts, arranged east to west, were Troops C and D, commanded by Captain Henry Jackson and Captain Edward S. Godfrey, respectively, but under Jackson's overall command. Completing the encirclement in a slight depression 160 yards northwest of the west end of the camp and guarding the west flank in support of Capron's dominating Hotchkiss battery stood Troop E, the so-called Gray Horse Troop, mounted, under Captain Charles S. Ilsley.

At the battery the gunners had readied their pieces for prompt use and zeroed them on the camp, while the crews had placed their ammunition nearby. Two more cavalry troops, B and K of Whitside's squadron, commanded, respectively, by Captains Charles A. Varnum and George D. Wallace, former West Point classmates who had served at the Little Bighorn, took position between the line of tents thrown up for the Lakotas (but not used by them) and the first squadron bivouac area, with B on the west and K on the east. These troops were held in reserve. Their horses remained behind on the picket lines near the first squadron bivouac with those of Troops A and I. Small reserve guard detachments flanked the expansive ground to replace sentinels as needed. All cavalrymen were armed with carbines and revolvers fully loaded, while the artillerymen wore holstered pistols.[9]

Forsyth's available troop complement at Wounded Knee, including the cavalry and artillery components and medical personnel but not including the scouts, numbered 36 officers and 436 enlisted men (472 total). Before them were approximately 370 people of Big Foot's camp, 120 of them considered warriors (males of fighting age). At least 49 of the soldiers were raw recruits who had joined the regiment as recently as December 6, with little training or experience. It was reported that some had never fired a weapon. Wallace's Troop K held most of the uninitiated (ten).

The day started clear, calm, sunny, and cold but grew warmer. The wind of previous days seems to have abated. "In nearby trees, the birds were chirping their matins," remembered a correspondent.[10] At the cook tent the civilians collected a meager breakfast of hardtack, bacon, and coffee left over from feeding the troops and sat to consume it while observing the morning's events. In a line west of Big Foot's tent stood several large brown wall tents complete with awnings that fronted the rows of white shelter tents occupied by the soldiers. Forsyth, Whitside, several staff officers and sergeants, and mixed-blood interpreters Philip F. Wells (on loan from Taylor's scouts) and John and William Shangrau, as well as the scout Little Bat Garnier, consulted there as they prepared to proceed with disarming Big Foot's band. Nearby stood Father Craft, garbed in his black cassock. The expansive acre to the south between Whitside's bivouac and the Indian encampment now became a designated assembly point and council area. Criers went forth, calling upon all the men in the camp to approach and hear what Colonel Forsyth had to say. The colonel wanted to separate the men from the camp so as not to alarm the women and children unduly. A group of spectators from the surrounding area had arrived that morning by horseback and buggy and were watching from positions north and east of the first squadron bivouac area.

The tribesmen, alerted to the army activity about them, were up early and had eaten their army rations. The women were generally happy—some even sang—and looked forward to moving on to Pine Ridge Agency. Yet the men approached the designated assembly area uneasily. They did so in groups, seemingly unarmed. Many of them had painted faces, signifying brave deeds or personal ornamentation, and wearing blankets or sheets over their clothing in the crisp air. Some actually turned back to their camp, despite Forsyth's dictum to listen to his words. Some stood. Others crouched or took seats on the dry grass in irregular semicircular rows facing the line of scout and headquarters tents several yards away and not far from Big Foot's tent near the middle of that line. Approaching the assembly, Forsyth stopped and asked Big Foot to attend the council. Being ill, the chief declined and remained in his tent. Forsyth, along with Whitside, several other officers, including Adjutant Loyd S. McCormick, and a few teamsters and interpreters, stood facing the assembly and waited while the Sioux men initiated a rite of filling and lighting pipes and passing them among themselves. A quick count disclosed 106 warriors present. The 14 missing were thought to be still in the camp or in Big Foot's tent. Whitside directed a search made of the camp, and others reluctantly approached the assembly area.

With Wells interpreting, Forsyth spoke firmly yet with conciliation, according to witnesses. He extended a greeting and remarked regretfully on the circumstances of the moment, telling the Indians that they were prisoners and as such must surrender all weapons. They would not be harmed, however, and would be compensated for their arms. Forsyth explained that wagons then en route from Pine Ridge Agency would take them and all their goods to a camp near the agency. He did not mention the plan to remove them to Omaha. The people would be treated well and given food. When no guns appeared to be forthcoming and the Indians claimed that they had none, Forsyth directed the men to go back to the camp in groups of twenty, retrieve all firearms, and deliver them back at the council. Members of the first group consulted among themselves and headed out. They were hesitant. Some later described their demeanor as petulant. The troops watched and waited, talking among themselves about the situation at hand. The remaining warriors waited quietly in the circle, with heads bowed.[11]

For Big Foot's people, this was the day of dread. Disarmament—the army's obligatory procedure for dealing with fugitive tribesmen—called for them to give up their Winchesters and other firearms, perhaps their most highly treasured personal items. Giving up their weapons represented the loss of the last vestige of freedom. That notion had obsessed the Sioux since the days after Custer's defeat when the government mandated the yielding of guns and ponies as prerequisites for their submission to federal authority and incarceration on the Great Sioux Reservation. Many of the people had fled to Canada with Sitting Bull to avoid the "disarm and dismount" edict. As an army officer who had served with the Seventh Cavalry continuously since 1876 put it, "to the Indian a gun is the most cherished of all earthly possessions. The cost almost precludes the possibility of any one Indian buying more than one gun during a lifetime. . . . The Indian [moreover] recognizes the superiority of the white man's gun over his bow and arrow for hunting purposes." The Sioux and Cheyennes who surrendered in the wake of the fighting in 1876–77 gave up their weapons at the agencies then or in 1880–81, when those who had gone into Canada came back. Many later purchased arms and ammunition from government-licensed traders for hunting purposes. As Dr. McGillycuddy had observed, when the army had required the Lakotas to disarm in the past it "usually resulted in their turning in a 'museum of guns,' that is, all the antiquated pieces they could gather up, but keeping or concealing the good ones."[12]

So it was at Wounded Knee. As they returned to their camp under instructions to deliver up their firearms and other weapons, the men were upset and ill disposed to do so. Something else perhaps intensified those feelings. Word may have leaked from the army command, perchance through Indian scouts, that the people would be removed to the railroad and taken away in boxcars. Army plans indeed specified their removal to Omaha, but at least one scribe surmised that they would be shipped south to the dreaded Indian Territory—something the Tetons had been fearful of for decades. The possibility had been discussed repeatedly in conjunction with surrenders and treaty agreements going back to the 1870s. Despite all this, most of the Lakota men returned to the council ground after what seemed an excessive length of time. Reporter Charles Allen noted an "independent swagger" in some, while others in their war paint and painted ghost shirts appeared "conspicuously grim of visage." Just a few took their seats. Most simply stood rather insolently to await more words from Forsyth. Some of the women, wearing blankets, now tagged along with their husbands to await resumption of the meeting. Southeast of the gathering eight or ten boys wearing gray wool school uniforms played leapfrog among themselves. People came and went from the assembly until Colonel Forsyth again began speaking. He asked the group if they had brought in their guns. He told them to deliver them to a sergeant and several privates at the west edge of the council area. The men complied, turning in several firearms. Troops then escorted those disarmed men to a location north of the assembly, where they took seats on the ground.[13]

Allen noticed that the men delivering firearms represented a poor class among the Lakotas. As he put it, they seemed "lax, spiritless, shabbily dressed. Their ghost shirts were either plain or daubed with inartistic characters."[14] He and others observed that the guns surrendered were old and worthless—"blunderbusses," said one soldier. Most eyewitness accounts say that the Indians turned in two relic muzzleloaders. Other accounts suggest that several useless guns were surrendered. These were none of the firearms that Whitside's soldiers had seen the warriors brandish proudly the day before east of Porcupine Butte. Now Big Foot was lifted by the hospital steward and an Indian man. He was brought from his tent to the front center of the assembly and placed in a kneeling position to ask that his people obey Forsyth's orders and keep the peace. He talked with some of his men and explained to Forsyth through Wells that they had no guns, that all had been destroyed at Cheyenne River before they left.[15] At Whitside's suggestion and Forsyth's direction, Troops B and K, some 110 strong, wearing overcoats and armed with carbines and pistols, marched afoot down either side of the council area to its rear. There they established themselves between the assembly and the north side of Fast Horse Road adjacent to the Indian camp. The units fronted inward at right angles to each other in something of an expanded V- or U-shaped formation, with Troop B facing somewhat northeast and Troop K roughly northwest, toward the assembly and both perhaps thirty paces behind the semicircle. Each unit, arranged in ranks and with two or more yards between files, extended about 75–100 yards in its formation and fairly flanked the area occupied by the Lakota men. Their purpose was to provide a cordon to keep the Lakota men from heedlessly leaving the council and going to their camp. Even then some Lakotas tried to push their way through the soldiers and depart. Forsyth, with Philip Wells interpreting loudly, addressed their evident deception and lectured them about their faithlessness in carrying through with surrendering their weapons. According to Forsyth's adjutant, his words were greeted "with the sullen defiance so often displayed by strikers during labor troubles." At about this time Captain Varnum indicated to Whitside that some of his men had informed him that the warriors had guns beneath their blankets. Whitside responded: "We will search them when you are through with the village."[16]

As Forsyth admonished the excited people, two squads of soldiers each from Troops B and K started into the Indian camp to make a thorough search for weapons. They did so on orders from Whitside and were led by Captains Varnum and Wallace, along with interpreters Little Bat and John Shangrau.[17] The mission was carefully controlled. The respective squads began at either end of the camp and worked toward the middle. The hunt was thorough but not without incident, as Lieutenant Mann explained:

> The enlisted men were not allowed to go inside the tents and only took the arms as we handed them out. The squaws were sitting on bundles concealing guns and other arms. We lifted them as tenderly and treated them as nicely as possible. Had they been the most refined ladies in the land, they could not have been treated with more consideration. The

squaws made no resistance, and when we took the arms they seemed to be satisfied.[18]

The soldiers shook bags and parfleches, opening them when they heard metallic sounds. They looked everywhere, including under hay in wagons and among campfire ashes, seizing anything that might be construed as a weapon, including a variety of knives, bows and arrows, axes, hatchets, crowbars, war clubs, tent stakes, awls, and scissors, as well as ammunition. Captain Wallace, a veteran of the Battle of the Little Bighorn, picked up a stone-headed war club as a curio on the east side of the camp and carried it along with him. Despite Mann's statement, some of the women concealing weapons under them had to be forcibly moved by the soldiers. They often left the lodges and wickiups in disarray, further antagonizing the people, including the men in the assembly who overheard the cries and wails of the protesting women. It was yet another irritant.

The soldiers reportedly found forty-five guns, many damaged or otherwise unserviceable and some dismantled. They brought them back to the council area to be transferred by wagon to a deposit site northwest of the assembly toward earthworks fronting Capron's battery. Young Second Lieutenant Guy H. Preston, normally with the Indian scouts, supervised the deposit and stood astride the growing stack on the west side of the circle to keep fellow officers from taking souvenirs.[19] Another weapons pile was started at the front of the assembly just west of Big Foot's tent. Most of the soldiers returned from the camp with the retrieved items, but a few lagged behind or remained in the camp without authority. Throughout the search the women hurriedly continued to pack up their belongings, apparently expecting to leave soon. At the council, someone called out loudly to Forsyth that the camp search had been completed.

Attention now focused directly on the men in the circle. Because 120 warriors had been counted, a large number of firearms remained to be located. Concluding that they were hidden with loaded cartridge belts under blankets draped on or held by the Lakotas in front of him, Forsyth directed his men to search the warriors individually. Many of the Indians in council had been standing. Father Craft and at least a few soldiers noticed that they were indeed armed. Forsyth spoke calmly. To carry out the search, he told the Lakotas to return to their camp by passing through the gap south of the assembly formed by the apex of Troops B and K, where a search detail composed of Wallace, Varnum, and six soldiers, and supervised by Whitside would personally inspect each for concealed weapons as well as ammunition. To the rear of the troops, at the fringe of the camp, stood a number of women and elderly people carefully observing the proceedings. Father Craft moved through the crowd, speaking affably and giving out cigarettes. Because of the overwhelming nature of the army force and its weaponry, no one expected trouble. It was 9:15 A.M.[20]

One of the Lakotas circling within the council area was believed by officers to be a medicine man. Later variously identified as Yellow Bird, Black Fox, Black Coyote, Sits Straight, Good Thunder, Shakes Bird, Hose-Yanka, and Good-for-Nothing, he had a green-painted face, a war bonnet, and an elaborate ghost shirt. Since the village search began, he had been carrying on a gradually rising harangue against the proceedings, performing Ghost Dance exercises, and scooping up dirt and tossing it toward the soldiers. Forsyth had paid him little regard. As reporter Charles Allen explained: "He would take up hands full of dirt and scatter it, then hold up his hands as if momentarily expecting the earth to open and swallow up the troops."[21] After Forsyth announced the search of individuals, however, the man's tenor abruptly changed to fomenting resistance to the plan. Arguing against the advice of both Forsyth and Big Foot, he moved excitedly among the young men, most of whom were in the rear of the assembly, raising his hands to the sun while imploring them to defy the soldiers. Some of the troops openly laughed at his conduct. Interpreter Wells, standing with Forsyth before Big Foot's tent, told the colonel that the man was calling on the ghost-shirted warriors to resist and saying the soldier bullets would not harm them. After much difficulty Forsyth induced the medicine man to sit.[22] With crucifix in hand and speaking in Lakota, Father Craft tried to settle the fidgeting people down and to promote compliance with Forsyth's edict. Tension reigned nonetheless.

Some of the Indians stood hesitatingly or began moving about. Some moved into line as the search commenced. Wells recalled that "Major Whitside said to me [to] tell the Indians that it is necessary that they should be searched one at a time; this while he stood off to the side with five or six soldiers." The older Indians, Wells said, assented willingly by answering "How," as the search began.[23] The lines between the units now pulled together and moved to close down the opening between them. With foreboding, Lieutenant Mann, rejoining the troop from the Indian camp with Captain Wallace and their enlisted helpers, told the Troop K soldiers to be ready for trouble. Wallace, too, apparently told his men that if the Indians broke they would run for the ravine. If shooting erupted, he said, his men should hit the ground and return fire from a prone position. Varnum had given similar instructions.

The Indians by now faced generally south. Mann's men stood six or eight feet from them—too close. Mann now told them to fall back. They did so until about twenty-five feet separated the two groups. The abrupt movement startled the Indians, and events unfolded quickly. The impassioned medicine man was again on his feet. He renewed his loud tirade and broke into Ghost Dance movements, repeatedly advising his listeners to "Be brave," and to "Stand up and be brave."[24] As he did so, a number of the older Lakotas were searched and moved through the opening between the troop units. Father Craft said later: "I went up to them and tried to reassure them, but very few listened to me."[25] At this point eyewitness accounts differ on particulars. Varnum said that he and Whitside had gone through about twenty men but collected only cartridges in a hat. Others said that several firearms had been confiscated. Still others maintained that when one or two sergeants either reported seeing rifles or wrenched a rifle from beneath an Indian's blanket the medicine man, who had been grabbing sand and rubbing it on his head, suddenly stooped, grasped a handful, and tossed it heavenward. Some recalled that this movement was accompanied by his letting loose on a high-shrieking eagle-bone whistle. A mounted Lieutenant Robinson saw the man lurch toward the rear of the line with eight or ten warriors and spurred his horse to within a few feet, motioning them back. But it was too late, and Robinson quickly pulled his horse away. Captain Varnum, overseeing the search with his troop a short distance to the west, caught the movement from the corner of his eye as a simultaneous commotion erupted in the circle. "Look out!" he screamed. "They've broken!"[26]

In a flash all was tumult. What happened next took but seconds but would mark memory and history forever. A single gunshot pierced the air. Some officers, enlisted men, and Lakotas later said that they had heard it. Wells, who was with Forsyth, wheeled about quickly to see a soldier drop. While some of the Indians motioned excitedly toward the camp's white flag, perhaps five or six young warriors flung aside their blankets and turned, revealing lever-action Winchesters. Several more shots rang out and were followed almost instantly by a devastatingly massive volley of gunfire—at least fifty shots together, said Whitside—as the Indians turned against the surprised men of Troops B and K in their front and the soldiers

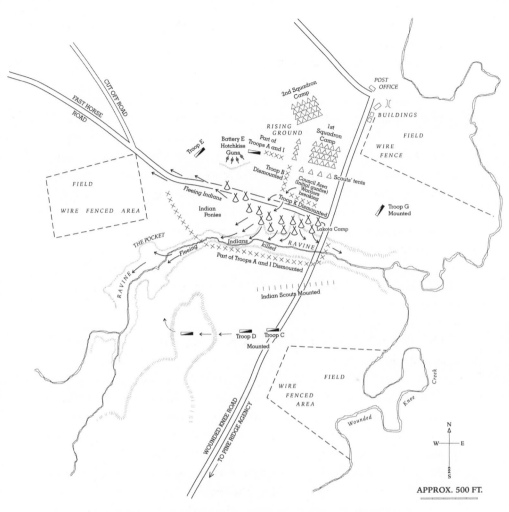

Map 5. The Wounded Knee Massacre, December 29, 1890.
Map by Robert G. Pilk.

instantaneously responded. Varnum remembered "one deafening crash" that felled twenty-five or thirty Indians at once and dropped soldiers in their tracks. Reporter Cressey wrote: "In a moment the whole front was a sheet of fire above which the smoke rolled, obscuring the central scene from view."[27] As Lieutenant Preston remembered, "the Indians fired outward in all directions as along the spokes from the hub of a wheel. Soldiers also fired inwardly."[28] Some later declared that the first shot came when the sergeant or sergeants grappled with a warrior for his weapon. Others said that a deaf or demented youth fired the opening shot. The incident may have been one and the same.

Lieutenant Mann described the moment:

> In front of me were four bucks[29]—three armed with rifles and one with bow and arrows. I drew my revolver and stepped through the line to my place with my detachment [of Troop K]. The Indians raised their weapons over their heads to Heaven as if in votive offering, then brought them down to bear on us. . . . Then they seemed to wait an instant. The medicine man threw a handful of dust into the air, put on his war bonnet, and then I heard a gun fired near him. This seemed to be the signal they had been waiting for and the firing immediately began. I ordered my men to fire and the reports were almost simultaneous.

Mann's observation is significant in that he was in the forefront of the opening action and provided one of the earliest personal accounts in a letter to his brother within days of the event.[30]

Father Craft had tried to quell the warriors when they first raised their weapons in unison. He recalled:

> I ran along the line of Indians & told them to stop & listen. . . . They laughed & lowered their guns . . . [but then] a young man . . . afterwards found to be Black Fox, a deaf man, who could not hear our words, & saw only the excitement . . . suddenly leveled his rifle on B Troop. . . . Before I could reach him the shot came, & the next second the Indians, excited by the shot, poured volley after volley into the lines of B & K Troops, their fire also mowing down like grass the crowd of their own women & children who stood in the camp looking on behind the soldiers. . . . They started to charge the two troops, towards their camp. . . . The soldiers kept cool & held their fire, until many had fallen & then received the order of their officers to return the fire, when it was clear that the fight could not be stopped.[31]

In the blur of confusion, unarmed Indians rushed to retrieve guns and ammunition from the deposit sites. As civilians and teamsters ran for cover, one of the first fatalities was Big Foot, who, in a nearly direct line from the soldiers, slumped from a sitting position before his tent, with a bullet through his neck and back.[32] Another quick fatality was the haranguing medicine man. Yet another early casualty was Philip Wells, who took a knife slash to his face, practically severing the tip of his nose, before he killed the warrior assaulting him. As he tried to pull away the flopping tip hanging by a shred of skin, Lieutenant Preston cried out, "My God, man! Don't do that! That can be saved!" Preston led him back to the hospital area, where several hasty stitches and a bandage from Dr. Ewing saved Wells's nose.[33]

In the meantime Father Craft was still trying to calm the Indians when he felt a bullet strike his foot. Almost simultaneously a piece of metal tore into his side as an Indian stabbed him from behind, slashing his lungs in what should have been a mortal wound. Still, he continued to administer absolution to the dying until he finally collapsed. During the melee the men of Troops B and K sustained quickly mounting casualties. Some dropped to a knee to return fire and reload, their single-shot weapons failing in close quarters against the warriors' fast-pumping magazine guns that produced the initial thunderous explosion heard by all. Said one officer: "I never in my life saw Springfield carbines worked so industriously as at that place."[34] Others pulled their revolvers and blazed away, the hand weapons being more effective in the moment. One trooper recalled: "After the first round, everybody used a revolver."[35] From the vantage point of the artillery position above the fray Private John W. Comfort watched the action below:

> In the first rush after the two troops and the warriors had poured their volleys into each other, I saw four warriors close on a cav[alry] serg't. Having no time to load, he used his carbine as a club. He went down but so did they from the fire that was focused on them from several points. A private in the act of loading his carbine was beset by a warrior who placed the muzzle of his Winchester right against the soldier's breast and fired. He killed the soldier but fell dead beside him.[36]

At the outbreak Lieutenant Preston fell to the ground and opened his revolver into the swirling throng: "It was a sure target, until the last shot or two, when through the gaps opened up by falling forms, soldiers appeared in range on the opposite side, so that I had to hold my fire for the moment. . . . It was clear that we had been killing each other."[37]

In their urgency the men of Troops B and K, however mindful of hitting their peers at close quarters, inevitably let fly bullets that likely struck not only warriors but comrades in distant alignments. Miraculously, the persons near Big Foot's tent, including Forsyth, Whitside, and Lieutenant Robinson's sixteen-year-old son, Ed, managed to avoid being hit by either the Indians or the soldiers. Reporter Cressey, who stood with Forsyth and Whitside "within touching distance" of the warriors at the outset of the clash, wrote that "the only thing that saved all three of us from instant death was that the Indians had their backs turned to us when they began firing."[38] A wounded soldier told a reporter several days later that "when the fight commenced the Indians were in the center with soldiers on all sides. . . . At the signal the Indians at once started the fight by firing on the soldiers. The latter were forced to shoot toward a common center and run the chances of shooting each other or else all be killed by the fire from the hostiles, and of course they chose the former alternative, and it is probable some of the soldiers were hit by shots fired by their own comrades."[39] In the early confusion some men likely hesitated to shoot for fear of contributing to the large number of trooper casualties. In the opening action twenty-six members of Troops B and K fell dead or wounded—the majority of army casualties at Wounded Knee. Among them was Captain Wallace, who received fatal shots to the stomach and head.[40]

Soldier Hugh McGinnis of K felt a bullet rip his arm. Another tore into his thigh, and a third hit his carbine. He "went spinning to the ground" and passed out. He next remembered that "the corpsmen moved rapidly among us and carried the wounded to a nearby knoll." McGinnis recalled: "They placed me with my head down the incline to keep the remaining blood near my heart. When the physician examined the gaping hole in my leg he said it looked like the bone had been smashed. I had ghastly visions of him sawing off my leg, but they had no time for such matters. . . . After administering first aid they carried me to one of the tents."[41]

Members of Troop I, located southeast of the firing, took casualties during the action but also sent rounds into the running warriors. Private Walter Crickett shot an Indian in the leg. "He returned my fire and struck my revolver which knocked me down, which saved me. . . . He didn't go much farther [because] our Capt. No[w]lan shot him through the heart."[42] In the initial volley Troop B, besides inflicting heavy casualties among the warriors, could have caused injury to comrades in guard positions beyond the agency road. Although the men of Troop G were unaffected, some of their horses were wounded, perhaps by such cross fire.

While Troops B and K bore the brunt of the opening attack, many of the Indian warriors' shots, as Craft observed, unconsciously flew into their own camp, with devastating results. The shots struck onlookers and family members out of sight beyond the soldiers and further hidden by rapidly billowing gun smoke.[43] An officer remarked: "Every shot that did not kill a soldier must have gone through their village."[44] As the fighting intensified, the surviving warriors armed with pistols and knives stormed into the soldiers clustered near the gap, using rifles as clubs as they struggled to break through the cordon and gain the ravine beyond the camp. A warrior stabbed Sergeant James Ward of Troop B in the shoulder just before another trooper shot the Indian with his revolver.

Each side flailed against the other, but the troops could not fully deflect the rush: some of the desperate Lakotas breached the ranks. "The charge on the lines was beaten back, but some broke through," remembered Craft. As they swept by, the soldiers still standing and kneeling instinctively pivoted, blindly delivering fire after the Indians plunging through the smoky shroud toward the ravine. Their bullets killed and wounded fleeing warriors and camp occupants alike, thereby compounding the Lakotas' own devastation by visiting more destruction on noncombatants converging on the ravine, which was quickly crowded in with warriors, women, and children.[45] Most of the Sioux fighters fell dead or wounded in the council area during the initial firing of soldiers of Troops B and K, many of whose shots indeed struck more than one target in the tightly compressed setting. Or they died in their effort to breach the line. In the unfolding chaos some escapees darting and stumbling through the camp ducked behind buggies and dead animals to fire back at the soldiers. Panicked horses raced in all directions as they tore across the field. Because of the scant breeze and a seeming inversion layer preventing its dispersal, the voluminous smoke lingered over the ground. From the east and southeast marksmen from Troops A, I, and G, now all dismounted and lying prone, targeted barely distinguishable "warriors"—in fact, men, women, the elderly, children, likely even animals—some of whom were moving east across the murky terrain toward Wounded Knee Creek.[46] These troops shortly halted human movement toward the stream and forced most of the survivors to turn west up the ravine, which then became a deadly trap.[47] Private Edward Edmunds of Troop G wrote that his troop "dismounted and followed up the braves that sought the ravine for protection. Volley after volley was poured into the Indians in the ravine with deadly effect. . . . The troops . . . shot down every Indian that showed up."[48] Others fired into the horses to ferret out warriors hiding there. An artilleryman from his hilltop vantage summarized the deadly riot:

A single shot followed immediately by a volley right in the faces of the troopers, a mad rush, hand to hand, shooting, stabbing, clubbing. Soldiers, warriors, squaws and children all mixed. Horses hitched to Indian wagons dashing wildly about. Tepees upset on fire, everybody running, some for shelter and safely, some in pursuit of a foe, the outside lines of troopers pouring in a rapid fire. All this time the artillerymen on the hill were standing, lanyard in hand, guns shotted with canister, waiting for their comrades of the cav[alry] to get clear from amidst the Indians.[49]

The beginning of the action occupied fewer than twenty minutes. In seven or eight minutes, said one cavalryman, "every Ind[ian warrior] in sight had been shot down."[50] Killed and wounded braves and soldiers lay sprawled on the assembly ground, some still struggling with each other. But closer to the ravine lay more bodies, nearly all Indians and most of them noncombatants. Preston remarked: "Where had been so many people was an area strewn with dead and writhing forms so thickly placed it was difficult to get about." Wounded Indians, he said, "were firing now and then from the heap."[51] However unpremeditated their actions may have been (and we have no compelling evidence otherwise), during these critical moments when the men of B and K swiveled and fired at the breaking warriors—shooting not only at them but through them to the noncombatants beyond—the tenor of the soldiers' initial actions ceased to be defensive. What happened at Wounded Knee evolved quickly into purposeful yet indiscriminate killing. It became a full-fledged massacre.

At last freed by the warriors' movement, the sentinel sharpshooters on the margins of the field opened a surge of gunfire against those on the flat of the camp where dense roiling smoke, blankets, and other garments combined to obfuscate distinctions between men and women, old and young, and even animals. No single officer exercised control, and the shooting momentarily escalated as all personal constraint and self-possession fell away. Although some reportedly counseled their men against targeting noncombatants, this advice seems to have come later and not during the throes of the pell-mell opening action. "At last they had a target and took full advantage of it, rapid fire," stated Preston.

It was, of course, excited fire, too, and much of it misdirected. Many of the fleeing bucks fell in their tracks but also many squaws toppled over. At once, officers began shouting above the din to stop the fire, warning that they were killing women and children. I was one who shouted, too. Then the fire stopped, and in that strange silence were ejaculations from all sides, *My God!* giving voice to horror at what had happened, . . . the killing of women with papooses on their backs.[52]

Private Eugene S. Caldwell of Troop D wrote his family: "I did not like to see the squaws killed, but they were as bad as the bucks after the fight started. Some of the men went wild; they would shoot men or women. The officers tried to stop them, but it was of no use; they would shoot any one they saw with a gun. . . . Some of the men went around and shot every Indian that was able to do any damage."[53]

As the frantic women fled, some in desperation sought help from the soldiers. A man from Troop I remembered a woman running up to him, a baby on her back. She said something unintelligible, pointing to the infant, "as if afraid that she would be shot." While the trooper stood there, "a bullet hit her in the bridge of the nose, killing her instantly."[54] It was probably shortly after this stage of the action that Forsyth, who had removed himself to the battery, sent off a hurried report via Lieutenant Preston to General Brooke:

On attempting to disarm the persons of the bucks they made a break, which resulted in a hot fight lasting from about 9.15 until about 9.45. About fifteen soldiers are wounded and a few killed. The number of Indians killed & wounded not known but believed to exceed the loss on our side. The ones who escaped have fled up the ravines to the west— pursued by three troops. . . . This dispatch is indefinite but is as accurate as I can give, as we are still engaged in clearing out the adjacent ravines.[55]

As bad as the action had become, more formidable ruin awaited. It came from the Hotchkiss Mountain Battery poised on the northwest rise. Each of the four pieces was capable of firing five or six rounds per minute or together as many as twenty-plus rounds in that time.[56] After the remaining men of Troops B and K, along with those of Troop G, at last withdrew to rally in the left rear of the guns on the hill (many of them had raced directly toward the ordnance, further delaying its entry into action), the four cannon unleashed a barrage of shrieking canister that shredded tipis and improvised shelters, extinguishing whatever life remained in the camp area. Artillery Private John Comfort described the opening fire: "Finally the way was clear. Crack-crash went the 4 guns sending their canister tearing into the mass of warriors, squaws, children & horses. It was a terrible thing to do but the warriors were mixed with the squaws, and were firing rapidly with their Winchesters, and squaws were seen to kill wounded soldiers."[57]

Captain Capron admitted to killing women and children with the Hotchkiss guns. "It was impossible to avoid it, as it was impossible to distinguish man from woman; they all seemed to be firing. . . . I continued to shoot at any parties that were shooting at our troops. . . . It was impossible to prevent killing squaws."[58] The captain sent a canister against tepees fifty yards away and percussion shell against "Indians and their ponies" as far as 2,500 yards away. In one instance a Hotchkiss round was directed at a conical army tent believed to be harboring a warrior who had periodically sniped at the soldiers through slits in the canvas. He killed at least three. A soldier who volunteered to approach the tent and look inside ran up, cut open the canvas, and was shot dead. Troops sent a volley into the tent. Then "a Hotchkiss gun was brought up, and a couple of shells exploded in the tent," wrote Lieutenant Mann.[59] The tent was then surrounded with hay and burned. "When everything was over," said a witness, "we found only a charred corpse."[60] In another instance Private William F. Bailey of Troop A watched as a Hotchkiss gun opened on a wagon filled with women and children trying to negotiate the far bank of the gulch and get away. "The shell on exploding on the wagon killed or wounded the whole load."[61] The blast tore the wagon, horses, and occupants to pieces in a bursting yellow cloud of debris. Another witness said that "the sight was as if a pile of rags had been thrown into the air. All were killed except a small baby."[62]

The roaring artillery bombardment continued for half an hour, intermixed with musketry from the periphery of the field. A correspondent recorded his impression: "It was a war of extermination now with the troopers. It was difficult to restrain . . . [them]. Tactics were almost abandoned. About the only tactic was to kill while it could be done whenever an Indian could be seen. Down into the creek [ravine] and up over the bare hills they were followed by artillery and musketry fire, and for several minutes the engagement went on, until not a live Indian was in sight."[63]

Finally the shooting ended. One soldier recalled: "The bugles [sic] sounded 'Cease Firing,' but many of the men were up in the hills, and now and then a shot was heard. Colonel Forsyth looked very white as he gave orders to see if any of the women who lay thick around were alive. . . . Of course the camp-liar was in his glory, but who shot the squaws was not known, at least no one boasted of it."[64] When it was over, the dead and wounded lay strewn throughout the assembly and camp areas, ravine, and beyond.

When the shooting broke out in the council area, the few soldiers and others who had remained searching for weapons in the camp without authority became targeted. Little Bat and reporter Allen were among those there. Allen likened it to "the activity of good dry popcorn in a hot pan."[65] Both men ran. The sergeant major of the Seventh Cavalry and another soldier were killed there, while the regimental quartermaster sergeant received a shot that tore away his chin and lower teeth. Some of those who were wounded found their way to the artillery position and were directed to the nearby field hospital for attention. Meanwhile those soldiers south of the big ravine took preventative action. Members of the sentinel guard of Troops A and I rallied across the ravine opposite the southeast corner of the Indian camp, while others sought protected areas northwest of the camp. When the Indians ran toward the ravine Captain Nowlan permitted women and children to pass. But when warriors appeared, he told his men to "give it to them."[66] Godfrey's Troop D and Captain Jackson's Troop C took position behind rising ground. Taylor's Indian scouts in their front, originally mounted in line beyond the chain guard, seem to have scattered at the outbreak. Most headed for shelter in or near the ravine with part of the guard. Some of the scouts passed south through Godfrey's line, others went north and east of the agency road, and some fled to the hills southwest of the camp, where they captured loose ponies. Quite likely their reaction came in response to shooting by soldiers and Lakotas directed at the assembly ground.[67]

Godfrey described the initial outbreak from his vantage: "The quiet was suddenly broken by a shot, and after a very short interval there came two or three more shots, followed by a continuous fusillade. . . . The whole village was in commotion, and in a short time the mass of Indians started in our direction. The troops on the ridge opposite us opened fire on them with small arms and Hotchkiss guns. As the mass neared the deep ravine some bullets ricocheted to our position."[68] Jackson, a hard-bitten veteran with Civil War experience dubbed "Old Hickory" by his men, recalled the outset of the shooting: "For ten or fifteen minutes it was as heavy a fire as I have ever experienced."[69] He promptly pulled his troop back to the far edge of a small field, while Godfrey removed his to a hill rising on his left, where the men dismounted in skirmish order behind the crest. They opened on Indians trying to flee by the agency road, while fire from the battery killed noncombatants there as well as in Wounded Knee Creek. "It seemed to me only a few seconds till there was not a living thing before us," Godfrey recalled. "Warriors, squaws, children, ponies and dogs—for they were all mixed together. . . . I believe over thirty bodies were found on our front."[70]

Both D and C troops exchanged shots with the running tribesmen until Godfrey sent half his men under Second Lieutenant Selah R. Tompkins to cover the ravine and keep Indians from escaping by that route. Crossing over on existing cow trails, surviving warriors with women and children fled the artillery fire only to meet troops now shooting into them from the south bank. Here Lieutenant Garlington, operating with Troop A on the periphery of the action, was himself wounded in the right arm but continued with his men.[71]

According to First Sergeant Ragnar, his Troop K, arrayed in skirmish order, proceeded up the floor of the large ravine to the positions held by D and C on the south side.

> Here we found [the dead after the fighting] . . . in big heaps, piled on each other. Women, the children in their arms, young and old, horses and mules in various positions, broken carts and clothing. More scattered, the warriors lay on their faces, still clutching their weapons. There lies a whole family, except the father, under an overturned cart body, with the horses still in the shafts; with their legs crushed they are writhing in agony. There a papoose cries by its mother's breast which, cold and insensible, can nourish it no more; there lies a young girl with her long hair sticky of blood, hiding her mutilated face. . . . And here—here rests the beautiful young squaw whom yesterday I offered a cigarette—dying, with both her legs shot off. She lies there without wailing and greets me with a faint smile on her pale lips.[72]

When the Hotchkiss guns fell silent, mounted soldiers attempted to seek out those still in the ravine and head off others en route to hills and gullies to the west. As many as thirty people, mostly women who had avoided the mounted troops, found sanctuary in a deep and heavily wooded subordinate washout, later known as the "pocket." It was more than an acre in size and located off the north side of the main gorge as it trended southwest, about 330 yards west of the center of the camp and perhaps 500 yards from the assembly area.[73] Because their position abutted old cattle crossings of the primary ravine, these Indians were soon surrounded by prone skirmishers of Troops C, D, and G, who sent lively barrages at them from thirty or forty yards away. At one point First Lieutenant Edwin P. Brewer took a risk to enter the pit and extract a number of women and children unharmed. The warriors, however, who had excavated an area beneath the bank, would sporadically charge up the steep interior slope, fire, and duck back to elude rounds from the soldiers. They succeeded in killing one cavalryman, Private Jan DeVreede of Troop C, who rolled over the bank into the pit when shot. As the troops pulled back, one of Lieutenant Hawthorne's pieces manned by Corporal Paul H. Weinert was advanced down the slope and through the Sioux camp to open fire against these people. Its thundering shells prompted a sharp response from the Indians. Hawthorne received a painful wound to the groin. If the officer's pocket watch had not deflected the bullet, the injury would have been fatal.

As an artillery crewman carried Hawthorne away, Weinert continued to advance and shell the occupants: "I . . . ran the gun fairly into the opening of the ravine and tried to make every shot count. . . . The wheels of my gun were bored full of [bullet] holes. . . . Once a [Hotchkiss] cartridge was knocked out of my hand just as I was about to put it in the gun, and it's a wonder the cartridge didn't explode."[74] A second gun was brought forward. But before it deployed Captain Capron directed both pieces back to the hill. The fight was largely over. Private Small remembered: "We threw another volley into the ravine, and then everything was quiet. We . . . finely [sic] got in the rear of this Hole where the shots came from, and we found a young Indian in the hole, about 16 years old. His head was almost shot off, his Winchester in his hands still pointed in our direction." With Taylor's scouts interpreting, Jackson's troops eventually captured twenty-three of the holdouts, many of them wounded, and sent for a wagon to haul them in. Six warriors had been killed in the pocket.[75] The combat at Wounded Knee then slackened into desultory firing surrounding the pursuit of people who had managed to flee.

When the first shooting erupted, a body of women and children (with perhaps some men) boarded wagons and took off northwest with the Indians' pony herd, skirting a fence and ascending the hill to reach Fast Horse

Road west of the assembly ground. As artilleryman Comfort related, the "herd of horses . . . dashed from the camp, some 70 or 80 of them ridden. . . . They chose the worst [route], and came tearing directly toward the guns . . . endeavoring to reach the rough broken country [to the north]. The guns after ex[h]austing their canister used percussion shell continuing their fire until what was left of the flying Indians were [sic] hid from view."[76] Nearby, Troop E of the Seventh, flanking the artillery, stood poised to shoot but at Lieutenant Horatio G. Sickel's direction did not fire. As the fighting in his front wound down, Forsyth sent Troops C, D, and G to pursue those people, capture them, and if necessary kill the men. Captain Godfrey took half his troop and marched beyond the ridge about five miles, moving generally northwest on the trail. But the Indians had scattered. The captain kept on, approaching a wooded vale, but saw no immediate trace of the people. The incident that followed haunted Godfrey for the rest of his life.

While moving down the valley of White Horse Creek with flankers out, the soldiers at last came upon a small body of Indians trying to run and hide in a clump of bushes. The captain dismounted his men as skirmishers and called out to the people but got no response. He told his men to advance until they saw Indians and called out again and again "How, cola! Squaw, papoose, cola!" but received no answer. Godfrey finally ordered his men to commence firing, and they sent forth a volley into the bushes that yielded screams of terror and Godfrey's abrupt command to cease firing. The men raced to the place from which the cries had emanated. "There I found one squaw and two children in the agonies of death and what appeared to be a man, sprawled face down, clothed with civilian clothes, and with coat turned over his head, perfectly quiet, and I supposed dead." As the party turned to depart, one of the flankers, a recruit named Maurice Carey, perceiving movement in the man, suddenly pulled his gun and shot him in the head. Godfrey then noticed that the victim was in fact a boy who appeared to be in his teens. Back at Pine Ridge Agency the next day, a contrite and tearful Carey told Godfrey that he had been frightened and fired on impulse. "I was shocked by the tragedy, but thought Carey had acted from fright and the well-known sentiment in the Army at that time to take no chance with a wounded Indian."[77]

Godfrey's detachment started back. Perhaps three miles from the Lakota camp and army bivouac, near the head of the large ravine that ran down to Wounded Knee Creek, they encountered Jackson's troop. Away in the distance toward Pine Ridge Agency the soldiers sighted six Indians approaching who appeared to be agency policemen. They advanced and shook hands with the officers and rode back a way then turned suddenly and fired at them. Immediately after this apparent signal some 150 warriors appeared—ostensibly some of Two Strike's Brulés from the agency—and began shooting at the soldiers from three sides. Both troops returned fire while Jackson dispatched a courier to Forsyth for help. A running fight commenced over several hundred yards. When Captains Ilsley and Edgerly appeared with their men, the warriors retired. No casualties occurred among the troops, although during the action Jackson's twenty-three prisoners were abandoned by the soldiers and escaped to the Brulés. Forsyth dispatched the news to Brooke when Jackson and the others returned to the army command and reported their activities.[78] Anticipating further retaliatory Indian attacks, especially from Brulés as Jackson had experienced, Forsyth raised a simple breastwork around the guns on the hill using sacks of flour, grain, and bacon together with hardtack boxes and placed his wagons end to end in a manner to protect the animals.

Across the field an absolute cease-fire took place when Forsyth finally yelled: "Quit shooting at them[!]" The word quickly circulated. By 1:30 P.M., while doctors and medics attended the wounded of both sides at the field hospital raised near the first squadron bivouac, soldiers had collected the army dead in a row. Nearby the men pitched several tents to accommodate the women and children, raising the walls to afford them a breeze in the warming day. Casualties among the troops engaged numbered sixty-five killed and wounded, including five officers. In addition, an Indian scout named High Back Bone had been killed, apparently mistaken for a Ghost Dancer who charged the troops, while interpreter Wells, Father Craft, and the off-duty Lieutenant Kinzie, Second Infantry, had all been wounded. In a note to Brooke Forsyth requested ambulances. Two of the injured enlisted men would die in transit to the agency, and another four would perish subsequently, boosting total army fatalities to thirty-six.[79] The extent of the Indian dead had yet to be determined. Private Flynn of Troop A roamed the sanguinary field looking for survivors. As he later wrote:

I came across a dead squaw and a little papoose who was sucking on a piece of hardtack. I picked up the little papoose and carried it in my arms. A little way farther on, I found another dead squaw and another papoose. I picked it up, too, and brought them over near the hospital tent, where there were a number of Indian women. As I came over to where they were, I met a big, husky sergeant who said, "Why didn't you smash them up against a tree and kill them? Some day they'll be fighting us." I told him I would rather smash him than those little innocent children. The Indian women were so glad that I saved the papooses that they almost kissed me.[80]

Elsewhere, however, the scenes evoked horror and profound sadness. Dead and dying horses lay strewn over the site amid rubble from the camp and the army positions. A private of Troop G, one of four litter bearers trained to assist the injured in combat, told of treating "bad cases." "There was one big brave who was shot in the stomach by a ricochet bullet." The man's intestines were protruding, he said, and "had to be pushed back and bandaged the best we could until we could get him into the Agency. One Indian boy that I bandaged . . . was hit . . . in the thigh, making a tearing wound—not so deep as tearing and ugly. I had to pull the sides together and bandage. The little fellow never made a groan."[81]

As the smoke cleared, reporter Allen located the students who had been frolicking at the outset. "On that spot of their playful choice were scattered the prostrate bodies of all those fine little Indian boys, cold in death. . . . Avoidance of the first death-dealing volleys was impossible. . . . They must have fallen like grass before the sickle."[82] Occasionally, the killing continued. An Oglala Scout named Walking Bull found three wounded tribesmen there on the ground, telling them not to be deceived because he wore a uniform. "I want to save you," he told them, whereupon one of them shot the scout in the leg, grazing him. Walking Bull told the man, "I came to save you, but you have no ears," and shot him dead.[83] Interpreter Wells similarly walked over the deadly plain where the camp had stood and so many had perished. When he called on the motionless to raise their heads if alive, about a dozen Lakotas responded. One warrior lifted himself on an elbow and called Wells to him, pointing at the dead medicine man. As Wells related:

He raised himself a little higher, raised his closed fist, pointing it towards the dead Indian, shot out his fingers, which is amongst Indians a deadly insult, . . . [then] speaking as though to the dead man: "If I could be taken to you I would stab you!," then turning to me said, "He is our murderer!"[84]

One of the Indians remained in a sheltered ravine and refused all efforts to extricate him. Forsyth decided to abandon him rather than risk further casualties.

The remainder of the command packed equipment for return to the agency. Much matériel and forage had to be abandoned, although officers and men managed to pull souvenirs from the destroyed camp. Private Nosheim Feaster of Troop E took a painted buffalo hide with him. The troops emptied the ration wagons, lined their floors with bags of oats covered with hay and blankets, and loaded the wounded soldiers, making them as comfortable as possible. In the meantime the civilian transport wagons that had been sent to carry Big Foot's people to the railroad had arrived. Teamsters were now employed to move casualties and equipment and to build litters. The dead soldiers were borne forward, while a sergeant identified each man and his unit for the reporters present, who then repaired to Mousseau's old store building to ready their dispatches. The bodies lay in the chilling air under blankets of canvas, faces exposed. Wallace's corpse was shrouded in an American flag. Indian scouts helped stack them into wagons for the trip, and several wounded soldiers had to ride with them. Wounded Lakota men, women, and children, in addition to a number of women and children who were mostly uninjured, also traveled under guard in some of these wagons. "There were constantly passing groups of two to five or more wounded Indian women and children, moaning, crying, or weeping silently," Allen reported. "Frequently a young girl could be seen hopping on one foot, supported on one side by a woman less disabled and on the other by a trooper. . . . Where the shot had passed between the knee and ankle, a protruding bone was disclosed at every step."[85]

The Indian dead could not immediately be buried and would be left on the field for later disposition. Some probably feigned death until the soldiers left.[86] Nor did Forsyth, in his hurry to depart before dark, have time to get an accurate count of all the Indian fatalities. Of immediate significance to the army command, however, was the number of warriors slain in the encounter. Forsyth prepared such an accounting for General Brooke, who next day sent the information on to Miles, who forwarded it to Washington:

Colonel Forsyth says 62 dead Indian men were counted on the plain where the attempt was made to disarm Big Foot's band, and where the fight commenced. On other parts of the ground were 18 more. This does not include those killed in ravines where dead warriors were seen but not counted. Six were brought in badly wounded and six others wounded were with a party of 23 men and women which Captain Jackson had to abandon when attacked by about 150 Brulé Indians from the Agency. . . . This accounts for 92 men killed [and wounded] and leaves but few alive and unhurt.[87]

Lieutenants Garlington and Hawthorne rode in one of the two ambulances, Father Craft and a wounded sergeant in the other. "The transportation for these four was bad enough," wrote Adjutant McCormick, "but it was heavenly when compared with the springless jolt of the freight wagon."[88] As a chill settled, the protracted column pulled out over the road about 4 P.M., leaving the Indians' white flag waving dissonantly over the ruinous scene. "One of the sad sights as the troops left the field," observed one reporter, "was the wounded cavalry horses struggling to their feet and neighing to their old comrades as the column marched away."[89] The journey through the darkness was slow. Lanterns were not allowed for fear of impending attack. The safety of the wounded required focused examination of the country ahead and on either side. Indian scouts herded approximately 150 captured ponies at the rear. Burning homes and prairie fires could be seen far in the distance on every side. The tired and famished command, with its lurching conveyances bearing anguished cargo, reached Pine Ridge Agency near half past nine. Upon arrival Forsyth reported to General Brooke: "Big Foot's party has practically ceased to exist."[90] As the soldiers returned to their respective camps around the agency, the severely wounded were taken to the divisional field hospital, where troops had stacked cordwood high around the tents as protection from bullets. The injured Lakotas were removed from the wagons into tents and soon after carried into the Holy Cross Chapel, which had been hastily converted into a hospital ward.[91]

Elsewhere at the agency confusion reigned. Four companies of the Second Infantry had been packed and ready, awaiting word from Forsyth to start for Gordon as escort to the surrendered Big Foot people. Then came the muffled booming of cannon in the distance. A few hours later runners appeared. When Lieutenant Preston and a cavalry soldier arrived around 11 A.M. with official news for Brooke, an alarm was sounded. Word quickly spread that when the fighting erupted at Wounded Knee "the Cavalry began shooting in every direction, killing not only Indians but their own comrades on the other side of the circle." The companies of the Second and Eighth Infantry prepared for action, along with two 3.2-inch cannons and a Gatling gun, helped by agency employees and Indian police.[92]

When word of the slaughter reached the agency via Indian messengers, the agency Lakotas and those Stronghold people camped at the Mission—now uncertain, frightened, and restless—dismantled their lodges, loaded up, and vacated the area en masse. Altogether, some three thousand Indians—particularly the dissident Oglalas of Little Wound and the Brulés under Two Strike and Crow Dog, along with frightened men, women, and children from the camp of "friendlies" who had been forced to go with them—began moving quickly. Caravan-like, they passed north down White Clay Creek and away from the agency, dumping their worldly belongings by the roadside to speed their way. Some of these people were part of the large party encountered by Jackson, Godfrey, and Edgerly in the wake of the fighting at Wounded Knee. Others joined Short Bull's followers to reclaim protection in the Badlands. By early afternoon the exodus was well underway. Friendly Indians such as Chief American Horse and his followers stayed, but they moved their lodges closer to the soldiers' camps. Red Cloud's people first equivocated then took their departure too. The old chief was virtually kidnapped.

Brooke meanwhile ordered companies formed and batteries prepared to meet an attack. Shooting at last broke out when about two hundred of Two Strike's warriors, seeking reprisals from the hills west of the schoolhouse, briefly fired into the agency about 2 P.M. and again at 4, wounding five soldiers. The attackers also set fire to several cabins and some hay west of the agency. When the Indian police interdicted their efforts many of their bullets went into the Oglala camp, further impelling the exodus. Terrified schoolchildren remained locked inside the building walls during the havoc. Father Jutz told of warriors torching government day schools down White Clay Creek and burning homes of whites wed to Lakota women. General Brooke notified settlers in Rushville and elsewhere to prepare for defense and directed his artillerymen to relocate from near White Clay Creek to an eminence south of the agency to better command approaches and to receive support from the infantry companies. The presence of eight big guns placed strategically around the agency buildings kept the warriors at bay until they disappeared into the western hills. That night the troops raised entrenchments around critical points, including the government school harboring the excited children. Brooke's refusal to permit the troops to shoot back at the Sioux angered his men but likely thwarted a more intense fusillade that might have produced ever-higher losses, including Indian women and children. After the commotion attending Forsyth's arrival with the Wounded Knee casualties and their placement in medical environments, things settled down. By 1 A.M. all was quiet at Pine Ridge Agency.[93]

24. Major Samuel M. Whitside

Major Samuel Whitside commanded the first squadron of the Seventh Cavalry, credited with capturing Big Foot and his people near Porcupine Butte on December 28, 1890, and leading them to the army camp at Wounded Knee Creek. Miles later blamed Whitside for placing the Indians near the ravine and for perilously disposing his force about them, an arrangement that Forsyth retained. Whitside played a major role in the disarmament immediately preceding the massacre and later commanded the regiment during Forsyth's suspension. Whitside retired from the army in 1902 as a brigadier general. Courtesy of the Fort Huachuca Museum.

25. Colonel James W. Forsyth, 1891

Colonel James Forsyth of the Seventh Cavalry was a West Point graduate who had served in the Civil War and in the West. Forsyth's performance at Wounded Knee and in the Mission Fight incensed General Miles, who removed him from command and ordered a thorough investigation, much to the chagrin of Washington authorities, who subsequently exonerated him. Courtesy of the University of Washington Libraries.

26. *Opening of the Fight at Wounded Knee*

This illustration by Frederic Remington appeared in *Harper's Weekly* on January 24, 1891. Remington based it on conversations with Seventh Cavalry participants during his visit to Pine Ridge soon after Wounded Knee. Author's collection.

In the photograph, handwritten text reads:

Father Craft The Hero of
Wounded Knee Fight
Coby Righted Jan 1st 1891
N.W. Photo Co Chadron Neb
122

27. Father Francis M. Craft

Jesuit missionary Father Francis Craft, here in his cassock with crucifix, accompanied Colonel Forsyth's battalion to Wounded Knee. On the morning of December 29, 1890, Craft tried to calm the excited men in the council area before the shooting erupted there. He received two wounds in the ensuing chaos, including a severe knife wound to his lungs, which he survived. Courtesy of the Denver Public Library and Paul Harbaugh.

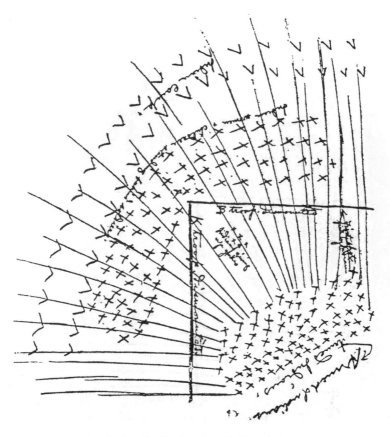

28. Father Craft's diagram of Wounded Knee

Father Craft's illustration of the opening action at Wounded Knee, indicating how the Indians' initial gunfire tore through the Troop B and K positions and into the camp area beyond, is important documentation explaining the earliest casualties among noncombatants. This illustration appeared in the *Catholic Standard and Times*, November 22, 1913. Author's collection. A similar rendering by Craft in early 1892 appears in Foley, *At Standing Rock and Wounded Knee*, p. 309.

29. Captain George D. Wallace

South Carolinian captain George Wallace, forty-one, commanded Troop K at Wounded Knee. A West Point graduate and Little Bighorn veteran, Wallace stood with his men at the south extremity of the council circle on the morning of December 29, 1890, one of the first fatalities as gunfire erupted. Courtesy of Glenwood J. Swanson.

31. Artillery battery

Battery E, First Artillery, with its four Hotchkiss cannon firing canister and explosive shell, caused devastation at Wounded Knee, destroying Big Foot's camp and killing and injuring many people. Battery members pose here days before the engagement. Captain Allyn K. Capron stands at far left, next to Private John W. Comfort, whose 1892 letter provided details of the artillery assault. To Comfort's left is Second Lieutenant Harry L. Hawthorne, who would suffer a debilitating wound while in the "pocket" of the large ravine. Lying at front right is Corporal Paul H. Weinert, who rolled his gun into the pocket, firing against Indians who sought refuge there. Both men received Medals of Honor. Author's collection.

30. Captain Edward S. Godfrey (*opposite*)

Captain Edward Godfrey, here arrayed in full dress uniform, took part in every major Indian engagement of the Seventh Cavalry since the regiment's inception in 1866. At Wounded Knee he commanded Troop D, initially operating south of the ravine that adjoined the Lakota camp. His men's killing of a Lakota woman and her children later that day at White Horse Creek boosted the horror of Wounded Knee and generated further controversy for the Army. Courtesy of the Denver Public Library and Paul Harbaugh.

32. Interior of the Episcopal church hospital

Wounded Indians, mostly women and children, were brought into Pine Ridge Agency on the evening of December 29, 1890. The Reverend Cook offered his Holy Cross Episcopal Church as a hospital for them over the next several weeks. This interior image shows patients resting on the hay-covered floor with army doctors and caregivers in attendance as Christmas decorations adorn the walls. Photo by George Trager. Courtesy of Paul Harbaugh.

"Bloody Pocket" "In which" The
Mission Fight" occured, Dec 30th 1890.
P.R. Res S.D.

33. Area of the Mission Fight

This view shows the rugged terrain at Colonel Forsyth's northernmost point of advance down White Clay Creek during the Mission Fight of December 30, 1890. Initiated by overly apprehensive Seventh Cavalry troops in the wake of Wounded Knee, the action further evinced Forsyth's ineptness in failing to extricate his command, facing minimal Lakota resistance, without help from the Ninth Cavalry. Photo by Clarence G. Moreledge. Courtesy of the Denver Public Library.

34. Post-massacre view: The council area at Wounded Knee

This view southeast from the hilltop mass grave area and former Hotchkiss gun position shows Lakota bodies being removed from the assembly ground, where the shooting broke out as Forsyth tried to disarm the Indians. Troop B, Seventh Cavalry, took position on the far side of the road in the immediate foreground and extended to the right, beyond the centermost tipi frame. Troop K occupied a line prolonged east, near side but parallel to the topmost road. The tipi frames mark Big Foot's camping ground, where assorted bodies yet remain scattered, while the broad ravine used by the fleeing Indians is largely obscured at the far right. Courtesy of Paul Harbaugh.

35. Post-massacre view: Broad overview of the Wounded Knee ground

This view to the northwest beyond thicketed Wounded Knee Creek, above center, shows the far distant body-gathering party silhouetted on the terrain near the former Indian camp north of the dry ravine and below the snow-covered hill where the Hotchkiss guns stood on December 29, 1890. The council area where the shooting erupted is still farther to the right (at the center, above the large trees along the creek), while buildings clustered in the distance are a store and the Wounded Knee Post Office. Courtesy of Paul Harbaugh.

36. Post-massacre view: Area of the Indian camp in the field at Wounded Knee

At least three Sioux fatalities can be discerned amid the blanket clutter in the foreground of this picture of Big Foot's camp after Wounded Knee. In the near distance lie the remains of a wagon (left of the tipi frame with a soldier standing inside); other camp debris resulting from the Hotchkiss assault lies scattered over the ground. This view to the south shows the dry ravine beyond the camp where many Indians sought shelter and were killed and, at the distant left and center, the road over which the troops returned to Pine Ridge Agency with their dead and wounded. Courtesy of Paul Harbaugh.

37. Post-massacre view: The medicine man in death

The medicine man who harangued the soldiers, tossing dirt skyward during the rising dispute in the council circle, lies dead and frozen amid the rubble six days later. He and the man to his upper right have been turned over, creating their grotesquely shaped appearance, while the body to the medicine man's immediate right has apparently not yet been so disturbed. The carbine was placed by the photographer or by an assistant. Courtesy of Paul Harbaugh.

38. Post-massacre view: Destroyed wagon in gulch

When soldiers surveyed the field days after the massacre, they examined the deep ravine adjacent to Big Foot's camp where so many Lakotas perished, including whole families. This view shows a typical farm wagon destroyed by raking fire from the Hotchkiss guns, its box tossed to the side with other wreckage and human fatalities. Courtesy of Paul Harbaugh.

Gathering up the Dead at the Battle of Wounded Knee, S.D.

39. Post-massacre view: Gathering the dead

Collection of the dead for their mass burial proceeded on January 3, 1891. In this view frozen bodies are being gathered by laborers from the ravine south of the former Indian camp and placed in a wagon for transport to the grave site. An empty wagon waits, along with mounted officers watching from the north edge of the ravine. Courtesy of Paul Harbaugh.

40. Post-massacre view: Mass burial scene

Burial of the Lakotas killed at Wounded Knee occurred on January 4, 1891, when mixed-blood and Mexican workers piled at least 146 mostly frozen corpses of men, women, and children into a broad trench and covered them with earth. Contractor Paddy Starr stands at left inside the grave overseeing the undertaking, while armed infantrymen pose with workmen bearing spades at the top of the low hill from which days before Hotchkiss guns had delivered canister and shell into the Lakota camp. Courtesy of Paul Harbaugh.

41. General Colby and Lost Bird

Two weeks after Wounded Knee Brigadier General Leonard W. Colby of the Nebraska
state militia adopted one of several infants who survived the slaughter. Colby and his
wife raised the girl, Lost Bird, whose subsequent life was full of heartbreak and despair.
Through acts of utmost benevolence, however, Lost Bird today lies at peace with her
people. Courtesy of Paul Harbaugh.

42. Buffalo Bill and others in front of quartermaster office, Pine Ridge Agency

This group of Indians, army officers, and scouts is posed before the Pine Ridge Agency quartermaster office in mid-January 1891. Among those present are Chief Young Man Afraid of His Horses (in a white sheet, center) and, following to the right, Department of the Platte medical director Dallas Bache; Colonel William R. Shafter, First Infantry; Captain James C. Ayres, department chief ordnance officer; and the ubiquitous Colonel William F. ("Buffalo Bill") Cody, here representing the Nebraska National Guard. Courtesy of Paul Harbaugh.

43. Delegation to Washington, 1891

Members of the 1891 delegation to Washington, D.C., included several prominent chiefs and other figures in the events surrounding Wounded Knee. *First row, left to right:* High Hawk (Miniconjou), Fire Lightning (Oglala), Little Wound (Oglala), Two Strike (Brulé), Young Man Afraid of His Horses (Oglala), Spotted Elk (Oglala), Big Road (Oglala). *Second row:* F. D. Lewis, He Dog (Oglala), Spotted Horse (Oglala), American Horse (Oglala), George Sword (Oglala), Louis Shangrau, Baptiste Pourier. *Third row:* David Zephier, Hump (Miniconjou), High Pipe (Brulé), Fast Thunder (Oglala), the Reverend Charles S. Cook, P. T. Johnson. Photo by C. M. Bell. Courtesy of South Dakota State Historical Society.

44. The Plenty Horses trial

The trial of Plenty Horses, confessed slayer of Lieutenant Casey, ended on May 28, 1891, with an acquittal. After the trial participants posed for photographer L. T. Butterfield in Sioux Falls. *Left to right, foreground:* Tom Flood, Living Bear, Plenty Horses, and Bear That Lays Down. *Second row, sitting:* Peter Richard, Broken Arm, Jack Red Cloud, He Dog, and Philip F. Wells. *Standing:* W. B. Sterling, Captain John M. Ballance (counsel for the United States), William Rowland, White Moon, F. C. Fry, Chris Mathison, Rock Road, Mr. Thompson, George P. Nock, and D. E. Powers. Author's collection.

45. The Wounded Knee Memorial at Fort Riley, late 1890s

The Wounded Knee and Drexel Mission Memorial dedicated at Fort Riley in 1893 honored the officers and enlisted men killed at Wounded Knee and the Mission Fight. In later years the monument was modified (the large foundation and steps removed) and relocated on the post. Most of the army dead from Wounded Knee rest in the cemetery at Fort Riley. Courtesy of the Nebraska State Historical Society. (*Inset:* The memorial as it appears today at the intersection of Sheridan Road and Heubner Road, Fort Riley, Kansas. Photo courtesy of Paul L. Hedren.)

46. Senator Francis H. Case

South Dakota representative and later senator Francis Case introduced legislation in the 1930s and 1940s seeking to recompense
Lakota survivors of Wounded Knee and their descendants for
losses sustained there. Prolonged army resistance to Case's bills for
redress, together with prevailing economic realities in the midst
of the Great Depression followed by the onset of World War II,
ensured that the compensation initiative would go unfulfilled.
Courtesy of the South Dakota State Historical Society.

47. Dewey Beard and his brothers

Surviving brothers White Lance (Daniel Horn Cloud), Joseph Horn Cloud, and Dewey Beard (Iron Hail) in 1907. White Lance received four wounds and Iron Hail two, while other family members perished in the massacre at Wounded Knee. Over his long life Dewey Beard, who had also survived Little Bighorn, became an enduring symbol of the old days among the Sioux. In the twentieth century he fought to gain redress for his fellow Sioux for Wounded Knee, testifying before Congress to that end in 1938. Courtesy of the Nebraska State Historical Society.

48. The mass grave at Wounded Knee

The historic mass grave at Wounded Knee today is enclosed by a chain link fence. At the far right stands the monument raised in 1903 through the efforts of Joseph Horn Cloud and inscribed with the names of heads of families of those who were killed. At the left front is the grave and headstone for Lost Bird, reinterred at the site in 1990. The mass grave is part of the Wounded Knee Catholic community cemetery. Courtesy of Paul Harbaugh.

TWELVE

Place of the Big Killings

All people have impressions about events that have shaped them. The Lakota Sioux are no exception. Lakota testimony about the grim events of December 29, 1890 (both immediate and reminiscent statements) constitutes an important body of information. These personal insights are crucial for those who survived and for the relatives and friends of those who did not and others. Taken together, the accounts show how deadly the action became as it quickly intensified from an apparently first shooting by warriors into a defensive reaction by troops before climaxing in an unchecked and devastating slaughter of innocents. Although one might hesitate to use the word "bloodlust" to explain what happened at Wounded Knee, the term is a clear reflection of how the events must have seemed to the Indians involved, particularly noncombatant women, children, and elderly men.

Unlike their predecessors of the 1860s and 1870s in the wilds of early Dakota, Wyoming, and Montana, many in the Lakota generation who experienced Wounded Knee had known reservation life for more than two decades. Through education and day-to-day contact with whites, they had become increasingly conversant in English. Moreover, because these Lakotas were in closer physical proximity to whites, their statements were sought out and recorded. Thus Lakota survivor accounts have been gathered and accumulated since the time of the events at Wounded Knee, with their volume and content becoming ever richer. Taken together, they provide clear images of what happened from individual points of view. Redundancy of detail in these testimonies demonstrates honesty and tends to validate accuracy. Drawing on these valuable resources, the following composite narrative based on Lakota reminiscences attempts to tell the story from their perspective.[1]

After they arrived with Whitside's soldiers at Wounded Knee Creek (Cankpe Opi Wahkpala) on the night of December 28, the people grew tense. They became especially anxious when the troops placed the chain of sentinels around them. Alice Ghost Horse recalled: "My mother and I went down the creek to go to the bathroom and pick up some sticks for the fire but two soldiers were following us around and they appeared to be drunk. They were saying bad words to us. . . . Some of the young men were detailed to watch the soldier guards all night." Many did not sleep, and some felt a sense of foreboding. "All night long the soldiers had lights [lanterns] and were working at something," remembered young Paul High Back. "We could hear the noise and rattle of iron being moved around and it made us all very nervous." Lakota survivors recalled one or more Indian criers announcing the council of the men with Colonel Forsyth and telling the women to ready the wagons to start for the agency. Assembling at the designated council ground, the older men took seats in front, not far from Big Foot's army tent. The younger men grouped together toward the rear. They recalled hearing Forsyth and some of the officers asking for the Indians' guns and seeing interpreters John Shangrau and Philip Wells in the circle translating the proceedings.[2]

After the request for some of the men to return to the camp and bring back their guns, they complied and deposited twenty-five of the arms in a pile near the front of the assembly area. But the officer in charge (either Forsyth or Whitside) demanded more. Big Foot responded that they had no more guns, but the officer told him that he would have to search the camp. The ailing chief concurred. According to the Miniconjou Joseph Horn Cloud, then sixteen years old, the soldiers went to the camp: they "took sacks out of wagons and emptied them on the ground." The soldiers went into tents, he said, "and everywhere [else,] examining, picked up some old shot guns, knives, tomahawks, arrows and awls; and they searched the persons of the women." Alice Ghost Horse said of the search: "They were really rude about it, they scattered our belongings all over the ground." A Miniconjou named Long Bull insisted: "We did not want to fight. The soldiers said we must give up our guns and some of us did. I had no gun.

Then the soldiers went into the tepees and kicked the beds about and upset everything a great deal. Some Indians had guns under their blankets [at the assembly], hiding them, for an Indian thinks much of his gun. The soldiers used the Indians very roughly and made them mad, until by and by 'Sits Straight' (the medicine man) gave the signal to shoot."[3]

At length the officer called for disarming the men in the council, saying, as Horn Cloud recalled, "I want the same number of soldiers to stand in front of the Indians and take their cartridges out of their guns and cock them and aim at their foreheads and pull the triggers. After this you will be free." After this confusing statement, he told the Indians that they would proceed to Pine Ridge Agency. The threatening actions and talk stressed the men, some of whom urged the others to be courageous in the circumstances before them. Big Foot called for calm, advising that they do nothing to make the situation worse. He was so sick that he could not sit erect and had to lie down on the ground repeatedly. Horn Cloud said that Captain Wallace told him to alert the women to saddle their horses and move the wagons. Otherwise there would be trouble, because "that officer [presumably Forsyth] is half shot [drunk]." A medicine man moved around the council area, waving his arms and singing Ghost Dance songs. Indians and troops alike reported another man moving about, singing the same songs.[4]

After the main search of the camp, the soldiers had begun moving around the council area taking guns from individuals. Horn Cloud and his thirty-two-year-old brother, Iron Hail, reported that a young deaf man named Black Coyote (sometimes called Black Fox) held his gun over his head with both hands. Horn Cloud said that he was complaining that the gun "had cost him a good deal of money, that if anybody wanted it he must pay for it, for he would not give it up without pay." Two sergeants grabbed his arms, while a third wrestled the gun from him. "Just as the struggle between him and the sergeants began," Horn Cloud remembered, "someone cried: 'Look out! Look out!' These words were scarcely uttered when the gun went off elevated in the air at an angle of about 45 degrees." Instantly, Horn Cloud said, "there was a volley from the soldiers standing around the circle. These shot the men in the back." When the shooting started, Horn Cloud said, "the women ran to the ravine. The shooting was in every direction. Soldiers shot into one another. Many Indians in the circle were killed. Many of them mingled with the soldiers behind them, picking up guns from dead soldiers and taking cartridge belts. They took guns they had turned over and the cartridge belts that they had turned over with them." Iron Hail protested that the young man had intended to put his gun down and had not pointed the weapon at anyone. But "all the soldiers standing around fired at once, just like one gun," he said, and then "everybody was rolling and kicking on the ground." He added that "the soldiers were firing on the Indians & stepping backwards & firing." In the quickly diffusing smoky haze it became impossible to see anybody or anything. "There was no wind to clear it away," Horn Cloud said. "It hung like a pall over the field. Through rifts in the smoke heads and feet would be visible. Women were killed in the beginning of the fight just the same as the men were killed."[5]

In an account taken within days of Wounded Knee, a brother of Big Foot named Frog was among those hospitalized for injuries received in the melee. He was at the assembly, he said, seated near the front of the Miniconjou leader's tent. "Then a lot of soldiers got in between us (the men) and our camp, separating us (the men) from the women and children." Frog and the older men turned over their guns on request. "I saw an Indian with a gun under his blanket and the soldiers saw it at the same time, and they took it away from him," he said. Frog listened to the medicine man's incantations then pulled his blanket over his head until he heard loud talking. "I uncovered my head, and saw every one had arisen on his feet, and I heard a shot coming from where the young Indians stood. Shortly after that I was shot down, and I laid there as I fell. The firing was so fast and the smoke and dust so thick I did not see much more of the fight until it was over." Frog then heard Philip Wells speaking to those on the ground. It was Frog who made a gesture of "most bitter hatred and contempt" at the body of the medicine man.[6]

Similarly, an Oglala named Help Them, who had traveled from Cheyenne River with Big Foot's people, told how the medicine man had been performing Ghost Dance maneuvers:

He stopped, turned around facing a crowd of young Indians (who were standing together with their guns concealed under their blankets) and spoke to them, but I could not hear what they said, though I heard them all answer "How." Shortly after I heard a white man saying something in excited tones, which I could not understand, and . . . I saw some of the Indians throw off their blankets and raise their guns, [and] one of the Indians fired a shot. . . . As I turned around, I heard a few shots following the first. Then the firing began so fast, I could not tell what happened after that.[7]

Another early statement by Hehakawanyakapi (Elks Saw Him) reported much the same. He had surrendered his Winchester. A soldier was taking bullets from his cartridge belt when a gunshot sounded. He watched a warrior throw off his sheet blanket. Hehakawanyakapi hit the ground when the general shooting started. As he sprang up to run, bullets struck him in both legs. Like the other wounded, he was later treated in the makeshift ward in the Episcopal church at Pine Ridge.[8]

Private Spotted Horse, an army scout who witnessed the beginning of the encounter, said that the first shot came from a young Indian man and killed an army officer. "As soon as this shot was fired, the Indians immediately began drawing their knives and they were exhorted from all sides to desist, but this was not obeyed. Consequently, the firing began immediately on the part of the soldiers." In the account that he gave to the Oglala Black Elk, Dog Chief told of the disarmament of two armed Indians (one of them named Yellow Bird) who wore white sheets in the council, with only their eyes showing. When an officer attempted to take Yellow Bird's rifle, the gun went off as the two men wrestled on the ground. "This fellow did not want to give up his gun, and did not intend to shoot the white man at all—the gun just went off." In the fighting that followed, Dog Chief said, Yellow Bird was the man who occupied the army tent and shot several soldiers before he himself was killed and the tent was burned.[9]

High Back maintained that before the shooting began two Indians with guns were targeted by cavalry troopers who advanced to take their weapons. "Suddenly," he reported, "all the rest of the soldiers raised their guns and fired right into us." Miniconjou Andrew Good Thunder said that when Black Coyote started acting up, telling the men with guns to discard their blankets, this was reported to Big Foot. The chief "said not to do what Black Coyote advised, as he [Big Foot] expected to locate there [meaning at Pine Ridge] & didn't want any trouble." When this was repeated to Black Coyote, he threw his blanket aside "& put a cartridge into his gun & two soldiers began backing up begging him to put his gun down." Good Thunder said that Black Coyote then "shot one of the soldiers who was backing up. I saw this." Good Thunder also recalled seeing Father Craft "in the midst of us with both hands up saying something but I did not hear what. . . . We had tried to avoid trouble but it seemed that through Black

Coyote's disobedience . . . we got right into the middle of it. I was wounded in several places. My own sister was killed there. Three of my nephews were killed there. . . . I managed to run to a coulee & some of us fought our way and escaped."[10]

A mixed-blood Oglala named Zella Vespucia had carried mail from the agency to Whitside's command the previous day. As a witness to the disarmament, he said that when the proposal was finally made to search the men in the assembly "there were about twenty-one on one side who gave up their guns very peacefully":

When the soldiers stepped over to the next gang and began to disarm them there was a young man by the name of His Dog who had a gun and objected to give it up. He had been quite intimate with the medicine man. When His Dog refused to give up [his gun] he fired a shot. Then all of the rest of the Indians fired a volley before the soldiers did anything. Then some of them said, "Look out!," several times. Then one buck with a painted ghost shirt on shot and Capt. Wallace staggered back. By that time an Indian came up behind him, and taking from his hand a war club . . . struck him several blows on the cranium until he fell dead on the ground. . . . I don't say that from hearsay, but I was in the center of the fight without any arms to fight with, except a belt full of cartridges. . . . When they killed Capt. Wallace they did not cease shooting, but became all the worse. I heard a man, who after the battle I found out was Lieut. Nicholson, say two or three times: "Don't shoot squaws," and after that several others repeated the same words.[11]

In one of the most comprehensive Indian statements, Horn Cloud said of the initial shooting: "It was just like a hail-storm with shots in all directions." In the confusion, "all we thought about . . . was to get away," said High Back. "The morning was cloudy and damp and the smoke from the guns did not rise but settled right on us. From then on nothing could be seen very plain. The soldiers were rushing around shooting all of us that they could see to shoot." He was hit in the hand as he dashed blindly through the cloud. In the combat Iron Hail, armed with only a knife, sought to get a gun and rushed a soldier so closely the man fired his carbine right next to the warrior's ear, momentarily deafening him. In the rising smoke the Indian yanked the gun away, stabbing the man. He grabbed Iron Hail by the throat before the Lakota knifed him repeatedly until he died. Iron Hail then took the gun and sprinted toward the ravine behind the camp. He was wounded before he got there, however, with an injury that severely debilitated his right arm. He finally shot a soldier but received a flesh wound in the leg as he entered the gulch. Others who broke through the soldiers raced with the women and children into the ravine and then ran in either direction. Iron Hail encountered soldiers and other fleeing Indians several times as he headed west up the dry wash, where he ultimately witnessed his own mother killed. "Soldiers on both sides of the ravine shot at her and killed her." Iron Hail saw "lots of women and children lying along the ravine, some alive and some dead." He told some young men to "take courage and do all they could to defend the women," but "an awful fire was concentrated on them now and nothing could be seen for the smoke. In the bottom of the ravine the bullets raised more dust than there was smoke, so that they could not see one another." Horn Cloud recalled that some with babies excavated hollows inside the ravine in which to hide them. Women and infants were killed together. "One mother lay dead," he said, "her breast covered with blood from her wound, and her little child was standing by her and nursing."[12]

Lakota survivor accounts of the furious action inside the council area are scarce. Many if not most of the Sioux men present were killed in that circle. Only those warriors who broke through the soldier cordon at the breach between Troops K and B and lived or already lay wounded on the field were able to describe how the fighting began. Beyond the thunderous explosion of the initial firing, which many of the people in the area of the Sioux camp clearly recalled hearing, most other survivor accounts described the action as it gravitated to the big ravine and beyond, where soldier targeting of noncombatants intensified.

Alice Ghost Horse remembered the cavalrymen "shooting at every Lakota who was running and it didn't matter if you were a child or woman. They shot you anyway. . . . We fled into the ravines where the plum bushes were the thickest and dived in like frightened rabbits. The gun fire was pretty heavy and people were hollering for their children and children were crying everywhere." Her father went back to help the others but soon returned wounded in the leg. He took Ghost Horn's young brother and moved down the ravine, telling her and her mother that he would return for them. "Soon afterwards my father came crawling back . . . and said 'they killed my son' and started to cry so we cried a little bit. . . . My father said we should move to a better hiding place but my mother objected again, saying we should all die here together. She told me to stand up so I did but my father pulled me down." They crawled to a deeper part of the ravine, then Ghost Horse's father left again to help others. More people took shelter in the ravine. "Four of them died right there, but there was nothing anybody could do," Ghost Horse said. One man who arrived "told us that my father was killed instantly. We all cried for a little bit because the soldiers were still firing their rifles at anything that moved." Ghost Horse and her mother remained hidden in the brush in the deep recesses of the ravine until late afternoon when the sounds of gunfire slackened.[13]

The wounded High Back also made it to the ravine, where he sought safety by crawling beneath the bodies of other casualties. Still, he took more bullets. Peter One Skunk, struck in the head by a bullet during the soldiers' opening volley, also made his way to the ravine and hid. He eventually caught a horse and broke free from the turmoil. When his horse was killed, One Skunk played dead and was left alone by the troops. In time he caught another horse and got away.

Elsewhere, as the action continued, some of those who headed west in the ravine found protection in the acre-sized gulch area known as the "pocket." They included Horn Cloud, several of his brothers, and several cousins, along with two old men, a woman named Helena Long Bull, and her small son. One brother, William Horn Cloud, was killed in the pocket. Several more received wounds there, and one named White Lance was badly injured but subsequently recovered. Iron Hail said that he killed at least five soldiers while in the pocket. When the soldiers brought a Hotchkiss gun forward to fire directly at these people, it became "a storm of thunder and hail." "There went up from these dying people," he said,

a medley of death songs that would make the hardest heart weep. . . . The death song is expressive of their wish to die. . . . It expresses that the singer is anxious to die, too. At this time I am unable to do anything more, and I took a rest, telling my brothers to keep up courage. The cannon were pouring in their shots and breaking down the banks which were giving protection. . . . The soldiers were pretty close to the edge of the bank and these kept up a continual fire . . . . Even if there was no more shooting, the smoke was so thick that the wounded could not live for it; it was suffocating. The Hotchkiss had been shooting rapidly and one Indian had got killed by it. His body was penetrated in the pit of the stomach by a Hotchkiss shell, which tore a hole through his body six inches in diameter. The man was insensible, but breathed for an hour when he expired. At the same time this man was shot, a young woman . . . was shot through between the shoulders. . . . [I] heard a laugh and looked at her and she was smiling, all unconscious that she was wounded. The next moment a young man was shot down right in front of this woman. When the man fell, his bow and arrows fell all around on the ground.[14]

Regaining his strength, Iron Hail soon moved farther up in the pocket. He found women and children, all wounded, in a pit dug to protect them from the troopers shooting at them from above. "In this same place," he recounted, "was a young woman with a pole in hand and a black blanket on it. When she would raise it up the soldiers would whistle and yell and pour volleys into it." Recalling his own baby, Iron Hail told the women that he would fight for them, that he did not care if he died there, "for the infants were all killed now, and he would like to die among the infants." He managed to shoot and kill yet another soldier and to knock one more from his horse. Iron Hail stayed in the pocket for a time. But as the sun went down he cautiously crept out and got away as soldiers intermittently fired at him from distant points.[15]

In the meantime Joseph Horn Cloud had somehow escaped from the pocket. He related how many women and children ran north and then west along Fast Horse Road. They became targets for nearby cavalrymen, who killed some there; others managed to traverse a nearby fenced field, where more were shot down. Horn Cloud moved fluidly through the area and collected numerous horses that he distributed to others to aid their escape. He fought troops to the west and overheard the arrival of the Pine Ridge Indians, who managed to free the prisoners captured from the pocket and took some of them back to the agency. Several captives raced back to the ravine, where soldiers killed three of them. Iron Hail also encountered several of the Pine Ridge Oglalas on horses and went with them, soon meeting his brother Horn Cloud, who told him that his father was also dead. Of eleven family members at Wounded Knee, Horn Cloud and Iron Hail lost their mother (Yellow Leaf) and father (a headman named Horned Cloud); and two brothers (Sherman and William). Iron Hail lost his wife (Wears Eagle, also known as White Face), killed at the scene, and would lose his infant son, Wet Feet, who within a short time would die from illness contracted during the massacre. Iron Hail's cousin, Pretty Enemy, who lived with the family, also died there. Iron Hail suffered two wounds in the fighting, while another brother, Daniel, received four. Iron Hail and Horn Cloud proceeded west from the upheaval at Wounded Knee to a point near the mission and then headed north to join the Stronghold people along White Clay Creek as they withdrew from the agency area. When they arrived, those people were crying and singing death songs and shook hands with them. As night descended at Wounded Knee, small knots of surviving Lakotas made their way north through draws and creek bottoms in the gathering chill.[16]

Other Lakotas present that day offered their own observations. A man named White Lance (no relation to Horn Cloud and Iron Hail) also told of the gathering of the men and the pile of surrendered guns that accrued near the center of the assembly:

> It was understood that just as soon as all the guns were stacked in the center we were to continue on to Pine Ridge Agency. Big Foot was placed right in the doorway of the tent and I stood right to his left side. I could see that there was commotion among the soldiers and I saw on looking back they had their guns in position ready to fire. There were two officers in the center; the one that was standing to the left gave a command in a loud voice, then [after the initial outburst of shooting] we couldn't see anything for smoke. The smoke was so dense I couldn't see anything so I didn't make a move, just stood there. When it cleared up a little . . . I saw Big Foot lying down with blood on his forehead and his head to the right side. . . . I went a little ways then. I was knocked down. I was unconscious for a little while. I was shot then and wounded and I went to this little wide cut bank [the ravine?] and there I found that we were surrounded by soldiers. Some [of us were] already wounded, some dead, but [they] continued to fire on us. . . . I stayed there all day with these young fellows, boys then, and since then I have been unable to use my left arm but I struggled along.[17]

When the shooting started at the council ground, twelve-year-old James Pipe on Head had just delivered tobacco to Big Foot, his ailing grandfather, who was prostrate in the center of the circle. The old chief had just told the boy to return to his grandmother in the camp. At the eruption of firing, "I started to run towards the hillside [on the west]," Pipe on Head said. "I came across a little boy. I took the little boy by the hand and all at once someone came on the side of me and took hold of my hand. This woman was my mother. She had a baby on her back, my sister, but this girl that she was carrying . . . was shot. While we were running we saw on the ground dust flying [and] some of the bullets struck near us." But James and his mother managed to escape and survived.[18]

Rough Feather, who was about twenty-two at Wounded Knee, remembered looking back and seeing the soldiers aiming their guns at the men in the assembly. "It sounded much the sound of tearing canvass, when they fired," he said. "As I heard the crash I became unconscious. Something struck me. As I was standing there I happened to look up and the smoke was awfully dense, but I could now make out a face right in front of me." Rough Feather followed the man, who soon engaged a soldier hand-to-hand in trying to bolt through the troops to reach the ravine. Another soldier struck Rough Feather in the chest with his carbine, painfully wounding him. But the warrior broke through toward the ravine before a man named Ghost Bear urged him to lie down on the flat where many of the men as well as women had fallen. After the firing ceased, Rough Feather heard Philip Wells, the interpreter known as the Fox, speak to those on the ground: "All of you that are still alive get up and come on over, you will not be molested or shot at any more." Fearful, Rough Feather lay still until Wells repeated the directive. Then Rough Feather got up and helped load a wagon with wounded from the scene, including one that he believed was the wife of Big Foot.[19]

Another survivor was Medicine Woman, a Lakota also known as Mrs. Mousseau, who was in the camp when the soldiers ransacked it looking for guns and other weapons. When the shooting broke out, "the smoke was awful thick," she recalled.[20] "I was wounded at the first fire, but I was so scared I did not feel it. My husband was killed there and my little girl, and a little boy baby on my back was [also] killed by a bullet which also broke my elbow, so that I dropped the body." As she and her mother sought to escape, they carried a dead child with them. All of this occurred as they fled through the camp toward the ravine. "The soldiers followed us up and kept firing," Medicine Woman said. She and her mother ascended the dry ravine but eventually turned back and returned to Wounded Knee Creek. They moved downstream, where they spent the night in a snowstorm before taking shelter for two days in a shack. "We didn't have anything to eat or drink and we were found in that condition by the Indian Scouts [*sic*] and were taken to the Agency."[21]

A youth named Edward Owl King, like so many others, fled west up the ravine after the shooting started. "There were some ponies, women and children shot down and scattered, and while running I stepped on them." He gained the pocket, which "wasn't a very deep place, and that was where many of the Indians were shot and killed. I was shot too, but did not die." Owl King reported that a soldier pulled him out of the pocket, but troops again fired at him when he and others began ascending a hill. Another Indian rescued him, taking him into a deep recess, where he remained until dark. "I was a boy, my sister and mother were killed. I was the only survivor of the family."[22]

Other women participants included Nellie Knife and Mrs. Rough Feather. Nellie Knife was packing that morning while the men attended the council. "All at once I heard an awful noise. As the shots were fired the women and children ran for a safe place to hide. I ran toward the flat and as I ran I saw many people were already killed. I was running with a young girl named Brown Ear Horse, but she got shot so I went on and left her." She passed the wife of One Skunk, who was also wounded and screaming. "I could not help her as the bullets were flying thick and I wanted to get to a safe place. . . . After the firing stopped . . . I returned to see if I could find any of my people. My mother-in-law, my sister-in-law and many brothers were dead. . . . My father-in-law, Little Bull, was alive but his leg was broken."[23] Likewise, after the gunfire opened Mrs. Rough Feather saw "nearly all the people on the ground bleeding." In sheer terror, she ran for safety with the others to the ravine south of the camp, following them up the gulch while "bullets flew all around us. . . . I was not hit one time, [but] my father, my mother, my grandmother, my older brother and my younger brother were all killed. My son who was two years old was shot in the mouth [and] that later caused his death."[24]

When young Henry Jackson heard the initial crash of guns, he and his mother had just been loading a wagon in the camp. They began running as a bullet hit her in the head, killing her instantly. Jackson's sister, running ahead, came back for him. They started into the large ravine that was filling with fleeing people and moved up the gulch with the crowd until they were helped out. "I have never said anything about this," said Jackson. "I didn't like to on account of my mother who was shot right with me and it appears that it just happened this morning [ca. 1936–37]; it makes me feel sad."[25]

Like so many others, John Little Finger, also known as Yellow Horn, rushed to reach protection in the big ravine. "When I reached the ravine

. . . there was [*sic*] a lot of Indians following [west] up the ravine and I was with them, and on each side . . . soldiers were shooting down on us until we got so far we couldn't go any further, as a line of soldiers got in front of us." These people took refuge in the washout called the pocket, where the soldiers continued shooting at them until Indian scouts called to them to come out. Most of them then submitted. Little Finger, however, had been shot in the leg and foot and instead crawled some distance before emerging on a flat of land. He spotted the mounted warriors from Pine Ridge Agency who had responded to the distant shooting. As the soldiers headed east, Little Finger got away with those Indians and was taken to the agency, away from the day's horror.[26]

Some participants provided focused data on one or more aspects of their time at Wounded Knee. Nearly all Lakota accounts allude to the density of smoke in the assembly area at the outbreak of shooting. Peter Stand remembered how unbearably incapacitating it became and how many of the Indians benefited from the concealing cloud. "As the volley was flying into us, we couldn't see anything—everything was smoking from then on; this valley was just covered with smoke, so I didn't see anything. Right after the volley was fired, I heard somebody bellow in Indian for them to throw themselves flat on the ground, so I did as he announced." Stand soon after got lost in the smoke as he tried to orient himself to the camp. He ran into one person then another before reaching the camp and the ravine, where he and others dug a trench. There he stayed for the duration of the shooting. After the soldiers left, he and other survivors started west up the ravine on foot.[27]

Many accounts cite the upper ravine as promising early shelter from the soldiers' guns as well as a means to get away from the opening turmoil to reach potential hiding places. The ravine also served eventually as a lifeline to any help that might arrive from Pine Ridge, such as those warriors who managed to get away with the captured women and children. Charley Blue Arm said that the "cannons on the hill . . . were firing at the Indians that were trying to escape, and the bullets hit the dirt all around us and, of course, that made us run faster, for we knew that they were trying to kill all of us." Blue Arm reached the ravine and moved up it to a point "where the bullets could not reach us." He said that the people lay concealed there "all day until the sun went down." When the soldiers were gone, "we went out to hunt for our people." He added: "We were all tired out and frightened and besides we were worried about our relatives."[28]

Elaine Goodale remembered that she and several teachers were preparing presents and candy bags for the children at the Episcopal church in Pine Ridge Agency that morning. A muted "distant thunder" abruptly "sent cold shivers down our backs," she remembered. "Within an incredibly short time came first reports of the slaughter at Wounded Knee. We were told, indeed, that the cavalry had been cut off from reaching us and that we were at the mercy of a maddened horde of Indians!"[29]

Among others at the agency who heard the muffled sound of discharging Hotchkiss guns was the Oglala Black Elk. "I knew from the sound that it must be wagon-guns (cannon) going off." As the shooting persisted, he donned the ghost shirt that he had earlier fashioned, with a flaming rainbow and red lightning streaks. He painted his face red, placed an eagle feather in his hair, and started for Wounded Knee. He took no weapon, only his sacred bow, which made him impervious to bullets. As he rode from the agency, Black Elk drew a number of companions to him. After a while they reached a high ridge, from which they saw in the distance the area with the ravine cutting the terrain. The Hotchkiss guns still blazed away. They could see troops posted about the high ground while others fired at the people in the gulch. Black Elk's party saw women with children—those who had emerged from the pocket—clustered under a bank with cavalry guarding them. Out of sight, the warriors sang a song of courage before charging directly toward the soldiers, who fired at them and fled. The warriors rescued the women and children and sent them to safety. Black Elk by himself, in a measure of his bravery, later charged the soldiers, who fired many bullets at him. "I ran my horse right close to them, and then swung around. Some soldiers across the gulch began shooting at me too, but I got back to the others and was not hurt at all." He added: "I had to hold my bow in front of me in the air to be bullet-proof but just as I had gotten over the hill after completing my charge, I let my bow down and I could feel some bullets passing through my ghost dance shirt near my hip."[30]

Soon more Lakotas from the agency appeared. All the warriors charged the troops, who fell back along the high ground. As Black Elk recalled,

> We followed down along the dry gulch. . . . Dead and wounded women and children and little babies were scattered all along there where they had been trying to run away. The soldiers had followed along the gulch, as they ran, and murdered them. . . . Sometimes they were in heaps because they had huddled together, and some were scattered along.

Sometimes bunches of them had been killed and torn to pieces where the wagon guns hit them. . . . There were two little boys at one place in this gulch [actually the boys were about fifteen years old]. They had guns and they had been killing soldiers all by themselves. We could see the soldiers they had killed. The boys were all alone there and they were not hurt. These were very brave little boys.[31]

After the army command pulled out with the dead and wounded soldiers and wounded Lakotas, Black Elk and the others returned to help and to survey the scene. "Men and women and children were heaped and scattered all over the flat at the bottom of the little hill where the soldiers had their wagon-guns, and westward up the dry gulch all the way to the high ridge, the dead women and children and babies were scattered." Black Elk, his heart heavy from what he had seen, returned to the vicinity of Pine Ridge Agency then followed down White Clay Creek to reach the Oglalas who had departed that day. He and a companion, Red Crow, brought with them two babies that they had rescued at Wounded Knee.[32]

When it was finally over, and the cavalrymen started away with lumbering wagons and ambulances bearing casualties from Wounded Knee, those Lakotas who were still alive and able to move picked themselves up and helped others off the field. Among them were Alice Ghost Horse and her mother as well as High Back. They had hidden for hours in dense thickets at the bottom of the large dry ravine. Stepping around bodies of people and animals and listening to those weeping and crying for relatives and water, they found their way to Wounded Knee Creek and started north through the cold and uncertain night. High Back recalled finding several women and children, some of them wounded. The survivors agreed to split into three groups so that they would not all be found together if the soldiers came back. The party traveling with Alice Ghost Horse and her mother numbered about thirteen. On the morning of December 30 the group paused on a hill to rest beneath wind-driven clouds now threatening a storm. Boys nearby spied approaching riders, which sent the people scrambling into coulees, but the riders proved to be Lakotas. On their arrival, they all shook hands and cried together. A woman offered dried meat to the riders, who had not eaten in over a day. They pressed on to the northwest as wind and storm clouds graduated into a blizzard, forcing the group into a vacant cabin. There they built a fire and stayed warm through the night. The next day they advanced through blowing snow, making their way toward the secure and impervious highlands. Eventually they came upon a mixed village of Brulés and Oglalas that included the Ghost Dance stalwart Short Bull.

On the day of the massacre Short Bull and his immediate followers were moving south up White Clay Creek on the trail of those from the Stronghold who had preceded them in going into the agency. His people also had heard the shooting of the Hotchkiss guns far to the east. As they caught up with the others near the Holy Rosary Mission, they learned the shocking news that Big Foot's band had been wiped out. Short Bull's own cousin Many Wounds, who had fled the scene, appeared in the village with a gunshot wound to his shoulder. After most of the Stronghold Indians began withdrawing from the vicinity of the agency and the mission amid continuing reports of the slaughter, Short Bull and his followers rode the next morning to Wounded Knee, where they were among the first to inspect the site. Short Bull located an uncle who had been wounded, and his people collected forty injured survivors. They placed some in a vacant building, from which other Indians retrieved them for medical help at the agency. Salvaging discarded farm wagons, Short Bull returned with the others to his camp, where Alice Ghost Horse and her party soon joined them. Those traveling with High Back also met some of the Stronghold people, who came out to see what was happening. "They were very angry and in a very hostile mood," Ghost Horse recalled. "They took care of us and took us over to their camp."[33]

Through their individual and family perspectives, Lakota accounts dramatically personalize the events at Wounded Knee. They impart important knowledge of how individuals and groups reacted, interacted, succumbed, and endured. These accounts amplify and sometimes correct conclusions found in government documents. Most of all, they add strength and a broader dimension and provide empathy. They describe all aspects of the experience, from the night of the Indians' arrival to the morning council and multiple searches for weapons, the outbreak of shooting, the killing on the plain and in the dry ravine, the opening of the Hotchkiss guns and the fighting in the pocket, the departure of soldiers from the field, the exodus of survivors, and the arrival of others not immediately involved. They add context, emphasis, and depth to the story of Wounded Knee.

In his own research on Wounded Knee, the avocational historian Walter M. Camp, after lengthy interviews and correspondence with tribal participants, offered succinct thoughts about how the situation in the assembly area managed to evolve into a massacre. His conclusions afford something of a window into Lakota views of the event in the early twentieth century:

The Ind[ian]s say that, as a whole, they were not inclined to resist giving up guns. When the soldiers were disarming [them] just before firing began, it was the intention generally to give up the guns & they were doing so. There were, however, among them two discontented Ind[ian]s who kept up an agitation to resist, but they had no sympathy from the rest of the Ind[ian]s, and several times they were told to keep still. Nevertheless those two kept declaring that they would not surrender their guns and they were very bitter to see that the rest were doing so, and they could not be made to keep still. One of them kept calling out in a loud voice (the one whom the white men took for a medicine man) and throwing dirt on his shoulders. He had a gun cocked under his blanket and a knife, and when, at length, a soldier came up to search him, he drew his gun and shot the soldier through, and then began cutting with his knife. The fight then started generally. These two loud Ind[ian]s were both wild from ghost dancing, and the one who fired the shot was known to be temporarily insane if not permanently so. The Ind[ian]s blame no one but themselves for starting the fight. The two Ind[ian]s referred to were the cause of it. They blame the soldiers for wanton killing. The gatling gun [*sic*: Hotchkiss guns] was turned on the lodges, killing women and children, who were entirely innocent and knew nothing of what was taking place where the disarming was going on. As soon as the firing commenced they tried to get away and many were killed on the flat south of the battlefield while driving off in wagons. A squaw with a baby on her back was killed on the road to the agency 1¼ miles from the battlefield.[34]

Despite whatever variances and vagaries may exist among the Indian and army participant accounts, somewhere within them lies the truth of Wounded Knee. While the record left by the soldiers and their officers frequently relates a bureaucratic slant, it is often legitimized by the personal tribal views. Within both sets of accounts, all aspects of what we know about Wounded Knee are exposed, from horrific beginning to tragic end. Discrepancies between army and Indian accounts mainly concern the outbreak of shooting in the assembly or council area. Few known Lakota statements mention the throwing aside of blankets by armed warriors at the inception of the shooting—probably because the majority of warriors in the council area were killed by the soldiers in the outburst of gunfire. Many if not most Lakota recollections came from women and other noncombatants (many of them children at the time) who stood outside the council area, at the edge of the camp, or elsewhere behind the cordon of soldiers of Troops B and K of the Seventh Cavalry. Consequently, their firsthand perception of the action began with the shooting, ultimately directed toward and into the camp itself. Sadly, we have no Indian statements regarding the heartrending killings of Elk Creek's wife and children on White Horse Creek northwest of Wounded Knee, which at least symbolically constituted the closing action. It was unquestionably a carryover of the slaughter five miles back. Beyond Lieutenant Godfrey and the men who committed that desolately conspicuous deed, no witnesses survived.

Of the 370 or so Lakota people arrested by Major Whitside east of Porcupine Butte and escorted to Wounded Knee, as many as 200 and perhaps more certainly died violently there or at another place from wounds received (a large number of others apparently received wounds and survived). Within days 146 bodies were gathered and hastily interred. After December 29 family members retrieved others for burial elsewhere. Shortly thereafter fourteen more bodies (including those succumbing from wounds at the Episcopal church) boosted the total of positively known dead to 160. While an official army report the following February raised the likely number to 200, the final tally might indeed have been higher. Nor were all the dead Sioux on the site interred on January 3–4; as late as January 12, a Sixth Cavalry private at the scene beheld "old and young of both sexes that were not [yet] buried." Efforts to chronicle the names and exact number of fatalities have proceeded over the ensuing decades. Yet beyond the figures cited above and well-considered approximations, the precise number of Lakotas killed at Wounded Knee has been—and remains—impossible to determine. As survivor John Little Finger, a grandson of Big Foot, noted, whatever the total, the day's events rendered Wounded Knee "the Place of the Big Killings."[35]

THIRTEEN

Direct Corollaries

As rumors and excitement swept through Pine Ridge Agency on the morning of December 29, General Brooke quickly telegraphed the unsettling news of Wounded Knee to General Miles's headquarters in Rapid City. Miles relayed it to his staff and subordinates in the field and notified the adjutant General in Washington. When Brooke told Miles of the Indians stampeding west from the agency, the division commander redoubled his orders to have troops occupy the Stronghold to prevent Short Bull, Kicking Bear, and their compatriots retaking it. Late that day Brooke, alarmed over Colonel Henry's whereabouts, sent a courier to warn him of a possible Indian attack: "Take every precaution and do not allow your command to be scattered. Use your scouts and be sure to avoid disaster." Miles did not yet know the gravity of what had happened at Wounded Knee, but he sensed that its occurrence just as the Stronghold occupiers at last verged on submission—in his words—only "prolonged the disturbance and made a successful termination more difficult." As more information became available, Agent Royer wired Commissioner Morgan that 300 Indians and several soldiers had been killed at Wounded Knee. Miles posted himself at the telegraph office in Rapid City to learn every particular of the event that he could from Brooke. He wanted to know casualty figures for both sides, numbers of those who escaped, and the direction in which they had gone. He also wanted to know more about the attack on Pine Ridge Agency.[1]

Miles later wired details of the affair to the adjutant general in Washington, telling him that many of the Indians had fled. "Last night everything looked favorable for getting all the Indians under control," he said; but "since [the] report from Forsyth, it looks more serious than at any time." With Brooke's concurrence, Miles prepared to send troops to guard the settlements along the upper Cheyenne River and in the southeastern Black Hills. He placed other troops to flank any movements by Indians in that direction.[2]

Much of Miles's knee-jerk planning went unfulfilled as more information came to bear. In the end he settled on his previous course, pressing components of his command toward and along the White River to force fleeing Indians back toward the agency and to keep them from moving north and west. Already Colonels Carr and Offley were maneuvering their troops toward the White. Colonel Sanford and others would join the effort, patrolling south and east of the upper Cheyenne as they advanced toward the White River and the agency. Colonels Sumner and Merriam would maintain their earlier positions along the lower Cheyenne to intercept any Indians breaking southwest. After briefly considering a move directly overland to Pine Ridge Agency, Miles made arrangements to leave Rapid City by train late on December 30. He would assume direct command at Pine Ridge Agency the following day. Clearly frustrated by the turn of events, he confided to his wife: "All my efforts to prevent a war appear to have been destroyed by the action of Lt. Col. Sumner and Col. Forsyth. That affair of the Seventh Cavalry is yet a mystery. It has placed over 3,000 Indians in a hostile attitude and it may result in a serious campaign. Forsyth's reports have been very indefinite and misleading." He squelched as premature a telegram from Schofield praising the Seventh Cavalry's "splendid conduct," and the commanding general presently withdrew it after clarification.[3]

Apprehension gripped Pine Ridge Tuesday morning following a long night in which random whoops and rifle shots jolted pickets awake. During reveille Brooke announced the loss from heart failure of popular captain William Mills, Second Infantry, whose striker had found him in his tent "in a kneeling position by the bed stone dead." Medical personnel at headquarters struggled to complete an accurate list of casualties to wire to Fort Riley. Officers' wives there were said to be almost frantic. At 6 A.M. Major Henry rode in with Troops F, I, and K, Ninth Cavalry, following their scouting venture. They settled into their old camp, having traveled more than eighty miles since the morning of December 29, including a visit to the vacated

Stronghold, which officers described as "an absurd place" where the vaunted entrenchments amounted to but "a few flimsy piles of dirt." After receiving word of Wounded Knee from Brooke, Henry led a forced march that evening, hoping to avoid attack. Traveling through a cold moonless night, they sought to reach the agency forty miles away. Henry's thirty-two-wagon baggage train, under Captain John S. Loud, had Troop D as an advance guard, but it fell more than an hour behind the remainder of the squadron. Sensing opportunity, a large band of warriors struck the train about two miles northeast of the agency along the road leading southwest from Cheyenne Creek near the ford off Wolf Creek. Roughly halfway between the Holy Rosary Mission and the agency, the Indians killed one member of the advance guard. Loud quickly deployed his first platoon along a ridge in front of them. "For a few minutes it was hot," Loud recalled, "but D Troop just did itself proud and the Indians soon withdrew." Loud strengthened his position with material from the train and sent a courier, who reached the agency at about 8 A.M. to report the attack.[4]

Amid the sound of "Boots and Saddles," Henry and his men, some on horses not yet saddled, raced out to relieve the train together with Forsyth and both Seventh Cavalry squadrons, sending a few gunshots and rounds from the Hotchkiss piece as they went. First Sergeant Ragnar of Troop K of the Seventh said that one of the Hotchkiss shells knocked two Indians from their ponies. "Both men and steeds tumbled down," he said, "torn to pieces by the splinter[s]. It was an excellent shot at the distance of two thousand feet." Having dared approach so close to the agency, the Indians (suspected to be Two Strike's followers) soon departed. The troops escorted the wagons the rest of the way to the agency. The dead soldier was believed shot "by an Indian dressed in the uniform of a cavalry soldier, with the yellow lining of his overcoat boldly displayed over his back." However the Indian was dressed, the attack on the wagon train clearly revealed the Lakotas' mounting outrage over the previous day's slaughter at Wounded Knee.[5]

The Indians' anger proved combustible. Less than an hour later, "Boots and Saddles" again sounded, eliciting "curses not only deep but loud" from the troops as columns of rising smoke to the north told of the two-year-old mission being under attack. Major Henry begged off, owing to the worn condition of his command. Forsyth and the Seventh, with Whitside and Captain Ilsley leading the squadrons and accompanied by a mule-drawn Hotchkiss gun of Capron's Light Battery E, galloped four miles north to learn that Brulés had set two log schoolhouses and some empty Indian cabins ablaze—perhaps as a ploy to draw the troops into an ambush. As the soldiers ate lightly of proffered fare at the mission, Forsyth consulted with authorities there and sent word to Brooke of the findings, telling him that Henry's command was not needed. But as Forsyth prepared to start back, "Little Bat" Garnier, who was with the scouts of the advance guard, informed him of loud shooting by heavy guns farther down the broad valley of White Clay Creek. The colonel, spotting more smoke to the northwest and aware that Colonel Sanford's troops were operating near White River in that direction, sent a hurried request for Henry's assistance. At about 11:30 A.M. Forsyth galloped northwest a mile to ascertain the source of the gunfire and to seek out the Brulés and Oglalas believed to have ignited the buildings. Soon after Forsyth's departure, about a dozen warriors going to the nearby White Bird camp passed by and fired random shots at the mission.[6]

As Forsyth advanced with his command, the plain narrowed considerably. Across a dilapidated bridge Lieutenant Preston's ten Lakota scouts soon flushed some fifty warriors from hills and ravines at the right and left front. The advance guard and units of Major Whitside's first squadron (Troops A, B, I, and K) quickly drove the Indians away. But within minutes a larger body appeared on hills to the southwest and opened fire on the command, momentarily diverting the troops. Soon shots came from other directions as well. Fearing possible attack from the rear, Forsyth managed to deploy his squadrons (Ilsley with Troops C, D, E, and G on the left; Whitside, with Troops A, B, I, and K on the right) along a ridge crest in front (northwest) and advanced them in extended skirmish order. Anticipating still more resistance, the colonel now dispatched a message directing Henry to "report here to me as soon as possible. Am about two (2) miles beyond the mission. One soldier wounded now." Soon afterward he sent another message and then dispatched Lieutenant Preston, who met Henry en route and told him that "the 7th were in a bad fix—to hurry up." The two sides exchanged brisk long-range shooting over the next hour. At one point several men of Troop D started to the rear for ammunition. As they returned, Private Jesse G. Harris wrote that Captain Henry J. Nowlan of Troop I "asked me where we were going, and the men carrying the boxes told him Captain Moylan [had] ordered them to take it to A Troop." When Nowlan directed them to turn it over to him, the men hesitated. "The Captain pointed his .45 Colt at them, and they left the boxes. . . . We found out afterwards that half his men had only one round of ammunition [left]."[7]

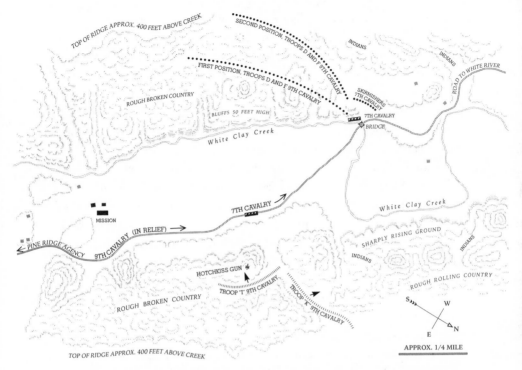

Map 6. The Mission Fight, December 30, 1890. Map by Robert G. Pilk.

Forsyth found maneuver difficult. He was in a natural cul-de-sac, confined by towering pine-covered ridges enclosing a thicketed terrain with wire fences. Small parties of Indians fired fleetingly on his men, only to vanish and redirect fire against either his flank or his rear. On Forsyth's left, Ilsley's four troops faced west and south, having taken sharp fire from those directions. On his right, warriors occupied a commanding hill that the colonel had targeted as well as several scattered log buildings in the area. The protracted exchange accounted for several army casualties. Capron's Hotchkiss piece in the meantime sparingly lobbed percussion shell at parties of Sioux negotiating hills from 800 to 3,000 yards away on either side of the valley. After a time Forsyth consulted with several of his officers and then directed the orderly retirement of his squadrons and artillery. Their position had been precarious. As First Sergeant Ragnar of Troop K later summed it up: "A sure thing is that before long we were exposed to cross-fire. . . . Unless we wanted to be shot down we had to abandon our positions; to advance was impossible. Thus we retired step by step during which my new troop leader,

Lieutenant Mann, was mortally wounded, whereupon I took command of the troop." Private Clarence Allen of Troop G of Ilsley's squadron recollected that as the command pulled back, "some of the boys were inclined to walk fast enough to get out of line and, when one would, you would hear some of the good ones give him a good cussing out to stay in line." Father Jutz watched the unfolding action from the mission more than a mile away. Seeing the troops in apparent retreat, he hurried off a note to Brooke telling him of Forsyth's predicament and need for prompt assistance.[8]

Major McCormick reported later that Forsyth strove to extricate Whitside's command first, "leaving Ilsley's squadron in position until Whitside could occupy one in rear, when Ilsley was to withdraw to the rear of Whitside." But the movement encouraged the Indians. Owning the high ground, they continually outflanked Forsyth on the ridges dominating either side of the valley. Over Whitside's objection, Captain Varnum raced his men up a steep rise to cover the withdrawal of Troop A then gradually pulled back after an intensive exchange with warriors. Private Walter R. Crickett remembered:

> We . . . had orders to mount, but had scarcely left our position when they seemed to spring up out of the ground. The hills was [sic] alive with them, and it [firing] commenced in real earnest. Such confusion you never saw. . . . After some pretty hot fighting we drove them back and commenced a steady retreat. . . . The man [Private Dominic Francischetti] that was killed we had to leave behind, as [we] was hard pushed. . . . When the body was recovered two [sic: seven] days later, he was horible [sic] mutilated, his hands, ears, [and] nose cut off, scalp gone and eyes full of [gun]powder. It was a shocking sight to see.[9]

Although Ilsley's troops helped cover the withdrawal, Forsyth doubtless welcomed the arrival of Henry's squadron at 1:30 P.M. with yet another Hotchkiss gun. "Colonel Henry [was] in the lead, every Trooper yelling like a mad-man, their horses at full speed," wrote Private Comfort of the First Artillery. (En route near the mission, Henry's command had encountered many of Forsyth's led horses rushing by uncontrollably with Lieutenant Robinson in pursuit.) Henry described Forsyth's position as "in a sort of pocket, north of [the] bridge. Indians were in the ravines and houses firing on them. To retreat they would have had to pass a narrow gorge commanded at all points." Troops D and F of the Ninth, under Captains John S. Loud and Clarence A. Stedman, respectively, dismounted and charged the high ridges southwest of the bridge and deployed there. Troops I and K, under Captain Henry H. Wright and Lieutenant Alexander W. Perry, assumed similar stations on the southeast. Wright and Perry bolstered Second Lieutenant John L. Hayden's fast-shooting Hotchkiss gun, placed atop a commanding knoll to target warriors occupying the houses and ravines in front and to keep others from assembling. Fire from this Hotchkiss and these troops eventually drove the Indians away. "Between *you and me*," Captain Loud wrote his wife later that day, "the 7th had got in a very tight fix—and we brought them out." In sum, the soldiers of the Ninth managed to drive back the Indians on the adjoining heights and protect Forsyth's retirement. Wrote Crickett: "I think . . . if it hadn't of been for the 9th Cav it would of gone very hard with us, as we was completely surrounded." When the Lakotas pulled away within half an hour of Henry's arrival, the Seventh retired without further incident. The action closed about 3 P.M. The men reached Pine Ridge Agency an hour later to find soldiers of the Second Infantry on the point of moving to their assistance. As Major Henry calculated his relief movement, "the zeal of action of officers and men—and the hearty cheers given by the 9th after every successful Hotchkiss shot—had I believe an enhancing effect upon the 7th and a corresponding demoralizing effect upon the Indians."[10]

Miles was clearly disappointed on learning of the so-called Mission (or White Clay Creek) Fight. It only intensified the bad feelings among the Lakotas in the immediate wake of Wounded Knee. "These two affairs," he concluded, ". . . seriously complicated the situation and increased the difficulty of suppressing the outbreak." In the Mission Fight the army eventually suffered two fatalities: First Lieutenant James D. Mann, Seventh Cavalry, who had survived Troop K's opening brawl at Wounded Knee and whose wound in the Mission Fight would prove fatal; and Private Dominic Francischetti of Troop G, whose body was not immediately recovered, as Private Crickett noted. Six enlisted men were wounded, among them First Sergeant Ragnar of Troop K, who returned to Pine Ridge Agency with the others in an army ambulance. Private Comfort, who had fought in numerous Indian engagements over a lengthy military career, said: "I never saw a fight with Indians where such rapid and continuous firing was indulged in, by both Troops [*sic*] and Indians, resulting in such slight loss."[11]

Several men would receive Medals of Honor for their performance during the Mission Fight; Captain Charles A. Varnum secured one years later

(1897) for distinguished service during the withdrawal of Forsyth's command. Some accounts indicate that large numbers of Lakotas died in the Mission Fight, but precise official figures for Indian casualties remain unknown. Personnel at the mission came to understand that no Indians had been killed or wounded. The number of Indian attackers may have been low. As Philip Wells maintained, despite Henry's extrication of Forsyth's command, "the Seventh Cavalry was in no danger, as there were only a few Indians on the hills." Wells's view was borne out later when Miles assigned Captain Frank Baldwin of the Fifth Infantry—the general's aide and confidant—to learn the magnitude of the Indian force present in the Mission Fight. Although unofficial estimates ranged wildly from fewer than a hundred to a thousand and more, Baldwin concluded that the soldiers faced "only scattering parties, . . . in all not more than 100 warriors at any one time." Nonetheless, press coverage highlighted Henry's rescue of Forsyth's besieged command, which in the wake of Wounded Knee would ultimately reflect on Forsyth's competency at both affairs. In another respect, press coverage emphasized the Seventh's appreciation of the Ninth Cavalry's Buffalo Soldiers, thereby fostering a lingering ambiance of racial harmony in both units.[12]

Lakota perspectives on the Mission Fight are decidedly rare. One who was there was Little Horse, an Oglala, who stated that the force was composed of Oglalas and Brulés, many without firearms. Little Horse said that when Forsyth's command withdrew some of the young men "went back to camp to try and urge the rest to come out, . . . [saying] the soldiers are on the run, and we can kill them all as they go back to the agency; but none of the other Indians would join us." Philip Wells, who had connections among the Pine Ridge Oglalas and interpreted for the army, learned that many of the warriors involved were ones from the Stronghold who had gone into the agency or nearly done so but had pulled back north after learning the news of Wounded Knee. Others had left the agency later on the night of December 29. They found shelter in the broken lands a dozen miles to the north and several miles east of White Clay Creek. Most who appeared north of the mission the next day—perhaps thirty or forty—were inexperienced young men who rejected cautionary advice from their elders. Some had attended schools like Carlisle and Hampton in the East. As Wells explained, "They fired from one side, then ran to another place and fired, then repeated this in another place." When the Buffalo Soldiers arrived and took control, "the boys scattered and hid, and the affair was done." Wells learned that the elders had charged the youths to gather intelligence but to not fight the soldiers. Wells said that one of three Indians wounded in the Mission Fight died.[13]

Another wounded in the action was the Oglala leader Black Elk. Appalled and angered over what he had seen and heard at Wounded Knee, Black Elk joined a war party of the Stronghold people and headed south up White Clay Creek on December 30. The warriors could hear shooting in the distance and rode west to a high ridge. They observed the fighting and saw Indians on either side of the stream shooting at the troops. The party moved forward and partly ascended the back of the high hill that had been Forsyth's initial objective. Black Elk then sought spiritual guidance, secured his rifle, and, over protestations from his colleagues, charged to the top of the hill, with his arms outstretched as he vocalized a personally empowering goose sound. "All this time," he recounted, "the bullets were buzzing around me and I was not touched." As he reached the top, however, fear interceded momentarily. A glancing soldier bullet nearly knocked Black Elk to the ground before he controlled his mount and dashed back behind the crest. The shot had ripped across his belly. A friend bound the wound and ushered Black Elk away, telling him to go home. He was taken to the Stronghold in the Badlands, where he healed, one of the few identified Sioux participants in the Mission Fight.[14]

Troops arriving back at Pine Ridge after the lengthy encounter found the infantry command manning picket posts in all directions while occupying rifle pits and other light entrenchments raised to protect the agency offices. An ordnance complement guarded the offices, while an outlying chain guard further enhanced the defenses. Army authorities believed that further attacks were imminent. The wounded in the day's fight joined Wounded Knee casualties (one more of whom would die during the night) at the Divisional Field Hospital. Surgeon Major Albert Hartsuff administered the hospital under the supervision of surgeon Lieutenant Colonel Dallas Bache (medical director, Department of the Platte, and acting medical director, Division of the Missouri in the Field). With a staff of hospital corpsmen assisting, they labored in huge floored tents with stoves and beds capable of accommodating sixty patients. Wounded Knee soldiers underwent treatment for frightful injuries that the doctors said resulted from being shot at unusually close range. Father Craft was with them for a while but soon relocated to the Catholic schoolhouse at the agency. Although weak, he was sitting upright and conversing within a few days. Visitors to the hospital tents found them "a model of neatness" and the patients hopeful, though some injuries would yet prove fatal. Even Quartermaster Sergeant Campbell, whose entire chin had been blown away at Wounded Knee, leaving him speechless, was expected to recover. He scribbled notes to medical personnel addressing his needs. Doctors Hoff, Ewing, and Glennan had attended the most serious of the Wounded Knee casualties in the field and then continued care at the hospital after reaching the agency. Ewing later provided detailed information on the treatment accorded the most severe injuries: gunshot wounds to the head and body.[15]

Winter returned in full force the next day with a harrowing whiteout. Beneath the whipping canopy, the Seventh Cavalry moved out to bury colleagues lost in Monday's engagement. Since their return from the Mission Fight, men of the Seventh had labored to fashion crude pine coffins. Now they pulled the frozen bodies from the wagons and laid them in a single row before loading them in the boxes, clad as they fell, "booted and spurred, . . . some with terrible bullet holes in their faces and others with their clothing torn where the missiles had pierced their body [sic]." At two o'clock the shrunken legion of the Seventh, all in heavy overcoats, armed and mounted, and with an assisting squad of infantry led by Colonel Forsyth and Major Whitside, escorted a convoy of fifteen mule-drawn army wagons bearing the deceased to a hill in the cemetery southeast of Pine Ridge Agency. There they consigned them to eternity. As howling winds all but obliterated the scene from onlookers, thirty army dead from Wounded Knee were interred in shallow graves arranged in rows of six. (Within days the remains of the single enlisted man killed in the Mission Fight would join them.) Reverend Cook briefly officiated, but the time-honored military firing salute was omitted so as not to alarm those Lakotas still camped at the agency. Instead "soft notes from the bugle and the wail of the storm whispered the last loving goodbye." The following day, at his family's request, the Indian scout High Back Bone, killed by the troops at Wounded Knee, was buried with full military honors next to the dead soldiers in the Pine Ridge cemetery. His comrades were all in attendance, with the Reverend Cook and Lieutenant Taylor presiding. Captain Wallace's remains had already gone to Fort Robinson bound for delivery on January 2 to Fort Riley en route to their final resting place near the officer's South Carolina home. Distraught, Forsyth wrote his daughter: "I am deeply depressed by the number of gallant officers and brave men of my command who are suffering and have passed beyond the river of Life. If I could call them back I would gladly die for them."[16]

Lakota survivors might have thought much the same of their own victims. Over succeeding days attention shifted to those lying prostrate and frozen beneath drifts eighteen miles northeast of the agency as well as the sufferers now healing in the makeshift ward in the Episcopal church. On New Year's Day Dr. Eastman, the agency physician, along with a group of Taylor's Indian scouts and other Indians appeared with wagons on the still snowy Wounded Knee field looking for more survivors. With great emotion—even as antagonized Brulés fired on them from afar—they found and saved eleven people, two wounded but sheltered in a local hut, and—incredibly—two men and five women (one of them blind) scattered hopelessly in gullies and still alive since the slaughter three days earlier. Perhaps most miraculously, they located two swaddled infants lying by their mothers' corpses. All of these people, and most surprisingly the babies, had outlasted long, cold, uncertain hours as well as the previous day's raging snowstorm. The babies found ready acceptance among the wives of the scouts, while the two wounded adults likely joined those in the Episcopal church and the others went to the Lakota camp at the agency. In a letter to a Boston friend, Eastman described the field:

> It was a terrible and horrible sight, to see women and children lying in groups, dead. . . . Some of the young girls [had] wrapped their heads with shawls and buried their faces in their hands. I suppose they did that so that they would not see the soldiers come up to shoot them. At one place there were two little children, one about 1 year old, the other about 3, lying on their faces, dead, and about thirty yards from them a woman lay on her face, dead. . . . In front of the tents, which were in a semi-circle, lay dead most of the men.[17]

Eastman counted eighty bodies of men in the area of the council circle. "It took all of my nerve to keep my composure in the face of this spectacle and of the excitement and grief of my Indian companions, nearly every one of whom was crying aloud." Deputy Marshal Bartlett was there that day. He described the scene as "wholesale murder." "I tell you dead Injuns laid around pretty thick. The worst of it was so many women and kids killed."[18]

More survivors were found on January 3 after units of the Ninth Cavalry (Troops A and G) and Eighth Infantry (Company A) marched in from Rosebud Agency at Brooke's direction, searching en route for possible escapees from Big Foot's band. Initially fired upon by angry Brulés roaming the vicinity, these soldiers not only participated in the collection and burial of the bodies in a mass grave but raised entrenchments and remained in the immediate area until the middle of the month. Captain Foliat A. Whitney of the infantry inspected the ground and reported finding 212 dead on the field. "A great number of bodies have [already] been removed," he said. "Since the snow, wagon tracks were made near where it is supposed dead or wounded Indians had been lying." He noted that both the camp and the bodies "had been more or less plundered," although since his arrival he had carefully prohibited such activity. (Whitney's figures, as well as those of most other fatality accountings for Wounded Knee, inexplicably remain at odds with each other.) That same day Major Whitside and Major J. Ford Kent, inspector-general of the Division of the Missouri, arrived with Second Lieutenant Sydney A. Cloman, First Infantry, and an escort of twenty men. Cloman would help draft the official army map of the action site.[19]

The next day they were joined by Captain Frank D. Baldwin, whom Miles had appointed acting assistant inspector general. The Fifth Infantry officer had reached Pine Ridge Agency on January 3, noting in his diary "much excitement here over the killing of so many women & children by Forsyth['s] com[man]d." Probably Miles's closest professional friend, Baldwin had served the divisional commander since their time together in the Red River War on the southern plains in 1874–75 and during the Sioux campaign of 1876–77. Like Miles, Baldwin had risen from the enlisted grades. He claimed a distinguished Civil War record but unlike his mentor held two Medals of Honor for his Civil War and Indian wars service. Baldwin would factor importantly in the army's closing operations in South Dakota. On January 4 his purpose at Wounded Knee—like Kent's—was to conduct a preliminary investigation of the ground. "It was an awful sight," he said, "women, children, some of the latter nursing. Children lying dead, they having been shot." Baldwin spent the next several days gathering information about the fighting there.[20]

With the burial party came reporters and photographers. Carl Smith, correspondent for the *Omaha World-Herald,* surveyed the scene that day and wrote a riveting column about the horrors he viewed. "Children just of an age to play tag in a city, and young men and old gray-haired women and warriors" had died, he wrote. He saw "boys, down to the ages of 10 and 11, who wore the gaudy painted ghost shirts . . . . These children lay everywhere, half buried under the snow which had fallen to conceal the blood stains which made their trappings of paint and fringe so piteous." Elsewhere "the slain were piled in heaps in some instances, in others they lay in isolated places. Where they lay in heaps they had fallen in heaps. In one square of less than half an acre there were forty-eight bodies stiffened by the frost." One corpse with "the look of a demon" drew special attention. "The face was painted a horrible green. . . . Blood had mingled with the paint and washed red rivers in the coating." He was recognized as the multi-named medicine man whose invective some Indians and soldiers believed had instigated the butchery and whose body had been castigated after the end of the shooting. "His hands were clenched, and his body seemed to have a tense appearance. One hand was raised in the air. The arm had frozen in that position." Nearby in a circle of ashes rested what remained of the flame-consumed tent of the sniper who had perished after shooting several soldiers. A short distance away lay the stiffened and overcoated body of Big Foot, his head yet bound in a scarf that he wore on the morning of December 29. As Smith described, "a wandering photographer propped the old man up, and as he lay there defenseless his portrait was taken."[21]

Photographer George Trager, along with others, took many views depicting the iced-up corpses after they had been pulled from the ground where they had fallen to assume graphically grotesque appearances. In their relative ease of availability in late 1890, the vivid descriptions by photographers and reporters on the scene demonstrated not only the effortless access to once-distant places like Wounded Knee but technical innovations to help spur public interest and consumption.

Paddy Starr, a mixed-blood scout who had witnessed the opening action, received the burial contract: two dollars for each body interred. Thirty or so Mexican and mixed-blood Sioux laborers with three wagons—all guarded by the troops—completed their work on January 4. Special agent Cooper of the Bureau of Indian Affairs was on hand to determine an accurate count of the bodies for the Interior Department. At the top of the low-lying hill, above where the Hotchkiss guns had spewed their rounds on December 29, the workers dug a 5-foot-deep trench 72 feet long by about 6 feet wide in a north-to-south alignment. Then they hauled and tossed into it the remains of the Indian dead. The soldiers clustered behind the trench while a photographer took their picture. Some in quest of souvenirs stripped ghost shirts from the bodies. One man recalled that Big Foot had been placed at the head of the grave. A Chadron newspaper reported the burial of 152 people—including 84 men and 63 women and children. The paper reported that 5 victims had previously been interred there by the Indians themselves. Other dead had been carted off for burial elsewhere—purportedly enough to raise the total Indian fatalities to at least 200. As mentioned, the army's formal number in the mass grave was modified to 146—82 men and 64 women and children; Starr had tendered an invoice for $292.00. Some survivors came to resent the government's failure to provide individual graves for the victims, most of whom had been friends and family members.[22]

Medical attention over the next days and weeks focused not only on the army wounded but also on those in the Episcopal chapel of the Holy Cross at Pine Ridge, which functioned as a temporary infirmary for the injured and dying Lakotas brought from Wounded Knee. The small frame and steepled structure normally accommodated local congregations. But when Forsyth's command came in on the night of December 29 the Reverend Cook graciously turned it over for emergency use by the injured Lakotas, whose numbers would diminish within days. Christmas wreaths and garlands still adorned the walls. A streamer emblazoned "Peace on earth, goodwill to men" draped from the rafter above the pulpit highlighted the improbable irony of it all. In order for the church to accommodate the wounded Indians, workmen removed the pews and covered the floor with a foot of loose hay. Soldiers carefully placed the incoming men, women, and children in two rows on blankets resting atop the hay. This was subsequently changed to army bedsacks filled with hay to help control the litter. Smoking was forbidden. Most assumed their beds quietly, but one tiny boy called repeatedly for *mini,* meaning water. As the child finally swallowed a cupful, part of the liquid gushed from a bloody wound in his neck. Another lad had lost his eyesight from a bullet entering his temple behind one eye and exiting directly through the other. Nearby a wounded girl screamed for attendants to remove her blooded Ghost Dance dress. "It is worthless!" she cried. While Surgeon Hartsuff and his staff immediately cared for the army wounded, he sent morphine to the Indian patients along with beef extract for making soup. Dr. Eastman and female agency employees, including school supervisor Elaine Goodale, tended them into the early hours of the morning and often assisted the medical officers throughout the following days. Years later Goodale recalled: "The glowing cross in the stained glass window behind the altar looked down in irony—or in compassion—upon the pagan children struck down in panic flight."[23]

Thirty-six afflicted individuals (thirty-four direct from Wounded Knee on December 29 and two arrivals on January 9) crowded virtually all areas of the building—alcove, chancel, sanctuary, and vestry. Twenty of them were males and sixteen were females, including children. Bandages and linen dressings stood on the lectern. Major Edmond Butler of the Second Infantry, who had asked the Reverend Cook for use of the church, oversaw preparations there and made tents available for an overflow of wounded Sioux. Assistant surgeon Captain Henry S. Kilbourne was placed in charge of the wounded prisoners, assisted by assistant surgeon Captain Frank J. Ives. Dr. Ives initially treated the Lakotas and was soon joined by Dr. Eastman, the Reverend Cook and his wife, Jessie, and volunteer assistants such as Elaine Goodale. Ives took down the names of the patients, briefly recorded the nature of their wounds, and in some cases indicated the outcome of their condition, as shown in this sampling:

No. 1. Has-a-dog, age 17. Gunshot wound upper lobe of left lung. Jan. 5—Hemorrhage—died.

No. 5. Child, female—[age] 6. "Holy bone" Comp'd fracture upper third left thigh

No. 7. Mrs Big-foot. Two flesh wounds upper third left thigh. . . . Both suppurating. Died of Pneumonia

No. 8. Squaw [name indecipherable]. Flesh wounds, right thigh. Wound right side penetrating abdomen. . . . Died Jan. 10th, 6:45 A.M.

No. 12. Man—shot many times. [Age] 36. 1. Severe flesh wound right side, fragment of shell. 2. Wound right foot below joint. 3. Wound through left ankle joint. . . . Jan. 5, Suppuration—Wound dressed. [Jan.] 6. Wound in side looking well; . . . other wounds dressed—looking well.

[No.] 18. Baby—male—1 year, with Mother. 1. Gunshot wound through left buttocks. 2. Gunshot wound through scrotum. Both wounds made by same ball. Jan. 5. Suppuration in both—hernia left testicle dressed. [Jan.] 9. Transferred to Indian Camp.

[No.] 23. Last-Man, [age] 40. Gun shot wound through abdomen—lay on the field until the 5th Jan. Died Jan. 6, at 8 A.M.

[No.] 31. Child, 5. "Steals a running horse." Gun shot injury over left scapular dorsum. Left side of neck & lower floor of mouth carrying away part of inferior maxilla right side.[24]

Over succeeding days, relatives and friends of the wounded survivors tried to take them from the care of the doctors and attendants, but mostly without success. Some of the older patients rejected all medical assistance and advice from the doctors, especially regarding necessary operations, and calmly died. Yet others showed up days later, received outpatient attention, and immediately returned to their families. One report claimed that two women had appeared along the road from Wounded Knee on January 11 as they crawled toward the agency thirteen days after being wounded. In spite of statments that almost all of the wounded Indians died, such was not the case; of thirty-eight reported casualties, only seven (less than one-fifth) of those receiving treatment at the Episcopal church hospital perished. On January 3 many of the Lakota casualties were removed from the church to the Catholic school one block away.[25]

Besides the church and school buildings, structures of the Oglala boarding school at Pine Ridge also incurred heavy use in the days following Wounded Knee. Sioux women found sustenance and shelter there, sleeping on the floors and consuming food from its kitchens. For weeks soldiers also made repeated use of its facilities, notably its bakery. In addition, much comforting material—clothing, dining ware, bedding—went directly to the Episcopal church for use by the wounded Indians. Staples such as bread and soup from the school also became mainstays for those patients for several weeks. To help alleviate congestion in the church ward, Father Jutz offered in early January to care for wounded Indian children at the mission school. Dr. Eastman's many appeals for help from the Indian Rights Association in Philadelphia as well as other beneficent organizations resulted in material and monetary contributions to aid the recovery of the survivors. Despite Eastman's own rattled convictions following what he had witnessed in the days preceding and following Wounded Knee, he continued his service as agency physician to the Lakotas at Pine Ridge for two more years.[26]

As it focused on the Indian and soldier casualties in the immediate wake of Wounded Knee, the army medical service received high-priority public attention and for a time served as an unceasing corollary to the devastating action. The patients quartered in the army field hospital—the first such facility established for evacuation and treatment since the Civil War—drew significant press notice. Among newsmen at the scene, the correspondent and nationally known artist Frederic Remington conversed with a number of injured soldiers and filled a column as well as pages containing his illustrations for readers of *Harper's Weekly*. During succeeding days medical director Bache pressed for increased readiness for more casualties in what looked to be a prolonged campaign with further fighting. He called initially for more help, including a hospital steward to replace the man killed at Wounded Knee, and urged the assembly at Pine Ridge of a fifteen-man company of enlisted corpsmen.

With the surgeon general's blessing, within days Bache sent requests throughout the country for medical furniture, supplies, and personnel, which brought a new complement of army surgeons to South Dakota to help meet new exigencies. Space for future casualties necessarily became mandatory. To that end, on January 4, the tented wards of the divisional hospital were largely vacated as the majority of convalescent soldiers departed for their home stations to complete their recuperation. (Those who returned to Fort Riley benefited from the kindness of army novelist and former army captain Charles King, who directed his publisher to ship copies of his books to the wards there to help the men "while away the tedium of long hours in the hospital.") But more deaths occurred at Fort Riley. Lieutenant James Mann, shot in the lower back during the Mission Fight, succumbed from his injury on January 15. He was interred next day in the post cemetery. Two more hospitalized enlisted men also died from injuries received at Wounded Knee. As preparations for anticipated contingencies proceeded at Pine Ridge Agency, executives of a newly completed Soldiers' Home at nearby Hot Springs, South Dakota, tendered their facility for use. That offer, along with the availability of services at Forts Robinson and Niobrara as well as other regional posts, would more than fulfill the needs of the army medical establishment should the campaign be extended.[27]

FOURTEEN

Close Out

The news of Wounded Knee spread quickly. Within hours it streamed through newsrooms across the nation. The first and most accurate reports were those hurriedly written in the field by the three newsmen who happened to be present—Will Cressey of the *Omaha Bee*, William F. Kelley of the Lincoln, Nebraska, *State Journal*, and Charles W. Allen of the *Chadron Democrat* and stringer for the *New York Herald*. They all sent their columns forth for transmittal from Rushville as soon as Forsyth's stricken command reached Pine Ridge. Rushville had only one telegrapher. Under a mutually agreed upon earlier rotation scheme, Kelley's on-the-scene dispatch was first to hit the wire some time around midnight. His paper, the *State Journal*, disseminated a bulletin via the United Press news agency. When Chicago requested a detailed account, Kelley's story went forward. Other correspondents at Pine Ridge provided information obtained from these reporters, other witnesses, and participants. Within hours headlines across the country told surprised citizens of the affair at Wounded Knee.

The *Omaha Bee*, which had covered the growing crisis for weeks, led with "A Bloody Battle—The Seventh Cavalry Encounters the Indians on Porcupine [*sic*] Creek—Brave Capt. Wallace among the Slain—Big Foot's Entire Band Almost Exterminated by the Soldiers." South Dakota's *Sioux Falls Argus-Leader* called it "A Big Fight. . . . Twenty-Five Soldiers and 300 Indians Are Killed. . . . Panic Reigns Supreme Near Wounded Knee." In the East the *Philadelphia Inquirer* led with "The Awful Massacre" in reference to the "SEVENTH CAVALRY'S HEAVY LOSS," while the *New York Times* reported "A FIGHT WITH THE HOSTILES—*BIG FOOT'S TREACHERY PRECIPITATES A BATTLE.*" Besides the dailies, the illustrated weeklies made the most of their artists' talents; within weeks Remington drew scenes for *Harper's Weekly.* J. M. McDonough for *Frank Leslie's Illustrated Newspaper* and Daniel Smith for the *New York Daily Graphic* did similarly.[1]

Reactions differed. Many editors (and readers) blamed the events on a combination of circumstances related to the government's handling of Indian affairs. In particular they blamed the land and rations issues that had compelled certain of the Sioux to embrace a peculiar religion perceived as ultimately contributing to violence. Others blamed the army's presence, which many thought had exceeded what was required to maintain peace. Some quite understandably saw Sitting Bull's death as a murder and its aftermath, following a host of contributing causes, as having provoked the climactic event at Wounded Knee. Frank Baum, of the *Aberdeen Saturday Pioneer,* who had so recently called for extermination of the Sioux, repeated his rhetoric and mordantly termed the loss of so many soldiers "a disgrace to the war department [*sic*]."[2]

Miles's uncle-in-law, General Sherman, fumed over the disaster. A long-time hardliner and architect of military policy against the Sioux after the Civil War, he believed that the people had gotten their just desserts. A month shy of his own demise, Sherman told Mary Miles privately to encourage her husband "to so act that never again will the Sioux dare to disturb the program of the country." Implicitly critiquing Miles, Sherman wrote: "If . . . some squaws were killed, somebody has made a mistake, for squaws have been killed in every Indian war . . . [and] in a fight the coolest man cannot distinguish female from male." Regarding the Indians' presumed imminent surrender, he railed that "they have defied the power of the Government and should be severely whipped."[3]

Countering Sherman's rant, Herbert Welsh of the Indian Rights Association offered an impartial assessment but conceded that "in a fierce sanguinary hand-to-hand fight common soldiers would become unrestrainable." He urged, moreover, that the Ghost Dance leaders be punished and that progressive Sioux who suffered losses because of the Ghost Dancers' actions be compensated. Welsh soon asked General Crook's former aide, Captain John G. Bourke, to investigate what had happened at Wounded Knee. In the process Louis Shangrau, who had been there, confirmed that the soldiers had "murdered them . . . in ravines, gulches, or other places."[4]

The earliest accounts charged Big Foot with duplicity and held him responsible. They also mourned the dead of the heroic Seventh Cavalry. Within days, however, as the casualty figures became clear, press attention focused on the unusually large numbers of Lakota women and children who had apparently died at the hands of the troops. What had happened to generate those losses? As early as January 17, for example, the *Washington Post* reported that education supervisor Elaine Goodale had told Commissioner Morgan what she had learned from the Indians themselves: although an officer called out "Don't shoot the squaws," "the men were doubtless too much excited to obey." She believed that the killing of women and children was "deliberate and intentional."[5] Questions also arose regarding the large number of cavalrymen killed and wounded at the outset of the shooting and whether Forsyth's close-in and enveloping placement of his command had contributed to those losses by causing some soldiers to fire across the council area into each other. The matter consumed the talk of officers and enlisted men in the Pine Ridge Agency community for hours and days, including those present at Wounded Knee who must have generated it. Press representatives would have had ready access to their conversations.[6]

Some concluded that revenge had motivated the excessive killing of non-combatants. They assumed that the Seventh Cavalry maintained a rancor against the Sioux because of the regiment's defeat at the Little Bighorn River fourteen years earlier. The press naturally relished that explanation and spread it, with the consequence that it has remained part of the causal equation for Wounded Knee ever since, perhaps the commonsense denouement. Its plausibility appeared even before the engagement occurred. Upon Big Foot's surrender the day before the killings, a newsman for the *Chicago Inter-Ocean* reported that "not a few" Seventh Cavalrymen "murmured their regrets that they could not pay off some of the unsettled scores of 1876." In its initial coverage of Wounded Knee on December 30, the first line in the same paper's story read: "The Seventh Cavalry are revenged, but with some loss." Two days later the *Chadron Democrat* editorialized: "We glory in the revenge of the Seventh, although they sustained a heavy loss, and notwithstanding there may have been but few in the late fight left who belonged to the Seventh during Custer's life." The *Junction City Republican*, adjacent to Fort Riley, home of the regiment, proclaimed: "The slaughter is on the other foot this time, and Custer and his boys are avenged after an interval of fourteen years. . . . It is a gratification to know that it was the Seventh horse that avenged the death of its old commander."[7]

Only five officers and eleven enlisted men who participated at Little Bighorn were present at Wounded Knee.[8] But many came to believe, as did Elaine Goodale, that "the Seventh Cavalry, Custer's old command, had an old grudge to repay." Indeed rumors flew around the army camp at Pine Ridge Agency that some soldiers shouted "Remember Custer!" as Wounded Knee unfolded. Interpreter John Shangrau said that a lieutenant on the hill near the Hotchkiss guns declared: "We've got our revenge now." The officer was perhaps from the First Artillery and not the Seventh Cavalry, however, and his conclusion may have come too early in the fighting to be credible, but it is conceivable.[9]

Nearly two weeks after the event Major Whitside directed Philip Wells, the mixed-blood interpreter, to learn the truth. "I found no evidence that the soldiers said that," Wells reported. Artillery Private John Comfort concurred. In a lengthy account of Wounded Knee for his brother in 1892, Comfort wrote: "A great amount of stuff was published in the Newspapers [sic] of the fight accusing the 7th Cav of purposely butchering everything in sight, out of revenge for the massacre [sic] of Custer and his men in '76 . . . and that the men of the 7th raised the cry of 'Remember Custer.' That was and is pure nonsense, there was no battle cry of any sort raised."[10]

Yet in the continuing aftermath the notion of retribution endured, probably not altogether without merit, and the regiment became known in some circles as "the famous 'bloody Seventh.'" One of the first professional journal accounts of the army experience of 1890–91, written by an Eighth Infantry officer who was present at Wounded Knee and Pine Ridge Agency after the action, editorialized as follows:

> I can understand the sudden rage of the soldiers at the action of the Indians [unexpectedly firing on them] on this occasion, and I am not inclined to withhold some justification to [toward] the 7th Cavalry, who still carried the memory of Custer and the Little Big Horn, especially as they had orders to destroy the Indians in case they resisted, yet the destruction of Indian life was carried to a most distressing length.

Thus did the "revenge" concept begin, stabilize, and persist.[11]

With such claims and reactions swirling about, General Miles felt all the more urgency to reach the seat of the crisis and take charge of operations personally. Shortly past noon on Tuesday, December 30, he and his staff arrived by train at Chadron, Nebraska, along with four companies of the First Infantry, recently stationed at Hermosa and Oelrichs. The infantrymen brought needed wagons to be outfitted with teams at Chadron. While most of the foot troops set out to bivouac along Beaver Creek twenty miles away, the divisional commander and his retinue took quarters for the night in the new Hotel Chadron adjoining the railroad depot. Still agitated over the army losses, he sent a message to the adjutant general's office with revised figures then wrote Brooke, telling him that "some one [*sic*] seems to be suppressing facts." Promptly at 4 the next morning Miles headed for the agency through falling snow, reaching there just as the burial ceremony for the fallen soldiers concluded.[12]

Assuming command, Miles moved into the agent's frame residence and office lately occupied by General Brooke and directed Brooke to prepare to go afield the following day. "His presence made it lively for everybody," remarked Private Comfort. Miles at once vigorously set about protecting the agency, ordering additions and improvements to the entrenchments that Brooke had established. Substantial fortifications of earth and logs supported by Gatling guns and other artillery completed an outer line on ridges and hills broadly encircling the agency as far north as three-quarters of a mile. Rifle pits and breastworks graced hillocks closer. "Now the Indians cannot reach the buildings without carrying the earthworks first," wrote a newsman. "For the first time the women and children and non-combatants feel protected." Within a few days a large trench—its crest lined with bags of dirt as a breastwork—had been excavated west of the government school, where a Hotchkiss gun masked with foliage stood ready to sweep the valley in all directions.[13]

Miles surveyed the surrounding area too and met principals in the community who could help facilitate his objective to end the conflict quickly and peacefully. (Father Jutz found him "a very noble man, but not as friendly as General Brooke.") On arrival Miles learned that those agency Indians who had stayed behind after the others had vamoosed continued to profess friendship toward the government. They were mostly mixed-bloods but included many aged, sick, and injured as well. Most of them occupied small camps south of the agency. Miles also learned of the arrival from Medicine Root Creek the previous night of seventy-three Hunkpapa refugees of the Sitting Bull Fight. Some of them had fled Sumner's soldiers near the Cheyenne, and all of them were seeking to overtake Big Foot's band. Army scouts found them on December 27 and brought them to Pine Ridge, where the Indian police helped disarm them, placed them under military guard, and only later informed them of the killings at Wounded Knee.[14]

Once he had secured the place, Miles sought to halt further bloodshed and terminate the increasingly costly operation in South Dakota. He placed several thousand troops at his disposal strategically to encircle all the frustrated Indians and block escape routes north and west leading off the reservation. He then slowly contracted the line toward the large encampment of the disaffected, pressing the people toward the agency. As he had explained to Brooke: "That high table land [Stronghold] was ordered occupied by three companies of Infantry, so that there is no chance of their returning there. A small force can hold the agency, and a larger portion of the command should be kept to the west of them [the Indians] and endeavor to hold them on the reservation." On Miles's authority, Brooke was to oversee this grand maneuver personally. Thus, at 11 A.M. on New Year's Day, Brooke and his staff set out for Beaver Creek in Nebraska, southwest of Pine Ridge Agency, en route to White River with the men of the Second Infantry contingent under Colonel Frank Wheaton and Colonel Henry's Ninth Cavalry squadron. "From the expression on the faces of the officers and men as they pulled out through the snow and bitter cold," noted a reporter, "it was evident that they didn't relish General Miles' order."[15]

Brooke's objective was to facilitate the field dispositions, of which Wheaton and Henry would be part, and to coordinate with components under Sanford, Offley, and Carr to thwart Lakota movements west or north and bring Miles's design to fruition. "It is important," he directed, "that no Indians be permitted to cross north of White River and to confine them as much as possible to the valley of White Clay [Creek]." Brooke still entertained hopes of salvaging something of his earlier plan, hoping to "arrange for a simultaneous movement of all the troops and attack [the Indians] from all points at a time to be fixed." Miles told Brooke that those officers "should be fully apprised of the situation and impressed with the importance of maintaining an effective line with available reserves, as well as to keep out reconnoitering and scouting parties in their fronts, the object being to . . . gradually . . . force the Indians into the Agency."[16]

To help execute his plan, Miles summoned from Chicago his assistant adjutant general, Lieutenant Colonel Henry C. Corbin, who took the train west on January 4 as Miles's chief of staff. Miles also made adjustments to his outer perimeter, sending units of the First Cavalry and Twentieth

Infantry at Fort Keogh to the Little Missouri River to cooperate via a First Cavalry outpost at Camp Crook with Major Carroll's command near Slim Buttes in northwestern South Dakota. Elsewhere, Colonel Merriam and the Seventh Infantry were en route to the forks of the Cheyenne River, while Sumner continued to patrol that stream, ready to intercept Indians fleeing north and west.[17]

Within days a squadron of the Seventh Cavalry under Ilsley started out to join Henry's men near the mouth of Beaver Creek on White River, as the relieved First Infantry companies marched into the agency. The Fifth Cavalry troop at Oelrichs shifted toward Pine Ridge as the other units of the Seventh remained at the agency along with the Eighth and First Infantrymen. There the Seventh troopers, rejoined by Ilsley's men, would constitute the south line of defense. More men of the First Infantry reached Pine Ridge on January 1 to help erect the new defenses, and units of the Sixteenth and Twenty-First infantry regiments from Utah Territory were expected soon. (Four companies of the Sixteenth reached Fort Robinson from Fort Douglas on January 3, destined for duty near Oelrichs and Pine Ridge Agency; the four companies of the Twenty-First remained at Fort Robinson.)

On January 8 corpulent and gouty Colonel William R. Shafter, First Infantry, arrived and took charge of all troops at the agency. Augmenting Miles's hopes for stemming the conflict, late word suggested a schism among the Indians camped down White Clay Creek that had impelled Red Cloud, Big Road, and Little Wound to seek to return to Pine Ridge Agency with their people at first opportunity. Their efforts were stymied by Two Strike, Short Bull, Kicking Bear, and their followers, who had maliciously threatened them and repeatedly cut their wagon harnesses to prevent their leaving. Miles also learned that warriors had killed a white government herder, Henry Miller, ten miles below the agency. Many of those cattle had been appropriated while the warriors destroyed more day schools and a church along White Clay Creek and threatened further violence.[18]

On January 1, as Miles's forces under Brooke departed Pine Ridge Agency to assume their respective stations and Colonel Carr's Sixth Cavalry settled into its assigned place below White River, the final armed confrontation between Lakotas and the soldiers in the so-called Ghost Dance War played out near the mouth of Grass Creek, entering White River from the south. Troop K of the Sixth, some fifty men strong, was to have escorted Miles cross-country, and now ushered their three-wagon baggage train along the valley of the White. They were now bound for Carr's camp on lower Wounded Knee Creek, six miles above the streams' confluence. Near noon, when warriors from the Lakota assemblage on lower White Clay Creek approached, troop commander Captain John B. Kerr and Second Lieutenant Robert L. Howze hurriedly clustered the wagons on sharply rising ground forming the angle between White River and the west bank of the mouth of Grass Creek. Kerr, a distinguished army marksman and gold medal winner, quickly sent off two riders to Carr's camp, dismounted his force, corralled his horses in a gully behind the knoll, and braced to meet the closing Sioux. The men hurriedly threw up breastworks, augmenting them with their bedrolls pulled from the wagons.

Perhaps fifty warriors in two columns advanced over the snow-covered ground, letting loose war cries and taunts to distract the command while fifty more Lakotas closed around them on foot from other directions below in the lightly wooded bottom of White River. In time the Indians succeeded in surrounding the soldiers, some firing volleys from the north side of the White. The two sides shot at each other from a long distance for approximately two hours before reinforcements from Carr's command under First Lieutenant Benjamin H. Cheever, Jr. (Troop A) and Major Tulius C. Tupper (Troops F and I) splashed through the icy waters of the White River to approach from the northeast and drive the warriors away with assistance from Carr and the rest of the command (Troops H and G). As night fell the column escorted Kerr and Troop K to the camp on Wounded Knee Creek. One government horse was killed, but no soldiers were injured in the action. Carr maintained that four Indians had been killed and four wounded and that three equipped cavalry mounts had been captured. Indian sources later said that two of their warriors were wounded and that they made off with five cavalry horses before returning to the large camp on White Clay Creek. Within months the army awarded Medals of Honor to Kerr, Howze, and Cheever as well as to three enlisted participants.[19]

Rumors of the engagement at Grass Creek quickly filtered back to Pine Ridge Agency, telling of the cavalry mounts held in the grand Sioux encampment now estimated by agent Royer to include some 3,000 men, women, and children. Miles realized that as part of his design for ending the conflict peacefully he must exercise diplomacy and open communication with those Indians. To do so he invited the chiefs to come to the agency and talk. A protracted exchange ensued in which Miles courted the chiefs, telling them: "I shake hands with all of you." Drawing on his past experience, he wrote familiarly, saying that he knew many of them, especially those who had surrendered to him on the Yellowstone River years before. But he addressed them forcefully:

> I expect all Indians to come to me when I send for them, and that is what I came here for. I would rather be a friend of the Indians than their enemy. If they all come in and do whatever I say, and as the Great Father at Washington wants them to do, they will have no trouble. The safe road is the road toward the Agency. A great many troops are on all sides . . . , but not a shot will be fired or a hand raised against any if they do as I direct them.[20]

Miles also sought to reassure Red Cloud and the agency chiefs: "The Indians that fired upon the troops [at Wounded Knee] and fired into the Agency caused you all to run away. . . . I might ask what is the matter with the Indians? It is the acts of a few that have caused all the trouble. All this occurred before I came here. You need not fear any of the soldiers as long as you do as I tell you. It is the acts of the few that have caused all the trouble."[21]

When Red Cloud demanded that Secretary Noble and Commissioner Morgan (as well as the vice president) come and settle the situation, Miles responded that President Harrison had vested all authority in him. "I am chief in command," Miles said, adding: "all this is in your hands. . . . You may send in six men to speak to me, and I will send them back to your camp again. You can all come in, and you may be sure I shall do what is right." In other messages Miles allowed that Red Cloud could "speak to the Secretary of the Interior, as well as the Great Father, but all the Indians must come in first and do as I tell them."[22]

Miles's efforts paid off. On January 5, within days of opening a dialogue, five Oglala representatives (Big Road, Little Hawk, Jack Red Cloud, and High Hawk, led by He Dog) appeared at his headquarters ready to talk. Complimenting Miles's former truthfulness with the Sioux, He Dog told his colleagues that "he was a friend of ours, which is the reason we came here to-day to see him." Addressing Miles, he said: "My friend, we ask you to put us on a good road . . . because we have confidence in you." He Dog asked that Miles restrain his soldiers, take them away, and understand that "this trouble was caused by people from a different agency," meaning the Rosebud Brulés. "We do not want to have any trouble." Drawing a parallel with the surrenders in Montana, Miles reminded the Sioux that "you came into our camp on the Yellowstone and came alongside of the troops and no one was hurt. You must do the same thing now. . . . The sooner they come in, the sooner the trouble will end." With that the five leaders returned to their camp, and Miles expressed confidence that the council would lead to a peaceful solution.[23]

Indeed the meeting with the friendly Oglala chiefs would prove instrumental to a final settlement. Since his arrival at Pine Ridge, Miles had acted purposefully and swiftly. Within days he informed General Schofield in Washington of the new military landscape unfolding to hasten the Indians' submission: "Nearly all of [the] 6th and 9th Cavalry and 2d and 17th Infantry, with 100 Indian scouts, are practically on 3 sides of them along Beaver [Creek], White River, and Porcupine [Creek], with Genl. Brooke in command; this may hold them in check. I am in close communication with them, and have informed them the only safe road is toward the agency, and about half are anxious to come in; the others are making desperate efforts to keep all at war." With an accord with the Oglalas seemingly at hand, Miles again called for the appointment of military officers as agents at all the affected stations, insisting that their presence and the semblance of military control after the Indians surrendered would be fundamental to maintaining the peace. His request won quick approval, and the general received notice to that effect within days.[24]

Miles also hoped that his dialogue with the Sioux would quell unrest among citizens in the region, primarily those in southwestern South Dakota and northwestern Nebraska who were understandably aroused and apprehensive in the aftermath of Wounded Knee. South Dakota governor Mellette sent more arms and ammunition to selected communities as many upgraded their defenses. Northwest of Pine Ridge Agency, townspeople of Buffalo Gap began work on a blockhouse, while at Hermosa, near Rapid City, the people raised a large log and sod bulwark called Fort Buckingham. Residents of Hill City instituted home guard patrols, and Colonel Day and the Dakota militia continued service despite Miles's fears that the unit might complicate his operations. When destitute families from Bad River showed up at the agency seeking relief, Miles requested more army rations and fuel for quartering them. The general also asked that agents along the Fremont, Elkhorn, and Missouri Valley Railroad keep settlers posted with recent and correct information. Citizens fleeing Oelrichs after Wounded Knee took refuge at Fort Robinson.

Communities along the railroad in Nebraska received telegraphed warnings from Pine Ridge Agency about possible Indian incursions. As rumors flew, couriers notified settlers in outlying areas. Soon destitute families arrived in Rushville and Hay Springs, seeking quarter in churches and public buildings. In Chadron 130 families sought relief. As in South Dakota, a few communities in Nebraska established home guard units. Others built defensive works, refitted earlier ones, or occupied stone houses to wait out alarms. A woman in Sheridan County took her own life when she erroneously believed that the Sioux were close at hand.[25]

Telegrams from Nebraska citizens to Governor John M. Thayer prompted his requests to the War Department for guns and ammunition. General Schofield suggested that arms be delivered to the state militia, which the governor might "organize and place under proper military control." In fact the Nebraska National Guard, composed of volunteers and with no appropriation from the legislature (although later reimbursed), prepared to take the field in support of regular troops in the area south of the Pine Ridge and Rosebud reservations. More formalized than South Dakota's local militia, the Nebraska force consisted of two infantry regiments, each ten companies strong, one cavalry troop, and an artillery battery, in all more than 800 officers and men. During the post–Wounded Knee excitement in Nebraska, Brigadier General Leonard W. Colby, a Union army veteran and commander of the state guard units, received notice from Thayer to ready the Nebraska National Guard for field service in response to the clamor from the northwestern counties. On January 5 Colby established his headquarters at Rushville and over the following days posted companies of the first and second regiments at Crawford, Valentine, Rushville, Cody, Gordon, Harrison, and Hay Springs. Supplied with breech-loading arms and ammunition and outfitted to protect against the cold and fulfill their mission, the troops took station "in readiness to march for defense against Indian depredations." Buffalo Bill Cody, commissioned a brigadier general in the state guard and as acting aide-de-camp to the governor, arrived at Rushville and rode off to Pine Ridge Agency on special duty to apprise Colby of developments there as they might affect Nebraska residents.[26]

Colby and his staff devised a strategy to monitor the territory south of Pine Ridge Reservation running east-to-west for 150 miles and north-to-south for 50 miles. The area embraced the route of the Fremont, Elkhorn, and Missouri Valley Railroad from Harrison near the Wyoming line to Valentine on the east, roughly between the White River and the Sand Hills.

Officers of the companies designated for the various town locations were responsible for assessing local conditions and reporting to brigade head-quarters. To protect citizens further, Colby established a line of earthwork-fortified camps north of the railroad, closer to the perceived Indian threat, and assigned forces to railroad stations and communities in each area. A network of mounted couriers hired from among the citizenry assured com-munications with all segments of the line. For two weeks the guard ful-filled an essential function, buttressing the regulars in discouraging Sioux incursions while boosting the area's economy and easing fears among the populace. On January 5 a large group of Sioux camped south of the agency on the portion of reservation extending into Nebraska. The guardsmen, in-terpreting the movement as an effort to circumvent the army and join other Indians in the Badlands, turned them back without difficulty. Beyond that, about the only campaign excitement for the "tin soldiers," as they called themselves, was the accidental shooting death of a private at Gordon on January 12.[27]

As General Miles sought to contain and control the Brulés and Oglalas gathered below Pine Ridge Agency, more controversy arose over Wounded Knee. He had told Schofield of his concerns over that affair: "large numbers of soldiers were killed and wounded by fire from their own ranks, and a very large number of women and children were killed in addition to the In-dian men."[28] Schofield reported to secretary of war Proctor, who consulted with President Harrison. The commanding general then wired Miles that the president "hopes that the report of the killing of women and children in the affair at Wounded Knee is unfounded, and directs that you cause an immediate inquiry to be made and report the results to the Depart-ment. If there was any unsoldierly conduct, you will relieve the responsible officer."[29]

Already incensed over Forsyth's performance, which had negated his hope of ensuring peace without further bloodshed (and reflected negatively on his own management), Miles resolved to examine the colonel's handling of affairs at Wounded Knee, now with seeming presidential concurrence. Miles no doubt believed strongly that Forsyth's inexperience and ineptitude had brought on the disaster but certainly also hoped that such a course would deflect criticism from himself. As Major Whitside wrote to his wife: "The settlement of the Indian trouble has been a failure . . . and now some one [sic] must . . . be sacrificed and from appearances Gen. F[orsyth] is the man selected."[30]

Focusing on Forsyth's troop disposition, which apparently had caused his men to shoot into their own ranks at the outbreak, as well as the excessive casualties among Sioux women and children, Miles informed a baffled General Schofield of his decision to proceed with a full investigation of what had happened. On January 4 he abruptly relieved Forsyth from command (for the moment to be succeeded by Whitside) and designated a court of inquiry headed by Major Jacob Ford Kent, acting inspector-general in Ruger's Department of Dakota, and Captain Frank Baldwin, Miles's acting assistant inspector-general and judge advocate of the Division of the Missouri. Together they would probe the matter immediately.[31] To his wife Miles wrote privately: "I think Col. Forsyth's actions about the worst I have ever known," remarking that a second lieutenant could have done better in the situation. Later he told her Forsyth was "utterly incompetent and unfit" and had caused "a useless slaughter of innocent women and children."[32]

When Forsyth heard of Miles's decision, he minced no words in distressing over his circumstance to his daughter: "I have been under such a mental strain for the past month that I feel about used up, and now comes this attack upon my life's record by this man Miles. From the time I got here I knew that some one [sic] would be selected as a scapegoat, . . . but I did not believe that I was to be selected by Providence to carry the load. I shall do everything in the world to protect myself, and the officers of the regiment are all indignant at the course pursued by Gen'l Miles, and are with me to a man. . . . I feel confident that I will come out of it all right." He later wrote: "[Recently arrived Major John M. Bacon, Seventh Cavalry,] told me that Brooke was my friend, but I doubt this."[33]

Upon learning of Miles's action, however, General Schofield warned that the president had only intended for him "to inquire into the facts and in the event of its being disclosed that there had been unsoldierly conduct, to relieve the responsible officer."[34] Despite his gaffe, Miles forged ahead. Miles's decision countered War Department protocol regarding relief of an officer during a campaign and further nettled his superiors. It also angered officers of the Seventh Cavalry, who stood behind their commander. The field court began on January 7 and completed its work eleven days later. Kent and Baldwin (Miles's old colleague, whose appointment clearly compromised the court's objectivity) visited the various unit camps with an appointed recorder to examine witnesses. Colonel Forsyth attended all the sessions. In all, Kent and Baldwin questioned twenty officers, including General Brooke and Colonel Forsyth, as well as interpreter Wells, Father

Craft, and two wounded Lakotas (Frog, a brother of Big Foot, and Help Him) whose statements were translated by Wells and the Reverend Cook. On January 10 Baldwin jotted in his diary: "Eliciting little Evidence [*sic*]. Too many people are not anxious to give Evidence."[35] Regarding Forsyth's placement of his troops at Wounded Knee, most junior officers concurred that nobody had anticipated an outbreak because of the command's superior strength and weaponry over the Indians on December 29; nor were they inclined to criticize Forsyth's decisions.

On that point, however, Dr. Ewing, who declared that he "saw the whole thing, was close at hand, [and] within from 5 to 10 feet of the principals," testified that some soldiers were killed by the fire of others. "I base it from the position of the troops," he said. "The most injury was inflicted upon Captain Wallace's Troop K, and there was another troop which suffered almost as severely. I think it was Captain Varnum's Troop B. One out of every 8 was wounded or killed, taking the number of troops to be 50 strong each. There were about 25 killed from all the troops, and a large number wounded." Ewing concluded: "Located as the troops were, and firing as they did, it was impossible not to wound or kill each other."[36]

On the issue of the excessive number of noncombatant losses, the officers stressed that they had tried not to shoot women and children and had repeatedly called out to their men to that effect. But in the dense smoke and running confusion it was often impossible to distinguish between warriors and others. Forsyth, who testified on his own behalf on January 11, maintained: "I made a judicious disposition of the troops under my command . . . so placed my troops as to make their power most effective in case of resistance, and at the same time to prevent any unnecessary destruction of or injury to non-combatants. I permitted no mixture of my command with this armed body of Indians, except such as was, in my judgment, necessary to effect their disarmament." Forsyth perhaps more revealingly wrote his daughter: "There was no possible chance of getting the guns from the Indians without a fight, and fight they did."[37]

In their report Kent and Baldwin presented no sharply drawn conclusions. Each officer filed a separate opinion. Major Kent's views were largely objective, while Baldwin's tended more to Miles's known thinking. As Whitside said in a letter to his wife, Baldwin's presence ensured that "the report of the Board will probably be in accordance with the will or desires of Gen. M. instead of the facts in the case as shown by the evidence adduced."[38] While both critiqued Forsyth's placement of Troops B and K between the council area and the Indian camp, Baldwin noted that "the relative position of K and B Troops made it impossible for them to deliver their most effective fire upon the fleeing warriors without endangering the lives of each other." Moreover, he said, "It was impossible for the troops outside the immediate vicinity of the first outbreak and at the most critical moment of the day to open fire without endangering the lives of the men of K and B Troops." Furthermore, a fusion of evidence suggested that the violent outcome of the attempted disarmament had been totally unforeseen by army leaders present (a conclusion contradicted at least by Forsyth in his comment to his daughter on January 4) and that the affair at Wounded Knee had been an accident wholly grounded in unanticipated and regrettable circumstances.[39]

Late in the proceedings, at Miles's direction, the board solicited Brooke's testimony, particularly inquiring into the department commander's dissemination of Miles's recurrent directive for officers to prevent their commands from becoming "mixed up with the Indians," to "hold them all at a safe distance" and to "guard against surprise or treachery." Brooke told the board that he had instructed both Forsyth and Whitside to keep Big Foot's followers "at a distance," although Forsyth denied he had received such instructions. Brooke earlier had told Miles, "My verbal instructions to him [Forsyth] on the evening of the 28th were to take every precaution to prevent the escape of any of Big Foot's band, and to be particularly careful in disarming them."[40]

Although the court of inquiry delivered its findings on January 18, Miles would not submit his approval until January 31, following his return to Chicago. "There is a general feeling," reported Forsyth's brother-in-law, "that he [Miles] is up a stump, and cannot get evidence satisfactory to him upon which to base an adverse report." And in something of an understatement, Forsyth wrote: "It is my belief that the report made by the Kent Board was not at all satisfactory to Gen'l Miles."[41] Still fuming, the general endorsed the report but wrote a stinging indictment of Forsyth, insisting that his "incompetency and neglect . . . should not pass unnoticed." "The testimony elicited shows . . . Colonel Forsyth had received repeated warnings as to the desperate and deceitful character of Big Foot's Band of Indians, and repeated orders as to the exercise of constant vigilance to guard against surprise or disaster under all circumstances." He added: "These warnings and orders were unheeded and disregarded by Colonel Forsyth."[42]

As for the placement of troops, Miles, citing Lieutenant Cloman's map, asserted that "at the beginning of the outbreak not a single company of the troops was so disposed as to deliver its fire upon the warriors without endangering the lives of some of their own comrades. It is in fact difficult to conceive how a worse disposition of the troops could have been made." Furthermore, "the testimony goes to show that most of the troops were forced to withhold their fire, leaving the brunt of the affairs to fall upon two companies [Troops B and K] until such warriors as had not been killed broke through or overpowered the small force directly about them, and reached the camp occupied by their women and children."[43] Miles did not directly comment upon the excessive numbers of casualties among women and children, apparently tolerant of the witnesses' explanations of what had happened, though noting that the Hotchkiss guns had directed their fire on the camp. (Kent had blamed the excessive deaths of women and children on the Indians who had initially fired into their own people.)

In the end, the Washington hierarchy united against Miles and his projected censure of Forsyth. General Schofield proclaimed that the report indicated that the officers and men had used "great care . . . to avoid unnecessary killing of women and children," that the Seventh Cavalry had performed with "excellent discipline" and "great forbearance," and that "the interests of the military service do not . . . demand any further proceedings in this case." Secretary of War Proctor, citing Kent and Baldwin in noting that "the evidence fails to show that a single man of Colonel Forsyth's command was killed or wounded by his fellows," agreed and ordered Forsyth's restoration to command "by direction of the President."[44]

In refusing to endorse proposed citations for Forsyth and Whitside ten months later, Miles forwarded to Schofield a blistering rejoinder. In it he amplified his view of the army's performance at Wounded Knee and took both men to task:

To commend subordinate officers and soldiers for restraining and withholding their fire in the early part of an engagement, when they, by the orders of their superior officers, had been so placed that their fire would have had "deadly effect" upon their comrades would be somewhat unusual; yet the actions of such officers as Captains Moylan, Capron, and Godfrey, and Lieutenants Garlington, Hawthorne, Sickel, and others, did much to retrieve the actions of Major Whitside and Colonel Forsyth, who were responsible for placing and retaining the command in such a fatal position, resulting . . . in the useless waste of many lives. Instead of commendation, Major Whitside deserves serious condemnation: First, for camping a body of Indians close to a deep ravine, where they were allowed to escape, or in case they should take refuge in the ravine, cause a useless loss of life in dislodging them. Second: By making so fatal a disposition of his command . . . that the line of fire of *every* troop and the artillery was directly towards its own camp or comrades.

Miles believed that the entire command, including the artillery, "should have been so placed that all might have fired upon the warriors who did not give up their arms, without endangering the soldiers' lives or the lives of over two hundred innocent people."[45]

The remainder of his diatribe Miles leveled at Forsyth: "Colonel Forsyth is equally deserving of censure for permitting and continuing such a disposition of his command in the presence of a body of armed Indians. The pretence that no danger was apprehended does not justify any officer in permitting his command to be uselessly jeopardized. He is also responsible for the way in which his command was handled after the first fire occurred." Miles concluded: "The recommendations for brevets or for honorable mention for such field officers is . . . an insult to the memory of the dead, as well as to the brave men living."[46]

Without question, the ongoing debate regarding Forsyth's conduct at Wounded Knee cast a long shadow over the army's closing weeks of campaign activity on Pine Ridge Reservation. The court of inquiry seemed to provide little but a façade to protect and enhance Miles's public persona. In exonerating Forsyth, it indeed provided bountiful historical data but most immediately furnished ammunition to exacerbate army political infighting and assure abundant fare for prolonged news consumption.[47] When asked for a statement about the outcome from reporters, Miles said only: "What I did I would do again under the same circumstances."[48]

Miles further commenced an investigation of the Mission Fight and Forsyth's role in it. His division inspector-general, Colonel Edward M. Heyl, submitted a report on January 28 in which he opined that Forsyth had not secured the high ground with skirmishers before Major Henry's relief troops arrived on the scene and that Forsyth's advance position had not been judiciously selected to preclude warriors from taking position on the hills to his rear. Heyl concluded: "Had it not been for the timely arrival of Maj. Henry with his battalion of the 9th Cavalry, the result would have in all probability been very serious."[49] It is possible that Miles held off submitting his endorsement of the Wounded Knee report to see what blame, if any, against Forsyth might derive from Heyl's scrutiny of the mission action. The division commander affixed and forwarded none; but his vendetta continued. In his annual report filed in September 1891 a still-angry Miles skewered Forsyth and thus his regiment with the following remarks on the mission encounter:

On December 30 a small band of Indians came near the Catholic Mission, 4 miles from the military camp at Pine Ridge [Agency], and set fire to one [*sic*] of the small buildings. Col. Forsyth, with eight troops of the Seventh Cavalry and one piece of artillery, was ordered by Gen. Brooke to go out and drive them away. He moved out, the Indians falling back before his command with some skirmishing between the two parties, until they had proceeded 6 miles from the camp at Pine Ridge. There the command halted without occupying the commanding hills, and was surrounded by the small force of Indians. Skirmishing between the two parties followed. . . . Fortunately Maj. Henry, with four troops of the Ninth Cavalry and one Hotchkiss gun, was in the vicinity, and moved at once at the sound of the guns. Upon arriving on the ground he made proper disposition of his troops by occupying the adjacent hills and drove the Indians away without casualty, thereby rescuing the Seventh Cavalry from its perilous position. . . . For his conduct on that day and the previous day Col. Forsyth was relieved from command.[50]

Nor had Miles forgotten about Colonel Sumner's earlier oversight with Big Foot. In a confidential statement, he severely critiqued that officer's negligence:

Big Foot once a prisoner should not have been allowed to escape, and . . . Colonel Sumner should have prevented such escape by using his entire command effectively. It appears that . . . after the Indians surrendered, . . . they were allowed to go wherever they wished without guard, and the troops were marched several miles distant from that place to camp. . . . To say the least, this was very poor judgment on Colonel Sumner's part. . . . [In retrospect,] Colonel Sumner's action in this case brought about a most serious complication of affairs in other parts of the field of operations, by making it possible for the entire hostile element to effect a concentration, and necessitated the using of nearly the entire mounted force of troops in the field to accomplish (& not without great loss of life), and what was so completely within the grasp of Colonel Sumner, without bloodshed.[51]

As the investigation of Colonel Forsyth's role at Wounded Knee dragged into mid-January, Miles relentlessly tightened his command around the Sioux, seeking a firm yet amenable end to the crisis without further violence. He issued Brooke strict orders: "Make all arrangements for moving the line forward simultaneously . . . , either pressing the Indians towards the agency, or following them should they move to the agency or elsewhere. In case [of] any attempt to break away, they must be followed by a strong mounted command, with the utmost vigor." Miles also sent troops up Grass and Wounded Knee Creeks to assure that no Indians had remained behind or somehow evaded the advancing line. Brooke would further "submit to this Headquarters a daily report giving the exact locality of each command, where they will camp each night, and the amount of supplies on hand."[52]

Brooke, in turn, issued instructions to his unit commanders along White River to dispense sage advice about engaging Indians: "Indians will always flank an advancing line if practicable to do so. Troops must employ the same methods and endeavor to flank Indians from positions taken by them. Care must be taken not to expose troops in massed bodies, as a shot fired at a mass will be more destructive than at individuals. Great care must be taken not to waste ammunition. No firing must be permitted except at an enemy." He urged that engaged troops fire from prone positions or from positions best shielded from enemy fire.[53]

With scouts, commanders, and most of his men dispersed to camps along the line of White River and its tributaries, General Miles resolved to continue his dialogue with the former Stronghold people—mostly Brulé former occupants of the Badlands retreat now joined by Oglala defectors from the agency. On January 1 a body of about one hundred came in, most of them women and children. Several more came in the next day. But despite Miles's meeting with the chiefs on January 5, the Indians remained frightened and angry, still venting their outrage over the slaughter of Big Foot's followers as they argued among themselves over what to do. Perhaps indicating a building momentum, however, on the day after the meeting seventy more needy women and children appeared at the agency, having slipped away from the White River encampment. Some of Buffalo Bill's former show Indians who made daily visits to the camp probably facilitated this. One of them reported that Red Cloud's band was kept under guard. The old chief wanted to come back but needed someone to help bring him. A trickle effect had begun. Two days later seventy-five more straggled into the agency, including men. It appeared that total submission was imminent.[54]

Late in the afternoon of January 7, the same day that testimony in the Forsyth case got underway, violence again marred Miles's yearned-for peaceful settlement. Word quickly spread that First Lieutenant Edward W. Casey, Twenty-Second Infantry, a widely known and respected officer commanding two troops of Cheyenne scouts lately arrived from Montana, had been killed north of the agency (eight miles above the mouth of White Clay Creek) while reconnoitering No Water's Oglala camp. Casey was forty years old, a West Point graduate, and a member of a prominent military family. In 1876–77 he had served in Miles's campaign against the Lakotas and Northern Cheyennes and had participated in the final major engagement of the Great Sioux War. Casey had studied Indian culture and enjoyed a deserved reputation for working with the people. On the day he died Casey, accompanied by a Cheyenne scout named White Moon, had passed near a group of Brulé Sioux butchering cattle. After a brief exchange with several of them, he and White Moon had continued on their way. They were presently joined by two Indians that he believed friendly and shortly afterward by a mixed-blood named Pete Richard, a son-in-law of Red Cloud, who carried a warning from the chief that Casey was in great danger. As Richard and Casey turned their horses to depart, a shot rang out from one of the Indian's Winchesters, striking the officer in the head and knocking him from his saddle. Plenty Horses, the nineteen-year-old Brulé who killed Casey, had been a student at the Carlisle Indian School. He abruptly wheeled his horse and proceeded to the Brulé camp. Later that day, Casey's scouts, sporting war paint and with their ponies' tails knotted ready for fighting, rode out at sundown and retrieved their commander's body. It had been stripped but not mutilated. Captain Baldwin mourned Casey as a "gallant brave friend." On learning of his death, Casey's artist friend Frederic Remington, who had just left Pine Ridge to return east, bemoaned: "The Indians who murdered him did away with a man who was their sincere friend. . . . He probably owed his death to his wonderful courage, which sometimes took him into places of extreme danger." Casey's body was shipped by train for burial in the family plot near Wickford, Rhode Island, on January 12.[55]

Four days later, in a spasm of unwarranted brutality unrelated to Casey's killing, an elderly Oglala man named Few Tails from the Pine

Ridge Reservation was ambushed and murdered by citizens along the Belle Fourche River (North Fork of the Cheyenne) near the mouth of Alkali Creek. Few Tails, his wife, Clown, and another tribesman named One Feather, with his own wife and two children, had been hunting wild game in the Black Hills with permission from Agent Royer and had missed the Wounded Knee trouble. En route home with two wagons loaded with meat, the party was suddenly set upon near Bear Butte by five citizens led by three brothers named Culbertson who shot to death Few Tails, twice wounded his wife, and killed the horses drawing his wagon. In the fracas One Feather broke away with his wagon and family. He told his wife, who had also been wounded, to fly with the children in the wagon, while he held off the thugs with his Winchester. One Feather soon caught up with his family. When the Culbertson bunch once more overtook them, however, One Feather again fended them off as his family fled in the wagon. All finally reached the distant agency. In the meantime, the wife of Few Tails survived a frigid night despite her wound. With help from good ranchers, she reached Pine Ridge Reservation. There she encountered Colonel Carr's troops on Wolf Creek, who fed her and took her by ambulance for treatment at the agency. An examination of the ground where the initial attack took place concluded that "the Indians were quietly going along this trail when they were fired on from . . . ambush. . . . It looks very much like murder in cold blood." Days after the Few Tails killing, Indians from the Cheyenne River Reservation located his body and buried it near the place where he died.[56]

The killings of Lieutenant Casey and Few Tails created dismay and new fears for army and Lakotas alike and threatened the anticipated peace settlement at Pine Ridge Agency. While word of Few Tails had not yet circulated, news of Casey's death at the hands of a Brulé spread quickly, precipitating a tremendous row between the Oglalas and Brulés when some Oglalas plotted to bolt the encampment. Upset over the incident that he had tried to avert, Red Cloud determined to get back to the agency. During the night of January 7, escorted by his son and daughter and perhaps 200 others, including He Dog, White Hawk, and their families, Red Cloud stole away in arctic conditions as angry Brulés fired their weapons after them. Red Cloud's party reached the agency cold but unscathed. Lieutenant Taylor recalled the occasion:

About dawn a scout reported that Red Cloud was coming, and soon a stealthily moving figure could be distinguished against the skyline. In course of time the old chief, assisted by scouts, staggered into camp. He was placed on a box in my tent close to a Sibley stove in which a fire burned. A squaw and a young girl had accompanied him, as his eyesight was failing him and he experienced difficulty in walking alone—all in a tremble, cold, wet, exhausted, hardly able to articulate. . . . Accordingly, I gave him a drink of good whiskey. . . . He took from his clothing a pistol and handed it to me saying it had belonged to Lieutenant Casey. . . . Red Cloud then proceeded to describe the situation among the hostiles in full, giving as his opinion that they would soon give up and come into the agency.[57]

Coincidentally, on the same day and much to Miles's satisfaction, Young Man Afraid of His Horses, the powerful Oglala chief and government ally who had been hunting in the Big Horn Mountains for several weeks, arrived back at the agency and met with the general. Miles had effected his early return by rail. The chief's wise and respected counsel as well as his stature and friendly demeanor had an instant calming effect on the people, and things moved quickly thereafter. More Oglala women and children also reached the agency that day, some escorted by Ninth Cavalry troopers. A correspondent observed that "the trader's stores are filled with men, women and children for the first time since the battle." Late on January 9, Young Man Afraid of His Horses visited the Oglala camp and received assurances that the rest would come in soon. Yet the signals remained mixed. Lieutenant Taylor obtained letters sent by Short Bull and Kicking Bear attesting to their intent to turn themselves in the next day and to camp near the Catholic mission, but it did not happen. Miles told reporters: "Things cannot remain as they are. Those people," he said of the Brulés, "must come to some conclusion and act upon it or, however much I regret it, I must move upon them." Notably, former agent Daniel Royer departed Pine Ridge that day, guarded by a detachment of policemen. Captain Francis E. Pierce, First Infantry, replaced him in an acting capacity in accordance with Miles's request as sanctioned by the Interior Department. (Agents were not directly replaced at the other agencies, as Miles had requested; at those stations, however, the designated officers were directed to "exercise such military supervision and control" without disrupting the agents' administration.)[58]

On January 10 a hefty load of provisions was sent to the distant Indian assemblage. On January 11, as the arc of soldiers drew ever nearer and rumors swirled of an impending attack on the agency that night, Miles boldly directed scouts Frank Grouard and Yankton Charley into the camps to deliver an ultimatum for the Indians to yield. The ultimatum precipitated a nighttime council in which the Sioux leaders deliberated yet again on what course to take. With food in short supply, harsh weather, and troops closing in around them, they finally decided to move immediately toward the agency while their chiefs would confer with Miles at a given point. If conditions then warranted, they would submit and turn in their weapons. Many feared to do so, however, and reports told of warriors burying or otherwise concealing their guns while en route to the agency.

Rather than create a crisis over disarmament, Miles had decided to delegate this activity to the leaders of the respective tribes. In the interim he had established guard posts at all roads into the agency, beyond which armed Indians were not permitted. Moreover, he planned to segregate the seemingly friendly Oglalas from the more radical Brulés and promoted the departure of the Brulés for Rosebud Agency as soon as possible.

On January 12 the Indian caravan got underway, and the couriers took the news to Miles. The chiefs presently sent word that they desired to meet the general the next day. Their rapprochement was further confirmed in a message from Brooke. Cautiously hopeful, Miles addressed Brooke: "From men that have been in the camp I learn that they are yet wild and excitable and talk a great deal about the Wounded Knee affair, but it is hoped that in a few days they will learn that the military are not going to do anything but what is right."[59]

By mid-afternoon the advance of the Indians was accompanied by the discharging of guns and turbulent demonstrations. Most of the remaining Oglalas as well as the Brulés finally halted within two miles of the agency and only one-half mile from army pickets guarding the northernmost earthworks. Indian camps with tipis, dogs, and ponies stretched along either side of White Clay Creek under a pine-topped bluff all the way back to the mission. "That day," wrote Father Jutz, "we had so many visitors that the bread basket and the coffee kettle grew much too small." All told, said Father Perrig, "we counted 734 armed men. There were undoubtedly about 1,000 women and children and more than 2,000 horses. . . . Right behind them came the van of General Brooke's troops." The troops threw up their tents near the mission farm (essentially the same tract where Forsyth's engagement of December 30 had occurred).[60]

Miles had forewarned Brooke to "take every precaution against creating an alarm or any unauthorized attack, and avoid bringing on an engagement."

On advancing, Brooke's soldiers pressed so closely that at one point, an observer recalled, "one of the reds came charging back waving a white sheet and excitedly pleaded for the soldiers not to come so fast because it was frightening and annoying the Indians." That evening Miles notified Washington of the developments, concerned over the Indians' fears that "their arms will be taken away and then all treated as those on Wounded Knee." Brooke bridled over the language, believing that the statement insinuated that "the arms of Big Foot's band were taken from them and the band massacred. I do not think the Major General commanding intended to give this impression. . . . He may [want to] correct what is to me an intimation to that effect." Miles did not revise his remark, however. Instead he told Cody to inform General Colby of the imminent settlement and that he might now withdraw all the Nebraska troops (Colby personally arrived at Pine Ridge late on January 14).[61]

Events moved quickly, though tentatively, thereafter. On January 13, a clear sunny day, another Wounded Knee soldier was buried in the agency cemetery. By then word of the killing of Few Tails had arrived to rouse and infuriate the Oglalas, although Miles met with several chiefs to allay their frenzy. In the Brulé camp fractiousness erupted among the younger warriors, who refused to part with their arms. Young Man Afraid of His Horses arrived among them to announce an imminent dispersal of government rations and to request ten chiefs to council with Miles, an invitation that produced further quarreling over the arms matter. When allowed into the agency, the Indians were expected to submit to agency regulations and directions of the military agent. The enclosing troops that night camped within six miles of Pine Ridge Agency and now fairly encircled it. Miles's forces were at the agency, Carr approached the area of the beef corral on the east, Brooke was directly north, and Wheaton was stationed along the western extremities. Miles sent word for his commanders to watch for escapees and to take measures to intercept or pursue them. "The whole field force was within striking distance," acknowledged an officer.[62]

On January 14, after extensive discussions between Miles and Young Man Afraid of His Horses and between that chief and the Oglala and Brulé leaders, the meeting with the chiefs proceeded. During the day Sioux leaders Little Wound, Calico, Big Road, Crow Dog, Turning Bear, Two Strike, Kicking Bear, Lance, High Pipe, High Hawk, and Eagle Pipe (four Oglalas and seven Brulés—Short Bull did not attend) agreed on a disarmament whereby the Indians would turn over their arms to their respective leaders to be tagged for monetary reimbursement. They would move their people to designated sites on the west side of White Clay Creek and return their children to school. Miles announced these developments to Schofield, telling him that "they have a large number of wounded women and children, which creates a most depressing feeling among the families, and a desperate disposition among them." Despite his overall optimism, as a military safeguard Miles directed a "strictly confidential" note to Brooke, urging him to "so dispose your command that, should it be required, you can enclose the hostile camp on three sides, with the least possible delay. Your line and Colonel Shafter's cannot be more than four miles apart. Between eight and nine hundred men are in the hostile camp and, should they endeavor to escape, the commands should be so placed as to be all effective at the same time."[63]

January 15 continued warm and sunny. Around noon the Oglalas and Brulés began advancing along White Clay Creek to their designated grounds west and south of the agency buildings. Private Charles W. Hayden, General Miles's standing orderly, witnessed the extraordinary happening: "The Hostiles numbering 3000 came in today bringing with them quite a number of wounded. . . . It was a grand sight to see so many comeing [sic] in in one long column with their war paint and feathers on[—]big, little, old, and young. Squaws and Poppoosses [sic], some walking, some in wagons, on ponies, on travoix and every way." Miles and his staff, along with General Colby, watched from horseback atop a rise that the Indians had to pass over in their approach. In the entrenchments nearby soldiers and artillery pieces stood poised for action. Baldwin described the occasion as a "grand display of their warriors both mounted & on foot." The line stretched back for several miles. The warriors advanced in pairs, carrying few guns and mostly war clubs, as if marching in review.[64]

Many of the returning Oglalas joined with "friendlies" already at the agency, and most assumed stations along the west bank of White Clay Creek. The Brulés at first camped separately near Red Cloud's house, also west of the creek, but soon moved to join the Oglalas, forming a grand cantonment fully a mile and a half long, stretching west to the bluffs on which they posted guards. When established, the camp numbered about 750 tipis with at least 3,500 people, with thousands of ponies and hundreds of wagons, buggies, and dogs.

On the appointed plain the arriving warriors turned in their firearms through their chiefs, as clerks tagged them for payment. But only a few were initially submitted, and the chiefs agreed to surrender others the next day to agent Pierce. Many observers believed that the guns presented were in the same antiquated condition as those delivered earlier at Wounded Knee, while the worthy repeaters had been stashed for later retrieval. Miles wisely did not order a search.

At the start of the disarmament Kicking Bear, principal architect and practitioner of the Lakota version of the Ghost Dance as well as the epitome of symbolism in the movement, took center stage. As described by correspondent Kelley, "Kicking Bear . . . strode forward with haughty step and form erect, with folded arms; he sternly eyed the military commander; defiance faced defiance for the moment; but in recognition of submission, this proud savage humbly laid his carbine at the feet of General Miles." Despite initial optimism, when all was done, over the next several days fewer than 200 guns had been collected and the camp at Pine Ridge Agency had swelled to more than 6,000 people.[65]

A lavish feast followed. In the afternoon the chiefs from Wednesday's meeting conversed with Miles, who assured them that the government would improve on its treaty commitments. Short Bull met privately with Miles at his headquarters, where he "surrendered freely" his Winchester rifle. The general most likely vowed to promote the Brulés' wish to remove permanently to Pine Ridge in appropriate offices. In the meantime Brooke advanced his troops in skirmish order from below the mission. Part of his command camped north of the Indian assemblage on the west side of the creek, while another part moved to flank the Indians on the southwest. In the entrenchments near the agency soldiers with artillery closely checked the Sioux. Miles notified Schofield that the crisis was over and that the troops could now be deployed elsewhere. The army occupation indeed appeared at an end.[66]

The following days offered respite and consolidation for Indians and soldiers alike and afforded a measure of relaxation long missing in either camp over recent weeks. On the day after the massive submission of the Oglalas and Brulés, Miles set the stage for the return of the Brulés to Rosebud Agency. At a council with tribal leaders on January 17 he called for their further disarmament and discussed the Brulés' desire to remain at Pine Ridge. Captain Jesse Lee, their appointed military agent, consoled the Brulés, saying: "I am here to do the bidding of the Great Father and General Miles. . . . I speak from my heart and would like to see as many Brulés . . . [at Rosebud] from here to help me." In February some 700 of the Brulés departed for Rosebud with Lee.[67]

Significantly, Miles also started the Northern Cheyennes on the way to Montana, twelve years after their arrival at Pine Ridge Agency. He sent many off early to Oelrichs, the first stop toward their destination. "They seem to be afraid of the Sioux," wrote diarist Hayden. Indeed many Cheyennes had signed the divisive land agreement. Others had served as scouts for the army in the late difficulties, both with Taylor's recruits and with those arriving from Fort Keogh with Lieutenant Casey. Anticipating danger from the Sioux, Miles urged the Cheyennes' early departure. Many Cheyennes also feared that the Sioux would steal their ponies. Moreover, most Cheyenne families at Pine Ridge were ready to head home to the reservation established for their relatives in 1884. The move, accepted by Morgan as commissioner of Indian Affairs, represented a temporary military expedient. But Miles remained sanguine that the action would become permanent. Although some of the people chose to remain at Pine Ridge, where they had local interests, approximately 400 Northern Cheyennes under Little Chief and Standing Elk set off with Captain Ewers to Fort Keogh and reached there in early February. After further negotiations, most of the Cheyennes eventually reunited permanently with their relatives and friends at the Tongue River Reservation near the community of Lame Deer.[68]

Within days of the massive surrender at Pine Ridge the grisly discovery of the remains of four apparently innocent Lakota dead along White Horse Creek, fourteen miles northeast of the agency, rekindled the horror of Wounded Knee. On January 20 Captain Baldwin and surgeon William H. Gardner rode out to investigate and bury the bodies. Riding with them were Red Hawk, the Pine Ridge policeman who had found the dead and identified them as his sister and her children; War Bonnet, an elderly Sioux guide with his face painted red; an interpreter; and two reporters, George H. Harries of the *Washington Evening Star* and Mrs. Teresa Howard Dean of the *Chicago Herald,* both late arrivals to Pine Ridge. The party was escorted by Company A, First Infantry, under First Lieutenant Thomas H. Barry. The men were bundled in heavy brown canvas coats, armed with rifles slung on their backs, and mounted on Indian ponies. Several Indian scouts ranged ahead and around the small column as it advanced.

The day was cold and windy, and the party passed hours crossing the infinite rolling prairie to reach the rough wooded breaks near White Horse Creek. They gained the site of the killings at 11 A.M. At the bottom of a ravine the dead lay face down in the brush, "frozen stiff," as Baldwin's orderly wrote, having been covered by snow and blowing leaves for three weeks.

A broken doll lay nearby. An examination took careful note of how each person died. The two girls, ages seven and nine, had been shot in the lungs. Their arms were frozen across their faces as they had tried to block the shootings from view. The boy, twelve, had been shot in the head, "leaving a bloody hole as large as a dollar." Their mother, Walks Carrying the Red, had been married to a man named Elk Creek, who was not present. Her face was frozen to the ground. She had been killed by a bullet "which commenced at the right shoulder and ended somewhere in the lower abdominal region. From the wounded shoulder a sanguinary flood had poured until her worn and dirty garments were crimson-dyed." The soldiers dug a three-foot grave at the crest of the hill overlooking the scene. Lifting the children's bodies, they carried them up the slope while Red Hawk, weeping silently, covered the remains of his sister with several yards of white linen brought for the occasion. She was then brought forward and placed in the grave. Her children were placed on either side and upon her. The infantrymen filled the grave and mounded the top.[69]

An examination of the surrounding ground disclosed an expended Springfield cartridge casing along with shod horseshoe impressions and booted footprints, strong evidence of army involvement. Most incriminating, however, were the powder burns. An investigation found that the deaths had resulted from "a volley delivered near enough to them to have powder-burned *each* [emphasis added]." It was assumed by most present that the killings had occurred within a day or two of Wounded Knee.[70]

The bodies were of course the four victims of Captain Edward Godfrey's afternoon sortie on December 29, as his detachment scoured the country west of the Wounded Knee field for escapees. Godfrey had briefly described the killings during his testimony before the Forsyth board. Baldwin sat on the board, asked questions, and listened as a participating member. Certainly he must have deduced who the dead were immediately upon learning the circumstances of the killings, in addition to weighing the evidence found at the site that supported a supposition of army responsibility. The incident delayed Godfrey's promotion to brigadier general until months before his retirement in 1907 and thereupon prevented his advancement to major general.

In March, at Secretary Proctor's direction, a formal investigation into the White Horse Creek affair proceeded under the auspices of the inspector-general, Department of the Missouri, the military jurisdiction that included Godfrey and his soldiers at Fort Riley. After considering testimony from the captain and the men who committed the killings, General Miles endorsed the results to Schofield and Proctor. He concluded that "Captain Godfrey was not responsible for this crime" because of the prevailing belief that the victims had come from the camp of Big Foot near Wounded Knee Creek. In fact, they had been neither Miniconjous nor Hunkpapas, but Oglalas from Pine Ridge. Although Secretary Proctor had earlier acknowledged that the killings had no connection with Wounded Knee, in a larger way—coming directly on its heels—they epitomized the worst aspects of that affair. In the weeks and months ahead, as word of the killings at White Horse Creek circulated, the episode would further tarnish the army's reputation at Wounded Knee and lend material credence to the perception of Wounded Knee as a blatant massacre in the public mind. References to Wounded Knee must consciously embrace these killings. They would not have happened otherwise.[71]

On January 18 Miles issued a lengthy congratulatory message to his command in which he assessed the campaign. He closed by expressing "his thanks and highest appreciation of the loyal and efficient service that has been rendered."[72]

Three days later the various army commands, except the First Infantry (which remained to protect the agency offices), moved their tents, belongings, and animals several miles out on the Rushville road. With excitement and full of frivolity to be returning to their home assignments, the men aligned their units opposite a broad plain and arrayed in a line of battle stretching for two miles. "The Infantry is on the extreme right, then the Artillery and then the Cavalry," noted Lieutenant Piper of the Eighth Infantry. Reporting to Brooke, he observed: "the General was very full of fun and laughed and joked with me for several minutes. I never saw him in such good humor. Must be that he is as glad the war is over as we are." Indeed, the army's formal presence at Pine Ridge Agency concluded on Thursday, January 22. It was a frigid, blustery day with portents of snow and dust storms, but not without a spectacular troop parade designed to impress upon the Indians the military power of the federal government. Implicit was a warning against further disruption. "It was," agreed newsman Harries, "a plain, practical showing of strength."[73]

As if acknowledging the new condition, General Miles, sans mustache, in a black campaign hat and navy blue greatcoat, passed down the line astride a sleek black charger at 11 A.M. With him were his staff and escort as nearly 3,000 soldiers and officers stood rigidly garbed in campaign dress.

Civilian teamsters and laborers also took part. Onlookers included agency employees and spectators in carriages and on horseback from the Nebraska communities and as far away as Rapid City. On distant ridges witnesses discerned many Lakota men who turned out to watch the display. The review commenced with General Brooke and his staff, followed by Lieutenant Taylor and his Oglala and Cheyenne scouts. Then came Colonels Shafter and Wheaton and the First and Second infantry regiments, the men advancing in blue overcoats and fur caps, decked out with arms and equipment. The First Infantry band stepped forward playing martial airs, followed by the Seventeenth Infantry and Capron's light battery of the First Artillery, replete with the Hotchkiss guns that had dealt such ruinous blows at Wounded Knee. Their attendants shivered before the mounting gale in blouses, fur caps, and gauntlets.

Miles doffed his hat to Colonel Carr, who had the honor of leading the self-styled cavalry brigade, which included, besides his own Sixth Cavalry, Colonel Sanford's professed Leavenworth battalion, a composite of troops from the First, Second, Fifth, and Ninth Cavalry regiments. Major Henry's Buffalo Soldiers, said one report, were "the leading feature of the parade." The men, straight in their saddles, arrayed in heavy fur overcoats, and with their carbines poised in salute, drew a hearty wave from Miles. When Major Whitside and the Seventh Cavalry soldiers rode by, the band struck up "Garryowen," the regiment's famous marching song. The troopers, with blue capes tossed back to expose yellow linings, raised their carbines in salute. "They had not shaved since they left their home garrisons, . . . [and] were as gaunt as greyhounds," recalled a private. It was obvious that the Seventh, its ranks noticeably thinned by recent casualties, received the strongest attention from the spectators. "A second lieutenant, with a bandaged head, was the only officer of little K Troop; and bringing up the rear was B Troop, with one-third of its men either in graves or hospital cots." Colonel Forsyth, who had commanded the Seventh in the defining engagement, remained exiled and watched, dismounted, from a distance. "As I am not a soldier," he wrote his daughter, "I am not required to be present."[74]

Following the parade of fighting troops, all other contributory aspects of the military undertaking received due recognition, including the Hospital Corps, represented by its men and eight ambulances. In its trail followed a mixed cavalcade of hundreds of heavily laden pack animals and at least 116 four-mule and six-mule and other transport vehicles. They seemed to extend forever. Of the pageantry, the *Harper's Weekly* correspondent concluded: "The column was almost pathetically grand, with its bullet-pierced gun-carriages, its tattered guidons, and its long lines of troopers and foot-soldiers facing a storm that was almost unbearable. It was the grandest demonstration by the army ever seen in the West; and when the soldiers had gone to their tents, the sullen and suspicious Brulés were still standing like statues on the crests of the hills."[75]

In such manner the country's then-largest post–Civil War military operation, with all its units, manpower, and collateral resources, abruptly ended. Within a week the South Dakota legislature would call for complete disarmament of the Indians and prohibition of all further arms sales to them. Although the legislators also called for more federal troops and armaments "to prevent further bloodshed and devastation," the occupation of Pine Ridge Reservation was for all practical purposes finished. The campaign was done.[76] The army took only a few days to withdraw its forces. Most units returned to home stations. Others traveled to new assignments. After the withdrawal the Lakotas were left to pick up the pieces of their shattered existence and in large measure fend for themselves. They had lost much through the upheaval in material, spiritual, and human terms. In the vestiges of the Ghost Dance movement it remained to be seen what, if anything, they might salvage from the ordeal. For the Miniconjous and Hunkpapas, who had experienced so much human loss, as well as for the Brulés and Oglalas, who shared in the wreckage, the horror of Wounded Knee would linger long, yielding further uncertainty and despair for the people.

FIFTEEN

Aftermath

When General Miles and his staff with a dozen Sixth Cavalrymen departed the reservation for Chicago on a special train heading east from Rushville, they took with them a large body of Sioux Indians. The Lakotas accompanying Miles included leaders bound for Washington to meet with President Harrison and other officials about the events at Wounded Knee. Also headed east but guarded by cavalrymen rode the Ghost Dance principals, including Short Bull and Kicking Bear. Their fate was detention at Fort Sheridan, Illinois, to remove their influence from the reservation communities.

Back at Pine Ridge, the weeks after Wounded Knee became intensely cold with frequent snowfall. "We have had 12 snowstorms in 30 days," wrote an officer. "Nothing but snow can be seen." "In 10 years so much snow has not fallen, nor has there been such continuous cold weather, the thermometer being as low as 40 degrees below zero." Until they were returned to their agencies at Standing Rock and Cheyenne River, most of the Wounded Knee survivors hunkered through the frigid temperatures with Oglalas and Brulés who had afforded them comfort after the massacre or remained in hospital care until they had recovered sufficiently to go home. Following their submission, it is likely that at least some of the people found fleeting shelter in the large government boarding school, sleeping in hallways and rooms and eating available school food stores.[1]

The passing days and weeks saw a rapid return to normalcy at Pine Ridge. The government boarding school, for example, resumed operation within days of Wounded Knee. Most Sioux people at the agency had not readily embraced the Ghost Dance and thus easily returned to the fold. Although the Oglalas mourned the devastating human losses of their Miniconjou and Hunkpapa relatives, their own suffering had been comparatively marginal. As designated by white authorities, the "disturbances" at Pine Ridge had yielded the loss of several day schools burned and difficulties hiring teachers as well as delays in annuities. Yet by late summer 1891 the military agent could remark that barring further detrimental influence by the traditionalists "the Indians are gradually getting into a better state of feeling, and the restoration of confidence is beginning to appear." Divisive feelings remained between conservatives and progressives, however, and they were bound to linger. Agent Wright at Rosebud reported: "The collision and results at Wounded Knee . . . will not soon be forgotten. Indians have learned that it is dangerous to oppose by force, the law of the Great Father." Wright optimistically believed that Brulés there experienced promising results in farming and in stockraising, despite their losses during the "disturbance." The agent reported that schooling, "notwithstanding the interruption," was proceeding satisfactorily.[2]

Within weeks of the Lakota submission, cavalrymen trudged through deep snows and freezing weather escorting most of the remnant of Big Foot's followers back to Cheyenne River Agency along the Missouri. Only four troops of the Ninth Cavalry, four of the Sixth, and Shafter's seven First Infantry companies, about 600 soldiers in all, camped south of Pine Ridge Agency along the Rushville road after January 25. Most of them remained for less than two months. General Brooke and his staff departed in early February. Surgeon John V. Lauderdale with two subordinates took charge of all medical responsibilities. Lauderdale described attending an Episcopal service and noticing "one of the little boys that was shot in the face at Wounded Knee. . . . He sat with his head all bound up." In mid-January a dozen wounded Lakotas still occupied straw-filled bedsacks on the floor of the church hospital. Uncomfortable and declining surgery, some left to improve or die with friends in the nearby camps. On February 5 the sole remaining Sioux patient departed. On February 18 the last soldier casualty of Wounded Knee, a leg amputee, left for Fort Riley.[3]

Elsewhere, while two companies of infantry continued at Rosebud Agency, units afield headed to home stations at Forts Meade, Yates, and

Robinson and to posts near Omaha, Denver, Cheyenne, and Leavenworth, to Utah, and eventually to California. Instead of returning to the Southwest, Carr's Sixth Cavalry was reassigned to Fort Niobrara. After the withdrawal, they and troops at Forts Yates, Meade, Robinson, and Bennett maintained more distant watch over the Indians, initially through the on-site military agents and their staffs at Pine Ridge, Rosebud, and the other reservations. The last soldiers left Pine Ridge Agency on July 27, 1891.

Recruitment of Lakota and Cheyenne scouts meanwhile transitioned into the experimental enlistment of Indian men into cavalry and infantry units beginning in 1891. Five such companies subsequently served in the Department of Dakota, while six more saw duty in the Department of the Platte, most consisting of Lakotas from the Sioux reservations. Although many deemed the enlistments an acculturating success (nearly 800 Indians had joined by late 1891), the closing of the frontier left them with little to do. As many recruits registered discontent with military life, the army hierarchy grew disenchanted with the program and ended it in 1895.[4]

Those soldiers leaving the Pine Ridge and Rosebud reservations in late January made the most of their opportunities. Having just been paid in the field, the majority of the men exited Indian country as quickly as they could, making for the seamier side of army life—the saloons of Rushville, Chadron, and Valentine and the local fleshpots.[5] When troops of the Ninth Cavalry and Eighth Infantry landed in Chadron en route to Fort Robinson, Private Hettinger recollected: "The boys proceeded to decorate the town a bright red. . . . [and] never noticed the 18 inches of snow that fell during the night until they looked for their equipment the next morning." Twenty-First Infantrymen headed home from Rosebud Agency and reached Valentine on January 27. "Several of their number indulged too freely in 'red-eye,' causing many of them to become acquainted with black eyes in a beastly row and knock-down among themselves." As drunken troops of the Seventeenth Infantry departed Chadron by train, some crawled through the windows of the cars. One who was trying to pass between the cars fell onto the tracks and was cut in two by the wheels. Many soldiers leaving the reservations got caught in severe blizzards that delayed their arrival home. In such manner Eighth Infantry companies reached Fort McKinney, Wyoming, in early February, to be greeted by a local band and the appreciative flag-waving citizens of Buffalo.[6]

Although the Seventh Cavalry drew the privilege of departing first, its return trip to Fort Riley proved disastrous. The decimated regiment, along with the First Artillery troops, fed, watered, and loaded their animals and left Rushville on Saturday, January 28, aboard two trains. One bearing the first squadron with Major Whitside and Colonel Forsyth, the section of Fourth Artillery, the hospital corpsmen, and the remaining dozen wounded pulled away late that afternoon. The other left about nine that night. Two engines powered the later train, carrying Ilsley's squadron as well as Captain Capron's First Artillery battery and all their ordnance. The train had four coaches for the cavalrymen, a fifth for the artillerymen, and a Pullman coach for the officers, all followed by two flatcars carrying cannon, fourteen stock cars loaded with horses, and five boxcars bearing the soldiers' luggage and equipment, besides a caboose. They traveled through the night and all the next day, stopping occasionally for meals. At Fremont, Nebraska, they unloaded, fed, watered, and reloaded the horses then rumbled into the night along the Union Pacific line, passing through Lincoln and Beatrice by 9 the next morning and then into Kansas.[7] Reaching Fort Riley early Monday afternoon, the first train was met by a throng of well-wishers and the regimental band.

The second train carrying the Seventh was not so fortunate. Private Hayden, who was aboard, detailed in his diary the horrendous accident that befell it that afternoon as it coursed along the same track toward Manhattan:

I understand our Conductor was to have side tracked us at Erving to let a Passenger train by, but it seems he thought he could make the next Station and side track there. So we pulled out, and were running along at a common rate of speed, and just as we arrived at Florina [Florena], where there is nothing but a side track, and on a curve and nearly level ground we were met by the other train of two coaches and one mail & baggage car combined, and as neither Train had distance enough to stop in, there was a terrible collision and two Soldiers were launched into Eternity, besides about 40 more who were more or less injured. . . . About half of our troop was injured, some being cut by broken glass, others struck by flying timbers or scalded with hot water and escaping steam from the Engine. But none were fatally injured. . . . There was no Passengers killed, but two or three were injured. The Officers' car was knocked over on its side with four big Cannons jammed up against its end, having been thrown from the flat cars (which were all mashed into kindling wood and lying on the opposite side of [the] track) by the weight of the long Stock train behind them. The Artillery lost one man and five or six horses. The other soldier belonged to the 7th. There was a Farmer [who] lived close to the Track and he kindly opened his house to as many of the injured soldiers as its size would accommodate, where they were kept and tended until a Train arrived to take them to the Fort.[8]

The accident had occurred thirty-three miles north of Manhattan when the troop train was reportedly "sailing along" at 30 miles per hour. The men gained Fort Riley at 6:30 A.M. Tuesday morning. Seventeen officers and enlisted men received injuries in the crash, mostly bruises and contusions. Some injuries were severe, however, including those to Captains Ilsley and Godfrey, who suffered a severe sprain of his left leg. This impairment left him with a pronounced and enduring limp (it was said that Godfrey had leaped from the locomotive cab, rupturing the knee ligaments and disabling him ever after). At least four victims (not including Godfrey) filed suit against the Union Pacific for damages totaling $9,500.[9]

Notwithstanding the problems getting home, troops of the Seventh Cavalry reaped ovations from crowds in St. Louis a few weeks later as they rode on horseback in General Sherman's funeral cortege. The black horse "Biff" from Troop D and Wounded Knee drew the honor of bearing Sherman's empty saddle, boots, and spurs. Forsyth, by then restored to command, was hero of the hour and evoked cheers and wild applause from spectators along the route.[10]

A cheering throng had also greeted Miles's four-coach train arriving at Chicago the night of January 27. While the general's debarking party distracted the people, fourteen of the Indians and their interpreters stealthily exited through an opposing door to be shuttled via waiting vehicles to a Washington-bound train. While Miles and his officers acknowledged "three cheers and a tiger," the surprised Lakotas still aboard raised curtains to peer at the raucous crowd "with sullen, sober faces." In a short time the train headed to Fort Sheridan and there discharged twenty-four Ghost Dance leaders, as well as three Sioux women and two interpreters, on another platform packed with curious onlookers. There the armed cavalry detachment, braced in buffalo coats, formed in front, rear, and flanks and marched the party to provisionally appointed tents to house them. "Tell them," an officer addressed an interpreter, "that they will be treated kindly, that blankets will be issued to them to-night, and fresh beef and flour in the morning. A sentinel will be placed on guard to prevent white people from annoying them. The Indians will be free to visit any part of the grounds, and the soldiers will not interfere with them. These are the orders of General Miles." The troops then occupied nearby vacated officer quarters as a sentry was posted within twenty feet of the Indian tents.[11]

The Ghost Dance leaders remained at Fort Sheridan until spring. "While there," related Short Bull, "we were often visited by Gen[era]l Miles, who with all the officers there made us as comfortable as could be, doing all in their power for us." Miles, however, had turned the "crowd of outlaws," as he called them, over to a Department of the Interior special Indian agent sent to Rushville to escort the chiefs (and, some believed, to dilute the military influence over them). "What will be done with them hereafter," said Miles, "it would be impossible for me to determine."[12]

With Miles's concurrence, however, Buffalo Bill Cody engineered consent from Secretary Noble in March 1891 to include the Fort Sheridan Sioux in his upcoming European tour. Over objections from Indian rights activists, most of the Lakotas in custody, including Short Bull and Kicking Bear, obliged and shortly set sail for Antwerp, Belgium, with the Wild West show, along with forty-three more from Pine Ridge. As one wag observed, "The Indians at Fort Sheridan are in the nature of a cross between a nuisance and a white elephant to both the war and interior [sic] departments, and it is understood Secretary Noble was only too glad to get rid of them."[13]

In early May Cody wrote Miles, telling him that "Kicking Bear and Short Bull receive $30 [per month]. Haven't got a sick Indian. They enjoyed the ocean voyage." Cody fawningly quoted the Indians as saying of the recent trouble: "You brought more [soldiers] than they ever seen [sic] before, and it frightened them. Their young men lost courage, and they surrendered without killing lots of people, which they intended doing. They say there is no use to fight you. You have too many soldiers." Soon afterward Cody sent two of the Indians with "lung disease" home to Pine Ridge. "They have been sick ever since leaving Chicago."[14]

The Lakotas who continued on from Chicago with a special agent reached Washington on Thursday, although substantive business did not occur immediately. The fourteen delegates selected by General Miles from Pine Ridge, Rosebud, and Cheyenne River included Young Man Afraid of His Horses, George Sword, American Horse, Little Wound, Big Road, Hump, Two Strike, High Pipe, and High Hawk. Those arriving from the other reservations included John Grass from Standing Rock and White Ghost and

Mad Bear from Crow Creek and Lower Brulé. Red Cloud did not accompany the group, perhaps because of his poor vision, as he attested, but more likely because his influence was waning among the Oglalas. Interpreters going to Washington included the Reverend Cook, Baptiste Pourier, and Louis Shangrau. Major John Burke, Cody's publicity manager and special friend to the Oglalas, also attended. While they awaited their audience, the visitors spent time shopping and sightseeing, including elevator rides to the top of the Washington Monument. "They were much interested in what they could see from the narrow windows at the top," noted a reporter, ". . . and some of them were loath to come down." In the interim since Wounded Knee Congress on January 19 had passed legislation incorporating most of the recommendations of the 1889 Sioux Land Commission, including a considerable appropriation for beef for the Lakotas.[15]

On February 7, in a small crowded room in the Interior Department building, Secretary Noble sat attentively at a long desk, surrounded by politicians, press representatives, a stenographer, and curious family members. The Indians, decked in ill-fitting white man's apparel—in waistcoats, shirts, collars, and neckties, and with hats in hand—occupied tightly spaced rows of office chairs. As Secretary Proctor and Commissioner Morgan listened nearby, Noble opened by welcoming the Sioux to tell of the recent trouble and other criticisms, saying that he "wants you to talk to him as a friend and will meet you in the same spirit."[16]

By preselection only a few Indians spoke. With Cook interpreting, the progressive John Grass addressed conditions at Standing Rock and told the secretary that civilians should continue as agents there and that the Indian police had controlled things well. He wanted to consult with President Harrison about the Indians' future. American Horse spoke of local problems, asking for compensation for property losses during the recent trouble and urged doing away with the boundary between Pine Ridge and Rosebud. Among other things, he registered concern over the Carlisle school, said the government had made errors trying to "civilize" the people, and called for opportunities for Indians to obtain positions of trust and responsibility on the reservation wherever possible.

Young Man Afraid of His Horses told of education and employment concerns of the Oglalas. Then Two Strike, Hump, Hollow Horn Bear, and Medicine Bull each spoke, addressing similar concerns and expectations regarding the land agreement. Hump, in particular, referenced the loss of his Miniconjou people at Wounded Knee and asked for consideration for the survivors. In closing Noble explained that the troubling $100,000 cut from the Sioux appropriation had been accidental and that the government meant only to do what was right. He concluded the session with the customary assurances of continued friendship. At its core the meeting was a précis to the meetings programmed for the next week with Morgan. Journalist David Graham Phillips abstracted the proceedings for *Harper's Weekly*, perhaps reflecting more white hopes than what the Indians truly had in their hearts. "They plead for a chance to be civilized," he wrote. "The war-path shall be no more. The tomahawk, the pillage, the war whoop, the cautious trail over the trackless prairie—all are out of date, as traditional as Cooper's Mohicans. The council fire is exchanged for the steam radiator of a government office. The Indian affects cigars, and buys clothes from Baxter Street. He wishes to raise crops and chickens, and to elect municipal officers. Sitting Bull died none too soon."[17]

Wounded Knee dominated much of the agenda with Commissioner Morgan on Wednesday, February 11. Turning Hawk, Sword, Spotted Horse, and American Horse spoke of events at Pine Ridge leading to the massacre, including the Ghost Dance, the initial exit of the Brulés from Rosebud Agency toward Pine Ridge and the presence of soldiers there that drove them to seek shelter in the Badlands. They spoke of the coming of Big Foot's Miniconjous and the Hunkpapa people who had fled Standing Rock in the wake of Sitting Bull's killing. They also told of Wounded Knee. "When the guns were taken and the men thus separated [in the council area] there was a crazy man, a young man of very bad influence and in fact a nobody, among that bunch of Indians [who] fired his gun, and of course the firing of a gun must have been the breaking of a military rule of some sort, because immediately the soldiers returned fire and indiscriminate killing followed." Most of the recollection was hearsay, for few Oglalas had participated, yet they had the gist of the story correct. Spotted Horse, however, was a voluntary scout and had been present. Noting that the first shot had killed an officer, he said that the warriors started to pull out their knives. "They were exhorted from all sides to desist, but this was not obeyed." The soldier ranks then immediately opened fire.[18]

Turning Hawk described the ensuing action as it had been told to him:

All the men who were in a bunch were killed right there, and those who escaped that first fire got into the ravine, and as they went along up the ravine for a long distance they were pursued on both sides by the soldiers and shot down, as the dead bodies showed afterwards. The women were standing off at a different place from where the men were stationed, and when the firing began those of the men who escaped the first onslaught went in one direction up the ravine, and then the women who were bunched together at another place went entirely in a different direction through an open field, and the women fared the same fate as the men who went up the ravine.[19]

American Horse provided his understanding of the events by reiterating the layout:

The men were separated as has already been said from the women, and they were surrounded by the soldiers. Then came next the village of the Indians and that was entirely surrounded by the soldiers also. When the firing began, of course the people who were standing immediately around the young man who fired the first shot were killed right together, and then they [the troops] turned their guns, Hotchkiss guns, etc., upon the women who were in the lodges standing there under a flag of truce, and of course as soon as they were fired upon they fled, the men fleeing in one direction and the women running in two different directions. So that there were three directions in which they took flight.[20]

American Horse continued:

There was a woman with an infant in her arms who was killed as she almost touched the flag of truce, and the women and children, of course, were strewn all along the circular [*sic:* crescent-shaped] village until they were dispatched. Right near the flag of truce a mother was shot down with her infant; the child not knowing that its mother was dead was still nursing, and that was especially a very sad sight. The women as they were fleeing with their babes on their backs were killed together, shot right through, and the women who were very heavy with child were also killed. All the Indians fled in these three directions, and after most all of them had been killed a cry was made that all those who were not killed or wounded should come forth and they would be safe. Little boys who were not wounded came out of their places of refuge, and as soon as they came in sight a number of soldiers surrounded them and butchered them there.

American Horse believed that the massacre had compromised him as a loyal supporter of the government. "I have come to Washington with a very great blame on my heart. Of course it would have been all right if only the men had been killed; we would feel almost grateful for it. But the fact of the killing of the women, and more especially the killing of the young boys and girls who are to go to make up the future strength of the Indian people, is the saddest part of the whole affair and we feel it very sorely."[21]

Turning Hawk expanded on American Horse's point about loyalty to the government. The whole affair distressed all the Lakota people, he said, but it particularly troubled those "who did all that they were able to do in the matter of bringing about peace." They "are very much hurt at heart." He spoke of the role of Young Man Afraid of His Horses in bringing many Oglalas back to the agency and suggested that a lot of the loyalists' property had been lost during the "great whirlwind out there."[22]

The Sioux met with the president in the East Room of the Executive Mansion the next afternoon. The diminutive Harrison, whose policy toward the tribes embraced precepts of the Dawes Act, spoke candidly. "It has been a great grief to me that some of the people represented by you have recently acted badly. . . . You can get nothing by war except punishment. You must understand by this time that you are too weak to contend against the United States in war. . . . You must tell your young men to spend their money or trade their ponies for something that is good for them and not for rifles." The president shook hands with each of them, but the Indians left Washington the next day disappointed. After the visit Commissioner Morgan directed the Sioux reservation agents to explain clearly what was due to the people under existing treaties, including the agreement of 1889. They were to be reassured that money would be available for their rations and annuities and other assistance. The agents should make them understand that Congress had appropriated funds to pay for the money that the Indians previously had been shorted. Material losses experienced by the so-called loyal Indians as a result of the events surrounding Wounded Knee would also be covered, and the Oglalas would be reimbursed for the ponies taken from them in 1876.[23]

Within weeks the government made good on the immediate annuities promised to the people. But neither they nor their descendants ever received full benefits prescribed in the land act of 1889. Problems with the issue of rations and annuities persisted. Long-term drought deterred settlement in South Dakota, and the pledged $1.25 per acre continued for only three years. Potential homesteaders stayed away. As of 1898 less than 1 million of the 9 million acres relinquished by the Sioux in accordance with the act had been apportioned to settlers. The guaranteed $3,000,000 permanent fund dwindled, due to both the collapse of the anticipated land boom and the government's failure to compute interest. Although several hundred thousand additional acres were negotiated from the Rosebud Brulés in 1904, the Lakotas never received full compensation for their land. When they brought suit against the government in 1935 for monies due them through educational clauses of the Treaty of 1868 and the Act of 1889, the Court of Claims and the Supreme Court rejected their appeal. From 1942 through 1948 the Indians petitioned for principal and interest from the sale of their lands; the courts again denied them, arguing that the government had already expended on the Sioux a figure in excess of the requested amount. The legal battle continued. As late as the 1960s litigation proceeded before the Indian Claims Commission, seeking to rectify injustices to the Lakotas by the land commission of 1889.

As for the boundary between Rosebud and Pine Ridge reservations, an 1892 agreement relocated it from the mouth of Pass Creek east to the mouth of Black Pipe Creek on White River and from there due south to the Nebraska line. Indians residing in the affected area could choose either agency as their official home and relocate there by an appointed date.[24]

Disturbed feelings among the Lakotas on the reservations in the aftermath of Wounded Knee did not easily subside, and time only worsened the despair. Routine hardships continued, including those related to assuring sufficient food and clothing for families, caring for children, unemployment following the army's departure, nursing the sick and wounded, and burying the dead. The trauma just overlaid the protracted feelings of hopelessness facing an uncertain future. Many Sioux remained inconsolable over the human toll of the recent violence, especially women and children and friends and families lost. Colonel Shafter wrote Miles on the matter, describing the people as being in an "unsettled state of mind," almost akin to listlessness, though "desirous of behaving themselves and doing as they are told." He added: "There are all sorts of wild rumors as to what is to be done to them and as to what is being done to those at Chicago. They hear that the Indians there are to be kept in prison & some of them killed—and until the Indians get back from Washington they will remain in their present doubt as to their future." Compounding all that, starvation returned. At the end of January Dr. Lauderdale, who remained at Pine Ridge Agency, wrote his wife: "Those of us on the spot can tell . . . [Commissioner Morgan] that . . . the [beef] issue has fallen short at least one or two hundred pounds on every head of cattle, and the consequence has been that the Indians have suffered for food."[25]

The returning delegation was itself dejected when its members got back to their respective reservations. Miles complained that "these men have been ignored, discouraged and disaffected." Insightfully, he noted: "The danger is not now from the hostile element, the leaders of which are either dead or under military surveillance, but from those who have heretofore been loyal." He called on the government immediately to rectify the increasingly dire food situation at Pine Ridge. The cattle were so hungry that the beef was often unfit for distribution. "I dislike to call attention to these matters," Miles wrote the Adjutant General, "but the peace of the future seems to render it imperative." Other observers noted that the attitude of the Sioux might portend more trouble in the spring. But in spite of the persistent malaise, life at Pine Ridge and elsewhere went on much as before. The people would struggle through, although still more children left the reservation to be educated at Carlisle, again with the misgivings of parents.[26]

In April 1891 Captain Charles G. Penney, acting agent at Pine Ridge, told of groups and individuals from Standing Rock, Cheyenne River, and the other agencies who were constantly visiting the mass grave at Wounded Knee and walking the field to find the places where relatives had fallen. "They cry and howl and work themselves and my people [Oglalas] into a sad state of mind," Penney wrote to Commissioner Morgan, recommending that he "stop these people from leaving their proper reservations. You may expect trouble from this cause unless it is stopped." The commissioner obliged with a directive to other agents. Second Lieutenant John J. Pershing, Sixth Cavalry, whose command had recently buried sixty-two horses at Wounded Knee, reported a band of Miniconjous from Cheyenne River as practically "living on the battlefield" and recommended that they be "arrested and sent out of the country." Similarly, Agent A. T. Lea described those people "hunting up the spots over the hills where the Indians fell in the fight, and marking them with sticks and sod"—in effect the earliest attempt at memorializing the site.[27]

The sorrowful Miniconjou and Hunkpapa relatives evolved an interest in establishing a permanent monument at the site. In the past, relatives of Lakotas, Cheyennes, and other tribes had placed small rock cairns on fields where their people (usually family members) had been wounded or died in combat with troops. Indian desire for something lasting was perhaps inspired by the July 1893 dedication at Fort Riley, Kansas, of a twenty-five-foot tall granite and limestone memorial to the fallen officers and men of the Seventh Cavalry and Hospital Corps at Wounded Knee and Drexel Mission, erected from contributions totaling nearly $2,000. The dedicatory proceedings included a dress parade of the Seventh Cavalry with Colonel Forsyth in attendance, light artillery drills, orations, and a band concert. More than 5,000 visitors had attended the events. The Indians' own wish for a permanent memorial to their Wounded Knee dead was formalized by a petition generated in June 1897, apparently planned for submittal to the Bureau of Indian Affairs. Employees of that office reportedly supported the concept "in view of the extenuating circumstances of the fight, and as a simple token of recognition of the valor of the tribe." Some even interpreted the plan to raise such a monument along the lines of government-sponsored structures as an indicator of the "civilizing" influence.[28]

Whatever the mix of motivations, the objective was realized with the raising of a substantial polished granite memorial beside the mass grave overlooking the massacre site. Joseph Horn Cloud, whose family had been almost totally destroyed there nearly thirteen years earlier, oversaw erection of the monument to the dead Lakotas of Wounded Knee on May 28, 1903. The stone cost about $400, and Horn Cloud managed the financial subscription for its creation and placement. The names of the forty-six heads of families killed there were neatly inscribed on the dark gray side panels by a contractor in Lincoln, Nebraska. A statement summarized the event, telling of Big Foot and concluding with the notation: "Many innocent women and children who knew no wrong died here." On Memorial Day a gathering of survivors from across the Sioux reservations took place, when the grave was blanketed with flowers. Throughout the Wounded Knee community people offered prayer and feasted. A concrete curbing and fenced enclosure eventually surrounded the entire plot.[29]

Over subsequent years family members and other generations of relatives have been buried adjacent to the mass grave in what is now known as the Wounded Knee Community Cemetery. By mid-century other changes had largely transformed the scene from its appearance on December 29, 1890. In 1930 a small white-frame Catholic church was built southeast of the grave. Soon afterward, across the ravine 700 feet to the south, in the area where troops had operated on that fatal day, a combination souvenir store, post office, and private museum flourished. At various places on the massacre site informational markers raised by the state, along with several other dwellings, proliferated. (The Sacred Heart Church was destroyed and the store-museum complex burned in 1973 during the American Indian Movement occupation there. Another Catholic church was built close by in 1975.) The historical integrity of the Wounded Knee site was marred forever with the construction of Bureau of Indian Affairs Highway 27, which runs directly through the locations of the 1890 Indian camp and the appointed council ground where the initial shooting erupted.[30]

In October 1906, three years after the placement of Joseph Horn Cloud's Wounded Knee monument, the dead soldiers buried eighteen miles away in the Pine Ridge cemetery were disinterred for removal to other sites off the reservation. Most of them went to Fort Riley for reburial in the post cemetery, although some had been exhumed earlier and shipped to family plots in cemeteries across the nation. The army contracted with a Chadron undertaker to exhume the bodies and prepare them for delivery to the Kansas post. Someone who worked on the project confirmed that the soldiers "were buried in the clothing they were wearing at the time when they fell, including uniform, gloves, overcoat, spurs, with personal effects including signet ring, watch, and other possessions such as small amounts of money." Government headstones placed at each grave since 1891 were likewise transported to Fort Riley and re-placed with the reburials. The body of Trooper Charles Haywood of the Ninth Cavalry, killed during the attack on the wagon train on December 30, went to Fort Robinson for burial in the post cemetery, while that of the Oglala scout High Back Bone, accidentally killed by the troops at Wounded Knee, remained in the Pine Ridge Cemetery.[31]

A lingering legal issue in the aftermath of Wounded Knee involved the prosecution of the Brulé youth Plenty Horses for the killing of Lieutenant Casey during the period preceding the Indians' surrender at Pine Ridge Agency. A detachment of Oglala scouts under Second Lieutenant Sydney A. Cloman, First Infantry, had arrested Plenty Horses without difficulty on February 8 in the camp of his grandfather Corn Man along White Clay Creek, perhaps eight miles from the White River. Cloman turned the youth over to the military camp commander at the agency. Plenty Horses and a Sioux man named Young Skunk, accused in the killing of government herder Henry Miller, were sent in custody to the Fort Meade guardhouse. A federal grand jury indicted Plenty Horses for murdering Casey on the Pine Ridge Reservation based on his own confession to the deed. But because of existing prejudice in the Black Hills communities federal Judge Alonzo J. Edgerton, over protest, changed the venue to the U.S. District Court at Sioux Falls, in eastern South Dakota. Edgerton and Judge Oliver P. Shiras both officiated at the opening of the trial of Plenty Horses, with Shiras presiding. U.S. district attorney for South Dakota William B. Sterling led the defense.

The proceeding began on April 23 in a packed courtroom and ended six days later in a hung jury, as jurors split over murder and manslaughter convictions. The new trial opened on May 25, when Captain Baldwin appeared as a witness in lieu of General Miles. Baldwin's testimony turned on Casey's reconnoitering of the No Water camp during a state of war and the circumstance that Plenty Horses consequently had been arrested and held as a prisoner of war. A bevy of witnesses testified in the case, including Pete Richard and the Cheyenne scout White Moon, who were present when the killing occurred. But it was Baldwin's statement supporting the existence of a state of war that sealed the verdict three days later after Shiras's direction to the jury in favor of acquittal (over Judge Edgerton's dissent). Following the verdict, Plenty Horses became an instant celebrity and signed autographs. Anticipating a similar verdict, the government dropped its prosecution of Young Skunk for the killing of Henry Miller.[32]

The Plenty Horses verdict also influenced the trial of the murderers of Few Tails, a prosecution that General Miles had demanded. A grand jury in May returned indictments in the crime charging five citizens, including the Culbertson brothers, all of whom were promptly arrested. Because the crime had been committed off the reservation, it would be prosecuted in the state courts. The Indian Rights Association provided funding for the prosecution. The trial began on June 22 in the Meade County Court at Sturgis, presided over by Judge Charles M. Thomas before a jury of twelve area farmers and ranchers. State district attorney Sterling, who had defended Plenty Horses, now prosecuted the accused. Testifying before a full courtroom, Clown, the wife of Few Tails, explained the killing of her husband and identified one of the Culbertsons as having been among the white men visiting the Indian campsite the night before the attack. She bared her wounds, including her mutilated breast, an action that stirred sympathies among observers in her favor. One Feather, whose whereabouts were unknown, did not testify. Several of the defendants claimed that Few Tails and his party had belonged to a band of horse-thieving Indians operating in the area and that he had been killed and the others wounded from return fire by the cowboys as they protected their stock. On July 2 the case went to the jury, which predictably acquitted the defendants in record time. Many blamed the verdict in the Plenty Horses case. Beyond the Black Hills, tabloids charged racism. The local state's attorney agreed, acknowledging that "a white man cannot be convicted for the killing of an Indian" in Meade County, South Dakota.[33]

Subsequent years at Pine Ridge and the other reservations were not easy, although such distinguished visitors as U.S. Civil Service commissioner Theodore Roosevelt reported otherwise. After touring several Sioux reservations in 1892, he reported on general improvements in Indian farming at Pine Ridge, stock raising, employment, and education and commented at length on notably enhanced beef procurement and issue processing techniques over those that had been practiced formerly. But Roosevelt also noted general discontentment at Pine Ridge, together with rumors of recommenced Ghost Dancing there. Indeed, the Ghost Dance enjoyed something of a small-scale resurgence among the Lakotas, despite having been severely discredited at Wounded Knee. The dance and its figurative and literal elements survived in traditional as well as renewal formats. The dance, of course, had widely occurred in other parts of the plains without the tragic results that had accompanied its practice among the Lakotas.

As early as March 1891 secretive ritual meetings took place among select bodies of steadfast conservative Sioux still committed to the return of the buffalo and the old lifeways. Many fashioned ghost shirts and bows and arrows in preparation for hunting the beasts. Some Yanktonai Sioux on Standing Rock Reservation adhered to the Ghost Dance in 1891. Captain Lee learned of the practice of the dance at Rosebud and so informed his superiors. A revised date of July 4, 1891, was set for the millennium. When that failed to occur the believers nonetheless continued to believe. Agent Penney at Pine Ridge noted in his annual report "a considerable number of very conservative Indians, medicine men and others, who still insist upon a revival of the Messiah craze and ghost dancing." Although special agent A. T. Lea believed the Ghost Dance among the Sioux "has proved to be one of the most demoralizing agencies that has ever come among them," for some of the people it retained influence and offered hope.[34]

While the dance never regained its pre–Wounded Knee following, it survived in modified form. Kicking Bear and Short Bull introduced its precepts to other reservations as late as 1902, and it spread into Canada. Sioux in Saskatchewan practiced a modified form, accenting upright living, into the 1960s. Ghost Dance songs and vestiges of other elements of the traditional movement endure on the Lakota reservations today, often with reconfigured worldviews to meet the stresses and challenges of modern generations.[35]

For the army officers and soldiers who served at Wounded Knee, substantial recognition came in the form of citations and decorations for distinctive performance in the line of duty. The government had promptly bestowed such laurels on individually recognized Seventh Cavalry and Battery E, First Artillery, soldiers for their service at Wounded Knee Creek and the Mission Fight at White Clay Creek. Commendations for officer and enlisted participants for service throughout the broader campaign were liberally granted. A few officers received nominations for brevet promotion. Those recommended for brevet honors for Wounded Knee and/or White Clay Creek service included Whitside (nominated by Forsyth), Capron (nominated by Forsyth), Hawthorne (nominated by Capron), and Forsyth (nominated by General Merritt). The officers never received them, probably because of Miles's intervention.[36]

Five enlisted men received the coveted Certificate of Merit, a large vellum document signed by the president on recommendation of each man's commanding officer attesting to his distinguished service and according him two dollars extra in his monthly pay. The most debatable recognition for service at Wounded Knee, however, was presentation of Medals of Honor, based on then-existing and simply stated criteria for awarding of such medals "to officers or enlisted men who have distinguished themselves in action." Authorized during the Civil War, as of 1890 the Medal of Honor remained the sole medal providing for such individualized honorable service and consequently was more frequently awarded. In effect, it was the predecessor to the Distinguished Service Cross, Distinguished Service Medal, Bronze Star, Silver Star, and Purple Heart of later generations. Three officers and fourteen enlisted men received the medals strictly for duty at Wounded Knee Creek. One additional private received his medal for service at both Wounded Knee and White Clay Creek. All belonged to the Seventh Cavalry except one officer (Hawthorne) of the Second Artillery and three enlisted men from Capron's Battery E of the First. In addition, one officer and two men of the Seventh received the medal exclusively for their service at White Clay Creek, while two others of the regiment received medals for service vaguely defined as related to the Sioux Campaign of 1890, which ostensibly included service at Wounded Knee and/or the Mission Fight. No one received the award posthumously.[37]

Among the nineteen specific awardees for Wounded Knee (out of twenty-five nominated), citations varied. Some awards detailed specific actions. Private Joshua B. Hartzog of Battery E was cited, for example, for going "to the rescue of the commanding officer [Lieutenant Hawthorne], who had fallen severely wounded, picked him up, and carried him out of range of the hostile guns." Other citations gave no clear definition beyond "distinguished," "conspicuous," or "gallant" conduct in battle, or "distinguished bravery." Despite the seemingly arbitrary nature of their issue, the Wounded Knee Medals of Honor survived review in 1916 when a War Department board headed by the retired General Miles reversed 911 previous awards. The board permitted the Wounded Knee medals to stand, based upon existing criteria at the time in which they were granted.[38]

Each soldier's immediate superior officer, usually the troop commander, was responsible for recommending Medals of Honor for Wounded Knee service. Among the first to submit nominations of subordinates were Captain Henry J. Nowlan of Troop I, Seventh Cavalry, and Captain Allyn Capron of Battery E, First Artillery. An insightful commentator for the *Junction City Republican* noted: "Captains Nowlan and Capron were the only two officers who presented the names of men who displayed great bravery during the late Sioux war. There are many more who deserve like recognition if their officers would exert themselves a little." Other troop commanders obviously followed suit. Some believe that the army institutionally delivered so many Medals of Honor for Wounded Knee service to provide a pretense of legitimacy for the killing of women and children there and to counter rising negative publicity. (The army likely termed the event the "Battle of Wounded Knee" for the same reason, even though soldiers on the scene and nearby at the time had recognized it as a massacre.) The complicity required for such a conspiracy undermines the argument, however. Given existing internal animosities and egos as well as the administrative levels and offices required to orchestrate it, such collusion seems nearly impossible. Moreover, we have no evidence that such artifice was ever contemplated, much less attempted. Seven of the Wounded Knee Medals of Honor were awarded in April 1891, with the remainder issued by late March 1895. (Many years later, in January 1925, Dr. John Van R. Hoff received the Distinguished Service Cross posthumously in recognition for his service at Wounded Knee treating injured soldiers and Sioux.)[39]

In hindsight, propriety might have dictated against conferral of Medals of Honor, regardless of the army's faulty premise that Wounded Knee was a battle, which the evidence cannot support. Given that wrongful basis (and in light of later revised criteria for the award that assuredly could have precluded its issue), it is hard to justify Medals of Honor for Wounded Knee. For many Lakotas, such recognition added insult to injury. Today they view the medals awarded to soldiers who killed and maimed innocent ancestors at Wounded Knee as so inappropriate that some have called for their rescission by the federal government.[40] Yet it is not so much the tendering of the medals to individuals (who may well have merited such award for their particular actions under certain circumstances) but rather the abhorrent nature of the Wounded Knee milieu that has driven efforts to deny the medals. Likewise, it is difficult to rationalize against judgments of personal distinction set by earlier and admittedly murky standards now generations removed. Because of the medals' individualized allocation rather than recognition being extended in the form of a unit citation, rescinding the medals seems unlikely.

Other laurels for officers took the form of promotion, as exemplified by Forsyth, Whitside, and Miles. Forsyth and Whitside, the two field grade officers at Wounded Knee, in time won promotion to general. Whitside became lieutenant colonel of the Third Cavalry in 1895 and colonel of the Tenth Cavalry in 1898. He attained the rank of brigadier general of volunteers in 1901 after service in the Spanish-American War and retired in 1902 as brigadier general, U.S. Army. As noted, Forsyth, who had withstood the humiliation of his brief removal from command of the Seventh Cavalry after Wounded Knee, succeeded to the grade of brigadier general only as he verged on retirement in 1907. Through seniority Miles became commanding general of the army in 1895, serving in that capacity through the Spanish-American War. Promoted lieutenant general in 1901, Miles retired in 1903.

Unit honors via distinctive assignments also constituted a form of recognition for troops who had been assigned to Pine Ridge Agency since November. The appearance of Forsyth with Seventh Cavalry units in Sherman's funeral procession represented an example of such special acknowledgment. Others included the designation of the regiment's Troops B and K as an escort to European royalty at the opening of the Chicago World's

Fair in 1893 and the reassignment of Colonel Henry with the Buffalo Soldiers of Troops A and K, Ninth Cavalry, to Fort Myer, Virginia, adjacent to the nation's capital, in the late spring of 1891.[41]

Some even had far less noble intentions than either the Indians or the army: people who sought and found ways to turn the horrors of Wounded Knee into personal gain. In the weeks and months that followed the conflict, particularly at Pine Ridge and Rosebud, traders and others sold items retrieved from the massacre site, the agencies, and other locations. Items tied to aspects of Lakota life, especially the Ghost Dance, proved profitable as well. Souvenir photographs of the massacre site and environs taken in early January were popular collectables, as well as garments, weapons, and related objects either stripped from the dead or in another manner associated with them and the site. Many of these legitimate items, as well as many lacking honest provenance, inevitably found their way into museums and private collections around the United States and abroad. Among the things scavenged from the frozen bodies of the Sioux before their mass burial on January 3 were weapons (mostly knives and war clubs), clothing (particularly ghost shirts and dresses, headdresses, and moccasins), and all other manner of personal adornment. Saddles, blankets, buffalo hides, pipes and pipe bags, beadwork, and other pieces of craftwork were stripped from the shattered tipis destroyed in the action or strewn across the field. Few collectors garnered honest specimens of the Indian firearms surrendered before the shooting broke out, but expended Hotchkiss cartridge casings apparently were traded. Members of the Nebraska National Guard even managed to visit the site of the Wounded Knee slaughter before returning home, proudly showing off bloodied and bullet-ridden Ghost Dance shirts and at least one scalp allegedly taken from a dead Sioux.

Store windows in Chadron and other communities—and in due course Omaha and Washington, D.C.—exhibited such curios said to have been retrieved at the scene. As news from Wounded Knee dominated the papers, demand for such items became a craze. One wit remarked: "If Gen. Miles had only given the relic hunters permission to visit the hostile camp there would have been no trouble about disarming the Indians." Some genuine articles from the site ended up in national museums such as the Smithsonian Institution, where they have lately been subject to repatriation measures. Many showcase pieces were contrived, peppered with air-rifle rounds and doused with chicken blood to ensure "battle" authenticity. In the weeks immediately after the massacre relic seekers acquired similar Lakota items at Pine Ridge Agency and other Indian communities. In later years Oglalas and other Sioux created and sold hand-fashioned Ghost Dance shirts and paraphernalia as well, so that pieces of dubious (and often fictitious) attribution have since proliferated, with many non–Wounded Knee artifacts turning up as "genuine" in museum collections nationwide and around the globe. Dime novels and flash-written histories often drawn from newspaper content fed popular culture, even as did post–Wounded Knee intellectual expressions. These included a profound chronicle by artist and former scout Amos Bad Heart Bull that depicted Oglala culture and history in more than 400 drawings and descriptions rendered between 1890 and his death in 1913.[42]

Lakota survivors of Wounded Knee, especially Miniconjous and Hunkpapas, became cherished reminders of the calamity. Tragedy and its memory touched all Lakotas. Some of the survivors relocated to the Pine Ridge community and became inspirational leaders in the struggle for recompense that extended well into the twentieth century. One Lakota who departed the reservation community within weeks of the massacre but came to symbolize the catastrophe and its aftermath for many was known simply as Lost Bird. Her given name was Waiting For Her, and she was born sometime during the late spring of 1890 on the Cheyenne River Reservation. Her parents, Crane Pretty Voice and his wife, Rock Woman, came south among the Miniconjou followers of Big Foot and were with their daughter in his camp on the morning of December 29. When the shooting erupted, they fled. After running some distance, they encountered an unattended horse-drawn wagon, got in, and raced away in the commotion. The vehicle flipped and tossed them out, leaving the baby unconscious. Believing her dead, the grieving mother swaddled her in a blanket and left her beside the overturned wagon as the couple continued their escape from Wounded Knee.

Two days later an elderly Sioux woman, finding the baby alive and crying on the field, turned her over to an Oglala man named White Butterfly, who had come out from Pine Ridge Agency. White Butterfly gave the baby to his brother, John Yellow Bird, a storekeeper at the agency. Soon afterward he made contact with Rock Woman, who identified the baby as her own. She told Yellow Bird that he could keep the child and on his invitation evidently stayed for a time at his house to nurse the baby. Two weeks later, when the Indians came in to Pine Ridge Agency to yield to Miles's soldiers, Brigadier General Leonard W. Colby of the Nebraska troops learned of the baby and sought to adopt her. He agreed to raise the child as his own and gave Rock Woman fifty dollars to conclude the agreement. Colby took the baby with him when he returned to his home at Beatrice, Nebraska, immediately petitioning the county court to adopt her legally.

A successful attorney in his civil profession, Colby had married British-born Clara Bewick, suffragist and editor of *Women's Tribune*. Although they named the child Marguerite Elizabeth, she continued to be known publicly as Lost Bird (Zintkala Nuni), a name that interpreter Philip Wells claimed to have given her. The Colbys solicitously called her Zintka. "She is my relic of the Sioux War and the Massacre of Wounded Knee," Colby told a visiting throng in 1891. Her early years with the Colbys, spent at intervals in Nebraska and Washington, D.C., where her parents worked, were at first loving and meaningful. The girl did well in school and traveled to England, where she learned to play the piano. She was regarded as something of a curiosity, however, and never fit in socially. As Zintka grew older, her life turned uneasy. Her history and background worked against her, as did parental absences, societal norms, racial attitudes of the day, susceptibility to illness, and perhaps physical abuse. Her mother enrolled the unhappy girl in boarding schools in South Dakota, where she faced a complicated self-identity grounded in two worlds, neither of which accepted her. When her adoptive parents divorced, Zintka traveled to South Dakota and briefly joined a Wild West show headed by Pete Culbertson, ironically a former defendant in the Few Tails case. Zintka became pregnant as a teen (perhaps by Colby), but the child was stillborn at the Nebraska reformatory where her father had placed her. She later went to live with her mother in Portland, Oregon, and married. The union failed almost immediately, however, after she contracted incurable and infectious syphilis from her husband.[43]

Zintka later found employment in early Hollywood as a movie extra and entertainer, worked for a time in Cody's Wild West show, and even traveled the vaudeville circuit. Distanced from her father and virtually destitute, Zintka married again and had two more children. One of them died. She gave away the other. In the meantime Clara Colby died in poverty in 1916. In the course of time everything in life failed for Zintka. Alienated from her adoptive father and other relatives, she and her husband moved to southern California in 1918, residing with his family until early in 1920. Wracked with syphilis and failing vision, she fell fatally ill and succumbed to complications of influenza at the age of twenty-nine. Seventy-one years later, through the efforts of writer Renée Sansom Flood and others, the earthly remains of Zintkala Nuni, exhumed from an unmarked California grave, were interred adjoining the mass grave atop the low hill overlooking the scene at Wounded Knee.[44] A plain granite headstone with her translated Lakota name, Lost Bird, and her inclusive dates, 1890 to 1920, marked her last resting place. She had endured a confused and stormy life. In the end Lost Bird had lost her real family, community, and culture and had become estranged from her adoptive family. A tragic victim of circumstance and of the difficulties of navigating a life between two cultures, she too was an unfeigned casualty of the massacre. In many ways she represented both the divide between cultures and the halting efforts to bridge them. She died, coincidentally, at a time of growing momentum for Wounded Knee survivors to seek justice for what had happened to them and their people on December 29, 1890.

SIXTEEN

Survivors

The Lakota survivors of Wounded Knee (*takini*)—the men, women, and children veterans of that day, along with their descendants—have become the keepers of the story of what happened to them.[1] As the years passed, however, most of the survivors spoke little of the events that took so many lives of their parents and grandparents, sons and daughters, brothers and sisters, aunts and uncles, cousins, nieces and nephews, other relatives, and friends. Non-Indian society commonly called Wounded Knee a "battle." In fact the only real battle to occur was in each Lakota's struggle to escape the onslaught and live.[2] The human loss was incalculable, as was the physical and emotional devastation. Entire families, *tiospayes,* and tribal societies were disrupted, notably at Cheyenne River and Standing Rock but also at Pine Ridge, Rosebud, and elsewhere. Virtually no one in the small reservation communities escaped the impact. The results have affected Lakota societal cohesion in every generation since. Broadly speaking, Wounded Knee and its related features constituted an existential plight embodying the worst elements of federal Indian policy regarding the Lakotas as a political and cultural entity.

Despite their immediate and long-standing grief, most of the people in time returned to everyday reservation society. They worked, raised families, attended schools and churches, and lived out their daily existence in the accustomed fashion, but as shaped by the new forces of acculturation. Some of the men continued as cowboys and stockmen and others as freighters, farmers, or agency workers. Most lived on a pittance and received government rations and annuities. Some enlisted in the Army's all-Indian units established for a few years in the 1890s or continued with one or another of the Wild West shows. Many survivors became the wise men and women of later generations, family teachers and exemplars that the young people looked up to for knowledge of their history and culture and for guidance. But it was never an easy life. The aura of Wounded Knee was always present.[3]

Most members of the survivors' fraternity stayed close to home, venturing only occasionally beyond the reservation community—on invitation or to participate with others in regional or national events. Some survivors attended the Trans-Mississippi Exposition in Omaha in September 1898, for example: along with Cheyennes, Arapahos, and Kiowas, they took part in dances before crowds of enthusiastic spectators at an Indian village set up for the purpose. The Sioux reportedly performed "the first ghost dance ever given in a civilized community," as one newspaperman put it. The dance was "not the hopping around an electric light designated as a war dance," he said, "but the real ghost dance led by the famous ghost dancers of the last Sioux Indian war, the survivors of Wounded Knee." Escorting the dancers from the attending tribes, anthropologist James Mooney of the Smithsonian Institution's Bureau of American Ethnology observed that "this dance is not a hostile movement. . . . By its strange character, . . . the whites interpreted the frenzied actions of the Sioux to be a war dance and took the initiative which really brought about the war." Through the press, Mooney seemed to speak almost apologetically to those who remembered the fears generated by Wounded Knee. "No alarm need be felt," he urged, "over the Indians who have gone into trances or over any of the actions of the Indians, for, like a fairy story, all will come out well in the last chapter." When at last the dance got underway, Geronimo, the imprisoned Apache leader then attending the exposition under auspices of the federal government, joined in the proceedings enthusiastically.[4]

Years later a number of the Wounded Knee survivors took part in a motion picture filmed at Pine Ridge in 1913 on the very scene of the massacre, with several of the original army officers on hand replicating their roles in the saga of 1890–91. Largely an epic paean to William F. Cody's career, the film was directed by Theodore Wharton. The project was the brainchild of Cody, whose long-running Wild West show was then in financial straits. He received loans totaling $20,000 from prominent Denver investors

Harry H. Tamman and Fred G. Bonfils, proprietors of the *Denver Post,* while the Essanay Film Company in Chicago provided technical support.

Planned as a visual spectacle of western history dealing with the Indian conflicts and sanctioned by both the War Department and Interior Department, the enterprise garnered attention not only because of Cody's role as organizer and featured player but also due to the appearance of noted figures who had served in key positions during the events surrounding Wounded Knee. Advisors and actors playing themselves included retired lieutenant general Nelson A. Miles and former junior officers (now all retired generals) Frank D. Baldwin, Jesse M. Lee, and Marion P. Maus. Also in the film was former Seventh Cavalry Troop E commander Horatio G. Sickel, Jr., whose unit had been on the hill at Wounded Knee and who now as a colonel commanded Fort Robinson. Sickel brought with him an artillery piece and three troops of the Twelfth Cavalry to portray period soldiers in the re-creation of the Wounded Knee sequence in the film. "Nothing like this has ever been done before," observed retired brigadier general Charles King, the army novelist. King, who also served as advisor, publicist, and probable scene writer, played himself in part of the production. "Nothing to equal it will perhaps ever be done again," he said. He was quite right, of course. How could anything like it ever be done again?[5]

The Indian contingent consisted of some 300 people, many of whom had appeared in the Wild West show, including Short Bull, Woman's Dress, No Neck, Flat Iron, Black Elk, and others well known to Cody. But those hired from the communities on the Pine Ridge and Rosebud reservations included Miniconjou survivors of Wounded Knee, some of whom had been severely injured during the fighting almost a quarter-century earlier. A report in the *Rapid City Journal* stated with fair accuracy that "some of the Indians who participated in the battle . . . played the same part today [October 13, 1913] they took in the battle of 23 years ago." Prominent among the Lakota veteran participants were Miniconjous Joseph Horn Cloud and his brother Dewey Beard, known as Iron Hail in 1890. Both brothers had been severely wounded and had lost most of their family in the fighting. They appeared in the reconstructed action sequences (Beard even wearing his old ghost shirt), along with mixed-blood interpreter Philip Wells, who had his nose practically severed in the action.[6]

At one point a number of the Indians met with Miles at what was then Pine Ridge Reservation agent John Brennan's house. As Melvin R. Gilmore, an ethnologist from Nebraska, recounted:

Among the speakers were Woman's Dress and Short Bull. It was pathetic to hear them recounting the sad affair and their attitude to the present project of representing historic events. They wanted to leave a true record. I was especially gratified to hear the reply of Gen. Miles. He told them that he had always been ashamed whenever he heard the name Wounded Knee. He said the affair was deplorable, unjustifiable, uncalled-for, unnecessary, and avoidable, that he had relieved the colonel who was in command of the Seventh and that he had never had a command again in his Department. That he [Miles] had issued orders to avoid conflict, not to fire on the Indians unless fired upon and under no circumstances to kill any women or children.

As Brennan said hopefully, the purpose of the movie was to "present historical events which paved the way to racial peace between red and white."[7]

Produced over several weeks in the fall of 1913, *The Indian Wars* included more than the events at Wounded Knee. Also depicted were engagements such as Summit Springs, Colorado (1869), and Warbonnet Creek, Nebraska (1876). Cody reenacted his original participation in both. Miles, it turned out, was a stickler for accuracy. Therefore neither he nor Cody took part in the restaging of events at Wounded Knee, despite unfair criticism that they had tried to be movie heroes by acting in the scene. The filming began with Whitside's meeting with Big Foot near Porcupine Butte and the army's escort of the Indians to Wounded Knee Creek. The next day tension appeared as soldiers and Indians reluctantly fired on each other using blanks. Scripting of the action seems to have included Wallace's death and the stabbing of Father Craft as well as re-creation of the next day's combat near the Catholic mission. Evidently the massacre segment was fairly accurate; one reviewer noted that "the white man was the aggressor. . . . The red men were crowded down into a great ravine where lines of bullets sent them to death in scores." Despite his propensity for exactness, Miles, still bitter over the massacre, protested the inclusion of this segment in the film and objected to the showing of dead women and children, who were evidently not portrayed.[8]

While the filming proceeded, Miles remained at the agency, refusing even to visit the site. Some of the Indians resisted re-creating the massacre sequence so near the mass grave. During the filming Lakota women and children wailed and sang death songs as warriors dropped before the soldiers' blank rounds. Observed a witness: "Many of them broke into tears as the vividness of the battle recalled that other time when lives were really lost." Miles's only appearance came when he re-created his part in the Grand Review segment, filmed at Rushville, while General Lee appeared ushering the Brulés off to Rosebud, as he had done in 1891. Regardless of the hype coming out of Pine Ridge after the filming, some Lakotas who took part said that the motion picture was inaccurate and that "they had done only what they had been told to do . . . [and had been] silenced and hustled into line by the picture manipulators." Dewey Beard wrote to Walter Camp: "They took it as they wished and therefore many false action was [*sic*] made." A major objection was that the producers had distorted history by portraying the Indians as having an equal number of guns as the soldiers.[9]

When completed the film consisted of six one-reel segments, the last containing cherubic scenes of Indians progressing into modern American life through education, farming, and industry. Initial screenings of the integrated parts took place in Washington, D.C., early in 1914. Government officials including the secretaries of the War Department and Interior Department and the commissioner of Indian Affairs attended. The film's national premiere—touting Buffalo Bill's moving picture appearance—occurred in Denver, followed by presentations around the country in cities such as Omaha, Milwaukee, and Eau Claire, Wisconsin. The film even had public showings in Chadron and Alliance, Nebraska. It was not a sensation despite its featured performers and content, although it went into limited national release late that year. After its opening tour the film appears to have been put into long-term storage. The few copies, including those sent to the government, likely disintegrated owing to their nitrate-based properties. Cody, who had been an omnipresent figure in the real-life drama surrounding Wounded Knee as well as in the celluloid version, died early in 1917. Only a snippet of *The Indian Wars* is known to exist today.

By their own participation, the Lakotas again drew media notice and public attention to what they had endured: the trauma and loss that Wounded Knee had come to represent in the national consciousness. Indeed their complaints about one-sidedness and their interest in assuring accuracy of the movie depictions spoke to awakening Indian concern about getting those events recorded correctly, not only for history but for more immediate reasons. As victims and survivors, they remained hopeful of reparation for the tragic wrong perpetrated against them, as had been implied by the Miniconjou chief Hump before Secretary Noble as far back as the Washington meeting of February 1891.

Interest among the reservation communities in obtaining restitution for fatalities and injuries persisted well into the twentieth century. These were long-standing grievances, principally among the Miniconjous and Hunkpapas but including others similarly affected. Precedent for compensation already existed. Within months of Wounded Knee Lakotas from Pine Ridge Agency—the so-called friendly Sioux, most of them progressive Indians who had rejected the reactionary Ghost Dance and its adherents and remained under agency control—had sought reimbursement for losses incurred during the opening days of the army campaign. Their outlying homes and property had been pillaged, mostly by Brulés stampeding from Rosebud Agency.

In consequence Congress moved on March 3, 1891, to devote $100,000 to be "immediately available, for prompt payment to the friendly Sioux and legal residents on the Sioux reservations for property destroyed or appropriated by the roving bands of disaffected Indians during the recent Sioux trouble." Within a month special agent James A. Cooper (who had been on hand at Pine Ridge throughout the crisis) turned up at the Oglala agency with the task of collecting and adjudicating depredation claims. He wanted to know about all manner of damaged property—housing, furniture, equipment, tools and farm implements, together with livestock destroyed, stolen, or otherwise lost by the Pine Ridge Indians and legal white residents on the reservation because of the Ghost Dancers. In pursuit of his assignment, Cooper also visited Cheyenne River, Standing Rock, and Rosebud, as well as the Tongue River Reservation in Montana for Northern Cheyenne claims.[10]

All affiants swore that during the hostilities they had been loyal to the government. Each of the 755 affidavits contained a deposition by the applicant affirming loyalty together with a list of articles for which the applicant should be compensated, accompanied by a statement verified by two witnesses. More than 600 claims were filed from Pine Ridge alone, and it took Cooper almost a year to complete his investigation. He journeyed to Washington in February 1892 to turn in the claims. The submitted petitions (even after a 10 percent reduction required to cover their processing) tallied well beyond the money authorized, so Cooper scaled back the figures to reach $97,647. By late summer all claimants had received the adjusted amount due them.[11]

The legislation compensating those people who did not participate in the Ghost Dances did not of course extend to the massacre victims. The material losses of the survivors were great, although not immediately recognized, while their human losses were immeasurable. Yet in a significant and broadly reaching pronouncement based on increased knowledge of the circumstances foreshadowing Wounded Knee, the army hierarchy through General Schofield concluded in 1891 that the majority of the resident populations of the affected reservations had not been "out of amity" with the government. "A careful consideration of all the circumstances of this uprising among the Sioux," stated Schofield, "seems to justify the opinion that no considerable number of them had seriously intended to engage in hostilities against the United States, unless driven to such a course by unbearable hardship, or in self-defense against the military operations ordered for their subjection." The army's conclusions gave hope. In apparent anticipation of one day obtaining relief for losses sustained during the trouble, some surviving followers of Big Foot began documenting their family and personal deprivation for future consideration. Wounded Knee survivors Joseph and Daniel Horn Cloud, for example, registered lost property at Cheyenne River owned by their father, Horned Cloud, who had been killed in the massacre, for which they hoped to be compensated. Their brother, Iron Hail, known also as Dewey Horn Cloud and Dewey Beard, similarly listed his own property losses at Cheyenne River and registered their estimated values. When some individuals living on the Cheyenne River Reservation in the early 1900s filed for property lost during 1890–91, however, inspector James McLaughlin pronounced them "ridiculously absurd." McLaughlin, formerly superintendent at Standing Rock Reservation, declared that "members of Big Foot's band . . . and . . . the stampeders from the Cheyenne River Reservation to Pine Ridge Agency in December 1890" who submitted claims were not entitled to compensation under the March 3, 1891, act that provided for payment to the "friendly Sioux."[12]

Ultimately it was the long-retired General Miles, still projecting his distinguished military bearing, who provided impetus for the compensation of the Wounded Knee survivors. Miles had never wavered in his views on the massacre. "I have never felt that the action was justified, and believe it could have been avoided," he wrote in 1911. Six years later, on learning of the presence of representatives of the remnant of Big Foot's people in the capital, the seventy-seven-year-old general addressed a letter to commissioner of Indian Affairs Cato Sells, endorsing their efforts for relief: "The least the Government can do is to make a suitable recompense to the survivors who are still living for the great unjustice that was done them and the serious loss of their relatives and property—and I earnestly recommend that this may be favorably considered by the Department and by Congress and a suitable appropriation be made." Early in 1920 Miles escorted several Lakotas to Sells's office, calling on the commissioner to support an act "of imperative importance and justice . . . to atone in part for the cruel and unjustifiable massacre of Indian men and innocent women and children at Wounded Knee." The visit prompted action. Soon afterward inspector McLaughlin, himself now seventy-eight, journeyed to the Cheyenne River, Standing Rock, and Pine Ridge reservations, seeking information to support a request to Congress for remedial assistance for the Lakotas.[13]

McLaughlin's task enhanced the survivors' quest for compensation. Although he believed that the Indians' faith in the "absurdity" of the Ghost Dance was their own fault, the former agent now comprehended their suffering and believed that they should receive assistance. His report, prepared during the summer of 1920, detailed seventy-five incident cases involving losses, while providing valuable historical data about property destruction at Wounded Knee that itemized the people's material possessions such as clothing, shelter, wagons, animals, arms, tools, and horse and camp equipment, all of which had been fundamental to their existence in 1890. In strictly human terms the value of McLaughlin's work escalated exponentially because the cases provided essential clues about ancestry and genealogical interrelationships. By identifying family members who died or were wounded and later perished from their injuries or who lingered sick for months, years, and even decades, his investigations gave insight into the coherence of Lakota group infrastructure. They also revealed the intragroup dynamics of the devastation and its long-term toll upon survivors and families.[14]

McLaughlin's report presented incisive testimony on the personal lives of people. In one case he noted:

Afraid of Enemy, of Cherry Creek [on Cheyenne River Reservation], aged 66 years, stated that he [was at Wounded Knee and] received 6 slight wounds and one serious gunshot wound, from a rifle bullet which entered his breast at the right nipple and passed out under the right shoulder, from which he bled profusely from his mouth and nose as well as from the wound. He showed me the scars of his wounds, [and] he also stated that his wife was wounded in the left thigh from which wound she recovered and died on White Clay Creek, Pine Ridge reservation, about 12 years ago; that his son named Scares the Hawk, 19 years of age, was also wounded but lived about 5 years after receiving that wound. He further stated that he had 10 horses and 2 colts with him, all of which were either killed or appropriated by others as he never saw any of them afterwards; that he also had set of harness, farm wagon, 2 saddles, tepee, full camping outfit and 2 rifles which he turned over to the military, all of which property was lost to him and never recovered.[15]

In another instance McLaughlin wrote:

Daniel Blue Hair of Cherry Creek [on Cheyenne River Reservation], aged 45 years, stated that he was at Wounded Knee with his father, mother, sister, a married brother with wife and child, all of whom were killed in that conflict except himself; that he was wounded in the left thigh; he stated that his father's name was "His Wounded Hand," and that the family had 26 horses with them when they reached Wounded Knee Creek, 24 of which horses were killed in the fight and the other 2 found by him before returning to Cherry Creek about 3 months later; that the family had set of harness, wagon, tepee, bedding and cooking utensils, all of which were lost there and nothing ever recovered except the 2 horses subsequently found.

In still another case McLaughlin recorded:

John Little Finger, of White Clay District [on Pine Ridge Reservation], aged 46 years, stated that . . . he was of the party of Cheyenne River Indians . . . under the leadership of his grandfather Big Foot and became involved in the Wounded Knee disaster of December 29, 1890 . . . ; that he himself was wounded in the right thigh, also in right foot; that his uncle Short Haired Bear and 3 of his children were killed in the conflict and his wife died about one year later from shock, fright and exposure at Wounded Knee, and that his uncle Long Bull was also killed outright in the melee. He further stated that said Short Haired Bear had 13 horses with him and Long Bull 4 horses, all of which were killed or lost to them, and that each of his said uncles had a set of harness, wagon, tepee, and full campaign outfit with them at Wounded Knee, all of which property was lost there and never recovered by any of their relatives.

McLaughlin noted:

Black Hair, aged 64 years, of White Clay District [on Pine Ridge Reservation], stated that he was in the Wounded Knee affair and received 7 wounds in the conflict (he showed me the scars in both legs, left arm and back of his neck); that the wife he had at that time was killed outright, also his 5 year old son was killed and 7 year old son wounded, from the effects of which he died 2 years later; that he had with him at Wounded Knee 4 horses, set of harness, wagon, tepee, and camping outfit, all of which was lost to him there and none of the property ever recovered.

McLaughlin concluded: "Thirty years have elapsed since that occurrence [*sic*] and . . . I am . . . strongly of the opinion that the peace of mind of the Sioux and interests of the government would best be subserved by not agitating the matter further at this late date, but should it be determined, as a matter of justice, to reimburse the Indians for the horses and other property lost to them in that unfortunate affair, an appropriation approximating $20,000 would, in my judgment, be necessary to reasonably compensate them for the losses there sustained." Notwithstanding the sentiment from McLaughlin, none of the plethora of bills in Congress during the 1920s and early 1930s addressing wide-ranging Indian claims formally undertook relief for the Wounded Knee victims. McLaughlin, who had grown to favor such atonement, died suddenly in 1923. Nelson Miles, perhaps the survivors' greatest champion, followed in 1925. Their silence brought a temporary halt in the promising effort.[16]

Vacationing in the Black Hills in August 1927, President Calvin Coolidge came to Pine Ridge Agency, where an all-Indian band played *The Star-Spangled Banner* and hundreds of Indians arrayed in traditional dress performed a selection of dances. Older Sioux men presented him with a memorial claiming the Black Hills as their own but broached nothing of the emerging matter of compensation for Wounded Knee survivors. The president had traveled by train from his vacation lodge in Custer State Park to Rushville, ironically motoring from there to the agency over almost exactly the same route taken by Brooke's soldiers in 1890. He thanked the Indians for their service in World War I. His remarks highlighting their recently legislated citizenship addressed their efforts to rise from "the hunter stage" in adjusting "to the new order of things."[17]

Four years later the Lakotas at Pine Ridge organized an advocacy group called the Survivors of the Wounded Knee Massacre. Hoping to formalize the means to gain congressional support, they began meeting each summer at the site. Agency superintendent James H. McGregor supported their efforts, although he acknowledged that their attempts to gain recognition in Washington were "feeble" because of racial prejudice and the Indians' inability to present their grievances properly. McGregor sought to enlist the support of commissioner of Indian Affairs John Collier in the Lakotas' behalf "to show the world that this was a real massacre, and not a battle." Although South Dakota's Democratic second district congressman Theodore B. Werner at last introduced a bill (H.R. 11778) to mitigate the claims of Wounded Knee survivors and their descendants, his measure drew little notice with the onset of the Great Depression and efforts by Congress to respond to the crisis.[18]

Despite the national predicament, Francis H. Case, elected as Werner's Republican successor in 1936, made vigorous attempts to fulfill the survivors' objective. Sidestepping the emerging factionalism between survivors at Cheyenne River and Pine Ridge, Case conscientiously tried to advance the Lakotas' cause, often visiting with the people in South Dakota during adjournment. With help from the Lakotas' tribal attorney Ralph H. Case (distinct from Francis Case), the congressman presented an indemnity bill in the House of Representatives on January 11, 1937, "to liquidate the liability of the United States for the massacre of Sioux Indian men, women, and children at Wounded Knee on December 29, 1890." Made controversial by U.S. Army opposition, Case's measure, H.R. 2535, called for heirs to receive $1,000 for each person killed and the same amount to those wounded or, if deceased, to their heirs. With concurrence from the House Indian Affairs Committee, the congressman sought endorsement for his legislation from the Interior Department. Commissioner Collier appeared supportive, terming the event a "massacre" and "a mournful phase of Indian history, now forty-six years in the past."[19]

News of Case's bill energized reservation survivor groups, which still included forty-four victims. Many of his aggrieved Lakota constituents submitted individual claims to the congressman, all seeking restitution. Mrs. Nellie Knife, sixty-seven, of Cherry Creek sent a handwritten appeal in questionnaire format: "Q. Were you wounded or injured? A. No, I wasn't but the gun smoke got in my lungs, and [I] also swallowed dead person's blood and my health has not been good since. Q. Did the soldiers intend to shoot you or kill you? A. Yes." She and her witnesses pressed their thumbprints on the document. Members of the survivors' association at Pine Ridge asked for donations to support delegates going to Washington to testify on behalf of the bill. Survivors at Cheyenne River and Pine Ridge even drafted their own version of a bill requiring payments of $20,000 "to [heirs of] women with child killed at the Massacre."[20]

In April 1937 Sioux tribal council members appeared without notification at congressional and Interior Department offices in Washington. "I do not know whether a hearing can be had for them right now," observed

Congressman Case, "but at least they can see some of the officials." In the meantime Pine Ridge survivors president James Pipe on Head notified Case that he and Dewey Beard would be available to testify before Congress in regard to H.R. 2535. Case appeared optimistic but forewarned the Indians: "The fate of the bill will depend upon the reaction of Congress to the President's current affection for economy." Endorsing the measure, acting Interior secretary Charles West suggested: "The massacre can be viewed both as an injury to the individuals who were killed or wounded, and as an injury to the entire Sioux Tribe. Redress, therefore, could be attempted through the method of pensioning individuals, or through creating some new advantage for the tribe as a whole, as, for example, a more generous relief to the indigent and infirm, or the establishment of an orthopedic hospital for all the Sioux, etc., etc."[21]

Following West's statement, Congressman Case notified James HiHawk (formerly spelled High Hawk), corresponding secretary and later president of the Cheyenne River survivor group, of the cautionary signals. "A large membership of the House showed its hostility towards any Indian legislation," he wrote. "It may be that the only possibility will be to get a bill which provides for some general reimbursement for the Tribe without any individual claim compensation." The Indians resisted this approach. Disarray now appeared within the survivor organizations over who would represent the groups. A suggestion from HiHawk that the matter might better be addressed before the Court of Claims led the two Cases to urge delay of the proceedings until the following year. "The time has run against us on this matter," wrote Ralph Case, "and . . . it is now quite impossible to hold an effective hearing with delegates present and develop the story of the Wounded Knee Massacre, as we hoped last winter. I feel that the only way this matter can receive due public attention is to let the matter rest during the remainder of the present session of Congress." He urged that arrangements be made for a delegation and hearing "very early in the session beginning January next." The congressman notified the survivor groups of the decision as his bill went into abeyance. Although the Bureau of Indian Affairs supported it, the office tepidly conceded that "its chances of passing the present Congress do not appear to be great."[22]

The survivor groups anxiously awaited the next regular session of Congress, beginning in January 1938. Although the War Department (through its acting secretary) discounted the Indians' appeal, citing Lakota responsibility for what had happened at Wounded Knee, the House Committee on Indian Affairs at last programmed the long-awaited hearing on

Representative Case's bill. At the subcommittee's proceeding on March 7, the congressman and the Sioux tribal attorney presented the case for compensating the victims and their heirs. The vivid testimony of James Pipe On Head and Dewey Beard, speaking for the associations, brought home for many the horrors of that day more than forty-seven years earlier. Their statements, grounded in personal experience, together with Pipe On Head's graphic paintings depicting the appearance of the Wounded Knee field before and after the eruption of shooting, clearly impressed the attendees. James Pipe On Head later submitted an adjunct statement to subcommittee members: "The survivors and descendants of those who were killed are really suffering today. The conditions on the reservation are terrible and if the Government would at least pay the survivors and the descendants . . . the whole will be forgotten. . . . We want to ask Congress to give H.R. 2535 a very serious consideration."[23]

Two months after Beard and Pipe On Head had returned to South Dakota, the subcommittee reconvened to hear a representative of the War Department oppose the bill. Colonel Russell H. Brennan was chief of budget and legislative planning in that office. He told the members that "the Department's theory is that the Government should not pay damages for any injury inflicted during a fight with enemies of the Government." Brennan was ill prepared, and his knowledge of what had happened was vague and even incorrect in places. He pointed out the Indians' treachery in firing on the soldiers "with the result that many Indians were killed, as well as many squaws." He discounted General Miles's view that a massacre had occurred at Wounded Knee, chalking it up to a presumed declining mental condition of the aged officer. Brennan did not know that Miles had indeed termed it a "a horrible massacre of women and children" and "a useless slaughter" in 1891. When pressed by Representative Case on other matters, notably on the extraordinary number of women and children killed, Brennan professed ignorance and suggested that a revenge motive likely existed within the Seventh Cavalry. Case also questioned the judgment of sending that regiment to Wounded Knee. Brennan and some members feared the implications of a compensation measure. Paying such claims, he said, "would establish a dangerous precedent" that would "throw it open to the War of 1812, the Civil War, and other wars." Before the meeting adjourned, several Sioux from Pine Ridge who were visiting the capital on other business spoke briefly. James Grass, a former army scout, recalled the mass burial at Wounded Knee: "We buried old men and old women; women that were still with child and even infants. We saw those children, perfectly harmless, who could not even harm anyone, that were killed; even little infants. About 2 miles up the ravine along the creek there were people lying dead. . . . We picked them up and buried them, . . . and there were many women."[24]

While Congressman Case drew encouragement for his legislation from supporters such as Elaine Goodale Eastman, who had helped treat the Lakota wounded in the church hospital, the effort to redeem the Indian sufferers expired in committee, a victim of Depression-era politics. Reelected in 1938, Case reintroduced the bill (H.R. 953) at the start of the Seventy-Sixth Congress. The War Department again pressed its institutional opposition, declaring that what had occurred was a battle and again recommending adverse action on the bill. Harold L. Ickes, secretary of the Interior, informed chairman Will Rogers that "the Acting Director of the Bureau of the Budget has advised that the proposed legislation would not be in accord with the program of the President." In July 1939, more than a year after his appearance before the subcommittee, Dewey Beard dictated a message to Case: "I am growing older. My wounds are making it more difficult to get around every day and I am badly in need of the money. I need the money now."[25]

Case tried again in 1940, this time placing the measure on the House consent calendar, where it received objections from several House members and died on January 3, 1941, when the Congress adjourned. Many other Lakotas inquired about the Wounded Knee indemnity legislation, only to learn that their hoped-for redress would not be forthcoming as Congress, now focused almost exclusively on a national defense agenda, demurred. Clearly frustrated, Case noted that the legislation "has always been opposed by the War Department on the grounds that it was a reflection upon the army if anything should be done," and "its passage was always blocked by the chairman of the Committee on Expenditures."[26]

The anticipated relief never appeared. After delays, amendments, and resistance thwarted Case's original measures, a bill introduced in the Senate (S. 1902) by South Dakota Democratic senator William J. Bulow received even less notice after Pearl Harbor and the country's entry into World War II. As time passed the number of survivors dwindled. Undeterred, Case renewed his effort, five years later arguing that compensating the Sioux would indicate the country's desire to resolve wrongs perpetrated against Indians throughout the United States (much in the manner that Japanese Americans and their heirs in 1988 would receive reparations for their forced internment during World War II). But Congress turned away from the Sioux, as it had done following passage of the Sioux Land Act of 1889. Case also suggested that the newly established Indian Claims Commission might process individual "claims of this type," although it never did. Indeed, no appropriation was ever forthcoming for the survivors' relief.[27]

Optimism faded. The survivors found themselves again victims of circumstance, their personhood downgraded as compassion and restitution offered in legislation was repeatedly deferred and denied. Time was running out. Old age and infirmities—many derived from Wounded Knee—took an increasing toll. In the 1940s and 1950s South Dakota newspapers regularly reported the deaths of Wounded Knee survivors, some more tragic than others. Nellie Knife, who had complained to Congressman Case about the suffocating gun smoke, died in 1946. A car accident in 1940 claimed a survivor named White Wolf, while survivor Benjamin B. Fox hanged himself in the Rapid City jail that same year. A toddler when the massacre occurred, Fox had been found beneath a blanket by his mother's body. He had lost other relatives at Wounded Knee as well. Fox attended Haskell Institute in Kansas, graduated from the Indian School in Rapid City, and later attended the School of Mines, where he was known as an exceptional athlete. He worked as an engineer at the Sioux sanatorium at the time of his death.

By the early 1950s only ten or so survivors remained alive, among them James Pipe on Head and Dewey Beard. Pipe on Head died in 1952 and was buried in the Micasa Presbyterian Church Cemetery in Oglala, South Dakota. Dewey Beard, ninety-three, the last of the Horn Cloud brothers and once known as Iron Hail, succumbed to old age on November 2, 1955, at his small tar-papered house in Kyle. Acknowledged as the last survivor of the Battle of the Little Bighorn as well as among the last Sioux participants at Wounded Knee, Dewey Beard was a remarkable touchstone to the distant past. While he never learned English, he had become an important advocate in the Sioux fight for compensation since his appearance before the subcommittee in 1938. Widely recognized across the state and nation, he had done much to promote tourism in South Dakota but had lost the use of his allotted property to an army aerial gunnery range during World War II. He lived mostly on state assistance. After his death his body was treated with herbs and his hair prepared according to age-old ritual. They buried Dewey Beard in an unmarked grave at the cemetery adjoining St. Stephen's Catholic Church near Kyle. A friend who was present noted that "as soon as that first shovel of dirt hit that coffin, the women started keening."[28]

Alice Ghost Horse, who as a young girl endured the mayhem that killed her brother and father and who left a comprehensive record of her travail that morning, died in 1964. James HiHawk, who later rendered important service organizing the survivors, passed two years later. Among the last survivors of Wounded Knee was Jessie Running Horse, whose parents were killed there. A Miniconjou born at Cheyenne River in 1888, she came south with Big Foot's followers in December 1890. Days after the massacre she had been one of the orphans found and taken to Pine Ridge, where George Sword and his wife took her in and raised her. In 1970, at age eighty-two and totally blind, Jessie Running Horse resided with her aging sons in a two-room cabin on the north edge of Pine Ridge. Her sole income was $40 per month from the lease of her land allotment. She died at Pine Ridge in 1977. Louisa Yellow Shield Motley outlived them all, dying at ninety-five on the Cheyenne River Reservation in 1979. She was buried in the Catholic cemetery at Cherry Creek. Now only the descendants remained. Many of their offspring fought for the United States in two world wars and later conflicts.[29]

The memory of Wounded Knee persisted among the Lakota survivors, like an untreated sore. It still haunts the people.[30] Although the federal government has returned sacred objects and remains retrieved from the site under existing repatriation laws,[31] issues still linger as to why the deaths of so many noncombatants occurred at all, even concerns about whether what happened represented ethnic cleansing. Certainly the Sioux Land Commission and its aftermath, including the rise of the Ghost Dance among the Lakotas, served as a catalyst for what happened. But strategic failure occurred at Pine Ridge Agency in misidentifying a need for troops, resulting in the overreaction that brought them onto the reservations only to aggravate conditions.

Questions about the massacre itself loom even larger. No premeditated intent seems to have existed. Indeed plans were in place: the trains were being readied to move Big Foot's people to Omaha. The explosive intensity of the violence must in part rest with the inordinate number of untrained troops arrayed in opposition to the Sioux and with Colonel Forsyth's failure to manage his command suitably. But the events that followed the initial exchange in the council area remain not only numbingly horrifying but largely inexplicable. In the hurriedly escalating fog-of-war scenario the critical tactical failure lay in permitting the Indians to break through the soldier cordon formed by Troops B and K. That collapse of control escalated the conflict at flash speed by redirecting the reacting soldiers' gunfire into the noncombatants beyond and tilting the ensuing action into a scene of uncontrollable riot. The increasing density of the gun smoke coupled with the excessively lengthy shooting inside and particularly outside the council area aggravated the breakdown. As a result many more Sioux, especially women and children, were slated to die in and along the big ravine and among subordinate gullies and hillocks as they sought to flee the unfolding slaughter. It is also probable that Forsyth's actions in distributing his troops preceding the outbreak caused inadvertent deaths and injuries to at least some of his own men. That question might only be answered by exhumation and forensic analysis of their remains. While the federal government, mostly in response to efforts of the Wounded Knee Survivors association, expressed its "deep regret" to the Lakota descendants of victims on the centennial anniversary of the massacre, it has yet to offer a specific apology for the event.[32]

Coming at the conclusion of what white Americans call the frontier period in their history, Wounded Knee climaxed an era of intermittent warfare. Troops and Indians clashed throughout the trans-Mississippi West in a thirty-year on-again, off-again conflict that witnessed the government's decisive subjugation of the Indians. Wounded Knee came in the wake of several other massacres of Native peoples during that period—all of them, it should be noted, undeniably premeditated—as punitive forces operating under the auspices of the United States forcibly subjected the Indians to the national will. Wounded Knee followed Bear River in Washington Territory (present Idaho), where some 250 members of a village of Northwestern Shoshoni Indians died facing attacking troops in January 1863. It followed Sand Creek in Colorado Territory, where at least 150 Southern Cheyennes and Arapahos fell before guns of a federalized cavalry onslaught in November 1864. And it came after yet another army strike killed 250 Piegan men, women, and children at the Marias River in northwestern Montana Territory in January 1870.[33]

The circumstances leading to Wounded Knee two decades later differed markedly from these earlier engagements. But the results, occurring within the bounds of a long-established, civilly administered reservation, were practically identical. It is important to note that earlier conflicts in the West involved the resistance of Indians to being *placed* on reservations. But Wounded Knee involved the Lakotas' efforts to deal with critical survival issues facing them *on* their reservations. Wounded Knee therefore was not the last of the Indian wars, as it is frequently called. That distinction rightly belongs to the Apache outbreak preceding Geronimo's surrender in 1886. Wounded Knee was something different.[34]

We know the manner in which Wounded Knee occurred. The larger question of why it happened at all will probably remain unresolved. It likely could have been avoided with improved communication and greater tolerance and patience all around, unfamiliar concepts at the time when the government sought to impress its control over tribal populations. As people came to understand later, the nonviolent Ghost Dance was only a side issue. As Valentine McGillycuddy explained, "Had these people been well fed the ghost dance would never have been heard of. The dance and its ceremonies was like the voice of a feast to a starving man. . . . They cried for help from above, all other help having failed." Historian Walter Camp said it well: "While it was the Indians who were doing the dancing it was really the whites who saw the ghosts."[35]

Perhaps in the end it all came down to an early summer day in 1947 when survivor John Little Finger took his young grandson fishing at a small lake that had been built along White Clay Creek by the Civilian Conservation Corps Indian Department. As the old man adjusted his clothing to fish, he casually exposed the jagged scars where he had been struck by cavalry bullets on that awful morning more than half a century before. When the boy questioned him about the stark disfigurement, the grandfather answered simply, saying that the scars were where he had been shot. The boy looked up inquiringly, thought for a moment, and then, beyond the innocence of youth, spoke for the ages. "Grandfather," he asked, "why would anyone want to shoot you?"[36]

APPENDIX A

Treaty with the Sioux—Brulé, Oglala, Miniconjou, Yanktonai, Hunkpapa, Blackfeet, Cuthead, Two Kettle, Sans Arcs, and Santee—and Arapaho, [April 29,] 1868 [Ratified February 16, 1869]

Source: Kappler, *Indian Affairs: Laws and Treaties,* 2:998–1003

Articles of a treaty made and concluded by and between Lieutenant-General William T. Sherman, General William S. Harney, General Alfred H. Terry, General C. C. Augur, J. B. Henderson, Nathaniel G. Taylor, John B. Sanborn, and Samuel F. Tappen, duly appointed commissioners on the part of the United States, and the different bands of the Sioux Nation of Indians, by their chiefs and head-men, whose names are hereto subscribed [not included], they being duly authorized to act in the premises.

ARTICLE 1. From this day forward all war between the parties to this agreement shall forever cease. The Government of the United States desires peace, and its honor is hereby pledged to keep it. The Indians desire peace, and they now pledge their honor to maintain it.

If bad men among the whites, or among other people subject to the authority of the United States, shall commit any wrong upon the person or property of the Indians, the United States will, upon proof made to the agent and forwarded to the Commissioner of Indian Affairs at Washington City, proceed at once to cause the offender to be arrested and punished according to the laws of the United States, and also re-imburse the injured person for the loss sustained.

If bad men among the Indians shall commit a wrong or depredation upon the person or property of any one, white, black, or Indian, subject to the authority of the United States, and at peace therewith, the Indians herein named solemnly agree that they will, upon proof made to their agent and notice by him, deliver up the wrong-doer to the United States, to be tried and punished according to its laws; and in case they willfully refuse so to do, the person injured shall be re-imbursed for his loss from the annuities or other moneys due or to become due to them under this or other treaties made with the United States. And the President, on advising with the Commissioner of Indian Affairs, shall prescribe such rules and regulations for ascertaining damages under the provisions of this article as in his judgment may be proper. But no one sustaining loss while violating the provisions of this treaty of the laws of the United States shall be re-imbursed therefor.

ARTICLE 2. The United States agrees that the following district of country, to wit, viz: commencing on the east bank of the Missouri River where the forty-sixth parallel of north latitude crosses the same, thence along low-water mark down said east bank to a point opposite where the northern line of the State of Nebraska strikes the river, thence west across said river, and along the northern line of Nebraska to the one hundred and fourth degree of longitude west from Greenwich, thence north on said meridian to a point where the forty-sixth parallel of north latitude intercepts the same, thence due east along said parallel to the place of beginning; and in addition thereto, all existing reservations on the east bank of said river shall be, and the same is, set apart for the absolute and undisturbed use and occupation of the Indians herein named, and for such other friendly tribes or individual Indians as from time to time they may be willing, with the consent of the United States, to admit amongst them; and the United States now solemnly agrees that no persons except those herein designated and authorized so to do, and except such officers, agents, and employés of the Government as may be authorized to enter upon Indian reservations in discharge of duties enjoined by law, shall ever be permitted to pass over, settle upon, or reside in the territory described in this article, or in such territory as may be added to this reservation for the use of said Indians, and henceforth they will and do hereby relinquish all claims or right in and to any portion of the United States or Territories, except such as is embraced within the limits aforesaid, and except as hereinafter provided.

ARTICLE 3. If it should appear from actual survey or other satisfactory examination of said tract of land that it contains less than one hundred and sixty acres of tillable land for each person who, at the time, may be authorized to reside on it under the provisions of this treaty, and a very considerable number of such persons shall be disposed to commence cultivating the soil as farmers, the United States agrees to set apart, for the use of said Indians, as herein provided, such additional quantity of arable land, adjoining to said reservation, or as near to the same as it can be obtained, as may be required to provide the necessary amount.

ARTICLE 4. The United States agrees, at its own proper expense, to construct at some place on the Missouri River, near the center of said reservation, where timber and water may be convenient, the following buildings, to wit: a warehouse, a store-room for the use of the agent in storing goods belonging to the Indians, to cost not less than twenty-five hundred dollars; an agency building for the residence of the agent, to cost not exceeding three thousand dollars; a residence for the physician, to cost not more than three thousand dollars; and five other buildings, for a carpenter, farmer, blacksmith, miller, and engineer, each to cost not exceeding two thousand dollars; also a schoolhouse or mission-building, so soon as a sufficient number of children can be induced by the agent to attend school, which shall not cost exceeding five thousand dollars.

The United States agrees further to cause to be erected on said reservation, near the other buildings herein authorized, a good steam circular-saw mill, with a grist-mill and shingle-machine attached to the same, to cost not exceeding eight thousand dollars.

ARTICLE 5. The United States agrees that the agent for said Indians shall in the future make his home at the agency-building; that he shall reside among them, and keep an office open at all times for the purpose of prompt and diligent inquiry into such matters of complaint by and against the Indians as may be presented for investigation under the provisions of their treaty stipulations, as also for the faithful discharge of other duties enjoined on him by law. In all cases of depredation on persons or property he shall cause the evidence to be taken in writing and forwarded, together with his findings, to the Commissioner of Indian Affairs, whose decision, subject to the revision of the Secretary of the Interior, shall be binding on the parties to this treaty.

ARTICLE 6. If any individual belonging to said tribes of Indians, or legally incorporated with them, being the head of a family, shall desire to commence farming, he shall have the privilege to select, in the presence and with the assistance of the agent then in charge, a tract of land within said reservation, not exceeding three hundred and twenty acres in extent, which tract, when so selected, certified, and recorded in the "land-book," as herein directed, shall cease to be held in common, but the same may be occupied and held in the exclusive possession of the person selecting it, and of his family, so long as he or they may continue to cultivate it.

Any person over eighteen years of age, not being the head of family, may in like manner select and cause to be certified to him or her, for purposes of cultivation, a quantity of land not exceeding eighty acres in extent, and thereupon be entitled to the exclusive possession of the same as above directed.

For each tract of land so selected a certificate, containing a description thereof and the name of the person selecting it, with a certificate endorsed thereon that the same has been recorded, shall be delivered to the party entitled to it, by the agent, after the same shall have been recorded by him in a book to be kept in his office, subject to inspection, which said book shall be known as the "Sioux Land-Book."

The President may, at any time, order a survey of the reservation, and, when so surveyed, Congress shall provide for protecting the rights of said settlers in their improvements, and may fix the character of the title held by each. The United States may pass such laws on the subject of alienation and descent of property between the Indians and their descendants as may be thought proper. And it is further stipulated that any male Indians, over eighteen years of age, of any band or tribe that is or shall hereafter become a party to this treaty, who now is or who shall hereafter become a resident or occupant of any reservation or Territory not included in the tract of country designated and described in this treaty for the permanent home of the Indians, which is not mineral land, nor reserved by the United States for special purposes other than Indian occupation, and who shall have made improvements thereon of the value of two hundred dollars or more, and continuously occupied the same as a homestead for the term of three years, shall be entitled to received from the United States a patent for one hundred and sixty acres of land including his said improvements, the same to be in the form of the legal subdivisions of the surveys of the public lands. Upon application in writing, sustained by the proof of two disinterested witnesses, made to the register of the local land-office when the land sought to be entered is within a land district, and when the tract sought to be entered is within a land district, and when the tract sought to be entered is not in any land district, then upon said application and proof being made to the Commissioner of the General Land-Office, and the right of such Indian or Indians to enter such tract or tracts of land shall accrue and be perfect from the date of his first improvements thereon, and shall continue as long as he continues his residence and improvements, and no longer. And any Indian or Indians receiving a patent for land under the foregoing provisions, shall thereby and from thenceforth become and be a citizen of the United States, and be entitled to all the privileges and immunities of such citizens, and shall, at the same time, retain all his rights to benefits accruing to Indians under this treaty.

ARTICLE 7. In order to insure the civilization of the Indians entering into this treaty, the necessity of education is admitted, especially of such of them as are or may be settled on said agricultural reservations, and they therefore pledge themselves to compel their children, male and female, between the ages of six and sixteen years, to attend school; and it is hereby made the duty of the agent for said Indians to see that this stipulation is strictly complied with; and the United States agrees that for every thirty children between said ages who can be induced or compelled to attend school, a house shall be provided and a teacher competent to teach the elementary branches of an English education shall be furnished, who will reside among said Indians, and faithfully discharge his or her duties as a teacher. The provisions of this article to continue for not less than twenty years.

ARTICLE 8. When the head of a family or lodge shall have selected lands and received his certificate as above directed, and the agent shall be satisfied that he intends in good faith to commence cultivating the soil for a living, he shall be entitled to receive seeds and agricultural implements for the first year, not exceeding in value one hundred dollars, and for each succeeding year he shall continue to farm, for a period of three years more, he shall be entitled to receive seeds and implements as aforesaid, not exceeding in value twenty-five dollars.

And it is further stipulated that such persons as commence farming shall receive instruction from the farmer herein provided for, and whenever more than one hundred persons shall enter upon the cultivation of the soil, a second blacksmith shall be provided, with such iron, steel, and other material as may be needed.

ARTICLE 9. At any time after ten years from the making of this treaty, the United States shall have the privilege of withdrawing the physician, farmer, blacksmith, carpenter, engineer, and miller herein provided for, but in case of such withdrawal, an additional sum thereafter of ten thousand dollars per annum shall be devoted to the education of said Indians, and the Commissioner of Indian Affairs shall, upon careful inquiry into their condition, make such rules and regulations for the expenditure of said sum as will best promote the educational and moral improvement of said tribes.

ARTICLE 10. In lieu of all sums of money or other annuities provided to be paid to the Indians herein named, under any treaty or treaties heretofore made, the United States agrees to deliver at the agency-house on the reservation herein named, on or before the first day of August of each year, for thirty years, the following articles, to wit:

For each male person over fourteen years of age, a suit of good substantial woolen clothing, consisting of coat, pantaloons, flannel shirt, hat, and a pair of home-made socks.

For each female over twelve years of age, a flannel skirt, or the goods necessary to make it, a pair of woolen hose, twelve yards of calico, and twelve yards of cotton domestics.

For the boys and girls under the ages named, such flannel and cotton goods as may be needed to make each a suit as aforesaid, together with a pair of woolen hose for each.

And in order that the Commissioner of Indian Affairs may be able to estimate properly for the articles herein named, it shall be the duty of the agent each year to forward to him a full and exact census of the Indians, on which the estimate from year to year can be based.

And in addition to the clothing herein named, the sum of ten dollars for each person entitled to the beneficial effects of this treaty shall be annually appropriated for a period of thirty years, while such persons roam and hunt, and twenty dollars for each person who engages in farming, to be used by the Secretary of the Interior in the purchase of such articles as from time to time the condition and necessities of the Indians may indicate to be proper. And if within the thirty years, at any time, it shall appear that the amount of money needed for clothing under this article can be appropriated to better uses for the Indians named herein, Congress may, by law, change the appropriation to other purposes; but in no event shall the amount of this appropriation be withdrawn or discontinued for the period named. And the President shall annually detail an officer of the Army to be present and attest the delivery of all the goods herein named to the Indians, and he shall inspect and report on the quantity and quality of the goods and the manner of their delivery. And it is hereby expressly stipulated that each Indian over the age of four years, who shall have removed to and settled permanently upon said reservation and complied with the stipulations of this treaty, shall be entitled to receive from the United States, for the period of four years after he shall have settled upon said reservation, one pound of meat and one pound of flour per day, provided the Indians cannot furnish their own subsistence at an earlier date. And it is further stipulated that the United States will furnish and deliver to each lodge of Indians or family or persons legally incorporated with them, who shall remove to the reservation herein described and commence farming, one good American cow, and one good well-broken pair of American oxen within sixty days after such lodge or family shall have so settled upon said reservation.

ARTICLE 11. In consideration of the advantages and benefits conferred by this treaty, and the many pledges of friendship by the United States, the tribes who are parties to this agreement hereby stipulate that they will relinquish all right to occupy permanently the territory outside their reservation as herein defined, but yet reserve the right to hunt on any lands north of North Platte, and on the Republican Fork of the Smoky Hill River, so long as the buffalo may range thereon in such numbers as to justify the chase. And they, the said Indians, further expressly agree:

  1st. That they will withdraw all opposition to the construction of the railroads now being built on the plains.
  2d. That they will permit the peaceful construction of any railroad not passing over their reservation as herein defined.
  3d. That they will not attack any persons at home, or travelling, nor molest or disturb any wagon-trains, coaches, mules, or cattle belonging to the people of the United States, or to persons friendly therewith.

4th. They will never capture, or carry off from the settlements, white women or children.

5th. They will never kill or scalp white men, nor attempt to do them harm.

6th. They withdraw all pretence of opposition to the construction of the railroad now being built along the Platte River and westward to the Pacific Ocean, and they will not in future object to the construction of railroads, wagon-roads, mail-stations, or other works of utility or necessity, which may be ordered or permitted by the laws of the United States. But should such roads or other works be constructed on the lands of their reservation, the Government will pay the tribe whatever amount of damage may be assess by three disinterested commissioners to be appointed by the President for that purpose, one of said commissioners to be a chief or head-man of the tribe.

7th. They agree to withdraw all opposition to the military posts or roads now established south of the North Platte River, or that may be established, not in violation of treaties heretofore made or hereafter to be made with any of the Indian tribes.

ARTICLE 12. No treaty for the cession of any portion or part of the reservation herein described which may be held in common shall be of any validity or force as against the said Indians, unless executed and signed by at least three-fourths of all the adult male Indians, occupying or interested in the same; and no cession by the tribe shall be understood or construed in such manner as to deprive, without his consent, any individual member of the tribe of his rights to any tract of land selected by him, as provided in article 6 of this treaty.

ARTICLE 13. The United States hereby agrees to furnish annually to the Indians the physician, teachers, carpenter, miller, engineer, farmer, and blacksmiths as herein contemplated, and that such appropriations shall be made from time to time, on the estimates of the Secretary of the Interior, as will be sufficient to employ such persons.

ARTICLE 14. It is agreed that the sum of five hundred dollars annually, for three years from date, shall be expended in presents to the ten persons of said tribe who in the judgment of the agent may grow the most valuable crops for the respective year.

ARTICLE 15. The Indians herein named agree that when the agency-house or other buildings shall be constructed on the reservation named, they will regard said reservation their permanent home, and they will make no permanent settlement elsewhere; but they shall have the right, subject to the conditions and modifications of this treaty, to hunt, as stipulated in Article 11 hereof.

ARTICLE 16. The United States hereby agrees and stipulates that the country north of the North Platte River and east of the summits of the Big Horn Mountains shall be held and considered to be unceded Indian territory, and also stipulates and agrees that no white person or persons shall be permitted to settle upon or occupy any portion of the same; or without the consent of the Indians first had and obtained, to pass through the same; and it is further agreed by the United States that within ninety days after the conclusion of peace with all the bands of the Sioux Nation, the military posts now established in the territory in this article named shall be abandoned, and that the road leading to them and by them to the settlements in the Territory of Montana shall be closed.

ARTICLE 17. It is hereby expressly understood and agreed by and between the respective parties to this treaty that the execution of this treaty and its ratification by the United States Senate shall have the effect, and shall be construed as abrogating and annulling all treaties and agreements heretofore entered into between the respective parties hereto, so far as such treaties and agreements obligate the United States to furnish and provide money, clothing, or other articles of property to such Indians and bands of Indians as become parties to this treaty, but no further.

[Executed on April 29, 1868, by the seven commissioners of the United States and the various chiefs and headmen of the Brulé, Oglala, Miniconjou, Hunkpapa, Yanktonais, Blackfeet, Two Kettle, Sans Arc, and Santee bands of Sioux Indians.]

APPENDIX B

Ghost Dance Leaders Recommended for
Arrest and Confinement

PINE RIDGE RESERVATION: Agent Daniel F. Royer's list for arrest and confinement "for a certain period in some prison off the reservation. The following are some of the worst element belonging to the Ghost Dances and are considered by the police the prime leaders." (*Source:* Royer to Acting Commissioner of Indian Affairs R. V. Belt, November 25, 1890, NA, RG 393, Entry 3779, Department of the Platte, Letters Received, 1890–91)

Residence, White Clay Creek, South Dakota
Kicking Bear, His Fight, Torn Belly, Red Cloud, Jack Red Cloud, Little, Back, Red Star, Clown Horse, Bear Bone, Charging Wolf, Medicine Pipe, Fighter, Paint, Little Bull, Little Killer, Flat Iron, Long Visitor, Female Elk Voice Walking, Spotted Elk, Weasel Bear, Short Bull, Iron Hawk, No Water, Scabby Face, Runs Above, Fire Thunder, Blue Handle, Big Road, Feather on Head, Six Feathers, Shell Boy, Eagle Dog, Cherry Stone, Singing Bear, Flying Horse, War Bonnet, Dreaming, Little Moon, Lone Bull, Red Horse, Bad Yellow Hair

Residence, Porcupine Creek, South Dakota
Standing Elk, Thunder Hawk, Blue Cloud, Jumping Eagle, White Mountain, White Belly, Bad Ree, Little Elk

Residence, Medicine Root Creek, South Dakota
Broken Arm, Big Foot, Yellow Bear, Top Bear, Little Wound, White Eyes, One Bear, Conquering Bear, Comes in Front, Runs On, Two Tails, Around the Head, Good Thunder

Wounded Knee Creek, South Dakota
Black Elk

ROSEBUD RESERVATION: Special Agent E. B. Reynolds's list (*Source:* Reynolds to Commissioner of Indian Affairs, November 21, 1890, in U.S. Congress, Senate, *Letter from the Secretary of the Interior*, December 11, 1890, p. 28)

Short Bull, Mashes-the-Kettle, Two Strike, Crow Dog, Little Eagle, Turning Bear, White Horse, Lance, Big White Horse, White Thunder, Brave Bird, Fins Bird, Born-in-the-Day, Left Hand Bear, White Face Crow, Good Voice, White Crane, Walking Fast Horse, Swift Crocker, Elk Tooth, Turtle Rib

CHEYENNE RIVER RESERVATION: Agent Perrain Palmer's list (*Source:* Palmer to Commissioner of Indian Affairs, November 21, 1890, in U.S. Congress, Senate, *Letter from the Secretary of the Interior*, December 11, 1890, p. 28)

Pump [Hump], Big Foot, Lodog [Low Dog], Blackfeed [Blackfeet?], and Pretty Hawk

APPENDIX C

Standing Rock Police Who Arrested Sitting Bull

"Names of the U.S. Indian Police of Standing Rock Agency, N.D. constituting the force which arrested 'Sitting Bull' at his camp on Grand River, 40 miles south west of Standing Rock Agency, on the morning of December 15, 1890. All are full-blood Sioux Indians." (*Source:* James McLaughlin Papers, South Dakota State Historical Society, Microfilm Roll 35)

Henry Tatankapah (Bull Head), First Lieutenant, *Dead*
Charles Kashlah (Shave Head), First Sergeant, *Dead*
Marcellus Chankpidutah (Red Tomahawk), Second Sergeant
James Wambdichigalah (Little Eagle), Fourth Sergeant, *Dead*
John Wambdi (Eagle Man), Fifth Sergeant
Thomas Tunkah (Stone Man), Private
Louis Wahpahah (Hat), Private
Hugh Chetahohonko (Swift Hawk), Private
Paul Akicitah (Afraid of Soldier), Private, *Dead*
Luke Ptasah (White Buffalo), Private
Alexander Hochokah (Middle), Private, *Wounded*
Eugene Akichitahchigala (Little Soldier), Private
Joseph Brown Wolf (Brown Wolf), Private
Paul Hantaymaza (Iron Cedar), Private
John Ishnawichah (Lone Man), Private
Oliver Hehakawaketo (Looking Elk), Private
Dennis Wahpahaichu (Take the Hat), Private
George Iron Star (Iron Star), Private

Richard Runninghawk (Running Hawk), Private
Afraid of Hawk, Special Police
White Bird, Special Police
Hawk Man No. 1, Special Police, *Dead*
Magpie Eagle, Special Police
Iron Thunder, Special Police
Paints Brown, Special Police
Weasel Bear, Special Police
Rooster, Special Police
High Eagle, Special Police
Good Voiced Eagle, Special Police
Red Bear, Special Police
Bad Horse, Special Police
Cross Bear, Special Police
Black Pheasant, Special Police
John Armstrong, Special Police, *Dead*
One Feather, Special Police
Walking Shooter, Special Police
Good Voiced Elk, Special Police
Cetanwicaste (Hawk Man No. 2), Special Police
Brown Man, Special Police
Gabriel Wanblihota (Gray Eagle), Volunteer
Otter Robe, Volunteer
Spotted Thunder, Volunteer
Young Eagle, Volunteer

APPENDIX D

U.S. Army Casualties, Sioux Campaign, 1890

WOUNDED KNEE CREEK, DECEMBER 29, 1890

Sources: Muster Rolls of the Seventh Cavalry, October 31, 1890, to December 31, 1890; Muster Roll, Light Battery E, First Artillery, October 31, 1890, to December 31, 1890; "Copy of Muster Roll, Company A. Indian Scouts enlisted at Pine Ridge Agency, South Dakota"; memo, Major and Surgeon Albert Hartsuff, "Sick & wounded to be returned to Station," January 3, 1891, all in NA, RG 393, part 1, Entry 3783, Letters and Telegrams Sent by the Medical Director's Office, December 1890–January 1891; Ewing, "The Wounded of the Wounded Knee Battle Field," pp. 41–49; *Junction City Republican,* January 23 and 30, 1891, and March 13, 1891.

KILLED

No.	Name	Rank	Unit
SEVENTH CAVALRY			
1.	Richard W. Corwine	Sgt. Major	
2.	Arthur C. Dyer	Sergeant	Troop A
3.	Henry Frey	Saddler	Troop A
4.	George P. Johnson	Private	Troop A
5.	James Logan	Private	Troop A
6.	Michael Reagan	Private	Troop A
7.	Dora S. Coffey	1st Sgt.	Troop B
8.	Charles H. Newell	Corporal	Troop B
9.	Ralph L. Cook	Private	Troop B

10. John Costello	Private	Troop B
11. William S. Mezo	Private	Troop B
12. Jan DeVreede	Private	Troop C
13. Frank T. Reinecky	Private	Troop D
14. Robert H. Pettles	Sergeant	Troop E
15. August Kellner	Private	Troop E
16. Albert S. Bone	Corporal	Troop I
17. Gustave Korn	Blacksmith	Troop I
18. Pierce Cummings	Private	Troop I
19. James E. Kelly	Private	Troop I
20. Daniel Twohig	Private	Troop I
21. Bernhard Jehnder	Private	Troop I
22. George D. Wallace	Captain	Troop K
23. William T. Hodges	Sergeant	Troop K
24. William Adams	Private	Troop K
25. William F. McClintock	Private	Troop K
26. John M. McCue	Private	Troop K
27. Joseph Murphy	Private	Troop K
28. Philip Schwenkey	Private	Troop K

HOSPITAL CORPS

| 29. Oscar Pollack | Steward | |

INDIAN SCOUTS

| 30. High Backbone | Private | Co. A |

WOUNDED

No. Name	Rank	Unit	Remarks

SEVENTH CAVALRY

1. Charles Campbell	QM Sergt		Gun shot wound lower jaw
2. Ernest A. Garlington	1st Lieut.	Troop A	Gun shot wound right arm
3. Alvin H. Hazlewood	Sergeant	Troop A	Wounds left chest and arm; died of pneumonia 3/11/91
4. Harry L. Duncan	Private	Troop A	Pistol shot wound to face

5. Herman Gromberg	Private	Troop A	Died of wounds 12/30
6. Daniel McMahon	Private	Troop A	Gun shot wound right foot
7. Adam Neder	Private	Troop A	Gun shot wound right shoulder
8. John C. Gresham	1st Lieut.	Troop B	Unspecified wound
9. William H. Toohey	Sergeant	Troop B	Gun shot wound right ankle
10. James Ward	Sergeant	Troop B	Knife wound right back
11. Harry A. Forrest	Corporal	Troop B	Died of wounds 12/29
12. Marvin C. Hillock	Private	Troop B	Gun shot wound left foot
13. William S. Kirkpatrick	Private	Troop B	Gun shot wound right leg
14. Francis Lewis	Private	Troop B	Gun shot wound right wrist
15. John McKenzie	Private	Troop B	Gun shot wound left shoulder
16. Harry B. Stone	Private	Troop B	Gun shot wound left arm; died 1/13/91
17. William H. Green	Private	Troop C	Gun shot wound left thigh
18. Ervin Schriver	Private	Troop C	Gun shot wounds both thighs
19. George York	Wagoner	Troop D	Gun shot wound left shoulder
20. John F. Trith	Sergeant	Troop E	Wounds right shoulder, arm
21. George Loyd	Sergeant	Troop I	Shot through right lung

22. Henry Howard	Sergeant	Troop I	Gun shot wound left shoulder; died 1/23/91
23. Gottlob Hipp	Private	Troop I	Gun shot wound right knee
24. Harvey Thomas	Private	Troop I	Gun shot wound left shoulder
25. Harold L. Clifton	Corporal	Troop K	Wounds, chest and forearm
26. James Christianson	Trumpeter	Troop K	Gun shot wound of thorax
27. William J. Davis	Private	Troop K	Fracture, lower right leg
28. George Elliott	Private	Troop K	Gun shot wound, right leg; died 1/13/91
29. Christ H. Martin	Private	Troop K	Flesh wound, left leg
30. Hugh McGuinnis	Private	Troop K	Wounds left thigh, right arm
31. Samuel F. Smith	Private	Troop K	Flesh wound, left calf
32. Edward A. Sullivan	Private	Troop K	Gun shot wound left shoulder
33. Frederick F. Yader	Private	Troop K	Gun shot wound right shoulder
SECOND ARTILLERY			
34. Harry L. Hawthorne	2nd Lieut	Lt. Batt. E, 1st Art	Gun shot wound right groin
INDIAN SCOUTS			
35. Philip Wells	Interpreter		Knife wound to face
SECOND INFANTRY			
36. John Kinzie	1st Lieut		Gun shot contusion left ankle

ATTACK ON WAGON TRAIN, DECEMBER 30, 1890

Source: Regimental Returns of the Ninth Cavalry, December 1890, NA Microfilm 744, Roll 90.

No. Name	Rank	Unit	Remarks
NINTH CAVALRY			
Charles Haywood	Private	Troop D	Killed

WHITE CLAY CREEK (MISSION FIGHT), DECEMBER 30, 1890

Sources: Muster Rolls of the Seventh Cavalry, October 31, 1890, to December 31, 1890, NA Microfilm 744, Roll 74; telegram, Miles to AG, January 3, 1891, NA Microfilm 983, "Sioux Campaign," 1890–91, Roll 1, p. 792.

No. Name	Rank	Unit	Remarks
SEVENTH CAVALRY			
Killed			
Dominic Francischetti	Private	Troop G	
Wounded			
1. Marvin C. Hillock	Private	Troop B	Gun shot wound left foot
2. William S. Kirkpatrick	Private	Troop B	Gun shot wound right leg
3. Peter Claussen	Private	Troop C	Gun shot wound left buttock
4. William Kern	Private	Troop D	Gun shot wound to face
5. Richard J. Nolan	Farrier	Troop I	Gun shot wound right foot
6. James D. Mann	Lieut	Troop K	Gun shot wound lumbar area; died 1/15/91
7. Theodore Ragnar	1st Sergt	Troop K	Gun shot wound left leg

APPENDIX E

U.S. Army Estimate of Lakota Casualties at Wounded Knee

Source: NA Microfilm 983, "Sioux Campaign," 1890–91, Roll 2, p. 1075

HEADQUARTERS DIVISION OF THE MISSOURI,
Chicago, Illinois, February 5th, 1891

To the
Assistant Adjutant General,
Division of the Missouri,
Chicago, Ill.

Sir: —

From the most reliable information obtainable, I collected the following relative to Big Foot's band of Indians:—

January 4, 1891, there were buried on the battle field [*sic*] at Wounded Knee Creek, eighty-two men and sixty-four women and children. Captain Whitney, who was in command of the troops near battle field January 4, 1891, states that there was undoubted evidence of the removal of twenty-six bodies of dead Indians, and there was no doubt in his mind but that at least forty bodies of dead Indians had been moved from battle field between December 29th, 1890 and January 4th, 1891.

I proceeded January 20th, 1891, with a small detachment of troops up White Horse Creek, to a point three miles west of the battle field [*sic*] and buried one Indian woman, two girls and one boy, who had been killed on the day of the battle at Wounded Knee. A day or two prior to this, an Indian scout reported as having found the bodies of two warriors who had been shot. These were buried by the scouts. About the same time, reliable reports through Captain Ewers was [*sic*] received, that the body of one warrior had been found and buried by a party of scouts.

There was received in the post hospital, Pine Ridge up to January 25th, 1891, eight adult males, twelve children males, eleven adult females, five children females. Seven of the foregoing died in hospital of wounds and two adult females were cared for at Gennies' [*sic*] ranch.

Captain Ewers reports that he has trace of some seventy surviving members of Big Foot's bank, but is unable to give positive information as to their whereabouts, condition or sex. As soon as he secures the information it will be furnished.

SUMMARY

Killed on the battle field, or died of wounds,	warriors . . .	85
" " " " "	noncombatants . . .	68
Killed on the battlefield, or died of wounds, sex and		
	Age not known . . .	47
		200

Wounded and received in Hospital at Pine Ridge.

Adults, males	8
Children, males	12
Adults, females	11
Children, females	5
	36

Seven of the foregoing died in hospital.

Scattered among other bands of Indians, exact whereabouts, condition or sex not known, although the major portion of whom are believed to be wounded 70

Grand total 306

Very respectfully,
Your obedient servant,
FRANK D. BALDWIN,
Captain, 5th Infantry.

1st Endorsement.

Hdqrs. Division of the Missouri,
Chicago, Feby. 9, 1891.

Respectfully forwarded to the Adjutant General of the Army for file with previous reports on same subject.

NELSON A. MILES,
Major General,
Commanding.

APPENDIX F

Lakota Casualties

Wounded Knee Creek, December 29, 1890

Source: Adapted from Jensen, "Big Foot's Followers at Wounded Knee," which readers might consult for additional information.

Killed Outright or Died within Days from Wounds Received

The following list accounts for many names of Lakotas reportedly killed or died from wounds received at Wounded Knee. Whereas Big Foot's band numbered only approximately 370 individuals, many of whom survived, it is apparent that much probable duplication exists owing to persons being known by more than one name (as indicated occasionally below), persons listed with no names, inexact translation of names, inaccuracy of sources, or other source-inherent discrepancies.

Afraid of Bear (No. 1), adult male, age 28
Afraid of Bear (No. 2), adult male, age 75
Afraid of Nothing Bear (Bear Fool), male age unknown
Appears Twice, female age unknown
Arousing Squirrel, adult female
   Her mother
Ashes, adult male

Bad (Bear) Woman's son, age unknown
Bad Braves, male age unknown
Badger, adult female, wife of Long Bull No. 2
Bad Owner Without Rope, adult male
   His wife
Bad Spotted Eagle, adult male, age 64
Bad Wound, age unknown, son of Shoots The Right
Bear Comes and Lies, adult male
Bear Don't Run, adult male, age 45
Bear Lays Down, adult male, age 30
   His wife
Bear Parts (Cuts) Body, adult male
   His son, unknown age
Bear Sheds His Hair, adult male, age 61, possibly not killed
   His son, Runs Behind, age 13
   His mother-in-law
Bear Skin Vest, adult male
   His baby daughter
Bear That Shoots, male age unknown
   His mother
Bear With Small Body, adult male, age 30
   His wife, age 29
   His son, Takes Away Enemy, age 11
Bear Woman, adult female
Beaver, daughter (?), age 9, of Elk Woman
Benefactress, female age unknown
Big Foot (Spotted Elk), adult male, age 65
   His wife, Sinte-chigela, age 60
   His daughter, Brings White (White Horse Woman), age 20
Big Skirt (Shirt), adult male
Big (Loud) Voice Thunder, adult male, age 20
   His wife, age 20
   His child, gender unknown
Birds Belly, female age unknown
Bird Wings, age and gender unknown
Black Flutes, male child, age unknown
Black Fox (Coyote), adult male, age 33
   Brings White, his daughter, age 2

Black Hair's wife, name unknown
    Her son, name unknown, age 5
    Her child, name unknown
Black Hawk, adult male, age 77
Blind, female age unknown
Blue American, adult male
Blue Spotted, son (?) of Goggle Eyes, age 8
Bo Blue, adult female, age 60
Break Arrow With Foot, male age unknown
Brings Choice, male age unknown
Brings Earth to Her, female age unknown
Brings The Woman, adult male
Broken Arm, adult male
Broken Arrow, adult male
    His wife
Brother of Charles Blue Arm (No. 1), age unknown
Brother of Charles Blue Arm (No. 2), age unknown
Brown, FG, age and gender unknown
Brown Beaver, adult male son (?), age 23, of Elk Woman
Brown Bull, adult male, age 68
    His wife, age 67
    His son, Bird Shaker, age 23
Brown Ear, sister of High Back, age unknown
Brown Ear Horse, female, age unknown, possibly not killed
Brown Hoops (Hoop), adult male
    His son, age unknown
    His daughter, age unknown
Brown In Ears, adult female
    Her son, age unknown
Brown Leaf, female age unknown
Brown Turtle, adult male
Brown Woman, adult female, age 46
Buckskin (Bells In) Breech Clout, adult male, age 50
Burnt Thigh, female age unknown
Cannu, male age unknown
Cast Away And Run, age and gender unknown
Cedar Horse, age 8, daughter of Red Eagle

Charge [?] Near The Lodge, adult male
Charge At Them, age and gender unknown
   His mother, age unknown
Charger, male age unknown
Chase In Winter, age and gender unknown
Chief Woman, age and gender unknown
Close To Home, Louis, adult male, possibly not killed
Clown, female age unknown
Comes Last, male age unknown
Confiscate Arrow, male age unknown
Cottonwood, adult male, age 22, son of Hair Pipe
Courage (Courageous) Bear, adult male
   His wife
   Fat (child?), age and gender unknown
   George, male age unknown
Cow Buffalo Horn, adult male
Crazy Bear, adult male, possibly not killed
Daughter of Mrs. Brings White Horses, age unknown
Deaf, adult female, age 69
Disturbs Ahead, male age unknown
Drops Blood, Mrs., adult female
   Her son, male age unknown
   Her son, male age unknown
Eagle Body (Her Eagle Body), age unknown, daughter of Red Eagle
Eagle Hawk Bear, or Hawk Bear, adult male
   His daughter, 12
   His son, 6
Eagle Wing (Wing Eagle), adult male, possibly not killed
Elk Creek, adult male
   His wife
Elk Tooth (Her Elk Tooth), wife of Hard To Kill or Young Bear
Fair Woman, wife of Goggle Eyes, age 50
Fat Bear's mother, name unknown
Feather Earring, adult male
   His son, age unknown
Feather Man, female age unknown
First, female age unknown

First Born, age 67, mother of Brown Turtle

Flying Hawk, female age unknown

Fool Bear, adult male, age 36, possibly not killed

Frost On Her, age 12, son of Industrious Bear

Ghost Dog, male age unknown

Goggle (Eye) Eyes, adult male, age 62

Good Bear (No. 1), elderly adult male

Good Bear (No. 2), young adult male

   His wife

   His son, age unknown

Good Enemy, adult female

Good Hawk, adult male

   His wife

Good Pipe, age 6, daughter of Elk That Looks, possibly not killed

Grease Leg Bone, adult male

Grey Hand, adult male, possibly not killed

Grey In Eye (Eyes), male age unknown

Grey Thunder, male, age 17

Handsome, female age unknown

Happens, adult male

Hard To Kill's (Young Bear's) mother

Has Scarlet, female age unknown

Has The Bell, adult male

Hat, adult male, age 25

His daughter, Makes Presents, age 1

Hawk Flying, adult male

He (Male) Crow, adult male

Head Woman, age 21, Bear Don't Run's adult daughter

Heart of Timber, male age unknown

Her Good Cloud, female age unknown

Her Sacred Blanket, female age unknown

High Hawk, adult male, age 51

   His wife, Bear Woman, age 46

   His daughter, age unknown

His Fight, adult male, age 41

His Wounded Hand, adult male

   His wife, age unknown

   His daughter, age unknown

Horn Cloud (Horned Cloud), adult male, age 52
    His wife, Yellow Leaf, age 51
    His son, William Horn Cloud, age 14
    His son, Sherman, age unknown
    His daughter (niece?) Pretty Enemy, age 17?
Horses Ghost, adult male, age 40
    His son, White Horse, age 6
Hunts Alone, adult male, age 50
Hunts The Enemy By Night (Hunts The Enemy), adult male, age 29, poss. not killed
I Shot The Bear, elderly male, age 81
I Shot The Hawk, adult male age 41
Important Man, adult male, age 45
    His wife, age 34
Industrious Bear (Audacious Bear), adult male, age 61
Iron American, Mrs.
Iron Eyes, adult male
    His wife, Plenty Horses
    His son, Albert Iron Eyes
Has A Dog, unknown age and gender (child of Iron Eyes?)
Pretty Woman, age 15 (daughter of Iron Eyes?)
Red Shirt Girl, unknown age and gender (child of Iron Eyes?)
White Day, adult female, age 22 (daughter of Iron Eyes?)
    Son of White Day, child
Kills, male age unknown
Kills Assiniboine, male age unknown
Kills Crow Indian, male age unknown
Kills First (Killed First, Kills Him First), adult male, age 49
    His son, Wounded In Winter, adult male, age 20
    His daughter, Shoots The White, age 5, possibly not killed
    His daughter, White Mule, age 3, possibly not killed
Kills In Bush, adult male, age 31
    His son, Mad, age 5
Kills Seneca, age and gender unknown
Kills Tincup, adult male
Kills Who Stand In Timber, adult male
    His wife
Kyle, Charles, adult male

Lap, Mrs.

Last Man, adult male, age 40

Last Talking, adult female

Leg, adult male, age 61

Light Hair, female age unknown

Little Body Bear, adult male

   His wife

   His son

   His daughter, baby

Little Elk, adult male

   His wife

Little Water, adult male, age 36, possibly not killed

   His wife, White Face, age 39, possibly not killed

   His son, Sacred Blanket, age 7, possibly not killed

   His son, Animal, age 6, possibly not killed

   His daughter, The Voice, age 17, possibly not killed

   His daughter, Not Stingy, age 4, possibly not killed

Living Bear, age and gender unknown

Lodge Knapkin, age and gender unknown

Lodge Skin, age and gender unknown

Log, adult male

Lone Child, female age unknown

Long Bull (No. 1), adult male

Long Medicine, age and gender unknown

Made To Stand, male, age unknown

Male Eagle, adult male

   His wife, Roan Horse Woman or Short Woman

   His daughter, Runs After Her, age 2

   His son, Edward or Warrior, adult male, age 21

   His son, Two Arrows, adult male, age 19

Mangy Elk, adult male, age 42

Mercy To Others, age and gender unknown

Miniconjou, female age unknown

Mule's Daughter, adult female

Near Lodge, male age unknown

Nest, female age unknown

No Ears, age and gender unknown

Not Afraid Of Lodge (Camp), female age unknown

Not Go In Among, male age unknown

One Feather, adult male
   His son, male age unknown
Ones Call, age 15, daughter of Frog
Owl King, Mrs.
   Her son, age unknown
   Her son, age unknown
   Her daughter, age unknown
Pass Water In Horn, age and gender unknown
Pawnee Killer, age 17, Bear Don't Run's adult son
Peaked, male age unknown
Picket Horse, age and gender unknown
Plain Voice, adult female, age 21
Poor, age 10, son of Industrious Bear
Pretty Bear, adult male, age 36
Pretty Hawk, adult male
   His wife
   His baby, Whitewoman, possibly not killed
Pretty Voice Elk, male age unknown, possibly not killed
Pretty White Cow, age 5, daughter of Black Shield
Produce (From), adult female
Rattles, female age unknown
Rattling Leaf, female age unknown
Really Woman's son, age unknown
Red Buffalo, Bear Sheds His Hair's adult daughter, age 25
Red Eagle, adult male, 50
Red Ears Horse, age and gender unknown
   Sister, age unknown
Red Fish, adult male, possibly wounded
   His wife
Red (Scarlet) Horn, adult male, age 28
Red Juniper, adult female
Red Other Woman, age and gender unknown
Red Shell, male child
Red Water Woman, age and gender unknown
Roots Its Hole, age and gender unknown
Running In Lodge, male age unknown
Running Standing Hairs, adult male
   His wife
   His daughter, age unknown

Runs After, adult male
Runs Off With Horse, age unknown
Runs Off With Horses, male age unknown
Sacred Face, female age unknown
Sacred In Appearance, male age unknown
Scabbard Knife, adult male
    His wife
Scares The Bear, adult male
    His wife, Yellow Bird Woman
    His grandchild, unknown age and gender
    His grandchild, unknown age and gender
Scarlet Calf, adult female
    Her son, age unknown
    Her son, age unknown
Scarlet Otter, female age unknown
Scarlet Smoke, adult female
Scarlet White Buffalo, female age unknown
Scatter (Scatters) Them, adult male
Shaving Bear, adult male
    His four children, age and gender unknown
She Bear or Cheyenne Woman, age 54, wife of Black Hawk
Shot At Accurately, age and gender unknown
    His son, age unknown
Shoots Straight, adult male
Shoots The Bear, George, adult male, age 21
    His wife
Shoots The Right, age and gender unknown
Shoots (With) The Hawk Feather, adult male
    His mother
Short Hair (Close Haired) Bear, adult male
    His three children
Shot In Hand, male age unknown
Singing Bull, adult male
    His wife
    His adult son, Ha-shi-ta, age 35
    His granddaughter, Scarlet Coat, age 7
Sister-in-law of Charles Blue Arm, age unknown
Sister of James Pipe On Head, age unknown, possibly not killed

Slippery Hide, male age unknown
Small Like (Bodied) Bear, age and gender unknown
Smoke Woman, age 51, wife of Industrious Bear
Spotted (Speckled) Chief, male age unknown
Spotted Elk (no. 2), adult male
    His wife
    His son, age 8
    His son, age 10
    His son, age 12
Spotted Thunder, adult male, age 49
Standing Bear, Chief, age and gender unknown
Standing Bear, adult male, age 67
Starts The Horse, male, age 7, son of Hair Pipe
Stone Hammer, Mrs.
    Her baby, unknown gender
Strike Scatter, age and gender unknown
    Her son, age unknown
Strong Fox (Tea), adult male, age 39
    His wife, age 31
    His son, The Guide (Quick), age 8
    His daughter, Brown Horn, age 9
Strong Tea, adult male, age 40
    His wife
Successful Spy, male age unknown
Sun In The Pupil, adult male
    His wife
Swift Bear, adult male
Swift Bird, adult male
    His wife
    His son, age unknown
    His son, age unknown
Takes (Away) The Bow, adult male
Takola Washaka, adult male
    His wife, Yellow Leaf Woman
    His child, age and gender unknown
The Ring, adult female, age 32, wife of Sole of Foot
Three, Henry, adult male, age 25
Thunder, adult male, age 27

Thunder Boy, son (?) of Goggle Eyes, age 15
Thunder Hawk Woman, female age unknown
To Laugh, adult female, age 65
Trotter, adult male, age 31
Trouble, age and gender unknown
Trouble In Front, Bear Sheds His Hair's adult son, age 22
Trouble In Love, Mrs.
Twin Woman, adult male, age 61
Unintentionally Brave, male age unknown
Up To His Waist, adult male, age 44
   His wife, age 50
   His son, Important Man, age 12
Used For Brother, male age unknown
Walking Bull, adult male, age 61
   His wife, age 51
Walks Red, elderly female, age 72
   Her son, Chief Boy, age unknown
War Is His, male age unknown
Water Snake, male age unknown
Wears Calf's (Calfskin) Robe, adult male, age 51
Wears Eagle (White Face), wife of Iron Hail/Dewey Beard
   Her son(?) Thomas, age unknown
   Her son Wet Feet (White Face)
Weasel, age 11, daughter of Long Bull No. 2
Weasel, male age unknown
Weasel Bear, adult male
Weasel Bear, or Weasel, age 16, daughter of Black Hawk
Whip, female age unknown
Whirlwind Bear, male age unknown
Whirlwind Hawk, adult male
   His wife
   His daughter, child
   His daughter, child
   His daughter, child
   His son, child
   His son, child
White American, age and gender unknown
White Beaver Woman, age and gender unknown
White Bull, adult male, age 61

His wife, Clown Woman, age 61
His daughter, Pretty Hair, age 11, possibly not killed
White Dog, brother of High Back, age unknown
White Face Sun, female child
White Feather, male age unknown
White Hat, male age unknown
White Man (No. 1), adult male
   His son, age 5
   His son, age 1
   His daughter, baby
White Man (No. 2), adult male
White Wolf, age and gender unknown
White Woman, age 50, wife of Bad Spotted Eagle
Wicaka-badeea, adult male
Wind, elderly female, age 78, possibly not killed
Wing, male age unknown
   His son, age unknown
Winter, age and gender unknown
Without Robe, age and gender unknown
Wolf (Dog) Skin Necklace, adult male, age 39
   His daughter, Scarlet Woman, age unknown
Wolf Eagle, adult male
   His son, Good Boy, age unknown
Wolf Ears, Edward, adult male, age 51
   His son, White, adult male, age 25
   His son, Feather Enemy, age 16
   His daughter, Medicine Lake Girl, age 5
Wood Shade, adult male
   His wife
Wounded Hand, adult male
   His wife, Comes Out Rattling
Yellow Bird, male age unknown
Yellow Buffalo Calf, age and gender unknown
Yellow Bull, adult male
   His wife, Humming
   His daughter, adult
   His daughter, adult
   Five grandchildren, ages and gender unknown
Yellow Robe, age and gender unknown

Yellow Turtle, adult male
Young Calf, male age unknown

WOUNDED AND LIVED

This list offers names for as many as 71 individuals who were wounded but survived. As above, name duplication, translation error, and other source problems likely exist.

Afraid of Enemy, adult male, age 37
 Wife, Brown Eyes, age 37
 Son, Scaring Hawk, age 5
Bear Gone, wife of Ashes
Bad (Bear) Woman, adult female
Wife of Bear Lays Down
Wife of Bear Skin Vest
Iron Hail (Dewey Beard)
Billy Woman, age and gender unknown
Black Hair's unnamed son, age 7
Kills the Fair, age 7, son (?) of Blind Woman
Blue Hair, age 14, unknown gender
Brings Plenty, adult female, age 26
Brown Sinew, adult male, age 23
Peter, male age unknown, son of Cow Buffalo Horn
Day, male age unknown
Dependable, adult female
Eagle Hawk Woman, wife of Eagle Hawk Bear
Elk Saw Him, adult male
Fish Boy, age 8, unknown gender
Frog, adult male, age 47
Wife of He (Male) Crow
Help Them (Helps Em Up), adult male, age 30
High Back, male age unknown
Long Woman, son of High Hawk, age 21
Kills In A Hurry, or James, age 5, son of High Hawk
Kills Twice, or Alex, age 12, son of High Hawk
Daniel Blue Hair, age 15, son of His Wounded Hand

Holds A Woman, female, age 16

Holy Bone, female, age 6

Daniel Horn Cloud, age 22, son of Horned Cloud

Howling Elk, adult female

   Her son, Sammey

Face, age 17, daughter of Industrious Bear

Iron Lavatta, Annie, female, age unknown

Kills Close To Lodge, Bertha, female, age 17

Holy Woman or Wakan, age 42, wife of Kills First

Wife of Kills (Killed) White Man

Liking, male, age 7

Little Bull, male, age 46

Little Finger, John, age 16

Looking Elk, adult male

   Wife, Lydia

Looks Back, female, age 18

Moves Over, Alice, age unknown

Wife of One Skunk

Owl King, Edward, or Fast Boat, child, son of Mrs. Owl King

Yellow Eyes, female, age 7, daughter of Pretty Shield

Put Away Moccasins, female age unknown

Her Black Horses or Her Gall, age 38, wife of Red Eagle

Red Fish, adult male, possibly not killed

Run Through His Hair Fussed, male age unknown

Runs Around Lodge, male, age 7

Sack Woman, female, age 40

White Cowboy, age 4, son of Sack Woman

Sloha main (Slohamani), adult female

Blue Whirlwind, female, age 44, wife of Spotted Thunder

White Buffalo Boy, male, age 4, son of Spotted Thunder

Spear, male, age 7, son of Spotted Thunder

Stands A Showing, female, age 78

Stands With, female, age unknown

Steals A Running Horse, age 5, sex unknown

Sunka Yatapi, male, age unknown

Swift Dog, male, age 57

Walking Buffalo, female, age 37

Weasel Bear, Louise, age 10

Medicine Woman, wife of White Man (No. 1)
Never Misses It, wife of White Man (No. 2)
Wife of Wolf Ears, age 50
Yellow Hair, male, age 10
Yellow Hair, adult male

WHITE HORSE CREEK, DECEMBER 29, 1890

Killed

Walks Carrying The Red, adult female age unknown
    Her son, age 12
    Her daughter, age 9
    Her daughter, age 7

APPENDIX G

Medals of Honor for the Pine Ridge Campaign, 1890–91

Source: The Medal of Honor of the United States Army, pp. 235–38.

MEDAL OF HONOR RECIPIENTS FOR SERVICE AT WOUNDED KNEE, DECEMBER 29, 1890

Austin, William G. Sergeant, Troop E, Seventh Cavalry
Clancy, John E. Musician (Trumpeter), Troop E, Seventh Cavalry
Feaster, Moshiem, Private, Troop E, Seventh Cavalry
Garlington, Ernest A., First Lieutenant, Troop A, Seventh Cavalry
Gresham, John C., Troop B, Seventh Cavalry
Hamilton, Mathew H., Private, Troop G, Seventh Cavalry
Hartzog, Joshua B., Battery E, First Artillery
Hawthorne, Harry L., Second Lieutenant, Second Artillery
Hobday, George, Private, Troop A, Seventh Cavalry
Hillock, Marvin C., Private, Troop B, Seventh Cavalry
Loyd, George, Sergeant, Troop I, Seventh Cavalry
McMillan, Albert W., Sergeant, Troop E, Seventh Cavalry
Sullivan, Thomas, Private, Troop E, Seventh Cavalry
Toy, Frederick E., First Sergeant, Troop G, Seventh Cavalry
Trautman, Jacob, First Sergeant, Troop I, Seventh Cavalry
Ward, James, Sergeant, Troop B, Seventh Cavalry
Weinert, Paul H., Corporal, Battery E, First Artillery
Ziegner, Hermann, Private, Troop E, Seventh Cavalry (also for White
    Clay Creek)

Medal of Honor Recipient for Service during the Attack on Ninth Cavalry Wagon Train, December 30, 1890

Wilson, William O., Corporal, Troop I, Ninth Cavalry

Medal of Honor Recipients for Service at White Clay Creek, December 30, 1890

Nolan, Richard J. Farrier, Troop I, Seventh Cavalry
Ragnar, Theodore, First Sergeant, Troop K, Seventh Cavalry
Varnum, Charles A., Captain, Troop B, Seventh Cavalry
Ziegner, Hermann, Private, Troop E, Seventh Cavalry (also for Wounded Knee)

Medal of Honor Recipients for Service at Grass Creek, January 1, 1891

Cheever, Benjamin H., Jr., First Lieutenant, Troop F, Sixth Cavalry
Howze, Robert L., Second Lieutenant, Troop K, Sixth Cavalry
Kerr, John B., Captain, Troop K, Sixth Cavalry
Knight, Joseph F., Sergeant, Troop F, Sixth Cavalry
Myers, Fred, Sergeant, Troop K, Sixth Cavalry
Smith, Cornelius C., Corporal, Troop K, Sixth Cavalry

Medal of Honor Recipients for Unspecified Service during the Sioux Campaign, 1890–91

Jetter, Bernhard, Sergeant, Troop K, Seventh Cavalry
Neder, Adam, Corporal, Troop A, Seventh Cavalry

General Miles's Congratulatory Message to His Troops at the Conclusion of the Sioux Campaign

Source: Army and Navy Journal, January 24, 1891.

HEADQUARTERS DIVISION OF THE MISSOURI,
In the Field, Pine Ridge, S.D. January 18, 1891.

GENERAL ORDERS,
   No. 3.

The Division Commander takes pleasure in announcing the satisfactory termination of hostilities in this Division. The disaffection among the Indians was wide spread [*sic*], involving many different tribes. The purposes of the conspiracy was to produce a general uprising of all the Indians in the coming spring. The hostile element of the Sioux Nation precipitated the movement by leaving the agencies, defying the authorities of the government, and destroying the property that had been given them for the purposes of civilization. They assembled in large force on almost impenetrable ground known as the Mauvaises Terres of South Dakota, and from that rendezvous marauding parties robbed both white citizens and friendly Indians on their reservation and through the adjacent settlements.

To check this insurrection, orders were given for the arrest of the chief conspirator, Sitting Bull, who was on the eve of leaving his reservation to join those above mentioned. This was done on the 14th of December last. After peacefully submitting to arrest by the officials of the government, he created a revolt, which brought to his assistance large numbers of his followers, who assailed the Indian police. This resulted in Sitting Bull's death, and the final arrest of three hundred of his people, thereby removing the principal part of the disaffected element from the Standing Rock Reservation.

The second arrest was that of Big Foot and his party, December 21st, 1890, who made their escape the following day. This band was composed of outlaws from different tribes, who defied the government officials.

While these measures were being carried into execution, the troops were quickly moved between the hostile element in their stronghold and the settlements, in such a way as to check their usual depredations, and give protection to life and property of the citizens. Nearly the entire force of troops in the Department of Dakota under General Ruger were judiciously placed where they would give the most protection to the settlements, and where they were enabled to intercept any body of hostiles should they escape. Brief delays were necessary to put the troops in proper position, as well as to give time for the work of disaffection to be carried on in the hostile camp and to strengthen the loyal element. Gradually the troops were moved to such positions as to render resistance of the hostiles useless, and they were forced back to the agency.

The escape of Big Foot and his party made their re-capture necessary. This was successfully done by a battalion of the 7th Cavalry and Lieutenant Hawthorne's detachment of artillery under Major Whitside, December 28th, 1890, after which they were marched seven miles to Wounded Knee, and at 9 o'clock, P.M., the command was joined by Colonel Forsyth with the second battalion of his regiment with two Hotchkiss guns under Captain Capron, 1st Artillery, and Lieutenant Taylor's Sioux scouts.

With this band of outlaws under control, the entire hostile camp moving in before the troops to surrender within a short distance of the agency, it was hoped and expected that this serious Indian difficulty would be brought to a close, without the loss of life of a single white man.

While disarming Big Foot's band, on the morning of December 29th, after a portion of their arms had been surrendered, they were incited to hostility by the harangues of one of their false prophets, and in their attack and attempt to escape, nearly all of the men were killed or wounded, and a serious loss of life occurred among the large number of non-combatants.

During the engagement, some one hundred and fifty young warriors left the village near the agency and went to the assistance of Big Foot's band, and were engaged with the troops, and returning, made a vigorous attack upon the agency, drawing the fire of the Indian police and scouts. This caused a general alarm, and upwards of three thousand Indians fled from the agency to the canyons and broken ground adjacent to White Clay Creek, and assumed a hostile attitude. The troops that were following however checked their further movements.

The attempts of some of the warriors to burn buildings near the agency the following day, resulted in a skirmish with the 7th Cavalry under Colonel Forsyth, promptly supported by Major Henry, 9th Cavalry.

On January 1, 1891, a spirited engagement occurred on White River between a body of warriors, numbering upwards of one hundred, and Captain Kerr's troops of the 6th Cavalry, in which the Indians were repulsed with loss, Major Tupper's battalion of Colonel Carr's command of the 6th Cavalry moving to Captain Kerr's support. This was followed by several skirmishes between the Indian scouts under Lieutenant Casey. While making a reconnoissance [sic], the service sustained a serious loss in the death of that gallant officer.

Within thirty days, more than one hundred of the most desperate and dangerous Indians who for years had been a disturbing element, and a terror to this north-western country, have been killed, and peace restored.

The troops under command of Brigadier General Brooke gradually closed their lines of retreat, and forced the hostiles by superior numbers back to the agency, where they are now under the guns of the command and the control of the military.

While the service has sustained the loss of such gallant officers and patriots as Captain Wallace, Lieutenants Casey, Mann, and the brave noncommissioned officers and soldiers, who have given their lives in the cause of good government, the most gratifying results have been obtained by the endurance, patience and fortitude of both officers and men.

The work of disarming the hostiles has been commenced, and will be continued by a portion of the command now in the field, and by the agency officials.

As soon as practicable, the troops will return to their stations, and will take with them the assurance that their services have been of great value to the country in suppressing one of the most threatening Indians [sic] outbreaks, and that they have been enabled to keep between the hostile Indians and the unprotected settlements to such an extent that not a citizen's life has been lost beyond the boundaries of the Indian reservations.

In announcing these facts, the Division Commander desires to express his thanks and highest appreciation of the loyal and efficient service that has been rendered. The mention of individual names, of either officers or soldiers for meritorious conduct will be deferred until sufficient time is given to ascertain each heroic act, in order that it may be properly recognized and duly rewarded.

BY COMMAND OF MAJOR GENERAL MILES:
H. C. CORBIN,
Assistant Adjutant General

OFFICIAL:

Eli L. Huggins
Captain 2d Cavalry, Aide-de-Camp.

APPENDIX I

List of Wounded Knee Survivors as of May 1941, Compiled by James Pipe On Head

Source: James Pipe On Head to Representative Francis H. Case, May 5, 1941, Francis H. Case Papers, Dakota Wesleyan University.

1. James Pipe on Head	(age) 62	Oglala, S.D.
2. Dewey Beard	76	Kyle, S.D.
3. Frank Sits Poor	62	Manderson, S.D.
4. Alice White Wolf	67	Pine Ridge, S.D.
5. Jessie Running Horse	52	Pine Ridge, S.D.
6. George Running Hawk	63	Wanblee, S.D.
7. Thomas Blue Leg	54	Wanblee, S.D.
8. George Blue Leg	56	Kyle, S.D.
9. Ella Ladeaux	66	Manderson, S.D.
10. Sylvia Looking Elk	86	Oglala, S.D.
11. Peter Stands	68	Oglala, S.D.
12. Julia Spider Backbone	62	Oglala, S.D.
13. Thomas Blindman	55	Oglala, S.D.
14. Charles Blindman, Sr.	57	Oglala, S.D.
15. Rough Feather	77	Kyle, S.D.
16. Jackson He Crow	61	Oglala, S.D.
17. Dora High Whiteman	60	Oglala, S.D.
18. Silas Afraid of Enemy	50	Oglala, S.D.
19. John Little Finger	66	Oglala, S.D.
20. Mrs. Young Bear	75	Porcupine, S.D.
21. Mrs. Haki kta win or LaVatta	61	Little Eagle, S.D.

22. Philip Black Moon	62	Red Scaffold, S.D.
23. Paul High Back	74	Popular, Mont.
24. John Spotted Bear	68	Little Eagle, S.D.
25. Jennie Knocks Him Down	70	Bull Head, S.D.
26. James Red Fish	61	Bull Head, S.D.
27. Blue Arm	67	Cherry Creek, S.D.
28. Carl or Jackson Kills Whiteman	66	Cherry Creek, S.D.
29. Edward Owekin (Owl King)	61	Cherry Creek, S.D.
30. Mrs. [Nellie] Knife	69	Dupree, S.D.
31. Julia Crane Pretty Voice	70	Howes, S.D.
32. Mrs. Widow or Good Shawl	75	Cherry Creek, S.D.
33. Mrs. Circle	63	White Horse, S.D.
34. Alex High Hawk	62	Howes, S.D.
35. James High Hawk [HiHawk]	55	Howes, S.D.
36. Jonas High Hawk	53	Howes, S.D.
37. Leon Holy	50	Cherry Creek, S.D.
38. One Skunk	74	Cherry Creek, S.D.
39. Francis Eagle–Little Crow	57	Howes, S.D.
40. Jackson Roan Horse	61	Howes, S.D.
41. Henry Roan Horse	56	Howes, S.D.

Notes

PROLOGUE

1. *Washington Post*, March 7, 1938 (weather and photo); *Rapid City Journal*, March 4, 1938; "Present the Bill for the Historic 'Wounded Knee Massacre,'" *American Weekly*, April 24, 1938 (including photo); "Wounded Knee Veterans," *Time*, 31 (March 14, 1938), p. 15 (including photo); *Rapid City Journal*, November 3, 1955; "The True Legend of Dewey Beard"; Francis H. Case to James Pipe on Head, March 10, 1938, Ralph H. Case Papers, Wounded Knee File, I. D. Weeks Library, University of South Dakota, Archives and Special Collections.

2. U.S. Congress, House, *A Bill to Liquidate the Liability of the United States for the Massacre of Sioux Indian Men, Women, and Children at Wounded Knee on December 29, 1890* (1937), pp. 1–2. Case's bill had been introduced in the House on January 11, 1937. The hearing by a subcommittee of the House Committee on Indian Affairs was approved on March 31, 1937. As of January 21, 1938, however, the members of the subcommittee had not yet been appointed, although Sioux delegates had been selected. Case to James Brown Dog, March 31, 1937; Case to Chairman, Committee on Indian Affairs, House of Representatives, January 21, 1938; various correspondence of Case with Louis Iron Hawk, James HiHawk, Henry Standing Bear, Charles Blindman, Sr. (aka Spotted Thunder), and James Brown Dog, representing the survivors' organizations, between January and May 1937. Dewey Beard and James Pipe on Head had been selected by the Pine Ridge group. See also Pine Ridge Agency Superintendent William O. Roberts to Case, February 15, 1938, and Roberts to Case, February 23, 1938, Francis H. Case Papers, Dakota Wesleyan University (hereinafter cited as Francis H. Case Papers).

3. Francis H. Case to Pipe on Head, March 10, 1938; U.S. Congress, House, Subcommittee on Indian Affairs, *Hearing on H.R. 2535*, pp. 7–16 (hereinafter cited as *Hearing on H.R. 2535*).

4. Ibid., pp. 18–19.

5. Ibid., p. 17. Pipe on Head's paintings appeared in *American Weekly*, April 24, 1938. "Tipi" versus "tepee," as per Larry Belitz, *The Buffalo Hide Tipi of the Sioux*, p. 3.

6. *Hearing on H.R. 2535*, pp. 22, 24.

7. Ibid., pp. 23, 32. The inserted data included a letter from Acting Secretary of the Interior Charles West to House Indian Affairs Committee Chairman Will Rogers, dated April 28, 1937; a letter from Acting Secretary of War Malin Craig, dated June 3,

1936 (both of these also reference earlier related legislation); as well as excerpts from the Fort Laramie Treaty of 1868; an article by General Hugh L. Scott; and lengthy extracts from Mooney, "The Ghost-Dance Religion."

8. *American Weekly*, April 24, 1938; *Time*, March 14, 1938, p. 12 (which includes a photo of a slight and intimidated looking John Collier with Pipe on Head and Beard). Collier referenced the visit of the Sioux delegation in an editorial that he penned for *Indians at Work* (April 1938). The Department of the Interior's endorsement of H.R. 2535 appeared in a report of the acting secretary on April 28, 1937. F. W. LaRouche to Francis H. Case, March 28, 1938, Francis H. Case Papers. Case sought publicity for the hearing and asked his aide to notify the *New York Times*, *Washington Post*, and first lady Eleanor Roosevelt of the survivors' presence in the capital. Penciled instructions on Roberts to Francis H. Case, February 23, 1938, Francis H. Case Papers.

9. Telegram, Case to Fred McKown, March 11, 1938, and Francis H. Case to Pipe on Head, March 10, 1938, Francis H. Case Papers.

10. Pipe on Head to Francis H. Case, May 4, 1938, Francis H. Case Papers.

Chapter 1. Wild Indians

1. DeMallie, "Sioux until 1850," p. 719 (map); Swanton, *The Indian Tribes of North America*, p. 283; Christafferson, "Sioux, 1930–2000," p. 830. The terms "Dakota" and "Lakota" mean "friendly, affectionate people" (p. 750).

2. DeMallie, "Sioux until 1850," pp. 748, 749–50, 756–60. A concise overview of the assorted Sioux tribes is found in McCrady, *Living with Strangers*, pp. xv–xvi. See also Bettelyoun and Waggoner, *With My Own Eyes*, pp. 118–19.

3. For detailed cultural and historical background on the Sioux, including the Lakotas, see Gibbon, *The Sioux;* DeMallie, "Sioux until 1850," pp. 718–60; Albers, "Santee"; DeMallie, "Yankton and Yanktonai"; DeMallie, "Teton"; Walker, *Lakota Society;* Hassrick, *The Sioux;* DeMallie and Parks, *Sioux Indian Religion;* Powers, *Oglala Religion;* Hyde, *Red Cloud's Folk;* Hyde, *A Sioux Chronicle;* Hyde, *Spotted Tail's Folk;* and Ostler, *The Plains Sioux and U.S. Colonialism.* An early history appears in Robinson, *A History of the Dakota or Sioux Indians.*

4. DeMallie, "Sioux until 1850"; Kappler, *Indian Affairs: Laws and Treaties* vol. 2 (Treaties), 588–96; Clowser, *Dakota Indian Treaties*, pp. 23 (map), 29–34; White, "The Winning of the West." Individual accountings of the seven Teton subtribes appear in DeMallie, "Sioux until 1850," pp. 755–60.

5. For specific treatment of these actions, see McChristian, *Fort Laramie*, pp. 69–88; and Paul, *Blue Water Creek and the First Sioux War.*

6. The beginning of the Minnesota uprising is detailed in Michno, *Dakota Dawn*, while the Sibley and Sully campaigns are thoroughly treated in Utley, *Frontiersmen in Blue*, pp. 261–80; and Josephy, *The Civil War in the American West*, pp. 94–154.

7. For Sand Creek, see Hoig, *The Sand Creek Massacre;* and Carroll, *The Sand Creek Massacre.*

8. For Sand Creek in the context of the emigrant trails, see West, *The Contested Plains.*

9. The fighting along the North Platte is precisely treated in McDermott, *Frontier Crossroads*, while Connor's expedition is detailed in McDermott, *Circle of Fire.* The Fort Sully accords appear in Kappler, *Indian Affairs*, 2:896–908.

10. For Fort Phil Kearny and related events, see especially McDermott, *Red Cloud's War*. See also Utley, *Frontier Regulars*, pp. 93–110, 122–25, 128–29; and Monnett, *Where a Hundred Soldiers Were Killed*.

11. Two treaties actually were concluded with the affected tribes: on April 29, 1868, with the "Brulé, Oglala, Miniconjou, Yanktonai, Hunkpapa, Blackfeet, Cuthead, Two Kettle, Sans Arcs, and Santee—and Arapaho," and on May 10, 1868, with the "Northern Cheyenne and Northern Arapaho." Kappler, *Indian Affairs*, 2:998, 1012.

12. Ibid., 2:998–1011 (quotations); *The Sioux Nation and the United States*, p. 3. See appendix A for the complete text of the Fort Laramie Treaty of 1868.

13. Ibid., p. 1002. See the discussion regarding elements of the treaty in Hedren, *Fort Laramie in 1876*, pp. 2–6.

14. Ibid. (emphasis added). For construed Lakota perspectives as well as legal issues stemming from the treaty, see especially Powell, "The Sacred Treaty,"; DeMallie, "Treaties Are Made between Nations"; and Jacobs, "The Sioux Nation and the Treaty."

15. U.S. Congress, Senate, Select Committee to Examine into the Condition of the Sioux and Crow Indians, *Report of the Special Committee of the United States Senate, Appointed to Visit the Indian Tribes in Northern Montana*, p. iii (hereinafter cited as *Report of the Special Committee of the United States Senate*).

16. DeMallie, "Teton," p. 797; Fritz, *The Movement for Indian Assimilation*, pp. 56–86; Fritz, "The Making of Grant's Peace Policy"; Utley, "The Celebrated Peace Policy of General Grant"; *Report of the Commissioner of Indian Affairs, 1873*, pp. 230, 231, 233, 243–44; *Report of the Commissioner of Indian Affairs, 1875*, pp. 737, 740, 746, 752, 756.

17. Utley, *The Indian Frontier of the American West*, pp. 178–80.

18. The Yellowstone encounters are treated in Lubetkin, *Jay Cooke's Gamble*. A complete account of the Black Hills venture appears in Frafe and Horsted, *Exploring with Custer*. Article 2 of the Fort Laramie Treaty of 1868 held that "no persons except . . . such officers, agents, and employees of the Government as may be authorized to enter upon Indian reservations in discharge of duties enjoined by law, shall ever be permitted to pass over, settle upon, or reside in the [reservation] territory described." Kappler, *Indian Affairs*, 2:998–99; *Report of the Commissioner of Indian Affairs, 1874*, p. 8 (quotation).

19. The Black Hills gold rush is thoroughly chronicled in Parker, *Gold in the Black Hills*, while government policy regarding the Black Hills, the unceded Indian lands, and the nontreaty Sioux is discussed at length in Hutton, *Phil Sheridan and His Army*, pp. 282–301; and Larson, *Red Cloud*, pp. 186–97.

20. The sequences of the Great Sioux War are described at length in the following works: Vaughn, *The Reynolds Campaign on Powder River;* Mangum, *Battle of the Rosebud;* Donovan, *A Terrible Glory;* Greene, *Slim Buttes, 1876;* Greene, *Morning Star Dawn;* Greene, *Yellowstone Command;* Greene, "Out with a Whimper"; and Hardorff, *The Surrender and Death of Crazy Horse*. For Crazy Horse's death and all its contributing implications and collateral repercussions among the Sioux, see especially Powers, *The Killing of Crazy Horse*. For army and Indian accounts of the actions, see Greene, *Battles and Skirmishes of the Great Sioux War;* and Greene, *Lakota and Cheyenne*. Comprehensive interpretations of the war and its various combats appear in Utley, *Frontier Regulars*, pp. 249–95; Robinson, *A Good Year to Die;* and Hedren, *Great Sioux War Orders of Battle*.

21. *Report of the Commissioner of Indian Affairs, 1876*, pp. xv (including quotation), 330–57 ("Report of the Commission Appointed to Obtain Certain Concessions from

the Sioux," including articles of agreement); *Report of the Commissioner of Indian Affairs, 1877*, pp. 17–18; Kappler, *Indian Affairs*, vol. 1 (Laws), 168–72; Manypenny, *Our Indian Wards*, pp. 324–25; *Sioux Nation and the United States*, pp. 4–5; Tallent, *The Black Hills*, pp. 95–98; Hyde, *Spotted Tail's Folk*, pp. 226–29; and Clowser, *Dakota Indian Treaties*, p. 234 (map). On March 3, 1871, Congress abolished the old treaty system, asserting that "hereafter no Indian nation or tribe within the territory of the United States shall be acknowledged or recognized as an independent nation, tribe, or power with whom the United States may contract by treaty." Fritz, *Movement for Indian Assimilation*, p. 84. Henceforth products of such negotiation would be termed "agreements." The Black Hills Agreement of 1876 and the long fight for restitution is detailed in Lazarus, *Black Hills/White Justice*. Although the Sioux won a $102,000,000 judgment in 1980, the tribe rejected the settlement (and its accumulated interest) and demanded the return of the Black Hills. Ortiz, *Great Sioux Nation*, p. viii. See also Ostler, *The Lakotas and the Black Hills*, particularly pp. 107–91.

22. Captain Ezra P. Ewers, "Report of Indians that surrendered or were captured through the exertions of the troops of the District of the Yellowstone," Fort Keogh, Montana Territory, December 15, 1881, Folder, Fifth Infantry, Ft. Keogh M.T., Box T-2, Fifth Infantry to August 1881, Nelson A. Miles Collection, Manuscript Division, U.S. Army Military History Institute, Army War College (hereinafter cited as Miles Collection). For the Canadian years of the refugee Lakotas and their ultimate surrender, see Bray, "'We Belong to the North'"; DeMallie, "The Sioux in Dakota and Montana Territories"; Manzione, *"I Am Looking to the North for My Life"*; McCrady, *Living with Strangers*, pp. 61–102; and Utley, *The Lance and the Shield*, pp. 183–233. Sitting Bull's submission is also related in Hedren, *Sitting Bull's Surrender at Fort Buford*. For the cycles of change enveloping the northern plains during the late 1870s through the 1880s, see Hedren, *After Custer*.

Chapter 2. New World

1. This included an area adjoining the north edge of the Great Sioux Reservation (below the south fork of the Cannonball River in present North Dakota) set aside via executive order on March 16, 1875, to support the Standing Rock Agency, which was located about ten miles north of the boundary. Royce, "Indian Land Cessions in the United States," part 2, p. 880, cession 581 on map "North Dakota and South Dakota 2." It should also be noted that several much smaller separate reserves had been designated earlier for Santee and Yankton-Yanktonai Sioux in the southeastern part of Dakota Territory, all east of the Missouri River. It was estimated that the modified Great Sioux Reservation after the Black Hills Agreement contained 21,735,846 acres. See also Hoover, "The Sioux Agreement of 1889 and Its Aftermath," p. 68.

2. E. Dalrymple Clark's transcription in Assistant Commissioner A. G. Irvine, North-West Mounted Police to Canadian Secretary of State Richard W. Scott, June 6, 1877 (including quotation), in "Papers Relating to the Sioux Indians of the United States, Who Have Taken Refuge in Canadian Territory," Public Archives of Canada, p. 27.

3. This synopsis of the land encompassing the modified Great Sioux Reservation is drawn from Schell, *History of South Dakota*, pp. 3–14; Fenneman, *Physiography of the Western United States*, pp. 67–69, 75–79, 86–91; Gries, *Roadside Geology of South Dakota*, pp. 170–71, 191–202; and O'Hara, *The White River Badlands*.

4. "Rosebud (formerly Spotted Tail) Agency, Dakota, October 1, 1878," Report of Special U.S. Indian Agent William J. Pollock, in *Report of the Commissioner of Indian Affairs, 1878*, pp. 534–36; "Rosebud Agency, Dakota, September 13, 1879," Report of U.S. Indian Agent Cicero Newell, in *Report of the Commissioner of Indian Affairs, 1879*, pp. 41–43; DeMallie, "Pine Ridge Economy," pp. 252–53. For the early months at Pine Ridge, see "Pine Ridge Agency, Dakota, October 15, 1879," Report of U.S. Indian Agent Valentine T. McGillycuddy, in *Report of the Commissioner of Indian Affairs, 1879*, pp. 37–40. For more on the uneasy relocations of the two agencies, see Hyde, *Spotted Tail's Folk*, pp. 260–66; Clow, "The Brulé Indian Agencies"; Larson, *Red Cloud*, pp. 221–25; Hyde, *Sioux Chronicle*, pp. 7–25; Olson, *Red Cloud and the Sioux Problem*, pp. 256–63; and Hedren, *After Custer*, pp. 63–65.

5. Hedren, *After Custer*, pp. 50–69; Utley, *Frontier Regulars*, p. 403; Mattison, *The Army Post on the Northern Plains*, pp. 2–3. For capsule histories of these posts, see Frazier, *Forts of the West*.

6. Anderson, "A History of the Cheyenne River Agency," p. 485.

7. Greene, *Fort Randall on the Missouri*, pp. 139–64; Utley, *Lance and the Shield*, pp. 234–47, 254–55; Pope, *Sitting Bull*.

8. DeMallie, "Teton," part 2, pp. 812–15; Utley, *Frontier Regulars*, p. 401; Hyde, *Sioux Chronicle*, pp. 30–31; Hagan, *Indian Police and Judges*, pp. 104, 111; U.S. Congress, Senate, Committee on Indian Affairs, *Letter from the Secretary of the Interior, in Response to Senate Resolution of December 13, 1888*, p. 3 (quotation).

9. Dobak, "Killing the Canadian Buffalo," p. 34; Smith, *The Champion Buffalo Hunter*, pp. 131–32, 189–90; *Omaha Bee*, December 28, 1890; Utley, *Lance and the Shield*, pp. 199–203. One of the last formal buffalo hunts took place in June 1882 and involved Sioux from Standing Rock Agency targeting animals west of the South Cannonball River and killing around 2,000 over several days. McLaughlin, *My Friend the Indian*, pp. 100–116; Punke, *Last Stand*, pp. 134–35; Hornaday, *The Extermination of the American Bison*, p. 512. See also Vestal, *Warpath*, pp. 238–40.

10. DeMallie, "Teton," part 2, pp. 812–15; Utley, *Frontier Regulars*, p. 401; Remington, "The Art of War and Newspaper Men," p. 58; Eastman, "The Ghost Dance War," p. 26 (quotation). For pre–Wounded Knee assessments of life on the Great Sioux Reservation, see the annual reports of the agents and missionaries concerning matters of industry, health, education, and control in *Report of the Commissioner of Indian Affairs, 1890*, pp. 41–64. See also Utley, *The Last Days of the Sioux Nation*, pp. 18–39.

11. Schell, *History of South Dakota*, p. 317; Anderson, "A History of the Cheyenne River Indian Agency," p. 486; Eastman, *Pratt, the Red Man's Moses*, p. 173 (quotation); Hall, *To Have This Land*, pp. 2, 5–7. For agreements with the Sioux regarding right-of-way for the Chicago, Milwaukee & St. Paul Railway and the Dakota Central Division of the Chicago and North Western Railway, see U.S. Congress, House, Committee on Indian Affairs, *Right of Way to Dakota Central Railway through Sioux Reservation, Dakota;* U.S. Congress, Senate, Committee on Indian Affairs, *Message from the President, Transmitting a Communication from the Secretary of the Interior of 4th Instant;* U.S. Congress, House, Committee on Indian Affairs, *Agreements with Sioux Indians.*

12. U.S. Congress, House, Committee on Indian Affairs, *An Agreement with the Sioux Indians, Dakota*, p. 1.

13. Ibid., p. 2.

14. Schell, *History of South Dakota*, p. 317; Anderson, "A History of the Cheyenne River Indian Agency," p. 486. Based on subsequent surveys, the land actually encompassed approximately 9,000,000 acres.

15. *Report of the Special Committee of the United States Senate*, p. iii.

16. Ibid., pp. iv, v, vi, vii, ix; U.S. Congress, House, Committee on Indian Affairs, *To Divide a Portion of the Reservation of the Sioux Nation of Indians in Dakota;* Hoover, "The Sioux Agreement of 1889," pp. 60–65; *Sioux Nation and the United States*, pp. 6–7; Schell, *History of South Dakota*, pp. 317–18; Anderson, "History of the Cheyenne River Indian Agency," pp. 486–90; Behrens, "In Defense of 'Poor Lo,'" pp. 158–59; Ostler, *Plains Sioux and U.S. Colonialism*, pp. 218–21. For the early years of the Indian Rights Association, see Hagan, *The Indian Rights Association*.

17. See the discussion of these interim measures in Behrens, "In Defense of 'Poor Lo,'" pp. 159–62; and Hagan, *The Indian Rights Association*, pp. 54–59.

18. Allotment proposals, like other presumed inducements toward civilization, stood on a premise of social evolution advocated by theorists like anthropologist Lewis Henry Morgan in the 1870s. These views formed the underpinnings of U.S. Indian policy grounded in pastoralism, education, and religion by the late 1870s and early 1880s. See Fritz, *The Movement for Indian Assimilation*, pp. 123–24; Forsyth, *Representing the Massacre*, pp. 12–17.

19. Hagan, *American Indians*, pp. 139–43; Hoover, "The Sioux Agreement of 1889," p. 65; *Report of the Special Committee of the United States Senate*, p. ii; Sweeney, "Indian Land Policy since 1887," pp. 258–62; Morgan, *The Present Phase of the Indian Question*, pp. 7–8 (quotation); *Sioux Nation and the United States*, pp. 7–11. (For background on Morgan, see "Thomas Jefferson Morgan, 1889–93," in Kvasnicka and Viola, *The Commissioners of Indian Affairs*, pp. 193–203.) A fine history of the allotment program is found in Banner, *How the Indians Lost Their Land*, pp. 257–90; but see also Deloria and Lytle, *American Indians, American Justice*, pp. 8–12; Fritz, *Movement for Indian Assimilation*, pp. 209–20; Priest, *Uncle Sam's Stepchildren*, pp. 177–97; and Washburn, *The Assault on Indian Tribalism*. See also Forsyth, *Representing the Massacre*, pp. 11–17. Between 1887 and 1934 nonallotted land purchased by the U.S. government, together with fee-patented lands sold by Indians at the end of the trust period, reduced Indian landholdings from 138 million to 55 million acres. Larson, *Red Cloud*, p. 252.

20. *Report of the Commissioner of Indian Affairs, 1888*, p. lxxiii.

21. Colonel Edward Hatch to Brigadier General John R. Brooke, July 19, 1888, John Rutter Brooke Papers, Historical Society of Pennsylvania, Box 8, Folder 1 (hereinafter cited as Brooke Papers).

22. Eastman, *Sister to the Sioux*, pp. 86–93; Olson, *Red Cloud and the Sioux Problem*, pp. 309–12; Larson, *Red Cloud*, pp. 252–54; *Sioux Nation and the United States*, pp. 11–17; Anderson, "History of the Cheyenne River Indian Agency," pp. 490–93; Behrens, "In Defense of 'Poor Lo,'" p. 162; Hagan, *Indian Rights Association*, pp. 59–62; Schell, *History of South Dakota*, p. 318; Sweeney, "Indian Land Policy since 1887," pp. 257–58; Ostler, *Plains Sioux and U.S. Colonialism*, pp. 221–28. See the report of the commission in U.S. Congress, Senate, Committee on Indian Affairs, *Letter from the Secretary of the Interior, in Response to Senate Resolution of December 13, 1888*, pp. 2ff. For Lower Brulé Agency with respect to Crow Creek, see Schusky, *The Forgotten Sioux*.

23. Larson, *Red Cloud*, pp. 254–56; Olson, *Red Cloud and the Sioux Problem*, p. 311; Utley, *Lance and the Shield*, pp. 274–77; Anderson, "History of the Cheyenne River Indian Agency," p. 493; Behrens, "In Defense of 'Poor Lo,'" pp. 163–64; *Report of the Secretary of the Interior, 1888*, p. lxiv (quotation); Greene, "The Sioux Land Commission of 1889," pp. 43–44.

24. Pine Ridge Oglala Council to the President of the United States, December 10, 1888, National Archives (NA), Record Group (RG) 75, Records of the Bureau of

Indian Affairs, Letters Received (file 31115–1888, enclosed in 716–1889), copy provided by Michael Her Many Horses. For background on Young Man Afraid of His Horses, see Hartley, "Dakota Images."

CHAPTER 3. BROKEN FAITH

1. *An Act to Provide for the Division of Dakota into Two States and to Enable the People of North Dakota, South Dakota, Montana, and Washington to Form Constitutions and State Governments and to Be Admitted into the Union on an Equal Footing with the Original States, and to Make Donations of Public Lands to Such States*, February 22, 1889, in Hosen, *Unfolding Westward in Treaty and Law*, pp. 311–20; U.S. Congress, Senate, Committee on Indian Affairs, *Joint Resolution and Memorial of the Legislative Assembly of the Territory of Dakota;* Behrens, "In Defense of 'Poor Lo,'" pp. 166–67; *Chadron Advocate*, June 28, 1889; *Report of the Commissioner of Indian Affairs, 1889*, p. 21 (quotation); Kappler, *Indian Affairs*, 1:328–39; *U.S. Statutes at Large*, 25, 888–99; Olson, *Red Cloud and the Sioux Problem*, p. 312. For the long prelude to statehood, see Lamar, *Dakota Territory, 1861–1889;* and Lauck, *Prairie Republic*. For the pony claims, see Clow, "General Philip Sheridan's Legacy." Much of this chapter has been adapted and modified from Greene, "Sioux Land Commission of 1889." For intriguing insight and solid analyses of the objectives and designs of the incoming Harrison administration with respect to Sioux land status vis-à-vis the Dawes legislation, expansive Republican politics, and tariff economics of the time, see Richardson, *Wounded Knee*, chapters 3–5.

2. Richardson, *A Compilation of the Messages and Papers of the Presidents*, vol. 11, 5480–81; *Report of the Commissioner of Indian Affairs 1889*, p. 20 (quotation); *New York Times*, May 9, 1889; *Yankton Daily Press and Dakotaian*, April 18, 1889; May 13, 1889 (hereinafter cited as *Yankton Daily Press*).

3. *New York Times*, May 6, 1889, and May 12, 1889; *Yankton Daily Press*, May 9, 1889 (quotation); *New York Times*, May 12, 1889; Johnston, *Federal Relations with the Great Sioux Indians of South Dakota*, p. 41.

4. *Yankton Daily Press*, April 24 and 25, 1889; *Biographical Directory of the American Congress*, pp. 907, 1777; *Yankton Daily Press*, May 15, 1889 (quotations).

5. Possibly the Indians themselves influenced Crook's selection. The commander at Fort Robinson, Nebraska, reported a demonstration by hundreds of Sioux in Crook's favor. Colonel Edward Hatch to Assistant Adjutant General (AAG), Omaha, March 4, 1889, NA, RG 48, Letters Received, cited in Olson, *Red Cloud and the Sioux Problem*, p. 313; *Yankton Daily Press*, April 24 and 26 and May 28, 1889 (quotation). For background on Crook, see Robinson, *General Crook and the Western Frontier;* Magid, *George Crook;* and Greene, "George Crook," pp. 246–72. The Crook/winter count connection is mentioned in Vestal, *Warpath*, p. 271.

6. U.S. Congress, Senate, Committee on Indian Affairs. *Reports Relative to the Proposed Division of the Great Sioux Reservation* (hereinafter cited as *Reports Relative to the Proposed Division of the Great Sioux Reservation*), pp. 16, 35; Schmitt, *General George Crook*, p. 284.

7. *Yankton Daily Press*, June 1, 1889; Schmitt, *General George Crook*, p. 284; *Advocate*, June 28, 1889 (quotation); *Reports Relative to the Proposed Division of the Great Sioux Reservation*, pp. 90–91; Utley, *Last Days of the Sioux Nation*, p. 49.

8. Standing Bear, *My People the Sioux*, pp. 210–11; *Reports Relative to the Proposed Division of the Great Sioux Reservation*, p. 45; Schmitt, *General George Crook*, p. 286.

Interpreter Philip F. Wells, who lived among the Lakotas and knew them well, maintained that in 1888 the people were only beginning to realize how the Black Hills had been stolen from them. Wells to Major General Hugh L. Scott, September 3, 1920, Thomas Odell Collection, Drawer 6, Folder 44, Special Collections, Leland D. Case Library, E. Y. Berry Library–Learning Center, Black Hills State University (hereinafter cited as Thomas Odell Collection).

9. *Reports Relative to the Proposed Division of the Great Sioux Reservation*, pp. 4, 17–18; DeLand, "The Sioux Wars," p. 430; Hyde, *A Sioux Chronicle*, p. 211; Standing Bear, *My People the Sioux*, p. 212; Schmitt, *General George Crook*, p. 285.

10. Schmitt, *General George Crook*, p. 286; Hyde, *A Sioux Chronicle*, pp. 206, 208, 211; *Reports Relative to the Proposed Division of the Great Sioux Reservation*, p. 50 (quotation).

11. *Reports Relative to the Proposed Division of the Great Sioux Reservation*, pp. 35, 51–52; Hyde, *A Sioux Chronicle*, pp. 209–10; Olson, *Red Cloud and the Sioux Problem*, p. 313; Robinson, *General Crook and the Western Frontier*, p. 299; Behrens, "In Defense of 'Poor Lo,'" pp. 168–70.

12. *Yankton Daily Press*, June 13, 1889.

13. *Advocate*, June 28, 1889.

14. Hyde, *Sioux Chronicle*, pp. 200–201, 212, 213; Priest, *Uncle Sam's Stepchildren*, p. 86; *Reports Relative to the Proposed Division of the Great Sioux Reservation*, p. 18; Agent Hugh D. Gallagher to Commissioner of Indian Affairs Thomas J. Morgan, August 28, 1890, in *Report of the Commissioner of Indian Affairs, 1890*, p. 49. The determined Bland had on at least one occasion been physically ousted from Pine Ridge Agency for his efforts with the Sioux. Copy of broadside notice effecting said removal, dated July 12, 1884, provided by Paul Harbaugh, Cherry Hills Village, Colorado. Bland edited a pamphlet entitled *A Brief History of the Late Military Invasion of the Home of the Sioux*. For background on Bland's efforts vis-à-vis allotment as an element of agrarian radicalism of the period, see Johnson, "Red Populism?" For more on Bland, see Cowger, "Dr. Thomas Bland." For allotment as a premier element of assimilation, see Hoxie, *The Final Promise*.

15. *Advocate*, June 28, 1889; *New York Times*, June 17, 1889 (first quotation); *Yankton Daily Press*, June 17, 1889; *Reports Relative to the Proposed Division of the Great Sioux Reservation*, pp. 18, 70, 79 (second quotation), 86–87; Hyde, *A Sioux Chronicle*, p. 214. Under their own Fort Laramie Treaty of 1868 the Cheyennes were authorized to live on the Great Sioux Reservation. See article 2, "Treaty with the Northern Cheyenne and Northern Arapaho," in Kappler, *Indian Affairs*, 2:1012.

16. *Reports Relative to the Proposed Division of the Great Sioux Reservation*, pp. 17, 87–93, 97.

17. Schmitt, *General George Crook*, pp. 286, 287; *Yankton Daily Press*, June 22 and July 5, 1889; Gallagher to Morgan, August 27, 1889, in *Report of the Commissioner of Indian Affairs, 1889*, p. 153; *Reports Relative to the Proposed Division of the Great Sioux Reservation*, pp. 51, 113, 114 (quotation), 116; Olson, *Red Cloud and the Sioux Problem*, pp. 317–19; Hyde, *Sioux Chronicle*, p. 217; Larson, *Red Cloud*, pp. 259–60; Johnston, *Federal Relations with the Great Sioux Indians of South Dakota*, p. 51. A mixed-blood Lakota at Pine Ridge charged that Crook had called upon whites married to Sioux women to sign "as representatives of their Indian wives who would receive allotments of land under the treaty." William Garnett interview in Jensen, *Voices of the American West*, 1:93. For American Horse's background, see Powers, *The Killing of Crazy Horse;* and "Dakota Images: American Horse," pp. 252–53.

18. Crook to Foster, August 27, 1889. Letterbook II, Item 14, pp. 20–22, George Crook Papers, Rutherford B. Hayes Memorial Library (hereinafter cited as George Crook Papers); Gallagher to Morgan, August 27, 1889, in *Report of the Commissioner of Indian Affairs, 1889*, p. 157 (first quotation); Olson, *Red Cloud and the Sioux Problem*, p. 318 (second quotation); Behrens, "In Defense of 'Po Lo,'" p. 170. On July 4 Red Cloud addressed citizens of Chadron, Nebraska, telling them that "the great father sent commissioners here to try and bulldoze me like a child and try to take my land away from me. . . . I did not sign the paper." *Advocate*, July 5, 1889.

19. *Reports Relative to the Proposed Division of the Great Sioux Reservation*, pp. 19, 122, 124, 129, 135 (quotation); Eastman, *Pratt, the Red Man's Moses*, p. 133; Schmitt, *General George Crook*, p. 287; Hyde, *Sioux Chronicle*, p. 219.

20. *Reports Relative to the Proposed Division of the Great Sioux Reservation*, pp. 20, 35, 143, 144 (first quotation), 151; *Executive Orders Relating to Indian Reservations*, p. 167; Royce, "Indian Land Cessions," part 2, pp. 918–19; *New York Times*, July 10, 1889; *Yankton Daily Press*, July 13, 1889; Hyde, *Sioux Chronicle*, p. 220; Schmitt, *General George Crook*, p. 287 (second quotation); Behrens, "In Defense of 'Poor Lo,'" p. 170.

21. *New York Times*, July 16, 1889; *Reports Relative to the Proposed Division of the Great Sioux Reservation*, pp. 20 (quotation), 35.

22. *Reports Relative to the Proposed Division of the Great Sioux Reservation*, pp. 20, 169; Schmitt, *General George Crook*, p. 287; Hyde, *Sioux Chronicle*, p. 221.

23. *Reports Relative to the Proposed Division of the Great Sioux Reservation*, pp. 20–21 (quotation); *New York Times*, July 20, 1889; Hyde, *Sioux Chronicle*, p. 222.

24. *Reports Relative to the Proposed Division of the Great Sioux Reservation*, pp. 21, 175–76, 180, 181, 184, 296; Schmitt, *General George Crook*, p. 287; Hyde, *Sioux Chronicle*, p. 223. McChesney and Randall collected 320 votes in addition to the 300 obtained by the commissioners. McChesney to James McLaughlin, August 26, 1889, in *Report of the Commissioner of Indian Affairs, 1889*, p. 135 (quotation); Anderson, "History of the Cheyenne River Indian Agency," pp. 494–96. The concurrence of such a strong dissenter as Chief Hump suggests that they employed extraordinary persuasion.

25. *Reports Relative to the Proposed Division of the Great Sioux Reservation*, pp. 21, 35; McLaughlin, *My Friend the Indian*, pp. 281–82; Wilkinson, "The Death of Sitting Bull," Don G. Rickey Papers, Western History Department, Denver Public Library, p. 1 (hereinafter cited as Rickey Papers, Denver Public Library); Johnston, *Federal Relations with the Great Sioux Indians of South Dakota*, p. 31.

26. *Reports Relative to the Proposed Division of the Great Sioux Reservation*, pp. 17, 187 (first quotation), 194–202; Wilkinson, "Death of Sitting Bull," pp. 1–2; McLaughlin, *My Friend the Indian*, p. 281; Schmitt, *General George Crook*, p. 288; McLaughlin to Morgan, August 26, 1889, in *Report of the Commissioner of Indian Affairs, 1889*, p. 169 (second quotation); *Reports Relative to the Proposed Division of the Great Sioux Reservation*, p. 206 (third quotation).

27. *Reports Relative to the Proposed Division of the Great Sioux Reservation*, p. 200.

28. Ibid., pp. 21; McLaughlin, *My Friend the Indian*, pp. 284–85; McLaughlin to Morgan, October 17, 1890, in *Report of the Commissioner of Indian Affairs, 1891*, 1:329; undated note by One Bull, Walter S. Campbell Papers, Box 105, Item 41, Western History Collection, University of Oklahoma Library (hereinafter cited as Campbell Papers); Loneman, "Sitting Bull's Address to the Silent-Eaters Protesting the Treaty [*sic*] of 1889," Campbell Papers, Box 104, Item 20; Vestal, *New Sources of Indian History*, p. 304 (quotation); statement by Mary Collins, Congregationalist missionary to the Sioux, Campbell Papers, Box 113, Item 4. This statement is similar, though not

identical, to one reproduced in Vestal, *New Sources of Indian History*, p. 72. There are inferences that John Grass was bribed to influence the Indians, although McLaughlin apparently was not complicit. See the typescript "Signing the Crook Treaty [*sic*]," pp. 2–3, Philip F. Wells materials, Thomas Odell Collection, Drawer 6, Folder 47. One report stated that Grass discussed the land matter with lawyers in Bismarck before switching sides. Ibid., pp. 68–69; *New York Times*, July 30 and August 7, 1889. See also Larson, *Gall*, pp. 208–209; Foley, *Father Francis M. Craft*, pp. 68–70; and Foley, *At Standing Rock and Wounded Knee*, pp. 266–70.

29. *Reports Relative to the Proposed Division of the Great Sioux Reservation*, pp. 209, 213; McLaughlin, *My Friend the Indian*, pp. 286–87; Schmitt, *General George Crook*, p. 288; Hyde, *Sioux Chronicle*, p. 227; *Yankton Daily Press*, August 7, 1889 (first quotation); *New York Times*, August 7, 1889 (second and third quotations); Utley, *Lance and the Shield*, pp. 277–79. For precise descriptions of land conveyed by the 1889 transaction, see Royce, "Indian Land Cessions," part 2, pp. 930–34; cessions 699, 700, 701, 702, 703, 704, 705, on map, "North Dakota and South Dakota 3," and cession 631 on map, "Nebraska."

30. *Yankton Daily Press*, August 7, 1889 (first quotation); McLaughlin, *My Friend the Indian*, p. 287; Hyde, *A Sioux Chronicle*, p. 227; *Reports Relative to the Proposed Division of the Great Sioux Reservation*, pp. 21 (second quotation), 113; Utley, *The Lance and the Shield*, pp. 278–79; Behrens, "In Defense of 'Poor Lo,'" pp. 171–72. See also the detailed coverage of the 1889 commission in Ostler, *The Plains Sioux and U.S. Colonialism*, pp. 228–38.

31. *Yankton Daily Press*, August 9, 1889; *New York Times*, August 8, 1889 (first quotation); *Reports Relative to the Proposed Division of the Great Sioux Reservation*, p. 21; *Report of the Secretary of the Interior, 1889*, p. xi (second quotation).

32. *Report of the Commissioner of Indian Affairs, 1891*, 1:32–35; and "Letters from Commissioner of Indian Affairs to Secretary of the Interior Relating to the Amount of Subsistence Supplies Issued to Sioux," in ibid., pp. 191–93ff.; *Reports Relative to the Proposed Division of the Great Sioux Reservation*, p. 24 (first quotation); Crook to Foster, August 27, 1889 (second quotation), letter book II, item 14, pp. 20–22. George Crook Papers; *Reports Relative to the Proposed Division of the Great Sioux Reservation*, p. 24 (third and fourth quotations). Adding to the problem, the reservation Sioux through the years had of necessity gradually inflated their census figures as a means to offset regular beef shrinkage between delivery and slaughter of their cattle. Coincidentally, even before the commissioners had arrived at Rosebud, some traditionalists on the reservation noted a new federal census underway and perceptively drew conclusions about an ensuing rations cut. Larson, *Red Cloud*, pp. 260–61. Senator Dawes stated that the beef reduction occurred through "some sort of hocus-pocus in the census," whereby the government had been issuing rations to 2,500 more Indians than existed. *Washington Post*, January 9, 1891.

33. *Report of the Commissioner of Indian Affairs, 1890*, p. 49 (quotation); *Reports Relative to the Proposed Division of the Great Sioux Reservation*, p. 218; Utley, *The Last Days of the Sioux Nation*, p. 56.

34. *Reports Relative to the Proposed Division of the Great Sioux Reservation*, pp. 218–33 (quotation on 232). For the matter of statehood vis-à-vis Indian land concerns, see Lamar, "Perspectives on Statehood," pp. 15–17. Relative populations of the new states in 1890 after crop failures and the resulting exodus were North Dakota 182,719 and South Dakota 328,808 (32,559 located in the Black Hills area). Briggs, "The Great Dakota Boom," p. 120.

35. *Reports Relative to the Proposed Division of the Great Sioux Reservation*, pp. 25–28, 30–31.

36. *New York Times*, August 11, 1889; *Yankton Daily Press*, August 24, 1889; *New York Times*, February 11, 1890 (first quotation); *U.S. Statutes at Large*, 26:1554–57; U.S. Army General Orders No. 16, February 15, 1890, in *General Orders and Circulars, Adjutant General's Office, 1890;* Johnston, *Federal Relations with the Great Sioux Indians of South Dakota*, p. 42; Green, "The Administration of the Public Domain in South Dakota," p. 160; Richardson, *A Compilation of the Messages and Papers*, 8:61–62, 95–97 (second and fourth quotations); *Harper's Weekly*, March 8, 1890 (third quotation); Royce, "Indian Land Cessions," p. 938.

37. *Report of the Secretary of the Interior, 1890*, p. xxv; *Report of the Commissioner of Indian Affairs, 1891*, 1:134, 182–91; *Eighth Annual Report of the Executive Committee of the Indian Rights Association*, p. 5; Gallagher to Morgan, August 28, 1890, in *Report of the Commissioner of Indian Affairs, 1890*, p. 49 (first quotation); McChesney to Morgan, August 25, 1890, in ibid., p. 42 (second quotation); *Report of the Commissioner of Indian Affairs, 1891*, 1:42, 133; *Twenty-First Annual Report of the Board of Indian Commissioners*, p. 61; Spencer to Morgan, August 23, 1889, in *Report of the Commissioner of Indian Affairs, 1889*, p. 160; McLaughlin's account in Burdick, *The Last Days of Sitting Bull*, p. 63. See especially the discussion in DeLand, "The Sioux Wars," pp. 429–38. For more contemporary insight on the commission's work and its results, see Tallent, *The Black Hills*, pp. 527–29; *The Sioux Nation and the United States*, pp. 16–27; "Why the Indians Fight," 391–93; and Richardson, "Some Observations upon the Sioux Campaign of 1890–91," pp. 517–19. For a modern assessment, see Marks, *In a Barren Land*, pp. 217–18, 221–22. An analysis of the reasons for the success of the 1889 commission in gaining approval of the Sioux is found in Hoover, "Sioux Agreement of 1889," pp. 66–67.

38. *Frank Leslie's Illustrated Newspaper*, December 20, 1890.

Chapter 4. Trauma

1. *Chadron Democrat*, March 13, 1890. Another description of a contemporary beef issue at Pine Ridge appears in the *Chicago Tribune*, November 28, 1890; see also "Old Timers Recall Indian Beef Issues," *Rapid City Journal*, June 18, 1950; and Eastman, *Sister to the Sioux*, pp. 59–60.

2. *Chadron Advocate*, November 21, 1890.

3. *New York Weekly Witness*, January 22, 1890; *New York Weekly Witness*, February 12, 1890; *New York Weekly Witness*, March 5, 1890 (first quotation); *Harper's Weekly*, March 8, 1890 (second quotation); Hall, *To Have This Land*, p. 11; *Harper's Weekly*, March 8, 1890 (third quotation).

4. Schell, *History of South Dakota*, pp. 155, 244–47, 250, 252; Lee, *Scotty Philip*, p. 118; Peter Iverson, *When Indians Became Cowboys*, pp. 66–67; "The Beginning of the Last Indian War," in "Accounts of Unidentified South Dakota Family during the Messiah War in 1890," Manuscript H88.32 3749A, South Dakota State Historical Society (hereinafter cited as SDSHS). Some semblance of life on the cattle range at Standing Rock and Cheyenne River reservations within a few years of the Sioux crisis period is conveyed in Blasingame, *Dakota Cowboy*, pp. 42–55, 116–17. For Pine Ridge Reservation, see especially Means, "'Indians Shall Do Things in Common'"; and Sanderson, "'We Were All Trespassers,'" pp. 52–53, 58. Estimated acreage of the six new

reservations was as follows: Standing Rock, 2,672,640; Cheyenne River, 2,867,840; Crow Creek, 285,521; Lower Brulé, 472,550; Pine Ridge, 3,155,200; and Rosebud, 3,228,160. *Reports Relative to the Proposed Division of the Great Sioux Reservation*, p. 41.

5. *Report of the Commissioner of Indian Affairs, 1890*, pp. 450–51. Non-Lakota reservations in eastern South Dakota were for the Sisseton and Wahpeton Sioux (1,509 people) and the Yankton Sioux (1,725 people). Ibid., p. 450.

6. American Horse and other Oglala chiefs to Secretary of the Interior John W. Noble, Pine Ridge Agency, March 6, 1890, NA, RG 75, File 8276, copy provided by Michael Her Many Horses (quotation); Richardson, "Some Observations on the Sioux Campaign of 1890–91," p. 519; Hyde, *Sioux Chronicle*, pp. 232–34.

7. *New York Times*, August 11, 1889 (Foster quotation); in *Report of the Commissioner of Indian Affairs, 1890*, pp. 36–64 (agents' quotations and reports); Eastman, "Ghost Dance War," p. 29 (final quotation).

8. More than 2,600 cases of measles were reported at the six agencies in 1888–89: most were at Standing Rock (922), Cheyenne River (481), Pine Ridge (465), and Rosebud (447). Influenza (1,198 cases) and whooping cough (551) reigned in 1889–90 and to a lesser degree in 1890–91 (526 cases of flu at Standing Rock). *Report of the Commissioner of Indian Affairs, 1889*, pp. 528–29, 536–37; *Report of the Commissioner of Indian Affairs, 1890*, pp. 39, 42, 44–45, 57, 482–505; *Report of the Commissioner of Indian Affairs, 1891*, 1:122–23, 130–31, 138–39; Schell, *History of South Dakota*, p. 320; Hyde, *A Sioux Chronicle*, p. 238.

9. U.S. Congress, House, *Letter from the Acting Secretary of the Treasury*, pp. 1–5.

10. Former Pine Ridge agent Valentine T. McGillycuddy explained the problem inherent in government distribution of beef to the people: "In October a beef is in its best condition, weighing say 1,100 pounds. In March it has shrunk to 700 pounds. The shrinkage is of the edible portions; hoofs, horns, bones and hide do not lose in weight. Five hundred pounds of the beef is not subject to being cooked, consequently the net amount in October is 600 pounds, while that of March is 200. No provision is made for the shrinkage, however. The department recognizes a beef as being simply a beef. So in winter when he needs food more, the Indian gets just about one-third the amount of beef he is supposed to have. Other rations are always short." *Omaha World-Herald*, November 28, 1890.

11. Harvey, "The Last Stand of the Sioux," p. 226; Tibbles, *Buckskin and Blanket Days*, p. 300; Hyde, *Sioux Chronicle*, pp. 230–31; American Horse et al. to Secretary of the Interior John W. Noble, Pine Ridge Agency, March 6, 1890, NA, RG 75, File 8276-1890, copy provided by Michael Her Many Horses (quotation); Buecker, "Fort Niobrara, 1880–1906," p. 314; Schubert, *Buffalo Soldiers, Braves, and the Brass*, p. 27; Larson, *Red Cloud*, p. 263; Richardson, "Some Observations upon the Sioux Campaign of 1890–91," pp. 518–19; Fritz, *Movement for Indian Assimilation*, pp. 218–19; Hedren, *After Custer*, pp. 130–31; Philip F. Wells to Major General Hugh L. Scott, September 3, 1920, Thomas Odell Collection. See also the views of Major General Oliver O. Howard regarding the beef issue crisis in Ellis, *The Indian Wars of the United States*, p. 399.

12. Jordan to Major General Nelson A. Miles, February 25, 1896, Charles Percival Jordan Papers, H74–42 SC61, vol. 1 (ledger), File Box 043, SDSHS. For the transfer debate as revived during the post–Civil War period, see Priest, *Uncle Sam's Stepchildren*, pp. 15–27; and Fritz, *The Movement for Indian Assimilation*, pp. 133–34. As an example of the Indians' deprivation regarding beef issues at Rosebud, Jordan calculated figures based on the reduced census of July 1, 1890, showing 5,354 persons on that reservation,

and demonstrated a deficiency in the beef ration of 489,804 pounds (based on three pounds per person per day) for the period July 1 to September 30. Similarly estimating for the period from October 1, 1890, to June 30, 1891, including the massive shrinkage that further reduced cattle weight through the winter, Jordan postulated a deficit of 885,116 pounds, thereby totaling a shortage of 1,374,920 pounds of beef for the entire fiscal year 1890–91. Jordan to Miles, February 25, 1896.

13. Quoted in "Sioux Women at Home," *Illustrated American*, January 31, 1891, pp. 484–85.

14. Schell, *History of South Dakota*, pp. 320–21; *New York Weekly Witness*, January 8, 1890 (quotation); *Washington Evening Star*, February 3, 1891; Hagan, *American Indians*, pp. 135–37; Priest, *Uncle Sam's Stepchildren*, pp. 150–51.

15. U.S. Congress, Senate, Committee on Indian Affairs, *Letter from the Secretary of the Interior, in Relation to the Affairs of the Indians*, pp. 1–7ff. (which thoroughly airs the matter); Wells to Scott, September 3, 1920, in Thomas Odell Collection; Philip F. Wells, "Reminiscences," pp. 198–200, Thomas Odell Collection,; *Chicago Tribune*, November 22, 1890; "Report of Rosebud Agency," August 26, 1890, in *Report of the Commissioner of Indian Affairs, 1890*, p. 58; "Report of Rosebud Agency," August 27, 1891, in *Report of the Commissioner of Indian Affairs, 1891*, 1:412–13; Jordan to Jonathan T. Chumasero, April 21, 1890, Charles Percival Jordan Papers, H74–42 SC61, vol. 1 (ledger), File Box 043, SDSHS (hereinafter cited as Jordan Papers).

16. After Morning Star's death in 1883, the principal Cheyenne leaders at Pine Ridge had been Little Chief, Standing Elk, and Wild Hog (who died in 1889). The flight of the Northern Cheyennes is explained at length in Monnett, *Tell Them We Are Going Home;* Hoig, *Perilous Pursuit;* and Svingen, *The Northern Cheyenne Indian Reservation*, pp. 19–23, 88–89. See also Leiker and Powers, *The Northern Cheyenne Exodus in History and Memory*. Cheyenne population figures for Pine Ridge as of June 1, 1890, are found in "Report of Pine Ridge Agency," August 25, 1890, in *Report of the Commissioner of Indian Affairs, 1891*, 1:50, while notice of Wild Hog's death appears in the *Chadron Democrat*, August 15, 1889.

17. "Report of Pine Ridge Agency," August 25, 1890, in *Report of the Commissioner of Indian Affairs, 1891*, 1:53; *Letter from the Secretary of the Interior, in Relation to the Affairs of the Indians*, pp. 7–10, 147, 159–85; Buecker, *Fort Robinson and the American West*, p. 172; Schubert, *Buffalo Soldiers, Braves, and the Brass*, p. 25; U.S. Congress, Senate, Committee on Indian Affairs, *Message from the President of the United States, Transmitting a Letter from the Secretary of the Interior Relative to the Use of Funds*; U.S. Congress, Senate, Committee on Indian Affairs, *Message from the President of the United States, Transmitting a Letter of the Secretary of the Interior and Documents*, pp. 15–18; *Chicago Tribune*, November 10, 1890; *Chadron Democrat*, May 1, 1890; "Sioux Women at Home," p. 485. For a study of Cheyennes who continued to live with the Oglalas at Pine Ridge, see Starita, *The Dull Knifes of Pine Ridge*.

18. "Report of Pine Ridge Agency," August 25, 1890, p. 54; *Chadron Democrat*, April 10, 1890 (quotations).

19. *Harper's Weekly*, March 29 and April 5, 1890 (first quotation); Bourke, *On the Border with Crook*, p. 486 (second quotation).

20. Red Cloud (through James A. Finley, Indian Trader, Pine Ridge) to Noble, May 30, 1890, NA, RG 75, File 1756-1890 (quotations); Forsyth, *Representing the Massacre*, pp. 18–19; Bryde, *Modern Indian Psychology*, p. 382. For more on causes, see Mooney, "Ghost-Dance Religion," pp. 825–42.

CHAPTER 5. SEEKING TO ENDURE

1. Goody, "Time," 16:41 (quotation), as cited in McDermott, "Wounded Knee," p. 250; and Thrupp, *Millennial Dreams in Action*, p. 12.

2. Adapted from "Prophet," in Hodge, *Handbook of American Indians North of Mexico*, 2:309–10. See also Overholt, *Channels of Prophecy;* and Thrupp, *Millennial Dreams in Action*, p. 32.

3. Weslager, *The Delaware Indians*, p. 242; Mooney, "Ghost-Dance Religion," pp. 662–69; Sugden, "Neolin"; Gibson, *The American Indian*, p. 473; Lanternari, *The Religions of the Oppressed*, pp. 115–24; Montour, "Handsome Lake"; Underhill, *Red Man's America*, p. 108; Hagan, *American Indians*, pp. 24–25, 53; Gibson, *The American Indian*, pp. 473–74. For Handsome Lake, see also Wallace, *The Death and Rebirth of the Seneca;* Edmunds, "Shawnee Prophet (Tenskwatawa)"; Edmunds, *The Shawnee Prophet;* Josephy, *The Indian Heritage of America*, pp. 316–19; Josephy, *The Patriot Chiefs*, pp. 131–73; Hagan, *American Indians*, pp. 56–59; Lanternari, *Religions of the Oppressed*, pp. 124–25; Mooney, "Ghost-Dance Religion," pp. 670–91; and Gibson, *The American Indian*, pp. 474–75.

4. Lanternari, *Religions of the Oppressed*, pp. 127–31; Hagan, *American Indians*, p. 116; Miller, "Smohalla"; Gibson, *The American Indian*, pp. 475–76; Farb, *Man's Rise to Civilization*, pp. 262–64; Mooney, "Ghost-Dance Religion," pp. 708–11. See also Ruby and Brown, *Dreamer-Prophets of the Columbia Plateau*.

5. Hämmäläinen, *The Comanche Empire*, pp. 337–39; Lanternari, *Religions of the Oppressed*, pp. 141–42; Nye, *Carbine and Lance*, pp. 189–92, 268–70; Hagan, *American Indians*, p. 130; *Chicago Tribune*, November 9, 1890; Calloway, "Sword Bearer and the 'Crow Outbreak' of 1887"; Jones, *A Battle at Little Bighorn*. Other examples of Indian prophets in history are Pope (Pueblo), Kenekuk (Kickapoo), Tavibo (Paiute), and Nakaidoklini (Apache). Josephy, *Indian Heritage of America*, p. 298; Josephy, *Patriot Chiefs*, pp. 63–94; Underhill, *Red Man's America*, p. 203; Lanternari, *Religions of the Oppressed*, p. 126; Farb, *Man's Rise to Civilization*, pp. 261–62; Mooney, "Ghost-Dance Religion," pp. 701–707.

6. Scott, *Some Memories of a Soldier*, pp. 147–49 (see Scott to Post Adjutant, Fort Sill, Oklahoma Territory, December 16, 1890; and "Essay for the Fort Sill Lyceum, March 1892. Subject: The 'Messiah Dance' in the Indian Territory," both in Hugh L. Scott Papers, Box 75, I, Reports File, Library of Congress); Berthrong, *The Cheyenne and Arapaho Ordeal*, pp. 138–39. The notion of the existence of an Indian messiah and an accompanying "Ghost Dance" appears to have had a certain universality at about this time when tribal cultures faced dire existence on assorted reservations throughout the West. See Fletcher, "The Indian Messiah," p. 60. An in-depth account of the adaptive nature of Ghost Dances among Indian people (notably in the Great Basin but with decided influences beyond) is found in Smoak, *Ghost Dances and Identity*. On Porcupine's experience, see Mooney, "Ghost-Dance Religion," pp. 793–96 (quotations); *New York Times*, November 11, 1890; *Deseret News*, July 12, 1890; *Deseret Weekly*, December 27, 1890; *Omaha Bee*, November 18, 1890; and Marquis and Limbaugh, *The Cheyennes of Montana*, pp. 128–29. The account of an Arapaho named Sitting Bull appears in *Deseret News*, November 15, 1890, while the experiences of Arapahos and Shoshonis, among other tribes, are explicated in Mooney, "Ghost-Dance Religion"; but see also Trenholm, *The Arapahoes, Our People*, pp. 283–88; Fowler, *Arapahoe Politics*, p. 102; and Trenholm and Carley, *The Shoshonis*, pp. 296–98. In 1890 the Arapaho Sitting

Bull journeyed to the Darlington Agency in the Indian Territory to preach about the messiah. Wheeler, *The Frontier Trail*, p. 318; Scott, *Some Memories of a Soldier*, p. 152.

7. Mooney, "Ghost-Dance Religion," pp. 819–20; Hyde, *Sioux Chronicle*, p. 239. Some sense of the way in which word of a messiah spread through the plains region is conveyed in an article about Captain Richard H. Pratt's views, which mentions dissemination of the news as learned from some of his Carlisle students, including a copy of a letter written from a Cheyenne at Pine Ridge to a relative at the Darlington Agency in the Indian Territory. *New York Times*, November 24, 1890.

8. See *Chicago Tribune*, November 9, 1890, including an interview with Smoholla by Captain Eli L. Huggins, Second Cavalry. Valentine T. McGillycuddy stated that the Oglala chief Little Wound ascribed first knowledge of the new messiah among his own people to the Northern Cheyennes. *New York Times*, November 14, 1897.

9. Mooney, "Ghost-Dance Religion," p. 771.

10. Ibid., pp. 764–74 (including quotations); Andersson, *The Lakota Ghost Dance of 1890*, pp. 24–29. Initial information about Wovoka was derived from Mooney's visit with him early in January 1892 and from a meeting between Wovoka and army scout Arthur Chapman, arranged at the direction of the War Department, in December 1890. Mooney, "Ghost-Dance Religion," p. 766; Smoak, *Ghost Dances and Identity*, pp. 169–71. The most comprehensive and authoritative treatment of Wovoka appears in Hittman, *Wovoka and the Ghost Dance*. Although this significant volume remains unindexed, some of the information about Wovoka's father is from pp. 29–34. The long-standard biography is Bailey, *Wovoka*, but this should now be used in conjunction with Hittman's work, at the least. Other elements that contributed to Wovoka's thinking are considered in McCann, "The Ghost Dance"; but see also Overholt, "The Ghost Dance of 1890." For several interpretations of Wovoka's message, see Ostler, *Plains Sioux and U.S. Colonialism*, pp. 243–50. See also the discussion of attributes of Mormonism as being among the origins of the Ghost Dance in Smoak, "The Mormons and the Ghost Dance of 1890," pp. 269–94.

11. These changes included the introduction of horses into their society, the thriving of the Sun Dance in their ritual lifeways, domination by whites who aggregated in their midst (including various government prohibitions), loss of the buffalo, and their introduction/transition to reservation existence. DeMallie, "The Lakota Ghost Dance: An Ethnohistorical Account," pp. 390, 400–401. An early narrative of the Ghost Dance as it impacted the Sioux is found in Moorehead, "The Indian Messiah and the Ghost Dance."

12. "Selected Excerpts from the Diary of Reverend Aemilius Perrig, kept while at the St. Francis Mission on Pine Ridge, from 1 September 1889 to 13 March 1891" (draft typescript edited and annotated by John M. Carroll), Marquette University, entry for September 9, 1889 (hereinafter cited as Perrig Diary); Mooney, "Ghost-Dance Religion," p. 820. These attendees are taken from Hyde, *Sioux Chronicle*, p. 240, and are somewhat at variance with those given in Mooney, particularly in regard to agency origin. Possible misunderstanding may exist as to how many visits to the Paiutes were made by the Lakotas. Mooney, "Ghost-Dance Religion," pp. 819–20, described two (1889 and 1890) but emphasized one that departed in 1889 and returned in 1890, suggesting that the two might in fact be the same; Hyde, in *Sioux Chronicle*, p. 240, mentioned two visits, in 1889 and 1890, one on the heels of the other and in the winter, which seems improbable. Olson, *Red Cloud and the Sioux Problem*, p. 322, settled on one visit, which is probably correct. See also Andersson, *Lakota Ghost Dance of 1890*,

pp. 31–33 (which supports this view), as well as DeMallie, *The Sixth Grandfather*, pp. 256–58; and Neihardt, *Black Elk Speaks*, pp. 186–89, which mention two visits. Elaine Goodale wrote in her diary as early as July 23, 1889, that while camping in the Nebraska sandhills her party encountered a Pine Ridge man named Chasing Crane en route home from the Rosebud Agency. He reported that Christ had recently appeared to the Crows—the messiah had returned. Eastman, "Ghost Dance War," p. 28.

13. Mooney, "Ghost-Dance Religion," p. 820 (quotation); Andersson, *Lakota Ghost Dance of 1890*, pp. 34–40. The return of the buffalo was consistent with Lakota traditional beliefs regarding explanations for abundance or scarcity of the beasts and anticipation of the same. See DeMallie, "Lakota Ghost Dance," p. 391.

14. This is the "free rendering" of the messiah letter given to the Indians by Wovoka. See also the slightly variant versions given to the Arapahos and Cheyennes in Mooney, "Ghost-Dance Religion," pp. 780–81.

15. Eastman, "Ghost Dance War," p. 31 (quotation); Eastman, *Sister to the Sioux*, pp. 138–40. For Goodale Eastman, see Sargent, *The Life of Elaine Goodale Eastman*.

16. Sword, "The Story of the Ghost Dance," pp. 28–29 (including first quotation); Cooper, "Short Bull's Story of the Battle of Wounded Knee," pp. 205–12 (including second quotation). For Good Thunder's version as told to Goodale, see Eastman, *Sister to the Sioux*, pp. 143–44. For variants to these accounts, see also the partly hearsay recollection of the Oglala leader Black Elk, in DeMallie, *Sixth Grandfather*, pp. 256–57; and Neihardt, *Black Elk Speaks*, pp. 185–87. Additional Short Bull narratives referencing aspects of the visit to Wovoka and/or the dance among the Lakotas appear in Maddra, *Hostiles?*, pp. 192–218. Yet another account is given in the *Chicago Herald*, January 30, 1891. For background on George Sword, see Garrett-Davis, "Dakota Images: George Sword."

17. Definition of *wanagi wacipi* by Leonard Little Finger, National Register of Historic Places Registration Form for Wounded Knee National Historic Landmark, Wounded Knee, S.Dak., December 6, 1990, section 8, p. 31; Walker, *Lakota Belief and Ritual*, pp. 70–71; DeMallie, "Lakota Ghost Dance," p. 385; Eastman, "Ghost Dance War," p. 29 (quotation).

18. "Report of Pine Ridge Agency," August 28, 1890, in *Report of the Commissioner of Indian Affairs, 1890*, p. 49; Eastman, "Ghost Dance War," p. 31; Robinson, *History of the Dakota or Sioux Indians*, p. 462; Hyde, *Sioux Chronicle*, pp. 241–42; Olson, *Red Cloud and the Sioux Problem*, pp. 324–25; Perrig Diary, entry for August 24, 1890; Kelley, "The Indian Troubles and the Battle of Wounded Knee," p. 33. Details of Gallagher's confrontation with the dancers appear in Utley, *Last Days of the Sioux Nation*, pp. 92–93.

19. As the Ghost Dancing took hold on the Sioux reservations, one critic portrayed it as "the delusion which has taken possession of the minds of the wilder portion among the Indians"; quoted in Ellis, *Indian Wars of the United States*, p. 403. Vestal, *Warpath*, p. 233. Josephine Waggoner, a mixed-blood Hunkpapa who was married to a Fort Yates soldier, remembered that "throughout this period the Indians who were church members remained true to their respective beliefs, their ministers and priests advising against accepting the new creed. Those who belonged to no church were the ones who took up with the new religion"; quoted in Mason, "Chief Sitting Bull's Latter Days" (unpublished manuscript in folder H74.115, James McLaughlin Letter, 1920, Box 3473A, SDSHS).

20. Andersson, *Lakota Ghost Dance of 1890*, p. 21.

21. Kingsley Bray, e-mail to the author respecting Kicking Bird's background, December 10, 2012; Bray, "Pine Ridge Letters Shed New Light on the Battle of the Little Bighorn," pp. 39–42; Andersson, *Lakota Ghost Dance of 1890*, pp. 40–41, 50, 273; "Dakota Images: Short Bull." Kicking Bear's pictograph of the Battle of the Little Bighorn appears in Godfrey, *The Field Diary of Lt. Edward Settle Godfrey*, following p. 58.

22. "Report of Cheyenne River Agency," August 17, 1891, in *Report of the Commissioner of Indian Affairs, 1891*, 1:390; Hyde, *Sioux Chronicle*, pp. 242–43; Hall, *To Have This Land*, p. 31; Hollow, "The Sioux Ghost Dance of 1890," p. 41.

23. "Folk-Lore Scrap-Book," p. 160; Perrig Diary, entries for September 14, September 26, October 6, and October 19, 1890 (quotations).

24. DeMallie, *Sixth Grandfather*, p. 258; Neihardt, *Black Elk Speaks*, pp. 189–90; Andersson, *Lakota Ghost Dance of 1890*, pp. 41–47; Hyde, *Sioux Chronicle*, pp. 242–43; Robinson, *History of the Dakota or Sioux Indians*, p. 467; Schell, *History of South Dakota*, p. 321. Mrs. James A. Finley, wife of the trader at Pine Ridge Agency, indicated that the first dances apparently took place on that reservation in August. *Philadelphia Inquirer*, November 22, 1890.

25. *Chicago Tribune*, November 22, 1890 (quotation). This address, abbreviated here, was taken down by Captain Cyrus A. Earnest, Eighth Infantry, at Rosebud. See slight variants in *Philadelphia Inquirer*, November 22, 1890; *Omaha World-Herald*, November 22, 1890; "Report of Major General Miles," September 14, 1891, in *Report of the Secretary of War, 1891*, pp. 142–43; and Mooney, "Ghost-Dance Religion," pp. 788–89. In an autobiographical essay composed soon after the crisis ended, Short Bull referenced his speech thus: "One day while a dance was in progress I stood up in the centre and told all my people what the Messiah had done and said—the people kept the dancing up with a good will." Autobiographical essay entitled "As Narrated by 'Short Bull,'" trans. George Crager, 1891, p. 7 (manuscript #71.0019, Buffalo Bill Museum and Grave Archives at Lookout Mountain). This essay has been published in Maddra, *Hostiles?*, pp. 192–205. See also McDermott, "Wounded Knee," p. 253. For discussion on whether Short Bull's sermon was fabricated as an incentive for military intervention, see Ostler, *Plains Sioux and U.S. Colonialism*, pp. 295–97.

26. McLaughlin to Morgan, October 17, 1890, in *Report of the Commissioner of Indian Affairs, 1891*, 1:329; "Report of John M. Carignan" (undated, ca. 1891), in Vestal, *New Sources of Indian History*, pp. 1–2; McLaughlin, *My Friend the Indian*, pp. 185–91; Robinson, *History of the Dakota or Sioux Indians*, p. 467; Utley, *Last Days of the Sioux Nation*, pp. 97–98; Utley, *Lance and the Shield*, pp. 282–84; Pfaller, *James McLaughlin*, pp. 127, 131–34; Hagan, *Indian Police and Judges*, p. 99; Ostler, *Plains Sioux and U.S. Colonialism*, pp. 273–78; McLaughlin to Morgan, October 17, 1890, in *Report of the Commissioner of Indian Affairs, 1891*, 1:328–29 (quotations).

27. DeMallie, *Sixth Grandfather*, p. 258; Neihardt, *Black Elk Speaks*, p. 190; Sword, "Story of the Ghost Dance," pp. 30–31 (quotations).

28. Sword, "The Story of the Ghost Dance," pp. 30–31 (quotation); Grinnell, "Account of the Northern Cheyennes concerning the Messiah Superstition," p. 67; Steltenkamp, *Nicholas Black Elk*, pp. 60–62. See also the interview with Paul Beckwith, Smithsonian Institution, in *Washington Evening Star*, November 29, 1890.

29. DeMallie, *Sixth Grandfather*, pp. 258–65 (quotations); also Neihardt, *Black Elk Speaks*, pp. 194–96; and Steltenkamp, *Nicholas Black Elk*, pp. 60–64. Black Elk's biography appears in Steltenkamp, *Black Elk*.

30. Quoted in DeLoria, *Speaking of Indians*, pp. 81–83.

31. Vestal, *New Sources of Indian History*, pp. 43–44.

32. Unidentified observer's account in Daniel Dorchester, "Report of the Superintendent of Indian Schools," September 30, 1891, in *Report of the Commissioner of Indian Affairs, 1891,* 1:529–31.

33. First Lieutenant Marion P. Maus, in *Harper's Weekly*, December 6, 1890 (first quotation); Colby, "Wanagi Olowan Kin (The Ghost Songs of the Dakotas)," pp. 140 (second quotation)–41.

34. *The Word Carrier* 19 (November 1890), p. 30 (Collins quotations), as cited and quoted in DeMallie, "Lakota Ghost Dance," pp. 397–98 (quotation), 399. See also Andersson, *Lakota Ghost Dance of 1890,* pp. 48–65. Other white descriptions of the Ghost Dance include the reminiscence of Elaine Goodale in Eastman, *Sister to the Sioux*, pp. 148–50; Mrs. Z. A. Parker, *New York Evening Post*, April 18, 1891 (reprinted in *Journal of American Folk-Lore* 4 [April–June 1891]: 160–62); and Mrs. James A. Finley, wife of the trader at Pine Ridge, *Philadelphia Inquirer*, November 22, 1890 (with slightly different versions in Johnson, *Life of Sitting Bull and History of the Indian War of 1890–91*, pp. 258–60; and the *Graphic* [London], December 13, 1890); a Holy Rosary sister in Kreis, *Lakotas, Black Robes, and Holy Women*, pp. 89–90; Father Johann Jutz in ibid., pp. 156–60; and Elaine Goodale in Eastman, "Ghost Dance War," p. 32. Contemporary data also appear in "Ghost-Dances in the West," *Illustrated American*, January 17, 1891, pp. 327–33; and Moorehead, *The American Indian in the United States*, pp. 105–17. South Dakota cowman James "Scotty" Philip also observed a Ghost Dance: Lee, *Scotty Philip*, p. 173. For more details on the Lakota Ghost Dance and further assessment of its elements, see Utley, *Last Days of the Sioux Nation*, pp. 85–91; and Ostler, *Plains Sioux and U.S. Colonialism*, pp. 256–63.

35. Bartlett to Warren K. Moorehead, November 4, 1890, George Bartlett Letters, Warren K. Moorehead Papers (MS 106), Box 4, Ohio Historical Society (hereinafter cited as Moorehead Papers).

36. *Indian Helper*, December 5, 1890.

37. DeMallie, *Sixth Grandfather*, p. 265; Andersson, *Lakota Ghost Dance of 1890,* pp. 67–73; Mooney, "Ghost-Dance Religion," pp. 789–90; Neihardt, *Black Elk Speaks*, pp. 196–97; Steltenkamp, *Nicholas Black Elk*, p. 62; DeLoria, *Speaking of Indians*, p. 81; *Hot Springs Daily Star*, January 15, 1891; Paul, "Wounded Knee and the 'Collector of Curios,'" pp. 211, 212; *Friends of the W. H. Over Museum Newsletter* (undated, ca. 1980s); Lurie, *North American Indian Lives*, p. 57; Cooper, "Short Bull's Story," p. 211; Bryde, *Modern Indian Psychology*, p. 384; Hollow, "Sioux Ghost Dance of 1890," pp. 44–47. Elaine Goodale, who was present in the area, wrote that "after the troops appeared, it was asserted that the sacred garments were bullet-proof." Eastman, "Ghost Dance War," p. 33. This seems borne out in the lengthy descriptions of the shirts and dresses at a dance on about June 20, 1890, along White Clay Creek at Pine Ridge, which did not mention the bullet-stopping capability of the garments. Unidentified teacher's account in Daniel Dorchester, "Report of the Superintendent of Indian Schools," September 30, 1891, in *Report of the Commissioner of Indian Affairs, 1891,* 1:529–31. But Robert Higheagle recalled discussing the "bullet-proof" shirts at Standing Rock in the summer of 1890. Vestal, *New Sources of Indian History*, pp. 42–43. See also Kreis, *Lakotas, Black Robes, and Holy Women*, p. 89; and the discussion in Jensen, Paul, and Carter, *Eyewitness at Wounded Knee*, pp. 7–12. At least one account stated that the shirts were saturated in a special fluid to make them so resistant. In late November, at a dance held on Wounded Knee Creek on the Pine Ridge Reservation, a shirt-wearing dancer

reportedly urged his colleagues to test the shirts and to fire on him; when they did, the man fell mortally wounded. *Philadelphia Inquirer*, December 1, 1890. A pictographic portrayal of this incident appears in Ritzenthaler and Hunt, *Sioux Indian Drawings*, plate 27, "Testing the Ghost Shirt, Bullet Proof." See illustrations of typical shirts by a careful illustrator in "Sioux Ghost Shirts," in Hunt, *Indiancraft*, pp. 28–29. See also the photograph in Hamilton and Hamilton, *The Sioux of the Rosebud*, pp. 280–81, plate 208. For possible precepts on ghost shirt use among the Mormons, Shoshonis, Bannocks, and Arapahos, see discussions in Mooney, "Ghost-Dance Religion," pp. 790–91; and Smoak, *Ghost Dances and Identity*, p. 167; as well as the stimulating points in Ostler, *Plains Sioux and U.S. Colonialism*, pp. 279–88.

Chapter 6. Perception

1. *Chadron Democrat*, June 16 and July 7, 1887; July 10, 1890; November 29, 1888; *Chadron Advocate*, March 28 and July 11, 1890. See also Allen, *From Fort Laramie to Wounded Knee*, pp. 142–45; Scott, *Some Memories of a Paleontologist*, pp. 177–81.

2. Walter M. Camp Manuscripts, Manuscripts Department, Lilly Library, Indiana University, Box 4, File 3, Envelope 4, pp. 225–33 (hereinafter cited as Camp Manuscripts, Lilly Library).

3. "Report of Pine Ridge Agency," August 28, 1890, in *Report of the Commissioner of Indian Affairs, 1890*, pp. 49, 50, 51–53; "Map of the Country embraced in the recent Campaign against the Hostile Sioux Indians of Dakota," in *Report of the Secretary of War, 1891*, between 1:154 and 155; Allen, *From Fort Laramie to Wounded Knee*, pp. 49–71; history of Pine Ridge Reservation contained in National Archives Microfilm Publications pamphlet describing Microfilm 1229, "Miscellaneous Letters Sent by the Agents or Superintendents at the Pine Ridge Indian Agency, 1876–1914" (Washington, D.C.: National Archives and Records Service, 1983), pp. 3–4; Sprague, *Images of America: Pine Ridge Reservation*, pp. 7–8; Gagnon and White Eyes, *Pine Ridge Reservation*, p. 16; Ross, *A Brief History of Pine Ridge Reservation*, pp. 1, 2.

4. "Pine Ridge Agency," map in *Chicago Inter-Ocean*, January 10, 1891; Bailey, "Map of Pine Ridge Agency." Order of Indian Wars (OIW) Collection, U.S. Army Military History Institute, File No. X-8, William C. Brown materials; "Report of Pine Ridge Agency," August 28, 1890, p. 153; Zens, "The Educational Work of the Catholics among the Indians of South Dakota," p. 336. For further description of the agency and reserve, see *Indians Taxed and Indians Not Taxed*, p. 589; *Chadron Democrat*, October 11, 1888; *Chadron Democrat*, March 13, 1890; *Chicago Inter-Ocean*, November 29, 1890 (quotation). For an accounting of many of the residents of Pine Ridge Agency at the time, see especially Watson, "Pine Ridge, 1890–1891," pp. 1–6.

5. Sialm, "History, Holy Rosary Mission, Pine Ridge, S.D." (unpublished manuscript), Holy Rosary Mission, p. 82; Larson, *Red Cloud*, pp. 267–68, 270, 272–75; Hyde, *Sioux Chronicle*, pp. 239–40, 250–51; Olson, *Red Cloud and the Sioux Problem*, pp. 321–23; Camp Manuscripts, Lilly Library, Box 4, File 3, Envelope 4, pp. 225–33 (citing undated interview with Valentine T. McGillycuddy); "Report of Pine Ridge Agency," August 28, 1890, p. 53.

6. *Washington Evening Star*, November 29, 1890.

7. National Archives and Records Service Microfilm Publications pamphlet describing Microfilm 1229, pp. 4–5, and appendix B, "Agents Administering the Red Cloud/

Pine Ridge Agency and Their Predecessors," p. 9; Camp Manuscripts, Lilly Library, Box 4, File 3, Envelope 4, pp. 225–33; *National Tribune*, June 22, 1893; Phillips, "The Indian Ring in Dakota Territory," p. 366; Fritz, *Movement for Indian Assimilation*, p. 218; Hagan, *Indian Police and Judges*, pp. 90–91. For McGillycuddy's biography, see McGillycuddy, *McGillycuddy, Agent;* and Moulton, *Valentine T. McGillycuddy.* The Red Cloud–McGillycuddy running feud is detailed in Hyde, *Sioux Chronicle*, pp. 67–106; Larson, *Red Cloud*, pp. 217–51; and Olson, *Red Cloud and the Sioux Problem*, 265–307; *Chadron Democrat*, October 23, 1890. Senator Richard F. Pettigrew (R-SD) went after Gallagher and other Democratic agents after his election in 1889. Hendrickson, "The Public Career of Richard F. Pettigrew of South Dakota," p. 202.

8. Paper on Royer's background by Bob Lee, September 1972 (copy in the Vertical Files, SDSHS Library); "Public Career of Richard F. Pettigrew," p. 202. For an example of McGillycuddy's post–Pine Ridge meddling, see a letter in the *Black Hills Weekly Journal*, December 5, 1890. The successive appointment of Indian agents at Pine Ridge via patronage was addressed succinctly by the *St. Paul Pioneer Press:* "Here is an agency . . . where an agent who knows his duty and does it has been established for many years, and where the Indians have come to like him and to trust him. . . . Now comes a change of administration. For no reason in the world except to give a place to some political worker, this experienced man is removed and a green hand put in his place. Every time that this happens, the Government deliberately invites a disturbance that may cost many lives and is sure to cost many dollars." Quoted in the *Army and Navy Journal*, December 20, 1890. See also the commentary in *Harper's Weekly*, December 13, 1890.

9. *Chadron Democrat*, September 4 and 25, 1890; telegram, Brooke to Adjutant General (AG), June 18, 1890, NA, RG 75, Letters Received, cited in Olson, *Red Cloud and the Sioux Problem*, p. 324, n. 24; Kreis, *Lakotas, Black Robes, and Holy Women*, pp. 154, 158, 159 (Jutz quotations); Sisters of St. Francis Chronicles (typescript), pp. 3–4, Marquette University Archives. See also Jutz, "Historic Data on the Causes of the Dissatisfaction among the Sioux Indians in 1890"; *Chadron Democrat*, November 27, 1890 (first press quotation); Perrig Diary, entry for September 26, 1890 (quotation); *Omaha World-Herald*, November 22, 1890; *Aspen Weekly Times*, November 22, 1890; *Omaha Bee*, November 22, 1890 (last quotation), November 26, 1890.

10. Richardson, "Some Observations upon the Sioux Campaign," pp. 520.

11. *Omaha World-Herald*, December 5, 1890 (first Hollow Horn Bear quotation); Lieutenant Colonel John S. Poland to Assistant Adjutant General (AAG), Department of the Platte, November 29, 1890, in James McLaughlin Papers, Roll 34 (second Hollow Horn Bear quotation), SDSHS (hereinafter cited as McLaughlin Papers). For ration issue concerns at Rosebud, see Special Indian Agent E. B. Reynolds to Commissioner of Indian Affairs, November 28, 1890, McLaughlin Papers, Roll 3 (quotations). For a contemporary description of the Rosebud Agency and reservation, see *Indians Taxed and Indians Not Taxed*, pp. 588–89. A month later Hollow Horn Bear repeated his plea when he and 101 Brulés petitioned the president for food. Boyd, *Recent Indian Wars*, p. 233; U.S. Congress, Senate, *Letter from the Secretary of the Interior, Transmitting, in Response to a Senate Resolution of 2d Instant, a Communication*, December 11, 1890, p. 13, citing Reynolds to the Commissioner of Indian Affairs, November 2, 1890 (hereinafter cited as *Letter from the Secretary of the Interior*, December 11, 1890).

12. Richardson, "Some Observations upon the Sioux Campaign," p. 523; "Report of Rosebud Agency, August 26, 1890," in *Report of the Commissioner of Indian Affairs, 1890*, pp. 57, 60, 62; "Allotments of land in severalty, on the Rosebud Reservation,

made under the treaty of 1868, and now occupied by the allottees," McLaughlin Papers, Roll 34; "Report of Rosebud Agency, August 27, 1891," in *Report of the Commissioner of Indian Affairs, 1891,* 1:410, 411 (quotation), 412.

13. An Indian remembrance of this rumored arrival of soldiers at Rosebud Agency is found in Standing Bear, *My People the Sioux,* pp. 221–22. Special Agent Reynolds learned that Short Bull's timetable for the millennium had lately been advanced "to the new moon after the next one, or about December 11." Reynolds to the Commissioner of Indian Affairs, November 2, 1890, in *Letter from the Secretary of the Interior,* December 11, 1890, p. 13; Hyde, *Sioux Chronicle,* pp. 261–62. Wright's administration was fraught with ongoing corruption. For specific allegations respecting the cheating of his charges and immoral behavior by his employees toward Indian women, see E. A. Bridger, to Major General Nelson A. Miles, December 20, 1890. NA, RG 393, Entry 2546, Box 126. For historical pictorial coverage of Rosebud Reservation, see Sprague, *Images of America: Rosebud Sioux.*

14. "Report of Cheyenne River Agency," August 25, 1890, in *Report of the Commissioner of Indian Affairs, 1890,* pp. 42–46; "Report of Cheyenne River Agency, August 17, 1891," in *Report of the Commissioner of Indian Affairs, 1891,* 1:387–91; Hoxie, "From Prison to Homeland," pp. 3–6; Hyde, *Sioux Chronicle,* p. 258; Palmer to Commissioner of Indian Affairs Thomas J. Morgan, November 10, 1890, in *Letter from the Secretary of the Interior,* December 11, 1890, pp. 15 (quotation), 16; Anderson, "History of the Cheyenne River Indian Agency," pp. 501–502; Ghost Horse, "A True Story of What Happened at Wounded Knee in December 1890," undated typescript, copy in Author's Collection; *Omaha Bee,* November 13, 1890; *Chicago Tribune,* November 16, 1890; *Omaha World-Herald,* November 21, 1890; *Chicago Inter-Ocean,* November 27, 1890; Shunk (Mato Ska), "Reminiscing about the Dakota," p. 117; Palmer to Commissioner of Indian Affairs Morgan, November 28, 1890, and December 1, 1890. NA, RG 94, PRD Document File 1890, 5412 Sioux Troubles, Box 49. For a detailed contemporary description of the Cheyenne River Reservation, see *Indians Taxed and Indians Not Taxed,* pp. 584–85. A pictorial history of the Cheyenne River Reservation and its occupants is found in Sprague, *Images of America: Cheyenne River Sioux, South Dakota.*

15. Utley, *The Lance and the Shield,* pp. 285–87 (see also Vestal, *Sitting Bull,* p. 271–72; and Anderson, *Sitting Bull and the Paradox of Lakota Nationhood,* pp. 156–57, both of which indicate that Sitting Bull participated); *Army and Navy Register,* November 29, 1890 (first quotation); *Omaha World-Herald,* November 25, 1890 (second quotation).

16. *Harper's Weekly,* December 20, 1890; Camp Interview with Joseph R. DeLoria re: Ghost Dance and Sitting Bull Death, in Camp Manuscripts, Lilly Library, Box 5, Folder 12; *Deseret News* (Salt Lake City), November 8, 1890 (quotation). See also McLaughlin to Morgan, October 17, 1890, in *Report of the Commissioner of Indian Affairs, 1891,* 1:329. For period background on Standing Rock and its people, see *Indians Taxed and Indians Not Taxed,* pp. 519–26; Hagan, *Indian Police and Judges,* p. 97; Sprague, *Images of America: Standing Rock Sioux,* pp. 7–9.

17. McLaughlin, *My Friend the Indian;* also Pfaller, *James McLaughlin;* McLaughlin to Morgan, October 17, 1890, in *Report of the Commissioner of Indian Affairs, 1891,* 1:329 (quotation). See also Jensen, Paul, and Carter, *Eyewitness at Wounded Knee,* pp. 7–8.

18. Government communications took precedence over telegraphic transmission of outgoing newspaper reports. Among reporters present during the Pine Ridge crisis in

1890–91 were Alfred H. Burkholder, Charles W. Allen, Edgar F. Medary, local South Dakota and Nebraska reporters and stringers for the *New York Herald;* William E. Kelley for the *State Journal* of Lincoln, Nebraska; Thomas H. Tibbles, his Omaha wife Bright Eyes (Susette LaFlesche), and Carl Smith for the *Omaha World-Herald* and *Chicago Express;* Charles G. Seymour for the *Chicago Herald;* Irving Hawkins and Edward B. Clark for the *Chicago Tribune;* Dent H. Robert for the *St. Louis Post-Dispatch;* John A. McDonough for the *New York World;* Will Cressey and Charles H. Coppenharve for the *Omaha Bee;* the famous artist and illustrator Frederick Remington for *Harper's Weekly;* Guy Butler for the *Duluth Tribune;* R. J. Boylan for the *St. Paul Pioneer-Press;* George H. Harries for the *Washington [D.C.] Evening Star;* Warren K. Moorehead for the *Illustrated American;* Gilbert F. Bailey for *Chicago Inter-Ocean;* John Burns of Deadwood, stringing for the *Chicago Times;* and later Mrs. Teresa Howard Dean of the *Chicago Herald,* who was the first female war reporter; as well as others. Knight, *Following the Indian Wars,* pp. 313–14; Watson, "The Last Indian War"; Watson, "A Sketch of George H. Harries, Reporter of Wounded Knee," p. 73; *Middle Border Bulletin* 4 (Summer 1944): pp. 1–2; Tibbles, *Buckskin and Blanket Days,* pp. 300–301; *Chadron Democrat,* December 4, 1890 (first quotation); *Chicago Tribune,* December 1, 1890 (second quotation).

19. *Washington Evening Star,* November 20, 1890; *Omaha Bee,* November 20, 1890 (first three quotations); *Hot Springs Daily Star,* November 24 and 28, 1890; December 13, 1890 (fourth quotation); and December 24, 1890 (other quotations). Charles Allen recalled an arrangement with trader James Asay "for the privilege of using his long store counter for desk space, after business was closed for the night." Allen, *From Fort Laramie to Wounded Knee,* p. 167; see also ibid., pp. 178–81. For a focused account of media involvement, see Kolbenschlag, *A Whirlwind Passes.*

20. DeMallie, "Lakota Ghost Dance," p. 392 (quotation); Philip Wells to Major General Hugh L. Scott, September 3, 1920, Thomas Odell Collection, Philip Wells Materials; Tibbles, *Buckskin and Blanket Days,* p. 301.

21. Sarah Jane Osborne, "Memoirs of [a] Pennington Co. Resident," SDSHS, H92–85, Box 5510B, Travel in America; "Early Reminiscences of Early Ft. Pierre, 1883–1890, 1936," R. E. Curran Letters, SDSHS, H90–82, Box 3857B; F. A. Foster to father, December 10, 1890, typescript copy in the files of Fort Robinson Museum, Fort Robinson State Park (quotation).

22. Tallent, *The Black Hills;* Van Nuys, *The Family Band from the Missouri to the Black Hills; Omaha World-Herald,* November 23, 1890; *Chicago Inter-Ocean,* November 29, 1890; *Chicago Tribune,* November 29, 1890; Hall, *To Have This Land,* pp. 40 (citing *Black Hills Daily Times,* November 20, 1890), 48; *Black Hills Journal,* November 22, 1890; Schusky, *Forgotten Sioux,* p. 132; Tate, *The Frontier Army in the Settlement of the West,* pp. 114, 272. Chadron, Nebraska, residents called on the editors of two Omaha papers, the *Bee* and the *World-Herald,* to desist from publishing lies and falsehoods about the situations near Rosebud and Pine Ridge. The local paper called this "a move in the right direction" that will "probably not do any good." *Chadron Democrat,* November 27, 1890. Full coverage of the Sioux scare in South Dakota appears in Hall, *To Have This Land,* pp. 58–82; but see also Tarbell, "History of the South Dakota National Guard," pp. 424–32; and Cropp, *The Coyotes,* pp. 86–88.

23. *Black Hills Journal,* November 20, 1890; *Black Hills Weekly Times,* November 22, 1890; *Omaha Bee,* November 22 and 27, 1890; *Omaha World-Herald,* November 23, 25, and 28, 1890; *Sioux County Herald,* November 22, 1890 (quotation); *Gordon*

Journal, May 20, 1953; "Soddies to Satellites." See sketch of the Montrose Fort by David Anderson in the Manuscripts Department, Nebraska State Historical Society Archives; and Anderson, "'Fort' Montrose, Sioux County." This crude defense coincidentally stood on a site formerly fought over by Northern Cheyennes and U.S. troops in 1876, known as the Warbonnet Creek skirmish site. Similar "forts" were raised near Valentine, at Hay Springs, and in Beaver Valley near the former Spotted Tail Agency. Anderson, "'Fort' Montrose, Sioux County," p. 115n.

24. R. M. Tuttle to President Harrison, November 18, 1890, in *Letter from the Secretary of the Interior*, December 11, 1890, pp. 22–24; *Chicago Tribune*, November 18 and December 1, 1890; *Army and Navy Journal*, November 22, 1890; *Chicago Inter-Ocean*, December 1, 1890; telegram, November 18, 1890, Frank Zahn Collection, SDSHS (first quotation); *Army and Navy Register*, November 29, 1890 (second quotation); *Deseret News*, December 6, 1890; Watson, "Last Indian War," p. 208, n. 10. A sampling of the talk: "A friendly Indian just in [to Bismarck] from the Sioux reservation says that the forward movement has practically begun, it being the intention of the reds to first attack Fort Lincoln . . . and after slaughtering the troops there to descend upon the town of Mandan." *Ogdensburg (New York) Advance*, November 20, 1890. A North Dakota settler named Buckley reportedly stated that "every Indian on the reservation will shortly go on the warpath, and that they have got possession of Custer's rifles, which the United States army never found." *Chadron Advocate*, November 23, 1890. And a dispatch from Winnipeg cited Sioux Indians near Regina, North-West Territory, who "say they will shortly move across the American boundary at the request of their brethren there." *Chicago Inter-Ocean*, December 1, 1890. Thorough coverage of the North Dakota reaction is found in Pfaller, "Indian Scare of 1890."

25. Royer to Morgan, October 12, 1890, in *Letter from the Secretary of the Interior*, December 11, 1890, p. 5 (first quotation); *Report of the Commissioner of Indian Affairs, 1891*, 1:126, 127 (second and third quotations), 128; *Report of the Secretary of War, 1891*, p. 144. Former Pine Ridge agent Valentine T. McGillycuddy described Royer as "a gentleman totally ignorant of Indians and their peculiarities; a gentleman with not a qualification in his make-up calculated to fit him for the position of agent of one of the largest and most difficult agencies in the service to manage." McGillycuddy to Brigadier General Leonard W. Colby, Nebraska National Guard, January 15, 1891, in Colby, "The Sioux Indian War of 1890–'91," p. 179. On the matter of regional response to the Ghost Dance, see also Ostler, "Conquest and the State," pp. 220–24.

26. Tilford to Royer, October 17, 1890, cited in Schubert, *Buffalo Soldiers, Braves, and the Brass*, pp. 27 (first quotation), 194 n. 28; Royer to Morgan, November 8, 1890, in *Letter from the Secretary of the Interior*, December 11, 1890, p. 14 (second quotation); *Chadron Democrat*, November 27, 1890 (third quotation); Mooney, "Ghost-Dance Religion," p. 848; Hyde, *Sioux Chronicle*, pp. 261–62. See Dr. Charles A. Eastman's remembrance of a conversation with Royer in which the agent espoused his desire for an army presence. Eastman, *From the Deep Woods to Civilization*, p. 202. Later charges by his issue clerk portrayed Royer and chief clerk Bishop J. Gleason as debt-plagued "broken down politicians" who despite their recent arrival on the scene were well on their way to cheating the Indians of rations and viewed the imminence of troops as "a mammoth consumer—[hence] a safe destroyer [of evidence]." Jensen, *Voices of the American West*, 2: *Settler and Soldier Interviews*, 68–69 (hereinafter cited without volume title).

27. Tibbles, *Buckskin and Blanket Days*, p. 302; Cook, *Fifty Years on the Old Frontier*, p. 232; *Chadron Democrat*, November 27, 1890 (Hare quotation); Royer to Acting

Commissioner Belt, October 30, 1890, in *Letter from the Secretary of the Interior*, December 11, 1890, p. 10 (first Royer quotation); Royer to Morgan, November 8, 1890, in ibid., pp. 14–15 (second and third Royer quotation); *Omaha Bee*, November 16, 1890; *St. Paul Pioneer Press*, November 20, 1890; *Chicago Tribune*, December 1, 1890; Schusky, *Forgotten Sioux*, p. 134; Mooney, "Ghost-Dance Religion," pp. 848–49; Coleman, *Voices of Wounded Knee*, pp. 66–67; Pohanka, *Nelson A. Miles*, p. 185; Utley, *Last Days of the Sioux Nation*, p. 105; Wooster, *Nelson A. Miles and the Twilight of the Frontier Army*, p. 177. Although Miles urged that the Cheyennes be relocated to the Tongue River Reservation, the Indian Bureau resisted the recommendation, concerned that the Montana reserve was too small. Weist, *A History of the Cheyenne People*, p. 141.

28. The attempted arrest of Little is recounted by Robert O. Pugh, Royer's issue clerk, in Jensen, *Voices of the American West*, 2:70–71. The meeting in Royer's office on the night of November 10 is addressed in Eastman, *From the Deep Woods to Civilization*, pp. 216–18. Eastman recalled that "a visiting inspector" was present. Some historians have presumed that this was James A. Cooper, but he did not receive instructions to proceed from Kansas to Pine Ridge until November 15, five days after the meeting. See Belt to Cooper, November 15, 1890, and Cooper to Belt, same date, in *Letter from the Secretary of the Interior*, December 11, 1890, p. 21. The likely "inspector" at the meeting was special agent A. T. Lea, who had been present on the Pine Ridge Reservation taking a census of the Indians. There is also speculation that Royer hurriedly left Pine Ridge for Rushville with his family out of fear (see Hyde, *Sioux Chronicle*, pp. 264–65). Royer's wife later reported: "Dr. Royer went to Rushville when the trouble began because if he had called for the troops over the telephone line to [the telegrapher at] that place it would have precipitated a stampede among the settlers." *Chicago Inter-Ocean*, January 13, 1891. The following inclusive telegrams among Royer, Belt, Chandler, and the War Department, appear in U.S. Congress, Senate, *Letter from the Secretary of War*, pp. 16 (quotations)–21 (hereinafter cited as *Letter from the Secretary of War*). The telegram of November 15 from Royer to Belt is in the McLaughlin Papers, Microfilm Roll 35. See also *Report of the Commissioner of Indian Affairs, 1891*, 1:128.

29. *Omaha Bee*, November 16, 1890; telegram, Royer and Cooper to Commissioner of Indian Affairs, November 21, 1890, McLaughlin Papers, Roll 34; *Letter from the Secretary of War*, p. 16 (quotations).

30. *Chicago Tribune*, November 24, 1890; *Minneapolis Tribune*, November 24, 1890; *St. Paul Pioneer Press*, November 24, 1890; *Letter from the Secretary of War*, p. 18–19 (quotations).

31. *Letter from the Secretary of War*, p. 21.

32. Royer went to Fort Robinson on November 14. *Chicago Tribune*, November 16, 1890; Taylor, "The Surrender of Red Cloud." Agent Wright at Rosebud wired his superiors in Washington that his charges were "wild and Crazy," requiring the presence of 1,000 soldiers. Mooney, "Ghost-Dance Religion," p. 849. For Lea's conclusions, see Belt to Secretary Chandler, November 2, 1890, in *Letter from the Secretary of the Interior*, December 11, 1890, pp. 11–12; and Lea to Cooper, undated but ca. November 21, 1890, in ibid., p. 29 (first quotation); Lea to CIA Morgan, November 28, 1890, NA, RG 75, Special Case No. 188, NIS 176 Roll 4 (second quotation). See also telegram, Brooke to Assistant Adjutant General, November 22, 1890, Division of the Missouri, John Rutter Brooke Papers, Historical Society of Pennsylvania, Sioux Campaign 1890–91, vol. 1, pp. 69–70 (hereinafter cited as Brooke Papers). Trader Charles P. Jordan at Rosebud Agency suspected something nefarious in Lea's conclusions regarding the beef ration

imbroglio: "There is a history & reason behind Spec Agt Lea's reported representations that the Indians were not in need—& if *his* reason was shown up—and his extended employment @ $10. per diem in counting Indians & other facts be made known, his evidence would be impeached and a sensation might be created." Jordan to "Dear Charlie," December 17, 1890, Jordan Papers, H74.42 SC 61, vol. 1; Lea to Brigadier General John R. Brooke, November 22, 1890. NA, RG 393, Entry 3779, Department of the Platte, Letters Received, 1890–91 (third quotation).

33. Bartlett to Warren K. Moorehead, November 18, 1890, George Bartlett Letters, Moorehead Papers (MS 106), Box 4.

34. *Omaha World-Herald*, December 1, 1890. This article contains a rigorous critique of Royer, while a well-reasoned yet notional view of events leading to army intervention appears in Ostler, "Conquest and the State," pp. 227–35.

CHAPTER 7. DEPLOYMENT

1. Connelly, *John M. Schofield and the Politics of Generalship*, pp. 272–73; *Chicago Herald*, January 24, 1891; *New York Weekly World*, December 10, 1890 (quotation). Modern and contemporary treatments of Miles (1839–1925) and/or aspects of his career from which this background is drawn include Wooster, *Nelson A. Miles and the Twilight of the Frontier Army;* DeMontravel, *A Hero to His Fighting Men;* Pohanka, *Nelson A. Miles;* Johnson, *The Unregimented General;* Utley, "Nelson A. Miles"; "Major-General Nelson A. Miles," *Harper's Weekly*, April 18, 1891; Pond, "Major-General Nelson A. Miles"; Greene, *Yellowstone Command;* Greene, *Nez Perce Summer, 1877;* Thrapp, *The Conquest of Apacheria;* and DeMontravel, "General Nelson A. Miles and the Wounded Knee Controversy." Miles authored two autobiographies: *Personal Recollections and Observations of General Nelson A. Miles;* and *Serving the Republic*. A conjectural assessment of Miles's postulated efforts to shape the intervention appears in Ostler, "Conquest and the State," pp. 235–39.

2. For the army of the post–Civil War/Indian wars period, ca. 1865–98, see Coffman, *The Old Army*, pp. 215–404; Rickey, *Forty Miles a Day on Beans and Hay;* Foner, *The United States Soldier between Two Wars;* Merritt, "The Army of the United States"; and Greene, "Indian Wars of the Trans-Mississippi West, 1850s–1890s." The Miles quotation is from Miles to the Adjutant General (AG), November 28, 1890, in *Letter from the Secretary of War*, p. 11.

3. Data from "Report of the Quartermaster General," October 9, 1890, in *Report of the Secretary of War, 1890*, pp. 844, 848, 849, 850, 852, 854; "Report of Major General Miles," September 14, 1891, in *Report of the Secretary of War, 1891*, 1:148.

4. Fritz, *The Movement for Indian Assimilation*, pp. 18, 131–33; Wooster, *The Military and United States Indian Policy*, p. 89; Connelly, *John M. Schofield and the Politics of Generalship*, p. 271; Assistant Adjutant General Samuel Breck to Miles, October 31, 1890, in *Letter from the Secretary of War*, p. 3; Ruger to Assistant Adjutant General (AAG), Division of the Missouri, November 26, 1890, in ibid., pp. 9–10 (quotation); Ruger to AAG, Division of the Missouri, November 16, 1890, quoted in DeBarthe, *Life and Adventures of Frank Grouard*, pp. 207–208; *Omaha World-Herald*, November 18, 1890; *Army and Navy Register*, November 22, 1890; *Chicago Tribune*, November 1, 1890; *Chicago Inter-Ocean*, November 18, 1880; Harvey, "Last Stand of the Sioux," p. 230; Wooster, *Nelson A. Miles and the Twilight of the Frontier Army*, p. 178. Troops from

Fort Meade had been in the field since the spring of 1890 manning posts at Oelrichs, west of Pine Ridge, and at the forks of the Cheyenne River, west of the Cheyenne River Reservation. *Chadron Democrat*, November 27, 1890; Lee, *Fort Meade and the Black Hills*, p. 101; "Record of Events from Post Returns, Fort Robinson, Nebraska, 1890–1899," Fort Robinson Museum files, Fort Robinson State Park; *Black Hills Journal*, November 22, 1890; Lee, "Messiah War on Cheyenne River," p. 1; Scott, *Some Memories of a Paleontologist*, p. 178.

5. Harrison to Proctor, November 13, 1890, in *Letter from the Secretary of War*, pp. 4–5 (quotation); telegram, Belt to Agent McLaughlin, Standing Rock Agency, Fort Yates, North Dakota, November 14, 1890, Frank Zahn Papers, Archives and Manuscripts Division, State Historical Society of North Dakota; Winthrop, *Military Law and Precedents*, pp. 863–64; Hamilton, *Elementary Principles Connected with the Art of War*, pp. 344–45; Davis, *A Treatise on the Military Law of the United States*, pp. 327–29.

6. The Division of the Missouri, downsized effective September 1, 1890, was stripped of the departments of the Missouri and Texas, which became administered directly from the War Department. The State of Illinois, formerly part of the Missouri Department, was added to Miles's managerial sphere. General Orders No. 84, Headquarters of the Army, Adjutant General's Office, August 8, 1890, responding to the president's executive order of the same date, decreed the reconfiguration of the Division of the Missouri. *General Orders and Circulars, Adjutant General's Office, 1890; Report of the Secretary of War, 1890*, p. 182.

7. Bell, *Commanding Generals and Chiefs of Staff*, p. 86 (see also Connelly, *John M. Schofield and the Politics of Generalship;* and "John McAllister Schofield"); Schofield to Miles, November 14, 1890, in Letter from the Secretary of War, p. 5 (quotations).

8. Telegram, AAG Major Michael V. Sheridan to Brooke, December 1, 1890, NA, RG 393, Part 1, Entry 3782, Department of the Platte, Telegrams Received by Headquarters, 1890–91, Box 2; "Report of Brigadier General Brooke," September 5, 1891, in *Report of the Secretary of War, 1891*, p. 251; telegram, Miles to AG, January 16, 1891, plus endorsement from Schofield, January 20, 1891. NA Publication M983, "Sioux Campaign," 1890–91, Roll 1, p. 955; telegram, Miles to AG, January 19, 1891, ibid., p. 956; *General Orders and Circulars, Adjutant General's Office, 1891; Army and Navy Journal*, January 31, 1891; *Army and Navy Register*, January 31, 1891. Background on the Vermont-born Proctor, including his Civil War service, appears in Bell, *Secretaries of War and Secretaries of the Army*, p. 92.

Brooke's assistant adjutant general in Omaha was unable to find precedent authority by which Miles might declare Pine Ridge and Rosebud agencies belonging to the Department of the Platte "for all practical military purposes." This expediency lasted until January 27, 1891, when General Orders No. 9, Headquarters of the Army, specified that on "direction of the President all that portion of the State of South Dakota lying south of the forty-fourth (44th) parallel of north latitude is transferred to the Department of the Platte," with Brooke assuming command of "the territory and the troops serving therein." In 1895 the Department of the Platte was expanded to include the area between the forty-fourth and forty-fifth parallel west of the Missouri River. General Orders No. 45, Headquarters of the Army, July 23, 1895. *General Orders and Circulars, Adjutant General's Office, 1895.*

9. *Chicago Tribune*, November 17, 1890; "Report of Major General Miles," September 14, 1891, in *Report of the Secretary of War, 1891*, p. 145; *Army and Navy Journal*, November 22, 1890; Schofield to Miles, November 19, 1890, and November 24, 1890,

in *Letter from the Secretary of War*, pp. 7, 9 (quotations); *Black Hills Weekly Times*, November 22, 1890; *Harper's Weekly*, November 29, 1890.

10. *Chicago Tribune*, November 20, 1890; *Omaha World-Herald*, November 20, 1890 (quotation); *Washington Evening Star*, November 20, 1890. In fact Royer likely saw the need for his presence at Rushville, because the telegraph service between there and Pine Ridge had failed, with the wire down and needing repair, although a telephone line was still connected and evidently had been frequently used. Two Western Union operators arrived in Rushville in the meantime to help facilitate communication from the agency once Brooke established his headquarters there. W. P. McFarland to Brooke, November 21, 1890, NA, RG 393, Entry 3778; *Omaha World-Herald*, November 20, 1890; *Chadron Advocate*, November 21, 1890.

11. *Omaha World-Herald*, November 19, 1890.

12. The units with Brooke were Companies A, B, C, and D, Second Infantry. Troops F, I, and K, Ninth Cavalry, and Company C, Eighth Infantry, joined from Fort Robinson. Those with Smith at Rosebud were Troops A and G, Ninth Cavalry, and A, B, and H, Eighth Infantry. Regimental Returns of the Second Infantry, November 1890, NA Microfilm 665, Roll 23; Regimental Returns of the Ninth Cavalry, November 1890, NA Microfilm 744, Roll 90; Regimental Returns of the Eighth Infantry, November 1890, NA Microfilm 665, Roll 95; Wilson, "The Eighth Regiment of Infantry," p. 524; *Chicago Tribune*, November 19 and 20, 1890; *Washington Evening Star*, November 20, 1890; *New York Times*, November 22, 1890; *Boston Globe*, November 21, 1890; *Omaha World-Herald*, November 18, 1890; *Chadron Democrat*, November 20, 1890; *Hot Springs Weekly Star*, November 20, 1890; *Black Hills Journal*, November 20 and 21, 1890; *Chadron Advocate*, November 21, 1890; *Army and Navy Register*, November 22, 1890; Wilson, "The Attack on the Pine Ridge Indian Agency, S.D.," pp. 562–63; Richard T. Burns, "Infantry Operations at Pine Ridge," in Greene, *Indian War Veterans*, p. 196; Wright, "The Second Regiment of Infantry," p. 431; *Army and Navy Journal*, November 22, 1890 (quotation), and December 6, 1890; Buecker, "Fort Niobrara," p. 314. Private Edward Forrest, Company D, Second Infantry, remembered the trek from Rushville: "The night was dark; the weather very cold. We were not allowed to make a light [with matches]. When we came to a halt we would crowd together and mill about like cattle to get warm." "Service Account, Edward Forrest, 2nd U.S. Infantry, Dictated to His Wife, Mrs. Edith M. Forrest, about 1930." Edith M. Forrest File, Box 2, Folder 6, Indian Wars Widows Project Records, Jefferson National Expansion Memorial, National Park Service. The arrival of troops at Rosebud is described from the Brulé perspective in Standing Bear, *My People the Sioux*, p. 223, although its chronology in terms of surrounding events is somewhat skewed.

13. Morgan, "Reminiscences of My Days in the Land of the Ogalala [*sic*] Sioux," pp. 50–51.

14. Perrig Diary, entry for November 29, 1890; *Report of the Commissioner of Indian Affairs, 1891*, 1:128; *Chadron Advocate*, November 21, 1890; *Omaha World-Herald*, November 26, 1890; *Chicago Tribune*, November 29, 1890; Dougherty, "The Recent Indian Craze," pp. 576–77; *Omaha Bee*, December 3, 1890 (quotation).

15. Hyde, *Sioux Chronicle*, pp. 265–66; Eastman, *From the Deep Woods to Civilization*, p. 220; Leckie and Leckie, *The Buffalo Soldiers*, p. 273; *Chadron Democrat*, November 20, 1890 (quotation); Larson, *Red Cloud*, p. 273. An account of the movement of soldiers from Fort Niobrara to Rosebud Agency is found in August Hettinger, "Recollections of the Pine Ridge Campaign," in Greene, *Indian War Veterans*, pp. 199–201.

16. Some senior army officers grumbled when Miles pulled men from across the country. Brigadier General Wesley Merritt, commanding the abridged Department of the Missouri, was reportedly "put out by the sending of troops from his department . . . as he had [some of] the same trouble in his own department and did not want his troops taken away." Scott, *Some Memories of a Soldier*, p. 149.

17. Regimental Returns of the Ninth Cavalry, November 1890, NA Microfilm 744, Roll 90; Henry, "Adventures of American Army and Navy Officers," p. 1273; *Chicago Tribune*, November 19, 1890; Regimental Returns of the Second Infantry, November 1890, NA Microfilm 665, Roll 23; *Harper's Weekly*, July 27, 1895; *Omaha World-Herald*, November 24, 1890; Jocelyn, *Mostly Alkali*, p. 332; Buecker, "Fort Niobrara," p. 314 (the companies of the Twenty-First Infantry were A, C, G, and E); Garlington, "The Seventh Regiment of Cavalry," p. 264; Henry Daum, Company C, Eighth Infantry, to Mary Baumgard, November 25, 1890, in Jensen, "A Love Letter from Pine Ridge," pp. 47–48 (quotation).

18. Carr's command consisted of Troops A, C, D, E, F, G, H, and I. Regimental Returns of the Sixth Cavalry, December 1890, NA Microfilm 744, Roll 65; *Chicago Tribune*, December 10, 1890; *Omaha Bee*, December 8, 1890; undated clipping, *Albuquerque Citizen*, ca. December 2, 1890, Carr Papers; Carter, "The Sixth Regiment of Cavalry," p. 249; Carter, *From Yorktown to Santiago with the Sixth U.S. Cavalry*, pp. 256–57; King, *War Eagle*, pp. 239–40; John J. Pershing Memoirs, draft of chapter 5, pp. 86–87. John J. Pershing Papers, container 377, Manuscript Division, Library of Congress; Smythe, "John J. Pershing," pp. 237–43; Smythe, *Guerrilla Warrior*, p. 22.

19. See, for details, "Report of General Merritt," Department of Dakota, St. Paul, Minnesota, September 1, 1891 (after Merritt's assumption of command from the Department of the Missouri), which includes troop assignments under Brooke in the Department of Dakota in 1890–91, in *Report of the Secretary of War, 1891*, 1:162–76. For troop distribution, see also Chubb, "The Seventeenth Regiment of Infantry," p. 641; McRae, "The Third Regiment of Infantry," p. 450; Regimental Returns of the Seventh Infantry, December 1890, NA Microfilm 665, Roll 84; McIver, "The 7th U.S. Infantry in the Sioux Campaign of 1890–91," p. 23; Ebstein, "The Twenty-First Regiment of Infantry," p. 679; Richards, "The Sixteenth Regiment of Infantry," p. 632; Regimental Returns of the Fourth Artillery, November 1890, NA Microfilm 727, Roll 31; Regimental Returns of the Eighth Cavalry, November–December 1890, NA Microfilm 744, Roll 82; Abbot, "The Twelfth Regiment of Infantry," p. 572; Brinkerhoff, "The Fifteenth Regiment of Infantry," p. 627; Regimental Returns of the First Cavalry, December 1890, NA Microfilm 744, Roll 8; Regimental Returns of the Second Cavalry, December 1890, NA Microfilm 744, Roll 21; Regimental Returns of the Fifth Cavalry, December 1890, NA Microfilm 744, Roll 55; Camp Return of First Infantry, January 1891, NA Microfilm 665, Roll 90; *Valentine Republican*, December 12, 1890; *Army and Navy Journal*, March 7, 1891; "The First Regiment of Infantry," pp. 412–13; "Report of Operations Relative to the Sioux Indians in 1890 and 1891," in *Report of the Secretary of War, 1891*, pp. 179–81; *Army and Navy Journal*, December 6, 1890; *Army and Navy Register*, December 6, 1890; *New York Herald*, November 28, 1890; Schofield to Brigadier General David S. Stanley, December 3, 1890; and Schofield to Stanley, December 10, 1890; both in NA, Microfilm 983, "Sioux Campaign," 1890–91, Roll 1, p. 432.

20. Rickey, *Forty Miles a Day on Beans and Hay*, pp. 216, 227; Hettinger, "Recollections of the Pine Ridge Campaign," in Greene, *Indian War Veterans*, pp. 200–201 (quotation).

21. AAG, U.S. Army headquarters, to Miles, November 22, 1890, in *Letter from the Secretary of War*, p. 8 (first quotation); *Omaha World-Herald*, November 26, 1890; *Deseret News*, December 6, 1890 (second quotation); General Field Orders No. 5, Headquarters Department of the Platte in the Field, December 23, 1890, in "Field Orders Sioux Campaign 1890–91," Brooke Papers; *Chadron Advocate*, November 28, 1890 (third and fourth quotations); *Army and Navy Journal*, December 6, 1890; *Chicago Inter-Ocean*, November 29, 1890; Bad Heart Bull and Blish, *A Pictographic History of the Oglala Sioux*, p. 421; Taylor, "The Surrender of Red Cloud," p. 4. (Other Lakota and Cheyenne scout units would be recruited between January and June 1891, forming three other companies plus a detachment, and in December additional units composed of Cheyennes and Crows would join from Montana.) Copies of muster rolls for Indian scouts enlisted at Pine Ridge Agency and Camp Cheyenne, South Dakota, November 1890–April 1891. NA at Kansas City, RG 75 (Records of the Pine Ridge Agency), General Records, Main Decimal Files, Box 657, Folder 650; NA, RG 94 (Records of the Adjutant General's Office), Microfilm 233, pp. 853–55; *Chicago Tribune*, November 26, 1890; *Omaha World-Herald*, November 23, 1890; *Omaha Bee*, November 27, 1890. The military considered enlisting Pawnee Indians, who had served thus in campaigns against the Sioux during the 1860s and 1870s. "The Division Commander believes it would be desirable to have a strong force that are known to be hostile to the Sioux in that vicinity to aid the troops in intercepting raiding parties or move with a strong command of cavalry in case there should be a serious outbreak. Their presence through that country in uniform would give confidence to the settlers and at the same time prevent small parties committing depredations." The plan was never instituted, although the Cheyennes and Crows served Colonel Carr's troops. Telegram, Ruger to Carr, December 10, 1890, forwarding AAG, Division of the Missouri, to Ruger; also telegram, Carr to Ruger, December 11, 1890. NA, RG 393, Department of Dakota, Letters Sent, vol. December 4–31, 1890.

22. *Chadron Democrat*, September 25 and November 27, 1890; *New York World*, November 30, 1890; *Omaha World-Herald*, November 26, 1890; Allen, *From Fort Laramie to Wounded Knee*, pp. 153, 167; "Service Account, Edward Forrest, 2nd U.S. Infantry" (first quotation); *Chadron Advocate*, November 28, 1890 (second quotation). For the photographic side of events on the Sioux reservations in 1890–91 in a contemporary context, see Jensen, Paul, and Carter, *Eyewitness at Wounded Knee*.

23. Eastman, "The Ghost Dance War," p. 33.

24. "Statement of Military Service of John R. Brooke," March 29, 1889, Brooke Papers, Box 8, Folder 2; Heitman, *Historical Register and Dictionary of the United States Army*, 1:248; Powell, *Powell's Records of Living Officers of the United States Army*, pp. 88–89; *Army and Navy Journal*, November 29, 1890; Erisman and Erisman, "Letters from the Field," p. 29; Tibbles, *Buckskin and Blanket Days*, pp. 302–305; Warner, *Generals in Blue*, pp. 46–47. Information regarding Brooke's Apache combat experience with the Third Infantry in New Mexico Territory is in former Sergeant Major Charles F. Goldbeck to Brooke, September 4, 1888, Brooke Papers, Box 8, Folder 1. See also Brooke's journal of a scout against Apaches in the spring of 1869, Brooke Papers, Box 8, Folder 6.

25. *New York Times*, November 22, 1890.

26. Perrig Diary, entry for November 20, 1890; *New York Times*, November 23, 1890; *Chicago Tribune*, November 23, 1890; Kelley, *Pine Ridge 1890*, p. 36; telegram, AAG to Brooke, November 24, 1890, NA at Kansas City, RG 75, Pine Ridge Agency,

Controversies, 1867–1907, Entry 67 (first quotation); *Omaha Bee*, November 21, 1890 (second quotation); *Omaha World-Herald*, November 21, 1890; *Chicago Tribune*, November 21, 1890 (third quotation), and November 23, 1890; *Washington Evening Star*, November 21, 1890; *New York Times*, November 22, 1890; *Army and Navy Register*, November 22, 1890.

27. Kelley, *Pine Ridge 1890*, pp. 37, 40, 66; Allen, *From Fort Laramie to Wounded Knee*, p. 176; Perrig Diary, entry for November 25, 1890; *Chicago Tribune*, November 20, 1890 (quotation), and November 22, 25, and 28, 1890; *Omaha Bee*, November 22, 1890; *New York Times*, November 2, 1890; Eastman, "Ghost Dance War," p. 33; Kelley, "Indian Troubles and the Battle of Wounded Knee," p. 30.

28. Miles to AG, December 5, 1890. McLaughlin Papers, Roll 34 (quotation). On November 24 rancher Henry P. Smith on White River recorded that "a cour[i]er was sent to inform us of danger of an indian [*sic*] outbreak. As it was near midnight and we had become accustomed to such reports we thanked our informant and turned in to wait until daylight for further investigation." Smith noted "armed Rose Bud indians continually passed on their way to join the Pine Ridge indians who had stubbornly refused to give up the ghost dance." Smith and his neighbors found refuge in a nearby store and raised fortifications. Buecker, "'The Even Tenor of Our Way Is Pursued Undisturbed,'" pp. 209–10.

29. *Chicago Tribune*, November 22, 1890. For a slight variant, see also *Omaha Bee*, November 22, 1890.

30. *Chicago Tribune*, November 23, 1890 (quotation), and November 25, 1890; *New York Times*, November 23, 1890; *Omaha World-Herald*, November 23, 1890; *Omaha Bee*, November 24, 1890; *Chicago Tribune*, November 25, 1890.

31. Miles (through AG) to Brooke, November 18, 1890, and November 23, 1890. NA Microfilm 983, "Sioux Campaign," 1890–91, Roll 1 (first and second quotations), pp. 100, 738; *Nebraska State Journal*, November 26, 1890; *Omaha Bee*, November 26, 1890 (third quotation); Kelley, *Pine Ridge 1890*, pp. 38–39.

32. *Omaha Bee*, November 25, 1890 (including quotations); *Philadelphia Inquirer*, November 26, 1890; *Chicago Tribune*, November 29, 1890.

33. Brooke to AAG, Division of the Missouri, November 30, 1890. NA, RG 393, Department of the Platte, Letters Sent, 1866–98, PI 172, Entry 3722, vol. 19, pp. 159–63.

34. *Omaha World-Herald*, November 27, 1890 (for a reporter's conversation with Little Wound and Yellow Hair in which he learned of the recent death of Little Wound's daughter from starvation); Regimental Returns of the Seventh Cavalry, November 1890, NA Microfilm 744, Roll 74; Regimental Returns of the First Artillery, November 1890, NA Microfilm 727, Roll 7; "Scrapbook of Clippings and Pictures of Troop C with a History of Troop A, 1867–1932," NA, RG 391, Records of U.S. Regular Army Mobile Units, Cavalry, 7th Cavalry, 1866–1917, Entry 865; *Omaha World-Herald*, November 24, 1890; *Chicago Tribune*, November 25, 1890; *Army and Navy Journal*, November 29, 1890; *New York Times*, November 24, 1890; Lloyd S. McCormick, "Wounded Knee and Drexel Mission Fights, December 29th and 30th, 1890," U.S. 7th Cavalry Collection (Microfilm Roll 12), Little Bighorn Battlefield National Monument; Kelley, *Pine Ridge 1890*, pp. 51–53; Slaughter, "Time at Wounded Knee," in Greene, *Indian War Veterans*, p. 180; *Nebraska State Journal*, December 10, 1890; Mackintosh, *Custer's Southern Officer*. Troops F and H remained in garrison at Fort Sill, Indian Territory, while Troops L and M had been skeletonized (as with all

cavalry and infantry regiments) in September per General Orders No. 79, Adjutant General's Office, July 25, 1890. Chandler, *Of GarryOwen in Glory*, p. 80; *Junction City Republican*, December 5, 1890; Kelley, *Pine Ridge 1890*, p. 103. Historian George E. Hyde stated that word circulating among the Sioux was that the Seventh Cavalry had arrived seeking vengeance for Little Bighorn, an assertion without attribution. Hyde, *Sioux Chronicle*, p. 271.

35. *Black Hills Journal*, November 25, 1890; *Omaha Bee*, November 25, 1890; *Omaha World-Herald*, November 26, 1890; McGillycuddy, *McGillycuddy, Agent*, p. 262; Hall, *To Have This Land*, pp. 59, 60; Eastman, "Ghost Dance War," pp. 33–34 (quotation).

36. Brooke to AAG, Division of the Missouri, November 26, 1890, in *Letter from the Secretary of War*, p. 9; McGillycuddy to Walter M. Camp, December 5, 1919, Walter M. Camp Papers, Little Bighorn Battlefield National Monument; *Chicago Tribune*, November 25 and 28, 1890; *Black Hills Weekly Times*, November 29, 1890; *Omaha Bee*, November 26 and 27, 1890 *Chadron Democrat*, December 11, 1890; *Chicago Inter-Ocean*, November 29, 1890; *Chicago Tribune*, November 29, 1890 (quotations); *Omaha World-Herald*, November 30, 1890.

37. *New York Times*, December 2, 1890 (quotation); Kelley, *Pine Ridge 1890*, p. 45; Hall, *To Have This Land*, pp. 54–55, 57–58, 59, 66; McGillycuddy, *McGillycuddy, Agent*, p. 259.

38. *Omaha World-Herald*, November 23, 1890; *Omaha Bee*, November 24, 1890 (quotation), and November 25 and 26, 1890; "As Narrated by 'Short Bull,'" pp. 10–16; *Chicago Inter-Ocean*, November 29, 1890; *Hot Springs Daily Star*, December 2, 1890; Kelley, *Pine Ridge 1890*, pp. 61–62; Allen, *From Fort Laramie to Wounded Knee*, p. 175; Hall, *To Have This Land*, p. 73. The warrior estimate is from Royer and Cooper to Belt, November 30, 1890, in *Letter from the Secretary of War*, p. 46. For more on the tumult around Pine Ridge and Rosebud agencies in late November and early December 1890, see Hyde, *Sioux Chronicle*, pp. 268–72; Olson, *Red Cloud and the Sioux Problem*, pp. 327–28; Larson, *Red Cloud*, pp. 273–74. Of the 5,354 Brulé people at Rosebud, the agent projected 1,800 as absent. *Chicago Tribune*, December 3, 1890. For more specifics on the movements and dancing of the Brulés and certain Oglalas, see Neihardt, *Black Elk Speaks*, pp. 202–204; and DeMallie, *Sixth Grandfather*, pp. 267–69.

39. Brooke to wife, November 29, 1890, Brooke Papers, Box 8, Folder 4 (quotation); "Report of the Inspector-General of the Army," October 7, 1890, in *Report of the Secretary of War, 1890*, pp. 287–88 and supplement 4; *Army and Navy Journal*, December 13, 1890; *New York Times*, November 26, 1890; *Narrative Descriptions of the Named Campaigns of the U.S. Army*, p. 50. The troops assigned between November 1890 and February 1891 represented 36 percent of available cavalry and 21 percent of available infantry. See Russell, "Selfless Service," U.S. Army Command and General Staff College, pp. 67–68. For comparisons with the Great Sioux War, see Hedren, *Great Sioux War Orders of Battle*, pp. 165–66.

Chapter 8. Stronghold

1. *Omaha Bee*, December 3, 1890. Those arriving or en route to the Sioux reserves included four more cavalry troops under Lieutenant Colonel George B. Sanford for service at Oelrichs and nine under Carr at Rapid City, along with seven infantry

companies posted along the Fremont, Elkhorn and Missouri Valley Railroad between Oelrichs, Buffalo Gap, Piedmont, and Rapid City, plus seven more at Fort Sully on the Missouri.

2. Miles to the Adjutant General, December 12, 1890, enclosing Ruger to Miles, presumably same date. NA Microfilm 983, "Sioux Campaign," 1890–91, Roll 1, p. 511; *Chicago Tribune*, December 8, 1890; Traub, "Sioux Campaign—Winter of 1890-'91," pp. 55–56; DeLand, "The Sioux Wars," p. 450; Lee, "Messiah War on Cheyenne River," p. 2; Nankivell, *History of the Twenty-Fifth Regiment United States Infantry*, p. 46; *New York Herald*, November 28, 1890; Hagemann, *Fighting Rebels and Redskins*, pp. 86–87.

3. *Chicago Tribune*, November 27, 1890; Buecker, "'The Even Tenor of Our Way Is Pursued Undisturbed,'" pp. 208–12; Sheridan County Historical Society, *Recollections of Sheridan County, Nebraska*, pp. 280, 389, 478; *Deseret News*, December 20, 1890; Doan, "A Boy's Memory," p. 24; Western Union Telegraph Company telegrams dated November 22–December 7, 1890, variously from Henry W. Tinker, Governor Arthur C. Mellette, "Republican," Rapid City Mayor J. B. Dickover, and N. Steele, Paul Harbaugh Collection; *Chicago Tribune*, November 26 and December 2, 1890; *Omaha World-Herald*, November 27, 1890; *Chicago Inter-Ocean*, November 27, 1890; *Brooklyn Daily Eagle*, December 2, 1890; "As Narrated by 'Short Bull,'" pp. 12–13; *Omaha World-Herald*, December 3, 1890; Greene, *Fort Randall on the Missouri*, p. 171; *Black Hills Journal*, December 5 and 7, 1890; Poland to AAG, Department of the Platte, November 29, 1890, McLaughlin Papers, Roll 34; Allen, *From Fort Laramie to Wounded Knee*, p. 178; Hall, *To Have This Land*, pp. 74–75, 79–81; Koupal, *Our Landlady*, pp. 142–43. Among the ranchers whose property was plundered by Indians in the vicinity of Rosebud and Pine Ridge agencies in November and December were John Sweeny, William McGaa, John O'Rourke, Dick Stirk, William Valaazry, John Steele, Charles Cuny, John Davidson, Henry Kearns, Baptiste Pourier, and John Dwyer. *Omaha Bee*, December 7, 1890; *Black Hills Journal*, December 3, 1890; Kelley, *Pine Ridge 1890*, pp. 89–92. Some settlers criticized Brooke for doing nothing to curb the raiders or go after them, although at this juncture he clearly lacked such discretion. Kelley, *Pine Ridge 1890*, p. 74. A proper assessment of Judge Burns's role appears in Hall, "Reasonable Doubt," p. 75.

4. *Philadelphia Inquirer*, November 29, 1890; *Chicago Tribune*, December 1, 1890; *Deseret News*, December 13, 1890; Harrison to Noble, December 4, 1890. McLaughlin Papers, Roll 34; DeMontravel, *A Hero to His Fighting Men*, pp. 200–201; Proctor to Miles, December 1, 1890, Miles Collection; also in *Letter from the Secretary of War*, p. 12 (quotation).

5. Telegram, Miles to Brooke, December 2, 1890, NA, RG 393, part 1, Entry 3782, Department of the Platte, Telegrams received by Headquarters, 1890–91, Box 2; Noble to Morgan, December 1, 1890, ibid., p. 13 (quotation). The carte blanche authority document also appeared in *Report of the Commissioner of Indian Affairs, 1891*, 1:128–29; *Army and Navy Register*, December 6, 1890.

6. Schofield to Proctor, December 1, 1890, in *Letter from the Secretary of War*, p. 13; *Chicago Inter-Ocean*, December 3, 1890 (first quotation); *Deseret News*, December 13, 1890 (second quotation); *Army and Navy Register*, December 6, 1890 (Heyl quotations); *Chicago Inter-Ocean*, December 4, 1890.

7. "Report of Major General Miles, September 14, 1891," in *Report of the Secretary of War, 1891*, p. 145 (quotation); *Washington Post*, December 1, 1890; *New York Times*, December 1, 1890; *Philadelphia Inquirer*, December 1, 1890; *Chicago Tribune*, December

8, 1890; Baird, "General Miles's Indian Campaigns," p. 370. There was a suggestion that Miles somewhat modeled his plan after an Indian situation in the Indian Territory in 1884–85 that was dealt with by importing large numbers of troops to overawe the tribesmen, a strategy that then–commanding general Sheridan approved. *New York Times*, November 15, 1890.

8. Telegram, Royer to Belt, November 15, 1890, in *Letter from the Secretary of War*, p. 22; telegrams, Royer to Belt, November 26, 1890, November 27, 1890, and November 28, 1890, in ibid., pp. 39–44, 49; Cooper to Belt, in ibid., pp. 40 (quotations), 41–42, 44; AAG Division of the Missouri to Brooke, December 9, 1890, containing Noble to Proctor, December 3, 1890, containing Royer to Belt, November 25, 1890, NA, RG 393, Entry 3779, Department of the Platte, Letters Received, 1890–91; telegram, E. B. Reynolds to Commissioner of Indian Affairs, November 21, 1890, in *Letter from the Secretary of War*, p. 28; Palmer to Commissioner of Indian Affairs, November 21, 1890, in ibid., p. 28. See appendix B for the names contained in the documents from Pine Ridge and Rosebud agencies.

9. All of these items and others are graphically presented with detailed descriptions in *Specifications for Clothing*. Supplies ordered or on hand in the Department of the Platte in December 1890 included 3,000 woolen blankets, 500 additional horse covers, aparejos (pack saddles), fur gauntlets, horses and pack mules (and hired teams), manila rope, oats, hay, forage, tents, stovepipes, canvas overcoats, woolen stockings, 3,000 flannel shirts, 6,000 drawers, tools (farrier knives, pickaxes, hatchets, steel tongs, rasp files), cavalry forges, pack saddle blankets, mess pans, camp kettles, cross-cut saws, ambulances, wagons, wagon covers, field desks, and horse blankets. NA, RG 393, Department of the Platte, Entry 3887, Letters Received, 1866–91, Box 342; Brooke to AG, December 3, 1890, NA Microfilm 983, "Sioux Campaign," 1890–91, Roll 1, p. 428. Other items included 5,000 pairs of "seamless" wool boots and 1,000 buffalo overcoats. Telegrams, AG, Division of the Missouri, to Brooke, December 1, 1890; and AAG, Division of the Missouri, to Brooke, December 9, 1890, both in NA, RG 393, part 1, Entry 3782, Department of the Platte, Telegrams Received by Headquarters, 1890–91, Box 2. Every contributing post or office was required to submit a "Report of Expenses on Account of Indian Hostilities" in January 1891. NA, RG 393, Department of the Platte, Entry 3887, Letters Received, 1866–91, Box 282, 1891; Kelley, *Pine Ridge 1890*, p. 87 (quotation).

10. Rickey, *Forty Miles a Day on Beans and Hay*, pp. 249 (quotation), 251, 254, 257.

11. "Service Account of Louis Ebert, Troop A, 6th Cavalry, 1888," Don G. Rickey Papers (quotation); *Chadron Democrat*, December 11, 1890. Other documentation for issued clothing and equipment is found in Circular No. 1, December 9, 1890, Headquarters Department of the Platte, in the Field, Field Orders Sioux Campaign 1890–91, Brooke Papers; Bogan, "Field Order, 3rd Infantry, 1890," p. 188; Mackintosh, *Custer's Southern Officer*, p. 147; Pershing, draft of chapter 5, p. 87; Carter, *From Yorktown to Santiago*, p. 258; Eastman, *From the Deep Woods to Civilization*, p. 223; *Omaha World-Herald*, November 19 and 24, 1890; *Washington Evening Star*, February 10, 1891. A Twenty-First Infantry soldier at Rosebud Agency remembered that he carried an 1890-pattern entrenching knife: "a clumsy sword-knife about 10" [long] in a scabbard attached to our cartridge belt. I never once saw anyone use this 'thing' for any purpose." Remembrance of former private Walter C. Harrington, Twenty-First Infantry, Indian War Veterans survey form dated September 1954, Don Rickey, Jr., Indian Wars Veterans Project materials, U.S. Army Military History Institute, Army War College;

Breckons, "The Army Pack Train Service," p. 428. The abandonment of sabers and bayonets is addressed in *Report of the Secretary of War, 1891*, 26.

12. Telegram, AAG, Department of the Platte, to Brooke, December 4, 1890, NA, RG 393, part 1, Entry 3782, Department of the Platte, Telegrams Received by Headquarters, 1890–91, Box 2 (quotation); First Lieutenant Douglas A. Howard to Brooke, December 1, 1890, NA, RG 393, part 1, Entry 3779, Department of the Platte, Letters Received, 1890–91; Miles to Brooke, December 23, 1890. NA, RG 393, part 1, Entry 3782, Department of the Platte, Telegrams Received by Headquarters, 1890–91, Box 2; *New York Times*, December 15, 1891.

13. *New York Times*, November 23, 26, and 30, 1890 and December 1, 1890 (quotation).

14. *Chicago Tribune*, November 27 and December 7, 1890; *Omaha Bee*, November 29, 1890; Steltenkamp, *Nicholas Black Elk*, p. 64; *Omaha World-Herald*, November 27, 1890; Brooke to AG, December 1, 1890. NA Microfilm 983, "Sioux Campaign," 1890–91, Roll 1, p. 360; McGillycuddy letter in *Hot Springs Daily Star*, December 2, 1890; *Chicago Tribune*, December 1, 1890; *Chicago Tribune*, December 2, 1890; *Brooklyn Daily Eagle*, December 1 and 2, 1890; *New York Times*, December 2, 1890 (first quotation); *Omaha Bee*, December 2 and 5, 1890; *Chicago Tribune*, December 3, 1890 (second quotation); "Account Given by Indians of the Fight at Wounded Knee Creek, South Dakota, December 29, 1890," in *Report of the Secretary of the Interior, 1891*, p. 180; Neihardt, *Black Elk Speaks*, p. 204; DeMallie, *Sixth Grandfather*, p. 267. Reports placed the people at a spot called "Grass Basin," near the head of Battle Creek Draw on the northwest side of Cuny Table and west of the Stronghold. *Chicago Tribune*, December 3, 1890; *Army and Navy Journal*, December 20, 1890. It is stated that Short Bull took the advice of "the old crier," a Brulé who made such proclamations, to move to the Badlands. "As Narrated by 'Short Bull,'" p. 200. Chief High Hawk told Father John Jutz on December 2 that the Badlands encampment contained 500 lodges (approximately 3,500 people), mostly Brulés, but including as many as 30 lodges (about 200 people) of Oglalas. Perrig Diary, entry for December 2, 1890.

15. Gries, *Roadside Geology of South Dakota*, pp. 122–24; Froiland and Weedon, *Natural History of the Black Hills and Badlands*, pp. 177–78, 183, 186–87; *New York Times*, December 2, 1890; *Chicago Inter-Ocean*, December 7, 1890; Kelley, "The Indian Troubles and the Battle of Wounded Knee," pp. 35–36; Lautenschlager, *A History of Cuny Table, SD*, pp. 1–5; "As Narrated by 'Short Bull,'" p. 14; Dougherty, "The Indians of North America II," pp. 369–70; Bosma, "An Interview with Jim Mesteth," p. 20; Andersson, *Lakota Ghost Dance of 1890*, pp. 81–82; Utley, *Last Days of the Sioux Nation*, pp. 121–22. An untitled sketch map of the Stronghold area, ca. 1891, showing streams, springs, buttes and other landforms, Indian trails, wagon roads, and herd camps is located in the manuscript holdings of the U.S. Army Military History Institute. Guy V. Henry Collection, Box 1, "Wounded Knee" File. See also Cuny Table East Quadrangle, South Dakota–Shannon County. Galligo Table, a short distance northeast, is inexplicably and erroneously labeled "Stronghold Table" on this quad. The area of the Stronghold, later part of Badlands National Monument (today Badlands National Park), became a component of an air gunnery and bombing range during World War II. See untitled topographic map, Army Map Service, October 1957, showing Badlands Bombing Range, Rapid City Air to Air Gunnery Range, Black Hills State University, Special Collections, E. Y. Berry Collection.

16. Brooke to wife, December 1, 1890, Brooke Papers, Box 8, Folder 4 (first quotation); Jutz, "Historic Data on the Causes of the Dissatisfaction among the Sioux

Indians in 1890," pp. 319–20 (Jutz quotations); John Jutz interview with Walter M. Camp, September 28, 1914, Robert S. Ellison, Walter M. Camp Papers, Western History Department, Denver Public Library, WH1702, Box 1, FF137 (hereinafter cited as Ellison/Camp Papers).

17. Jutz, "Historic Data on the Causes of the Dissatisfaction," pp. 319–20 (quotation); DeMallie, *Sixth Grandfather*, pp. 268–69. Black Elk indicated that Jutz visited the Indians at another camp, after which the tribesmen ascended to the Stronghold location. Ibid., p. 269. Black Elk (or possibly Neihardt) further confused Jutz with Father Francis Craft, who did not participate in these events. Neihardt, *Black Elk Speaks*, p. 204n (Craft arrived at Pine Ridge Agency only on December 10 and played no role in Jutz's endeavor). Perrig Diary, entry for December 10, 1890; Foley, *Father Francis M. Craft*, p. 85. For other material presented, see also "Excerpts taken from the Diary of Holy Rosary Mission on the Battle of Wounded Knee," pp. 65–69 (copy of undated typescript, Marquette University, University Libraries, with accompanying letter dated November 15, 1989, provided by R. Eli Paul), p. 3; Perrig Diary, entries for December 2–6, 1890; Kreis, *Lakotas, Black Robes, and Holy Women*, pp. 142–46; Green, "German Missionary Participation during the Ghost Dance of 1890," pp. 31–33; Louis J. Goll, *Jesuit Missions among the Sioux; New York Times*, December 6 and 7, 1890; *Omaha Bee*, December 6 and 7, 1890; *Chicago Tribune*, December 6 and 7, 1890; *Black Hills Daily Times*, December 9, 1890; *Brooklyn Daily Eagle*, December 6, 1890; *Deseret News*, December 13, 1890; *Boston Daily Globe*, August 10, 1908; Kelley, *Pine Ridge 1890*, pp. 84–87, 93–95; Coleman, *Voices of Wounded Knee*, pp. 158–63; Hyde, *Sioux Chronicle*, pp. 274–75; Olson, *Red Cloud and the Sioux Problem*, pp. 328–29. Jutz had earlier received High Hawk, a Brulé chief, who told him that many of the Rosebud people simply wanted to move to Pine Ridge as had been arranged when the boundary between the reservations had changed. They had left Rosebud because of fear of the soldiers at that place. Jutz to Brook, December 3 (probably December 1 or 2), 1890, NA, RG 393, Entry 3779, Department of the Platte, Letters Received, 1890–91; *Chicago Tribune*, December 7, 1890. For a critical contemporary perspective on Jutz and the Catholic efforts around Pine Ridge, see "Priests and Indians," *Chicago Inter-Ocean*, January 22, 1891.

18. Jutz, "Historic Data on the Causes of the Dissatisfaction," pp. 319–20.

19. Perrig Diary, entries for December 15 and 18, 1890; Miles to AG, December 7, 1890, citing Brooke, NA Microfilm 983, "Sioux Campaign," 1890–91, Roll 1, p. 451 (quotation).

20. *Omaha Bee*, December 6, 1890; *Chicago Tribune*, December 9, 1890; *Omaha World-Herald*, December 13, 1890; *Chicago Tribune*, December 12, 1890 (including telegram, Brooke to Miles, December 11, 1890); *Chicago Tribune*, December 13, 14, and 16, 1890; *Chicago Inter-Ocean*, December 12, 1890; *Army and Navy Journal*, December 13 and 27, 1890; *New York Weekly Witness*, December 17, 1890; *Black Hills Journal*, December 25, 1890; *Hot Springs Daily Star*, December 12, 1890; Kelley, *Pine Ridge 1890*, pp. 76, 85–86, 97, 106–107, 121; DeMallie, *Sixth Grandfather*, p. 269; Neihardt, *Black Elk Speaks*, p. 204; Ostler, *Plains Sioux and U.S. Colonialism*, pp. 316–19; Louis Shangrau's account in "Sioux on the War-Path," pp. 266–70 (quotation on 269); a distillation of this piece appears in Moorehead, *The American Indian*, pp. 118–22.

21. Garnier to Brooke, December 10, 1890, and Garnier to Brooke, December 13, 1890, NA, RG 393, part 1, Entry 3779, Department of the Platte, Letters Received, 1890–91; Boyd, *Recent Indian Wars*, pp. 207–209, 236–38; Johnson, *Life of Sitting Bull*, pp. 414–20; Coleman, *Voices of Wounded Knee*, pp. 164–66. Short Bull's brief allusion

to the internal dispute at the Stronghold appears in "As Narrated by 'Short Bull,'" p. 15. His note to "Chief of Indian Scouts" is in the National Archives (copy provided by John D. McDermott). See also "Man Above's Interview," in Jensen, *Voices of the American West*, 1:240–41; Hyde, *Sioux Chronicle*, pp. 276–78; and the perceptive account of a Brulé woman who had been at the Stronghold, as interviewed by Bright Eyes, the wife of correspondent Henry Tibbles, in *Omaha World-Herald*, December 17, 1890. Shangrau (also spelled Shangraux and Shangreau) described the Stronghold thus: "Trenches are everywhere to be seen, and near the entrance exceed ten feet in depth and are very wide. On the farther side from the entrance there are two places where the hill slopes at an angle of thirty-eight or forty degrees. Of course, it would be out of the question for one to climb up such an incline, but the Indians might slide down safely in case they were compelled to retreat. All other sides of the plateau are perpendicular. Some rifle-pits have been excavated on the hills near at hand, and the Sioux, taking advantage of these, might harass the soldiers should the latter gain access to the camp." "[Shangrau] claims that the only way properly to assault the spot is by cannon. . . . If cannon can be brought near, so that shells can be thrown into the fort, he thinks the Indians will not be able to hold it." "Sioux on the War-Path," p. 268.

22. Hauk, "M. Brainard Poste," p. 25; First Lieutenant John F. McBlain, Ninth Cavalry, to Adjutant, Camp at Oelrichs, December 11, 1890, NA, RG 393, part 1, Entry 3779, Department of the Platte, Letters Received, 1890–91 (first quotation); telegram, Captain Camillo C. C. Carr, First Cavalry, to Adjutant First Lieutenant Fayette W. Roe, Third Infantry, December 7, 1890; and telegram, Carr to Roe, December 8, 1890 (second quotation), both in NA, RG 393, part 1, Entry 3782, Department of the Platte, Telegrams Received by Headquarters, 1890–91, Box 2; telegram, Lieutenant Colonel George B. Sanford to Roe, December 11, 1890, NA, RG 393, part 1, Entry 3782, Department of the Platte, Telegrams Received by Headquarters, 1890–91, Box 2; Allen, *From Fort Laramie to Wounded Knee*, p. 177.

23. Sanford to Brooke, December 11, 1890, transmitting McBlain report of Warren's ranch depredations, NA, RG 393, Entry 3778, Register of Letters Received in the Field at Pine Ridge, S.D., from November 21st, 1890 to January 24th, 1891, pp. 8–9; Captain Almond B. Wells, Eighth Cavalry, to Assistant Adjutant General, Department of Dakota, December 14, 1890, Brooke Papers, Sioux Campaign 1890–91, 1:329. The warrior killed at Daily's ranch was evidently the aforementioned Circle Elk, nephew of Short Bull and a Carlisle attendee. "As Narrated by 'Short Bull,'" p. 14; *Army and Navy Journal*, December 20, 1890. Scout Garnier reported to Brooke "a fight with some Cowboys and the Cowboys shot one of the Indians." Little Bat to Brooke, December 13, 1890, NA, RG 393, Entry 3779, Department of the Platte, Letters Received, 1890–91; Coleman, *Voices of Wounded Knee*, pp. 167–71. A participant account of the encounter appears in John B. McCloud, undated manuscript entitled "Reminiscence," Manuscript H76.15, Folder 1, Box 3564A (with McCloud ranch Home Guard enlistment roll attached), SDSHS; and hearsay accounts are found in G. E. Lemmon, "My Participation in and Recollections of the Sioux Uprising of 1890–91," Wyoming State Historical Research and Publication Division, MS-691, American Heritage Center, University of Wyoming; and an unreliable hearsay reminiscence in Yost, *Boss Cowman*, pp. 152–53. See also "Accounts of Unidentified South Dakota Family during the Messiah War in 1890," Manuscript H88.32, Box 3749B, SDSHS; Lee, *Fort Meade and the Black Hills*, pp. 106–108. For newspaper references to the Warren and Daily incidents and their aftermath, see *Black Hills Journal*, December 11, 13, 14, 17, and 18, 1890; *Black Hills Daily Times*, December 16, 1890; *Chicago Inter-Ocean*, December 15, 1890;

Chicago Tribune, December 14 and 15, 1890; *Philadelphia Inquirer*, December 18, 1890; *Omaha Bee*, December 14, 1890; *Omaha World-Herald*, December 9, 11, and 23, 1890. The most comprehensive secondary treatment of the Daily's Ranch encounter and related episodes is found in Hall, *To Have This Land*, pp. 89–94.

In an assertion made many years later former rancher Ed Lemmon claimed that while on a reconnoitering assignment Second Lieutenant Joseph C. Byron with twelve enlisted men perpetrated the killing of an entire "small band" of Indians somewhere in the vicinity of the west end of Cuny Table. Lemmon stated: "If this had been known at headquarters it would have been a court-martial case, so it was kept a secret." Yost, *Boss Cowman*, p. 151. There is not a hint of credible documentation to verify this alleged incident. Even if true, such a calamity could not have been kept hidden from the army hierarchy and from the record and thereby hushed up in a conspiracy of silence. The purported dozen enlisted men involved unquestionably could not have kept quiet about such an affair for the remainder of their lives or the remainder of their enlistments or the rest of their tour in South Dakota. Even more telling, no contemporary evidence from the Lakota perspective indicates that this event ever occurred. If such a "band" had indeed been massacred and thereafter simply vanished, the disappearance of such a group would have become known among relatives of the people at Pine Ridge and Rosebud, including among scouts, mixed-bloods, and agency employees and, through them, military personnel, to say the least. Lemmon's reminiscence entitled "My Participation in and Recollections of the Sioux Uprising of 1890–91" contains no allusion to this incident. Unfortunately, the unsubstantiated yet incendiary episode contained in *Boss Cowman* has found its way with added elaboration into otherwise well-intentioned volumes, where it is presented as gospel and as the basis for anti-government harangues. See Flood, *Lost Bird of Wounded Knee*, pp. 54–55; and Gonzalez and Cook-Lynn, *The Politics of Hallowed Ground*, pp. 175–77, 253.

24. The Belle Fourche River was also known as the North Fork of the Cheyenne; hence the area was often referenced as the forks of the Cheyenne.

25. *Omaha Bee*, December 11 and 13, 1890; *Black Hills Journal*, December 12, 13, and 19, 1890; *Black Hills Weekly Times*, December 20, 1890; *St. Louis Globe-Democrat*, December 18, 1890; Pershing, draft of chapter 5, pp. 87–88; "Service Account of Louis Ebert, Troop A, 6th Cavalry"; McRae, "The Third Regiment of Infantry," pp. 450–51; Special Field Orders No. 17, Headquarters Department of the Platte in the Field, Pine Ridge Agency, December 18, 1890 (regarding the dispatch of Taylor's scouts and the enlistment of replacements), NA, RG 393, part 1, Entry 3786, "U.S.A. Medical Department. Register of Patients," between 61 and 62; Special Field Orders No. 17, December 18, 1890, Headquarters Department of the Platte, in the Field, Field Orders Sioux Campaign 1890–91, Brooke Papers; Carr to "My dear Sister," January 7, 1891, Carr Papers; Regimental Returns of the Sixth Cavalry, December 1890, Microfilm 744, Roll 65; Carter, *From Yorktown to Santiago*, p. 258; King, *War Eagle*, pp. 240–42.

26. Regimental Returns of the Eighth Cavalry, April–June 1890, Microfilm 744, Roll 82; Regimental Returns of the Seventh Infantry, December 1890, Microfilm 665, Roll 84; McIver, "The 7th U.S. Infantry in the Sioux Campaign of 1890–91," pp. 23–24; Dixon to Ruger, December 15, 1890, NA Microfilm 983, "Sioux Campaign," 1890–91, Roll 1 (first quotation), p. 570. The names of the seventeen offenders were Slow Grower, Crazy Bear, Chasing Crane, Eagle Thunder, From Above, Gunny Sack Lodge, Bear Elk, Little Man, John Logan, Grinder, Running Rattler, Winter Chaser, Fool Elk, Button, Pretty Voice Hawk, Blue Dog, and Shooting. Ibid.; *Omaha Bee*, December 6 and 10, 1890; *Chicago Tribune*, December 7, 1890 (second and third quotations) and

December 9, 1890; Schusky, *Forgotten Sioux*, p. 132. For graphic location of the military commands, see "Map of the Country Embraced in the Recent Campaign against the Hostile Sioux Indians of Dakota Showing the Different Positions of Troops from the Beginning to the Surrender in January 1891," NA, RG 77, Records of the Office of the Chief of Engineers, War Department Map Collection, South Dakota 10, Cartographic Archives Collection.

27. Whitside to wife, December 11, 1890, Samuel M. Whitside Papers, U.S. Army Military History Institute, Army War College (first quotation; hereinafter cited as Whitside Papers); *Chicago Inter-Ocean*, December 15, 1890 (second quotation); Brooke to wife, December 3, 1890, Box 8, Folder 4, Brooke Papers (third quotation).

28. Slaughter, "Time at Wounded Knee," p. 180; Alexander W. Perry, "The Ninth United States Cavalry in the Sioux Campaign of 1890," in Carroll, *The Black Experience in the American West*, p. 252 (first quotation); *Junction City Republican*, December 26, 1890; Wilson, "Attack on Pine Ridge Indian Agency, S.D.," p. 563 (second quotation); Seventh Cavalryman Walter R. Crickett undated letter, ca. January 1891, copied from original in the American Museum in Britain, Claverton Manor, transcribed by Linda Robbins Coleman (third quotation; hereinafter cited as Crickett letter); Piper, "Extracts from Letters Written by Lieutenant Alexander R. Piper, 8th Infantry," pp. 1–3; "Private Diary of Warren Moorehead, Vol. XXI, Sept. 1st 1890 to [illeg.] 1891," entries for December 12 and 18, Moorehead Papers, MS 106, Box 19; *Omaha Bee*, November 27, 1890; *Chicago Tribune*, November 19, 1890; *Army and Navy Journal*, December 6, 1890; *Junction City Republican*, December 12, 1890; Hettinger, "Recollections of the Pine Ridge Campaign," p. 201 (fourth quotation); *Army and Navy Journal*, December 27, 1890. See also the remembrance of former private Walter C. Harrington, Twenty-First Infantry, Indian War Veterans survey form dated September 1954, Don Rickey, Indian Wars Veterans Project materials, U.S. Army Military History Institute, Army War College. The daily regimen at Rosebud Agency (and doubtless at Pine Ridge Agency too) was as follows: "[At reveille] the whole command turns out under arms, and the 1st sergeants call the roll, using a lantern to see by; the list of bugle calls during the day then are as follows: Reveille, 6 A.M.; breakfast, 6:15 A.M.; sick call, 7 A.M.; fatigue call, 7:30 A.M.; water call, cavalry, 11 A.M.; recall from fatigue and orderly call, 11:45 A.M.; mess call, 12 m; water call, cavalry, 2:45 P.M.; stable call and recall from fatigue, 3 P.M.; guard mount, 30 minutes before sunset; retreat, sunset; tattoo, 8 P.M.; taps at 8:30 P.M." Ibid. For the veritable plethora of daily perfunctory correspondence associated with army occupation of Pine Ridge and Rosebud agencies, see the three volumes "Telegrams Sent Headquarters in the Field, from December 26, 1890, to January 25, 1891"; and "Headquarters Dep't Platte. In the Field. Roughs of Field Correspondence. Pine Ridge Agency, 1890," vols. 1 and 2, NA, RG 393, Entry 3775. During these days Brooke obtained the ghost shirt belonging to Big Road and soon afterward the Ghost Dance dress of Big Road's wife, shipping both to Mrs. Brooke. Brook to wife, December 10, 1890, and December 11, 1890, Brooke Papers, Box 8, Folder 4.

29. Brooke to wife, December 5, 1890, Brooke Papers, Box 8, Folder 4; Kelley, *Pine Ridge 1890*, p. 88 (first quotation); Whitside to wife, December 14, 1890, Whitside Papers (second quotation); Brooke to wife, December 13, 1890, Brooke Papers, Box 8, Folder 4 (third quotation).

30. Brooke to Miles, December 11, 1890; and Brooke to Miles, December 14, 1890, contained in telegrams, Miles to AG, December 11 and 14, 1890; and telegram, Ruger to AAG, Division of the Missouri, December 14, 1890; all in NA Microfilm 983, "Sioux Campaign," 1890–91, Roll 1, pp. 534, 543 570; Brooke to AAG, Division of the

Missouri, March 2, 1891, Roll 2 (quotation), p. 1682. See also selected documents from this publication as transcribed and reproduced in Carroll, *To Set the Record Straight!*; Whitside to wife, December 15 and December 16, 1890, Whitside Papers (these letters indicate that Brooke planned his advance to begin on December 16); *Army and Navy Journal*, December 20, 1890; *Omaha Bee*, December 13 and 15, 1890; *Chicago Tribune*, December 15, 1890; Kelley, *Pine Ridge 1890*, pp. 116–17;

31. Brooke to Forsyth (through aide-de-camp), December 15, 1890, vol. 1, pp. 339–40 (first quotation); Brooke to Forsyth, December 15, 1890, p. 341; telegram, Brooke to Carr, December 15, 1890, p. 69 (second quotations); all in Brooke Papers, Sioux Campaign 1890–91, Circular No. 3, Camp at Pine Ridge Agency, S.D., December 16, 1890, Headquarters Department of the Platte, in the field (third quotation), copy in Brooke Papers, "Field Orders Sioux Campaign 1890–91"; *Army and Navy Journal*, December 27, 1890 (fourth quotation); Brooke to AAG, Division of the Missouri, December 15, 1890, NA Microfilm 983, "Sioux Campaign," 1890–91, Roll 1 (fifth quotation), p. 556. By December 14, 1890, Brooke was convinced by word from his scouts that certain of the Stronghold warriors from Two Strike's band had gone on the warpath "and the next thing to do is to go after them." Brooke to wife, December 14, 1890, Brooke Papers, Box 8, Folder 4.

32. For Miles's possible motives for his course in the 1890–91 campaign, see Ostler, *Plains Sioux and U.S. Colonialism*, pp. 301–306.

Chapter 9. Grand River

1. The removal of specific Indian leaders and their followers suspected by authorities of threatening or causing disruption on the frontier had been part of military rationale for much of the nineteenth century and remained a viable option within Lakota reservation environments in 1890. Examples of this practice in the West preceding the 1890–91 Sioux crisis included the imprisonment at Fort Leavenworth of Brulé leader Spotted Tail and other Lakotas in 1855; the imprisonment of Modocs at Alcatraz following their 1872–73 war; the incarceration at Fort Marion, Florida, of Comanches, Southern Cheyennes, Caddos, Southern Arapahos, and Kiowas in 1875; the removal to Fort Leavenworth and later the Indian Territory of Chief Joseph and the Nez Perce prisoners in 1877; the removal of the Northern Cheyennes to Indian Territory after the Great Sioux War; and the exile of Geronimo and his Apaches to Florida and successive venues beginning in 1886. From the government's perspective, the obvious intent was to remove perceived unruly influences as well as to discourage potentially obdurate leaders. See Utley, *Frontiersmen in Blue*, pp. 116–18; Thompson, *Modoc War*, p. 123; Lookingbill, *War Dance at Fort Marion*, pp. 5–9, 39–41; Greene, *Nez Perce Summer*, pp. 335–37; Leiker and Powers, *The Northern Cheyenne Exodus in History and Memory*, pp. 36–38; and Utley, *Geronimo*, pp. 221–54.

2. Palmer to Morgan, October 29, 1890, in *Letter from the Secretary of the Interior*, p. 9. Palmer also mentioned Low Dog, Blackfeet, and Pretty Hawk. Transcript of 16087, AGO, 1890, dated November 24, 1890, in NA Microfilm 983, "Sioux Campaign," 1890–91, Roll 1, p. 403.

3. Telegram, Palmer to Morgan, November 5, 1890 (first quotation); Palmer to Morgan, November 10, 1890 (second quotation); Palmer to Morgan, November 28, 1890; Palmer to Morgan, December 1, 1890, in *Letter from the Secretary of the Interior*, pp. 13, 15, 42, 46–47; Lee, *Fort Meade and the Black Hills*, p. 108.

4. *Omaha World-Herald*, November 21, 1890; *New York Herald*, November 24, 1890; *Omaha Bee*, November 21, 1890; *Deseret News*, December 6, 1890; *Chicago Tribune*, November 26 and 30, 1890; Palmer to Commissioner of Indian Affairs, December 1, 1890, NA Microfilm 983, "Sioux Campaign," 1890–91, Roll 1, pp. 438–40; *Chicago Tribune*, December 3, 1890; *Black Hills Daily Times*, December 5, 1890; *Army and Navy Register*, December 6, 1890. One of the purveyors of that knowledge was "Stepps the Cripple," a Shoshoni-Bannock man who had been with Chief Joseph's Nez Perces in 1877 but had fled into Canada, where he joined the Sioux with Sitting Bull and later surrendered with them in 1881.

5. Greene, *Yellowstone Command*, pp. 192–94, 196, 198, 208; Greene, *Nez Perce Summer*, pp. 262, 288, 316, 371. See Hump's account of his participation in the Lame Deer Fight, May 7, 1877, in Greene, *Lakota and Cheyenne*, pp. 145–47.

6. Miles to AG, December 10, 1890, NA Microfilm 983, "Sioux Campaign," 1890–91, Roll 1, p. 485; "Report of Major General Miles," September 14, 1891, in *Report of the Secretary of War, 1891*, p. 147 (first quotation); *Omaha World-Herald*, December 13, 1890 (second quotation); *Chicago Tribune*, December 15, 1890; *Army and Navy Journal*, February 14, 1891; *Army and Navy Register*, February 14, 1891; Richardson, "Some Observations upon the Sioux Campaign of 1890–91," p. 525; Mooney, "Ghost-Dance Religion," pp. 861–62; Ewers, *When the Army Still Wore Blue*, pp. 106–109; Johnson, *Unregimented General*, pp. 277–78; Lee, *Fort Meade and the Black Hills*, p. 108. Lieutenant Hale and Captain Ewers received citations for "specially meritorious acts" upon this occasion. Ewers's reads: "For gallant and meritorious services in traveling 60 miles through a country infested by hostile Indians, accompanied only by Lieutenant Hale . . . , and entering the camp of Chief Hump, an Ogallalla [*sic*] Sioux, on Cherry Creek, South Dakota, at the time when the Indians in the camp were in an excited and dangerous condition, pacifying the Indians, and changing their attitude from one of hostility and distrust to one of peace and confidence." General Orders, No. 100, Headquarters of the Army, Adjutant General's Office, Washington, December 17, 1891, *General Orders and Circulars, Adjutant General's Office, 1891*, p. 2 (also published in *Army and Navy Journal*, December 19, 1891).

7. Utley, *Lance and the Shield*, pp. 282–83, 286–92; *New York Weekly World*, January 8, 1890 (quotation); *Omaha World-Herald*, November 26, 1890. Collins, who came to know Sitting Bull well, quoted him as saying of the government: "They did not regard my wishes in selling the lands and opening the reservation. I will be chief. I can only be chief by keeping the people in a savage condition. If they become civilized, I shall go down." Olson, "Mary Clementine Collins, Dakotah Missionary," p. 77. Collins believed that Sitting Bull "and three or four other leaders" should be removed "away from the Indians and away from each other." "A few years in a prison learning English and a good trade would have a quieting influence upon the old man and his followers, whereas, if he dies, he will still be worshipped as a martyr." Ibid., pp. 77–78. For more on Collins, see Clow, "Autobiography of Mary C. Collins"; Jacobsen, "Mary Collins"; interview with Mary Collins, January 15, 1913, Camp Manuscripts, in Lilly Library, Box 6, Folder 3, Envelope 78, pp. 471–80.

8. Appointed a district farmer on the reservation to receive $10 per month, Sitting Bull, whose age was given as fifty-six, was described by a government Indian inspector as "no good" and as "stirring up a mess of some kind all the time." Report of Inspector James H. Cisney to the Bureau of Indian Affairs, September 23, 1890, McLaughlin Papers, Roll 34. Sitting Bull was dropped from the payroll on September 30, 1890.

McLaughlin to Morgan, October 1, 1890, McLaughlin Papers, Roll 34. For Weldon's anticipated role in the Sitting Bull community, see Weldon to Morgan, August 7, 1890. McLaughlin Papers, Roll 34. A comprehensive treatment of Weldon's work is found in Pollack, *Woman Walking Ahead;* but see also Pfaller, *James McLaughlin*, pp. 120–21, 126–27, 130–31.

9. McLaughlin to Morgan, October 17, 1890, McLaughlin Papers, Roll 35.

10. Ibid. (quotations); Utley, *Lance and the Shield*, pp. 285–86.

11. McLaughlin to Morgan, October 17, 1890, in *Report of the Commissioner of Indian Affairs, 1891*, 1:329–30; Utley, *Lance and the Shield*, pp. 287–89, 292–93; *Chicago Tribune*, November 24 and 29, 1890; *Chicago Inter-Ocean*, November 29, 1890; *New York Herald*, November 24, 1890; *Omaha World-Herald*, November 23, 1890; McLaughlin to Morgan, November 19, 1890, McLaughlin Papers, Roll 35 (this letter appeared in the *Chicago Tribune*, December 16, 1890); McLaughlin to Morgan, November 21, 1890 (quotation), McLaughlin Papers, Roll 35; McLaughlin to Morgan, December 4, 1890, ibid.

12. For Gall's position on the Ghost Dances and Sitting Bull, see Larson, *Gall*, pp. 212–15.

13. *Chicago Tribune*, November 14 and 30, 1890; *Washington Evening Star*, November 20, 1890; *Chadron Advocate*, November 21, 1890; *Omaha Bee*, November 21 and 24, 1890; Program, "Buffalo Bill's Wild West and Congress of Rough Riders of the World," 1893, C671, pp. 32–33, Nebraska State Historical Society Archives; *London Daily Chronicle*, November 25, 1890 (first quotation); arrest authorization and calling card, Miles to Cody, November 24, 1890 (second quotation), in the Buffalo Bill Museum and Grave Archives (see also Friesen, *Buffalo Bill*, p. 87).

14. Cody to Miles, December 3, 1890, Miles Collection.

15. Ibid. (quotations); Traub, "Sioux Campaign—Winter of 1890–'91," p. 59.

16. Telegram, McLaughlin to Morgan, November 28, 1890, *Letter from the Secretary of the Interior*, p. 11 (first quotation); telegram, Belt to McLaughlin, November 28, 1890, Frank Zahn Papers, State Historical Society of North Dakota (second quotation); telegram, Proctor to Miles, November 28, 1890, in *Letter from the Secretary of the Interior*, p. 12 (third quotation); telegram, Miles to Drum, November 30, 1890, in ibid. (fourth quotation).

17. Proctor to Miles, December 1, 1890, Miles Collection; also in *Letter from the Secretary of the Interior*, p. 12 (first quotation); "Report of Major General Miles," September 14, 1891, in *Report of the Secretary of War, 1891*, p. 145 (second quotation). See also Schofield to Miles, November 29, 1890, citing President Harrison's intention "not . . . to interfere with the military policy, but to prevent premature or inharmonious action." NA Microfilm 983, Roll 1, p. 347. Cody was accompanied on his mission by friends Frank ("White Beaver") Powell, Robert H. ("Pony Bob") Haslam, and John Keith, who knew Sitting Bull from the show. In common newspaper hyperbole of the day, no doubt further sensationalized by Cody himself, it was reported that "Buffalo Bill is sent out to get at the bottom of the Messiah craze, with almost unlimited authority to act." *New York Herald*, November 28, 1890. Indeed one officer at Fort Yates at the time believed that Cody was "merely making advertisement" with the project (Steele, "The Death of Sitting Bull," p. 6). Numerous accounts of the affair indicate that McLaughlin and Drum conspired to keep Cody intoxicated through the night with help from the post trader while McLaughlin pursued the countermanding of his orders and that the road meeting with Primeau with the message that Sitting Bull had

gone in by another route was only a ruse. Other first-person accounts of Cody's mission are McLaughlin, *My Friend the Indian*, pp. 209–11; Wilkinson, "The Death of Sitting Bull" (undated, but transcribed in July 1954) (a variant appears in Carroll, *The Arrest and Killing of Sitting Bull*, pp. 54–65); America Elmira Collins to Edith Warner Collins, December 9, 1890, America Elmira Collins Papers, MS 20255, State Historical Society of North Dakota. Newspaper reports appear in *Chicago Tribune*, November 28 and 30 and December 2 and 5, 1890; *Omaha Bee*, November 28, 1890; *Brooklyn Daily Eagle*, November 29 and December 1, 1890; *Chicago Inter-Ocean*, November 30, 1890; *Omaha Bee*, December 2 and 3, 1890; *Army and Navy Journal*, December 6, 1890; *Army and Navy Register*, December 13, 1890. Cody's melodramatic and embellished noncontemporary accounts appear in Cody, *True Tales of the Plains*, pp. 252–56; and Cody, *An Autobiography of Buffalo Bill*, pp. 304–13. They are replete with errors and Cody's self-aggrandizement (he referred to Drum as "Colonel Brown" throughout the latter rendering). Cody wrote that he later met President Harrison, who told him that "he had allowed himself to be persuaded against my mission in opposition to his own judgment, and said he was very sorry that he had not allowed me to proceed." Cody, *Autobiography*, p. 311.

18. *Brooklyn Daily Eagle*, November 29, 1890 (first, third, fourth, and fifth quotation); *Army and Navy Journal*, December 6, 1890 (second quotation). The call for Miles's removal appeared in the *Brooklyn Daily Eagle*, December 1, 1890. Secondary renditions of the Cody episode appear in Utley, *The Lance and the Shield*, pp. 293–95; Pfaller, *James McLaughlin*, pp. 139–46; *El Segundo Herald*, December 28, 1928 (reprinted as Brininstool, "Buffaloing Buffalo Bill"; and as Brininstool, "'Buffaloing' Buffalo Bill"); Vestal, *Sitting Bull*, pp. 280–82; Utley, *Last Days of the Sioux Nation*, pp. 123–26; account of John M. Carignan in Fiske, *Life and Death of Sitting Bull*, pp. 36–43; Russell, *The Lives and Legends of Buffalo Bill*, pp. 358–61; Johnson, *Unregimented General*, pp. 278–80; DeMontravel, *Hero to His Fighting Men*, pp. 200–202; Wooster, *Nelson A. Miles and the Twilight of the Frontier Army*, p. 181; Warren, *Buffalo Bill's America*, pp. 517–20; and Richardson, *Wounded Knee*, pp. 230–32. Cody was later paid $505.60 as reimbursement for his expenses. Russell, *Lives and Legends of Buffalo Bill*, p. 366.

19. Miles to Schofield, December 6, 1890, NA Microfilm 983, "Sioux Campaign," 1890–91, Roll 1, p. 448 (first quotation); Corbin to Adjutant General, U.S. Army, December 16, 1890, enclosing copy of his December 10 telegraph to Ruger, in ibid., p. 571 (second quotation).

20. See correspondence related to authority for the arrest in *Report of the Commissioner of Indian Affairs, 1891*, 1:333, and especially McLaughlin to Commissioner of Indian Affairs, December 24, 1890, in ibid., pp. 333–34; *Chicago Tribune*, December 2 and 6, 1890; *Omaha Bee*, December 2, 1890 (quotations) and December 12, 1890.

21. McLaughlin to Commissioner of Indians Affairs, December 24, 1890, in *Report of the Commissioner of Indian Affairs, 1891*, pp. 334–35 (including quotation). The text of John Carignan's letter along with McLaughlin's response, as well as McLaughlin's directive of December 14, are found in Vestal, *New Sources of Indian History*, pp. 13–16. Photos of the original English and Dakota-language messages as delivered and their envelopes appear in Vestal, *Sitting Bull*, opposite pp. 282 and 283. The postscript notation was occasionally omitted in later published renditions of McLaughlin's order, probably because of its inflammatory suggestion, and is only referenced contextually in the agent's report of August 26, 1891, in *Report of the Commissioner of Indian Affairs, 1891*, 1:325–40; it also appears in McLaughlin, *My Friend the Indian*, pp. 2187–18. See

also two slightly variant early drafts of the order written in McLaughlin's hand, each containing the postscript, in Mary Collins Family Papers, SDSHS, H80.14, Folder 15; and Hollow, "Sioux Ghost Dance of 1890," pp. 58–59. Just before the order went out, an effort orchestrated by Bishop Hare and Joseph DeLoria, Episcopalian prelate at Wakpala, that was to involve Gall, John Grass, and others to dissuade Sitting Bull from promoting the dances was underway; the plan was obviously abandoned with his imminent arrest. Camp interview with Joseph DeLoria, undated, Camp Manuscripts, Lilly Library, Box 5, Folder 12. Lakota sources maintain that Sitting Bull was not planning to leave Standing Rock Reservation. See the accounts of Four Blanket Woman and One Bull in Carroll, *Arrest and Killing of Sitting Bull*, pp. 70, 71.

22. Fechet's squadron consisted of Troops F (First Lieutenant Stephen L'H. Slocum and Second Lieutenant Matthew F. Steele) and G (First Lieutenant Enoch H. Crowder and Second Lieutenant Edward C. Brooks), Eighth Cavalry. Account of James Connelly in *Omaha World-Herald Sunday Magazine*, October 21, 1923).

23. Captain Fechet's report, December 17, 1890, in *Report of the Secretary of War, 1891*, pp. 197–99; Fort Yates Post Orders No. 247, December 14, 1890, in ibid., p. 199 (these orders were modified per discussion with Colonel Drum, as referenced in Fechet's report, p. 197); McLaughlin to Commissioner of Indian Affairs, December 24, 1890, in *Report of the Commissioner of Indian Affairs, 1891*, 1:336. "Rough Sketch of the Country Where the Fight between Indians and Indian Police Took Place," Standing Rock Agency, December 16, 1890; and untitled map of area where Sitting Bull was killed, showing roads, camps, streams, etc.; both in McLaughlin Papers, Roll 35; "Map of Standing Rock Reservation, Dak., Feby 10th 1890"; McLaughlin Papers, Roll 34; McLaughlin to Commissioner of Indian Affairs, December 24, 1890, in *Report of the Commissioner of Indian Affairs, 1891*, 1:335. Continued tipi use is noted in *Indians Taxed and Indians Not Taxed*, p. 524. For precise data locating Sitting Bull's cabin, see Otto P. Kopplin to Standing Rock Reservation Indian Agent James B. Kitch, November 9, 1917, and Kitch to Walter M. Camp, November 27, 1917, enclosing map of Township 20N, Range 25E, Black Hills Meridian, and sketch map of Township 20N, Range 25E, northeast quarter of southwest quarter, Section 26, in Ellison/Camp Papers, Box 2, FF 16 and OV FF 1; U.S. Geological Survey, Miscol NE Quadrangle, South Dakota–Corson County. For Bull Head's house, see Camp to Kopplin, December 3, 1917, enclosing Kopplin to Camp, December 6, 1917, in Ellison/Camp Papers, FF 149 (see also the maps in Robinson, *History of the Dakota or Sioux Indians*, pp. 279–80); "The Arrest and Killing of Sitting Bull, told by John Lone Man, one of the Indian Police ordered to arrest the Chief. Translated and Recorded by his relative, Robert P. Higheagle," in Vestal, *New Sources of Indian History* (quotation), p. 46 (hereinafter cited as Lone Man account). See also the map in Fechet, "The Capture of Sitting Bull," p. 191.

24. Comprehensive information including biographical data on the regular and special Indian policemen as well as the volunteer participants on the night of December 15, 1890, appears in Carroll, *Arrest and Killing of Sitting Bull*, pp. 157–76.

25. Lone Man account in Vestal, *New Sources of Indian History*, p. 50. Red Tomahawk kept the weapons, one a Model 1873 Springfield rifle (carbine?) said to have been taken from Custer's troops in 1876 and the other a Model 1873 Winchester, Serial No. 329499-B. A pistol of undetermined make and model and a trade knife with which Red Tomahawk claimed to have stabbed Sitting Bull were also taken. Red Tomahawk presented the firearms and knife to assistant secretary of the Interior Joseph M. Dixon in September 1924. Letter and affidavits reproduced in an article from an unidentified

newspaper, ca. March 1932, Vertical Files, "M-Indians-Tribes-Sioux," Montana Room, Parmly Billings Public Library. Red Tomahawk died in 1931 at the age of eighty-three.

26. Lone Man account in Vestal, *New Sources of Indian History*, pp. 50–51.

27. Ibid., p. 51.

28. Ibid.

29. Based on historic photos, Sitting Bull's cabin appears to have measured approximately 25 feet long by 15 feet wide with a slightly gabled roof. Like other cabins on the reservation, its roof was waterproofed with a layer of nonabsorbent clay soil atop which grass and weeds took root. The windows probably did not open, so ventilation was poor unless the door was opened. The floor was likely earthen. *Indians Taxed and Indians Not Taxed*, p. 524. Sitting Bull's horse is referenced in McLaughlin to Walter M. Camp, January 15, 1919, Ellison/Camp Papers, Box 1, FF 153. The description of activity in and around the cabin is based on the following sources: Lone Man account in Vestal, *New Sources of Indian History*, pp. 53 (quotation); McLaughlin to Morgan, December 24, 1890, in *Report of the Commissioner of Indian Affairs, 1891*, 1:335; affidavit of special policeman Shoots Walking, enclosed in Representative William Williamson to Doane Robinson, January 12, 1925, Sioux Miscellany Collection, SDSHS (hereinafter cited as Shoots Walking affidavit); Fred P. Caldwell to Walter M. Camp, June 6, 1914, Ellison/Camp Papers, Box 1, FF 130. In addition, this reconstruction has benefited from the following Lakota eyewitness sources: Lone Man account; "Story of Lone Man"; "Story of Tashima Topawin (Four Blanket Woman)"; account of Scares of Elk; and account of Mrs. One Bull, all ca. 1912 in Camp Manuscripts, Lilly Library, Box 5, Folder 1, 335–58, Envelope 41. These and other accounts by Gray Eagle, One Bull, Mrs. One Bull, Lone Man, Shoots Walking, Black Hills, Charging Bear, and Little Soldier are included in Carroll, *Arrest and Killing of Sitting Bull*, pp. 67–97. See also Francis Red Tomahawk (Red Tomahawk's son), "Sitting Bull's Life Ends in Tragedy"; Frank Bennett Fiske, "Spotted Bear," Frank Fiske Papers, Box 5, "Spotted Bear Folder," Archives and Manuscripts, State Historical Society of North Dakota. See additional material in *Oyate Ivechinka Woglakapi*, MS 868 (Regina Hayes); 869 (Philip Holy Rock); and 872 (William Thunder), pp. 53–55; account of One Bull in *Billings Gazette*, August 19, 1934. See also Robert High Eagle, "How Sitting Bull Was Made a Chief" (undated typescript), H. V. Johnson Cultural Center, pp. 35–36, 53–54. Readers might further consult the account by Sitting Bull's grandson: LaPointe, *Sitting Bull, His Life and Legacy*, pp. 102–12; as well as material online in the Alfred B. Welch Dakota Papers, at http://www.welchdakotapapers.com. Popular statements that Sitting Bull's horse from the Wild West show went into its old routine when the shooting erupted have been soundly discredited in Lemmons, "History by Unreliable Narrators."

There were charges that some of the policemen had been drinking before the encounter. Sitting Bull's wife, Four Robes, who was present during the affair, stated that "the police were intoxicated and used insulting language. They smelled of whiskey as though it had been spilled on their blouses." "Story of Tashima Topawin (Four Blanket Woman)," in Camp Manuscripts, Lilly Library, Box 5, Folder 1, Envelope 41, pp. 335–58. Private John F. Waggoner of the Eighth Cavalry, who was married to a mixed-blood Lakota woman and served under Fechet's command at the time, later reported that the police at the scene had been drinking. Campbell Papers, Box 104, Folder 14; Bettelyoun and Waggoner, *With My Own Eyes*, p. xix. See also Coleman, *Voices of Wounded Knee*, pp. 70, 86. But this is explicitly denied in the account of Black Hills contained in Carroll, *Arrest and Killing of Sitting Bull*, p. 90. Red Tomahawk claimed to have shot

Sitting Bull twice, "once through the left side and once through the head." *State-Line Herald* (North Lemmon, North Dakota), May 19, 1911. An undated imprint (probably ca. early 1930s) entitled "Red Tomahawk," composed by Frank Fiske (in Author's Collection) stated that the sergeant "carried a small revolver that he had taken from the chief. With this he shot Sitting Bull in the head." Private Alban Siegert, of Company G, Twelfth Infantry, viewed Sitting Bull's body and wrote: "A person could not recognize him at all so badly was he disfigured and all covered with blood." Siegert to "Dear friend Gaetke," December 17, 1890, Archives and Manuscripts Division, State Historical Society of North Dakota, ocm17998050. In 1914 a veteran soldier who examined Sitting Bull's remains soon after he was killed remembered that he had been shot in the left side as well as "in front and center of body about two inches below where neck joins body. I think it passed through lower part of collar bone [*sic*]. I am sure he was not shot in the head. His head was pounded all out of shape, but that happened after we got there. . . . I viewed the body of Sitting Bull on first reaching camp and outside of the two gunshot wounds he was not mutilated or pounded in the least. He had the forefinger of his left hand inserted full length in the wound in [his] side probable [*sic*] to stop the flow of blood." Fred P. Caldwell to Walter M. Camp, May 12, 1914 (and Camp to Caldwell, May 4, 1914), Ellison/Camp Papers, Box 1, FF 129. Someone who examined Sitting Bull's remains in 1908 at the time when the soldier dead were removed from the post cemetery to Keokuk, Iowa, following the closure of Fort Yates, also claimed that he had not been hit in the head: "The skull was never hit, or broken by any bullet, but it must have been battered with the butts of the guns, as it was in several pieces. . . . Some of the ribs had been broken and they looked as though they had been cut off by a shot, and also one of the shoulder blades had a hole through it which was no doubt done by a bullet." Frank J. Ecker to Walter M. Camp, May 25, 1914, Ellison/Camp Papers, Box 1, FF 128. (Ecker, who photographed the remains, further disproved a notion that the body had been destroyed by an application of quicklime. See Ecker to Camp, December 29, 1909, in Hammer, "Sitting Bull's Bones," pp. 7–8.) For a somewhat different configuration of persons on the scene at the killing of Sitting Bull, specifically countering the assertions of Red Tomahawk, see the Shoots Walking affidavit, which claimed that Bull Head alone killed Sitting Bull.

30. Wilkinson, "Death of Sitting Bull."

31. Ibid.

32. McLaughlin to Commissioner of Indian Affairs, December 16, 1890 (corrected version), McLaughlin Papers, Roll 35; McLaughlin to Commissioner of Indians Affairs, December 24, 1890, in *Report of the Commissioner of Indian Affairs, 1891*, 1:335–337; "Record of Events," Eighth Cavalry, December 1890, NA Microfilm 744; "Record of Events," Twelfth Infantry, December 1890, NA Microfilm 665. See also Brigadier General Thomas H. Ruger, "Report of Operations Relative to the Sioux Indians in 1890 and 1891," in *Report of the Secretary of War, 1891*, pp. 181–83. Eighth Cavalryman Albert J. Bloomer witnessed Hawk Man's arrival and his frantic yelling: "Hurry! Hurry! Indian police killed. Sitting Bull dead!" Quoted in a clipping from an unidentified newspaper, Rawlins Municipal Library; Bloomer account in Peterson, *The Battle of Wounded Knee*, pp. 13–14; Captain Fechet's report, December 17, 1890, in *Report of the Secretary of War, 1891*, pp. 197–99 (first quotation p. 198); Drum to AAG, Department of Dakota, February 27, 1891, in *Report of the Secretary of War, 1891*, pp. 194–97; "Names of the U.S. Indian Police . . . constituting the force which arrested 'Sitting Bull' . . ." compiled by McLaughlin, December 20, 1890, McLaughlin Papers, Roll 35; Drum to AAG,

Department of Dakota, December 17, 1890, Miles Collection; see also Fort Yates Post Orders No. 247, December 14, 1890, p. 199, Miles Collection. Lone Man's account in Vestal, *New Sources of Indian History*, pp. 48–54 (second quotation p. 54). The shirted warrior was Crow Woman. One of the policemen named Little Soldier shot at him too but also missed. Vestal, *New Sources of Indian History*, 33n. See also Drum to McLaughlin, February 26, 1891, with reference to this incident, in ibid. For the treatment of Sitting Bull's body, see Shoots Walking affidavit, pp. 2–3 (third quotation p. 2); Fred P. Caldwell to Walter M. Camp, May 12, 1914, and Camp to Caldwell, May 4, 1914, and May 18, 1914, Ellison/Camp Papers, Box 1, FF 129.

33. Indian recollections incorporated here, beyond those already cited, include Lee, "Messiah Craze and Wounded Knee," 8 (account of Clarence Grey Eagle). Other first-person accounts on which this passage is based are Steele, "The Death of Sitting Bull," pp. 7–11; the autobiographical account of Matthew F. Steele and interview in Carroll, *Arrest and Killing of Sitting Bull*, pp. 30–37; McLaughlin, *My Friend the Indian*, pp. 211–21; McLaughlin, *Account of the Death of Sitting Bull;* Fechet, "The True Story of the Death of Sitting Bull" (1898), pp. 182–89 (reprinted in Cozzens, *Eyewitnesses to the Indian Wars*); Fechet account in *Chicago Inter-Ocean*, November 24, 1900; Fechet, "Capture of Sitting Bull"; McLaughlin to Mary Collins, December 26, 1890; and Rev. George W. Reed to Collins, December 16, 1890, both in Mary Collins Family Papers, SDSHS, H80.14, Folder 15; Albert Bloom account in clipping from an unidentified newspaper, Vertical Files, Rawlins Municipal Library; account of John F. Waggoner, Twelfth Infantry soldier, undated (ca. 1930s), in Mason, "Chief Sitting Bull's Latter Days" (undated typescript, in Box 3473A, Folder H74.115, containing James McLaughlin letter, 1920), SDSHS; Von Ostermann, *The Last Sioux Indian War*, pp. 2–11; Matthew F. Steele, "Arrest and Death of Sitting Bull," in Greene, *Indian War Veterans*, pp. 171–72; Private Alban Siegert to "Dear friend Gaetke," December 17, 1890, Archives and Manuscripts, State Historical Society of North Dakota, ocm17998050. Dr. Chapin's treatment of the wounded in Lieutenant Matthew F. Steele to his mother, January 31, 1891, in Matthew Forney Steele Papers, Archives and Manuscripts, State Historical Society of North Dakota, MS 10115. The scene of Sitting Bull's cabin following the engagement is described by Sergeant George B. DuBois, Troop F, Eighth Cavalry, in "Two Letters Regarding Fort Yates and Sitting Bull's Death," in Greene, *Indian War Veterans*, p. 176 (originally published in *Winners of the West*, March 30, 1935). The seven people from the Sitting Bull community who were killed during the confrontation, including Crow Foot, remained unburied until Congregationalist missionary the Reverend Thomas L. Riggs and a party went out from the agency to do it. America Elmira Collins to Edith Warner Collins, January 13, 1891, America Elmira Collins Papers, 1890–91, Small Manuscripts Collection, MS 20255, State Historical Society of North Dakota. A witness to the burials stated that they occurred about a week later. "We . . . found the seven men in a little cabin. Two Crow and I dugged [*sic*] a grave large enough for all seven men, lined the grave with a tent and hauled the seven men one by one to the grave and covered them with another tent and covered that with dirt, after which Rev. Riggs said a short prayer." Simon J. Kirk Manuscript, H75.176, Folder 1, Box 3543A, SDSHS. Walter Camp wrote that "the Inds killed with Sitting Bull 12/15/1890 are buried just west of heap of stones about 50 ft. at edge of low bank" in the vicinity of the former location of Sitting Bull's cabin. Camp Manuscripts in Lilly Library, Box 6, Folder 5, 471–480, Envelope 80. A hearsay account of Sitting Bull's death, related by his brother-in-law Green Eagle to Northern Cheyenne James Tangled

Hair, is found in Marquis and Limbaugh, *Cheyenne and Sioux*, pp. 43–45. Readers might also consult the array of pertinent primary data presented in Coleman, *Voices of Wounded Knee*, pp. 180–224.

Contemporary newspaper accounts covering aspects of Sitting Bull's death and the subsequent action, all erroneous in many respects, appear in *Omaha Bee*, December 16 and 18, 1890; *New York Times*, December 16, 1890; *Brooklyn Daily Eagle*, December 16 and 17, 1890; *New York Weekly Witness*, December 17 and 24, 1890; *Omaha World-Herald*, December 17, 18, and 20, 1890; *Chicago Tribune*, December 17, 1890; *Hot Springs Daily Star*, December 17, 1890; *Black Hills Daily Times*, December 18, 1890; *New York World*, December 18, 1890; *London Daily Telegraph*, December 18 and 19, 1890; *Black Hills Journal*, December 28, 1890; *Chicago Inter-Ocean*, December 28, 1890. Secondary treatments valuable to this rendering are found in Utley, *Lance and the Shield*, pp. 291–307; Anderson, *Sitting Bull and the Paradox of Lakota Nationhood*, pp. 161–68; Pfaller, *James McLaughlin*, pp. 146–65; Vestal, *Sitting Bull*, pp. 282–314; Ostler, *Plains Sioux and U.S. Colonialism*, pp. 320–26; Pollack, *Woman Walking Ahead*, pp. 147–52; Mooney, "Ghost-Dance Religion," pp. 855–60; Falconer, "The Death of Sitting Bull," pp. 18–19, 22; Robinson, *History of the Dakota or Sioux Indians*, pp. 474–82; Hyde, *Sioux Chronicle*, pp. 288–90; Utley, *Frontier Regulars*, pp. 404–405; DeLand, "The Sioux Wars," pp. 455–63; Traub, "Sioux Campaign—Winter of 1890–'91," pp. 59–61; Traub, "The First Act of the Last Sioux Campaign"; Larson, "A Victor in Defeat," p. 44; Wiltsey, "Death on the North Plains," pp. 31–33; Robinson, *Doane Robinson's Encyclopedia of South Dakota*, pp. 867–71; A. T. Lea, "The Killing of Sitting Bull" (undated typescript ca. December 1910), A. T. Lea Papers, Item No. 6, Reg. No. 4026.6054, Archives, Gilcrease Museum; Johnson, *Life of Sitting Bull*, pp. 179–88; Boyd, *Recent Indian Wars*, pp. 240–42, 247–48; and Northrup, *Indian Horrors*, pp. 516–19.

34. Telegram, McLaughlin to Commissioner of Indian Affairs, December 15, 1890, in U.S. Congress, Senate, Committee on Indian Affairs, *Letter from the Secretary of the Interior, Relative to Granting Pensions and Medals*, pp. 8–9.

35. Miles to AG, December 15, 1890, NA Microfilm 983, "Sioux Campaign," 1890–91, Roll 1 (first quotation), p. 517; McLaughlin to Morgan, December 16, 1890, McLaughlin Papers, Microfilm Roll 35 (second quotation); Fechet, "True Story of the Death of Sitting Bull" (1898), p. 189.

36. Adapted from listing in *Report of the Commissioner of Indian Affairs, 1891*, 1:338; and McLaughlin, *Account of the Death of Sitting Bull*.

37. McLaughlin to Commissioner of Indian Affairs, December 19, 1890, McLaughlin Papers, Roll 35; Siegert letter, December 17, 1890; Albert Boomer account, in unidentified newspaper, Rawlins Municipal Library; Shufeldt, "Relics of Sitting Bull"; Fiske, *Life and Death of Sitting Bull*, pp. 52–57, including Edward Forte to Fiske, November 7, 1932, pp. 53–56; *Omaha World-Herald*, December 20, 1890; *London Daily Telegraph*, December 19, 1890; *White Pine Cone*, January 2, 1891. See also the account of John F. Waggoner, soldier at Fort Yates, who claimed that he was present at Sitting Bull's burial and that a mixture of muriatic acid and chloride of lime was poured into the casket, a statement seemingly unsubstantiated by later evidence. Waggoner's account is found in Mason, "Chief Sitting Bull's Latter Days." Denial of this claim appears in Fred P. Caldwell to Walter M. Camp, May 18, 1914, and Caldwell to Camp, June 6, 1914, Ellison/Camp Papers, Box 1, FF 130. The monument at the policemen's grave carries an inscription penned by McLaughlin: "These were killed at Grand River,

Standing Rock Indian Reservation Dec. 15, 1890 in a battle with hostile Indians while arresting the noted Chief Sitting Bull who was also killed in the fight. 43 policemen were opposed by 160 armed fanatical Ghost Dancers. This monument is erected by admirers of the loyalty and bravery of the U.S. Indian Police on that occasion." Camp Manuscripts in Lilly Library, Box 5, Folder 12. See the list of all Indian policemen involved in the arrest and killing of Sitting Bull in appendix C. An assemblage of items in the Heritage Center of the State Historical Society of North Dakota reflects the death of Sitting Bull, including a muslin ghost shirt attributed to him. Other artifacts include a Model 1859 U.S. Army cavalry sword with a bulky replaced wood grip and red trade cloth ribbon; the blade bearing Sitting Bull's rudely scratched signature; the police badges of Lieutenant Bull Head and Sergeant Little Eagle; a knife case that belonged to Spotted Horn Bull, who was killed in the Sitting Bull fight; two muslin ghost shirts and a shield collected at Sitting Bull's camp after his death on December 15, 1890; and the marble headstone from his grave, inscribed "Sitting Bull, Died Dec. 15, 1890. Chief of the Hunkpapa Sioux." Sitting Bull's grave, with a wooden marker, remained the only burial in the post cemetery after 1908, when the other dead were disinterred and removed to Keokuk National Cemetery. In 1921 the Standing Rock superintendent installed a four-by-eight-foot concrete slab over the grave, with a monument reading "Sitting Bull Died Dec. 15, 1890." There was interest in Bismarck for the chief to repose there. But when relatives requested in the 1920s that Sitting Bull be reburied at Grand River, a bill to that end introduced in the South Dakota legislature failed in committee. In 1953 the holy man's remains were controversially relocated to the west bank of the Missouri River opposite Mobridge, South Dakota, where a seven-ton granite monument carved by sculptor Korczak Ziolkowski now stands atop his grave. Standing Rock Superintendent Eugene D. Mossman to Commissioner of Indian Affairs, August 22, 1922, E. D. Mossman Papers, 1925–53, ocm17868968, Box 1, 280502.2Y, State Historical Society of North Dakota; Fiske, *Life and Death of Sitting Bull*, p. 61; *Mobridge South Dakota Chamber of Commerce 2006–2007 Directory of Information*, p. 38. See also Collins, "The Fight for Sitting Bull's Bones"; DeWolf, *The Saga of Sitting Bull's Bones;* and Edman, "Dakota Images: Sitting Bull." For a recent perspective, see *New York Times*, January 28, 2007.

In the flurry of public interest that followed Sitting Bull's death it was perhaps natural for his Grand River log cabin to draw notice. Almost immediately efforts began to secure the building and other personal effects of the medicine man for exhibition purposes, and the cabin ultimately appeared at the 1893 World's Fair in Chicago. Representatives Henry C. Hansbrough and Martin N. Johnson to Secretary of the Interior Noble, January 21, 1891; Senator Lyman R. Casey to Morgan, February 14, 1891; Johnson to Noble, March 13, 1891; and Acting Secretary of the Interior George Chandler to Commissioner of Indian Affairs Morgan, May 13, 1891. See especially McLaughlin to Morgan, March 6, 1891, stating that the cabin should be "purchased and exhibited not because it was Sitting Bull's house, but that the Indian police as officers of law and order made such a gallant and determined stand in upholding the government against their own race and kindred on the morning of Decr 15, 1890." These documents are in the McLaughlin Papers, Roll 34. In 1894 the cabin was at Coney Island, New York. Carignan to Walter M. Camp, August 1910, Camp Manuscripts, Lilly Library, Box 5, Folder 12, 412–16, Envelope 65.

38. *Chicago Tribune*, December 17, 1890; *Hot Springs Daily Star*, December 17, 1890; First Lieutenant Marion P. Maus, aide-de-camp, to Ruger, December 27, 1890,

Miles Collection; *Army and Navy Journal*, February 7, 1891; Noble to McLaughlin, December 30, 1890 (first quotation), to which McLaughlin complied in McLaughlin to Noble, December 30, 1890; Noble to Commissioner of Indian Affairs, December 31, 1890 (second quotation); McLaughlin to Morgan, January 23, 1891 (third quotation); all in McLaughlin Papers, Roll 35.

39. For the NIDA's concern that the remains of Sitting Bull had been desecrated, see Bland to Commissioner Morgan, December 24, 1890; McLaughlin to Commissioner Morgan, January 27, 1891; both in McLaughlin Papers, Roll 35; and Pollack, *Woman Walking Ahead*, pp. 153–56 and respective notes. The newspapers reporting Sitting Bull's demise acknowledged the coincident death in New Haven, Connecticut, on December 16 of Major General Alfred H. Terry, who had commanded field operations against Sitting Bull's Lakotas in 1876 and had headed the commission seeking the Lakotas' return from Canada in 1877. Terry had retired from the army in 1888. *Chicago Tribune*, December 17, 1890. For the award of pensions and medals, see McLaughlin to Commissioner Morgan, March 3, 1891, McLaughlin Papers, Roll 35; McLaughlin to Ruger, December 22, 1890. NA Microfilm 983, "Sioux Campaign," 1890–91, Roll 1, p. 778; Ruger to AG, January 1, 1890, ibid.; U.S. Congress, Senate, Committee on Pensions, *Families of Certain Indian Policemen*, pp. 1–12; *Washington Post*, May 24, 1908; U.S. Congress, House, Committee on Appropriations, *Medals for the Captors of Sitting Bull*.

40. *Army and Navy Journal*, December 20, 1890; *Omaha World-Herald*, December 17, 1890; *Omaha Bee*, December 17, 1890; *Harper's Weekly*, December 27, 1890 (first quotation); Koupal, *Our Landlady*, p. 147 (second and third quotations). See also Koupal, "On the Road to Oz," p. 93.

41. *Chicago Tribune*, February 4, 1891 (first quotation); *New York Times*, March 8, 1891 (second quotation).

42. *Chicago Tribune*, December 17, 1890.

43. U.S. Congress, House, Committee on Military Affairs, *Chief Sitting Bull* (1890); U.S. Congress, House, Committee on Military Affairs, *Chief Sitting Bull* (1891).

CHAPTER 10. PURSUIT

1. Telegram, Miles to AG, December 14, 1890, NA Microfilm 983, "Sioux Campaign," 1890–91, Roll 1, p. 543; Brooke to AAG, Division of the Missouri, March 2, 1891, ibid., pp. 1682–83; *Omaha Bee*, December 17, 1890 (quotation); untitled chronological abstract of correspondence pertaining to Major General Miles's operations against the Sioux Indians in South Dakota, December 14, 1890, to January 30, 1891, p. 1, Miles Collection (hereinafter cited as "Abstract of Correspondence"); Whitside to wife, December 16, 1890 and December 18, 1890, Whitside Papers; *Army and Navy Journal*, December 20 and 27, 1890. *Army and Navy Journal*, December 20, 1890, tentatively outlined Brooke's projected movement as follows: "At the date of our latest advices from the Indian country about 150 Indian warriors were located in the vicinity of the mouth [head] of Battle Creek on a high table land, commanded by a spur running toward the Cheyenne. Col. Carr was ordered to occupy this spur, and Col. Forsyth was expected to move in from White River Dec. 17, cover all points and drive the Indians towards Battle Creek or down the trail on Bad Water, about 20 miles south from Cheyenne River. The forces under Col. Forsyth consisted of the 7th Cavalry (eight troops),

the battalion 9th Cavalry (four troops), three Hotchkiss guns and one 3.2-in. field gun of Light Battery E, 1st Artillery, and 100 Indian scouts. He was ordered to demand the surrender of the Indians without conditions and, in the event of a refusal, to attack and, if possible, to destroy them. Prisoners were to be sent to Pine Ridge. It was hoped that Col. Carr would be able to co-operate with him from the north, covering from the north and east the road extending across the Bad Lands from the mouth of Wounded Knee Creek to Cheyenne River near the mouth of Rapid Creek. Col. Sanford, of the 9th Cavalry, was ordered to co-operate from the west, and he was at last accounts somewhere near the junction of White Clay Creek with the White River. This movement against the hostiles was suspended on Dec. 18 to give the friendly chiefs one more opportunity to bring in their people."

2. Telegram, Miles to Brooke, December 16, 1890 (from Long Pine, Nebr.) (first quotation); telegram, Miles to Brooke, December 16, 1890 (on train) (second and third quotations); telegram, Miles to Brooke, December 16, 1890 (from Norfolk Junction, Nebr.) (fourth and fifth quotations); all in NA, RG 393, part 1, Entry 2540, Military Division of the Missouri, Letters Sent by Headquarters in the Field, 1890–91. General Ruger late on December 15 wired Brooke that Miles had advised a suspension of Brooke's movement and notified Carr of the same. Telegram, Ruger to Brooke, December 15, 1890; and telegram, Ruger to Brooke, December 15, 1890; both in Brooke Papers, Sioux Campaign 1890–91, vol. 1, p. 344. Miles next outlined to Brooke a bizarre peace plan that he contrived, which would entail sending hostages to Omaha or some other place on a rotation basis to guarantee the good behavior of the different bands. Among other things, it also called for enlisting Indians in the army and hiring them in civilian jobs. "Should they commit any crimes and remain defiant and hostile they will be pursued by the troops until they are destroyed or entirely removed from the country."

3. Telegram, Miles to Brooke, December 16, 1890, NA, RG 393, part 1, Entry 3782, Department of the Platte, Telegrams Received by Headquarters, 1890–91, Box 2; Brooke to Miles, December 17, 1890, NA, RG 393, PI 172, Entry 3722, Department of the Platte, Letters Sent, 1866–98, vol. 19, pp. 87–88 (first quotation); telegram, Miles to Brooke, December 20, 1890, NA, RG 393, part 1, Entry 3782, Department of the Platte, Telegrams Received by Headquarters, 1890–91, Box 2 (second quotation).

4. Brooke to Ruger, December 16, 1890, Brooke Papers, Sioux Campaign 1890–91, vol. 1, p. 347 (first quotation); Brooke to wife, December 15, 1890 (second quotation); and Brooke to wife, December 17, 1890 (third quotation); both in Brooke Papers, Box 8, Folder 4. For more specifics of Brooke's plan for attacking the Stronghold, see Brooke to Miles, December 16, 1890, Brooke Papers, Sioux Campaign 1890–91, vol. 1, pp. 369–70.

5. Ruger to AG, October 19, 1891, "Report of Operations Relative to the Sioux Indians in 1890 and 1891," in *Report of the Secretary of War, 1891*, pp. 185–86; Brooke to wife, December 17, 1890, Brooke Papers, Box 8, Folder 4 (first quotation); Brooke to AAG, Division of the Missouri, March 2, 1891, NA Microfilm 983, "Sioux Campaign," 1890–91, Roll 1, pp. 1682–83; *Omaha Bee*, December 17 and 18, 1890; *Black Hills Journal*, December 18, 1890; *Deseret News*, January 3, 1891; "Abstract of Correspondence," pp. 1–2; Miles to Brooke, December 16, 1890; Miles to Day, December 18, 1890 (second quotation); both in NA, RG 393, part 1, Entry 2540, Military Division of the Missouri, Letters Sent by Headquarters in the Field, 1890–91.

6. *Black Hills Journal*, December 24 and 25, 1890; *Omaha Bee*, December 19 and 20, 1890; *Omaha World-Herald*, December 20, 1890; *Chicago Inter-Ocean*, December 20,

1890; *White Pine Cone*, December 26, 1890; "Report of Brig. Gen. Merritt," September 1, 1891, in *Report of the Secretary of War, 1891*, p. 168; "Abstract of Correspondence," pp. 2 (quotation), 3, 9; *Chicago Tribune*, December 17, 1890; *Army and Navy Journal*, December 27, 1890, and January 24, 1891; *Army and Navy Register*, December 27, 1890; Wilkinson, "The Death of Sitting Bull"; Albert Bloomer account in Peterson, *The Battle of Wounded Knee*, p. 14; "Tabular Statement of Campaigns, Expeditions, and Scouts made from Fort Keogh, Mont. During the quarter ending December 31st, 1890" (also for quarter ending March 31, 1891), NA, RG 393, part 1, Entry 1204, Tabular Statements for Campaigns, Expeditions, and Scouts, 1883–93; "Service of Troop H, 8th Cav., Sioux War, 1890–1891," Colonel Joseph A. Gaston to the Adjutant General, U.S. Army, December 31, 1926, original typescript copy in Author's Collection; Oskaloosa M. Smith, "The Twenty-Second Regiment of Infantry," in Rodenbough and Haskin, *Army of the United States*, p. 690; Robert P. Page Wainwright, "The First Regiment of Cavalry," in Rodenbough and Haskin, *Army of the United States*, p. 172; Smith, Wassell, and Appleton, *History of the Twenty-Second United States Infantry*, p. 14.

7. See Miles's interview comments in the *Black Hills Journal*, December 18, 1890, and the *Omaha Bee*, December 18, 1890. Miles's quotations regarding Sioux lands appear in telegram, Miles to Schofield, December 19, 1890, NA Microfilm 983, "Sioux Campaign," 1890–91, Roll 1, p. 585; DeMontravel, *A Hero to His Fighting Men*, p. 203; Miles to Mary Miles, December 20, 1890, in Johnson, *Unregimented General*, p. 282 (quotation).

8. Brooke to wife, December 20, 1890, Brooke Papers, Box 8, Folder 4; *Army and Navy Journal*, December 20, 1890 (quotations); Alberts, *Brandy Station to Manila Bay*, pp. 178, 284–85. For Miles's presidential interests, see DeMontravel, *Hero to His Fighting Men*, pp. 198, 208, 324, 331–32, 340, 361–62; and Wooster, *Nelson A. Miles and the Twilight of the Frontier Army*, pp. 181–82, 238–39, 243, 251–53. General Merritt knew full well Miles's difficult history with Oliver O. Howard over credit for closing the Nez Perce War in 1877, notwithstanding his sly hint. His assessment of Miles's nonuse of troops from Major General Howard's Division of the Atlantic was to an extent justified.

9. *New York Times*, December 19, 1890; *White Pine Cone*, December 26, 1890; *Chicago Inter-Ocean*, December 20, 1890; Agent Palmer to Morgan, December 17, 1890, NA Microfilm 983, "Sioux Campaign," 1890–91, Roll 1, pp. 623–24; Palmer to Morgan, December 22, 1890, ibid.; telegram, Ruger to AG, December 23, 1890, enclosing Hurst to Ruger, December 22, 1890; Ruger to AAG, Division of the Missouri, March 26, 1891; all in McLaughlin Papers, Roll 35; Hale to Post Adjutant, Fort Bennett, December 26, 1890, in *Report of the Secretary of War, 1891*, pp. 200–201; Hurst to AAG, Department of Dakota, January 9, 1891, in ibid., pp. 201–202 (quotations); "Record of Events," Twelfth Infantry, December 1890, NA Microfilm 665, Roll 138; Palmer to Morgan, December 22, 1890, NA Microfilm 983, "Sioux Campaign," 1890–91, Roll 1, p. 601; *Army and Navy Journal*, December 27, 1890; Anderson, "History of the Cheyenne River Indian Agency," pp. 502–503; Abbot, "Twelfth Regiment of Infantry," p. 573; Robinson, *Doane Robinson's Encyclopedia of South Dakota*, pp. 872–74; Lee, "Messiah War on Cheyenne River," p. 4; Robinson, *History of the Dakota or Sioux Indians*, pp. 484–86.

10. Figures for the Hunkpapas who submitted differ confusingly among sources. The number given here is taken from Hale's report, in *Report of the Secretary of War, 1891*, p. 201. Other Hunkpapas from Standing Rock also joined at Fort Bennett, until 227 were transferred to Fort Sully on December 30. Hurst's report in ibid., p. 202. See also Brigadier General Thomas H. Ruger, "Report of Operations Relative to the Sioux

Indians in 1890 and 1891," in ibid., p. 184. Background on Big Foot is drawn from miscellaneous notes in the Camp Manuscripts, Lilly Library, Box 4, Folder 4, Envelope 5, pp. 233–43, (Cheyenne River, 1915); Box 4, Folder 14, Envelope 35, pp. 307–314 (Cheyenne River, 1916); Box 5, Folder 1 (1912); Box 6, Folder 6, Envelope 81, pp. 485–487 (Cheyenne River, 1912); High Eagle, "How Sitting Bull Was Made a Chief," p. 34; "Big Foot, Miniconjou," http://www.americantribes.com/Lakota/BIO/Bigfoot -Miniconjou.htm; Kappler, *Indian Affairs*, 2:1005. Greene, *Yellowstone Command*, pp. 99, 108, 109, 150, 151, 260 n. 39, 262 n. 4, 264 n. 8, 265 n. 14, 267 n. 23; Hyde, *Sioux Chronicle*, p. 258. Miniconjou John Long told Camp that Spotted Elk (Big Foot) was not present at the Little Bighorn in 1876. Camp Manuscripts, Lilly Library, Box 4, Folder 14. In 1921 Mrs. James Pipe on Head told James McLaughlin that Big Foot was sixty-five years old at the time of Wounded Knee. James McLaughlin to Commissioner of Indian Affairs Cato Sells, January 12, 1921, p. 10, Wounded Knee Compensation Papers, SDSHS, Box 3564A, H76.24, Folder 14.

11. Sumner had been charged to protect settlers in the vicinity while watching over Big Foot; his command consisted of Troops C, D, and I, Eighth Cavalry; Company F, Third Infantry; and two Hotchkiss guns.

12. The delegates sent from Big Foot to the Sitting Bull refugees were Black Coyote, Iron Hail, Pretty Hawk, Henry One Eye, Daniel Horn Cloud, Bear-Part-Body, Brown Turtle, Brown Beaver, Wing, and Bear-Comes-and-Lies Down. Joseph Horn Cloud's statement in "The Truth of the Wounded Knee Massacre," p. 244 (originally published in the *Lincoln Daily Star*, January 25, 1914). Captain Philip Reade of the Third Infantry, who was present, recalled part of Big Foot's conference with Sumner on December 21. When the chief inquired of Sumner, "Why do you come among my people armed?" Sumner responded: "Sitting Bull was a great chief, and he was killed while resisting arrest. You are a great chief. You have been to Washington and seen the power of the country. Why are you sheltering refugees from among Sitting Bull's braves? And why are you moving East? It is my business to go armed. You, too, are armed, but the great chief, General Miles, says you must keep peace." *Army and Navy Register*, May 16, 1891. For the movements of Merriam and Sumner, see Merriam to AAG, Department of Dakota, January 30, 1891, in *Report of the Secretary of War, 1891*, pp. 203–23; and particularly the following subordinate communications within that document: Ruger to Merriam, December 18, 1890, p. 204; Miles to Commanding Officer, Fort Bennett, December 24, 1890, pp. 209–10; Merriam to Miles, December 25, 1890, p. 210; Sumner to Merriam, December 26, 1890; Regimental Returns of the Seventh Infantry, December 1890, NA Microfilm 665, Roll 84; Regimental Returns of the Eighth Cavalry, December 1890, NA Microfilm 744, Roll 82. See also Maus to Sumner, December 17, 1890, NA, RG 393, part 1, Entry 2540, Military Division of the Missouri, Letters Sent by Headquarters in the Field, 1890–91; and "Abstract of Correspondence," p. 2 (quotation). See also telegram, Sumner to Miles, December 18, 1890, p. 229; Sumner to AAG, Department of Dakota, December 18, 1890, p. 230; Sumner to Carr, December 19, 1890, p. 231; Maus to Sumner, December 23, 1890, pp. 231–32; Sumner to Miles, December 21, 1890 (two dispatches), p. 232; Sumner to Miles, December 22, 1890 (four dispatches), p. 233; and Sumner to Miles, December 23, 1890 (two dispatches), p. 234.

13. Sumner to AAG, Department of Dakota, February 3, 1891, in *Report of the Secretary of War, 1891*, pp. 223–28. Sumner reported: "I concluded that one of two things must happen—I must either consent to their going into their village or bring on a fight; and, if the latter, must be the aggressor, and, if the aggressor, what possible reason could I produce for making an attack on peaceable, quiet Indians on their reservation and

at their homes, killing perhaps many of them, and offering, without any justification, the lives of many officers and enlisted men." Ibid., p. 225. See also Brigadier General Thomas H. Ruger, "Report of Operations Relative to the Sioux Indians in 1890 and 1891," in *Report of the Secretary of War, 1891*, pp. 184–85. Background on Sumner is found in Heitman, *Historical Record and Dictionary of the United States Army*, 1:936. For a personal version of these events, see the account of Captain Edward A. Godwin, Troop D, Eighth Cavalry, in Von Ostermann, *Last Sioux Indian War*, pp. 12–19. Sumner's father, as colonel of the First Cavalry, had fought in the army's first major encounter with Cheyenne Indians in 1857. See Chalfant, *Cheyennes and Horse Soldiers*, pp. 174–219.

14. Interview, Andrew Good Thunder, July 12, 1912, Camp Manuscripts, Lilly Library, Box 6, Folder 14, Envelope 90, pp. 521–32 (quotation). Another detailed account is found in "Joseph Horn Cloud's Interview," in Jensen, *Voices of the American West*, 1:193–94.

15. Telegram, Miles to AG, Washington, D.C., December 22, 1890, NA Microfilm 983, "Sioux Campaign," 1890–91, Roll 1, p. 604; "Abstract of Correspondence," p. 8; telegram, Maus to Brooke, December 21, 1890, NA, RG 393, part 1, Entry 3782, Department of the Platte, Telegrams Received by Headquarters, 1890–91, Box 2; *Omaha Bee*, December 23, 1890 (quotation).

16. Sumner to Miles, December 22, 1890, in *Report of the Secretary of War, 1891*, p. 233 (first quotation); Sumner to Miles, December 23, 1890, in ibid., p. 234 (second quotation); Miles to Sumner, December 24, 1890, in ibid., pp. 234–35 (third quotation).

17. "Statement of Felix Benoit," January 18, 1891, in ibid., pp. 237–38 (first quotation); Sumner to Merriam, December 27, 1890, in ibid., pp. 210–11 (second quotation); telegram, Sumner to Miles, December 24, 1890, NA, RG 393, part 1, Entry 1167, Department of Dakota, Letters Sent, 1890–1904; Miles to Sumner, December 24, 1890, in *Report of the Secretary of War, 1891*, p. 235 (third quotation); Merriam to AAG, Department of Dakota, January 30, 1891, in ibid., pp. 210, including Sumner to Merriam, December 27, 1890, pp. 210–11; Maus to Merriam, December 27, 1890, in *Report of the Secretary of War, 1891*, p. 212 (fourth quotation); Merriam to Sumner, December 28, 1890, in *Report of the Secretary of War, 1891*, p. 213; Miles to Brooke, December 24, 1890, RG 393, part 1, Entry 3782, Department of the Platte, Telegrams Received by Headquarters, 1890–91, Box 2 (fifth quotation).

18. Maus to Sumner, December 27, 1890, p. 214 (first quotation); Sumner to Merriam, December 26, 1890, p. 215; Miles to Sumner, December 24, 1890, p. 235 (second quotation); all in *Report of the Secretary of War, 1891*; and Miles to AG, December 24, 1890, NA Microfilm 983, "Sioux Campaign," 1890–91, Roll 1, p. 608 (third quotation). For Sumner's movement and its result, see also *Black Hills Journal*, December 25, 1890; *Army and Navy Register*, December 27, 1890; Mooney, "Ghost-Dance Religion," pp. 864–65; Allen, *From Fort Laramie to Wounded Knee*, pp. 183–85; Traub, "Sioux Campaign—Winter of 1890–'91," pp. 62–66; Shockley, "The Affair at Wounded Knee," pp. 39–41; Utley, *Last Days of the Sioux Nation*, p. 186ff.; Lee, *Fort Meade and the Black Hills*, pp. 112–14; Hall, *To Have This Land*, pp. 120–22; Lee, "Messiah War on Cheyenne River," pp. 4–7; and Hyde, *Sioux Chronicle*, pp. 294–97; Ostler, *Plains Sioux and U.S. Colonialism*, pp. 328–30; and Andersson, *Lakota Ghost Dance of 1890*, pp. 150–53.

19. Sumner to AAG, Department of Dakota, February 3, 1891, in *Report of the Secretary of War, 1891*, p. 227 (first quotation); Horn Cloud's statement of October 24, 1913, in "Truth of the Wounded Knee Massacre," pp. 243–44; *Washington Evening*

Star, January 28, 1891 (comments by Long Bull and Hump); Good Thunder interview (fourth quotation). See also Edward Ashley interview notes, July 10, 1914, Walter Mason Camp Papers, Brigham Young University (hereinafter cited as Camp Papers, BYU), Box 4 (Microfilm Roll 3). John Dunn's report of his meeting with Big Foot on December 23 indicated that they had mentioned fighting in a contextual sense but not literally or necessarily imminently. Dunn's statement, January 17, 1891, in *Report of the Secretary of War, 1891*, p. 236. Some thought that Big Foot's intensifying illness, which evolved into pneumonia, let him be swayed by younger men who wanted to unite with the Ghost Dancers on Pine Ridge Reservation. Lee, "Messiah War on Cheyenne River," p. 7. For more on the discussions among the Indians on their decision to leave, including Big Foot's procrastination, see "Joseph Horn Cloud's Interview," in Jensen, *Voices of the American West*, 1:194–95. See also Ostler, *Plains Sioux and U.S. Colonialism*, pp. 330–31.

20. Telegram, Miles to Brooke, December 26, 1890, NA, RG 393, part 1, Entry 3782, Department of the Platte, Telegrams Received by Headquarters, 1890–91, Box 2 (first quotation). See Carr's official report of his regiment's activities in Carr to AAG, Department of the Platte, April 20, 1891, in NA Microfilm 983, "Sioux Campaign," 1890–91, Roll 2, pp. 14–17 (hereinafter cited as Carr's report, April 20, 1891); Carter, *From Yorktown to Santiago*, p. 259 (second quotation); King, *War Eagle*, p. 243–44 (including third quotation); Carr to "My dear Sister," January 7, 1891, Carr Papers (fourth quotation); John J. Pershing, "Memories," draft of chapter 5, pp. 89–90, John J. Pershing Papers, Manuscript Division, Library of Congress, Container 377; *Omaha Bee*, December 20, 1890; *Omaha World-Herald*, December 25, 1890; *Black Hills Journal*, December 26, 1890; Smythe, *Guerrilla Warrior*, pp. 22–23; Smith, *Don't Settle for Second*, p. 14; Grant C. Topping, "On the Pine Ridge Campaign," in Greene, *Indian War Veterans*, p. 195; Maus to Carr, December 28, 1890, attached to incomplete handwritten account by Carr in respect to the pursuit of Big Foot, unknown origin, Carr Papers. See Frederic Remington's essay "A Merry Christmas in a Sibley Tepee," perhaps partly reminiscent of aspects of Carr's sojourn in December 1890. *Harper's Weekly*, December 5, 1891.

21. Carter, *From Yorktown to Santiago*, pp. 259, 261; *Black Hills Journal*, December 24, 1890; incomplete handwritten account by Carr in respect to the pursuit of Big Foot, unknown origin. The Regimental Returns of the Sixth Cavalry for December 1890 inexplicably omitted normally requisite information pertaining to Carr's scout; the troops involved were not identified therein, although it is certain that Troops C, D, F, H, I, and K took part. For Merriam's role in the unfolding operations, see Ballard, *Commander and Builder of Western Forts*, pp. 135–40.

22. "Abstract of Correspondence," pp. 12, 13; telegram, Brooke to Miles, December 24, 1890, Brooke Papers, Sioux Campaign 1890–91, vol. 1, p. 506 (quotation).

23. Telegram, Miles to Brooke, December 26, 1890, NA, RG 393, part 1, Entry 3782, Department of the Platte, Telegrams Received by Headquarters, 1890–91, Box 2. Eighth Cavalry officer Captain Argalus G. Hennisee specifically tallied 333 people with Big Foot, including 38 of Sitting Bull's followers, of whom 14 were warriors. Sumner to Miles, December 22, 1890, in *Report of the Secretary of War, 1891*, p. 233, with assumed reference to Sumner to AAG, Department of Dakota, February 3, 1891, in ibid., p. 224. The most thorough and credible discussion of the size and composition of Big Foot's band between the time of its departure from Cheyenne River on the night of December 23–24 to the chief's surrender on December 28, 1890, and immediately thereafter,

is found in Jensen, "Big Foot's Followers at Wounded Knee," pp. 194–97. For the heliograph, see *Black Hills Daily Times*, December 25, 1890; and Lee, *Fort Meade and the Black Hills*, p. 116. The Hopkins incident is recounted in *Omaha Bee*, December 23, 1890 (first quotation) and December 24, 1890; *Omaha World-Herald*, December 23, 1890; *Chadron Democrat*, December 25, 1890; *Army and Navy Journal*, December 27, 1890 (second quotation); *Omaha Bee*, December 28, 1890; and Hyde, *Sioux Chronicle*, pp. 282–83.

24. For the Stronghold people, see Perrig Diary, entry for December 27, 1890; *Omaha World-Herald*, December 27, 1890; *Chicago Inter-Ocean*, December 22, 1890; *Black Hills Journal*, December 24 and 25, 1890; *Washington Evening Star*, December 27, 1890; Miles to AG, December 25, 1890, NA Microfilm 983, "Sioux Campaign," 1890–91, Roll 1, p. 609; Miles to AG, December 27, 1890, ibid., p. 616; *Philadelphia Inquirer*, December 29, 1890 (quotations); *New York Times*, December 29, 1890; *Chicago Inter-Ocean*, December 29, 1890. (Earlier on Christmas Day, before news of the capitulation of Short Bull and Kicking Bear had arrived, Miles had devised a substantive contingency plan to "drive out or destroy any body of Indians in those Bad Lands" if necessary. "A good snow storm would be to our advantage," he wrote. Telegram, Miles to Brooke, December 25, 1890, NA, RG 393, part 1, Entry 3782, Department of the Platte, Telegrams Received by Headquarters, 1890–91, Box 2.)

25. "Extracts from Letters Written by Lieutenant Alexander R. Piper, 8th Infantry," p. 4; McGinnis "I Was There!," p. 8 (also published in *Junction City Daily Union*, June 7, 1961, and substantially the same as "I Took Part in the Wounded Knee Massacre"); *Junction City Republican*, December 26, 1890; Lindberg, "Foreigners in Action at Wounded Knee," pp. 172–73 (first quotation); Roger Phillips, "George and Alice Hatch Family," in Sheridan County Historical Society, *Recollections of Sheridan County, Nebraska*, p. 342; "Private Diary, Sept. 1st 1890 to [illeg.] 1891," Moorehead Papers (MS 106), Box 19, vol. 21 (second and following quotations). A lengthy account of the Seventh Cavalry's Christmas revelry at Pine Ridge Agency appears in *Chicago Inter-Ocean*, December 28, 1890. For the Indians' receipt of meager disbursements on December 24, see Coleman, *Voices of Wounded Knee*, pp. 254–56; *Junction City Republican*, February 6, 1891. It is probable that officers and enlisted men obtained access to spirits from trader James Asay. "William Peano's Interview," in Jensen, *Voices of the American West*, 1:235–36.

26. Eastman, *Sister to the Sioux*, pp. 151–52.

27. Regimental Returns of the Ninth Cavalry, December 1890, NA Microfilm 744, Roll 90; telegram, Miles to Brooke, December 24, 1890, NA, RG 393, part 1, Entry 3782, Department of the Platte, Telegrams Received by Headquarters, 1890–91, Box 2; Brooke to Henry, December 27, 1890, 9 A.M., NA, RG 393, Entry 3773, vol. 2 of 3, "Letters Sent Headquarters in the Field. From December 19th, 1890. To January 9th, 1891," p. 26; *Omaha Bee*, January 1, 1891; *Army and Navy Journal*, January 3, 1891; "William Denver McGaa's Interview," in Jensen, *Voices of the American West*, 1:25–51; *Army and Navy Journal*, January 24, 1891; *Army and Navy Register*, December 27, 1890; *Omaha World-Herald*, December 25, 1890; *Omaha Bee*, December 25, 1890; *Chicago Inter-Ocean*, December 25, 1890; *Black Hills Daily Times*, December 27, 1890; Guy V. Henry, "Sioux Indian Episode," *Harper's Weekly*, July 27, 1895, pp. 1273–74; Perry, "The Ninth United States Cavalry in the Sioux Campaign," pp. 252–53; Leckie and Leckie, *Buffalo Soldiers*, p. 274; Rickey, "An Indian Wars Combat Record," p. 10 (quotation from "Annapolis Centenarian Recalls Last Stand of Sioux," in clipping from

unidentified newspaper, April 1963); telegram, Brooke to Miles, December 26, 1890; telegram, Brooke to Miles, December 26, 1890; both in NA, RG 393, PI 172, Entry 3722, Department of the Platte, Letters Sent, 1866–98, vol. 19; Buecker, *Fort Robinson and the American West*, pp. 176–77; telegram, Brooke to Miles, December 26, 1890, NA, RG 393, PI 172, Entry 3722, Department of the Platte, Letters Sent, 1866–98, vol. 19. Brooke had feared that Henry's movements in the area might defeat the attempt to coax in the Stronghold occupants. Brooke to Ruger, December 24, 1890, Brooke Papers, Sioux Campaign 1890–91, vol. 1, p. 512. Henry's wounding is described in Mangum, *Battle of the Rosebud*, pp. 79–80.

28. Joseph Horn Cloud's statement in "Truth of the Wounded Knee Massacre," p. 245; "Joseph Horn Cloud's Interview," in Jensen, *Voices of the American West*, 1:195–96; Sheldon, "Ancient Indian Fireplaces in South Dakota Bad-Lands," p. 44; Hall, *To Have This Land*, pp. 123–24.

29. Ghost Horse, "A True Story of What Happened at Wounded Knee in December 1890," pp. 11–12.

30. Good Thunder interview. Details of Big Foot's route southwest from White River using early twentieth-century place-names are found in George Little Dog to Walter M. Camp, June 15, 1916, Camp Manuscripts, Lilly Library, Box 4, Folder 9, 282–95, Envelope 11: "On the White river up the river from Will Jacobs ranch is the place where Big foot band crosses and they went on and camp at now where Nelson Shangreau ranch is. And they move and camp over to Red Water Creek at Bill Garnette [*sic*] ranch. And they move on after the next day to Medicine root creek at Two Crows ranch. After the next day they move on to the American Horse creek at where that government day school is now [1916] located. And the next day they move to Porcupine Creek near Wet Hep (Sichay [illeg.]) ranch. And the next day [December 28] they got caught under the Porcupine Butte." For other accounts, see Iron Hail (Dewey Beard, also known as Dewey Horn Cloud), "The Ghost Dance and Wounded Knee Fight," in Walker, *Lakota Society*, p. 160; "Dewey Beard's Interview," in Jensen, *Voices of the American West*, 1:213–15.

31. Telegram, Miles to Brooke, December 26, 1890, NA, RG 393, part 1, Entry 3782, Department of the Platte, Telegrams Received by Headquarters, 1890–91, Box 2.

32. Brooke (Roe) to Forsyth, December 26, 1890, NA Microfilm 983, "Sioux Campaign," 1890–91, Roll 1, p. 757; telegram, Brooke to Miles, December 26, 1890, NA, RG 393, part I 172, Entry 3722, Department of the Platte, Letters Sent, 1866–98, vol. 19 (first quotation); Brooke to Forsyth, December 26, 1890; Brooke to Poland, December 26, 1890, and Brooke to Poland, December 27, 1890; Forsyth's Diary, December 26, 1890, and December 27, 1890; all in NA, RG 393, Entry 3773, "Letters Sent. Headquarters in the Field. From December 19th, 1890. To January 9th, 1891" (second quotation).

33. Whitside to wife, December 26, 1890, Whitside Papers; Regimental Returns of the Seventh Cavalry, December 1890, NA Microfilm 744, Roll 74; NA, RG 94, Records of the Adjutant General's Office, Muster Rolls of the Seventh Cavalry, Troops A, B, C, D, E, G, I, and K, December 31, 1890, and Muster Roll, Light Battery E, First Artillery, October 31, 1890, to December 31, 1890, NA, RG 94, Box 1252; *Omaha Bee*, December 27 and 28, 1890; *Omaha World-Herald*, December 27, 1890; *Chicago Inter-Ocean*, December 28, 1890; Chandler, *Of GarryOwen in Glory*, p. 81 (officer veterans of the Little Bighorn present at Wounded Knee were Captain Myles Moylan, Captain Charles A. Varnum, Captain Edward S. Godfrey, Captain Winfield Scott Edgerly,

Captain Henry J. Nowlan, and Captain George D. Wallace); Brooke to Whitside, December 27, 1890, Brooke Papers, Sioux Campaign 1890–91, vol. 1, p. 573; Crickett letter; First Sergeant Theodor Ragnar (Theodor Ling-Vannerus), quoted in Lindberg, "Foreigners in Action at Wounded Knee," p. 173 (quotation).

34. McGinnis, "I Was There!," p. 8; Kelley, "Indian Troubles and the Battle of Wounded Knee," p. 40; Kelley, *Pine Ridge 1890*, pp. 175–78; NA, RG 94, Samuel M. Whitside Appointment, Commission, and Personal (ACP) File (hereinafter cited as Whitside ACP File); Powell, *Powell's Records of Living Officers*, pp. 641–42; Heitman, *Historical Register and Dictionary of the United States Army*, 1:1031; Russell, "Selfless Service," pp. 9–64; Whitside to Brooke, December 27, 1890 (two messages), NA, RG 393, part 1, Entry 3778, "Register of Letters Received. In the Field at Pine Ridge, S.D. From November 21st, 1890. To January 24th, 1891," pp. 22–23; Brooke to Whitside, December 27, 1890, p. 28; Brooke to Whitside, December 27, 1890, 3 A.M., p. 24; Brooke to Whitside, December 27, 1890, 7:50 A.M., p. 25 (quotation); all in NA, RG 393 "Letters Sent. Headquarters in the Field. From December 19th, 1890. To January 9th, 1891"; Whitside to Brooke, December 27, 1890, NA, RG 393, part 1, Entry 3779, Department of the Platte, Letters Received, 1890–91. Whitside sent this message from Wounded Knee at 7 P.M. on December 27; it reached Brooke's headquarters at Pine Ridge Agency at 9:55 P.M., an approximate courier delivery time of three hours to cover the distance of about eighteen miles in the dark. Whitside also had access to a Signal Corps station established three miles northeast of the agency and heliographed at least one message to Brooke on December 27: ibid. For the scouting on December 27, see also Brooke to AAG, Division of the Missouri, March 2, 1891, in Carroll, *To Set the Record Straight!*, p. 11; First Lieutenant Charles W. Taylor to Brooke, December 27, 1890, NA, RG 393, part 1, Entry 3779, Department of the Platte, Letters Received, 1890–91. See also "Abstract of Correspondence," pp. 16–17; Garlington, "The Seventh Regiment of United States Cavalry," pp. 33–34, draft typescript in the Edward S. Godfrey Papers, Container 6, Manuscript Division, Library of Congress. See also Garlington, "Seventh Regiment of Cavalry," p. 265.

35. Whitside to Brooke, December 27, 1890, NA, RG 393, part 1, Entry 3778, "Register of Letters Received. In the Field at Pine Ridge, S.D. From November 21st, 1890. To January 24th, 1891," p. 23.

36. First Lieutenant James D. Mann to his brother, December 29, 1890, quoted in Arnold, "Ghost Dance and Wounded Knee," p. 21 (hereinafter cited as Mann letter).

37. Mann to AAAG, Headquarters Department of the Platte, in the Field, December 28, 1890. Brooke Papers, Sioux Campaign 1890–91, vol. 1, p. 603; First Lieutenant John C. Gresham account in *Harper's Weekly*, February 7, 1891; *Daily Nebraskan*, December 30, 1890; Whitside to AAAG, Headquarters, Department of the Platte, in the field, December 26, 1890. NA, RG 393, Entry 3779, Department of the Platte, Letters Received, 1890–91; Trooper Charles Franklin account in *Rocky Mountain News*, January 29, 1933 (quotation).

38. Lindberg, "Foreigners in Action at Wounded Knee," p. 174 (quotation); one witness stated that shortly after the arrest of the tribesmen "many of them . . . crowded around the guns and the artillery detachment. . . . Then came the usual handshaking, in which the Indian delights. . . . They rubbed their hands over the [Hotchkiss] guns in a very friendly way": Lieutenant Harry L. Hawthorne, "Vivid Description of Warpath Life," in undated account (ca. 1891) in *Newport (Kentucky) Times-Star* (hereinafter cited as Hawthorne, *Times-Star* account).

39. Lindberg, "Foreigners in Action at Wounded Knee," pp. 74 (Sergeant Ragnar's real name was Ragnar Theodor Ling-Vannerus), 174 (first quotation); *Omaha Bee*, December 29, 1890 (second quotation).

40. Whitside to Brooke, December 28, 1890, NA, RG 393, Entry 3779, Department of the Platte, LR, 1890–91 (quotation); Whitside to Adjutant, Seventh Cavalry, January 1, 1891, NA Microfilm 983, "Sioux Campaign," 1890–91, Roll 1, pp. 822–23; *Army and Navy Journal*, January 24, 1891; *Chicago Inter-Ocean*, December 29, 1890; NA, RG 391, Records of U.S. Regular Army Mobile Units, Cavalry—7th Cavalry, 1866–1917, Entry 865, "Scrapbook of Clippings and Pictures of Troop C with a History of Troop A, 1867–1932." Garnier is identified as the likely interpreter at the meeting in High Back, "Paul High Back's Version of the Disaster of Dec. 29, 1890 at Wounded Knee," p. 2. John Shangrau stated that he interpreted for Whitside. "John Shangrau's Interview," in Jensen, *Voices of the American West*, 1:261 (see also interviews of Joseph Horn Cloud and Dewey Beard in ibid., 1:196–98, 215–17). One early secondary account stated that Lieutenant Hawthorne desired to place his guns on a nearby knoll but that Whitside preferred them at front center. Scott, "Wounded Knee," p. 9. Captain Varnum remembered: "My Troop B and K Troop were dismounted in line with the other two troops, mounted, behind them." Carroll, *I, Varnum*, p. 22. Brooke immediately wired news of the capture to Miles, who forwarded it on to the War Department. Telegram, Miles to AG, December 28, 1890; interview of Major Samuel M. Whitside, January 7, 1891, pp. 656–64, 707–709 (hereinafter cited as Whitside interview); and interview of Captain Myles Moylan, Seventh Cavalry, January 7, 1891, pp. 664–67; all in NA Microfilm 983, "Sioux Campaign," 1890–91, Roll 1, p. 626. First Lieutenant James D. Mann, who stayed in the Wounded Knee camp when Whitside departed to meet Big Foot, reported the development to Brooke in a penciled note dispatched at 1:30 P.M. on December 28, 1890. Mann told Brooke: "We have in camp here two of their [Big Foot's] men holding them as prisoners." NA, RG 393, Entry 3779, Department of the Platte, Letters Received, 1890–91. First Sergeant Ragnar also noted the arrival of these prisoners. Lindberg, "Foreigners in Action at Wounded Knee," p. 174.

41. Good Thunder interview.

42. Beard, "Ghost Dance and Wounded Knee Fight," pp. 161–62. See also Beard's more detailed remembrance in "Dewey Beard's Interview," in Jensen, *Voices of the American West*, 1:215–17.

43. Joseph Horn Cloud's statement, "Truth of the Wounded Knee Massacre," pp. 245–46 (quotations). For other tribal accounts of the army arrest of Big Foot's followers, see "Statement of Hehakawanyakapi" (undated but likely January 7, 1891), Philip F. Wells Materials, D6, F41, Thomas Odell Collection; "Statement of Dewey Beard," March 12, 1917, stamped received, Office of Indian Affairs, April 13, 1920, Exhibit Item 31678, Records of the Bureau of Indian Affairs (copy provided by Michael Her Many Horses); "Statement of Hehakananyakapi" (ca. 1920), stamped January 14, 1921, NA, RG 75; Ghost Horse, "True Story," p. 12; High Back, "Paul High Back's Version of the Disaster," p. 2; Frank Thomson to "Mr. Nye," November 28, 1968, citing Amos Fasthorse's account, Frank Thomson Papers, Drawer 31, Folder 2, Leland D. Case Library Black Hills State University. See also DeMallie, *Sixth Grandfather*, p. 270 (Black Elk's reminiscence of Big Foot's route). An illuminating hearsay reminiscence by Dewey Beard's granddaughter appears in "Celane Not Help Him," in Penman *Honor the Grandmothers*, p. 16. See also Celane Not Help Him, "What Happened at Wounded Knee, 1890," *Lakota Times*, October 16, 1990; Coleman, *Voices of Wounded Knee*, pp. 261–66; and Ostler, *Plains Sioux and U.S. Colonialism*, pp. 334–36.

44. This description of the arrest of Big Foot's band and movement to Wounded Knee is also drawn from the following personal accounts: Allen, *From Fort Laramie to Wounded Knee*, p. 184; Kelley, "Indian Troubles and the Battle of Wounded Knee," pp. 40–41; Ragnar in Lindberg, "Foreigners in Action at Wounded Knee," pp. 174–75; McGinnis, "I Was There!," pp. 8–9; Robinson, "Recollections of Gen. W. W. Robinson, Jr." (undated typescript, Item 12518, Little Bighorn Battlefield National Monument; Gresham in *Harper's Weekly*, February 7, 1891; "Battle of Wounded Knee. Extracts from an account written for publication by Lieut. T. Q. Donaldson, Jr.," pp. 2–3, Camp Papers, BYU, Box 5 (Microfilm Roll 4) (quotation; hereinafter cited as Donaldson, "Battle of Wounded Knee"); Whitside to Adjutant, Seventh Cavalry, January 1, 1891, NA Microfilm 983, "Sioux Campaign," 1890–91, Roll 1, pp. 822–23; account of Scout Patrick Starr, *Sioux Falls Argus Leader*, December 27, 1937; Coughlan, *Varnum*, pp. 24–25; Crickett letter, p. 3; Garlington to Chief, Historical Section, Army War College, April 4, 1931, in Carroll, *A Seventh Cavalry Scrapbook*, p. 2 (hereinafter cited as Garlington letter); account of Private Charles Franklin, Troop A, Seventh Cavalry, in *Rocky Mountain News*, January 29, 1933.

45. Telegram, Brooke to Miles, December 28, 1890 (3:45 P.M.); Miles to Brooke, December 28, 1890 (quotation); both in Brooke Papers, Sioux Campaign 1890–91, vol. 1, p. 605; Brooke to Henry, December 28, 1890, NA, RG 393, Entry 3773, vol. 2 of 3, "Letters Sent Headquarters in the Field. From December 19th, 1890. To January 9th, 1891," p. 33; *Chicago Inter-Ocean*, December 29, 1890. See also Mooney, "Ghost-Dance Religion," p. 867; Traub, "Sioux Campaign—Winter of 1890–'91," p. 67; Shockley, "Affair at Wounded Knee," pp. 41–42; and Ostler, *Plains Sioux and U.S. Colonialism*, pp. 336–37. In 1920 a number of Lakotas applied for compensation for personal articles lost at Wounded Knee, including at least thirty-four tipis, suggesting that more were present there or that many simply were not raised, perhaps based on the Indians' expectation that they would be moved to Pine Ridge Agency. Besides their shelter and horses, other property in the village included weapons, saddles, packsaddles, camping outfits, cooking utensils, travois, parfleches, clothing, bedding, horse equipment, buffalo robes, and deerskins. McLaughlin to Commissioner of Indian Affairs Cato Sells, January 12, 1921, Wounded Knee Compensation Papers, H76.24, Box 3564A, Folder 14, SDSHS.

CHAPTER 11. BLOODBATH

1. The second squadron consisted of the regimental headquarters and staff and Troops C, D, E, and G—10 officers and approximately 210 men. Troops manning the Hotchkiss brace belonged to Light Battery E, First Artillery, commanded by Captain Allyn Capron, while the Cheyenne and Oglala scouts were commanded by First Lieutenant Charles W. Taylor, Ninth Cavalry, assisted by Second Lieutenant Guy H. Preston, also of the Ninth.

2. Forsyth to AAAG, Headquarters, Department of the Platte in the field, December 31, 1890, NA, RG 393, Entry 3779. Department of the Platte, Letters Received, 1890–91 (hereinafter cited as Forsyth's report, December 31, 1890); Regimental Returns of the Seventh Cavalry, December 1890, NA Microfilm 744, Roll 74; Chandler, *Of GarryOwen in Glory*, p. 81; Regimental Returns of the First Artillery, December 1890, NA Microfilm 727, Roll 7; Muster Roll, Light Battery E, First Artillery, October 31, 1890, to December 31, 1890, and Muster Roll, Companies A–D, "Indian scouts

enlisted at Pine Ridge Agency and Camp Cheyenne, South Dakota," NA, RG 75, Pine Ridge Agency, South Dakota, General Records, Main Decimal Files, Folder 650 (Box 657), NA at Kansas City; *Junction City Republican*, November 28, 1890; Tibbles, *Buckskin and Blanket Days*, p. 309; Donaldson, "Battle of Wounded Knee," p. 4; McCormick, "Wounded Knee and Drexel Mission Fights, December 29th and 30th, 1890," U.S. 7th Cavalry Collection (Microfilm Roll 12), pp. 7–8, Little Bighorn Battlefield National Monument; Brooke to Miles, undated (ca. December 29, 1890), NA, RG 393, Entry 3773, "Letters Sent Headquarters in the Field. From December 19th, 1890. To January 9th, 1891," vol. 2 of 3 (quotation).

3. Garlington, "The Seventh Regiment of United States Cavalry," draft copy, pp. 33–34; James R. O'Beirne to Proctor, November 24, 1890, NA Microfilm 983, "Sioux Campaign," 1890–91, Roll 1, p. 208; *New York Sun*, November 2, 1890; Foley, *Father Francis M. Craft*, p. 85; Foley, *At Standing Rock and Wounded Knee*, p. 293. With Brooke's permission, Craft apparently trailed after Forsyth's column and reached Wounded Knee around 11 P.M. He stated that he went to "be of some service by going among the Indians and reassuring them." Craft interview in NA Microfilm 983, "Sioux Campaign," 1890–91, Roll 1, pp. 721–25. His biographer states that Craft arrived with the soldiers "and a few civilian spectators" near midnight. Foley, *Father Francis M. Craft*, p. 87. For background on Forsyth, see NA, RG 94, James W. Forsyth Appointment, Commission, and Personal File; Heitman, *Historical Register and Dictionary of the United States Army*, 1:430; and Forsyth, "General James William Forsyth," pp. 45–58 (including quotation).

The *Army and Navy Register*, February 14, 1891, published a letter from Forsyth to the adjutant general in which Forsyth addressed his experience with Indians: "I was present and took part as a staff officer with General Sheridan in the Cheyenne and Arrapahoe [*sic*] campaign in the winter of 1868–9. Was designated by General Sheridan as his representative, with Colonel John E. Smith, in the Sioux expedition in, I think, the winter of 1873. As lieutenant colonel, I commanded eight troops of the First Cavalry in the Bannock campaign, and had an engagement in the John Day Valley. The closing out of the campaign . . . was entrusted to me by General Howard, who returned to his headquarters. This does not include my familiarity with the Indians and Indian military affairs, gained as the confidential officer of Lieutenant General Sheridan through a period of 10 years, concerning many tribes and over a large extent of territory." For Forsyth's service in the Bannock conflict, see Brimlow, *The Bannock Indian War of 1878*, pp. 146, 155–56. The road to the Wounded Knee community followed the road to Rosebud Reservation and branched northeast four miles from Pine Ridge Agency. See "Map of a Portion of South Dakota, Showing the Country Adjacent to the Pine Ridge & Rosebud Indian Agencies," NA, RG 77, Headquarters Map File, Q734-3.

4. "Abstract of Correspondence," pp. 16–17; telegram, Miles to Brooke, December 26, 1890 (first quotation); telegram, Miles to Brooke (congratulatory), December 28, 1890; and telegram, Miles to Brooke, December 28, 1890; all in NA, RG 393, part 1, Entry 3782, Department of the Platte, Telegrams Received by Headquarters, 1890–91, Box 2; Brooke to Whitside, December 29, 1890, 8:30 A.M., NA Microfilm 983, "Sioux Campaign," 1890–91, Roll 1, p. 755 (congratulatory); Brooke to Whitside, December 29, 1890, 8:30 A.M., NA, RG 393, Entry 3773, "Letters Sent Headquarters in the Field. From December 19th, 1890. To January 9th, 1891," vol. 2 of 3 (congratulatory) (also in Whitside ACP File); First Lieutenant Fayette W. Roe to Whitside, December 29, 1890, 7 A.M., p. 34 (second quotation), NA, RG 308; Brooke to

Wheaton, December 29, 1890, ibid., pp. 32, 35 (third quotation). Brooke arranged for the trains with his staff in Omaha. Acting adjutant general Major Michael Sheridan wired Brooke: "The trains with proper locomotive power [to transport "three hundred seventy indians [*sic*] and their plunder"] will be [ready at Gordon] on the 30th. . . . The two trains combined in one will make thirty one [*sic*] cars & the railroad officials say it will be impossible to move this many cars in less than two sections no matter how much engine power they have in the above calculation. It is presumed that there are no Indian ponies." Telegram, Sheridan to Brooke, December 29, 1890, NA, RG 393, part 1, Entry 3782, Department of the Platte, Telegrams Received by Headquarters, 1890–91, Box 2; "Extracts from Letters Written by Lieutenant Alexander R. Piper, 8th Infantry," p. 5.

5. Whitside to Adjutant, Seventh Cavalry, January 1, 1891; Whitside interview; Forsyth to AAAG, Department of the Platte, December 28, 1890, NA, RG 393, Entry 3779, Department of the Platte, Letters Sent, 1890–91; Private John W. Comfort to "'Brother Chess,'" April 5, 1892, p. 3 and map, John W. Comfort Papers, Box 1, Department of Rare Books and Special Collections, Princeton University Library, Princeton University (hereinafter cited as Comfort letter, April 5, 1892). See Comfort's biography in Olmsted, "John W. Comfort"; Gresham in *Harper's Weekly*, February 7, 1891 (first quotation); Donaldson, "Battle of Wounded Knee," p. 4; Tibbles, *Buckskin and Blanket Days*, pp. 309–10; Crickett letter, p. 3; Garlington letter, p. 3. Captain Henry Jackson of Troop C wrote that the squadron "went into bivouac without tents, as we took nothing with us. Luckily Lieut. Waterman [of Whitside's squadron] asked me to sleep in his tent, which I did, with Dr. Hoff, Lieuts. Donelson [Donaldson] and Sickel. We kept warm all night, but did not sleep a bit owing to the hard ground." Jackson in *New York World*, January 7, 1891. Likewise, Captain Edward S. Godfrey spent the night in Captain George D. Wallace's tent. Godfrey to Chief, Historical Section, Army War College, May 29, 1931, Edward S. Godfrey Collection, U.S. Army Military History Institute, Army War College; Scott, "Wounded Knee," p. 10; Shockley, "The Affair at Wounded Knee," p. 42; Hawthorne account in *Times-Herald* (ca. 1891); Slaughter, "Time at Wounded Knee," p. 181 (second quotation).

6. Tibbles, *Buckskin and Blanket Days*, pp. 309–10; Cook, *Fifty Years on the Old Frontier*, p. 235; Allen, *From Fort Laramie to Wounded Knee*, p. 127 (quotation).

7. Allen, *From Fort Laramie to Wounded Knee*, p. 190 (quotation). About a dozen civilians were present at Wounded Knee, including the reporters. "Meded Swigert's Interview," in Jensen, *Voices of the American West*, 2:20. For Stirk's commentary on the presence of whiskey, see ibid., 2:288–89. Judge Eli S. Ricker, who interviewed many civilian, military, and tribal participants at Wounded Knee and discovered evidence that the officers had imbibed whiskey the night before the engagement, nonetheless stated: "I have tried to find out if the officers were not drunk that morning hoping there might be as poor an excuse as intoxication for the sins of omission and commission; but beyond the conviviality of the night before preceding the battle nothing could be established." Ibid., 2:62. Former lieutenant Guy H. Preston verified that liquor had been consumed, "but not by all and sundry, but by a few convivial, or more likely, weary souls." Preston, "Letter from Brigadier General Guy H. Preston, April 5, 1931," p. 32 (hereinafter cited as Preston letter). Former private William J. Small of Troop G years later took umbrage at reports of drunk soldiers at Wounded Knee. He admitted that the men imbibed when in the garrison, "but not when you were in the field. . . . Our good[-]hearted Captain [Edgerly] . . . was like a mother to his men and god help

the man who would get drunk in line of duty. He would not have him in the outfit." He added: "When people say we were drunk and Boozing [*sic*] tell them they are crazy." Small to George W. Webb, Chairman, National Indian War Veterans Association, 1932, SDSHS, William J. Small Collection, H2010-029 (hereinafter cited as Small Collection). (Small was reacting to a luridly flawed rendering of Wounded Knee in Robert Gessner, *Massacre: A Survey of Today's American Indian* [New York: Jonathan Cape and Harrison Smith, 1931], pp. 414–18.)

8. *Omaha World-Herald*, November 23, 1890; Allen, *From Fort Laramie to Wounded Knee*, map opposite p. 127, p. 189; McFarland map in Jensen, *Voices of the American West*, 2:2 and opposite p. 210; Hade map, "Scene of the Fight with Big Foot's Band, Dec. 29th 1890," NA Microfilm 983, Roll 1, following p. 650 (hereinafter cited as Hade-Cloman map); Lea, sketch map of Wounded Knee engagement, A. T. Lea Papers, Gilcrease Museum, Special Collections Division, Item 4026.6055, Lea #7 (hereinafter cited as Lea sketch map); Craft, map entitled "Battle Field [*sic*] of Wounded Knee"; *Chicago Inter-Ocean*, January 7, 1891; Scott, "Wounded Knee," p. 10; Hyde, *Sioux Chronicle*, p. 298; Jim Gillihan (Tatonka Ska), "How Wounded Knee Got Its Name, and Related Historic Incidents" (typescript dated 1976), Vertical Files, SDSHS. The land lies within the NW quarter of Section 23, Township 36 North, Range 43 West, Sixth Principal Meridian, U.S. Geological Survey, Denby Quadrangle, South Dakota–Shannon County.

9. U.S. Naval Observatory Astronomical Applications Department (online: http://aa.usno.navy.mil/data/docs/RS_OneDay.html); Garlington letter, p. 3; Scott, "Wounded Knee," pp. 10–11; McCormick, "Wounded Knee and Drexel Mission Fights," p. 10; Hade-Cloman map; NA Microfilm 983, "Sioux Campaign," 1890–91, Roll 1, map following p. 650; Comfort letter, April 5, 1892, p. 4. A reporter for the *Omaha World-Herald* overheard part of a conversation between a lieutenant and Captain Ilsley questioning the "strange formation" of the troop placement. "I saw exactly what he meant," remembered Henry Tibbles. "If any troop should try to shoot any Indian, it must fire straight in the direction of some other army group stationed in that enclosing square." Tibbles, *Buckskin and Blanket Days*, p. 311.

10. Whitside to AAAG, Division of the Missouri, January 5, 1891, NA, RG 393, part 1, Entry 2546, Military Division of the Missouri, Letters Received, Box 126-7. One new enlistee had arrived on December 17. NA, RG 94, Muster Rolls of the Seventh Cavalry, October 31, 1890, to December 31, 1890; Hawthorne, "The Sioux Campaign of 1890–91" (1896), p. 186; Allen, *From Fort Laramie to Wounded Knee*, p. 191 (quotation).

11. "Paddy Starr's Interview," in Jensen, *Voices of the American West*, 1:237. Scout John Shangrau, who interpreted at the council, told Judge Eli S. Ricker in an interview in 1906 that when he broached the matter of giving up their guns, the Indian men requested Big Foot's opinion on the matter. Shangrau and two of the Indians spoke to the chief in his tent, who told them to "give them some of the bad guns, but keep the good ones." This apparently was done. "John Shangrau's Interview," in Jensen, *Voices of the American West*, 1:261–62.

12. McCormick, "Wounded Knee and Drexel Mission Fights," pp. 8–9 (first quotation); Stauffer, *Letters of Mari Sandoz*, pp. 269–70; McGillycuddy interview, Camp Manuscripts, Lilly Library, Box 4, Folder 14, Envelope 35, pp. 307–314 (Cheyenne River, 1916) (second quotation). "The Sioux were armed with three different kinds of guns: Winchester of pattern 1866 and caliber [.44 rimfire] . . . ; Winchester [Model 1873], caliber 38; and the Springfield carbine, caliber 45. The principal weapon was the

[magazine-loaded] Winchester, caliber 38, together with very few of the other patterns mentioned." Ewing, "The Wounded of the Wounded Knee Battlefield," p. 51.

13. Allen, *From Fort Laramie to Wounded Knee*, pp. 193–94.

14. Ibid., p. 195.

15. McGinnis, "I Was There!," p. 52 (quotation). According to Philip Wells, who interpreted this conversation between Big Foot and Forsyth, the colonel pointed out the favorable treatment that he had accorded the chief since the previous day, telling him that his denial of the weapons that Whitside's men had seen indicated his obvious deception. "You are lying to me in return for all my kindness to you," said Forsyth. Philip F. Wells interview, in NA Microfilm 983, "Sioux Campaign," 1890–91, Roll 1, pp. 711–12; "Philip Wells's Interview," in Jensen, *Voices of the American West*, 1:127–28.

16. McCormick, "Wounded Knee and Drexel Mission Fights," p. 11 (first quotation); assistant surgeon John Van R. Hoff interview, in NA Microfilm 983, "Sioux Campaign," 1890–91, Roll 1, p. 675; Whitside in NA Publication 983, "Sioux Campaign," 1890–91, Roll 1, pp. 667–68 (second quote).

17. A translated personal account by Swedish-born First Sergeant Theodore Ragnar of Troop K stated that at this juncture Forsyth told Big Foot that "fire would be opened at the camp unless the warriors did not immediately come back with their guns." Ragnar, in Malm, *The Last Battle of the Sioux Indians*, pp. 154–55 (see also Lindberg, "Foreigners in Action at Wounded Knee," p. 175). This statement is inconsistent with all other first-person narratives examined. It is the only one known suggesting such premeditative action on the part of the troops and might in fact have been embellished by Ragnar and/or his editor.

18. Mann letter.

19. In early January 1891 Forsyth received a request from Miles to "report what disposition was made of the arms taken from Big Foot's band in the recent engagement with your regiment." Forsyth responded: "Up to the time the fight began 45 guns had been secured. Most of these were old and worthless Winchesters. After the fight, and during it, 27 of the old guns were broken—some of them having the wooden parts burned off in a tent which caught fire. Of the remaining 18, Mr. Asay was loaned one for personal protection. Of the others, 13 are under my control. The foregoing accounts for forty-one of the forty-five taken. The other four I cannot account for." Maus to Forsyth, January 3, 1891, and Forsyth's reply in first endorsement, NA, RG 393, part 1, Entry 2546, Headquarters, Military Division of the Missouri, Letters Received, Box 126-7. Wounded Knee store owner Louis Mousseau stated that sixty-nine guns had been collected in the two piles: fifty-seven at the site below the hill and twelve at the pile near Big Foot's tent. "Louis Mousseau's Interview," in Jensen, *Voices of the American West*, 1:228. At least twenty-four surrendered firearms, mostly Winchesters, are evidently enumerated in the 1920 property inventory taken by James McLaughlin, to recompense Lakota survivors of Wounded Knee for their losses. Presumably the collection of these firearms resulted from their initial voluntary surrender at the outset of the meeting, the search of Indian property by soldiers that followed, and physical confiscation of the weapons immediately preceding the fighting. See McLaughlin to Sells, January 12, 1921 (copy in Wounded Knee Compensation Papers, H76.24, Box 3564A, Folder 14, SDSHS). A Winchester collected from a pile by correspondent Charles W. Allen was donated to the Nebraska State Historical Society museum in Omaha, where it reposes today. Paul, "Wounded Knee and the 'Collector of Curios,'" pp. 213–14.

20. Time as given in a dispatch from Forsyth to Brooke, December 29, 1890, NA, RG 393, Entry 3779, Department of the Platte, Letters Received, 1890–91.

21. *Chadron Democrat*, January 1, 1891.

22. Two weeks later Wells told investigators that the medicine man addressed the young men in the assembly thus: "Do not be afraid and let your hearts be strong to meet what is before you. We are all well aware that there are lots of soldiers about us and they have lots of bullets, but I have received assurance that their bullets cannot penetrate us; the prairie is large and the bullets will not go towards you; they will not penetrate you." Said Wells: "Then all these young bucks answered 'How' with great earnestness, this meaning that they were with him or would stand by him. I then turned to Major Whitside and said that man is making mischief, and repeated to him what he had said. He said go direct to General Forsyth and tell him about it, which I did. So he came along with me to the edge of the Indian circle of bucks and told me to tell that man then engaged in silent manoeuvres [*sic*] or incantations to sit down, but he kept on and paid no attention to the order, and when I translated it in Indian, Big Foot's brother-in-law said 'He will sit down when he gets around the circle,['] and when he reached the end he sat down." Wells interview, in NA Microfilm 983, "Sioux Campaign," 1890–91, Roll 1, p. 712; "Philip Wells's Interview," in Jensen, *Voices of the American West*, 1:128.

23. Wells interview, in NA Microfilm 983, "Sioux Campaign," 1890–91, Roll 1, p. 713.

24. "Richard C. Stirk's Interview," in Jensen, *Voices of the American West*, 2:288.

25. Craft interview, in NA Microfilm 983, "Sioux Campaign," 1890–91, Roll 1, p. 724.

26. McCormick, "Wounded Knee and Drexel Mission Fights," p. 13. Most accounts relate the outbreak similarly but with slight variations, apparently depending upon each witness's particular viewpoint.

27. *Omaha Bee*, December 30, 1890. Father Craft later indicated that the lone shot came from the vicinity of the left end of the Troop B line. See the map accompanying Craft to Editor, *Catholic Standard and Times*, November 22, 1913. As he put it positively and succinctly: "In the Wounded Knee fight the Indians fired first." *New York Freeman's Journal*, quoted in *Army and Navy Register*, January 17, 1891.

28. Preston letter, p. 30. Weeks later an unidentified Seventh Cavalry officer extended a compliment: "The way those Sioux worked those Winchesters was beautiful." Quoted in *Harper's Weekly*, January 24, 1891.

29. "Buck" refers to a male human being. It was a commonly applied colloquialism of eighteenth- and nineteenth-century America, often used pejoratively in reference to Indian and black males.

30. Mann letter. Lieutenant Mann survived the engagement only to be wounded during the White Clay Creek or so-called Drexel Mission fight the next day and perished from his injuries on January 15, 1891. See also Mann's comments in *Army and Navy Register*, February 28, 1891; and especially those of civilian witness Richard C. Stirk in Jensen, *Voices of the American West*, 2:288. Correspondent Henry Tibbles of the *Omaha World-Herald*, having been through Indian councils before and learned from several officers that the likelihood of trouble was nil, and believing that the numerical superiority of the troops over the warriors present militated against their resistance, had earlier decided to start back to Pine Ridge on the agency road. He had ridden for half an hour and had left the valley on a trail ascending some sand hills about seven miles from the Indian camp when he heard the initial shooting. "Suddenly I heard a single shot from the direction of the troops—then three or four—a few more—and

immediately a volley. At once came a general rattle of rifle firing." Tibbles, *Buckskin and Blanket Days*, p. 312. In *Omaha World-Herald*, December 30, 1890, Tibbles stated: "When seven miles away I heard heavy firing, which lasted half an hour, with frequent heavy volleys of musketry and cannon" (see also another account by Tibbles, *Omaha World-Herald*, January 6, 1891). Philip Wells clarified that the medicine man's action in tossing dirt into the air was no signal. As he walked around the council circle, said Wells, the medicine man "said 'Ha! Ha!,' an expression of regret that he would do something. He picked up the dust and threw it to illustrate that the bullets could not penetrate the ghost shirts. He showed that the bullets would pass as harmlessly as the wind carried dust away." Thomas E. Odell, "Comments of Philip F. Wells on Mr. W. R. Leigh's Information regarding the Wounded Knee Battle," Hot Springs Soldiers Home, December 27, 1942, Philip F. Wells Materials, D6, F41, Thomas Odell Collection.

An intriguing question concerns the number of warriors in the assembly who were in fact armed when the shooting at Wounded Knee started. When the gathering began, the men took seats on the ground. In such a position rifle-length firearms could not have been easily hidden, although handguns and knives might be so concealed. Of the twenty men who returned to the camp to retrieve guns, some likely brought back long arms hidden beneath their blankets or in half-leggings, accounting for some of those weapons present in the council when the shooting started. Those harboring long arms on their return would likely have remained standing until the shooting erupted in order to conceal them. Given these circumstances, hidden revolvers probably played a big part in what ensued, but the matter of exact numbers of Indian rifles and carbines present defies easy resolution.

31. Craft to James E. Kelly, March 13, 1891, as presented in Foley, *At Standing Rock and Wounded Knee*, p. 308 (this "Black Fox" did not refer to the medicine man). Craft corroborated years later: "The armed Indians fired upon the lines of K and B troops in one continued volley, mowing down not only the soldiers, but also the Indian women and children who stood in a dense crowd behind the soldiers." *Catholic Standard and Times*, November 22, 1913. Charles Tackett, a mixed-blood interpreter at Rosebud Agency, within days guided an army column to Wounded Knee to bury the dead. Tackett questioned wounded Lakota survivors, said Charles P. Jordan, who, in Jordan's words, "laid all the blame upon two young Indians who fired the first shots, that caused the other armed Indians to open upon the soldiers, the Indians then mingling among their women & children and continued the fire upon the troops." Jordan to "Dear Doctor," March 11, 1891, Jordan Papers.

32. "Louis Mousseau's Interview," in Jensen, *Voices of the American West*, 1:228–29. Despite accounts that say otherwise, correspondent Charles Allen stated that Big Foot was one of the last killed, in the afternoon when the shooting was largely over. "I saw Big Foot rise to a sitting posture from the ground where he had been lying on his back with his face to the glaring sun. . . . No sooner had he done so than—'Crack! Crack!' spoke a couple of rifles, and he fell back to the earth in actual death. Then his daughter . . . came running from the tent where she had been nursing him. . . . Another shot rang out and she fell dead at his side." (It is possible that Allen confused Big Foot with someone else.) Allen, *From Fort Laramie to Wounded Knee*, p. 205. See also *Chicago Inter-Ocean*, December 31, 1890.

33. *Sturgis Tribune*, May 25, 1934; Wells, "Ninety-Six Years among the Indians," p. 287 (quotation). Years later Wells sought a government pension for his service at Wounded Knee, receiving endorsement for his request from then-colonel Charles W.

Taylor, who had organized the first Indian scout company at Pine Ridge Agency. Taylor to the AG, December 17, 1913, Wells Materials, Thomas Odell Collection. Wells again filed for pension status fourteen years later. Survivor's Certificate (SC) 1573038, October 8, 1927, in White, *Index to Pension Applications for Indian Wars Service*, p. 895. A biography of Wells appears in *Westerners Brand Book* 3 (February 1947): 84–85.

34. Quoted in *Army and Navy Register*, February 28, 1891. Brigadier General Ernest D. Scott, whose perceptive study of Wounded Knee appeared simultaneously in 1939 in both *Cavalry Journal* and *Artillery Journal*, remarked: "The soldiers had the advantage of position, being at intervals of two or more yards on a quarter-circle. The Indians were within that curve and closely crowded. The soldiers had the disadvantage of the single-shot carbine, the Indians the advantage of the seven-shot repeating rifle. But the latter advantage ends with the emptying of the magazine; it is difficult to use the rifle as a single-loader and a soldier handy with the carbine could get in several shots in the time necessary to fill the magazine. . . . Attempts to reload their . . . Winchesters must have been fumbling at best; one may reasonably conclude that fighting [in the council area] was over for the Indians [at this stage of the combat] when they had emptied their magazines, perhaps in two or three minutes." Scott, "Wounded Knee," p. 16. Craft later told a reporter that in the thick of the fighting "he felt a sting in the back, and thought that a bullet had struck him. In the excitement he forgot it. He still kept shouting to the Indians to put their guns on the ground. . . . He felt a wave of dizziness and the blood trickling down his back. Just then a soldier came up to him and said: 'Father, hear my confession. I am dying.' He held out his arms to the soldier. With his head resting on the father's shoulder he was given absolution." *Chicago Herald,* January 31, 1891. Craft identified his knife-wielding assailant as Aimed at Him (Tantanyan Kuetpi). Foley, *Father Francis M. Craft,* p. 90.

35. Quoted in Ragnar, in Malm, *The Last Battle of the Sioux Indians,* p. 157.

36. Comfort letter, April 5, 1892. Comfort had seen Civil War service with the Pennsylvania volunteers and in 1865 joined the First Artillery for duty on the Mexican boundary until his discharge three years later. Reenlisting in 1870, he joined the Fourth Cavalry and fought Comanches and Kiowas on the Staked Plains, winning a Medal of Honor for his performance in an encounter at Lake Tahokay, Texas. He was subsequently promoted to sergeant and took his discharge in 1878. Comfort rejoined the First Artillery in 1885, reenlisted in 1890, and served as a private until discharged at his request for apparent age-related infirmities in November 1892. Olmsted, "John W. Comfort," p. 126.

37. Preston letter, p. 30.

38. *Omaha Bee,* December 30, 1890.

39. *Carbon County (Wyoming) Journal,* January 10, 1891. Other contemporary soldier accounts also maintain that because of the formation around the assembly area the men likely shot one another in the initial fusillade. Private Edward Edmunds of Troop G concluded: "I think that the most of our men were injured by our own cross-firing." Edmunds's letter to his father, December 31, 1890, *Washington Evening Star,* January 8, 1891. Another private wrote: "Our commanding officer is going to get a raking over the coals for the way that he managed the fight. If he had done what was right, we would not have lost one-fifth of the men that we did." Quoted in Northrup, *Indian Horrors,* p. 545. Reporter William F. Kelley stated: "The men [were] well-nigh frantic during the engagement, owing to the unfortunate way they were placed." Kelley, *Pine Ridge 1890,* p. 188. Robinson's son "was standing among the Indians when the firing began.

He managed to escape, got a gun and fought the thing out to a finish." *Omaha World-Herald*, January 15, 1891. For Ed Robinson, see also *Junction City Republican*, January 30, 1891. Father Craft was among those who reiterated that "the Indians, in firing upon K & B Troops, . . . shot down their own women & children who stood just beyond the soldiers. Most of the women & children were killed by this fire of the Indians, & others wounded, so that they died either on or near the [council] field." Craft did not believe that the soldiers purposefully killed women and children but that they "did everything in their power, & at their own risk, to prevent it." Craft to Assistant Secretary of War Robert Shaw Oliver, October 11, 1907, Godfrey ACP, NA, RG 94. See also Craft to Editor, *Catholic Standard and Times*, November 22, 1913, including a map.

40. Wallace's location on the field when he was killed is not altogether clear, with some accounts maintaining his presence with his troop and others suggesting that he was returning from searching the Lakota camp when he was shot; at least one more stated that he was found dead near Big Foot's tent. Mann letter. Early accounts reported that Wallace's head had been crushed by a war club. Private Daniel McDonnell of Troop I said he saw Wallace just before the shooting started, "walking along with an Indian stone hammer in his hand, making the remark that he was going to take that home to remember the occasion by. . . . Talk was to effect that after the first shot was fired some Indian grabbed the hammer from Wallace's hand and struck Wallace over the head with it." McDonald (McDonnell) Interview, March 10, 1911, Walter Camp Interview Notes, MS 57, Box 3 (Microfilm Roll 3), BYU. Dr. Ewing confirmed that Wallace had received "two cuts with a tomahawk or hatchet," neither of which fractured the skull. Ewing, "The Wounded of the Wounded Knee Battlefield," p. 41. See also the account of packer John W. Butler in Jensen, *Voices of the American West*, 2:23, and the discussion in Mackintosh, *Custer's Southern Officer*, pp. 154–56. Interpreter Philip Wells believed that Wallace had been killed accidentally by soldiers firing into each other across the assembly area. Wells to editor, *Rapid City Daily Journal*, January 10, 1914. Wells placed Wallace's death at the south periphery of the assembly area near his troop. Untitled sketch map, Wells Materials, D6, F48, Thomas Odell Collection. For Wallace's official obituary, published as Orders No. 21, Fort Riley, February 14, 1891, see McClernand, "Edward W. Casey," pp. 42–43.

41. McGinnis, "I Was There!," p. 52. When he died on March 22, 1965, Hugh McGinnis was the last soldier survivor of Wounded Knee.

42. Crickett letter, p. 4.

43. See Lakota firing lines as depicted in Craft's sketch map (1892), "Battle Field [*sic*] of Wounded Knee." See also Craft's map in *Catholic Standard and Times*, November 22, 1913. Father Craft, who was not active in the later stages of the encounter, believed that women (and presumably children) thus wounded by warriors and fleeing the opening standoff "afterwards fell on other parts of the field," a view not necessarily substantiated by soldier accounts. Ibid.

44. NA Microfilm 983, "Sioux Campaign," 1890–91, Roll 1, p. 671. Wells later wrote that by firing into Troop K to break through to gain the ravine the warriors "exposed their women and children to their own fire." Wells, "Ninety-Six Years among the Indians," p. 287.

45. Craft to James E. Kelly, March 13, 1891, cited in Foley, *At Standing Rock and Wounded Knee*, p. 308 (quotation). On this significant point, see Whitside's comment in NA Microfilm 983, "Sioux Campaign," 1890–91, Roll 1, p. 662: "When the Indians broke through the circle [of Troops B and K] and ran through the village mixed up

with the women and children, the soldiers [were] firing in the direction in which the Indians were going; as a natural consequence women and children were shot. . . . The women and children were never away from the immediate company of the bucks, after the break of bucks from the circle before alluded to." And Wells's remark: "The women and children in and around the tepees were not fired at [by the soldiers] until some five or six of the bucks ran amongst the women and children and began firing from there, and the fire of the soldiers was directed towards them." Ibid., p. 714.

46. An eyewitness reported that "the smoke seemed to cling to the ground and shrouded the struggle." *New York World*, January 2, 1891. Private Clarence Allen of Troop G recalled that when the shooting started "we went off our horses—some on one side, some on the other. Every fourth man was supposed to take the horses back but a lot of them didn't. The horses were simply turned loose and ran wherever they wanted to. As soon as we got off, we immediately laid down as quickly as we could and got a shot in." Allen, "My Experiences in the Seventh Cavalry Known as Custer's Regiment" (undated typescript manuscript), Phillips Materials, Western History Collection, University of Oklahoma Library, Don G. Rickey Papers, p. 8.

47. "Richard C. Stirk's Interview," in Jensen, *Voices of the American West*, 2:286 and map "Richard Stirk's Wounded Knee" and accompanying text, between pp. 210 and 211.

48. Edmunds's letter to his father, December 31, 1890, *Washington Evening Star*, January 8, 1891.

49. Comfort letter, April 15, 1892.

50. Stanislas Roy Interview (1909), Walter Camp Interview Notes, MS 57, Box 2 (Microfilm Roll 4), BYU.

51. Preston letter, p. 30.

52. Ibid., p. 31. See Ricker's interpretation of what happened in Jensen, *Voices of the American West*, 2:60–61. A period definition of "massacre" described it as "the killing of human beings by indiscriminate slaughter, murder of numbers with cruelty or atrocity, or contrary to the usages of civilized people; cold-blooded destruction of life; butchery; carnage." Wilhelm, *A Military Dictionary and Gazetteer*, p. 310. Note that the definition encompasses neither intent nor purpose, only the act itself.

Philip Wells recalled months later that the many recruits accompanying the army command "could not tell squaws from bucks, and consequently shot them both. I defy any man to pick the squaws from among the bucks in a group of Indians at a distance of 100 feet who has not had considerable experience among them." *Sioux City Journal*, May 5, 1891.

53. Quoted in Northrup, *Indian Horrors*, p. 545.

54. McDonald (McDonnell) interview, March 10, 1911. On the matter of being a massacre, it is important to specify that at least one junior infantry officer at Pine Ridge, doubtless reflecting peer gossip in the immediate wake of the event, penned his wife an accurate private briefing on Wounded Knee on December 30, noting that "several [warriors] who were slightly wounded killed soldiers treacherously *so none were spared* [by the troops] *after that*. The squaws were as bad as the men . . . like she-devils. . . . General Brooke is very sanguine and thinks yesterday's *massacre* will be sufficient. That's what he thought at Reveille [on December 30; emphases added]." "Extracts from Letters Written by Lieutenant Alexander R. Piper, 8th Infantry," pp. 6–7. Similarly, photographer Clarence G. Moreledge, who was at Pine Ridge during this time, wrote only two days after the event that the "'Wounded Knee Massacre' is said to be the hardest fight since the 'Custer Massacre.'" Moreledge to Warren K. Moorehead, December 31, 1890. Moorehead Papers, MS 106, Box 19.

55. Forsyth to Brooke, December 29, 1890, NA, RG 393, Entry 3779, Department of the Platte, Letters Received, 1890–91. Another hastily scribbled message perhaps went forward via one of Taylor's scouts: "Gen Brooke[:] Big Foot's band practically destroyed! Capt Wallace killed. Lieut Garlington wounded. 20 soldiers killed & wounded[.] Indians fired on troops while being disarmed[.] [signed] Taylor comdg scouts[.]" This note reached the agency at 12:30 P.M. NA, RG 393, Entry 3779, Department of the Platte, Letters Received, 1890–91.

56. Each piece with its compressed-steel carriage weighed only 337 pounds, so that single units with their components and ammunition could be transported by four mules. The guns fired percussion-fuzed two-pound fixed 1.65-inch shells that, exploding on impact, could violently rake a targeted enemy with fragmented shards. They also delivered tinned canister cartridges, each of which strafed targets with as many as thirty one-half-inch lead balls. The guns employed a bolt-operated breech-loading/ejection system and had an effective range of 4,200 yards. Muzzle velocity was 1,298 feet per second. Introduced by then colonel Miles in the 1870s for use in Indian combat, the guns first saw action during the Nez Perce War. Each piece required two cannoneers to service it. "Report of the Chief of Ordnance, October 1, 1880," in *Report of the Secretary of War, 1880*, 3:132–34, 219–20; Farrow, *Farrow's Military Encyclopedia*, 2:57; *Chicago Inter-Ocean*, January 18, 1891; *New York Times*, December 15, 1891; Greene, *Nez Perce Summer*, pp. 287–88. Approximate rate of fire is based on time for discharge, recoil, realignment, and resighting of each piece: thus perhaps ten seconds or so between shots. I am grateful to Daniel Cullity for this estimate.

57. Comfort letter, April 15, 1892. James Mooney learned of the effect of the canister on one woman he met in 1891. She "had received fourteen wounds, while each of her two little boys was also wounded by her side." Mooney, "Ghost-Dance Religion," p. 869.

58. NA Microfilm 983, "Sioux Campaign," 1890–91, Roll 1, p. 699. See the excerpt from Capron's report in an endorsement for the mountain gun in *Descriptive Catalogue of War Material Manufactured by the Hotchkiss Ordnance Company, Limited*, p. 23. Capron would himself be killed by a bullet to the heart while serving with the Rough Riders at Las Guásimas, Cuba, on June 24, 1898.

59. Mann letter. Capron indicated that the canister was fired into the tent. *Descriptive Catalogue of War Material*, p. 23.

60. Quoted in Lindberg, "Foreigners in Action at Wounded Knee," p. 177. The tent had belonged to the scout Garnier, who had left his weapon there when he went into the Indian camp to interpret for the soldiers collecting guns. Cook, *Fifty Years on the Old Frontier*, pp. 197–98.

61. William F. Bailey interview (1909), Walter Camp Interview Notes, MS 57, Box 4 (Microfilm Roll 3), BYU.

62. "Meded Swigert's Interview," in Jensen, *Voices of the American West*, 2:19.

63. *Omaha Bee*, December 30, 1890.

64. *Chicago Inter-Ocean*, January 20, 1891; also quoted in Northrup, *Indian Horrors*, p. 549.

65. Allen, *From Fort Laramie to Wounded Knee*, p. 197. Scout John Shangrau maintained that he also was still in the village when the firing erupted. "John Shangrau's Interview," in Jensen, *Voices of the American West*, 1:262.

66. NA Microfilm 983, "Sioux Campaign," 1890–91, Roll 1, p. 701.

67. On this point, see "Paddy Starr's Interview," in Jensen, *Voices of the American West*, 1:237–38, and "Standing Soldier's Interview," in ibid., 1:243–44. Regarding the

scouts, see also First Lieutenant Fayette W. Roe to Forsyth, February 16, 1891 (particularly the seventh endorsement by Lieutenant Godfrey), Brooke Papers, Box 9.

68. Godfrey to Chief, Historical Section, Army War College, May 29, 1931, Edward S. Godfrey Collection, U.S. Army Military History Institute, Army War College.

69. *New York World*, January 7, 1891.

70. Godfrey, "Cavalry Fire Discipline," p. 259.

71. Former private Andrew M. Flynn of Troop A, Seventh Cavalry, who was a trained medic, provided details of Garlington's treatment. See his reminiscence "An Army Medic at Wounded Knee," in Greene, *Indian War Veterans*, pp. 187, 189. Another account stated that Garlington was wounded on the rise near the Hotchkiss guns. "Wounded Knee Statement of Charles W. Allen," in Jensen, *Voices of the American West*, 2:14, 15.

72. Quoted in Lindberg, "Foreigners in Action at Wounded Knee," pp. 176–77.

73. The "pocket" is precisely delineated on the Hade-Cloman map. It also appears on the map accompanying the John Comfort letter, April 5, 1892, but is inexplicably represented as being on the south side of the large ravine.

74. Quoted in Beyer and Keydel, *Deeds of Valor*, 2:325. See citations for Hawthorne, Weinert, and other artillerymen in *Army and Navy Register*, March 21, 1891.

75. Small to George W. Webb, 1932 (quotation); Forsyth's report, December 31, 1890; Roe to Forsyth, February 16, 1891, 6th endorsement by Captain Edgerly, Brooke Papers, Box 9. Perspectives of Northern Cheyenne scouts at Wounded Knee appear in Marquis and Limbaugh, *Cheyenne and Sioux*, pp. 42–43; and Marquis, *A Warrior Who Fought Custer*, pp. 335–37.

76. Comfort letter, April 15, 1892.

77. Godfrey to Chief, Historical Section, Army War College, May 29, 1931.

78. Forsyth to Brooke, December 29, 1890, NA, RG 393, Entry 3779, Department of the Platte, Letters Received, 1890–91.

79. Wells, "Ninety-Six Years among the Indians," p. 288 (quotation); Regimental Returns of the Seventh Cavalry, December 1890, NA Microfilm 744, Roll 74; Regimental Returns of the First Artillery, December 1890, NA Microfilm 727, Roll 7; "Report of the Surgeon-General," September 22, 1891, in *Report of the Secretary of War, 1891*, p. 600; "Muster Roll, Company A. Indian Scouts." For specifics on the casualties, see appendix D.

80. Flynn, "An Army Medic at Wounded Knee," p. 189. Indeed the saving of women and children by troops or others is frequently mentioned. See, for example, Father Craft to Judge Eli S. Ricker, January 16, 1907, in Jensen, *Voices of the American West*, 2:22–23.

81. Allen, "My Experiences in the Seventh Cavalry," pp. 9–10.

82. Allen, *From Fort Laramie to Wounded Knee*, p. 206.

83. Odell, "Comments of Philip F. Wells."

84. NA Microfilm 983, "Sioux Campaign," 1890–91, Roll 1, p. 715; "Philip Wells's Interview," in Jensen, *Voices of the American West*, 1:129–30 (quotation). See also Allen, *From Fort Laramie to Wounded Knee*, p. 206. One witness stated that soldiers killed at least one of those who sat up. "Paddy Starr's Interview," 1:238.

85. Allen, *From Fort Laramie to Wounded Knee*, pp. 207–208 (quotation); telegram, Miles to AG, December 30, 1890, NA, RG 393, part 1, Entry 2540, Military Division of the Missouri, Letters Sent by Headquarters in the Field, 1890–91; Mackintosh, *Custer's Southern Officer*, p. 161; *Heritage Auction Catalog*, Auction 681, November 10, 2007, p. 127.

86. Philip Wells stated that he forbade the soldiers from moving the dead, perhaps because he understood that the families might later claim them. Odell, "Comments of Philip F. Wells."

87. Telegram, Miles to AG, December 30, 1890, NA, RG 393, part 1, Entry 2540, Military Division of the Missouri, Letters Sent by Headquarters in the Field, 1890–91. Forsyth maintained that but "for the attack by the Brules, an accurate count [of all the Indian dead] would have been made." Ibid.

88. McCormick, "Wounded Knee and Drexel Mission Fights," p. 14.

89. *Chicago Inter-Ocean*, December 31, 1890.

90. Brooke to Miles, December 29, 1890, 9:25 P.M., Brooke Papers, Sioux Campaign 1890–91, vol. 1, p. 652.

91. Morning Report, Divisional Field Hospital, Pine Ridge Agency, S.D., December 30, 1890, NA, RG 393, part 1, Entry 3789. "Morning Reports of Sick at Kearney, Nebr., Camp George Crook, Nebr., and Field Hospital, Pine Ridge, S. Dak., Aug. 1889–Jan. 1891"; Eastman, *From the Deep Woods to Civilization*, pp. 233–34; Tibbles, *Buckskin and Blanket Days*, pp. 321–22.

92. Letter from an unidentified carpenter at Pine Ridge, March 1, 1891, SDSHS, Item H75.157; "Extracts from Letters Written by Lieutenant Alexander R. Piper, 8th Infantry," entry for December 29, 1890 (quotation). Father Jutz stated that "the shooting at Wounded Knee could be heard at our Mission. An Indian of the neighborhood . . . ran excitedly to our house to call my attention to it." Jutz, "Historic Data," p. 324. Agent Royer notified Commissioner Morgan at 12:37 P.M. Telegram, Royer to Commissioner of Indian Affairs, December 29, 1890, McLaughlin Papers, Roll 35 (see also Morgan to Secretary of the Interior, December 30, 1890, NA Microfilm 983, "Sioux Campaign," 1890–91, Roll 1, p. 638). At 11:30 A.M. Brooke disseminated the news of Wounded Knee through Miles to the army command. Brooke to Miles, December 29, 1890, Brooke Papers, Sioux Campaign 1890–91, vol. 1, p. 636; Miles to AG, December 29, 1890, NA Microfilm 983, "Sioux Campaign," 1890–91, Roll 1, p. 632. Word of the disaster reached Fort Riley at 3 P.M. on December 29, just on the heels of receipt of word of Whitside's success in capturing Big Foot. *Junction City Republican*, January 2, 1891; telegram, Miles to AG, December 29, 1890, forwarding Brooke to Miles, December 29, 1890, NA Microfilm 983, "Sioux Campaign," 1890–91, Roll 1, p. 624.

93. Telegram, Brooke to Miles, December 29, 1890, 10:15 P.M., Brooke Papers, Sioux Campaign 1890–91, vol. 1, p. 654; *Omaha World-Herald*, January 4, 1891; Wilson, "The Attack on the Pine Ridge Indian Agency," pp. 565–68; "Extracts from Letters Written by Lieutenant Alexander R. Piper, 8th Infantry," p. 6; Moreledge to Moorehead, December 31, 1890, Moorehead Papers, MS 106, Box 19; *National Tribune*, June 22, 1893; Eastman, *From the Deep Woods to Civilization*, pp. 229–33; Eastman, *Sister to the Sioux*, p. 156; Tibbles, *Buckskin and Blanket Days*, pp. 317–21; Morgan, "Reminiscences of My Days in the Land of the Ogalala [sic] Sioux," pp. 55–56; *Philadelphia Inquirer*, December 31, 1890; Brooke to Miles, January 5, 1891, Brooke Papers, Sioux Campaign 1890–91, vol. 1, pp. 761–62; telegram, Cooper to Commissioner Morgan, December 30, 1890, McLaughlin Papers, Roll 35. See also "William Peano's Interview," in Jensen, *Voices of the American West*, 1:233–35. At the mission Father Jutz learned of the fighting from Indians in the morning, probably within an hour of when it started. A Sioux man who had been shot three times at Wounded Knee appeared at one of the camps near the agency. Perrig Diary, entries for December 29 and 30, 1890; Jutz, "Historic Data," p. 324; account of Captain Augustus W. Corliss, Eight Infantry, in *Denver Post*, November 15, 1903; *Omaha Bee*, January 1, 1891. Elaine Goodale wrote

that when the word circulated the Sioux camps "melted away like snow-banks in April. The brown hills were instantly alive with galloping horsemen and a long line of loaded wagons disappeared in the distance." Eastman, "Ghost Dance War," p. 36. Red Cloud's forced departure is described in Red Cloud to W. J. Pollock, February 5, 1891, NA, RG 75, Letters Received, NIS 176 (Microfilm), Roll 3. See also Larson, *Red Cloud*, p. 280.

In addition to the sources quoted or otherwise cited above, this account of Wounded Knee has benefited from material in the following primary materials by participants and eyewitnesses: Whitside to AAAG, Division of the Missouri in the field, January 5, 1891, "Statement[,] Strength of 7th Cavalry at Battle of Wounded Knee Creek S.D. Dec 29 1890," NA, RG 393, part 1, Entry 2546, Military Division of the Missouri, Headquarters, Letters Received, Box 126-7; Hawthorne, *Times-Star* account; Philip Wells's accounts in *Sioux City Journal*, May 5, 1891, and in *Winners of the West* (January 1939); Carroll, *I, Varnum*, pp. 22–23; Sedgwick Rice interview (undated). Walter Camp Interview Notes, MS 57, Box 3 (Microfilm Roll 3), BYU; Colonel Charles W. Taylor Interview, February 6, 1912, Walter Camp Interview Notes, MS 57, Box 6, Folder 9, Envelope 85, pp. 494–95 (Microfilm Roll 5), BYU; Bailey (first name unknown) interview (undated). Walter Camp Interview Notes, MS 57, Box 4 (Microfilm Roll 3), BYU; Colonel John Van R. Hoff interview, October 13, 1912, Ellison/Camp Papers, Box 1, FF 49; First Lieutenant Ezra B. Fuller to unidentified recipient, December 30, 1890, eBay Auction #250696000024, October 12, 2010; Green A. Settle to "My Dear Comrade," February 28, 1936, Don C. Rickey Files; Robinson, "Recollections of Gen. W. W. Robinson, Jr."; NA, RG 391, Records of U.S. Regular Army Mobile Units, Cavalry—7th Cavalry, 1866–1917, Entry 865, "Scrapbook of Clippings and Pictures of Troop C with a History of Troop A, 1867–1932"; Kelley, "Indian Troubles and the Battle of Wounded Knee," pp. 41–44; Document 2.6, "The Indian Wars in South Dakota," in Kreis, *Lakotas, Black Robes, and Holy Women*, pp. 151–52. In addition to previously cited maps, see "Scene of the Fight with Big Foot's Band Dec. 29, 1890," NA, RG 77, War Department Map Collection, South Dakota 17. (Three versions of this map with largely imperceptible differences exist; one has been cited as the Hade-Cloman map. The third appears in NA Microfilm 983, "Sioux Campaign," 1890–91, Roll 1, following p. 650.) See also "Wounded Knee Battlefield, based on the map of Lieutenant Thomas Q. Donaldson," in Mooney, "Ghost-Dance Religion," plate 97, following p. 868. Useful sketch maps include "Map Furnished by Col. Forsythe [*sic*], 7th Cav, of Action of 29 Dec 1890." NA, RG 77, War Department Map Collection, South Dakota 30; map, A. T. Lea Papers, Gilcrease Museum; Stanislaus Roy, map, "Battle of Wounded Knee"; map by Philip F. Wells (marked on the back "Felix Fly" and "One Feather"), Wells Materials, D6, F48, Thomas Odell Collection; the aforementioned map by John Comfort; and the maps by Father Craft in Foley, *At Standing Rock and Wounded Knee*, pp. 303, 309, 312.

Contemporary newspaper accounts not previously cited appear in *Army and Navy Register*, January 3, 1891; *Army and Navy Journal*, January 3, 17, and 24, 1891, and February 7, 1891; *New York Times*, December 29, 1890; *Junction City Republican*, February 6, 1891; *Chicago Inter-Ocean*, December 30, 1890, and January 7, 1891; *Omaha Bee*, December 31, 1890; *New York Herald*, December 31, 1890; *Philadelphia Inquirer*, December 31, 1890; and *Harper's Weekly*, February 7, 1891.

The following secondary works contain important elements and insights in respect to facets of the Wounded Knee engagement: Utley, *Last Days of the Sioux Nation*, pp. 200–30; Mattes, "The Enigma of Wounded Knee"; Mattes, *Special Site Report on Wounded Knee Battlefield;* Utley, *Frontier Regulars,* pp. 406–408; Scott, "Wounded Knee," pp. 9–24; Shockley, "The Affair at Wounded Knee," pp. 42–44; Mackintosh, *Custer's Southern Officer,* pp. 151–55; DeBarthe, *Life and Adventures of Frank Grouard,* pp. 238–40; Harvey, "Last Stand of the Sioux," pp. 232–33; Rickey, *Forty Miles a Day on Beans and Hay,* pp. 274–77, 287–89, 313, 317, 320; Traub, "Sioux Campaign— Winter of 1890–'91," pp. 67–71; and Robinson, *History of the Dakota or Sioux Indians,* pp. 491–99. See also Shaw, "The Battle of Wounded Knee."

Chapter 12. Place of the Big Killings

1. For information of the status of education and English usage among Indians at Cheyenne River and Standing Rock in 1889 and 1890, see "Report of Cheyenne River Agency," August 5, 1890 (pp. 42–44), and "Report of Standing Rock Agency," August 26, 1890 (pp. 37–38), in *Report of the Commissioner of Indian Affairs, 1890;* "Report of Cheyenne River Agency," August 17, 1891 (1:388–89, especially pp. 391–92), and "Report of Standing Rock Agency," August 26, 1891 (1:326–27), in *Report of the Commissioner of Indian Affairs, 1891.* Data respecting the uses and importance of Indian testimony appear in Greene, *Lakota and Cheyenne,* pp. xxi–xxiii. It has been suggested that Lakota veterans of Wounded Knee perhaps contrived compliant rather than defiant narratives of their recollections of the massacre. Ostler, *Plains Sioux and U.S. Colonialism,* p. 340. This most likely would have occurred during the 1920s–1940s as impending compensation legislation promoted the creation of survivors' organizations at the Pine Ridge and Cheyenne River reservations.

2. Ghost Horse, "True Story," p. 12; High Back, "Paul Highback's Version of the Disaster," p. 2.

3. Horn Cloud's account in Jensen, *Voices of the American West,* 1: 199; Ghost Horse, "True Story," p. 12; Long Bull's account in *Washington Evening Star,* January 28, 1891. A statement prepared by Lakota survivors in September 1915 supported this unfolding scenario. It said that the men were called to council at 8 A.M. and that the "army leader that met Big Foot yesterday [Whitside] said: Yesterday when I saw you, I seen that all of you men had guns. You will give me those guns." The men brought forth guns, some from the camp. "As they were putting their guns in the pile someone blew a whistle and all the army men loaded their guns as one." Then "an army leader sitting atop a dark bay horse gave the order to shoot and they started shooting." Statement entitled "Dec. 29, 1890," signed by Peter One Skunk, Jessie Sunka Luzahan (Jessie Running Horse?), Alex High Hawk, Charles Blue Arm, Solomon Afraid of Enemy, and Daniel Blue Hair. Camp Manuscripts, Lilly Library.

4. "Joseph Horn Cloud's Interview," in Jensen, *Voices of the American West,* 1:198– 204 (quotations on 199 and 200).

5. Joseph Horn Cloud's statement of October 24, 1913, in "Truth of the Wounded Knee Massacre," in Jensen, *Voices of the American West,* 1:200, 247 (first and second quotations); see also a truncated and somewhat different account by Horn Cloud contained in a typescript statement given on March 12, 1917, during a compensation hearing (NA, RG 75, copy provided by Michael Her Many Horses); "Dewey Beard's Interview," in Jensen, *Voices of the American West,* 1:217–26; Iron Hail, "The Truth of the Wounded Knee Massacre" (statement of November 27, 1913), in Jensen, *Voices of the American West,* 1::248–51 (third quotation on 249).

6. "Statement of Frog, of Big Foot's Band," January 7, 1891 (interpreted by Philip F. Wells, witnessed by the Reverend Charles Smith Cook), in NA Microfilm 983, "Sioux Campaign," 1890–91, Roll 1, pp. 717–18.

7. "Statement of 'Help Them,'" January 7, 1891 (interpreted by Philip F. Wells, witnessed by the Reverend Charles Smith Cook)," ibid., pp. 719–20.

8. "Statement of Hehakawanyakapi," undated but likely January 7, 1891 (signed by Reverend Charles Smith Cook and Philip F. Wells), Philip F. Wells Materials, D6, F41, Thomas Odell Collection. The accounts of Frog, Help Them, and Hehakawanyakapi also appeared in Wells, "Ninety-Six Years among the Indians," pp. 290–93.

9. Spotted Horse's remark in "Account Given by Indians of the Fight at Wounded Knee Creek, South Dakota, December 29, 1890," February 11, 1891, in *Report of the Commissioner of Indian Affairs, 1891*, 1:180 (also reproduced in Mooney, "Ghost-Dance Religion," p. 885); Dog Chief account through Black Elk in DeMallie, *Sixth Grandfather*, pp. 270–71.

10. High Back, "Paul High Back's Version of the Disaster," p. 2; interview, Andrew Good Thunder, July 12, 1912, Camp Manuscripts, Lilly Library, Box 6, Folder 14, Envelope 90, pp. 521–32.

11. Account of Zella Vespucia, *Washington Evening Star*, January 27, 1891 (Vespucia had been a signer of the 1889 land agreement: see *Reports Relative to the Proposed Division of the Great Sioux Reservation*, p. 269).

12. Joseph Horn Cloud's statement of October 24, 1913, in "The Truth of the Wounded Knee Massacre," p. 247; High Back, "Paul High Back's Version of the Disaster of Dec. 29, 1890, at Wounded Knee," pp. 2–3; Joseph Horn Cloud, sketch map of the Wounded Knee site, ca. 1904, Ricker Collection, MS8, Nebraska State Historical Society (see also the Joseph Horn Cloud map in Jensen, *Voices of the American West*, following 1:272); Jensen, *Voices of the American West*, 1:222 (Iron Hail quotations). The Ricker interviews of Joseph Horn Cloud and Dewey Beard also appear in Danker, *The Wounded Knee Interviews of Eli S. Ricker* (reprint from *Nebraska History* 62 [Summer 1981]: 164–79, and 180–200, respectively). Other interviews with Dewey Beard (Iron Hail—also known as Beard and Dewey Horn Cloud) appear in Walker, *Lakota Society* (a statement given to Pine Ridge Agency physician Walker between 1896 and 1914), pp. 157–68; a typescript statement given on March 12, 1917, during a compensation hearing (NA, RG 75; copy provided by Michael Her Many Horses); and McGregor, *The Wounded Knee Massacre from the Viewpoint of the Sioux*, pp. 103–107. A recollection essentially ascribed to Dewey Beard, written by Pine Ridge Agency physician Dr. James R. Walker and apparently fictionalized for dramatic effect, appeared in Beach, "Wounded Knee." The alternative names for Beard's sister and wife appear in Maurice Frink to "Dear John," December 9, 1969, James R. Walker Manuscripts, Collection 653, FF 245, Item 9, Colorado Historical Society. For more on Dewey Beard and his experiences, see Utley, "Wounded Knee and Other Dark Images."

13. Ghost Horse, "True Story," pp. 12–13.

14. One Skunk account in *Rapid City Daily Republican*, December 29, 1938, and *Newcastle News Letter-Journal*, August 17, 1939; Iron Hail, "Truth of the Wounded Knee Massacre" (statement of November 27, 1913), 248–51; Dewey Beard interview in Jensen, *Voices of the American West*, 1:224 (quotation).

15. "Dewey Beard Interview," in Jensen, *Voices of the American West*, 1:224.

16. "Joseph Horn Cloud's Interview," 1:198–204 (quotation on 203).

17. "Statement of John White Lance re: the Wounded Knee Massacre of 1890," December 12, 1975 (copy provided by Michael Her Many Horses); account of White

Lance in McGregor, *The Wounded Knee Massacre*, pp. 118–19 (quotation) (photocopy provided by Michael Her Many Horses); all personal statements from this source were derived from typescript testimony assembled in support of a bill drafted during the second session of the 74th Congress in 1936–37, seeking compensation for the massacre.

18. Account of James Pipe on Head in McGregor, *Wounded Knee Massacre*, pp. 108–109.

19. Account of Rough Feather in ibid., pp. 110–11.

20. Account of Mrs. Mousseau (Medicine Woman) in ibid., pp. 113–14; account of Mrs. Mousseau given on October 29, 1913, in "The Truth of the Wounded Knee Massacre," pp. 251–52.

21. Account of Mrs. Mousseau in "Truth of the Wounded Knee Massacre," pp. 251–52. If there were indeed heroes on the army side at Wounded Knee, they most certainly were among the Indian scouts who tried to protect and save some of their people when things got out of hand.

22. Account of Edward Owl King in McGregor, *Wound Knee Massacre*, pp. 116–17.

23. Account of Nellie Knife in ibid., pp. 138–39.

24. Account of Mrs. Rough Feather in ibid., pp. 127–28.

25. Account of Henry Jackson in ibid., pp. 119–20.

26. Account of John Little Finger in ibid., pp. 120–22.

27. Account of Peter Stand in ibid., pp. 123–24.

28. Accounts of Dog Chief and James High Hawk in ibid., pp. 133–36; account of Charley Blue Arm in ibid., p. 138 (quotations).

29. Eastman, *Sister to the Sioux*, p. 160.

30. Neihardt, *Black Elk Speaks*, pp. 207–14 (including first quotation); DeMallie, *The Sixth Grandfather*, pp. 272–74 (including second quotation). (For a critique of Black Elk's remembrance, see Steltenkamp, *Nicholas Black Elk*, pp. 69–70.)

31. Neihardt, *Black Elk Speaks*, p. 210.

32. Ibid. Philip Wells maintained that by and large "women and children did not fight [at Wounded Knee]. They were busy getting away in order to save their lives." Odell, "Comments of Philip F. Wells." Within months Brulé chief Hollow Horn Bear at Rosebud Agency suggested that some of the Wounded Knee Indian dead were in fact mixed-blood children fathered years earlier by soldiers at Fort Laramie. *Army and Navy Register*, March 14, 1891.

33. High Back, "Paul High Back's Version of the Disaster," pp. 2–3; Ghost Horse, "True Story," pp. 13–14 (quotation); "As Narrated by 'Short Bull,'" pp. 16–18. For the versions of others who were present at Wounded Knee, see the accounts of Louise Weasel Bear, George Running Hawk, Bertha Kills Close to Lodge, Donald Blue Hair, Afraid of the Enemy, Frank Sits Poor, Richard Afraid of Hawk, and Joseph Black Hair, in McGregor, *Wounded Knee Massacre;* and that of Ellis Standing Bear in Standing Bear, *My People the Sioux*, pp. 231–32. Hearsay or secondary accounts passed down from participants and eyewitnesses may not possess the immediacy and likely accuracy of those by persons who were on the scene in 1890. But these accounts, particularly from those only one generation removed from the event, nonetheless possess ephemeral value that can be interpretively useful among families in recalling, conveying, and preserving recollections of what happened. Among the best are Celane Not Help Him, re: Iron Hail/Dewey Bear, in Penman, *Honor the Grandmothers*, pp. 14–23; Jensen and Paul, National Register of Historic Places Registration Form, with statements of Celane Not Help Him, re: Iron Hail/Dewey Beard, August 1, 1990; Leonard Little Finger, re: John Little Finger, July 14, 1990; Leona Broken Nose, re: James Pipe on Head, August

1, 1990; and Birgil Kills Straight, re: Daniel White Lance, July 14, 1990. See also Celane Not Help Him, re: Iron Hail/Dewey Beard, *Lakota Times*, October 16, 1990; Wounded Horse, "Dewy Girl Was There"; Turning Hawk, American Horse, and George Sword (none of whom were present at Wounded Knee), in *Report of the Commissioner of Indian Affairs, 1891*, 1:179–81; and report of Elaine Goodale, January 12, 1891, *Washington Post*, January 17, 1891. Although of a secondary nature, the last two citations contain solid information about Wounded Knee obtained close to the event from persons who were present. A useful though somewhat editorialized montage incorporating both participant and hearsay Lakota accounts appears in Coleman, *Voices of Wounded Knee*, pp. 279–341.

34. Camp Manuscripts, Lilly Library, Box 6, Folder 13, Envelope 78, "Data on monument and notes of Battlefield and fight from Indian side" (1910). It is clear today that the Hotchkiss fire did not take place until the cavalry shooting in the council area was finished.

35. Private Hartford G. Clark, Troop G and Band, Sixth Cavalry, January 1891 Diary, Don G. Rickey Papers (hereinafter cited as Clark Diary), entry for Monday, January 12, 1891 (first quotation); interview with Leonard Little Finger, April 21, 2010, Sacred Hoop School, Oglala, South Dakota (second quotation). For discussion of the numbers of Indians present and killed, see Mooney, "Ghost-Dance Religion," pp. 870–71. For the army's February 1891 estimate of Indian casualties, see appendix E. An unavoidably imprecise tabulation containing more than 800 entries that nonetheless helps personalize the Lakotas' presence and losses at Wounded Knee appears in Jensen, "Big Foot's Followers at Wounded Knee," pp. 201–209, and accounts for perhaps 71 Lakotas wounded who survived (a subjective list of Lakota casualties derived from Jensen's compilation appears in appendix F). Among early listings of casualty data, see especially Perain P. Palmer, "Number and names of Indians absent and not drawing Rations at Cheyenne River Agency S.D., December 22, 1890" (which includes names of heads of families and sizes of families), December 28, 1890, NA at Kansas City, RG 75, Cheyenne River, Book 364; "Approximate Census of the Sioux Indians belonging to the Cheyenne River reservation who were in the battle of Wounded Knee and as yet at Pine Ridge Agency S.D., taken January 30, 1891" (lists names, sex, age, and whether living or dead, including a Black Fox, age 33, as "Dead"), NA, RG 75; copy in Wounded Knee Compensation Papers, SDSHS, H76.24, Folder 16, Box 3564A; Joseph Horn Cloud, "Names of those killed at the Wounded Knee Massacre, Pine Ridge Agency, South Dakota, December 29, 1890" (ca. 1907), in Jensen, *Voices of the American West*, 1:204–208 (also included in Danker, *Wounded Knee Interviews*, pp. 176–79); "List of Indians Killed and Wounded at Sioux Massacre, December 29, 1890," with collateral papers, filed by Joseph Horn Cloud, April 14, 1920 (incorporates lists compiled in 1917 and 1918 and includes people living at Pine Ridge, Cheyenne River, and Standing Rock), Wounded Knee Compensation Papers, SDSHS, H76.24, Box 3564A. See also James W. Wengert, "Wounded Knee Killed or Subsequently Died of Wounds," James Wengert Military Medical Collection, Pritzker Military Library.

Chapter 13. Direct Corollaries

1. "Abstract of Correspondence," pp. 17–18; Brooke to Miles, December 29, 1890, Brooke Papers, Sioux Campaign 1890–91, vol. 1, p. 636; telegram, Miles to AG, December 29, 1890, NA Microfilm 983, "Sioux Campaign," 1890–91, Roll 1, p. 633;

telegram, Miles to AG, December 29, 1890 (forwarding Brooke's message), ibid., p. 634; *Sioux Falls Argus-Leader*, December 30, 1890; *Washington Evening Star*, December 30, 1890; *Chicago Inter-Ocean*, December 31, 1890; Brooke to Henry, December 29, 1890, NA, RG 393, Entry 3775, vol. 2 of 3, "Letters Sent Headquarters in the Field. From December 19th, 1890. To January 9th, 1891" (first quotation); "Report of Major General Miles," September 14, 1891, in *Report of the Secretary of War, 1891*, 1:150 (second quotation).

2. Miles to AG, December 29, 1890 (Item 265); Miles to AG, December 29, 1890 (Item 263) (quotation); both in NA, RG 393, part 1, Entry 2540, Military Division of the Missouri, Letters Sent by Headquarters in the Field, 1890–91; Royer to Morgan, December 30, 1890, NA Microfilm 983, "Sioux Campaign," 1890–91, Roll 1, p. 638. See also telegram, A. T. Cooper to Commissioner of Indian Affairs, December 30, 1890, in Morgan to Noble, December 31, 1890, in NA Microfilm 983, "Sioux Campaign," 1890–91, Roll 1, p. 639.

3. "Abstract of Correspondence," p. 18; telegram, Miles to Brooke, December 29, 1890 (Item 260); telegram, Miles to Brooke, December 29, 1890 (Item 261); telegram, Miles to Brooke, December 29, 1890 (Item 262); telegram, Miles to AG, December 29, 1890 (Item 263); telegram, Miles to Commanding Officer, Fort Meade, December 29, 1890 (Item 272); all in NA, RG 393, part 1, Entry 2540, Military Division of the Missouri, Letters Sent by Headquarters in the Field, 1890–91; telegram, Miles to AG, December 30, 1890, enclosing Brooke to Miles, same date; telegram, Aide-de-Camp Marion Maus to Commanding Officer, First Infantry, Hermosa, South Dakota, December 29, 1890 (Item 268); both in NA Microfilm 983, "Sioux Campaign," 1890–91, Roll 1, p. 635; telegram, Maus to First Lieutenant Thomas Connolly, December 29, 1890 (Item 275), ibid.; Johnson, *Unregimented General*, pp. 288–89 (including first quotation, December 30, 1890); telegram, Schofield to Miles, December 30, 1890, with note of January 2, 1891; telegram, Miles to Schofield, January 1, 1891, p. 785; both in NA Microfilm 983, "Sioux Campaign," 1890–91, Roll 1, p. 641 (second quotation).

4. Regimental Returns of the Ninth Cavalry, December 1890, NA Microfilm 744, Roll 90; "Extracts from Letters Written by Lieutenant Alexander R. Piper, 8th Infantry," p. 7 (first quotation); telegram, AAG, Department of the Platte, to Brooke, December 30, 1890, NA, RG 393, PI 172, Entry 3722, Department of the Platte, Letters Sent, 1866–98, vol. 19, p. 129; telegram, urgent request dated December 29, 1891, Fort Riley, for list of killed and wounded, NA, RG 393, Headquarters, Department of the Platte, Letters Received, 1890, Box 152; "Augustus W. Corliss's Interview," in Jensen, *Voices of the American West*, 2:325–26; Henry to First Lieutenant Fayette W. Roe, January 17, 1891, NA, RG 393, part 1, Entry 3779, Department of the Platte, Letters Received, 1890–91; *Army and Navy Journal*, May 29, 1892 (second quotation); "Sketch of Location of Attack on Wagon train under escort of Capt. J. S. Loud 9th Cavalry near Pine Ridge Agency, Dec. 30, 1890, drawn by Major Guy V. Henry, 9th Cav.," in NA Microfilm 983, "Sioux Campaign," 1890–91, Roll 2, p. 1715; Crickett letter, p. 6; McCormick, "Wounded Knee and Drexel Mission Fights," p. 15; Kelley, *Pine Ridge 1890*, p. 192; *Harper's Weekly*, July 27, 1895; *Chicago Inter-Ocean*, December 31, 1890; *New York Herald*, December 31, 1890; Loud to wife, December 30, 1890, in Erisman and Erisman, "Letters from the Field," pp. 32–33 (third quotation); Allen, *From Fort Laramie to Wounded Knee*, pp. 215–16; Loud to wife, December 30, 1890, in Erisman and Erisman, "Letters from the Field," p. 34 (fourth quotation).

5. Ragnar (Ling-Vannerus), in Lindberg, "Foreigners in Action at Wounded Knee," p. 178 (first quotation); Alexander W. Perry, "The Ninth United States Cavalry in the

Sioux Campaign of 1890," in Carroll, *Black Military Experience in the American West*, p. 252 (second quotation); *Army and Navy Journal*, January 10, 1891. Secondary treatments appear in Brady, *Indian Fights and Fighters*, p. 353; Buecker, "'The Men Behaved Splendidly,'" p. 61; Buecker, *Fort Robinson and the American West*, p. 177; Leckie and Leckie, *The Buffalo Soldiers*, p. 276; Kenner, *Buffalo Soldiers and Officers of the Ninth Cavalry*, p. 127.

For specifics of Henry's route through the Badlands environs, see Henry to AAG, Department of the Platte, December 26, 1890 (Dispatches Nos. 62 [including sketch map] and 64), and Henry to AAG, Department of the Platte, December 27, 1890 (Dispatch No. 67), NA, RG 393, Entry 3779, Department of the Platte, Letters Received, 1890–91. The trooper killed was Private Charles Haywood of Troop D, who also lost his horse as well as his carbine, revolver, cartridge belt, and holster, "captured from his remains." Regimental Returns of the Ninth Cavalry, December 1890, NA Microfilm 744, Roll 90. The courier who rode for help was Corporal William O. Wilson, Troop I, later recognized for his courageous feat with Battalion Order No. 13, January 1, 1891, which was "read to each troop of this [squadron] command," with copies furnished to Wilson and Ninth Cavalry regimental headquarters. *Army and Navy Journal*, January 17, 1891. Wilson received a Medal of Honor for bravery in September 1891. *The Medal of Honor of the United States Army*, p. 237 (see appendix G). For details of Wilson's deed, see Amos, *Above and Beyond in the West*, pp. 36–39; and Schubert, *Voices of the Buffalo Soldiers*. See citations for conduct of officers in *Army and Navy Journal*, January 31, 1891.

6. In sending forward Henry's squadron, Brooke cautioned Forsyth against trying to round up the Indians "unless you see your way clear to making a clean sweep." Brooke to Forsyth, December 30, 1890, Brooke Papers, Box 9. For the Mission Fight, see General Brooke's testimony, January 28, 1891, including two notes, Forsyth to Brooke, December 30, 1891, in NA Microfilm 983, "Sioux Campaign," 1890–91, Roll 2, pp. 1081–83; Brooke to Forsyth, 1 P.M., December 30, 1890, ibid., p. 1082; and also Forsyth's rather uncharitable dictated memorandum describing the Mission Fight (in which he noted Henry's seeming delay: "it seemed to me that he had been unnecessarily long in coming"). Forsyth to Bell, March 5, 1891, James W. Forsyth Papers, Yale University, Beinecke Rare Book and Manuscript Library, series II, "Wounded Knee Papers," WA MSS S-1404; Regimental Returns of the Seventh Cavalry, December 1890, NA Microfilm 744, Roll 74. This account is based on the following sources: Mooney, "Ghost-Dance Religion," pp. 875–76. Chandler, *Of GarryOwen in Glory*, p. 81; Regimental Returns of the Ninth Cavalry, December 1890, NA Microfilm 744, Roll 90; Regimental Returns of the First Artillery, December 1890, NA Microfilm 727, Roll 7; Capron's report in *Descriptive Catalogue of War Material*, p. 23; Garlington, "The Seventh Regiment of United States Cavalry," draft copy, pp. 37–38; Jutz, "Historic Data," pp. 324–26; Jutz interview with Walter M. Camp, September 28, 1914, Ellison/Camp Papers, Box 1 FF 137; Perrig Diary, pp. 39–40; Forsyth's Diary, entry for December 31, 1890; Forsyth to AAAG, Department of the Platte, December 31, 1890, NA, RG 393, Entry 3779, Department of the Platte, Letters Received, 1890–91 (No. 100); Forsyth to Brooke, December 30, 1890, NA, RG 393, Entry 3779, ibid. (No. 86); Perry, "Ninth United States Cavalry in the Sioux Campaign of 1890," p. 254; field note, Forsyth to Brooke, December 30, 1890, NA, RG 393, Entry 3779, Department of the Platte, Letters Received, 1890–91 (No. 89) (quotation).

7. "Philip Wells's Interview," in Jensen, *Voices of the American West*, 1:160–63; Second Lieutenant Guy H. Preston's testimony, January 24, 1891, in NA Microfilm 983,

"Sioux Campaign," 1890–91, Roll 2, pp. 1085–89; Major Guy V. Henry's testimony, January 24, 1891, ibid., pp. 1083–85; Major Guy V. Henry's report of the Mission Fight in Henry to Roe, January 17, 1891, NA, RG 393, part 1, Entry 3779, Department of the Platte, Letters Sent, 1890–91 (including first, second, and fourth quotations); Jesse G. Harris remembrance in Rickey, *Forty Miles a Day on Beans and Hay*, p. 298 (third quotation).

8. Ragnar, in Lindberg, "Foreigners in Action at Wounded Knee," pp. 178–79 (first quotation); Allen, "My Experiences in the Seventh Cavalry," p. 13 (second quotation); Jutz to Brooke, December 30, 1890, NA Microfilm 983, "Sioux Campaign," 1890–91, Roll 2, p. 1083.

9. McCormick, "Wounded Knee and Drexel Mission Fights," pp. 15–16 (first quotation); Coughlan, "Charles Albert Varnum," pp. 86–87; Crickett letter, pp. 6–7 (second quotation). Dr. McGillycuddy told Walter Camp that the Indians mutilated Francischetti's body terribly, "scalping it and shooting arrows into his abdomen, cutting off fingers & toes and cutting off the privates & sticking them in the mouth. Says the Indians who did this did it in revenge for an Indian who was scalped at Wounded Knee by a white man." McGillycuddy comments, Camp Manuscripts, Lilly Library, Box 4, Folder 3, 225–233, Envelope 4; McGillycuddy, *McGillycuddy, Agent*, p. 271.

10. Comfort letter, April 5, 1892 (first quotation); Major Guy V. Henry's report of the Mission Fight in Henry to Roe, January 17, 1891, NA, RG 393, part 1, Entry 3779, Department of the Platte, Letters Sent, 1890–91 (second and fifth quotation). Loud to wife, December 30, 1890, in Erisman and Erisman, "Letters from the Field," p. 34 (third quotation); Crickett letter, pp. 6–7 (fourth quotation); "Sketch [Map] of the Scene of the Mission Fight, December 30th 1890," NA Microfilm 983, "Sioux Campaign," 1890–91, Roll 1, p. 1098; "John Shangrau's Interview," in Jensen, *Voices of the American West*, 1:263–64; Allen, *From Fort Laramie to Wounded Knee*, pp. 215–16; *Army and Navy Journal*, January 31, 1891; Document 2.6 ("The Indian Wars in South Dakota"), in Kreis, *Lakotas, Black Robes, and Holy Women*, pp. 153–54.

11. "Report of Major General Miles," September 14, 1891, in *Report of the Secretary of War, 1891*, p. 150 (first quotation); telegram, Miles to AG, January 3, 1891, giving soldier casualties for the White Clay Creek engagement, NA Microfilm 983, "Sioux Campaign," 1890–91, Roll 1, p. 792 (see appendix D for a list of army casualties); Comfort letter, April 5, 1892 (second quotation).

12. Odell, "Comments of Philip F. Wells" (first quotation); Baldwin to Miles, August 24, 1891 (second quotation)), Miles Collection. For Indian numbers at the Mission Fight, see also the testimony of Father Jutz (p. 1089), the Reverend Cook (pp. 1089–90), John Shangrau (pp. 1090–91); Louis Shangrau (p. 1091); and the Oglala Little Horse (pp. 1091–92) in NA Microfilm 983, "Sioux Campaign," 1890–91, Roll 2. For description of the warm feelings between men of the Seventh and Ninth generated in the wake of the Mission Fight, see *Washington Evening Star*, February 5, 1891, which contains an in-depth profile of the Buffalo Soldiers' performance there and elsewhere. The *Sturgis Weekly Record*, January 23, 1891, called attention to the Ninth's heroic role in the Mission Fight. For Medal of Honor recipients for White Clay Creek, see appendix G. (For Varnum's achievement and award, see *Medal of Honor of the United States Army*, p. 237; *Junction City Republican*, February 6, 1891; *Army and Navy Journal*, February 14, 1891; and Carroll, *I, Varnum*, p. 23.)

Other sources contributing to this account of the Mission Fight include the following letters in the Forsyth Papers, Yale University, Series II, "Wounded Knee Papers," WA MSS S-1404: Colonel Edward M. Heyl, Inspector General, to AAG, Division of the Missouri, January 28, 1891 (Item 3-51); Whitside to Forsyth, March 11, 1891 (3-56); First Lieutenant Loyd S. McCormick to First Lieutenant James F. Bell, June 8, 1895 (1-19); Captain William W. Robinson to Forsyth, March 1, 1896 (2-27); Major Myles Moylan to Forsyth, April 10, 1896 (2-28); First Lieutenant William J. Nicholson to Forsyth, June 12, 1896 (2-30); McCormick to Bell, July 29, 1896 (2-31); Captain Charles A. Varnum to Forsyth, July 30, 1896 (2-31); McCormick to Bell, August 9, 1896 (2-32); Captain Edward S. Godfrey to Forsyth, August 10, 1896 (2-32); McCormick to Bell, August 12, 1896 (2-32); Brooke to Forsyth, August 25, 1896 (2-32); Trumpeter Charles Grill, Fourth Cavalry, to Bell, September 30, 1896 (2-33); and First Lieutenant Sedgwick Rick to Forsyth, July 16, 1897 (2-43). See also Stanislaus Roy Interview (1909); "Extracts from Letters Written by Lieutenant Alexander R. Piper, 8th Infantry," p. 7; William J. Small to George W. Webb, 1932, Small Collection; Kreis, *Lakotas, Black Robes, and Holy Women*, pp. 153, 167–68; *Army and Navy Register*, January 3, 1891; *Army and Navy Journal*, January 3, 10, and 17, 1891; *Chicago Inter-Ocean*, December 31, 1890, and January 1, 2, and 8, 1891; *Omaha Bee*, December 31, 1890; *Omaha World-Herald*, January 1 and 15, 1891; *Black Hills Daily Times*, January 3, 1891; *New York Times*, January 3, 1891; *Deseret News*, January 10, 1891; *Sioux County Journal*, January 15, 1891; *Sturgis Weekly Record*, January 23, 1891; *Harper's Weekly*, February 7, 1891; Kelley, *Pine Ridge 1890*, pp. 190–91; Richardson, "Some Observations upon the Sioux Campaign of 1890–91," p. 527; Mooney, "Ghost-Dance Religion," pp. 875–76; Ellis, *Indian Wars of the United States*, pp. 421–22; Robinson, *History of the Dakota or Sioux Indians*, pp. 499–500; Beyer and Keydel, *Deeds of Valor*, 2:326; Traub, "Sioux Campaign—Winter of 1890–'91," pp. 71–71; Brady, *Indian Fights and Fighters*, pp. 353–54; Von Ostermann, *Last Sioux Indian War*, p. 26; Utley, *Last Days of the Sioux Nation*, pp. 237–40; Buecker, "'The Men Behaved Splendidly,'" pp. 61–63; Leckie and Leckie, *The Buffalo Soldiers*, pp. 275–76; Buecker, *Fort Robinson and the American West*, p. 178; and Hyde, *Sioux Chronicle*, p. 306.

13. Little Horse's statement, January 24, 1891, in NA Microfilm 983, "Sioux Campaign," 1890–91, Roll 2, p. 1091 (first quotation); "Philip Wells's Interview," in Jensen, *Voices of the American West*, 1:162–63 (second quotation).

14. Neihardt, *Black Elk Speaks*, pp. 214–16 (quotation); DeMallie, *Sixth Grandfather*, pp. 276–78; Steltenkamp, *Nicholas Black Elk*, pp. 70–71. Lieutenant Preston learned that nine Indians had been wounded in the Mission Fight, none of whom died. Two of their ponies were killed and another wounded. Preston to AAG, Department of the Platte, January 7, 1891, Brooke Papers, Sioux Campaign 1890–91, vol. 1, p. 785.

15. *Omaha World-Herald*, December 25, 1890, and January 1, 1891; *New York Times*, January 4, 1891; *Washington Post*, January 4, 1891; "Organization Medical Department, in the Field, Pine Ridge Agency, S.D.," NA, RG 393, part 1, Entry 3784, Letters Sent. And Endorsements. List of Div. Field Hosp. Corps Men and Company of Hos. Corps; Special Field Orders No. 12, Headquarters Department of the Platte, in the Field, December 12, 1890, Field Orders Sioux Campaign 1890–91, Brooke Papers; *Chadron Advocate*, January 2, 1891 (quotation); *Army and Navy Journal*, February 28, 1891; Ashburn, *A History of the Medical Department of the United States Army*, pp. 144–45; *New York Herald*, December 31, 1890; *Chicago Inter-Ocean*, January 1, 1891; Ewing, "Wounded of Wounded Knee Battlefield," pp. 42–46. Father Craft asked that if his wound proved mortal he would be buried in the mass grave among the Indian dead of Wounded Knee. Foley, *At Standing Rock and Wounded Knee*, p. 316. Secretary Proctor wired Brooke: "If father craft [*sic*] has been killed have his body embalmed & sent

to genl Jas R. Obierne acting supt of emigration [*sic*] new york city[.]" NA, RG 393, part 1, Entry 3782, Department of the Platte, Telegrams Received by Headquarters, 1890–91, Box 2. A few weeks later a reporter described Craft as "very pale. . . . He will not admit that his wound was anything but an accident." *Chicago Herald*, January 31, 1891. Wounded Knee represented a baptism of fire for the army's Hospital Corps, newly organized in 1887; one of their own, steward Oscar Pollack, died in the fighting while treating casualties.

16. Walter R. Crickett letter, p. 8; *Chicago Inter-Ocean*, January 1, 1891; Peterson, *The Battle of Wounded Knee*, pp. 26–27; *Chadron Advocate*, January 2, 1891 (first quotation); "Service Account, Edward Forrest, 2nd U.S. Infantry"; Burns, "Infantry Operations at Pine Ridge," in Greene, *Indian War Veterans*, p. 197; *Omaha Bee*, January 1, 1891; *Sioux Falls Argus-Leader*, January 3, 1891; *Army and Navy Register*, January 3, 1891; *Boston Daily Globe*, January 2, 1891 (second quotation); *Washington Evening Star*, January 2, 1891; *Chicago Inter-Ocean*, January 2 and 4, 1891; *Chadron Democrat*, January 8, 1891; *Black Hills Daily Times*, January 3, 1891; "Plot Showing Location of Graves of U.S. Soldiers at Pine Ridge Cemetary [*sic*] South Dakota," drawn by L. H. Bigelow, Fort Robinson, Nebraska, May 1906, Little Bighorn Battlefield National Monument, Accession No. 16580; *Junction City Republican*, January 9, 1891; Forsyth's Diary, January 1, 1891 (third quotation). Justification for the burial of the soldiers at the agency is contained in General Orders No. 29, Headquarters of the Army, Adjutant General's Office, March 10, 1891, *General Orders and Circulars, Adjutant General's Office, 1891*, paragraph 155. Wallace's remains "were met at the [Fort Riley] depot by light battery A, Second artillery [*sic*], and conveyed on a caisson to the cavalry administration building where they remained until the arrival of the east bound train Saturday afternoon [January 3, 1891]. Every available man in the post was drawn up in line at the depot and upon the arrival of the train presented arms while the Seventh cavalry band played a beautiful dirge. The captain's gray horse was draped in mourning and led by Jack Hackett, an old trooper of L troop. Col. R. M. Wallace, a brother of the captain, accompanied the remains to Yorkville, S.C." *Junction City Republican*, January 9, 1891.

17. *Chadron Democrat*, January 8, 1891; *Omaha Bee*, January 2, 1891; *New York Times*, January 3, 1891; *Chicago Inter-Ocean*, January 20, 1891; Almon, "I Saw the Wounded Knee Massacre," p. 26; *Chicago Inter-Ocean*, January 4, 1891; Eastman to unknown recipient, Boston, January 3, 1891, in *Cheyenne Daily Leader*, January 11, 1891 (quotation).

18. Eastman, *From the Deep Woods to Civilization*, p. 238 (quotation); Utley, *The Last Days of the Sioux Nation*, pp. 2–3. As late as early February Colonel Shafter reported finding two more women survivors. "They had built a shelter and had been living ten miles from the battle field [*sic*]. One was wounded in the arm, the other was unhurt." "Abstract of Correspondence," p. 54. Bartlett's comments appear in Bartlett to Warren K. Moorehead, January 24, 1891, and January 10, 1891, Moorehead Papers, MS 106, Box 4. In 1977 ninety-six-year-old Jim Mesteth, an Oglala, recalled going to the site as a nine-year-old with his family to remove bodies and find survivors. "I just seen them laying here and there all over, men, women, and kids." He added: "Some, two or three babies, was alive. Their mothers were dead. So we brought them in [to Pine Ridge]." Bosma, "An Interview with Jim Mesteth," pp. 18, 19.

19. Brooke to Poland, December 29, 1890, Brooke Papers, Sioux Campaign 1890–91, vol. 1, p. 657; Maus to Poland, January 3, 1891, NA, RG 393, part 1, Entry 2540, Military Division of the Missouri, Letters Sent by Headquarters in the Field, 1890–91;

"Abstract of Correspondence," pp. 22, 23; Richardson, "Some Observations upon the Sioux Campaign of 1890–91," pp. 529–30; Wilson, "The Eighth Regiment of Infantry," pp. 524–25; Regimental Returns of the Eighth Infantry, January 1891, NA Microfilm 665, Roll 138; Regimental Returns of the Ninth Cavalry, January 1891, NA Microfilm 744, Roll 90; Hettinger, "Recollections of the Pine Ridge Campaign and Wounded Knee," pp. 205–207; "Paddy Starr's Interview," in Jensen, *Voices of the American West*, 1:23; *Sioux Falls Argus Leader*, December 27, 1937; Whitney to AAAG, Department of the Platte, January 3, 1891, in NA Microfilm 983, "Sioux Campaign," 1890–91, Roll 1, p. 824 (also in *Army and Navy Journal*, January 24, 1891 (quotations); *Chicago Inter-Ocean*, January 5, 1891; *Chadron Democrat*, January 8, 1891; Maus to Lieutenant Colonel James S. Casey, First Infantry, January 1, 1891, NA, RG 393, part 1, Entry 2540, Military Division of the Missouri, Letters Sent by Headquarters in the Field, 1890–91.

20. Diary of Frank D. Baldwin, December 1890–January 1891, Department of Manuscripts, Huntington Library, entry for January 2, 1891 (quotations; hereinafter cited as Baldwin Diary). For Baldwin, see Steinbach, *A Long March;* and Greene, *Yellowstone Command.*

21. *Omaha World-Herald*, January 5, 1891 (quotations); *Madison Daily Leader*, January 2, 1938; *Rapid City Daily Republican*, January 5, 1937; *National Tribune*, December 6, 1934; Mooney, "Ghost-Dance Religion," pp. 876–78; Torrey, *Early Days in Dakota*, pp. 224–25; Utley, *Last Days of the Sioux Nation*, pp. 2–4; *Chadron Democrat*, January 8, 1891. For representative photographic depictions of the dead Lakotas, see Jensen, Paul, and Carter, *Eyewitness at Wounded Knee*, pp. 49, 105–17. Other photographers on the scene of the aftermath included Clarence G. Moreledge, Solomon D. Butcher, W. R. Cross, J. C. H. Grabill, and J. E. Meddaugh. Ibid., pp. 40, 43, 45, 49–50, 57–58, 60.

22. "Paddy Starr's Interview," 1:238–39; *Omaha Bee*, January 3, 1891; *Chicago Inter-Ocean*, January 4, 1891; *Rapid City Daily Republican*, December 29, 1938; Robinson, *A History of the Dakota or Sioux Indians*, p. 501; *Chadron Democrat*, January 8, 1891; Jensen, "Big Foot's Followers at Wounded Knee," p. 198; McGregor, *Wounded Knee Massacre*, p. 82. Private Hartford G. Clark, who arrived on the scene with Sixth Cavalry troopers more than a week later to find Sioux yet unburied, noted that "I got a pair of leggings off one of the warriors' legs—everybody was looking out for relics." Clark Diary, entry for Monday, January 12, 1891. For known names of Indian dead, see appendix F. A schematic plat entitled "Massacre Grave Site," probably ca. 1930s, gave a measurement of 75 feet by 9 feet for the trench, while a recent assessment, including the enclosing fence raised in 1990, placed the figure at 80 by 12.5 feet.

23. "List of Indian wounded received into Hospital," NA, RG 393, part 1, Entry 3784, "Letters Sent. And Endorsements. List of Div. Field Hosp. Corps Men and Company of Hosp. Corps" (hereinafter cited as "List of Div. Field Hosp. Corps"); Tibbles, *Buckskin and Blanket Days*, pp. 322–24; Eastman, *From the Deep Woods to Civilization*, p. 238; Eastman, *Sister to the Sioux*, pp. 161–62 (quotations). Among those who helped nurse the wounded Indians were the following from the Pine Ridge community: Henry Red Shirt, Silas Fills Pipe, Thomas Tyon, Mrs. Thomas Tyon, Paul Eagle Bull, John J. Bissonet, Mrs. Red Rock, Mrs. Blunt Horn, Mrs. Eliza Last Horse, Mrs. Mary Fire Thunder. Charles Red Shirt to Francis H. Case, August 12, 1937, and November 30, 1937; Mary Fire Thunder to Case, June 6, 1940, Francis H. Case Papers, Wounded Knee Files, Dakota Wesleyan University. The historic Holy Cross Episcopal Church, erected at Pine Ridge Agency in the late 1880s, was replaced in 1924, when it

was removed to the Oglala community north of the agency as St. John's Church. It is still there today. *Reservation Round-Up*, pp. 1–2. For its years the structure remains in remarkably good condition, but its rural location will likely require a strong preservation commitment.

24. "List of Indian wounded received into Hospital"; Notebook, "Indians wounded in 'Fight at Wounded Knee' South Dakota, December 29, 1890. Treated by Frank J. Ives, Capt. & Asst. Surgeon, U.S.A.," SDSHS, H84–38, Wounded Knee Journal, Francis Joseph Ives Notebook, Box 3616B (list). Ledger pages in the hand of medical director (surgeon and lieutenant colonel) Dallas Bache, at slight variance with Captain Ives's notebook, account for thirty-five total Indian wounded. NA, RG 393, part 1, Entry 3783, Letters and Telegrams Sent by the Medical Director's Office, Dec. 1890–Jan. 1891; McGillicuddy, *McGillycuddy, Agent*, pp. 269–70; Dougherty, "The Indians of North America II," p. 373; DeWolfe, *The Life and Labors of Bishop Hare*, pp. 240–42; "Service Account, Edward Forrest, 2nd U.S. Infantry"; *Chicago Inter-Ocean*, January 12, 1891; *Omaha World-Herald*, January 2, 1891; *Chadron Advocate*, January 2, 1891; *Washington Post*, January 12 and 13, 1891; *Washington Evening Star*, February 7, 1891; Dr. James W. Wengert, Omaha Veterans Administration Hospital, to Richmond Clow, University of Montana, February 27, 1990 (copy provided by R. Eli Paul; Author's Collection); *Omaha Bee*, January 4, 1891.

25. The refusal of the wounded Indians to undergo surgery, in addition to their determination to abandon medical treatment on a whim, clearly frustrated the doctors. Lauderdale wrote of one of the injured girls: "[She] had gotten along so [well] that we had some hope of saving her, but her mother came along and the girl saw her and wanted to go to her tepee, and nothing would satisfy but she must go and we will probably hear of her death in a day or two. . . . It's strange that these stupid Indians become prejudiced against educated practice, and being without knowledge and patience they take their friends out of the care of those who can care for them and left to themselves to die. It is very unsatisfactory to us." Lauderdale to wife, February 5, 1891, in Green, *After Wounded Knee*, p. 111. "The wounds of the Indians were mostly severe and difficult to heal, as all capital operations were refused, notwithstanding repeated explanation and urging through missionaries, interpreters, and friends." "Report of the Surgeon-General, September 22, 1891," in *Report of the Secretary of War, 1891*, p. 601.

26. Daniel Dorchester, "Report of Inspection of Government Schools, Pine Ridge Reservation, S.D., May, 1891," pp. 1–2, NA, RG 75, Records of the Bureau of Indian Affairs, Pine Ridge Agency, Pine Ridge, South Dakota, Entry 67, Controversies, 1867–1907, NA at Kansas City; AAG Henry C. Corbin to Superintendent, Holy Rosary Mission School, January 9, 1891, NA, RG 393, part 1, Entry 2540, Military Division of the Missouri, Letters Sent by Headquarters in the Field, 1890–91; "Abstract of Correspondence," p. 38; "List of Div. Field Hosp. Corps"; Eastman, *From the Deep Woods to Civilization*, p. 243; Eastman, "Ghost Dance War," p. 37; Wilson, *Ohiyesa*, pp. 60–61.

27. Telegrams, December 30, 1890, AAG, Department of the Platte, to Commanding Officer, Fort Omaha, Nebraska; Colonel Bache, Pine Ridge Agency, S.D.; and Captain George Ruhlen, Assistant Quartermaster, Rushville, Nebraska, regarding medical equipment, NA, RG 393, PI 172, Entry 3722, Department of the Platte, Letters Sent, 1866–98, vol. 19, pp. 131–33; Wengert to Clow, February 27, 1990; *Harper's Weekly*, January 24 and February 7, 1891; *Army and Navy Register*, February 28, 1891; Memo, Major and Surgeon Albert Hartsuff, "Sick & wounded to be returned to Station," January 3, 1891; Bache to Post Surgeon, Fort Niobrara; both in NA, RG 393, part 1,

Entry 3783, Letters and Telegrams Sent by the Medical Director's Office, December 1890–January 1891; "List of Div. Field Hosp. Corps"; "Report of the Surgeon-General, September 22, 1891," in *Report of the Secretary of War, 1891*, pp. 574, 599–602; *New York Herald*, December 31, 1890; *Army and Navy Journal*, January 17, 1891; Forsyth's Diary, entries for January 3 and 4, 1891; *Junction City Republican*, January 16, 1891 (quotation), and January 23, 1891; *Junction City Republican*, January 30, 1891. On January 3, 1891, thirty-two sick and wounded soldier patients received clearance to transfer to post hospitals at their assigned stations. Memo, Major and Surgeon Albert Hartsuff, "Sick & wounded to be returned to Station," January 3, 1891, in NA, RG 393, part 1, Entry 3783, Letters and Telegrams Sent by the Medical Director's Office, December 1890–January 1891; "Abstract of Correspondence," p. 32. The twenty-two Seventh Cavalry and First Artillery wounded, including Lieutenants Garlington, Hawthorne, and Mann, reached Fort Riley at 4:30 A.M. on January 6, accompanied by assistant surgeon Glennan. The enlisted men went directly to the post hospital, while the officers went to rest in their quarters. *Junction City Republican*, January 9, 1891. Mann's obituary appears in *Twenty-Second Annual Reunion of the Association of the Graduates of the United States Military Academy*, pp. 49–50. Among medical personnel assigned to Pine Ridge for several weeks following the fighting was Major and Surgeon John V. Lauderdale, who had served for more than two decades with the army. Lauderdale's daily missives to his wife following his arrival at Pine Ridge on January 3, 1891, would provide significant contemporary commentary for the balance of the army presence on that reservation. Green, *After Wounded Knee*, p. 47.

Chapter 14. Close Out

1. *Omaha Bee*, December 30, 1890; *Sioux Falls Argus-Leader*, December 30, 1890; *Philadelphia Inquirer*, December 30, 1890; *New York Times*, December 30, 1890; Knight, *Following the Indian Wars*, p. 315; *Chadron Democrat*, January 8, 1891; statement of Hugh G. McVicker, *Nebraska State Journal*, January 19, 1941; Allen to Camp, October 22, 1913. Walter M. Camp Papers, Item 12525, Little Bighorn Battlefield National Monument; Huntzicker, "The 'Sioux Outbreak' in the Illustrated Press," pp. 314–22; Hines, "Pressing the Issue at Wounded Knee," pp. 31–37. Uses of the term "massacre" in the papers announcing the event were all in reference to the losses sustained by the Seventh Cavalry, such as the *Indianapolis Sentinel's* headline for December 30, 1890: "YET ANOTHER MASSACRE/The Sioux Once More Prove Treacherous/And Shoot Down a Number of Soldiers." The news did not appear in the *Pierre Daily Free Press* until December 31, fully two days after the event and on the back page beneath an entry titled "Pierre Potpourri." Schusky, *The Forgotten Sioux*, p. 135. The only tabloid devoting a one-page "extra" to the story was the *Hot Springs (South Dakota) Herald*, whose enterprising cub reporter, Edgar F. Medary, after hearing an account of the action from Colonel William R. Shafter of the First Infantry, rushed the news, typeset in a handpress, to Hot Springs residents at 6 A.M. on December 30. Elmo Scott Watson Papers, Newberry Library, Box 24, Folder 356.

2. Koupal, *Our Landlady*, p. 147, citing *Aberdeen Saturday Pioneer*, January 3, 1891 (quotation); Koupal, "On the Road to Oz," p. 96.

3. Sherman to Mary Miles, January 7, 1891, Nelson A. Miles Papers, Library of Congress, Manuscript Division, Container 4.

4. Welsh to Edward I. Bacon, January 23, 1891, in Hagan, *The Indian Rights Association*, pp. 120 (first quotation), 121; Bourke to Welsh, February 11, 1891, quoted in Porter, *Paper Medicine Man*, pp. 264 (second quotation), 331 n. 67.

5. *Washington Post*, January 17, 1891.

6. Firsthand accounts suggest that this view was commonly held in the ranks. See, for example, the December 29 statement of Lieutenant Piper to his wife, reflecting what must have been pervasive camp chatter: "the Cavalry began shooting in every direction, killing not only Indians but their own comrades on the other side of the circle [accompanied by a sketch diagram]." "Extracts from Letters Written by Lieutenant Alexander R. Piper, 8th Infantry," entry for December 29, 1890, p. 5. See also the letter of Eugene S. Caldwell of Troop E, Seventh Cavalry, who wrote his parents that "the way the soldiers were fixed they could not shoot for fear of killing one another." Quoted in Northrup, *Indian Horrors*, p. 544. A more detailed remark from a wounded cavalryman aboard the special train running to Fort Riley on January 4 indicated that the soldiers "were forced to shoot toward a common center and run the chances of shooting each other or else all be killed by the fire from the hostiles, and of course they chose the former alternative, and it is probable some of the soldiers were hit by shots fired by their own comrades, but it is not positively known that they were." *Omaha World-Herald*, January 6, 1891. (See later mention of the positioning of the soldiers in the previously cited accounts by Private McGinnis and First Sergeant Ragnar, both of Troop K: McGinnis, "I Was There!," p. 52; Lindberg, "Foreigners in Action at Wounded Knee," p. 175.)

7. *Chicago Inter-Ocean*, December 29, 1890 (first quotation), and December 30, 1890 (second quotation); *Chadron Democrat*, January 1, 1891 (third quotation); *Junction City Republican* (fourth quotation).

8. The officers were Moylan, Godfrey, Edgerly, Varnum, and Wallace. The enlisted men were chief trumpeter Sergeant William G. Hardy; Saddler Sergeant Otto Voit; Sergeant Stanislaus Roy, Troop A; Private George W. Wylie, Troop A; Sergeant Rufus D. Hutchinson, Troop B; Private John Hackett, Troop B; Sergeant John Dolan, Troop C; Farrier John Jordan, Troop C; Saddler John Donahoe, Troop E; Sergeant George Loyd, Troop I (wounded; suicide from despondency December 16, 1892); and Private Gustave Korn, Troop I (killed). NA, RG 94, Records of the Adjutant General's Office, Muster Rolls of the Seventh Cavalry, Troops A, B, C, D, E, G, I, and K, December 31, 1890; *Junction City Republican*, December 19, 1890, January 30 and February 6, 1891; *Kansas City Star*, December 19, 1892; Williams, *Military Register of Custer's Last Command*; Hammer, *Biographies of the 7th Cavalry*.

9. Goodale in *Washington Post*, January 17, 1891 (first quotation); "John Shangrau's Interview," in Jensen, *Voices of the American West*, 1:262 (second quotation). Shangrau had earlier given the Reverend Cook an account with similar overtones but different quoted remarks under unlike circumstances. Cited in Bland, *A Brief History of the Late Military Invasion of the Home of the Sioux*, p. 17. See also *New York Times*, February 12, 1891.

10. Odell, "Comments of Philip F. Wells" (first quotation); Comfort letter, April 5, 1892 (second quotation).

11. *Washington Post*, March 18, 1891 (first quotation); Richardson, "Some Observations upon the Sioux Campaign of 1890–91," p. 526 (second quotation). Miniconjou survivor Joseph Horn Cloud in 1917 stated that during the initial firing at Wounded Knee a white-haired soldier standing near him "cried out . . . 'remember

Custer, remember Custer.' Just about this time there was an old Indian woman running past him with some children following here [*sic*] and on her back was an Indian child. This white haired [*sic*] soldier after saying 'remember Custer' shot the old Indian woman down. On the second shot he shot one of the little children and then this other soldier who stood near by [*sic*] turned around and shot down the white haired soldier who was shooting the Indian children." Typescript statement given on March 12, 1917, during compensation hearing, NA, RG 75, copy provided by Michael Her Many Horses. Some Indians believed that the burial of their people in the long trench grave at Wounded Knee, "placed there by the soldiers who had killed them," offered further proof of their vengeance. McGregor, *Wounded Knee Massacre*, p. 82. On the revenge factor, see also Scott, "Wounded Knee," p. 22; Shaw, "Battle of Wounded Knee," p. 145; and Marshall, "Wounded Knee Revisited," p. 29.

12. *Chadron Democrat*, January 1, 1891; *Chadron Advocate*, January 2, 1891; telegram, Miles to AG, December 30, 1890, NA Microfilm 983, "Sioux Campaign," 1890–91, Roll 1, p. 646; *Army and Navy Journal*, March 7, 1891; Miles to Brooke, December 30, 1890, NA, RG 393, part 1, Entry 3782, Department of the Platte, Telegrams Received by Headquarters, 1890–91, Box 2 (quotation).

13. Comfort letter, April 5, 1892 (first quotation); Burns, "Infantry Operations at Pine Ridge," p. 197; *Omaha Bee*, January 1, 1891; *Omaha World-Herald*, January 1, 1891; *Chicago Inter-Ocean*, January 4, 1891 (second quotation).

14. *Washington Post*, January 4, 1891; *Omaha World-Herald*, January 9 and 16, 1891; *Chicago Inter-Ocean*, January 13, 1891; Brooke to AAG, Department of the Platte, December 31, 1891, NA, RG 393, PI 172, Entry 3722, Department of the Platte, Letters Sent, 1866–98, vol. 19, p. 159; Jutz, "Historic Data," p. 326 (quotation); Wooster, *Nelson A. Miles and the Twilight of the Frontier Army*, p. 186; Royer to Morgan, December 31, 1890, Hugh L. Scott Papers, Manuscript Division, Library of Congress, Reports File, Box 75; "William Garnett's Interview," in Jensen, *Voices of the American West*, 1:99–100; "Philip F. Wells's Interview," in ibid., 1:153–54; "Louis Mousseau's Interview," in ibid., 1:230; "Standing Soldier's Interview," in ibid., 1:242–45; Utley, *Last Days of the Sioux Nation*, pp. 241–43; Mooney, "Ghost-Dance Religion," p. 876. Miles originally planned to travel cross-country to Pine Ridge Agency escorted by a troop of Colonel Carr's Sixth Cavalry. News of Wounded Knee made him determined to travel more circuitously and by rail. Carr to "My dear Sister," January 7, 1891; *Black Hills Daily Times*, December 28, 1890; *Chicago Inter-Ocean*, December 31, 1890. A vividly detailed room-by-room description of Miles's quarters and offices at Pine Ridge Agency appears in the *Washington Evening Star*, January 30, 1891.

15. Kelley, "Indian Troubles and the Battle of Wounded Knee," pp. 44–45; *Army and Navy Journal*, January 10, 1891; Miles to Brooke, December 30, 1890, NA, RG 393, part 1, Entry 3782, Department of the Platte, Telegrams Received by Headquarters, 1890–91, Box 2 (first quotation); "Abstract of Correspondence," p. 20; telegram, Miles to AG, January 1, 1891; and Miles to Brooke, January 3, 1891; both in NA, RG 393, part 1, Entry 2540, Military Division of the Missouri, Letters Sent by Headquarters in the Field, 1890–91; Brooke's directive, January 4, 1891, in *Army and Navy Journal*, January 17, 1891; Forsyth's Diary, entries for January 1 and 2, 1891; Regimental Returns of the First Infantry, January 1891, NA Microcopy 744, Roll 9; *Omaha Bee*, January 2, 1891 (second quotation).

16. Roe to First Lieutenant Edward W. Casey, December 30, 1890, pp. 696–97 (first quotation); and Brooke to Carr, December 30, 1890, ibid., pp. 698–99 (second

quotation); both in Brooke Papers, Sioux Campaign 1890–91, vol. 1; Maus to Brooke, December 31, 1891, NA, RG 393, Entry 3779, Department of the Platte, Letters Received, 1890–91 (third quotation).

17. *Washington Evening Star*, January 2, 1891; *New York Times*, January 5, 1891; *Chicago Inter-Ocean*, January 5 and 7, 1891; telegram, AAG, Department of Dakota, to Commanding Officer, Fort Keogh, December 30, 1890, directing movements of the First Cavalry and Twentieth Infantry "for the purpose of scouting and intercepting any parties of Pine Ridge Indians trying to go north." NA, RG 393, part 1, Entry 1167, Department of Dakota Letters Sent, 1890–1904; telegram, Miles to Merriam, December 30, 1890, NA, RG 393, part 1, Entry 2540, Military Division of the Missouri, Letters Sent by Headquarters in the Field, 1890–91; Coe, "The Twentieth Regiment of Infantry," pp. 671–72; Wainwright, "The First Regiment of Cavalry," p. 172. For details of this movement, see Brimlow, *Cavalryman Out of the West*, pp. 137–41; and James E. Wilson, "Maneuvers in Montana during the Ghost Dance Crisis," in Greene, *Indian War Veterans*, pp. 215–20. See also Miles's broad overview and assessment of operations contained in telegram, Miles to AG, January 5, 1891, NA, RG 393, part 1, Entry 2540, Military Division of the Missouri, Letters Sent by Headquarters in the Field, 1890–91.

18. Regimental Return of the Fifth Cavalry, January 1891, NA Microfilm 744, Roll 55; First Lieutenant Edward W. Casey, Twenty-Second Infantry (camp of scouts on White River), to Captain Marion P. Maus, aide-de-camp to Miles, January 3, 1891, "Abstract of Correspondence," p. 25; *Chicago Tribune*, January 2, 1891; *Chicago Inter-Ocean*, January 9 and 10, 1891; *Chicago Inter-Ocean*, January 12, 1891; telegram, Miles to AG, January 2, 1891, p. 786; Morgan to Noble, January 3, 1891, p. 789; both in NA Microfilm 983, "Sioux Campaign," 1890–91, Roll 1; "Abstract of Correspondence," pp. 24, 30, 33; Corbin to Brooke, January 7, 1891, NA, RG 393, part 1, Entry 2540, Military Division of the Missouri, Letters Sent by Headquarters in the Field, 1890–91; Ebstein, "Twenty-First Regiment of Infantry," p. 679; Jocelyn, *Mostly Alkali*, pp. 332–34; Carlson, *"Pecos Bill,"* p. 149; *Chicago Inter-Ocean*, January 11, 1891; *Chadron Democrat*, January 8, 1891; *Army and Navy Journal*, January 3, 1891; *Army and Navy Register*, January 3, 1891; Hibbard, *Fort Douglas, Utah*, pp. 109, 111; *Omaha World-Herald*, January 1, 1891; Lee, *Fort Meade and the Black Hills*, p. 118.

19. Carr's report, April 20, 1891, pp. 20–21; "Abstract of Correspondence," pp. 22, 23, 25; Regimental Return of the Sixth Cavalry, January 1891, NA Microfilm 744, Roll 65; Record of Events, Master Roll, Troop K, Sixth Cavalry, February 28, 1891, NA, RG 94; Cornelius C. Smith, "The Last Indian War," pp. 17–21; see also the typescript Colonel C. C. Smith Reminiscence, p. 10, which is included in Smith, *Don't Settle for Second*, pp. 14–18; Carr to "My dear Sister," January 7, 1891; incomplete handwritten account by Carr in respect to the pursuit of Big Foot (unknown origin), Carr Papers; Pershing Memoirs, draft of chapter 5, pp. 91–92; Private Hartford G. Clark, Troop G and Band, Sixth Cavalry, January 1891, Clark Diary, entry for Thursday, January 1, 1891; Rhodes, "Diary Notes of the Brule–Sioux Indian Campaign," entry for January 1, 1891, pp. 21–22; Beyer and Keydel, *Deeds of Valor*, 2:327–32; Carter, "Sixth Regiment of Cavalry," p. 249; Carter, *From Yorktown to Santiago*, pp. 261–62; account based on the reminiscences of retired Sergeant Frederick Myers, in *Washington Evening Star*, December 31, 1939; Torrey, *Early Days in Dakota*, pp. 223–24; King, *War Eagle*, p. 245; Hall, *To Have This Land*, p. 139. The account of Black Elk, who took part, appears in DeMallie, *Sixth Grandfather*, pp. 278–79; and Neihardt, *Black Elk Speaks*, pp. 216–17. Brief news accounts of the action appear in *Washington Post*, January 4 and 5, 1891;

Omaha World-Herald, January 4, 1891; and *Chicago Inter-Ocean*, January 4, 1891. In the late spring of 1891 at Fort Niobrara Troop K of the Sixth Cavalry gave Major Tupper an inscribed presentation sword testifying to "their appreciation of his gallant services in the battle with Sioux Indians on White River, S.D., January 1, 1891." *Army and Navy Journal*, June 6, 1891. Captain William H. Carter's account of the action in "Sixth Regiment of Cavalry," p. 249, mentioned the killing of several wounded Lakotas by scouts after the withdrawal of the Indians. In historical documents and accounts the engagement is often said to have occurred on Little Grass Creek, although Little Grass Creek, an affluent of Grass Creek, joins that stream about twelve miles above (south of) its mouth. The area of the fight appears in U.S. Geological Survey, Section 25, Rockyford Quadrangle, South Dakota–Shannon County. For medal recipients, see appendix G.

20. *Omaha Bee*, January 4, 1891; *Chicago Inter-Ocean*, January 4, 1891; Miles to Brooke, December 30, 1890, NA, RG 393, part 1, Entry 2540, Military Division of the Missouri, Letters Sent by Headquarters in the Field, 1890–91; "Abstract of Correspondence," p. 23; Brooke to Red Cloud, Little Wound, Two Strike, Big Road, Crow Dog, No Water, Turning Bear, Calico, White Fan, Yellow Bear, Short Bull, He Dog, December 31, 1891, NA, RG 393, Entry 2546, Box 126 (also contained in Entry 3773, vol. 2 of 3, "Letters Sent Headquarters in the Field from December 19th, 1890, to January 9th, 1891," p. 47); Red Cloud to Brooke and Miles, ca. January 1, 1891; Red Cloud et al. to Miles, ca. January 1, 1891; both in NA, RG 393, Entry 2546; Miles to Red Cloud, January 1, 1891 (quotations), NA, RG 98, Military Division of the Missouri, Letters Sent Field Book, 1890–91 (copies in the James C. Olson Collection, Nebraska State Historical Society, MS51047); Red Cloud to Miles, ca. January 3, 1891, NA, RG 98, Military Division of the Missouri, Letters Sent Field Book, 1890–91 (copies in the James C. Olson Collection, Nebraska State Historical Society, MS51047). During the exchange Red Cloud asked Miles to send sugar, coffee, and tobacco to the Indian camp. "We bring the wounded [into the agency?] every day. I get your letter and I am happy. . . . I don't want any trouble." Red Cloud to Miles, undated, ca. early January 1891, NA, RG 393, Entry 2546, Box 126; Miles to Red Cloud, January 1, 1891, NA, RG 393, part 1, Entry 2540, Military Division of the Missouri, Letters Sent by Headquarters in the Field, 1890–91.

21. Miles to Red Cloud, January 2, 1891, NA, RG 98, Military Division of the Missouri, Letters Sent Field Book, 1890–91.

22. Miles to Red Cloud, January 1, 1891; and Miles to Red Cloud, January 4, 1891, both in NA, RG 98, Military Division of the Missouri, Letters Sent Field Book, 1890–91.

23. Telegram, Miles to AG, January 5, 1891, NA Microfilm 983, "Sioux Campaign," 1890–91, Roll 1, p. 810; "Conversation between General Miles and Sioux Indian Chiefs 'He Dog,' 'Big Road,' 'High Hawk,' 'Little Hawk,' and 'Jack Red Cloud,' January 5th, 1891, at Pine Ridge Agency, S.D." (He Dog quotations), NA, RG 393, part 1, Entry 2546, Letters Received, Military Division of the Missouri, Box 126; Miles to Big Road, He Dog, Little Hawk, Jack Red Cloud, and High Hawk, January 5 and (revised) January 6, 1891 (Miles quotation), NA, RG 393, part 1, Entry 2546, Military Division of the Missouri, Letters Sent by Headquarters in the Field, 1890–91; *Fremont (Wyoming) Clipper*, January 16, 1891. Several other Sioux also came in but did not attend the meeting, including Oglalas Left Hand Crane and Yellow Bear plus two unnamed Brulés. Yellow Bear apparently stayed at Pine Ridge when the others departed. *Omaha World-Herald*, January 6, 1891. See also *Sioux County Journal*, January 15, 1891, which appears to describe this council.

24. Telegram, Miles to Schofield, January 3, 1891, NA Microfilm 983, "Sioux Campaign," 1890–91, Roll 1, p. 795 (quotation); telegram, Miles to AGl, January 6, 1891, ibid., p. 825; *Washington Post*, January 4, 1891; *Sioux Falls Argus-Leader*, January 3, 1891; *Daily Boomerang* (Laramie, Wyoming), January 8, 1891. For Miles's initial request regarding replacement of the agents, see Miles to AG, December 11, 1890, NA Microfilm 983, "Sioux Campaign," 1890–91, Roll 1, p. 504; "Abstract of Correspondence," p. 31.

25. Hall, *To Have This Land*, pp. 126–28; telegram, Miles to AG, January 3, 1891, NA Microfilm 983, "Sioux Campaign," 1890–91, Roll 1, p. 801; *Omaha World-Herald*, January 7, 1891; Brooke to Captain George Ruhlen, December 29, 1890, NA, RG 393, PI 172, Entry 3722, Department of the Platte, Letters Sent, 1866–98, vol. 19; *Omaha Bee*, January 1, 1891; *Alliance Times-Herald*, June 18, 1926; *Rock County Leader*, January 3, 1952; *"Recollections" of Sheridan County*, pp. 152–53; *New York Herald*, December 31, 1890; Miles to AG, January 3, 1891, NA Microfilm 983, "Sioux Campaign," 1890–91, Roll 1, p. 796; "Abstract of Correspondence," pp. 24, 27, 29. Miles's notice to settlers appeared in the *Black Hills Daily Times*, January 8, 1891. See also Corbin to AAG, Department of the Platte, January 7, 1891, NA, RG 393, part 1, Entry 2540, Military Division of the Missouri, Letters Sent by Headquarters in the Field, 1890–91.

26. Telegram, County Clerk, Dawes County, to Thayer, December 30, 1891, in *Chadron Democrat*, January 1, 1891; telegram, Thayer to Secretary of War, January 4, 1891, and endorsement by Schofield, January 5, 1891, NA Microfilm 983, "Sioux Campaign," 1890–91, Roll 1, pp. 797–98 (first quotation); *Omaha Bee*, January 1, 2, 3, and 4, 1891; *Omaha World-Herald*, January 2 and 3, 1891; *Washington Evening Star*, January 2, 1891; Colby, "The Sioux Indian War of 1890–'91," pp. 158–61 (including second quotation, p. 157); "Abstract of Correspondence," p. 25; Hamilton, "Nebraska's National Guard in the Sioux War," pp. 317–19; telegram, Cody to Colby, undated but January 1891, NA, RG 75, Records of the Bureau of Indian Affairs, Pine Ridge Agency, Pine Ridge, South Dakota, Entry 67, Controversies, 1867–1907, NA at Kansas City; *Chicago Inter-Ocean*, January 8 and 9, 1891; Russell, *The Lives and Legends of Buffalo Bill*, pp. 366–67; Warren, *Buffalo Bill's America*, p. 381. Nebraska spent $42,000 in its effort. U.S. Congress, Senate, Committee on Military Affairs, *To Accompany S. 2476;* U.S. Congress, Senate, Committee on Military Affairs, *Expenses Incurred by Nebraska*. (These reports contain excellent maps showing the placement of Nebraska troops across Dawes and Sheridan Counties in 1891 in relation to sites on the Pine Ridge Reservation.)

27. *Chicago Inter-Ocean*, January 8, 1891; Sheldon, "Report on the Archives of the State of Nebraska," p. 380; Colby, "The Sioux Indian War of 1890–'91," pp. 162–63. Statements in this source regarding an engagement between regular cavalry and Indians on Wounded Knee Creek on January 5 (p. 164) appear vague, lack specificity as to unit and location, and are not supported in the "Record of Events" sections of the monthly regimental returns for the Sixth, Seventh, and Ninth Cavalry and most likely should be considered hyperbole. See also Hamilton, "Nebraska's National Guard in the Sioux War," p. 319. For their service Governor Thayer commissioned a bronze medal to be presented to officers and men who took part in the field campaign of 1891 (General Colby and the state adjutant general received gold versions). The award elicited jeering notice from the *Omaha Bee* (May 28, 1891): "A bloodless Indian campaign in which the militia did not catch sight of a hostile Indian is worthy of commemoration." For details and a list of recipients, see Ayres, "Indian Wars and Medals: The Sioux War of

1890–91 and the Nebraska Sioux War Medal" (recipients are listed in the April 1975 issue of *Medal Collector*); "Sword of General L. W. Colby," p. 261. Presentation of the medals took place at the annual encampment at Grand Island, Nebraska, in September 1891. *Fairbury Gazette*, September 12, 1891. Documents concerning the Nebraska troops during the Sioux campaign are found in the Nebraska State Historical Society. See especially RG 18, SG 2, Box 5, s. 1, Folder 13; Box 38, s. 4, Folder 157; and Box 92, s. 11, Folder 1 (Colby's reports). For more on the Nebraska troops, see *Historical Sketch: Omaha Guards*, pp. 31–32; Washington *Evening Star*, January 21, 1891; *Chadron Democrat*, January 8, 1891; *Nebraska City News*, January 9, 16, 23, and 30, 1891; *Sioux County Journal*, January 8, 15, and 22, 1891; *Fremont Weekly Herald*, January 8, 15, and 22, 1891; *Nebraska State Journal*, January 7 through January 17, 1891; *Norfolk Daily News*, January 13 and 21, 1891; *Gage County Democrat*, January 8, 15, 22, and 29, 1891; *Beatrice Republican*, January 10, 1891; *Fairbury Gazette*, January 10 and 17, 1891; *Beatrice Daily Express*, January 3, 5, 8, 9, 10, 12, 14, 16, 17, 19, 20, and 26, 1891; *Beatrice Daily Sun*, January 16, 23, and 30 and February 6, 1921; *Lincoln State Journal*, May 29, 1927; *Winners of the West*, July 30, 1930. Miles notified Cody of his intention to have troops from Fort Robinson occupy points in the Sand Hills to intercept any "outlaws" from among the Sioux seeking refuge there. Telegram, Miles to Cody, January 7, 1891, NA, RG 393, part 1, Entry 2540, Military Division of the Missouri, Letters Sent by Headquarters in the Field, 1890–91.

28. Miles to Schofield, January 1, 1891, NA Microfilm 983, "Sioux Campaign," 1890–91, Roll 1, p. 785; *Army and Navy Journal*, January 10, 1891 (quotation); *Washington Evening Star*, January 30, 1891.

29. Telegram, Schofield to Miles, January 2, 1891, NA Microfilm 983, "Sioux Campaign," 1890–91, Roll 1, p. 777 (quotation); "Abstract of Correspondence," p. 22.

30. Whitside to wife, January 5, 1891, in Russell, "Selfless Service," p. 141.

31. Telegram, Miles to Schofield, January 5, 1891, NA, RG 393, part 1, Entry 2540, Military Division of the Missouri, Letters Sent by Headquarters in the Field, 1890–91; Special Orders No. 8, Headquarters Division of the Missouri, In the Field, Pine Ridge, S.D., January 4, 1891, NA Microfilm 983, "Sioux Campaign," 1890–91, Roll 1, pp. 653–54; "Abstract of Correspondence," p. 28; *Washington Post*, January 5, 1891; *Washington Evening Star*, January 5, 1891; *Hot Springs Daily Star*, January 7, 1891. Officers at Pine Ridge generally denounced the action, grumbling that in the future "the death of each Sioux must be explained." *Cheyenne Daily Leader*, January 6, 1891. As for the charge of excessively killing noncombatants, the *Chadron Democrat* noted on January 8: "We doubt if any army officer could distinguish a squaw from a buck at a distance of ten paces." An *Omaha World-Herald* reporter at the agency related "a general impression . . . that General Schofield doesn't line with General Miles at all in this matter and that he regards General Miles . . . precipitate in causing Forsythe's [*sic*] relief from duty." At Fort Riley the news of Forsyth's relief was not taken lightly; the local paper groused: "If General Miles has been . . . the cause of Colonel Forsyth's suspension he will have to clear himself from the suspicion of having had his own ambition in view rather than the interests of the service." *Junction City Republican*, January 9, 1891; "Abstract of Correspondence," pp. 21, 26, 29 30.

32. Miles to Mary Miles, letters of January 6, 15, and 20, 1891, in Johnson, *Unregimented General*, pp. 289, 294 (quotations). Miles had solicited from Forsyth a statement regarding his engagements with Indians up to Wounded Knee. "Abstract of Correspondence," p. 47.

33. Forsyth Diary, January 4, 1891 (first quotation); ibid., January 6, 1891 (second quotation).

34. Telegram, Schofield to Miles, January 6, 1891, NA Microfilm 983, "Sioux Campaign," 1890–91, Roll 1, p. 828. This knowledge changed the level of the investigation, although its tenets remained much the same. Baldwin wrote on January 6: "To day [*sic*] I discovered that we could not act under the orders as a court of inquiry but only as [a court of] inspection and the orders have been modified accordingly and Col. Kent & myself proceeded with the investigation of the affair on Wounded Knee." Baldwin Diary, entry for January 6, 1891. The media continued to refer to the proceedings as a court of inquiry, however. Baldwin received the acting position after Miles learned that his division inspector "was taken ill in the field." Telegram, Miles to AG, January 1, 1891, NA, RG 393, part 1, Entry 2540, Military Division of the Missouri, Letters Sent by Headquarters in the Field, 1890–91; "Abstract of Correspondence," p. 31.

35. Baldwin Diary, entry for January 10, 1891.

36. "Report of the Investigation into the Battle at Wounded Knee Creek, South Dakota, Fought December 29th, 1890," in NA Microfilm 983, "Sioux Campaign," 1890–91, Roll 1, pp. 706, 707.

37. Ibid., pp. 709–10 (first quotation); comment to his daughter in Forsyth's diary, January 4, 1891 (second quotation).

38. Whitside to wife, January 15, 1891, in Russell, "Selfless Service," p. 142.

39. Miles to Kent and Baldwin, January 16, 1891. NA, RG 393, part 1, Entry 2540, Military Division of the Missouri, Letters Sent by Headquarters in the Field, 1890–91; "Abstract of Correspondence," p. 45. Baldwin's statement, January 13, 1891, NA Microfilm 983, "Sioux Campaign," 1890–91, Roll 1, pp. 728–29 (quotations).

40. Brooke to Miles, December 31, 1891, 10 P.M., NA, RG 393, Entry 3773, vol. 2 of 3, pp. 52–53, "Letters Sent Headquarters in the Field, from December 19th, 1890. To January 9th, 1891"; "Copy of Instructions to General John R. Brooke," NA Microfilm 983, "Sioux Campaign," 1890–91, Roll 1, p. 735; "Abstract of Correspondence," pp. 24, 46 (quotations).

41. Letter of Herman G. Dennison, included in Forsyth Diary, p. 17 (first quotation); Forsyth Diary, January 20, 1891 (second quotation).

42. Miles, 1st Endorsement to AG, January 31, 1891, NA Microfilm 983, "Sioux Campaign," 1890–91, Roll 1, p. 766.

43. Ibid., pp. 766–67 (quotations); *Washington Post*, February 13, 1891; *New York Times*, February 13, 1891; *Boston Daily Globe*, February 13, 1890.

44. Endorsements by Schofield, February 4, 1891, NA Microfilm 983, "Sioux Campaign," 1890–91, Roll 1, p. 768 (first quotation); endorsement by Proctor, February 12, 1891, in McCormick, "Wounded Knee and Drexel Mission Fights," pp. 17–20 (second quotation); *Washington Post*, February 13, 1891; *New York Times*, February 13, 1891; *Army and Navy Register*, January 17 and February 14, 1891; *Army and Navy Journal*, January 24 and February 14 and 28, 1891; *Junction City Republican*, February 20, 1891. Forsyth's 1895 thirty-eight-page rebuttal of the court's conclusions appears in "Statement of Brigadier General James W. Forsyth, U.S. Army, concerning the investigations touching the fights with Sioux Indians, at Wounded Knee and Drexel Mission, near Pine Ridge, S.D., December 29 and 30, 1890." James W. Forsyth Appointment, Commission, and Personal (ACP) File, NA, RG 94, Records of the Adjutant General's Office.

45. Miles to the Adjutant General, November 18, 1891, Miles Collection.

46. Ibid.

47. For more on the Forsyth action, see Garlington, "The Seventh Regiment of United States Cavalry," draft copy, pp. 38–39; Utley, *Last Days of the Sioux Nation*, pp. 245–48; Wooster, *Nelson A. Miles and the Twilight of the Frontier Army*, pp. 188–91; Johnson, *Unregimented General*, pp. 294–95; Steinbach, *A Long March*, pp. 158–61; Connelly, *John M. Schofield and the Politics of Generalship*, pp. 273–74; DeMontravel, *Hero to His Fighting Men*, pp. 204–206; DeMontravel, "General Nelson A. Miles and the Wounded Knee Controversy," pp. 34–37; Russell, "Selfless Service," pp. 88–90. For a participant's remarks, see also Hawthorne, "Sioux Campaign of 1890–91," pp. 215–16. Black Hills citizens started a subscription for a gold watch to be presented to Forsyth. *Black Hills Journal*, January 18, 1891. For procedures referencing courts of inquiry in 1891, see Winthrop, *Military Law and Precedents*, pp. 516–33.

48. *Omaha Bee*, February 13, 1891.

49. Heyl to AAG, Division of the Missouri, January 28, 1891, James W. Forsyth Papers, Yale University, Beinecke Rare Book and Manuscript Library, series II, "Wounded Knee Papers," WA MSS S-1404, Item 3-51. An unattributed letter in the *Army and Navy Journal*, February 7, 1891, stated: "Col. Heyl has been investigating the Indian Mission fight, and having a map made of same. The impression is, that the intention is to show that the 7th Cavalry, through mismanagement, were placed in a position of danger, but relieved by the 9th, and that Col. Forsyth exceeded his orders by going beyond the mission."

50. "Report of Major General Miles," September 14, 1891, in *Report of the Secretary of War, 1891*, 1:151.

51. Typescript draft, March 4, 1891, Miles Collection.

52. Corbin to Brooke, January 7, 1891 (first quotation); Corbin to Brooke, January 7, 1891 (second quotation); both in NA, RG 393, part 1, Entry 3779, Department of the Platte, Letters Received, 1890–91.

53. Roe to Commanding Officers on White River, January 4, 1890, Brooke Papers, Sioux Campaign 1890–91, vol. 1, p. 760.

54. Brooke to Carr, January 6, 1891, ibid.; *Chicago Inter-Ocean*, January 4, 1891; "Abstract of Correspondence," p. 35; telegram, Miles to AG, January 7, 1891, NA Microfilm 983, "Sioux Campaign," 1890–91, Roll 1, p. 885; *Omaha World-Herald*, January 7, 1891; *Black Hills Daily Times*, January 9, 1891. Lieutenant Preston of the Indian scout detachment wrote: "Red Cloud and [his] people wanted to return long ago but wounded squaws and children arriving from Wounded Knee have kept all [in the No Water camp] in a ferment of excitement." Preston to AAG, Department of the Platte, January 7, 1891, Brooke Papers, Sioux Campaign 1890–91, vol. 1, pp. 784–85.

55. First Lieutenant Benjamin L. Ten Eyck to Medical Director, Department of Dakota, January 7, 1891, NA Microfilm 983, "Sioux Campaign," 1890–91, Roll 1, p. 836; Brooke to Miles, January 6, 1891, vol. 1, p. 781; telegram, Miles to AG, January 7, 1891, p. 843; First Lieutenant Robert N. Getty to AAG, Department of Dakota, April 13, 1891, p. 838; telegram, AG John C. Kelton to Miles, January 8, 1891, p. 875; all in Brooke Papers, Sioux Campaign 1890–91; telegram, Corbin to Captain Eli L. Huggins, January 7, 1891, NA, RG 393, part 1, Entry 2540, Military Division of the Missouri, Letters Sent by Headquarters in the Field, 1890–91; *Report of the Commissioner of Indian Affairs, 1891*, 1:132 (also in *Report of the Secretary of War, 1891*), pp. 250–51; account of Scout Yankton Charley, in *Chicago Inter-Ocean*, January 10, 1891; *Washington Post*, January 9, 1891; *Chicago Inter-Ocean*, January 10, 1891; *Army and Navy Register*, January

10 and 17, 1891; *Army and Navy Journal,* January 17 and February 7, 1891; *Washington Evening Star,* January 31, 1891; Getty, "Death of Lt. Edward L. [*sic*] Casey," in Author's Collection; Baldwin Diary, entry for January 7, 1891 (first quotation); *Chicago Inter-Ocean,* January 9, 1891 (second quotation); McClernand, "Edward W. Casey"; Smith, "Twenty-Second Regiment of Infantry," p. 690; Frederic Remington, "Lieutenant Casey's Last Scout: On the Hostile Flanks with the Chis-Chis-Chash," *Harper's Weekly,* January 31, 1891; DeBarthe, *Life and Adventures of Frank Grouard,* pp. 242–43; Marquis, *Warrior Who Fought Custer,* p. 336; Frink with Barthelmess, *Photographer on An Army Mule,* pp. 116–19; Upton, *The Indian as a Soldier at Fort Custer,* pp. 22–23; and especially Utley, "The Ordeal of Plenty Horses." See also the coverage in DiSilvestro, *In the Shadow of Wounded Knee.* Details of the shooting are found in interviews with witnesses Pete Richard and Bear Lying Down in Second Lieutenant Sydney A. Cloman to Camp Adjutant, Pine Ridge Agency, February 21, 1891, NA Microfilm 983, "Sioux Campaign," 1890–91, Roll 2, pp. 1173–77; and Cloman to Camp Adjutant, Pine Ridge Agency, February 21, 1891, ibid., pp. 1171–73; "Abstract of Correspondence," pp. 34, 36, 37. For a sense of Casey's recent scouting activities, see telegram, Sanford to First Lieutenant Charles M. Truitt, December 30, 1890, Brooke Papers, Sioux Campaign 1890–91, vol. 1, p. 710.

56. Agent Pierce to AAG, Division of the Missouri, February 21, 1891, forwarding statements of One Feather, Red Owl (his wife), and Otter Skin Robe (his daughter), NA Microfilm 983, "Sioux Campaign," 1890–91, Roll 2, pp. 996–97; *Report of the Commissioner of Indian Affairs, 1891,* 1:132; *Report of the Secretary of War, 1891,* pp. 220–23 (particularly the report of Second Lieutenant Francis C. Marshall, January 13, 1891, p. 221 [quotation]); Carr to Roe, January 13, 1891, NA, RG 393, part 1, Entry 3779, Department of the Platte, Letters Received, 1890–91; "Abstract of Correspondence," pp. 43, 46, 49, 50, 51; press release regarding "Murder of Few Tails," Office of the Indian Rights Association, Philadelphia, Pennsylvania, March 31, 1891, contained in Anita S. Tilden, Office of Indian Affairs, to Thomas E. Odell, April 8, 1936; M. K. Sniffen, Indian Rights Association, to Odell, February 11, 1936; Emil Afraid of Hawk to James H. McGregor, March 11, 1936; Eb Jones, "The Murder of Chief [*sic*] Few Tails" (typescript manuscript dated December 30, 1937); all in Thomas Odell Collection, D9 F352; Lauderdale to wife, January 18 and 19, 1891, in Green, *After Wounded Knee,* pp. 77–79; Mooney, "Ghost-Dance Religion," pp. 889–90; Brown and Willard, *The Black Hills Trails,* pp. 125–27; Lee, *Fort Meade and the Black Hills,* pp. 123–26.

57. Baldwin Diary, entries for January 9 and 10, 1891; diary of Charles W. Hayden, Seventh Cavalry, White Swan Library, Little Bighorn Battlefield National Monument, entry for January 8, 1891 (hereinafter cited as Hayden Diary); *Chicago Inter-Ocean,* January 9 and 10, 1891; *Hot Springs Daily Star,* January 10, 1891; Preston to Adjutant, Battalion Second Infantry, January 8, 1891, Brooke Papers, Sioux Campaign 1890–91, vol. 1, p. 818; Taylor, "Surrender of Red Cloud" (undated typescript), Charles W. Taylor File, R-10 Order of Indian Wars Collection, U.S. Army Military History Institute, Army War College, pp. 4–5 (quotation).

58. "Abstract of Correspondence," pp. 36, 39, 40, 41; telegram, Miles to Major John L. Baird, January 2, 1891; telegram, Maus to Commanding Officer, Oelrichs, S.Dak.; and telegram, Miles to R. R. Woods, Merino, Wyoming, January 3, 1891, all in NA, RG 393, part 1, entry 2540, Military Division of the Missouri, Letters Sent by Headquarters in the Field, 1890–91; *Black Hills Daily Times,* January 10, 1891; Royer to Morgan, January 6, 1891, McLaughlin Papers, Roll 34; "Extracts from Letters Written

by Lieutenant Alexander R. Piper, 8th Infantry," entry for January 8, 1891, p. 11; *Chadron Advocate*, January 9, 1891; *Army and Navy Register*, January 17, 1891; *Omaha World-Herald*, January 8, 9, 10 (first and second quotations), and 12, 1891; *Black Hills Daily Times*, January 11, 1891; President Harrison to Royer, January 8, 1891, NA Microfilm 983, "Sioux Campaign," 1890–91, Roll 1, p. 911; *Report of the Commissioner of Indian Affairs, 1891*, 1:131; Schofield to Miles, January 7, 1891, NA Microfilm 983, "Sioux Campaign," 1890–91, Roll 1, p. 904; Miles to Brooke, January 12, 1891, NA, RG 393, part 1, Entry 2540, Military Division of the Missouri, Letters Sent by Headquarters in the Field, 1890–91 (third quotation).

59. *Omaha World-Herald*, January 11, 1891; *Chicago Daily Inter-Ocean*, January 12 and 13, 1891; *Washington Post*, January 12 and 13, 1891; *Washington Post*, January 13, 1891; *Black Hills Daily Times*, January 13, 1891.

Agents were not directly replaced at the other agencies, as Miles had requested. At those stations, designated officers were to "exercise such military supervision and control" as necessary, without disrupting the agents' administration. General Order No. 2, Headquarters, Division of the Missouri, in the Field, January 12, 1891, as published in *Army and Navy Journal*, January 31, 1891 (quotation). Shortly after his departure from Pine Ridge, Royer wrote Brooke confidentially from Rushville, soliciting the general's estimation of his tenure as agent. "I do not want it for publication but to set me right with my friends. . . . Was I justified in asking for Troops?" Brooke answered vaguely the next day: "Your justification in asking for troops [was] fully made by the results of the past two months." Brooke responded to Royer's "Was I the cause of the Trouble?": "You were not the cause of the trouble." Brooke replied to Royer's "Did the Indians seem satisfied with me as their Agent?": "As far as I could learn the Indians seemed satisfied with you as Agent." To Royer's question "Was my administration of affairs at the Agency commendable?" Brooke answered: "Your administration of affairs here was honest, as far as I could see. Of course your administration was short and the word commendable could only be used as the result of a long and successful service." Royer wrote: "Do you think I am guilty of the cowardice charged to me? I was worried several times about the safety of my Family but out side [*sic*] of that I don't think I was ever scared." Brooke answered: "I do not think you were guilty of cowardice. I have no doubt but that you would have made a success of your work here had you entered upon it under different circumstances." Royer asked the general: "Please treat this private." Royer to Brooke, January 18, 1891, and Brooke to Royer, January 19, 1891, Brooke Papers, Box 9.

60. *Black Hills Daily Times*, January 15, 1891; DeBarthe, *Life and Adventures of Frank Grouard*, pp. 243–45; Larson, *Red Cloud*, p. 282; Olson, *Red Cloud and the Sioux Problem*, p. 332; *Chadron Democrat*, January 11 and 12, 1891; *Cheyenne Daily Leader*, January 11, 1891; Kelley, "Indian Troubles and the Battle of Wounded Knee," p. 46; Kreis, *Lakotas, Black Robes, and Holy Women*, pp. 168–69 (first quotation); Perrig Diary, entry for January 12, 1891 (second quotation).

61. Miles to Brooke, undated (ca. January 12), NA, RG 393, part 1, Entry 3779, Department of the Platte, Letters Received, 1890–91 (first quotation); Medary, "Reminiscences of the Ghost Dance War of 1890–91," p. 49 (second quotation); Baldwin Diary, entry for January 12, 1891; Hayden Diary, entry for January 12, 1891; Colby, "Sioux Indian War of 1890–'91," p. 169; *Omaha World-Herald*, January 13, 1891; telegram, Miles to AG, January 12, 1891, Brooke Papers, Sioux Campaign 1890–91, vol. 1, p. 899 (third quotation); Brooke to AAG, Division of the Missouri, January 13, 1891, ibid. (fourth quotation); "Abstract of Correspondence," p. 42. See also the retrospective of Brooke's movement by Edgar F. Medary published in the *Publisher's Auxiliary*, January 17, 1942.

62. Hayden Diary, entry for January 13, 1891; Baldwin Diary, entry for January 13, 1891; Perrig Diary, entry for January 13, 1891; *Omaha Bee*, January 20 and 21, 1891; Lauderdale to wife, January 13, 1891, in Green, *After Wounded Knee*, pp. 64–65; *Black Hills Daily Times*, January 14, 1891; *Washington Post*, January 13, 1891; *Chicago Inter-Ocean*, January 14, 1891; *New York Times*, January 13, 1891; *Omaha World-Herald*, January 20, 1891; Miles to AG, February 3, 1891. McLaughlin Papers, SDSHS, Roll 35; Corbin to Carr, January 13, 1891, NA, RG 393, part 1, Entry 3779, Department of the Platte, Letters Received, 1890–91; Dougherty, "Indians of North America II," p. 374 (quotation); Dougherty, "Recent Indian Craze," p. 577; Harvey, "Last Stand of the Sioux," p. 235. A good descriptive account of the movements and activities of the Sixth Cavalry troops directly preceding the surrender appears in the *Army and Navy Register*, January 17, 1891.

63. Hayden Diary, entry for January 14, 1891; Baldwin Diary, January 14, 1891; *Washington Evening Star*, January 14, 1891; *Washington Post*, January 15, 1891; *Omaha World-Herald*, January 15, 1891; *New York Times*, January 15, 1891; telegram, Miles to Schofield, January 14, 1891, quoted in *Sioux Falls Argus-Leader*, January 14, 1891 (first quotation); *Chicago Inter-Ocean*, January 15, 1891; DeBarthe, *Life and Adventures of Frank Grouard*, p. 245; Maus to Brooke, January 14, 1891, NA, RG 393, part 1, Entry 3779, Department of the Platte, Letters Received, 1890–91 (second quotation); Lauderdale to wife, January 14, 1891, in Green, *After Wounded Knee*, p. 67. Brooke responded to the confidential directive, thereby providing definitive knowledge of the placement of his troops at the finale: "I brought Colonel Wheaton's command, which consisted of four companies of infantry, to this point yesterday afternoon. There are now in this camp [at the mission] the Second Infantry, six companies Seventeenth Infantry, Sanford's Leavenworth battalion of four troops, Wells' 8th Cavalry battalion of two troops, Henry's 9th Cavalry battalion of four troops, three Hotchkiss guns, Getty's Cheyenne scouts and part of Taylor's scouts. One battalion of Carr's command is about twelve miles from here, on the head of White Horse creek [*sic*], the other two battalions are disposed between that and Whitney on Wounded Knee. . . . I think the disposition of the troops from here can enclose three sides of the Indian camp in an hour." Brooke to AAG, Division of the Missouri, January 14, 1891, Brooke Papers, Sioux Campaign 1890–91, vol. 1, p. 921.

64. Hayden Diary, entry for January 15, 1891 (first quotation); Baldwin Diary, entries for January 15 (second quotation) and 18, 1891.

65. Lauderdale to wife, January 15, 1891, in Green, *After Wounded Knee*, pp. 69–70; DeBarthe, *Life and Adventures of Frank Grouard*, pp. 245–46; Colby, "Sioux Indian War of 1890–'91," pp. 169–70; Kelley, "Indian Troubles and the Battle of Wounded Knee," p. 47 (quotation).

66. "As Narrated by 'Short Bull,'" p. 17 (quotation); *Omaha World-Herald*, January 16, 1891; *Black Hills Daily Times*, January 16, 1891; *Hot Springs Daily Star*, January 17, 1891; *Cheyenne Daily Leader*, January 16, 1891; Dougherty, "Recent Indian Craze," p. 577; *Report of the Secretary of War, 1891*, p. 152. Miles reported that the surrendering people numbered at least 4,000 and that the total number of Indians at the agency was close to 7,000, which seems too high. Miles to AG, January 15, 1891, NA Microfilm 983, "Sioux Campaign," 1890–91, Roll 1, p. 965.

67. Telegram, Miles to the AG, January 9, 1891, NA, RG 393, part 1, entry 2540, Military Division of the Missouri, Letters Sent by Headquarters in the Field, 1890–91; Miles to Schofield, January 16, 1891, NA Microfilm 983, "Sioux Campaign," 1890–91, Roll 1, p. 969; Maus to Brooke, January 21, 1891, NA, RG 393, part 1, Entry 3779,

Department of the Platte, Letters Received, 1890–91; Perrig Diary, entries for January 16 and 19, 1891; "Open air council and feast January 17th, 1891 in Ogallalla [*sic*] Camp 2.40 P.M.," NA, RG 393, part 1, Entry 2546, Military Division of the Missouri Headquarters, Letters Received, Box 126 (quotation).

68. "Report of Rosebud Agency," August 27, 1891, in *Report of the Commissioner of Indian Affairs, 1891*, 1:410; Captain Jesse M. Lee to CO, U.S. Troops in the Field, Pine Ridge Agency, January 31, 1891, NA Microfilm 983, "Sioux Campaign," 1890–91, Roll 2, p. 1060; *Hot Springs Daily Star*, January 19, 1891; "Extracts from Letters Written by Lieutenant Alexander R. Piper, 8th Infantry," entry for January 17, 1891, p. 13; *Black Hills Journal*, January 20, 1891; *Black Hills Daily Times*, January 20, 1891; Hayden Diary, entry for January 16, 1891 (quotation); Maus to First Lieutenant Lewis H. Strother, First Infantry, January 6, 1891, NA, RG 393, part 1, Entry 2540, Military Division of the Missouri, Letters Sent by Headquarters in the Field, 1890–91; "Abstract of Correspondence," pp. 39, 45, 46, 47; *Chicago Inter-Ocean*, January 12, 1891; *Black Hills Journal*, January 17, 1891; *Army and Navy Journal*, January 17, 1891; *Omaha World-Herald*, January 20, 1891; *New York Times*, January 20, 1891; U.S. Congress, Senate, *Message from the President of the United States, Transmitting a Letter of the Secretary of the Interior and Documents;* U.S. Congress, Senate, *Letter from the Secretary of the Interior, in Relation to the Affairs of the Indians*, pp. 7–10; Svingen, *The Northern Cheyenne Indian Reservation*, pp. 90–95; Stands In Timber and Liberty, *Cheyenne Memories*, pp. 262–63; Marquis, *Warrior Who Fought Custer*, 345; Marquis and Limbaugh, *Cheyenne and Sioux*, pp. 48, 49 n. 4; Ewers, *When the Army Still Wore Blue*, pp. 119–21. Ewers urged the union of the Northern Cheyennes removed to Fort Keogh from Pine Ridge with their kin at the Tongue River Reservation. See Ewers to the Adjutant General, U.S. Army, May 4, 1891. Elmo Scott Watson Papers, Newberry Library, Box 36, Folder 548.

69. Corbin to Brooke, January 19, 1891, NA, RG 393, part 1, Entry 2540, Military Division of the Missouri, Letters Sent by Headquarters in the Field, 1890–91; Corbin to AG, January 19, 1891, ibid.; Baldwin Diary, entries for January 19 and 20, 1891; Hayden Diary, entry for January 20, 1891; *Cheyenne Daily Leader*, January 20, 1891; *Washington Evening Star*, January 27, 1891 (first and second quotations); *Chicago Herald*, January 28, 1891; *Omaha World-Herald*, January 29, 1891; *Boston Daily Globe*, February 13, 1891; *Chadron Democrat*, February 26, 1891.

70. Captain Thomas H. Barry to Baldwin, November 24, 1891, Miles Collection (quotation); Miles to AG, February 3, 1891, McLaughlin Papers, SDSHS, Roll 35; Eastman, "Ghost Dance War," pp. 39–40; Jones, "Teresa Dean," pp. 661–62. Reporter Harries left an insightfully agonizing description of the bodies and burial that by association powerfully signified all that happened at Wounded Knee. Harries, "Tragedy at White Horse Creek."

71. Miles to AG, March 2, 1891, NA Microfilm 983, "Sioux Campaign," 1890–91, Roll 2, p. 1139; "Abstract of Correspondence," p. 56 (in which it is stated that "energetic action is to be taken to arrest [the] murderers of the Indian woman and three children buried by Captain Baldwin"); Johnson, "Tragedy at White Horse Creek: The Military Account" (reprinted with additions as "Tragedy at White Horse Creek: Edward S. Godfrey's Unpublished Account"). For more about this incident and its effect on Godfrey's career, see Proctor to Schofield, February 12, 1891, with second endorsement, Miles to AG, March 2, 1891, Miles Collection; Miles to Colonel William R. Shafter, November 19, 1891, William R. Shafter Papers, Manuscript Division, Library of Congress, Microfilm Roll 1, Frames 793–94; Godfrey statement dated June 26, 1904, William J. Ghent

Papers, Manuscript Division, Library of Congress, Box 25, File 27 (also in Godfrey ACP File, 6810 ACP 1890, NA, RG 94); Selah R. H. Tompkins to Godfrey, May 1, 1905, William J. Ghent Papers, Manuscript Division, Library of Congress, Box 21, File 27; *New York Sun*, October 10, 1907; Proctor to Schofield, February 12, 1891 (quotation). Godfrey's first formal statement on the matter appears in "Report of the Investigation into the Battle at Wounded Knee Creek, South Dakota, Fought December 29th, 1890," NA Microfilm 983, "Sioux Campaign," 1890–91, Roll 1, p. 677. Testimony in the March 1891 scrutiny appears in "Investigation of circumstances connected with shooting of an Indian woman and three children by U.S. Troops near the scene of the battle of Wounded Knee Creek," NA Microfilm 983, "Sioux Campaign," 1890–91, Roll 2, pp. 1135–58, which includes Miles's exonerating endorsement (pp. 1139–40). A biographical obituary of Godfrey is found in the *Putnam County (Ohio) Gazette*, March 16, 1933. As for Godfrey's remorse over what happened, it is telling that his ten-page West Point necrology, while highlighting his numerous Indian campaigns, made no mention of his part at Wounded Knee. Bates, "Edward Settle Godfrey."

72. General Orders No. 3, Headquarters, Division of the Missouri, in the Field, January 18, 1891, *Army and Navy Journal*, January 24, 1891 (quotation); General Field Orders No. 1, January 20, 1891, and General Field Orders No. 2, January 21, 1891, Field Orders Sioux Campaign 1890–91, Brooke Papers.

73. "Extracts from Letters Written by Lieutenant Alexander R. Piper, 8th Infantry," entry for January 22, 1891, p. 17 (first and second quotations); Hayden Diary, entry for January 22, 1891; *Black Hills Journal*, January 19, 1891; *Omaha Bee*, January 21 and 23 (third quotation), 1891.

74. *Washington Evening Star*, January 29, 1891 (first and third quotations); *Army and Navy Journal*, January 24, 1891; *Harper's Weekly*, February 7, 1891; Hettinger, "Recollections of the Pine Ridge Campaign and Wounded Knee," p. 212 (second quotation); Lauderdale to wife, January 22, 1891, in Green, *After Wounded Knee*, p. 83; Forsyth's Diary, entry for January 22, 1891 (fourth quotation).

75. Comfort letter, April 5, 1892; *Hot Springs Daily Star*, January 24, 1891; *Washington Evening Star*, January 30, 1891; *Harper's Weekly*, December 26, 1896 (quotation); Lauderdale to wife, January 25, 1891, in Green, *After Wounded Knee*, p. 89; "The First Regiment of Infantry," pp. 412–13; Carter, *From Yorktown to Santiago*, pp. 263–64; King, *War Eagle*, pp. 245–46; DeMontravel, "Nelson A. Miles and the Wounded Knee Controversy," pp. 42–43. Miles claimed that he commanded "in the vicinity of Pine Ridge 2,840 officers and men, including about 115 Indian scouts." Miles to AG, January 29, 1891, NA Microfilm 983, "Sioux Campaign," 1890–91, Roll 2, p. 1035. The complete text of Miles's congratulatory message appears in appendix H.

76. Joint Resolution of the South Dakota Legislature signed by Governor Arthur C. Mellette, January 29, 1891, McLaughlin Papers, Roll 35.

CHAPTER 15. AFTERMATH

1. *Army and Navy Register*, March 14, 1891 (quotations); Daniel Dorchester, "Report of Inspection of Government Schools, Pine Ridge Reservation, S.D., May, 1891," NA at KC, RG 75, Pine Ridge Agency, Controversies, 1867–1907, Entry 67.

2. Lauderdale to wife, January 6, 1891, in Green, *After Wounded Knee*, p. 56; "Report of Pine Ridge Agency," September 1, 1891, in *Report of the Commissioner of Indian*

Affairs, 1891, 1:409–10 (including first quotation); "Report of Rosebud Agency," August 27, 1891, in *Report of the Commissioner of Indian Affairs, 1891,* 1:410–17 (including second quotation).

3. General Field Orders No. 3, January 23, 1891, Field Orders Sioux Campaign 1890–91, Special Field Orders No. 4, January 20, 1891; Special Field Orders No. 8, January 24, 1891, pp. 1–4; all in Brooke Papers; Regimental Returns of the Ninth Cavalry, January and February 1891, NA Microfilm 744, Roll 90; Regimental Returns of the Sixth Cavalry, January and February 1891, NA Microfilm 744, Roll 65; "Abstract of Correspondence," pp. 54–55; Regimental Returns of the First Infantry, January and February 1891, NA Microfilm 744, Roll 9; Lauderdale to wife, January 23, 1891, p. 85; Lauderdale to wife, January 17, 1891, p. 74; Lauderdale to wife, January 25, 1891, p. 90 (quotation); Lauderdale to wife, January 26, 1891, p. 93; Lauderdale to wife, February 5, 1891, p. 110; Lauderdale to wife, February 18, 1891, p. 130; all in Green, *After Wounded Knee.*

4. For examples of goings-on at Pine Ridge and Rosebud during and after the army occupation (including weather matters, auctioning of government equipment, lawsuits, and humdrum court-martial activities), see *Army and Navy Journal,* February 21, March 14, and April 4, 1891; and *Chadron Democrat,* January 29, March 26, June 25, and July 25 and 30, 1891. For the innovation of Indian enlistment, see most notably Lee, "Warriors in Ranks," pp. 273–74, 280–82, 288–89, 297–302; Rickey, "Warrior-Soldiers"; Connelly, *John M. Schofield and the Politics of Generalship,* pp. 276–79; and Buecker, "Fort Niobrara," p. 316. For contemporary insights, see General Orders No. 28, March 9, 1891, in *General Orders and Circulars, Adjutant General's Office, 1891; Report of the Secretary of War, 1891,* pp. 14–16, 57–58, 81–82; *Report of the Commissioner of Indian Affairs, 1891,* 1:37–38, 413; *Report of the Secretary of War, 1894,* pp. 68–69; *Report of the Secretary of War, 1895,* p. 186; *Sioux Falls Argus-Leader,* March 27, 1891; *Army and Navy Journal,* May 9 and August 29, 1891; *Boston Herald,* November 15, 1892.

5. More than sixty years later Private Walter C. Harrington, Company G, Twenty-First Infantry, recalled the following incident: "When we evacuated the Rosebud Agency in March 1891, . . . we marched southward about 35 miles to Valentine, Neb., where we were to entrain. About a mile outside this village . . . was some sort of a 'joint' called the 'Hog Ranch' [house of ill repute]. All the men had plenty of money after their winter's stay at the Rosebud Agency, and made a hike en masse to the 'joint' referred to. They held up the train we were to take about 30 hours before they could be rounded up. I was the only enlisted man who stayed on the train, and I remember distinctly while sitting alone in the coach Lieut. Monroe MacFarlane [*sic:* Munroe McFarland] came through the car, and as I rose to salute him, he smiled and said: 'Harrington, you and I are the only decent men in the command.'" Remembrance of former private Walter C. Harrington, Twenty-First Infantry. Indian War Veterans survey form dated September 1954, Don Rickey, Jr., Indian Wars Veterans Project materials, U.S. Army Military History Institute, Army War College.

6. Brooke to Ruger, January 25, 1891, NA, RG 393, part 1. Entry 3722, Pl 172, Department of the Platte, Letters Sent, 1866–98, vol. 20, pp. 51–52; "Record of Events from Post Returns, Fort Robinson, Nebraska, 1890–1899" (copy in Fort Robinson Museum); *Army and Navy Register,* January 31, 1891; *Chadron Advocate,* January 23 and 30, 1891; *Chadron Democrat,* January 22, 1891; *Omaha Bee,* January 18, 1891; Carter, *From Yorktown to Santiago,* pp. 264–65; Hettinger, "Recollections of the Pine Ridge Campaign and Wounded Knee," p. 213 (first quotation); *Valentine Republican,* January 27,

1891 (second quotation); Erisman and Erisman, "Letters from the Field," pp. 41–42; Buecker, *Fort Robinson and the American West*, p. 179; Buecker, "Fort Niobrara," p. 318; Chubb, "Seventeenth Regiment of Infantry," pp. 641–42; *Chadron Advocate*, January 30, 1891; Hill, "Buffalo—Ancient Cow Town," p. 145; *Buffalo Bulletin*, August 18, 1949; Hill, letter in *Annals of Wyoming* 39 (October 1967).

7. Special Field Orders No. 6, January 22, 1891, Field Orders Sioux Campaign, pp. 1–2, Brooke Papers; Hayden Diary, entries for January 24 and 25, 1891.

8. Hayden Diary, entry for January 26, 1891.

9. Chandler, *Of GarryOwen in Glory*, pp. 81–82; *Fremont Weekly Herald*, January 29, 1891; *Beatrice Daily Express*, January 26, 1891; *Junction City Republican*, January 30, 1891 (quotation); *Washington Post*, November 21, 1891.

10. Brigadier General Wesley Merritt to AG, January 28, 1891, NA Microfilm 983, "Sioux Campaign," 1890–91, Roll 2, p. 1026; Forsyth to Brooke, February 2, 1891, Brooke Papers, Box 9; Application for Leave of Absence, Captain Edward S. Godfrey, March 6, 1891; statement of physical condition of Captain Edward S. Godfrey, January 28, 1892; both in Godfrey ACP, NA, RG 94; *Putnam County Gazette*, March 16, 1933; *Junction City Republican*, February 27, 1891; *Army and Navy Journal*, December 19, 1891.

11. Carlson, *"Pecos Bill,"* p. 153; *Washington Evening Star*, January 31, 1891; Lauderdale to wife, January 26, 1891, in Green, *After Wounded Knee*, pp. 91–92; *Chicago Inter-Ocean*, January 28, 1891 (first and second quotations); "As Narrated by 'Short Bull,'" p. 19; *Chicago Herald*, January 28, 1891 (third quotation). The Indians held at Fort Sheridan were the Brulés Short Bull, Scatter Bear, Horn Eagle, Sorrel Horse, Standing Bear, One Bull, Kills Close to Home, Run Sideways, Good Eagle, High Eagle, Wounded with Many Arrows, and Crow Cane (a woman); the Oglalas Kicking Bear, Coming Grunt, Breaks in Two, Revenge, His Hoarse Voice, Standing Bear, Brave, Takes the Shield Away, Hard to Hit, One Star, Bring a White Horse, White Beaver, and Biting Bear and Medicine Horse (women). *Chicago Herald*, January 29, 1891. (For variations of some of these names, see Captain Charles G. Penney to Morgan, March 28, 189, NA Microfilm 1282, Letters Sent to the Office of Indian Affairs by the Pine Ridge Agency, 1875–1914, Roll 147; and *Washington Evening Star*, January 31, 1891.) For details of the Indians' accommodations at Fort Sheridan, see *Chicago Herald*, January 29, 1891. A lengthy description of Miles's lavish homecoming reception at the Palmer House is in the *Chicago Herald*, January 31, 1891.

12. "As Narrated by 'Short Bull,'" p. 19 (first quotation); *Chadron Democrat*, January 22, 1891; *Chicago Herald*, January 29, 1891 (second quotation); *Castle Rock Journal*, March 18, 1891 (third quotation).

13. "Abstract of Correspondence," p. 45; Captain Penney to Morgan, March 28, 1891, NA Microfilm 1282, Roll 147; America Elmira Collins to Edith Warner Collins, March 29, 1891, America Elmira Collins Papers, State Historical Society of North Dakota, MS 20255; *Army and Navy Journal*, April 25, 1891; Cody to Miles, May 4, 1891, William F. Cody Papers, Manuscript Division, Library of Congress, Container 1 (quotation).

14. Cody to Miles, June 24, 1891, William F. Cody Papers, Manuscript Division, Library of Congress, Container 1.

15. Russell, *The Lives and Legends of Buffalo Bill*, p. 369. Warren, *Buffalo Bill's America*, pp. 382–87 (for Cody's views on Wounded Knee vis-à-vis his show and the European tour with the Fort Sheridan detainees); *Harper's Weekly*, May 9 and 30, 1891;

Commissioner Morgan resisted Cody's request for using the Indians and wrote a disclaimer: "My views regarding the so-called 'Wild West shows' as previously expressed have undergone no modifications whatever. During the year only one party [Cody's], and that by special instructions from the Department, has been allowed to take Indians for this purpose." *Report of the Commissioner of Indian Affairs, 1891*, 1:78. See also Short Bull's experience in "As Narrated by 'Short Bull,'" pp. 19–20. For controversies regarding Indian participation in Cody's show, see Warren, *Buffalo Bill's America*, pp. 366–74; Moses, *Wild West Shows and the Images of American Indians*, pp. 109–28; and Maddra, *Hostiles?*, pp. 63–111. For the 1891–92 tour, see ibid., pp. 122–90. Cody's show initially refused to depict the Wounded Knee engagement, likely because of the controversy that it had generated. But a competitor, Pawnee Bill's Historic Wild West, which included "Warlike Bands of Indians" among its attractions, featured a replication of "The Wounded Knee Fight" in its advertisements in 1893. *Washington Post*, September 22, 1893. By 1894, however, Cody's show in Brooklyn, New York, had added a Wounded Knee attraction. *New York Times*, May 10, 1894; *Chadron Democrat*, February 12, 1891 (quotation).

16. Telegram, AAG to Miles, January 15, 1891, NA Microfilm 983, "Sioux Campaign," 1890–91, Roll 1, p. 961; Bland, *Brief History of the Late Military Invasion*, pp. 11–14; Olson, *Red Cloud and the Sioux Problem*, p. 334; Larson, *Red Cloud*, pp. 283–84; *Chadron Democrat*, February 12, 1891 (quotation).

17. Greene, "The Sioux Land Commission of 1889," p. 71; *Washington Evening Star*, February 7, 1891; *Omaha Bee*, February 8, 1891; *Chadron Democrat*, February 12, 1891; *Harper's Weekly*, February 21, 1891 (quotation).

18. "Account Given by Indians of the Fight at Wounded Knee Creek, South Dakota, December 29, 1890," in *Report of the Commissioner of Indian Affairs, 1891*, 1:179–81 (quotations); *Omaha World-Herald*, February 12, 1891; Eastman, "Ghost Dance War," p. 40. See also Bland, *Brief History of the Late Military Invasion*, pp. 15–17.

19. "Account Given by Indians of the Fight at Wounded Knee Creek, South Dakota," p. 180.

20. Ibid.

21. Ibid., pp. 180–81.

22. Ibid., p. 181.

23. Calhoun, *Benjamin Harrison*, p. 112; *Omaha World-Herald*, February 13, 1891 (quotation).

24. *Omaha Bee*, February 14, 1891; Eastman, *Pratt, the Red Man's Moses*, pp. 185–86; Olson, *Red Cloud and the Sioux Problem*, p. 335; U.S. Congress, Senate, *Statements of a Delegation of Ogalalla Sioux;* U.S. Congress, House, *A Bill to Liquidate the Liability of the United States for the Massacre* (1938), p. 14; U.S., *Court of Claims Reports*, 84:25, 41; *U.S. Court of Claims Reports*, 97:397–98; *Report of the Commissioner of Indian Affairs, 1891*, 1:410, 412–13; *Report of the Secretary of the Interior, 1892*, pp. lii–liii; *Letter from the Secretary of the Interior, in Relation to the Affairs of the Indians*, pp. 1–7ff.; *Army and Navy Journal*, June 20, 1891 (for more on the boundary issue and the returning Brulés, see Shafter to Miles, February 12, 1891, and Pierce to Morgan, February 12, 1891, in NA Microfilm 983, "Sioux Campaign," 1890–91, Roll 2, pp. 1113, 1115–16); Utley, *Last Days of the Sioux Nation*, p. 274; Greene, "Sioux Land Commission of 1889," pp. 71–72.

25. Shafter to Miles, February 15, 1891, Nelson A. Miles Papers, Manuscript Division, Library of Congress, Container 4 (first and second quotations); Lauderdale to wife, January 30, 1891, in Green, *After Wounded Knee*, p. 103 (third quotation).

26. Miles to Adjutant General, March 13, 1891, McLaughlin Papers, Roll 35 (quotations); *Cheyenne Daily Sun*, March 21, 1891; Deloria, *Speaking of Indians*, p. 84; *Chadron Democrat*, March 13, 1891.

27. Telegram, Penney to Morgan, April 8, 1891, and telegram, Acting Commissioner Belt to agents at Standing Rock, Cheyenne River, Crow Creek and Rosebud Agencies, April 8, 1891, quoted in Belt to Noble, April 9, 1891, NA Microfilm 983, "Sioux Campaign," 1890–91, Roll 2, p. 1430 (first quotation); Captain Clarence M. Bailey, letter 2639, NA, RG 393, Entry 3730, Registers of Letters Received, Department of the Platte, 1866–98 (second quotation); Lea to Commissioner Morgan, April 13, 1891, McLaughlin Papers, Roll 30 (third quotation). Retired Captain Augustus W. Corliss, formerly of the Eighth Infantry at Pine Ridge, recalled "seeing the entire field covered with short sticks flying flags. The Indians had gone there and located the places where their relatives had been killed and marked them with flags." *Denver Post*, November 15, 1903; Mooney, "Ghost-Dance Religion," photo of Wounded Knee site opposite p. 875. Captain Penney relieved the ailing Captain Pierce as agent at General Schofield's direction. Special Orders No. 29, Headquarters of the Army, February 5, 1891, NA Microfilm 983, "Sioux Campaign," 1890–91, Roll 2, p. 1730.

28. *Army and Navy Journal*, July 29, 1893; *Kansas City Star*, July 29, 1893; *New York Times*, July 26, 1893. The Wounded Knee Monument stood west of Sheridan Avenue near Arnold Hall until 1925. It was then relocated without its limestone foundation and steps to the junction of Sheridan and Heubner roads, where it stands today. Pride, *The History of Fort Riley*, pp. 216–18; *New York Times*, June 18, 1897 (quotation).

29. Camp to Joseph Horn Cloud, April 12, 1912, and Horn Cloud to Camp, May 4, 1912. Item 12524B, Walter M. Camp Papers, Little Bighorn Battlefield National Monument; "Data on monument and notes of Battle-field & fight from Indian side (1910)," Camp Manuscripts, Lilly Library, Box 6, Folder 13, Envelope 89; McGregor, *The Wounded Knee Massacre*, pp. 82–84; Jensen, *Voices of the American West*, 2:56–58; "Markers at the Wounded Knee Battle Field"; Ferris, *Soldier and Brave*, p. 309; *Indian Country Today*, February 25, 1993.

30. Despite the protections normally accorded by National Historic Landmark (NHL) status (a Wounded Knee NHL was so designated in 1965 and a nomination documenting the encompassing land area was completed in 1990), in 2010 NHL monitoring personnel noted that "the area suffers from neglect." Jensen and Paul, National Register of Historic Places Registration Form; NHL Summary Listing Assessment for Wounded Knee, 2010.

31. "Plot Showing Location of Graves of U.S. Soldiers at Pine Ridge Cemetary [*sic*] South Dakota," Little Bighorn Battlefield National Monument; Peterson, *Battle of Wounded Knee*, pp. 26–27 (quotation); *Sioux Falls Argus-Leader*, October 6, 1906; Carroll, "The Search for the Soldier Dead at Wounded Knee," pp. 11–14; Carroll, "Wounded Knee Update."

32. Cloman to Camp Adjutant, Pine Ridge Agency, February 19, 1891, NA Microfilm 983, "Sioux Campaign," 1890–91, Roll 2, pp. 1165–68; Cloman to Camp Adjutant, February 20, 1891, ibid., pp. 1173–77; Cloman to Camp Adjutant, February 21, 1891, ibid., pp. 1171–73; "Abstract of Correspondence," p. 56 (Cloman received commendation for his action in arresting Plenty Horses in General Orders No. 100, Adjutant General's Office, December 17, 1891, *General Orders and Circulars, Adjutant General's Office, 1891*, p. 9); *Sturgis Advertiser*, February 26, 1891; Lauderdale to wife, February 18, 1891, in Green, *After Wounded Knee*, p. 131; William B. Sterling, U.S. District Attorney for

South Dakota, to Acting Agent Captain Charles G. Penney, March 30, 1891, NA, RG 75, Records of the Bureau of Indian Affairs, Pine Ridge Agency, Pine Ridge, South Dakota, Entry 3, NA at Kansas City; *Army and Navy Journal*, March 28, 1891; *Report of the Commissioner of Indian Affairs, 1891*, 1:132; *Army and Navy Register*, March 28, 1891; *Army and Navy Journal*, May 2, 1891; *New York Times*, May 30, 1891; *Washington Post*, June 1, 1891; *Chadron Citizen*, June 4, 1891; *Chadron Democrat*, June 4, 1891. The *Chadron Advocate*, June 5, 1891, editorialized: "The truth is that there was no fighting at the time Lieut. Casey was killed. It was as cold-blooded and unprovoked a murder as murder can be. If some enterprising frontiersman will take the first opportunity to put a Winchester bullet where it will do the most good to Plenty Horses, we will guarantee him an acquittal in Dawes county." Much of Baldwin's testimony appeared in the *Sturgis Weekly Record*, June 5, 1891. An officer stationed in Montana railed at the news of the acquittal of Plenty Horses: "What a shame that infernal, cowardly savage that assassinated him [Casey] was allowed to go free. That very same miserable Judge will probably be hollering again soon that the Indians are out, send troops! I hope he will be the first man killed the next time they go on the warpath." First Lieutenant Matthew F. Steele, Eighth Cavalry, to his mother, June 7, 1891, Matthew Forney Steele Papers, State Historical Society of North Dakota, Archives and Manuscripts, MS 10115. Detailed insights into the Plenty Horses trial are found in Hagan, *Indian Rights Association*, pp. 121–23; Connelly, *John M. Schofield and the Politics of Generalship*, pp. 274–75; Lee, *Fort Meade and the Black Hills*, pp. 130–37; and DiSilvestro, *In the Shadow of Wounded Knee*, pp. 159–77, 180–96.

33. *Report of the Commissioner of Indian Affairs, 1891*, 1:132; Herbert Welsh et al., Indian Rights Association, to Attorney General William H. H. Miller, March 29, 1891, John G. Bourke Papers, Box 2, Folder 16, Nebraska State Historical Society Archives; Wells, "Ninety-Six Years among the Indians," pp. 305–307; transcribed leaflets of the Indian Rights Association regarding the Few Tails case D8, F175; Matthew K. Sniffen, Indian Rights Association, to O'Dell, February 11, 1936, D9, F352; William G. Rice to O'Dell, March 25, 1940; all in Philip F. Wells Materials, Thomas Odell Collection; Alexander McCall to Commissioner of Indian Affairs Morgan, March 18, 1891 (quotation), in Utley, *Last Days of the Sioux Nation*, p. 267. For detailed insights into the Few Tails case, see Hagan, *Indian Rights Association*, pp. 121–24; Lee, *Fort Meade and the Black Hills*, pp. 130–31, 134–35, 137–42; and DiSilvestro, *In the Shadow of Wounded Knee*, pp. 179, 196–98.

34. Jensen, "Commissioner Theodore Roosevelt Visits Indian Reservations," pp. 89–94; Richmond L. Clow, "The Lakota Ghost Dance after 1890"; DeMallie, "Lakota Ghost Dance," pp. 401–402; "Report of Pine Ridge Agency," September 1, 1891, in *Report of the Commissioner of Indian Affairs, 1891*, 1:410 (first quotation); Lea to Commissioner of Indian Affairs, April 13, 1891, McLaughlin Papers, Roll 30 (second quotation).

35. DeMallie and Parks, *Sioux Indian Religion*, pp. 7–9; DeMallie, "Yankton and Yanktonai," p. 792. Occasional post–Wounded Knee flare-ups like the Two Sticks murders of white cowboys on the Pine Ridge Reservation in 1893 have been variably associated with attributes of Ghost Dancing but doubtless expressed an element of animosity carried over from the massacre. See *Chadron Citizen*, February 9, 1893; *New York Times*, February 5, 1893; Wells, "Ninety-Six Years among the Indians," pp. 307–10; Bad Heart Bull and Blish, *Pictographic History of the Oglala Sioux*, pp. 416–20; and Hall, "Reasonable Doubt."

36. *Junction City Republican*, February 27, 1891; *Army and Navy Journal*, December 19, 1891; Forsyth to AG, February 17, 1891; Commanding Officer's Report for Whitside, January 15, 1892; both in Whitside ACP File, NA, RG 94; Capron to Forsyth, January 1, 1891, in *Army and Navy Register*, March 17, 1891; Merritt to AG, February 28, 1891, in Forsyth ACP File, NA, RG 94; *Army and Navy Register*, March 21, 1891; *Washington Post*, April 3, 1891; Green, "The Medals of Wounded Knee," p. 203. In 1892 Captain Wallace won commendation for his service at Wounded Knee, "where, holding his ground against overwhelming odds, his death at the hands of the enemy terminated a notably honorable and useful career." General Orders No. 33, Headquarters of the Army, May 16, 1892, *Army and Navy Journal*, May 21, 1892. A brevet promotion was an honorary and nonpaying appointment to a rank above an officer's current regular rank or his previous brevet appointed rank, generally for singular acts during specified engagements. Wilhelm, *Military Dictionary and Gazetteer*, p. 73.

37. Wilhelm, *A Military Dictionary and Gazetteer*, p. 318; General Orders No. 100, Adjutant General's Office, December 17, 1891, *General Orders and Circulars, Adjutant General's Office, 1891*, pp. 4–9; *Army and Navy Journal*, December 19, 1891; *Regulations for the Army of the United States, 1889*, article 26, p. 18 (quotation).

38. *The Medal of Honor of the United States Army*, pp. 235–37 (quotation); Gleim, *US Army Gallantry and Meritorious Conduct*; Carroll, *The Seventh Cavalrymen Winners of the Medal of Honor*; Kerrigan, *American War Medals and Decorations*, pp. 3–4, 14–15, 20, 24, 35, 43. Regulations governing the award of Medals of Honor were tightened in 1901 to read: "In order that the Congressional medal of honor may be deserved, service must have been performed in action of such a conspicuous character as to clearly distinguish the man for gallantry and intrepidity above his comrades—service that involved extreme jeopardy of life or the performance of extraordinarily hazardous duty . . . and incontestible [*sic*] proof of performance of the service will be exacted." *Regulations for the Army of the United States, 1901*, article 25, p. 29. For details of the Wounded Knee medal awards, see especially Green, "The Medals of Wounded Knee," pp. 203–206, including the revised online version athttp://www.dickshovel.com/MedalsG.a.html. For descriptions of ceremonies in which the Medal of Honor was presented to Seventh Cavalrymen, see *Army and Navy Journal*, July 4 and 18, 1891; and *Harper's Weekly*, September 19, 1891. The list of Wounded Knee Medal of Honor recipients appears in appendix G.

39. *Junction City Republican*, March 13, 1891.

40. Steltenkamp, *Nicholas Black Elk*, p. 77; *Washington Post*, January 15, 1925; Foley, *Father Francis M. Craft*, pp. 91–93; Lee, "The Great Whitewash"; Lee, *Fort Meade and the Black Hills*, p. 120; *Lakota Times*, December 25, 1990, and December 25, 1998; "Medals of (Dis)Honor," Resolution SPO-01-163, Support the Action to Revoke the Congressional Medals of Honor to the Soldiers of the 7th Calvary [*sic*] at Wounded Knee; http://www.dickshovel.com/WKmassacre.html, National Congress of American Indians, November 2001 Annual Session, Spokane, Washington.

41. Heitman, *Historical Register and Dictionary of the United States Army*, 1:430, 708–709, 1031; Coughlan, *Varnum*, p. 27; *Washington Post*, March 18 and June 6, 1891; *New York Times*, June 15, 1891. Recommendations and memorials endorsing Forsyth's promotion to brigadier general are in Forsyth's ACP file, NA, RG 94. In June 1891 General Brooke solicited seventy-six "badges" to be awarded to certain Lakota leaders who were "among the most progressive of these Sioux" and who "assisted the military very greatly in many ways by their example of loyalty to the Government. It is believed

that a recognition of the services of these men would go far toward encouraging other Indians to change their mode of life." He added: "[These men] aided me very greatly at Pine Ridge last winter." Brooke to Quartermaster General Richard N. Bachelder, June 9, 1891, Brooke Papers, Box 9. It is not known if such badges were ever produced and awarded.

42. Jensen, Paul, and Carter, *Eyewitness at Wounded Knee*, pp. 47–60; Paul, "The Faraway Artist"; *Chadron Democrat*, January 8, 1891; *Stromsburg Headlight*, January 8, 1891; *Norfolk Daily News*, January 13, 1891; *Hot Springs Daily Star*, January 15, 1891; *Nebraska City News*, January 16 and 30, 1891; *Omaha World-Herald*, January 28, 1891; *Washington Evening Star*, February 2, 1891; *Chadron Advocate*, March 13, 1891; unattributed, undated handwritten note regarding Hotchkiss shell, ca. 1894, on stationery of Scarboro Mineral Water Company, Portland, Maine, provided by Thomas R. Buecker, curator, Fort Robinson Museum, 2007; *Middle Border Bulletin* 4 (Summer 1944): 2; Metcalf, "Two Relics of the Wounded Knee Massacre," pp. 1–2; *St. Louis Post-Dispatch*, January 29, 1891 (quotation); ca. 1930s catalog, Lyon Curio Store, Clinton, Nebraska, p. 3 (citing, for sale: "WAR SHIRTS—Ghost shirts made of muslin, decorated, such as were used in the Wounded Knee Battle. We have some very old ones.—[$]10.00"); *Indian Country Today*, November 23, 1994; *Omaha World-Herald*, August 2, 1999; Bad Heart Bull and Blish, *A Pictographic History of the Oglala Sioux;* Berlo, *Plains Indian Drawings 1865–1935*, p. 37. For more about Wounded Knee relics and the resulting curio industry, see especially Paul, "Wounded Knee and the 'Collector of Curios'"; Paul, "'Relics' of Wounded Knee"; and Klein, "Everything of Interest in the Late Pine Ridge War," pp. 55–62.

43. *Woman's Tribune*, September 12, 1891, cited in Flood, *Lost Bird of Wounded Knee*, p. 83.

44. Material regarding Lost Bird's parentage appears in Acting Commissioner of Indian Affairs A. C. Towner to Agent John R. Brennan, August 7, 1901; Office of Indian Affairs to Brennan, May 12, 1902; Brennan to Commissioner of Indian Affairs, June 14, 1902; and statements from White Butterfly (1902) and Yellow Bird (June 14, 1902), related to the 1901 application by Clara Bewick Colby for her enrollment at the Cheyenne River Agency to insure Lost Bird's tribal rights, including a land allotment. John R. Brennan Scrapbook, John R. Brennan Family Papers, SDSHS, H72.002, Flat Box 028; Acting Commissioner of Indian Affairs to Secretary of the Interior, June 26, 1902, respecting the same, attached to James S. Rush, Civil Reference Branch, National Archives, to Richard E. Jensen, Nebraska State Historical Society, July 19, 1991 (copy provided by R. Eli Paul). On the matter of her parentage, see also statement by A. T. Lea regarding Zintka Lanuni, January 1892 (Item 4026.6052), Late Special Agent Lea to Colby, December 15, 1892 (Item 3826.1457), and Colby to Lea, December 27, 1892 (Item 3826.1458), A. T. Lea Papers, Archives, Gilcrease Museum. Also for Lost Bird, see *Omaha Bee*, January 17, 1891; *Beatrice Daily Express*, January 19, 1891; *Chicago Herald*, February 2, 1891; *Washington Post*, January 1 and June 21, 1893; *Boston Daily Globe*, May 9, 1904; *Washington Post*, June 17 and 18, 1906; *Denver Field and Farm*, March 13, 1909; *Washington Post*, May 18, 1909; *Washington Post*, January 21, 1917; *Woman's Home Weekly*, January 27, 1917; *Sheridan (Wyoming) Enterprise*, October 4, 1913; *Denver Post*, May 12, 1929; Wells, "Ninety-Six Years among the Indians," pp. 295–96; and especially Flood, *Lost Bird of Wounded Knee*.

CHAPTER 16. SURVIVORS

1. The imprecise figure of 170 survivors is conjecturally derived from the known estimated number of Big Foot's people at Wounded Knee (370) minus at least 200 fatalities.

2. Continued use of the term "battle," as registered constantly thereafter by the army, appears to have been an attempt by the War Department to give an iota of legitimacy after the fact to what transpired at Wounded Knee while inferring the denial of a massacre. Similarly, euphemisms such as "affair," "tragedy," and "incident," often used by whites, connote a desire not to confront the edgy reality of Wounded Knee as a massacre. These terms reflect something inexact, possibly as a panacea and thereby a more gently acceptable truth. It must be understood that motive, intent, or extenuating factors do not contribute to defining "massacre"; it is the act itself. See Charles Woodard, "A Massacre Is a Massacre Is a Massacre," *Lakota Times*, April 10, 1990.

3. Ruby, *The Oglala Sioux*, p. 16. Survivors who enlisted included Charles Blue Arm, Hard to Kills, James Axe, Felix Crane Pretty Voice, Daniel Blue Hair, and Fasunke Cigeila. Daniel Blue Hair to Walter Camp, March 8, 1916. Camp Papers, BYU, Box 2, Folder 2 (Microfilm Roll 3).

4. *Omaha World-Herald*, September 19 (quotations) and 20, 1898; *Omaha Bee*, September 19, 1898; Mooney, "Ghost-Dance Religion."

5. *Rapid City Journal*, June 15, 1969 (citing King).

6. *Rapid City Journal*, October 17, 1913.

7. Gilmore to C. S. Paine, October 17, 1913, Nebraska State Historical Society Archives, RG 14, S.G. 1, s. 1, Box 28 (first quotation); Brownlow, *The War, the West, and the Wilderness*, pp. 224–35 (including second quotation, cited from *Moving Picture World*, November 22, 1913).

8. *Chadron Journal*, October 10, 1913; *Chadron Journal*, October 17, 1913; *Rapid City Journal*, October 22, 1913 (quotation).

9. *Denver Post*, October 29, 1913; *Rocky Mountain News*, October 17, 1913 (first quotation); *Rapid City Journal*, September 14, 1952; *Rapid City Journal*, June 22 and July 6, 13 (citing *Scenic Observer*, October 24, 1913), 20, and 27, 1969; *Rapid City Journal*, July 20 and 27, 1969 Paul, "Buffalo Bill and Wounded Knee," pp. 183–85, 186, 188, 190; Warren, *Buffalo Bill's America*, pp. 537–40; Gilmore, "The Truth of the Wounded Knee Massacre," pp. 240–41 (including second quotation); Wells, "Ninety-Six Years among the Indians," pp. 297–302. For objections by the Lakotas to certain aspects of the filming, see also ibid., pp. 299–301, citing *Rapid City Journal*, January 4, 1914; and Russell, *The Lives and Legends of Buffalo Bill*, pp. 456–58. Beard to Camp, December 6, 1915, Camp Manuscripts, Lilly Library, Box 4, Folder 9, Envelope 11, pp. 282–295, (Pine Ridge) (third quotation). General Baldwin wrote Agent Brennan: "As you know, the General [Miles] did not go near that field, nor did Cody appear in a single instance [regarding the Wounded Knee scenes]." Baldwin to Brennan, December 6, 1913, photocopy in Author's Collection. Brennan noted: "Generals Miles, Maus, Baldwin, King, and Jesse M. Lee all remained at the Agency the day the pictures were taken at Wounded Knee. Cody was present assisting in the general directions of the work, but at no time did he pose before the moving picture camera." Brennan to Warren K. Moorehead, January 19, 1914, Letters Sent by Agents or Superintendents, Pine Ridge Agency, vol. 75, pp. 488–90, as cited by Paul, "Buffalo Bill and Wounded Knee," p. 190. See also Wells to Editor, *Rapid City Journal*, January 10, 1914. Philip F.

Wells Materials, D6, F44, Thomas Odell Collection. Of the participating officers, only Colonel Sickel had been at Wounded Knee, despite Father Craft's complaint to Walter Camp that "no officer who was present at the battle was present on the occasion of the reproduction by the moving picture firm." Craft to Camp, January 24, 1914, Ellison/Camp Papers, Box 1, FF 16.

10. *Report of the Commissioner of Indian Affairs, 1891*, 1:139; *Army and Navy Journal*, April 4, 1891 (quotation); *Report of the Commissioner of Indian Affairs, 1892*, p. 128; Paul, "Dakota Resources," pp. 212–23. This article contains a complete list of claimants and witnesses, citing material in Cooper to Morgan, May 16, 1891, as derived from NA, RG 75, Entry 561, Special Case No. 188, Records Relating to Sioux Property Claims, 1891–92, Boxes 1–46, enclosures 7805–92; see also U.S. Congress, Senate, Committee on Indian Affairs, *Claims of Friendly Indians*, pp. 1–14.

11. Cooper also considered claims of Cheyenne River Miniconjous who had gone to Fort Bennett in late December and who claimed losses of property from their homes around Cherry Creek. Pfaller, *James McLaughlin*, pp. 361–62.

12. *Report of the Secretary of War, 1891*, 1:56 (first quotation); U.S. Congress, Senate, Committee on Indian Affairs. *Indian Depredation Claims*, pp. 7–8; McLaughlin to Secretary of the Interior Richard A. Ballinger, April 6, 1910 (second quotation), photocopy provided by Michael Her Many Horses; Pfaller, *James McLaughlin*, p. 363. On April 15, 1896, the Horn Clouds recorded their estimated value for lost property on page 8 of a ledger at Holy Rosary Mission. Daniel Horn Cloud File, Biography Files, SDSHS. Government compensation for losses under comparable circumstances—or at least the promise of it—was not without precedent. After the Sand Creek Massacre in 1864, the government pledged in the Little Arkansas Treaty in 1865 to recompense Southern Cheyenne and Arapaho families for losses suffered there, though it never followed through. Greene, *Washita*, pp. 28–29.

13. "The War with the Messiah," p. 526 (first quotation; a similar quotation by Miles appears in Miles, *Serving the Republic*, p. 243); Miles to Cato Sells, March 13, 1917 (second quotation); Miles to Sells, April 12, 1920 (third quotation); Sells to Secretary of the Interior John B. Payne, May 4, 1920; Sells to McLaughlin, May 5, 1920; memorandum by McLaughlin, May 5, 1920; all in the Wounded Knee Compensation Papers, H76.24, Folder 14, Box 3564A, SDSHS.

14. McLaughlin to Commissioner of Indian Affairs Thomas J. Morgan, October 17, 1890, McLaughlin Papers, Roll 35.

15. Report of Inspector James McLaughlin, in McLaughlin to Sells, January 12, 1921, Wounded Knee Compensation Papers, H76.24, Folder 14, Box 3564A, SDSHS (quotation and quotations in following paragraphs below) (McLaughlin's rough notes for his report are in McLaughlin Papers, Roll 17). See also "List of Indians Killed and Wounded at Sioux Massacre, December 29, 1890," with accompanying papers, filed by Joseph Horn Cloud, April 14, 1920 (which incorporates lists compiled in 1917 and 1918 and includes people living at Pine Ridge, Cheyenne River, and Standing Rock reservations), McLaughlin Papers, Roll 17; and Pfaller, *James McLaughlin*, pp. 363–64.

16. McLaughlin to Sells, January 12, 1921.

17. *Kansas City Star*, August 14, 1927; *Buffalo Evening News*, August 18, 1927 (quotation).

18. McGregor to Collier, May 27, 1935 (quotation), enclosing "Program, Survivors of the Wounded Knee Massacre," June 19–21, 1935, and Collier to McGregor, June 15, 1935. NA, RG 75, Records of the Bureau of Indian Affairs Central Classified Files,

1907–39, Pine Ridge, 29681-1935–Pine Ridge–160, Box 60; McGregor, *Wounded Knee Massacre*, pp. 85–86. In a 1933 resolution several of the survivors wrote: "On the morning of December 29, 1890, Chief Big Foot and his band were compelled to disarm, and were herded in an uncivil way and surrounded by furnished armed soldiers, and without any further notice the Officer in Charge commanded 'fire' on the Indians, and thereupon slaughtered men, women, and children who were helpless. . . . The Surviving Members of the Association do hereby present as evidence those marks of the wounded men and women, together with their written statements." The resolution, signed by James Pipe on Head, Charles Blindman, Sr., Louis Iron Hawk, Richard A. O. Hawk, Jackson He Crow, Alfred Frog, Peter Stands, and John Little Finger, was sent to the commissioner of Indian Affairs on April 3, 1933. McGregor to Commissioner Charles J. Rhoads, April 3, 1933. The commissioner responded: "There is no authority of law to determine any claims of the nature mentioned, either by this Department or by the United States courts. The War Department claims that the Big Foot Band was hostile and that this was a battle instead of a massacre, in which case Congress might not be willing to pass legislation for the relief of any descendants of the Indians who participated in the battle." Commissioner John Collier to McGregor, May 8, 1933. NA, RG 75, Records of the Bureau of Indian Affairs Central Classified Files, 1907–39, Pine Ridge, 15190-1933–Pine Ridge–260.

19. *Biographical Directory of the American Congress*, p. 670; U.S. Congress, House, Subcommittee on Indian Affairs, *Hearing on H.R. 2535*, p. 1 (first quotation); Chenoweth, "Francis Case," p. 324; McGregor, *The Wounded Knee Massacre*, p. 86; James HiHawk to Francis Case, May 17, 1937, Francis H. Case Papers, Wounded Knee Files. The Department of the Interior's endorsement of H.R. 2535 appeared in a report of the acting secretary on April 28, 1937. Floyd W. LaRouche to Francis Case, March 28, 1938, Case Papers; *Indians at Work*, April 1938 (second quotation); Eastman, "Ghost Dance War," p. 41. Commissioner Collier made "certain derogatory statements" about the Seventh Cavalry at Wounded Knee in a national radio address delivered on December 4, 1939, and published in the *Washington Evening Star*, December 5, 1939. See *Proceedings of the Annual Meeting of the Order of Indian Wars*, pp. 8–11.

20. "Claim of Survivors made by Mrs. Nellie Knife," undated, ca. January 1937 (first quotation); Louie L. Lavatta to Francis Case, January 27, 1938; James Pipe On Head to Francis Case, April 14, 1937 (all in Francis H. Case Papers, Wounded Knee Files); "Indemnity Bill for the Massacre of Chief Big Foot and His Band, on December 29, 1890," drafted by "the living Survivors of Cheyenne River and Pine Ridge Reservations," a process "concluded at Wounded Knee, S.D., June 22, 1935." Photocopy provided by Michael Her Many Horses (second quotation).

21. See Louis Iron Hawk to Francis Case, January 18, 1937; James HiHawk to Francis Case, February 12, 1937; James HiHawk to Francis Case, April 26, 1937; Francis Case to James Pipe on Head, April 20, 1937 (first quotation); Francis Case to Louis L. Lavatta, April 26, 1937 (second quotation); West to Will Rogers, Chairman, House Committee on Indian Affairs, April 28, 1937 (third quotation); see also Francis Case to Robert Two Elk, May 6, 1937; all in Francis H. Case Papers, Wounded Knee Files. See the list of forty-one Wounded Knee Lakota Survivors as provided by James Pipe On Head in appendix I.

22. Francis Case to HiHawk, June 29, 1937 (first quotation); Ralph H. Case to Francis Case, April 29, 1937; HiHawk to Francis Case, May 26, 1937; HiHawk to Francis Case, June 5, 1937; HiHawk to Francis Case, June 26, 1937; Ralph H. Case

to Francis Case, July 9, 1937 (second quotation); HiHawk to Francis Case, June 26, 1937; Francis Case to HiHawk, July 10, 1937; all in Francis H. Case Papers, Wounded Knee Files; *Indians at Work*, August 1, 1937; *Washington Post*, August 8, 1937 (third quotation).

23. "Supplementary Written Statement of James Pipe-On Head," U.S. Congress, House, Subcommittee on Indian Affairs, *Hearing on H.R. 2535*, p. 21 (hereinafter *Hearing on H.R. 2535*).

24. *New York Herald Tribune*, March 31, 1938; *American Weekly*, April 24, 1938; Francis Case to James Pipe On Head, December 28, 1937, Case Papers, Wounded Knee Files; *Hearing on H.R. 2535*, pp. 7, 33–48 (including Brennan and James Grass quotations); Johnson, *Unregimented General*, pp. 294 (Miles quotations). Besides James Grass, Lakotas in attendance were Frank Wilson (president of the Oglala Sioux Tribe), Charles Little Hawk, James H. Red Cloud, Peter Bull Bear, Cornelius T. Craven, and Henry Standing Bear. *Hearing on H.R. 2535*, pp. 43–49.

25. Elaine Goodale Eastman to Francis Case, April 7, 1938, and July 19, 1939; Francis Case to James Pipe On Head, March 1, 1939; both in Francis H. Case Papers, Wounded Knee Files; U.S., Congress, House, *A Bill to Liquidate the Liability of the United States for the Massacre* (1939), pp. 1–3; U.S. Congress, House, *Liquidating the Liability of the United States for the Massacre;* J. M. Stewart, Director of Lands, Bureau of Indian Affairs, to Mary Anne Ouelette, July 11, 1938, and July 27, 1938, and Stewart to Representative Usher L. Burdick, October 1, 1940, NA, RG 75, Records of the Bureau of Indian Affairs Central Classified Files, 1907–39, Pine Ridge, 15190-1933–Pine Ridge–260; Ickes to Rogers, April 12, 1939 (first quotation); Beard to Francis Case, July 25, 1939 (second quotation); both in Francis H. Case Papers, Wounded Knee Files.

26. McGregor, *Wounded Knee Massacre*, pp. 90–91; Francis Case to John White Lance, March 10, 1941, Case Papers, Wounded Knee File. H.R. 953 had been amended to pay $1,000 only to persons totally disabled at Wounded Knee, with those only partially disabled to receive a graduated percentage of that amount. U.S. Congress, House, Committee on Indian Affairs, *Liquidating the Liability of the United States for the Massacre*, pp. 1–14; Francis Case to "Dear friend," July 19, 1939; Case to Boyd Leedom, November 22, 1947 (quotations); both in Francis H. Case Papers, Wounded Knee Files.

27. *Pierre Daily Capital Journal*, October 2, 1941. Regarding the 1940 effort Case wrote: "Too many members out of the 435 members make fun of all Indian Bills [*sic*] and go home and tell their people how much money they have saved without considering whether the bill is just or not." Francis Case to James Pipe On Head, June 10, 1940; Francis Case to Thomas Owns the Fire, March 31, 1941; Francis Case to Arthur R. Hudson, January 7, 1942; Case to Edward Owl King, February 25, 1946 (quotation); James HiHawk to Case, October 29, 1947; all in Francis H. Case Papers, Wounded Knee Files; Chenoweth, "Francis Case," p. 324–25; Lurie, "The Indian Claims Commission Act," p. 65.

Related measures for compensation, some involving referral to the Indian Claims Commission and/or Court of Claims, were introduced in 1951 (S. 2053, 82nd Congress), 1954 (H.R. 9304, 83rd Congress), 1955 (H.R. 4116, 84th Congress), 1958 (H.R. 5595, 85th Congress), 1975 (S. 1147, 94th Congress), and 1976 (S. 2900, 94th Congress). None passed. For more recent attempts, see U.S. Congress, Senate, Committee on the Judiciary, *Hearings before the Committee on the Judiciary*, pp. 75–79, 97–102; memorandum, Director, Congressional and Legislative Staff, January 23, 1976, Wounded Knee Compensation Papers, H76.24, Folder 14, Box 3564A, SDSHS. Regarding Wounded Knee claims before the Indian Claims Commission, see also

Ralph H. Case to Boyd Leedom, March 1, 1948, Ralph H. Case Papers, Wounded Knee File. Regarding survivor factionalism, see James E. HiHawk to Ralph H. Case, July 13, 1948, Francis H. Case Papers, Wounded Knee Files. The Interior Department allowed that the 1975–76 bills would be of little benefit because of elapsed generations: "It is expected that most of the original survivors, and surely all of those who died at Wounded Knee or shortly thereafter, died intestate, naming no specific heirs. Many of their descendants . . . also died intestate. Therefore, the 'Heir' in these cases may consist of the heirs-in-law of the original victims—nearly all their descendants. The amounts received by each such descendant would be a mere fraction of the $3,000 figure [proposed in the legislation for each Lakota killed or wounded or their heirs] and would bear no relation to whatever damages may have been suffered by such descendant. More important, in many instances the descendants have reached the fifth generation. The compensation to these individuals . . . at best would be a symbolic gesture." Assistant Secretary of the Interior John H. Kyl to Senator James O. Eastland, February 5, 1976, copy in author's possession. See also the U.S. Army report in Acting Secretary of the Army Norman R. Augustin to Senator James O. Eastland, August 28, 1975, pp. 19–23, copy in author's possession. See also Frazier, *On the Rez*, p. 100; and Forsyth, *Representing the Massacre of American Indians at Wounded Knee*, pp. 97–100, 126–32.

28. *New York Times*, April 14, 1940, and November 4, 1955; *Rapid City Journal*, September 16, 1940; *Sioux Falls Argus-Leader*, February 16 and November 4, 1955; *Rapid City Journal*, November 3, 1955; Burnham, "The True Legend of Dewey Beard" (quotation); *Rapid City Journal*, December 27, 1970.

29. Flood, *Lost Bird of Wounded Knee*, p. 314; *Flandreau Santee Sioux Tribe Monthly Newsletter* (March 2008): 17; Bureau of Indian Affairs, Branch of Realty, Pine Ridge, South Dakota; U.S. Congress, Senate, Committee on the Judiciary, *Hearings before the Committee on the Judiciary*, p. 449; http://www.findagrave.com/cgi-bin/fg.cgi.

30. Tim Giago, "Lakota Will Not Ever Forget Wounded Knee," *Omaha World-Herald*, December 29, 2007.

31. *Chicago Tribune*, September 17, 1998; *Omaha World-Herald*, October 1, 1998.

32. Gonzalez and Cook-Lynn, *The Politics of Hallowed Ground*, pp. 62–77, 358–59 (quotation); Forsyth, *Representing the Massacre of American Indians at Wounded Knee*, p. 214. Wounded Knee's significance in American history has been acknowledged with the site's designation in 1965 as a National Historic Landmark. Richard E. Jensen and R. Eli Paul completed the National Register of Historic Places Registration Form in December 1990. See http://pdfhost.focus.nps.gov/docs/NHLS/Text/66000719.pdf.

33. For Bear River, see Madsen, *The Shoshoni Frontier and the Bear River Massacre*. For Sand Creek, see Hoig, *Sand Creek Massacre*; and Greene and Scott, *Finding Sand Creek*. For the Marias River, see Wilson, "The U.S. Army and the Piegans"; and Ege, *"Tell Baker to Strike Them Hard!"*

34. Utley, *Indian Frontier of the American West*, p. 257. Sporadic civil disturbances required the presence of troops on Indian reservations after Wounded Knee. A notable example took place near Leech Lake, Minnesota, in October 1898, involving Chippewa Indians. See Greene, *Indian War Veterans*, pp. 220–27.

35. *Washington Evening Star*, January 22, 1891 (first quotation); Camp Manuscripts, Lilly Library, Miscellaneous Field Notes, Box 4, Folder 3, Envelope, pp. 4225–233 (second quotation).

36. Interview with Leonard Little Finger, April 21, 2010, Sacred Hoop School, Oglala, South Dakota.

Bibliography

MANUSCRIPT MATERIALS AND COLLECTIONS

American Museum in Britain, Claverton Manor. Bath, England
    Walter R. Crickett letter, ca. January 1891, transcribed by Linda Robbins Coleman.
Army War College. U.S. Army Military History Institute. Manuscript Division. Carlisle, Pennsylvania
    Don Rickey, Jr., Indian Wars Veterans Project materials.
    Edward S. Godfrey Collection.
    Eugene A. Carr Papers.
    Guy V. Henry Collection.
    Nelson A. Miles Collection.
    Order of Indian Wars Collection.
    Samuel M. Whitside Papers.
    William H. Bowen Papers.
Author's Collection. Arvada, Colorado
    Gaston, Joseph A., to the Adjutant General, U.S. Army, December 31, 1926. "Service of Troop H, 8th Cav., Sioux War, 1890–1891." Original typescript copy.
    Getty, Robert N. "Death of Lt. Edward L. [sic] Casey." Original typescript copy, ca. 1926.
    Ghost Horse, Alice. "A True Story of What Happened at Wounded Knee in December 1890." Undated typescript transcribed by John War Bonnet. Copy attached to letter, Richmond Clow, University of Montana, to R. Eli Paul, Lincoln, Nebraska, March 13, 1990.
Big Horn County Library. Hardin, Montana
    News clipping scrapbooks.
Black Hills State University. Leland D. Case Library, E. Y. Berry Library–Learning Center. Special Collections. Spearfish, South Dakota
    E. Y. Berry Collection.
    Frank Thomson Papers.
    Thomas Odell Collection.
Brigham Young University (BYU). L. Tom Perry Special Collections. Harold B. Lee Library. Provo, Utah
    Walter Mason Camp Papers.

Buffalo Bill Museum and Grave Archives at Lookout Mountain. Denver, Colorado
  "As Narrated by 'Short Bull.'" Trans. George Crager. 1891.
  Nelson A. Miles authorization to William F. Cody to arrest Sitting Bull. November 24, 1890.
Colorado Historical Society. Denver
  George B. DuBois Letters.
  James R. Walker Manuscripts.
Dakota Wesleyan University. George and Eleanor McGovern Library. Archives. Mitchell, South Dakota
  Francis H. Case Papers.
Denver Public Library. Western History Department. Denver
  Don G. Rickey Papers.
  Robert S. Ellison and Walter M. Camp Papers.
Don G. Rickey Papers. Evergreen, Colorado
Fort Robinson State Park. Fort Robinson Museum files. Crawford, Nebraska
  "Record of Events from Post Returns, Fort Robinson, Nebraska, 1890–1899."
Gilcrease Museum. Archives. Tulsa, Oklahoma
  A. T. Lea Papers.
Historical Society of Pennsylvania. Philadelphia
  John Rutter Brooke Papers.
Holy Rosary Mission. Pine Ridge, South Dakota
  Sialm, Placidus, S.J. Unpublished manuscript entitled "History, Holy Rosary Mission, Pine Ridge, S.D."
Huntington Library. Department of Manuscripts. San Marino, California
  Frank D. Baldwin Collection.
H. V. Johnson Cultural Center. Eagle Butte, South Dakota
  Robert High Eagle. "How Sitting Bull Was Made a Chief." Undated typescript.
I. D. Weeks Library. University of South Dakota. Archives and Special Collections. Vermillion, South Dakota
  John S. Painter Collection, Residual Papers. Wounded Knee Scrapbook, Sir Henry Wellcome.
  Oyate Ivechinka Woglakapi: The People Speak for Themselves, An Oral History Collection, vol. 4. American Indian Research Project, University of South Dakota, 1973.
  Ralph H. Case Papers.
  Wounded Knee Survivors Association Documents.
Indiana University. Lilly Library. Manuscripts Department. Bloomington
  Walter M. Camp Manuscripts.
John D. McDermott Collection. Rapid City, South Dakota
Library of Congress. Manuscript Division. Washington, D.C.
  Edward S. Godfrey Papers.
  Hugh L. Scott Papers.
  John J. Pershing Papers.
  Nelson A. Miles Papers.
  William F. Cody Papers.
  William J. Ghent Papers.
  William R. Shafter Papers.
Little Bighorn Battlefield National Monument. Crow Agency, Montana
  Diary of Charles W. Hayden, Seventh Cavalry. Photocopy.
  "Plot Showing Location of Graves of U.S. Soldiers at Pine Ridge Cemetary [*sic*] South Dakota."

Robinson, William W. "Recollections of Gen. W. W. Robinson, Jr., on the Battles of Wounded Knee and White Clay Creek." Item 12518. Undated typescript.

U.S. 7th Cavalry Collection. Microfilm Roll 12. Loyd S. McCormick, "Wounded Knee and Drexel Mission Fights, December 29th and 30th, 1890."

Walter M. Camp Papers.

Marquette University. Milwaukee, Wisconsin

Diary of Reverend Aemilius Perrig. Catholic Archives. Holy Rosary Mission Records (typescript).

"Excerpts Taken from the Diary of Holy Rosary Mission on the Battle of Wounded Knee" (typescript).

Sisters of St. Francis Chronicles (typescript).

Michael Her Many Horses Library and Collection. Wounded Knee, South Dakota

National Archives (NA). Washington, D.C.

James W. Forsyth, Appointment, Commission, and Personal File.

Microfilm 233. Register of Enlistments of Indian Scouts.

Microfilm 595, Roll 33. Contains "Approximate census of the Sioux Indians belonging to the Cheyenne River Reservation who were in the battle of Wounded Knee and are yet at Pine Ridge Agency, S.D., taken June 30, 1891."

Microfilm 665, Roll 9. Regimental Returns of the First Infantry, 1890–97.

Microfilm 665, Roll 23. Regimental Returns of the Second Infantry, 1884–92.

Microfilm 665, Roll 36. Regimental Returns of the Third Infantry, 1886–94.

Microfilm 665, Roll 84. Regimental Returns of the Seventh Infantry, 1885–95.

Microfilm 665, Roll 90. Camp Return of First Infantry, Jan. 1891.

Microfilm 665, Roll 95. Regimental Returns of the Eighth Infantry, 1883–92.

Microfilm 665, Roll 138. Regimental Returns of the Twelfth Infantry, 1886–96.

Microfilm 665, Roll 214. Regimental Returns of the Twentieth Infantry, 1890–97.

Microfilm 665, Roll 222. Regimental Returns of the Twenty-First Infantry, 1890–97.

Microfilm 665, Roll 230. Regimental Returns of the Twenty-Second Infantry, 1890–97.

Microfilm 665, Roll 256. Regimental Returns of the Twenty-Fifth Infantry, 1883–90.

Microfilm 727, Roll 7. Regimental Returns of the First Artillery, 1881–95.

Microfilm 727, Roll 31. Regimental Returns of the Fourth Artillery, 1878–92.

Microfilm 744, Roll 8. Regimental Returns of the First Cavalry, 1887–96.

Microfilm 744, Roll 21. Regimental Returns of the Second Cavalry, 1888–95.

Microfilm 744, Roll 55. Regimental Returns of the Fifth Cavalry, 1886–93.

Microfilm 744, Roll 65. Regimental Returns of the Sixth Cavalry, 1886–91.

Microfilm 744, Roll 74. Regimental Returns of the Seventh Cavalry, 1889–96.

Microfilm 744, Roll 82. Regimental Returns of the Eighth Cavalry, 1890–97.

Microfilm 744, Roll 90. Regimental Returns of the Ninth Cavalry, 1888–95.

Microfilm 983, Rolls 1 and 2, Sioux Campaign, 1890–91.

Microfilm 1282, Letters Sent to the Office of Indian Affairs by the Pine Ridge Agency, 1875–1914. 52 rolls.

Microfilm Roll 107. Fort Bennett, S.Dak., January 1881–December 1891.

Microfilm Roll 617. Returns from U.S. Military Posts.

Microfilm Rolls 0701–0801. Fort Meade, S.Dak., April 1890–January 1891.

Microfilm Roll 864. Fort Niobrara, Nebr., April 1880–December 1894.

Microfilm Roll 1029. Fort Robinson, Nebr., January 1885–December 1894.

Microfilm Roll 1240. Fort Sully, S.Dak., January 1885–October 1894.

Microfilm Roll 1477. Fort Yates, N.Dak., January 1885–December 1893.

Record Group 75. Records of the Bureau of Indian Affairs.

Record Group 77. Records of the Office of the Chief of Engineers.

Record Group 94. Records of the Office of the Adjutant General.

Record Group 391. Records of U.S. Regular Army Mobile Units, Cavalry.

Record Group 393. Records of United States Army Continental Commands.

Regular Army Muster Rolls. Seventh Cavalry, Troops A, B, C, D, E, G, I, K.

Samuel M. Whitside, Appointment, Commission, and Personal File.

National Archives at Kansas City. Record Group 75, Records of the Bureau of Indian Affairs. Pine Ridge Agency, Pine Ridge, South Dakota. Kansas City, Missouri

General Records, Main Decimal Files, Box 657, Folder 650.

"List of Indians absent and who have not reported for Rations to date. Cheyenne River Agency, S.D., December 29 '90." Cheyenne River Agency.

Muster Rolls, Companies A–D, Indian scouts enlisted at Pine Ridge Agency and Camp Cheyenne, South Dakota, November 1890–April 1891.

Pine Ridge Agency, Controversies, 1867–1907.

National Park Service. Jefferson National Expansion Memorial Archives. St. Louis, Missouri

Indian Wars Widows Project Records.

Nebraska State Historical Society Archives. Lincoln

Anderson, David. Sketch of Montrose Fort.

Eli S. Ricker Collection.

James C. Olson Collection.

John G. Bourke Papers.

Merrill J. Mattes Collection.

Nebraska National Guard in Sioux War, 1890–91, RG018.

Program, "Buffalo Bill's Wild West and Congress of Rough Riders of the World," 1893. C671.

Newberry Library. Chicago, Illinois

Midwest Manuscript Collection.

Elmo Scott Watson Papers.

Ohio Historical Society. Columbus

Warren K. Moorehead Papers.

Parmly Billings Public Library. Montana Room. Vertical Files. Billings, Montana

Paul Harbaugh Collection. Cherry Hills, Village, Colorado

Western Union Company telegrams, November–December 1890.

Princeton University. Princeton University Library. Department of Rare Books and Special Collections. Princeton, New Jersey

John W. Comfort Papers.

Pritzker Military Library, Chicago, Illinois

James Wengert Military Medical Collection.

Rawlins Municipal Library. Vertical Files. Pierre, South Dakota

Rutherford B. Hayes Memorial Library. Fremont, Ohio

George Crook Papers, Microfilm.

South Dakota State Historical Society (SDSHS). Library and Archives. Pierre

"Accounts of Unidentified South Dakota Family during the Messiah War in 1890." Charles Percival Jordan Papers.

Frank Zahn Collection.

James McLaughlin Letter, 1920.

James McLaughlin Papers. Microfilm.

John B. McCloud, "Reminiscence."

John R. Brennan Family Papers.

Letter from an unidentified carpenter at Pine Ridge, March 1, 1891.

Mary Collins Family Papers.

Mason, Nelson A. "Chief Sitting Bull's Latter Days."

Notebook, "Indians wounded in 'Fight at Wounded Knee,' South Dakota, December 29, 1890. Treated by Frank J. Ives, Capt. & Asst Surgeon, U.S.A."

Osborn, Sarah Jane. "Memoirs of a Pennington Co. Resident."

R. E. Curran Letters.

Simon J. Kirk Manuscript.

Sioux Miscellany Collection.

Travel in America.

Vertical Files.

William J. Small Collection.

Wounded Knee Compensation Papers.

State Historical Society of North Dakota. Archives and Manuscripts Division. Bismarck

America Elmira Collins Papers.

E. D. Mossman Papers.

Frank Fiske Papers.

Frank Zahn Papers.

Matthew Forney Steele Papers.

Private Alban Siegert Letter, December 17, 1890.

University of Colorado Libraries. Western History Collections. Boulder

William Carey Brown Papers.

University of Oklahoma Library. Western History Collection. Norman

Walter S. Campbell Papers.

University of Washington Libraries. Special Collections. Seattle

James W. Forsyth Family Papers.

University of Wyoming. American Heritage Center. Wyoming State Historical Research and Publication Division. Laramie

Lemmon, G. E. "My Participation in and Recollections of the Sioux Uprising of 1890–91."

U.S. Army Command and General Staff College. Fort Leavenworth, Kansas

Russell, Samuel L. "Selfless Service: The Cavalry Career of Brigadier General Samuel M. Whitside from 1858 to 1902." Master's thesis dated 2002.

Yale University. Beinecke Rare Book and Manuscript Library. New Haven, Connecticut

James W. Forsyth Papers.

GOVERNMENT PUBLICATIONS

Bell, William Gardner. *Commanding Generals and Chiefs of Staff: Portraits and Biographical Sketches of the United States Army's Senior Officers.* Washington, D.C.: Center of Military History, United States Army, 1987.

———. *Secretaries of War and Secretaries of the Army: Portraits and Biographical Sketches.* Washington, D.C.: Center of Military History, United States Army, 1982.

Biographical Directory of the American Congress, 1774–1961. Washington, D.C.: Government Printing Office, 1961.

Executive Orders Relating to Indian Reservations, from May 14, 1855 to July 1, 1912. Washington, D.C.: Government Printing Office, 1912.

Ferris, Robert G., ed. *Soldier and Brave: Historic Places Associated with Indian Affairs and the Indian Wars in the Trans-Mississippi West.* 2nd ed. Washington, D.C.: National Park Service, 1971.

General Orders and Circulars, Adjutant General's Office, 1890. Washington, D.C.: Government Printing Office, 1891.

General Orders and Circulars, Adjutant General's Office, 1891. Washington, D.C.: Government Printing Office, 1892.

General Orders and Circulars, Adjutant General's Office, 1895. Washington, D.C.: Government Printing Office, 1896.

Heitman, Francis B., comp. *Historical Register and Dictionary of the United States Army, from Its Organization, September 29, 1789, to March 2, 1903.* 2 vols. Washington, D.C.: Government Printing Office, 1903.

Hodge, Frederick Webb, ed. *Handbook of American Indians North of Mexico.* 2 vols. Washington, D.C.: Government Printing Office, 1910.

Hornaday, William T. *The Extermination of the American Bison.* Washington, D.C.: Government Printing Office, 1889.

Indians Taxed and Indians Not Taxed in the United States at the Eleventh Census: 1890. Washington, D.C.: Government Printing Office, 1894.

Kappler, Charles J., comp. and ed. *Indian Affairs: Laws and Treaties.* 2 vols. Washington, D.C.: Government Printing Office, 1904.

The Medal of Honor of the United States Army. Washington, D.C.: Government Printing Office, 1948.

Midwest Regional Office. National Park Service. *Special Site Report on Wounded Knee Battlefield, Pine Ridge Indian Reservation, South Dakota.* Omaha: U.S. Department of the Interior, August 1965.

Military Law and Precedents. 2nd ed. Washington, D.C.: Government Printing Office, 1920.

Narrative Descriptions of the Named Campaigns of the U.S. Army (Revolutionary War to Vietnam Conflict). Washington, D.C.: Department of the Army, ca. 1968.

National Archives and Records Service Microfilm Publications. Pamphlet describing M1229. Washington, D.C.: National Archives and Records Service, 1983.

National Park Service. *Draft Study of Alternatives and Environmental Assessment, Wounded Knee, South Dakota.* Denver: Denver Service Center, 1993.

"Papers Relating to the Sioux Indians of the United States, Who Have Taken Refuge in Canadian Territory." Governor General's Office. Public Archives of Canada, Ottawa, n.d. (circa 1879).

Regulations for the Army of the United States, 1889. Washington, D.C.: Government Printing Office, 1889.

Regulations for the Army of the United States, 1901. Washington, D.C.: Government Printing Office, 1901.

Report of the Commissioner of Indian Affairs, 1873. Washington, D.C.: Government Printing Office, 1874.

Report of the Commissioner of Indian Affairs, 1874. Washington, D.C.: Government Printing Office, 1875.

Report of the Commissioner of Indian Affairs, 1875. Washington, D.C.: Government Printing Office, 1875.

Report of the Commissioner of Indian Affairs, 1876. Washington, D.C.: Government Printing Office, 1876.

Report of the Commissioner of Indian Affairs, 1877. Washington, D.C.: Government Printing Office, 1877.

Report of the Commissioner of Indian Affairs, 1878. Washington, D.C.: Government Printing Office, 1878.

Report of the Commissioner of Indian Affairs, 1879. Washington, D.C.: Government Printing Office, 1879.

Report of the Commissioner of Indian Affairs, 1888. Washington, D.C.: Government Printing Office, 1888.

Report of the Commissioner of Indian Affairs, 1889. Washington, D.C.: Government Printing Office, 1889.

Report of the Commissioner of Indian Affairs, 1890. Washington, D.C.: Government Printing Office, 1890.

Report of the Commissioner of Indian Affairs, 1891. 2 vols. Washington, D.C.: Government Printing Office, 1891.

Report of the Commissioner of Indian Affairs, 1892. Washington, D.C.: Government Printing Office, 1892.

Report of the Secretary of the Interior, 1888. Washington, D.C.: Government Printing Office, 1888.

Report of the Secretary of the Interior, 1889. Washington, D.C.: Government Printing Office, 1889.

Report of the Secretary of the Interior, 1890. Washington, D.C.: Government Printing Office, 1890.

Report of the Secretary of the Interior, 1891. Washington, D.C.: Government Printing Office, 1891.

Report of the Secretary of the Interior, 1892. Washington, D.C.: Government Printing Office, 1892.

Report of the Secretary of War, 1880. Washington, D.C.: Government Printing Office, 1880.

Report of the Secretary of War, 1890. Washington, D.C.: Government Printing Office, 1891.

Report of the Secretary of War, 1891. Washington, D.C.: Government Printing Office, 1892.

Report of the Secretary of War, 1894. Washington, D.C.: Government Printing Office, 1894.

Report of the Secretary of War, 1895. Washington, D.C.: Government Printing Office, 1895.

Royce, Charles C., comp. "Indian Land Cessions in the United States." In *Eighteenth Annual Report of the Bureau of American Ethnology*, part 2, pp. 521–997. 2 parts. Washington, D.C.: Government Printing Office, 1899.

Specifications for Clothing, Camp and Garrison Equipage, and Clothing and Equipage Materials. Philadelphia: Philadelphia Depot of the Quartermaster's Department, 1889. Reprinted as *U.S. Army Uniforms and Equipment, 1889, By the Quartermaster General of the Army.* Lincoln: University of Nebraska Press, 1986.

Swanton, John R. *The Indian Tribes of North America.* Smithsonian Institution Bureau of American Ethnology, Bulletin 145. Washington, D.C.: Smithsonian Institution Press, 1952.

Twenty-First Annual Report of the Board of Indian Commissioners, 1889. Washington, D.C.: Government Printing Office, 1890.

U.S. Congress. House. *A Bill to Liquidate the Liability of the United States for the Massacre of Sioux Indian Men, Women, and Children at Wounded Knee on December 29, 1890.* H.R. 2535, 75th Cong., 1st sess., 1938.

———. *A Bill to Liquidate the Liability of the United States for the Massacre of Sioux Indian Men, Women, and Children at Wounded Knee on December 29, 1890.* H.R. 953, 76th Cong., 1st sess., 1939.

———. *Letter from the Acting Secretary of the Treasury, Transmitting an Estimate of the Appropriation to Meet a Deficiency in the Appropriation for the Support of Sioux Indians of Different Tribes, Subsistence and Civilization for the Fiscal Year 1891.* H. Doc. 52, 51st Cong., 2nd sess., 1890.

———. *Liquidating the Liability of the United States for the Massacre of Sioux Indian Men, Women, and Children at Wounded Knee.* H. Rept. 2317, 76th Cong., 3rd sess., 1940.

———. Committee on Appropriations. *Medals for the Captors of Sitting Bull.* H. Doc. 1272, 61st Cong. 3rd sess., 1911.

———. Committee on Indian Affairs. *Agreements with Sioux Indians.* H. Rept. 829, 48th Cong., 1st sess., 1884.

———. *An Agreement with the Sioux Indians, Dakota, for a Cession of a Part of Their Reservation to the United States.* H. Rept. 1536, 47th Cong., 1st sess., 1882.

———. *Right of Way to Dakota Central Railway through Sioux Reservation, Dakota.* H. Ex. Doc. 11, 48th Cong., 1st sess., 1883.

———. *To Divide a Portion of the Reservation of the Sioux Nation of Indians in Dakota into Separate Reservations.* H. Report 1724, 48th Cong., 1st sess., 1884.

———. Committee on Military Affairs. *Chief Sitting Bull.* H. Misc. Doc. 80, 51st Cong., 2nd sess., 1890.

———. *Chief Sitting Bull.* H. Report No. 3375, 51st Cong., 2nd sess., 1891.

———. *Expenses Incurred by Nebraska in a Raid by Sioux Indians.* H. Rept. 344, 54th Cong., 1st sess., 1896.

———. Subcommittee on Indian Affairs. *Hearing on H.R. 2535.* 75th Cong., 3rd sess., March 7 and May 12, 1938.

U.S. Congress. Senate. *Letter from the Secretary of the Interior, Transmitting, in Response to a Senate Resolution of 2d Instant, a Communication from the Commissioner of Indian Affairs Relative to the Alleged Armament of Indians in Certain States.* S. Ex. Doc. 9, 51st Cong., 2nd sess., December 11, 1890.

———. *Message from the President of the United States, Transmitting a Letter of the Secretary of the Interior and Documents Relative to the Condition of the Northern Cheyenne Indians.* S. Ex. Doc. 121, 51st Cong., 1st sess., 1890.

———. Committee on Indian Affairs. *Claims of Friendly Indians for Depredations Committed during the Pine Ridge Disturbance.* S. Ex. Doc. 93, 52nd Cong., 2nd sess., 1893.

———. *Indian Depredation Claims.* S. Report 1531, 55th Cong., 3rd sess., 1899.

———. *Joint Resolution and Memorial of the Legislative Assembly of the Territory of Dakota, Urging the Passage of the Pending Bill for the Opening to Settlement of a Portion of the Sioux Indian Reservation in Dakota.* S. Misc. Doc. 69, 50th Cong., 2nd sess., 1889.

———. *Letter from the Secretary of the Interior, in Relation to the Affairs of the Indians at the Pine Ridge and Rosebud Reservations in South Dakota.* S. Ex. Doc. 58, 52nd Congress, 1st sess., 1892.

————. *Letter from the Secretary of the Interior, in Response to Senate Resolution of December 13, 1888, Report Relative to Opening a Part of the Sioux Reservation.* S. Ex. Doc. 17, 50th Cong., 2nd sess., 1888.

————. *Letter from the Secretary of the Interior, Relative to Granting Pensions and Medals to Indians of the Standing Rock Agency.* S. Ex. Doc. No. 84. 52nd Cong., 1st sess., 1892.

————. *Letter from the Secretary of War, Transmitting, in Response to a Resolution of the United States Senate, a Letter from the Major-General Commanding the Army, Relative to Implements of Warfare Supposed to Be in the Possession of the Indians in Certain States.* Ex. Doc. 2, 51st Cong., 2nd sess., 1890.

————. *Message from the President of the United States, Transmitting a Letter from the Secretary of the Interior Relative to the Use of Funds for the Subsistence of Certain Northern Cheyenne Indians.* S. Ex. Doc. 212, 49th Cong., 1st sess., 1886.

————. *Message from the President, Transmitting a Communication from the Secretary of the Interior of 4th Instant, Submitting Draft of Bill "to Accept and Ratify Certain Agreements Made with the Sioux Indians and to Grant a Right of Way to the Chicago, Milwaukee and Saint Paul Railway Company through the Sioux Reservation in Dakota."* S. Ex. Doc. 20, 48th Cong., 1st sess., 1883.

————. *Reports Relative to the Proposed Division of the Great Sioux Reservation, and Recommending Certain Legislation.* S. Ex. Doc. 51, 51st Cong., 1st sess., 1890.

————. *Statements of a Delegation of Ogalalla Sioux before the Chairman of the Committee on Indian Affairs, United States Senate, April 29 and 30, 1897, Relative to Affairs at the Pine Ridge Agency, S. Dak.* S. Doc. 61, 55th Cong., 1st sess., 1897.

————. Committee on the Judiciary. *Hearings before the Committee on the Judiciary, United States Senate, . . . on S. 1147 and S. 2900, to Liquidate the Liability of the United States for the Massacre of Sioux Indian Men, Women, and Children at Wounded Knee on December 29, 1890.* 94th Cong., 2nd sess., February 5–6, 1976.

————. *To Accompany S. 463, to Reimburse the State of Nebraska the Expenses Incurred by that State in Repelling a Threatened Invasion and Raid by the Sioux in 1890–'91.* S. Rept. 45, 53rd Cong., 1st sess., 1893.

————. *To Accompany S. 2476, to Reimburse the State of Nebraska the Expenses Incurred by that State in Repelling a Threatened Invasion and Raid by the Sioux in 1890–'91.* S. Rept. 352, 52nd Cong., 1st sess., 1892.

————. Committee on Pensions. *Families of Certain Indian Policemen.* S. Rept. 1352, 58th Cong., 2nd sess., 1904.

————. Select Committee to Examine into the Condition of the Sioux and Crow Indians. *Report of the Special Committee of the United States Senate, Appointed to Visit the Indian Tribes in Northern Montana.* S. Rept. 283, 48th Cong., 1st sess., 1884.

U.S. Court of Claims Reports, 84. Washington, D.C.: Government Printing Office, 1937.

U.S. Court of Claims Reports, 97. Washington, D.C.: Government Printing Office, 1942.

U.S. Statutes at Large. Vols. 25, 26. Washington, D.C.: Government Printing Office, 1889, 1891.

Winthrop, William. *Military Law and Precedents.* 2nd ed. Washington, D.C.: Government Printing Office, 1920.

BIBLIOGRAPHY

BOOKS AND ARTICLES

Abbot, Charles W., Jr. "The Twelfth Regiment of Infantry." In Rodenbough and Haskin, *The Army of the United States*, pp. 555–74.

Abrams, Marc H., comp. and ed. *Newspaper Chronicle of the Indian Wars*. 16 vols. Brooklyn, N.Y.: Abrams Publications, 2010.

Albers, Patricia C. "Santee." In William C. Sturtevant (ed.), *Handbook of North American Indians*, vol. 13: *Plains*, ed. Raymond J. DeMallie, pp. 761–76. Washington, D.C.: Smithsonian Institution, 2001.

Alberts, Don E. *Brandy Station to Manila Bay: A Biography of General Wesley Merritt*. Austin, Tex.: Presidial Press, 1980.

Allen, Charles W. *From Fort Laramie to Wounded Knee: In the West That Was*. Ed. Richard E. Jensen. Lincoln: University of Nebraska Press, 1997.

Almon, Marvin. "I Saw the Wounded Knee Massacre." *True West* 3 (September–October 1955): 25–26.

Amos, Preston E. *Above and Beyond in the West: Black Medal of Honor Winners, 1870–1890*. Washington, D.C.: Potomac Corral of the Westerners, 1974.

Anderson, David. "'Fort' Montrose, Sioux County." *Nebraska History Magazine* 15 (April–June 1934): 114–15.

Anderson, Gary Clayton. *Sitting Bull and the Paradox of Lakota Nationhood*. New York: Longman, 1996.

Anderson, Harry H. "A History of the Cheyenne River Indian Agency and Its Military Post, Fort Bennett, 1868–1891." *South Dakota Report and Historical Collections* 28 (1956): 390–551.

Andersson, Rani-Henrik. *The Lakota Ghost Dance of 1890*. Lincoln: University of Nebraska Press, 2008.

Arnold, Frazer. "Ghost Dance and Wounded Knee." *Cavalry Journal* 43 (May–June 1934): 20–21.

Ashburn, P. M. *A History of the Medical Department of the United States Army*. Boston and New York: Houghton Mifflin Company, 1929.

Ayres, Anthony R. "Indian Wars and Medals: The Sioux War of 1890–91 and the Nebraska Sioux War Medal." *Medal Collector* 26 (March 1975): 3–28; and *Medal Collector* 26 (April 1975): 20–27.

Bad Heart Bull, Amos, and Helen H. Blish. *A Pictographic History of the Oglala Sioux*. Lincoln: University of Nebraska Press, 1967.

Bailey, Paul. *Wovoka: The Indian Messiah*. Los Angeles: Westernlore, 1957.

Baird, George W. "General Miles's Indian Campaigns." *Century Magazine* 42 (July 1891): 351–70.

Ballard, Jack Stokes. *Commander and Builder of Western Forts: The Life and Times of Major General Henry C. Merriam, 1862–1901*. College Station: Texas A&M University Press, 2012.

Banner, Stuart. *How the Indians Lost Their Land: Law and Power on the Frontier*. Cambridge, Mass.: Harvard University Press, 2005.

Bates, Alfred E. "The Second Regiment of Infantry." In Rodenbough and Haskin, *The Army of the United States*, pp. 153–72.

Bates, Charles Francis. "Edward Settle Godfrey." In *Sixty-Third Annual Report of the Association of Graduates of the United States Military Academy at West Point, New York, June 9, 1932*, pp. 58–68. Newburgh, N.Y.: Moore Printing Company, 1932.

Beach, Rex E. "Wounded Knee." *Appleton's Booklovers Magazine* (June 1906): 731–36.

Behrens, Jo Lea Wetherilt. "In Defense of 'Poor Lo': National Indian Defence Association and *Council Fire*'s Advocacy for Sioux Land Rights." *South Dakota History* 24 (Fall/Winter 1994): 153–73.

Belitz, Larry. *The Buffalo Hide Tipi of the Sioux.* Sioux Falls, S.Dak.: Pine Hill Press, 2006.

Berlo, Janet Catherine, ed. *Plains Indian Drawings 1865–1935: Pages from a Visual History.* New York: Harry N. Abrams, Publishers, 1996.

Berthrong, Donald J. *The Cheyenne and Arapaho Ordeal: Reservation and Agency Life in the Indian Territory, 1875–1907.* Norman: University of Oklahoma Press, 1976.

Bettelyoun, Susan Bordeaux, and Josephine Waggoner. *With My Own Eyes: A Lakota Woman Tells Her People's History.* Ed. and intro. by Emily Levine. Lincoln: University of Nebraska Press, 1998.

Beyer, W. F., and O. F. Keydel, eds. *Deeds of Valor.* 2 vols. Detroit: Perrien-Keydel Company, 1907.

Bland, Thomas A., ed. *A Brief History of the Late Military Invasion of the Home of the Sioux.* Washington, D.C.: National Indian Defence Association, 1891.

Blasingame, Ike. *Dakota Cowboy: My Life in the Old Days.* New York: G. P. Putnam's Sons, 1958.

Bogan, Alan. "Field Order, 3rd Infantry, 1890." *Military Collector and Historian* 45 (Winter 1993): 188.

Bosma, Boyd. "An Interview with Jim Mesteth." *Indian Historian* 11 (Spring 1978): 18–21.

Bourke, John G. *On the Border with Crook.* New York: Charles Scribner's Sons, 1891.

Boyd, James M. *Recent Indian Wars, under the Lead of Sitting Bull, and Other Chiefs.* N.p.: Publishers Union, 1891.

Brady, Cyrus Townsend. *Indian Fights and Fighters.* New York: McClure, Phillips and Company, 1904.

Bray, Kingsley M. *Crazy Horse: A Lakota Life.* Norman: University of Oklahoma Press, 2006.

———. "Pine Ridge Letters Shed New Light on the Battle of the Little Bighorn." *Ghost Herder: The Journal of the Friends of the Little Bighorn Battlefield* 1 (Summer 2011): 39–48.

———. "'We Belong to the North': The Flights of the Northern Indians from the White River Agencies, 1877–1878." *Montana The Magazine of Western History* 55 (Summer 2005): 28–47.

Breckons, J. A. "The Army Pack Train Service." *Recreation* 6 (May 1897): 426–28.

Briggs, Harold E. "The Great Dakota Boom, 1879–1886." In Janet Daley Lysengen and Ann M. Rathke (eds.), *The Centennial Anthology of North Dakota History, Journal of the Northern Plains*, pp. 109–31. Bismarck: State Historical Society of North Dakota, 1996.

Brimlow, George Francis. *The Bannock Indian War of 1878.* Caldwell, Idaho: Caxton Printers, 1938.

———. *Cavalryman Out of the West: Life of General William Carey Brown.* Caldwell, Idaho: Caxton Printers, 1944.

Brininstool, E. A. "Buffaloing Buffalo Bill." *Hunter-Trader-Trapper* 76 (April 1932): 17–19.

———. "'Buffaloing' Buffalo Bill: How the Post Commander of Fort Yates 'Put One Over' on Col. W. F. Cody." *Westerners Brand Book, 1945–46*, pp. 62–67. Chicago: n.p., 1947.

Brinkerhoff, H. R. "The Fifteenth Regiment of Infantry." In Rodenbough and Haskin, *The Army of the United States*, 610–28.

Brown, Jesse, and A. M. Willard. *The Black Hills Trails: A History of the Struggles of the Pioneers in the Winning of the Black Hills*. Rapid City, S.Dak.: Rapid City Journal Company, 1924.

Brownlow, Kevin. *The War, the West, and the Wilderness: A Celebration of the Great Silent-Movie Makers Who First Ventured Out of the Studios into Dangerous and Distant Places*. New York: Alfred A. Knopf, 1979.

Bryde, John F. *Modern Indian Psychology*. Vermillion: Institute of Indian Studies, University of South Dakota, 1971.

Buecker, Thomas R. "'The Even Tenor of Our Way Is Pursued Undisturbed': Henry P. Smith's Diary during the Ghost Dance Movement, 1890–91." *South Dakota History* 34 (Fall 2004): 197–236.

——. "Fort Niobrara, 1880–1906: Guardian of the Rosebud Sioux." *Nebraska History* 65 (Fall 1984): 300–325.

——. *Fort Robinson and the American West, 1874–1899*. Lincoln: Nebraska State Historical Society, 1999.

——. "'The Men Behaved Spendidly': Guy V. Henry's Famous Cavalry Rides." *Nebraska History* 78 (Summer 1997): 54–63.

Burdick, Usher L. *The Last Days of Sitting Bull*. Baltimore: Wirth Brothers, 1941.

Cabaniss, Charles H. "The Eighteenth Regiment of Infantry." In Rodenbough and Haskin, *The Army of the United States*, pp. 634–42.

Calhoun, Charles W. *Benjamin Harrison*. New York: Henry Holt and Company, 2005.

Calloway, Colin G. "Sword Bearer and the 'Crow Outbreak' of 1887." *Montana The Magazine of Western History* 36 (Autumn 1986): 38–51.

Carlson, Paul H. *"Pecos Bill": A Military Biography of William R. Shafter*. College Station: Texas A&M University Press, 1989.

Carr, G. Sam. "Two Years after Wounded Knee Chief Two Sticks and His Followers Were Ghost Dancing and More." *Wild West* 14 (July 2001): 10, 73–74.

Carroll, John M., ed. *The Black Military Experience in the American West*. New York: Liveright Publishing Corporation, 1971.

——, comp. *I, Varnum: The Autobiographical Reminiscences of Custer's Chief of Scouts*. Glendale, Calif.: Arthur H. Clark Company, 1982.

——, comp. *The Papers of the Order of Indian Wars*. Fort Collins, Colo.: Old Army Press, 1975.

——, comp. *The Sand Creek Massacre: A Documentary History*. New York: Sol Lewis, 1975.

——. "The Search for the Soldier Dead at Wounded Knee." *Frontier Times* 57 (August 1985): 10–16.

——, comp. *The Seventh Cavalrymen Winners of the Medal of Honor: The Indian Wars*. Bryan, Tex.: Privately published, 1978.

——, ed. *To Set the Record Straight!: The Real Story of Wounded Knee*. Bryan, Tex: Privately published, n.d.

——., comp. *The Unpublished Papers of the Order of Indian Wars*. Books 1–10. New Brunswick, N.J.: Privately published, 1977.

——, ed. *Who Was This Man Ricker and What Are His Tablets That Everyone Is Talking About?* Bryan, Tex.: Privately published, 1979.

——. "Wounded Knee—A Different View." *True West* 30 (July 1983): 12–18.

———. "Wounded Knee Update." *True West* 33 (January 1986): 32–33.

Carter, William H. *From Yorktown to Santiago with the Sixth U.S. Cavalry.* Baltimore, Md.: Lord Baltimore Press, 1900; reprint, Austin, Tex.: State House Press, 1989.

———. "The Sixth Regiment of Cavalry." In Rodenbough and Haskin, *The Army of the United States*, pp. 232–50.

Chalfant, William Y. *Cheyennes and Horse Soldiers: The 1857 Expedition and the Battle of Solomon's Fork.* Norman: University of Oklahoma Press, 1989.

Chandler, Melbourne C. *Of GarryOwen in Glory: The History of the Seventh United States Cavalry Regiment.* Annandale, Va.: Turnpike Press, 1960.

Chenoweth, Richard. "Francis Case: A Political Biography." *South Dakota Historical Collections* 39 (1979): 288–433.

Christafferson, Dennis M. "Sioux, 1930–2000." In William C. Sturtevant (ed.), *Handbook of North American Indians*, vol. 13, *Plains*, ed. Raymond J. DeMallie, part 2, pp. 821–39. Washington, D.C.: Smithsonian Institution, 2001.

Chubb, Charles St. John. "The Seventeenth Regiment of Infantry." In Rodenbough and Haskin, *Army of the United States*, pp. 634–42.

Clow, Richmond L., ed. "Autobiography of Mary C. Collins, Missionary to the Western Sioux." *South Dakota Historical Collections* 41 (1982): 1–6.

———. "The Brulé Indian Agencies, 1868–1878." *South Dakota Historical Collections* 36 (1972): 143–204.

———. "General Philip Sheridan's Legacy: The Sioux Pony Campaign of 1876." *Nebraska History* 57 (Winter 1976): 461–77.

———. "The Lakota Ghost Dance after 1890." *South Dakota History* 20 (Winter 1990): 323–33.

Clowser, Don C. *Dakota Indian Treaties: From Nomad to Reservation.* Deadwood, S.Dak.: Privately published, 1974.

Cody, William F. *An Autobiography of Buffalo Bill (Colonel W. F. Cody).* New York: Cosmopolitan Book Corporation, 1920.

———. *True Tales of the Plains.* New York: Empire Books Company, 1908.

Coe, John N. "The Twentieth Regiment of Infantry." In Rodenbough and Haskin, *The Army of the United States*, pp. 666–72.

Coffman, Edward M. *The Old Army: A Portrait of the American Army in Peacetime, 1784–1898.* New York: Oxford University Press, 1986.

Colby, Leonard W. "The Sioux Indian War of 1890–'91." In *Transactions and Reports of the Nebraska State Historical Society* 3, pp. 144–90. Fremont, Nebr.: Hammond Brown Printers, 1892.

———. "Wanagi Olowan Kin (The Ghost Songs of the Dakotas)." *Nebraska State Historical Society Proceedings and Collections* 1 (Second Series, 1895): 131–50.

Coleman, William S. E. *Voices of Wounded Knee.* Lincoln: University of Nebraska Press, 2000.

Collins, Dabney Otis. "The Fight for Sitting Bull's Bones." *American West* 3 (Winter 1966): 72–78.

Connelly, Donald B. *John M. Schofield and the Politics of Generalship.* Chapel Hill: University of North Carolina Press, 2006.

Cook, James H. *Fifty Years on the Old Frontier as Cowboy, Hunter, Guide, Scout, and Ranchman.* New Haven: Yale University Press, 1923.

Cooper, Courtney R. "Short Bull's Story of the Battle of Wounded Knee." *Red Man* (February 1915): 205–12.

Coughlan, Timothy M. "Charles Albert Varnum." In *Sixty-Seventh Annual Report of the Association of Graduates of the United States Military Academy at West Point, New York, June 11, 1936*, pp. 82–90. Newburgh, N.Y.: Moore Printing Company, 1936.

———. *Varnum: The Last of Custer's Lieutenants*. Bryan, Tex.: Privately published, 1980.

Cowger, Thomas. "Dr. Thomas Bland, Critic of Forced Assimilation." *American Indian Culture and Research Journal* 16 (March 1992): 77–97.

Cozzens, Peter, comp. *Eyewitnesses to the Indian Wars, 1865–1890*, vol. 4: *The Long War for the Northern Plains*. 5 vols. Harrisburg, Pa.: Stackpole Books, 2001–2005.

Cropp, Richard. *The Coyotes: A History of the South Dakota National Guard*. Mitchell, S.Dak.: Educator Supply Company, 1962.

"Dakota Images: American Horse." *South Dakota History* 11 (Summer 1981): 252–53.

"Dakota Images: Short Bull." *South Dakota History* 21 (Fall 1991): 332–33.

Danker, Donald F., ed. *The Wounded Knee Interviews of Eli S. Ricker*. Lincoln: Nebraska State Historical Society. (Reprint from *Nebraska History* 62 [Summer 1981].)

Davis, George B. *A Treatise on the Military Law of the United States*. 3rd ed. New York: John Wiley and Sons, 1915.

DeBarthe, Joe. *Life and Adventures of Frank Grouard* (1894). Norman: University of Oklahoma Press, 1958.

DeLand, Charles E. "The Sioux Wars." *South Dakota Historical Collections* 17 (1934): 177–551.

DeLoria, Ella. *Speaking of Indians*. New York: Friendship Press, 1944.

Deloria, Vine, Jr., and Clifford M. Lytle. *American Indians, American Justice*. Austin: University of Texas Press, 1983.

DeMallie, Raymond J. "The Lakota Ghost Dance: An Ethnohistorical Account." *Pacific Historical Review* 51 (November 1982): 385–405.

———. "Pine Ridge Economy: Cultural and Historical Perspectives." In *American Indian Economic Deveopment*, ed. Sam Stanley, pp. 237–312. The Hague: Mouton Publishers, 1978.

———. "The Sioux in Dakota and Montana Territories: Cultural and Historical Background of the Ogden B. Read Collection." In *Vestiges of a Proud Nation: The Ogden B. Read Northern Plains Indian Collection*, pp. 19–69. Burlington, Vt.: Robert Hull Fleming Museum, 1986.

———. "Sioux until 1850." In William C. Sturtevant (ed.), *Handbook of North American Indians*, vol. 13, *Plains*, ed. Raymond J. DeMallie, part 2, pp. 718–60. Washington, D.C.: Smithsonian Institution, 2001.

———, ed. *The Sixth Grandfather: Black Elk's Teachings Given to John G. Neihardt*. Lincoln: University of Nebraska Press, 1984.

———. "Teton." In William C. Sturtevant (ed.), *Handbook of North American Indians*, vol. 13, *Plains*, ed. Raymond J. DeMallie, part 2, pp. 794–820. Washington, D.C.: Smithsonian Institution, 2001.

———. "Treaties Are Made between Nations." In *The Great Sioux Nation*, ed. Ortiz, pp. 110–15.

———. "Yankton and Yanktonai." In William C. Sturtevant (ed.), *Handbook of North American Indians*, vol. 13: *Plains*, ed. Raymond J. DeMallie, pp. 777–93. Washington, D.C.: Smithsonian Institution, 2001.

DeMallie, Raymond J., and Douglas R. Parks, eds. *Sioux Indian Religion*. Norman: University of Oklahoma Press, 1987.

DeMontravel, Peter R. "General Nelson A. Miles and the Wounded Knee Controversy." *Arizona and the West* 28 (Spring 1986): 23–44.

———. *A Hero to His Fighting Men: Nelson A. Miles, 1839–1925*. Kent, Ohio: Kent State University Press, 1998.

DeWolf, Robb. *The Saga of Sitting Bull's Bones: The Unusual Story behind Sculptor Korczak Ziolkowski's Memorial to Chief Sitting Bull*. Crazy Horse, S.Dak.: Korczak's Heritage, 1984.

DeWolfe, Mark A. *The Life and Labors of Bishop Hare*. New York: Sturgis and Walton, 1912.

Dippie, Brian W. *The Vanishing American: White Attitudes and U.S. Indian Policy*. Lawrence: University of Kansas Press, 1982.

DiSilvestro, Roger L. *In the Shadow of Wounded Knee: The Untold Final Story of the Indian Wars*. New York: Walker and Company, 2005.

Doan, Fred. "A Boy's Memory." *Nebraska Farmer* 93 (June 2, 1951): 24–25.

Dobak, William A. "Killing the Canadian Buffalo, 1821–1881." *Western Historical Quarterly* 27 (Spring 1996): 33–52.

Donovan, James. *A Terrible Glory: Custer and the Little Bighorn, the Last Great Battle of the American West*. New York: Little, Brown and Company, 2008.

Dougherty, William E. "The Indians of North America II. Personal Experiences and the Fight at Wounded Knee." *Overland Monthly*, series 2: 19 (April 1892): 357–75.

———. "The Recent Indian Craze." *Journal of the Military Service Institution of the United States* 12 (1891): 576–78.

Eastman, Charles A. *From the Deep Woods to Civilization* (1902). Chicago: R. R. Donnelly and Company, 2001.

Eastman, Elaine Goodale. "The Ghost Dance War and Wounded Knee Massacre of 1890–91." *Nebraska History* 26 (January–March 1945): 26–42.

———. *Pratt, the Red Man's Moses*. Norman: University of Oklahoma Press, 1935.

———. *Sister to the Sioux: The Memoirs of Elaine Goodale Eastman, 1885–91*. Ed. Kay Graber. Lincoln: University of Nebraska Press, 1978.

Ebstein, Frederick H. E. "The Twenty-First Regiment of Infantry." In Rodenbough and Haskins, *The Army of the United States*, pp. 673–79.

Edman, Patricia A. "Dakota Images: Sitting Bull." *South Dakota History* 40 (Summer 2010): 204–205.

Edmunds, R. David. *The Shawnee Prophet*. Lincoln: University of Nebraska Press, 1983.

———. "Shawnee Prophet (Tenskwatawa)." In Frederick E. Hoxie, ed., *Encyclopedia of North American Indians*, pp. 584–85. Boston: Houghton Mifflin Company, 1996.

Ege, Robert J. *"Tell Baker to Strike Them Hard!": Incident on the Marias, 23 Jan. 1870*. Fort Collins, Colo.: Old Army Press, 1970.

Eighth Annual Report of the Executive Committee of the Indian Rights Association, 1890. Philadelphia: Office of the Indian Rights Association, 1891.

Ellis, Edward S. *The Indian Wars of the United States*. Chicago: J. D. Kenyon and Company, 1892.

Erisman, Fred, and Patricia Erisman. "Letters from the Field: John Sylvanus Loud and the Pine Ridge Campaign of 1890–1891." *South Dakota History* 26 (Spring 1996): 24–45.

Ewers, William L. *When the Army Still Wore Blue: The Military Life and Times of General Ezra P. Ewers*. Glendale, Ariz.: Privately printed, 1996.

Ewing, Charles B. "The Wounded of the Wounded Knee Battlefield, with Remarks on Wounds Produced by Large and Small Calibre Bullets." In *Transactions of the*

Second Annual Meeting of the Association of Military Surgeons of the National Guard of the United States. Held at Memorial Hall, St. Louis, Mo., on the 19th, 20th, and 21st of April, 1892, pp. 36–56. St. Louis: Becktold and Company, 1892. (Reprinted in *Boston Medical and Surgical Journal*, May 12, 1892.)

Falconer, W. A. "The Death of Sitting Bull." *Hunter-Trader-Trapper* 53 (March 1926): 18–22.

Farb, Peter. *Man's Rise to Civilization as Shown by the Indians of North American from Primeval Times to the Coming of the Industrial State*. Rev. ed. New York: E. P. Dutton Company, 1978.

Farrow, Edward S. *Farrow's Military Encyclopedia*. 3 vols. New York: Military-Naval Publishing Company, 1895.

Fechet, Edmond G. "The Capture of Sitting Bull." *South Dakota Historical Collections* 4 (1908): 185–93.

———. "The True Story of the Death of Sitting Bull." *Cosmopolitan* 20 (March 1896): 493–501.

———. "The True Story of the Death of Sitting Bull." *Publications of the Nebraska Historical Society* 7 (Lincoln: State Journal Company, 1898): 179–90.

Fenneman, Nevin M. *Physiography of the Western United States*. New York: McGraw-Hill Book Company, 1931.

"The First Regiment of Infantry," In Rodenbough and Haskin, *The Army of the United States*, pp. 401–13.

Fiske, Frank Bennett. *Life and Death of Sitting Bull*. Fort Yates, N.Dak.: Pioneer-Arrow Point, 1933.

Fletcher, Alice C. "The Indian Messiah." *Journal of American Folk-Lore* 4 (January–March 1891): 57–60.

Flood, Renée Sansom. *Lost Bird of Wounded Knee: Spirit of the Lakota*. New York: Scribner, 1995.

Foley, Thomas A., ed. *At Standing Rock and Wounded Knee: The Journals and Papers of Father Francis M. Craft, 1888–1890*. Norman: Arthur H. Clark Company, 2009.

———. *Father Francis M. Craft, Missionary to the Sioux*. Lincoln: University of Nebraska Press, 2002.

"Folk-Lore Scrap-Book." *Journal of American Folk-Lore* 4 (April–June 1891): 160–62.

Foner, Jack D. *The United States Soldier between Two Wars: Army Life and Reforms, 1865–1898*. New York: Humanities Press, 1970.

Forsyth, George A. "General James William Forsyth." In *Forty-First Annual Reunion of the Association of Graduates of the United States Military Academy, at West Point, New York, June 14th, 1910*, pp. 45–58. Saginaw, Mich.: Seemann and Peters, Printers and Binders, 1910.

Forsyth, Susan. *Representing the Massacre of American Indians at Wounded Knee, 1890–2000*. Lampeter, Wales: Edwin Mellen Press, 2003.

Fowler, Loretta. *Arapaho Politics, 1851–1978*. Lincoln: University of Nebraska Press, 1982.

Frafe, Ernest, and Paul Horsted. *Exploring with Custer: The 1874 Black Hills Expedition*. Custer, S.Dak.: Golden Valley Press, 2002.

Frazier, Ian. *On the Rez*. New York: Farrar, Straus, Giroux, 2000.

Frazier, Robert W. *Forts of the West: Military Forts and Presidios and Posts Commonly Called Forts West of the Mississippi River to 1898*. Norman: University of Oklahoma Press, 1965.

Friends of the W. H. Over Museum Newsletter. Undated, ca. 1980s.

Friesen, Steve. *Buffalo Bill: Scout, Showman, Visionary*. Golden, Colo.: Fulcum Publishing, 2010.

Frink, Maurice. "The Ghost Dance 'War' and the 'Battle' of Wounded Knee." *Westerners Brand Book, 1944*, pp. 115–35. Chicago: Chicago Corral of the Westerners, 1944.

Frink, Maurice, with Casey E. Barthelmess. *Photographer on an Army Mule*. Norman: University of Oklahoma Press, 1965.

Fritz, Henry E. "The Making of Grant's Peace Policy." *Chronicles of Oklahoma* 34 (Winter 1959): 411–32.

———. *The Movement for Indian Assimilation, 1860–1890*. Philadelphia: University of Pennsylvania Press, 1963.

Froiland, Sven G., and Ronald R. Weedon. *Natural History of the Black Hills and Badlands*. Sioux Falls, S.Dak.: Center for Western Studies, Augustana College, 1990.

Gagnon, Greg, and Karen White Eyes. *Pine Ridge Reservation: Yesterday and Today*. Interior, S.Dak.: Badlands Natural History Association, 1992.

Garlington, Ernest A. Letter to Chief, Historical Section, Army War College, April 4, 1931. In John M. Carroll (ed.), *A Seventh Cavalry Scrapbook*, pp. 1–6. Bryan, Tex.: Privately published, 1978.

———. "The Seventh Regiment of Cavalry." In Rodenbough and Haskin, *The Army of the United States*, pp. 251–67.

Garrett-Davis, Joshua. "Dakota Images: George Sword." *South Dakota History* 29 (Fall 1999): pp. 262–63.

Gesner, Robert. *Massacre: A Survey of Today's American Indian*. New York: Jonathan Cape and Harrison Smith, 1931.

"Ghost-Dances in the West." *Illustrated American*, January 17, 1891, pp. 327–33.

Ghost Horse, Alice. "A True Story of What Happened at Wounded Knee in December 1890." Trans. Sidney Keith. *Twin Light Trail* 2 (1992): 11–14.

Gibbon, Guy. *The Sioux: The Dakota and Lakota Nations*. Malden, Mass.: Blackwell Publishing, 2003.

Gibson, Arrell M. *The American Indian: Prehistory to the Present*. Lexington, Mass.: D. C. Heath and Company, 1980.

Gildersleeve, Clive A. "Story of the Gildersleeves at Wounded Knee, South Dakota." In *Reservation Roundup: Stories of Pioneers in the Settling of the Pine Ridge Area*, pp. 44–45. Shannon County, S.Dak.: Big Foot Historical Society.

Gilmore, Melvin R. "The Truth of the Wounded Knee Massacre." *American Indian Magazine* 5, no. 4 (1917): 240–52.

Gleim, Albert F., comp. *US Army Gallantry and Meritorious Conduct, 1866–1891*. N.p.: Planchet Press, 1986.

Godfrey, Edward S. "Cavalry Fire Discipline." *Journal of the Military Service Institution of the United States* 18 (September 1896): 252–59.

———. *The Field Diary of Lt. Edward Settle Godfrey, Commanding Co. K, 7th Cavalry Regiment, under Lt. Colonel George Armstrong Custer in the Sioux Encounter at the Battle of the Little Big Horn*. Ed. Edgar I. Stewart and Jane R. Stewart. Portland: Champoeg Press, 1957.

Goll, Louis J. *Jesuit Missions among the Sioux*. St. Francis, S.Dak.: St. Francis Mission, n.d.

Gonzalez, Mario, and Elizabeth Cook-Lynn. *The Politics of Hallowed Ground: Wounded Knee and the Struggle for Indian Sovereignty*. Urbana and Chicago: University of Illinois Press, 1999.

Goody, Jack. "Time: Social Organization." In David L. Sills, ed., *International Ency-clopedia of the Social Sciences*, vol. 16, p. 41. New York: Macmillan and Company and the Free Press, 1968.

Green, Adriana Greci. "German Missionary Participation during the Ghost Dance of 1890." *European Review of Native American Studies* 6, no. 1 (1992): 31–34.

Green, Charles Lowell. "The Administration of the Public Domain in South Dakota." *South Dakota Historical Collections* 20 (1940): 7–280.

Green, Jerry, ed. *After Wounded Knee: Correspondence of Major and Surgeon John Vance Lauderdale While Serving with the Army Occupying the Pine Ridge Indian Reserva-tion, 1890–1891*. East Lansing: Michigan State University Press, 1996.

———. "The Medals of Wounded Knee." *Nebraska History* 75 (Summer 1994): 200–208.

Greene, Jerome A., comp. and ed. *Battles and Skirmishes of the Great Sioux War, 1876–1877*. Norman: University of Oklahoma Press, 1983.

———. *Fort Randall on the Missouri, 1856–1892*. Pierre: South Dakota State Historical Society Press, 2005.

———. "George Crook." In Paul Andrew Hutton and Durwood Ball, eds., *Soldiers West: Biographies from the Military Frontier*, pp. 246–72. Norman: University of Oklahoma Press, 2009.

———. "Indian Wars of the Trans-Mississippi West, 1850s–1890s." In John M. Car-roll and Colin F. Baxter eds., *The American Military Tradition from Colonial Times to the Present*, pp. 101–25. New York: Rowman and Littlefield Publishers, 2007.

———, comp. and ed. *Indian War Veterans: Memories of Army Life and Campaigns, 1864–1898*. New York: Savas Beatie, 2007.

———, comp. and ed. *Lakota and Cheyenne: Indian Views of the Great Sioux War, 1876–1877*. Norman: University of Oklahoma Press, 1994.

———. *Morning Star Dawn: The Powder River Expedition and the Northern Cheyennes, 1876*. Norman: University of Oklahoma Press, 2003.

———. *Nez Perce Summer, 1877: The U.S. Army and the Nee-Me-Poo Crisis*. Helena: Montana Historical Society Press, 2000.

———. "Out with a Whimper: The Little Missouri Expedition and the Close of the Great Sioux War." *South Dakota History* 35 (Spring 2005): 1–39.

———. "The Sioux Land Commission of 1889: Prelude to Wounded Knee." *South Dakota History* 1 (Winter 1970): 41–72.

———. *Slim Buttes, 1876: An Episode of the Great Sioux War*. Norman: University of Oklahoma Press, 1982.

———. *Washita: The U.S. Army and the Southern Cheyennes, 1867–1869*. Norman: University of Oklahoma Press, 2004.

———. *Yellowstone Command: Colonel Nelson A. Miles and the Great Sioux War, 1876–1877*. Lincoln: University of Nebraska Press, 1991; reprint, Norman: University of Oklahoma Press, 2006.

Greene, Jerome A., and Douglas D. Scott. *Finding Sand Creek: History, Archeology, and the 1864 Massacre Site*. Norman: University of Oklahoma Press, 2004.

Gries, John Paul. *Roadside Geology of South Dakota*. Missoula, Mont.: Mountain Press Publishing Company, 1996.

Grinnell, George Bird. "Account of the Northern Cheyennes concerning the Messiah Superstition." *Journal of American Folk-Lore* 4 (January–March 1891): 61–69.

Gulliford, Andrew. "Repatriating Rifles from Wounded Knee." *Journal of the West* 42 (Winter 2003): 74–81.

Hagan, William T. *American Indians*. Chicago: University of Chicago Press, 1961.

———. *Indian Police and Judges*. Hartford: Yale University Press, 1966.

———. *The Indian Rights Association: The Herbert Welsh Years, 1882–1904*. Tucson: University of Arizona Press, 1985.

Hagemann, E. R., ed. *Fighting Rebels and Redskins: Experiences in Army Life of Colonel George B. Sanford, 1861–1892*. Norman: University of Oklahoma Press, 1969.

Hall, Philip S. "Reasonable Doubt: The Trial and Hanging of Two Sticks." *South Dakota History* 42 (Spring 2012): 63–87.

———. *To Have This Land: The Nature of Indian/White Relations, South Dakota, 1888–1891*. Vermillion: University of South Dakota Press, 1991.

Hamilton, Henry W., and Jean Tyree Hamilton. *The Sioux of the Rosebud: A History in Pictures*. Norman: University of Oklahoma Press, 1971.

Hamilton, William R. *Elementary Principles Connected with the Art of War*. Washington, D.C.: United Service Printing Company, 1887.

———. "Nebraska's National Guard in the Sioux War." *Outing* 27 (July 1896): 317–20.

Hämmäläinen, Pekka. *The Comanche Empire*. New Haven: Yale University Press, 2008.

Hammer, Kenneth. *Biographies of the 7th Cavalry June 25th 1876*. Fort Collins, Colo.: Old Army Press, 1972.

———. "Sitting Bull's Bones." *Research Review: The Journal of the Little Big Horn Associates* 15 (Winter 2001): 2–8, 31.

Hardorff, Richard G., comp. and ed. *The Surrender and Death of Crazy Horse: A Source Book about a Tragic Episode in Lakota History*. Spokane, Wash.: Arthur H. Clark Company, 1998.

Harries, George H. "Tragedy at White Horse Creek, or The Wounded Knee Tragedy: Its Causes and Lessons as Seen by a Newspaperman." Lecture reprinted in Robert B. Cormack, ed., *The 1963 All Posse-Corral Book of the Denver Posse of the Westerners*, pp. 74–87. Morrison, Colo.: Buffalo Bull Press, 1964.

———. "The Wounded Knee Tragedy: Its Causes and Its Lessons." *Denver Westerners' Roundup* (July 1962): 5–21.

Hartley, Rodger. "Dakota Images: Young Man Afraid of His Horses." *South Dakota History* 42 (Spring 2012): 94–95.

Harvey, Philip F. "The Last Stand of the Sioux." *Army and Navy Life* 12 (February 1908): 225–36.

Hassrick, Royal B. *The Sioux: Life and Customs of a Warrior Society*. Norman: University of Oklahoma Press, 1964.

Hauk, Joy K. "M. Brainard Poste." *Reservation Round-Up: Stories of Pioneer Days in the Settling of the Pine Ridge Reservation Area*, pp. 24–25. Shannon County, S.Dak.: Big Foot Historical Society, n.d.

Hawthorne, Harry L. "The Sioux Campaign of 1890–91." *Journal of the Military Service Institution of the United States* 19 (July 1896): 185–87.

——— "The Sioux Campaign of 1890–91." *Journal of the Military Service Institution of the United States* 20 (July 1897): 215–16.

Hedren, Paul L. *After Custer: Loss and Transformation in Sioux Country*. Norman: University of Oklahoma Press, 2011.

———. *Fort Laramie in 1876: Chronicle of a Post at War*. Lincoln: University of Nebraska Press, 1988.

———. *Great Sioux War Orders of Battle: How the United States Army Waged War on the Northern Plains, 1876–1877*. Norman, Okla.: Arthur H. Clark Company, 2011.

————. *Sitting Bull's Surrender at Fort Buford: An Episode in American History.* Williston, N.Dak.: Fort Union Association, 1997.

Hendrickson, Kenneth E., Jr. "The Public Career of Richard F. Pettigrew of South Dakota: 1848–1926." *South Dakota Department of History Report and Historical Collections* 34 (1968): 143–312.

Henry, Guy V. "Adventures of American Army and Navy Officers. IV—A Sioux Indian Episode." *Harper's Weekly*, July 27, 1895.

Hibbard, Charles G. *Fort Douglas, Utah, 1862–1991.* Fort Collins, Colo.: Vestige Press, 1999.

High Back, Paul. "Paul High Back's Version of the Disaster of Dec. 29, 1890, at Wounded Knee, as Told to John Williamson." *Wi-iyohi: Monthly Bulletin of the South Dakota Historical Society* 10 (June 1, 1956): 1–4.

Hill, Burton S. "Buffalo—Ancient Cow Town: A Wyoming Saga." *Annals of Wyoming* 35 (October 1963): 125–54.

————. Letter in *Annals of Wyoming* 39 (October 1967): 260.

Hines, Randy. "Pressing the Issue at Wounded Knee." *Wild West* 23 (December 2010): 28–37.

Historical Sketch: Omaha Guards, Company G, Second Regiment, N.N.G., Omaha Nebraska, 1887–1895. Omaha, ca. 1895.

Hittman, Michael. *Wovoka and the Ghost Dance: A Source Book for the Yerington Paiute Tribe.* Expanded ed. Ed. Don Lynch. Lincoln: University of Nebraska Press, 1990.

Hoig, Stan. *Perilous Pursuit: The U.S. Cavalry and the Northern Cheyennes.* Boulder: University Press of Colorado, 2002.

————. *The Sand Creek Massacre.* Norman: University of Oklahoma Press, 1961.

Hollow, Robert C. "The Sioux Ghost Dance of 1890." In *The Last Years of Sitting Bull*, pp. 39–48, 58–59. Bismarck: State Historical Society of North Dakota, 1984.

Hoover, Herbert T. "The Sioux Agreement of 1889 and Its Aftermath." *South Dakota History* 19 (Spring 1989): 56–94.

Hosen, Frederick E., comp. *Unfolding Westward in Treaty and Law: Land Documents in United States History from the Appalachians to the Pacific, 1783–1934.* Jefferson, N.Car.: McFarland and Company, Publishers, 1988.

Hoxie, Frederick E. *The Final Promise: The Campaign to Assimilate the Indians, 1880–1920.* Lincoln: University of Nebraska Press, 1984.

————. "From Prison to Homeland: The Cheyenne River Indian Reservation before WWI." *South Dakota History* 10 (Winter 1979): 1–24.

Hunt, W. Ben. *Indiancraft.* Milwaukee: Bruce Publishing Company, 1942.

Huntzicker, William E. "The 'Sioux Outbreak' in the Illustrated Press." *South Dakota History* 20 (Winter 1990): 300–321.

Hutcheson, Grote. "The Ninth Regiment of Cavalry." In Rodenbough and Haskin, *The Army of the United States*, pp. 280–87.

Hutton, Paul Andrew. *Phil Sheridan and His Army.* Lincoln: University of Nebraska Press, 1985.

Hyde, George E. *Red Cloud's Folk: A History of the Oglala Sioux Indians.* Norman: University of Oklahoma Press, 1937.

————. *A Sioux Chronicle.* Norman: University of Oklahoma Press, 1956.

————. *Spotted Tail's Folk: A History of the Brulé Sioux.* Norman: University of Oklahoma Press, 1961.

Iverson, Peter. *When Indians Became Cowboys: Native Peoples and Cattle Ranching in the American West.* Norman: University of Oklahoma Press, 1994.

Jacobs, Wilbur. "The Sioux Nation and the Treaty." In *The Great Sioux Nation*, ed. Ortiz, pp. 116–18.

Jacobsen, Ethel Collins. "Mary Collins." *Wi-Iyohi* 11 (September 1957): 1–4.

Jamieson, Perry D. *Crossing the Deadly Ground: United States Army Tactics, 1865–1899.* Tuscaloosa: University of Alabama Press, 1994.

Jensen, Richard E. "Big Foot's Followers at Wounded Knee." *Nebraska History* 71 (Fall 1990): 194–212.

———, ed. "Commissioner Theodore Roosevelt Visits Indian Reservations, 1892." *Nebraska History* 62 (Spring 1981): 85–106.

———, ed. "A Love Letter from Pine Ridge." *Nebraska History* 81 (Spring 2000): 47–48.

———, ed. *Voices of the American West.* 2 vols. (1: *The Indian Interviews of Eli S. Ricker, 1903–1919;* 2: *The Settler and Soldier Interviews of Eli S. Ricker, 1903–1919*). Lincoln: University of Nebraska Press, 2005.

Jensen, Richard E., R. Eli Paul, and John E. Carter. *Eyewitness at Wounded Knee.* Lincoln: University of Nebraska Press, 1991.

Jocelyn, Stephen Perry. *Mostly Alkali.* Caldwell, Idaho: Caxton Printers, 1953.

"John McAllister Schofield." In Roger J. Spiller, Joseph G. Dawson, and T. Harry Williams, eds., *Dictionary of American Military Biography*, vol. 3, pp. 956–60. 3 vols. Westport, Conn.: Greenwood Press, 1984.

Johnson, Alfred B. "The Seventh Regiment of Infantry." In Rodenbough and Haskin, *The Army of the United States*, pp. 498–510.

Johnson, Barry C. "Tragedy at White Horse Creek: Edward S. Godfrey's Unpublished Account of an Incident near Wounded Knee." *Brand Book* 19 (April–July 1977): 1–13.

———. "Tragedy at White Horse Creek: The Military Account of an Incident near Wounded Knee Creek by Capt. Edward S. Godfrey." Notes and an introduction by Barry C. Johnson. In Robert B. Cormack, ed., *The 1963 All Posse-Corral Book of the Denver Posse of the Westerners*, pp. 66–72. Morrison, Colo.: Buffalo Bull Press, 1964.

Johnson, Benjamin Heber. "Red Populism?: T. A. Bland, Agrarian Radicalism, and the Debate over the Dawes Act." In Catherine McNichol Stock and Robert D. Johnston, eds., *The Countryside in the Age of the Modern State: Political Histories of Rural America*, 15–37. Ithaca, N.Y.: Cornell University Press, 2001.

Johnson, Virginia Weisel. *The Unregimented General: A Biography of Nelson A. Miles.* Boston: Houghton Mifflin Company, 1962.

Johnson, W. Fletcher. *Life of Sitting Bull and History of the Indian War of 1890–91.* N.p.: Edgewood Publishing Company, Publishers, 1891.

Johnston, Sister Mary Antonio. *Federal Relations with the Great Sioux Indians of South Dakota, 1887–1933, with Particular Reference to Land Policy under the Dawes Act.* Washington, D.C.: Catholic University of America Press, 1948.

Jones, Brian. *A Battle at Little Bighorn: Being an Account of the Crow Outbreak of 1887.* London: English Westerners' Society, 1975.

Jones, Douglas C. "Teresa Dean: Lady Correspondent among the Sioux Indians." *Journalism Quarterly* 49 (Winter 1972): 656–62.

Josephy, Alvin M., Jr. *The Civil War in the American West.* New York: Alfred A. Knopf, 1991.

———. *The Indian Heritage of America.* New York: Alfred A. Knopf, 1968.

————. *The Patriot Chiefs: A Chronicle of American Indian Leadership.* New York: Viking Press, 1961.

Jutz, Johann. "Historic Data on the Causes of the Dissatisfaction among the Sioux Indians in 1890: The Ghost Dance Religion." *Woodstock Letters* 47 (1918): 313–27.

Kelley, William F. "The Indian Troubles and the Battle of Wounded Knee." In *Transactions and Reports of the Nebraska State Historical Society 4*, pp. 30–50. Lincoln: State Journal Company, Printers, 1892.

————. *Pine Ridge 1890: An Eyewitness Account of the Events Surrounding the Fighting at Wounded Knee.* Ed. and comp. by Alexander Kelley and Pierre Bovis. San Francisco, Calif.: Pierre Bovis, 1971.

Kenner, Charles L. *Buffalo Soldiers and Officers of the Ninth Cavalry, 1867–1898.* Norman: University of Oklahoma Press, 1999.

Kerrigan, Evans E. *American War Medals and Decorations.* New York: Viking Press, 1971.

King, James T. *War Eagle: A Life of General Eugene A. Carr.* Lincoln: University of Nebraska Press, 1963.

Klein, Christina. "Everything of Interest in the Late Pine Ridge War Are [*sic*] Held by Us for Sale." *Western Historical Quarterly* 25 (Spring 1994): 45–68.

Knight, Oliver. *Following the Indian Wars: The Story of the Newspaper Correspondents among the Indian Campaigners.* Norman: University of Oklahoma Press, 1960.

Kolbenschlag, George. *A Whirlwind Passes: News Correspondents and the Sioux Indian Disturbances of 1890–91.* Vermillion: University of South Dakota Press, 1990.

Koupal, Nancy Tystad. "On the Road to Oz: L. Frank Baum as Western Editor." *South Dakota History* 30 (Spring 2000): 49–106.

————, ed. and ann. *Our Landlady: L. Frank Baum.* Lincoln: University of Nebraska Press, 1996.

Kreis, Karl Markus. *Lakotas, Black Robes, and Holy Women: German Reports from the Indian Missions in South Dakota, 1886–1900.* Trans. Corinna Dally-Starna. Lincoln: University of Nebraska Press, 2000.

Kvasnicka, Robert M., and Herman J. Viola. *The Commissioners of Indian Affairs, 1824–1977.* Lincoln: University of Nebraska Press, 1979.

Lamar, Howard R. *Dakota Territory, 1861–1889: A Study of Frontier Politics.* New Haven: Yale University Press, 1956.

————. "Perspectives on Statehood: South Dakota's First Quarter Century, 1889–1914." *South Dakota History* 19 (Spring 1989): 2–25.

Lanternari, Victor. *The Religions of the Oppressed: A Study of Modern Messianic Cults.* Trans. Lisa Sergio. New York: Alfred A. Knopf, 1963.

LaPointe, Ernie. *Sitting Bull, His Life and Legacy.* Layton, Utah: Gibbs Smith, 2009.

Larson, Robert W. *Gall: Lakota War Chief.* Norman: University of Oklahoma Press, 2007.

————. *Red Cloud: Warrior-Statesman of the Lakota Sioux.* Norman: University of Oklahoma Press, 1997.

————. "A Victor in Defeat: Chief Gall's Life on the Standing Rock Reservation." *Prologue: Quarterly of the National Archives and Records Administration* 40 (Fall 2008): 36–45.

Lauck, Jon K. *Prairie Republic: The Political Culture of Dakota Territory, 1879–1889.* Norman: University of Oklahoma Press, 2010.

Lautenschlager, Virginia Irene. *A History of Cuny Table, SD, 1890–2002.* Ed. Katherine Bahr. Chadron, Nebr.: n.p., 2005.

Lazarus, Edward. *Black Hills/White Justice: The Sioux Nation versus the United States 1775 to the Present*. New York: Harper Collins Publishers, 1991.

Leckie, William H., and Shirley A. Leckie. *The Buffalo Soldiers: A Narrative of the Black Cavalry in the West*. Rev. ed. Norman: University of Oklahoma Press, 2003.

Lee, Robert. *Fort Meade and the Black Hills*. Lincoln: University of Nebraska Press, 1991.

———. "The Great Whitewash." *Empire Magazine* (*Denver Post*), December 31, 1950, pp. 8–9.

———. "Messiah Craze and Wounded Knee." *Wi-iyohi* 9 (May 1, 1955): 1–12.

———. "Messiah War on Cheyenne River." *Wi-iyohi* 17 (November 1, 1963): 1–8.

———. "Warriors in Ranks: American Indian Units in the Regular Army, 1891–1897." *South Dakota History* 21 (Fall 1991): 263–316.

Lee, Wayne C. *Scotty Philip: The Man Who Saved the Buffalo*. Caldwell, Idaho: Caxton Printers, 1975.

Leiker, James, and Ramon Powers. *The Northern Cheyenne Exodus in History and Memory*. Norman: University of Oklahoma Press, 2011.

Lemmons, William E. "History by Unreliable Narrators." *Montana The Magazine of Western History* 45 (Autumn/Winter 1995): 65–74.

Lindberg, Christer, ed. "Foreigners in Action at Wounded Knee." *Nebraska History* 71 (Fall 1990): 170–81.

Lomosits, Helga, and Paul Harbaugh. *Lakol Wokiksuye: Zur Geschichte der Plains von Little Bighorn bis Wounded Knee, 1868–1890*. Vienna: Jugend und Volk, 1990.

Lookingbill, Brad. *War Dance at Fort Marion: Plains Indian War Prisoners*. Norman: University of Oklahoma Press, 2006.

Lubetkin, M. John. *Jay Cooke's Gamble: The Northern Pacific Railroad, the Sioux, and the Panic of 1873*. Norman: University of Oklahoma Press, 2006.

Lurie, Nancy Oestreich. "The Indian Claims Commission Act." *Annals of the American Academy of Political and Social Science* 311 (May 1957): 97–110.

———. *North American Indian Lives*. Milwaukee: Milwaukee Public Museum, 1985.

Mackintosh, John D. *Custer's Southern Officer: Captain George D. Wallace, 7th U.S. Cavalry*. Lexington, S.C.: Cloud Creek Press, 2002.

Maddra, Sam A. *Hostiles?: The Lakota Ghost Dance and Buffalo Bill's Wild West*. Norman: University of Oklahoma Press, 2006.

Madsen, Brigham D. *The Shoshoni Frontier and the Bear River Massacre*. Salt Lake City: University of Utah Press, 1985.

Magid, Paul. *George Crook: From the Redwoods to Appomattox*. Norman: University of Oklahoma Press, 2011.

Malm, Einar. *The Last Battle of the Sioux Indians: With Lieutenant Ragnar Ling-Vannerus in the Battle against Sitting Bull during the Ghost Dance Conflict in Dakota 1890–1891*. Stockholm, Sweden: P. A. Norstedt and Sons, Publishers, 1929.

Mangum, Neil. *Battle of the Rosebud: Prelude to the Little Bighorn*. El Segundo, Calif.: Upton and Sons, 1987.

Manypenny, George W. *Our Indian Wards*. Cincinnati: Robert Clark, 1880; reprint, Sioux Falls, S.Dak.: Brevet Press, 1974.

Manzione, Joseph. *"I Am Looking to the North for My Life": Sitting Bull, 1876–1881*. Salt Lake City: University of Utah Press, 1991.

"Markers at the Wounded Knee Battle Field." *Wi-Iyohi: Monthly Bulletin of the South Dakota Historical Society* 10 (June 1956): 3–6.

Marks, Paula Mitchell. *In a Barren Land: American Indian Dispossession and Survival.* New York: William Morrow, 1998.

Marquis, Thomas B. *A Warrior Who Fought Custer.* Minneapolis: Midwest Company, 1931.

Marquis, Thomas B., and Ronald H. Limbaugh, comps. *Cheyenne and Sioux: The Reminiscences of Four Indians and a White Soldier.* Stockton, Calif.: Pacific Center for Western Historical Studies, University of the Pacific, 1973.

———. *The Cheyennes of Montana.* Algonac, Mich.: Reference Publications, 1978.

Marshall, S. L. A. "Wounded Knee Revisited." *Parameters* 3, no. 1 (1973): 23–29.

Mattes, Merrill J. "The Enigma of Wounded Knee." *Plains Anthropologist* 5 (May 1960): 1–11.

Mattison, Ray H. *The Army Post on the Northern Plains, 1865–1885.* Gering, Nebr.: Oregon Trail Museum Association, n.d.

McCann, Frank D., Jr. "The Ghost Dance, Last Hope of Western Tribes, Unleashed the Final Tragedy." *Montana The Magazine of Western History* 16 (Winter 1966): 25–34.

McChristian, Douglas C. *Fort Laramie: Military Bastion of the High Plains.* Norman, Okla.: Arthur H. Clark Company, 2008.

McClernand, Edward J. "Edward W. Casey." *Twenty-Second Annual Reunion of the Association of the Graduates of the United States Military Academy, at West Point, New York, June 12th, 1891,* pp. 47–49. Saginaw, Mich.: Seemann and Peters, Printers and Binders, 1891.

McCrady, David G. *Living with Strangers: The Nineteenth-Century Sioux and the Canadian-American Borderlands.* Lincoln: University of Nebraska Press, 2006.

McDermott, John D. *Circle of Fire: The Indian War of 1865.* Harrisburg, Pa.: Stackpole Books, 2003.

———. *Frontier Crossroads: The History of Fort Caspar and the Upper Platte Crossing.* Casper, Wyo.: City of Casper, 1997.

———. *Red Cloud's War: The Bozeman Trail, 1866–1868.* 2 vols. Norman, Okla.: Arthur H. Clark Company, 2010.

———. "Wounded Knee: Centennial Voices." *South Dakota History* 20 (Winter 1990): 245–92.

McGillycuddy, Julia B. *McGillycuddy, Agent.* Palo Alto, Calif.: Stanford University Press, 1941.

McGinnis, Hugh. "I Took Part in the Wounded Knee Massacre." *Real West* 9 (January 1966): 31–37.

———. "I Was There! The Wounded Knee Massacre" (as told to O. M. Glasgow). *True West* 8 (March–April 1961): 6–9, 52, 54.

McGregor, James H. *The Wounded Knee Massacre from the Viewpoint of the Sioux.* Baltimore: Wirth Brothers, 1940.

McIver, George W. "The 7th U.S. Infantry in the Sioux Campaign of 1890–91." In Carroll, *The Unpublished Papers of the Order of Indian Wars,* book 7, pp. 21–27.

McLaughlin, James. *Account of the Death of Sitting Bull and of the Circumstances Attending It.* Philadelphia: Indians Rights Association, 1891.

———. *My Friend the Indian.* Boston: Houghton Mifflin Company, 1926.

McRae, James H. "The Third Regiment of Infantry." In Rodenbough and Haskin, *The Army of the United States,* pp. 432–51.

Means, Jeffrey D. "'Indians Shall Do Things in Common': Oglala Lakota Identity and Cattle-Raising on the Pine Ridge Reservation." *Montana The Magazine of Western History* 61 (Autumn 2011): 3–21.

Medary, Edgar F. "Reminiscences of the Ghost Dance War of 1890–91." *Westerners Brand Book* (Chicago) 3 (September 1946): 45–47, 49–50.

Merritt, Wesley. "The Army of the United States." in *The Armies of To-Day: A Description of the Armies of the Leading Nations at the Present Time*, pp. 3–55. New York: Harper and Brothers, Publishers, 1893.

Metcalf, George. "Two Relics of the Wounded Knee Massacre." *Museum of the Fur Trade Quarterly* 2 (Winter 1966): 1–3.

Michno, Gregory F. *Dakota Dawn: The Decisive First Week of the Sioux Uprising, August 17–24, 1862*. New York: Savas Beatie, 2011.

Miles, Nelson A. "The Future of the Indian Question." *North American Review* 152 (January 1891): 1–10.

———. *Personal Recollections and Observations of General Nelson A. Miles*. Chicago: Werner Company, 1896.

———. *Serving the Republic*. New York: Harper and Brothers, Publishers, 1911.

———. "The War with the Messiah." *Cosmopolitan Magazine* 51 (September 1911): 522–33.

Miller, Christopher L. "Smohalla." In Frederick E. Hoxie, ed., *Encyclopedia of North American Indians*, pp. 600–603. Boston: Houghton Mifflin Company, 1996.

Mobridge South Dakota Chamber of Commerce 2006–2007 Directory of Information. Mobridge, S.Dak.: Mobridge Chamber of Commerce, 2006.

Monnett, John H. *Tell Them We Are Going Home: The Odyssey of the Northern Cheyennes*. Norman: University of Oklahoma Press, 2001.

———. *Where a Hundred Soldiers Were Killed: The Struggle for the Powder River Country in 1866 and the Making of the Fetterman Myth*. Albuquerque: University of New Mexico Press, 2008.

Montour, Ted. "Handsome Lake." In Frederick E. Hoxie, ed., *Encyclopedia of North American Indians*, pp. 230–31. Boston: Houghton Mifflin Company, 1996.

Mooney, James. "The Ghost-Dance Religion and the Sioux Outbreak of 1890." In *Fourteenth Annual Report of the Bureau of Ethnology to the Secretary of the Smithsonian Institution, 1892–93*, pp. 641–1136. Washington, D.C.: Government Printing Office, 1896.

Moorehead, Warren K. *The American Indian in the United States, Period 1850–1914*. Andover, Mass.: Andover Press, 1914.

———. "The Indian Messiah and the Ghost Dance." *American Antiquarian* 13 (May 1891): 161–67.

Morgan, Thisba Hutson. "Reminiscences of My Days in the Land of the Ogalala [*sic*] Sioux." *South Dakota Historical Collections* 29 (1958): 21–62.

Morgan, Thomas J. *The Present Phase of the Indian Question*. Boston: Frank Wood, 1891.

Moses, L. G. *The Indian Man: A Biography of James Mooney*. Urbana: University of Illinois Press, 1984.

———. *Wild West Shows and the Images of American Indians, 1883–1933*. Albuquerque: University of New Mexico Press, 1996.

Moulton, Candy. *Valentine T. McGillycuddy: Army Surgeon, Agent to the Sioux*. Norman, Okla.: Arthur H. Clark Company, 2011.

Nankivell, John H., ed. and comp. *History of the Twenty-Fifth Regiment United States Infantry, 1869–1926*. Denver: Smith-Brooks Printing Company, 1927.

Neihardt, John G., comp. *Black Elk Speaks: Being the Life Story of a Holy Man of the Oglala Sioux*. Ann. Raymond J. DeMallie. Albany: State University of New York, 2008.

Northrup, Henry Davenport. *Indian Horrors or Massacres by the Red Men*. Philadelphia: National Publishing Company, n.d. (ca. 1891). (Also published under the title *Indian Massacres and Savage Life*.)

Nye, Wilbur S. *Carbine and Lance: The Story of Old Fort Sill*. Norman: University of Oklahoma Press, 1937.

O'Harra, C. C. *The White River Badlands*. Bulletin No. 13. Rapid City: South Dakota School of Mines and Technology, 1920.

Olmsted, Merle C. "John W. Comfort: Portrait of a U.S. Regular, 1865–1892." *Military Collector and Historian* 20 (Winter 1968): 126–27.

Olson, Gary D. "Dakota Resources: The Richard F. Pettigrew Papers." *South Dakota History* 12 (Summer/Fall 1982): 182–87.

Olson, James C. *Red Cloud and the Sioux Problem*. Lincoln: University of Nebraska Press, 1965.

Olson, Louise P. "Mary Clementine Collins, Dakotah Missionary." *North Dakota History* 19 (January 1952): 59–81.

Ortiz, Roxanne Dunbar, ed. *The Great Sioux Nation: Sitting in Judgment on America*. 2nd ed. Lincoln: University of Nebraska Press, 2013.

Ostler, Jeffrey. "Conquest and the State: Why the United States Employed Massive Military Force to Suppress the Lakota Ghost Dance." *Pacific Historical Review* 65 (May 1996): 217–48.

———. *The Lakotas and the Black Hills: The Struggle for Sacred Ground*. New York: Viking Penguin, 2010.

———. *The Plains Sioux and U.S. Colonialism from Lewis and Clark to Wounded Knee*. Cambridge: Cambridge University Press, 2004.

Overholt, Thomas W. *Channels of Prophecy: The Social Dynamics of Prophetic Activity*. Minneapolis, Minn.: Fortress Press, 1989.

———. "The Ghost Dance of 1890 and the Nature of the Prophetic Process." *Ethnohistory* 21 (Winter 1974): 37–63.

Parker, Watson. *Gold in the Black Hills*. Norman: University of Oklahoma Press, 1966.

Paul, Andrea I. "Buffalo Bill and Wounded Knee: The Movie." *Nebraska History* 71 (Fall 1990): 182–90.

Paul, R. Eli. *Blue Water Creek and the First Sioux War, 1854–1856*. Norman: University of Oklahoma Press, 2004.

———. "Dakota Resources: The Investigation of Special Agent Cooper and Property Damage Claims in the Winter of 1890–91." *South Dakota History* 24 (Fall–Winter 1994): 212–35.

———. "The Faraway Artist." *Nebraska History* 71 (Fall 1990): 191–93.

———. "Wounded Knee and the 'Collector of Curios.'" *Nebraska History* 75 (Summer 1994): 209–15.

Penman, Sarah, comp. and ed. *Honor the Grandmothers: Dakota and Lakota Women Tell Their Stories*. St. Paul: Minnesota Historical Society Press, 2000.

Peterson, B. J. *The Battle of Wounded Knee*. Gordon, Nebr.: News Publishing Company, 1941.

Peterson, Nancy. "Interpreter Philip Wells: Wounded at Wounded Knee." *Wild West* 17 (August 2004): 23–30.

Pfaller, Louis L. *Guide to the Microfilm Edition of the Major James McLaughlin Papers.* Richardton, N.Dak.: Assumption College, 1969.

———. "Indian Scare of 1890." *North Dakota History* 39 (Spring 1972): 4–17.

———. *James McLaughlin: The Man with an Indian Heart.* Richardton, N.Dak.: Assumption Abbey Press, 1978.

"Philip F. Wells, 1850–1947." *Westerners Brand Book* 3 (February 1947): 84–85.

Phillips, George H. "The Indian Ring in Dakota Territory, 1870–1890." *South Dakota History* 2 (Fall 1972): 345–68.

Piper, Alexander R. "Extracts from Letters Written by Lieutenant Alexander R. Piper, 8th Infantry, at Pine Ridge Agency, South Dakota, to His Wife, Marie Cozzens Piper, at Fort Robinson, Nebraska, during the Sioux Campaign, 1890–91." In Carroll, *The Unpublished Papers of the Order of Indian Wars*, book 10, pp. 1–19.

Pohanka, Brian C., ed. *Nelson A. Miles: A Documentary Biography of His Military Career, 1861–1903.* Glendale, Calif.: Arthur H. Clark Company, 1985.

Pollack, Eileen. *Woman Walking Ahead: In Search of Catherine Weldon and Sitting Bull.* Albuquerque: University of New Mexico Press, 2002.

Pond, George E. "Major-General Nelson A. Miles." *McClure's Magazine* 5 (November 1895): 562–74.

Pope, Dennis C. *Sitting Bull: Prisoner of War.* Pierre: South Dakota State Historical Society Press, 2010.

Porter, Joseph C. *Paper Medicine Man: John Gregory Bourke and His American West.* Norman: University of Oklahoma Press, 1986.

Powell, Peter J. "The Sacred Treaty." In *The Great Sioux Nation*, ed. Ortiz, pp. 105–109.

Powell, William H., comp. *Powell's Records of Living Officers of the United States Army.* Philadelphia: L. R. Hamersly and Company, 1890.

Powers, Thomas. *The Killing of Crazy Horse.* New York: Alfred A. Knopf, 2010.

Powers, William K. *Oglala Religion.* Lincoln: University of Nebraska Press, 1975.

Preston, Guy H. "Letter from Brigadier General Guy H. Preston, April 5, 1931." In Carroll, *The Unpublished Papers of the Order of Indian Wars*, book 7, pp. 27–32.

Pride, Woodbury F. *The History of Fort Riley.* Privately published, 1926.

Priest, Loring Benson. *Uncle Sam's Stepchildren: The Reformation of United States Indian Policy, 1865–1887.* East Brunswick, N.J.: Rutgers University Press, 1942.

Punke, Michael. *Last Stand: George Bird Grinnell, the Battle to Save the Buffalo, and the Birth of the New West.* New York: Harper Collins, Publishers, 2007.

"Recollections" of Sheridan County, Nebraska. N.p.: Iron Man Industries, 1976.

Remington, Frederic. "The Art of War and Newspaper Men." In Peggy Samuels and Harold Samuels, eds., *The Collected Writings of Frederic Remington*, pp. 57–58. New York: Doubleday, 1979.

Reservation Round-Up: Stories of Pioneer Days in the Settling of the Pine Ridge Reservation Area. Shannon County, S.Dak.: Big Foot Historical Society, n.d.

Rhodes, Charles D. "Diary Notes of the Brule-Sioux Indian Campaign 1890–91 in South Dakota." In Carroll, *The Unpublished Papers of the Order of Indian Wars*, book 8, pp. 21–30.

Richards, William V. "The Sixteenth Regiment of Infantry." In Rodenbough and Haskin, *The Army of the United States*, pp. 629–33.

Richardson, Heather Cox. *Wounded Knee: Party Politics and the Road to an American Massacre.* New York: Basic Books, 2010.

Richardson, James D., comp. *A Compilation of the Messages and Papers of the Presidents, 1789–1897*. 20 vols. New York: Bureau of National Literature, 1897.

Richardson, Wilds P. "The Sioux Campaign of 1890–91." *Journal of the Military Institution of the United States* 20 (July 1897): 435–36.

———. "Some Observations upon the Sioux Campaign of 1890–91." *Journal of the Military Service Institution of the United States* 18 (May 1896): 512–31.

Rickey, Don, Jr. *Forty Miles a Day on Beans and Hay: The Enlisted Soldier Fighting the Indian Wars*. Norman: University of Oklahoma Press, 1963.

———. "Warrior-Soldiers: The All-Indian 'L' Troop, 6th U.S. Cavalry, in the Early 1890's." In Ray Brandes, ed., *Troopers West: Military and Indian Affairs on the American Frontier*, pp. 41–61. San Diego: Frontier Heritage Press, 1970.

Rickey, Don C. "An Indian Wars Combat Record." *By Valor and Arms: The Journal of American Military History* 2 (Fall 1975): 4–11.

Ritzenthaler, Robert E., and W. Ben Hunt. *Sioux Indian Drawings*. Milwaukee Public Museum Primitive Art Series No. 1. Milwaukee: Milwaukee Public Museum, 1961.

Robinson, Charles M. *General Crook and the Western Frontier*. Norman: University of Oklahoma Press, 2001.

———. *A Good Year to Die: The Story of the Great Sioux War*. New York: Random House, 1995.

Robinson, Doane. *Doane Robinson's Encyclopedia of South Dakota*. Pierre: Published by the author, 1925.

———. *A History of the Dakota or Sioux Indians*. Pierre: South Dakota State Historical Society, 1904; reprint, Minneapolis: Ross and Haines, 1967.

Rodenbough, Theophilus F., and William L. Haskin. *The Army of the United States: Historical Sketches of Staff and Line with Portraits of Generals-in-Chief*. New York: Maynard, Merrill, and Company, 1896.

Ross, Ralph H. *A Brief History of Pine Ridge Reservation: A Pictorial Description*. N.p., 1909.

Ruby, Robert H. *The Oglala Sioux: Warriors in Transition*. New York: Vantage Press, 1955; reprint, Lincoln: University of Nebraska Press, 2010.

Ruby, Robert H., and John A. Brown. *Dreamer-Prophets of the Columbia Plateau: Smoholla and Skolaskin*. Norman: University of Oklahoma Press, 1989.

Russell, Don. *The Lives and Legends of Buffalo Bill*. Norman: University of Oklahoma Press, 1960.

Sanderson, Nathan B. "'We Were All Trespassers': George Edward Lemmon, Anglo-American Cattle Ranching, and the Great Sioux Reservation." *Agricultural History* 85 (Winter 2011): 50–71.

Sargent, Theodore D. *The Life of Elaine Goodale Eastman*. Lincoln: University of Nebraska Press, 2005.

Schell, Herbert S. *History of South Dakota*. Lincoln: University of Nebraska Press, 1961.

Schmitt, Martin F., ed. *General George Crook: His Autobiography*. Norman: University of Oklahoma Press, 1946.

Schubert, Frank N. *Buffalo Soldiers, Braves, and the Brass: The Story of Fort Robinson*. Shippensburg, Pa.: White Mane Publishing Company, 1993.

———. *Voices of the Buffalo Soldiers: Records, Reports, and Recollections of Military Life and Service in the West*. Albuquerque: University of New Mexico Press, 2003.

Schusky, Ernest L. *The Forgotten Sioux: An Ethnohistory of the Lower Brule Reservation*. Chicago: Nelson Hall, 1975.

Scott, Ernest D. "Wounded Knee: A Look at the Record." *Field Artillery Journal* 29 (January–February 1939): 5–24. Also published in *Cavalry Journal* 48 (January–February 1939): 18–30.

Scott, Hugh Lennox. *Some Memories of a Soldier.* New York: Century Company, 1928.

Scott, William Berryman. *Some Memories of a Paleontologist.* Princeton, N.J.: Princeton University Press, 1939.

Shangrau, Louis. "Sioux on the War-Path." *Illustrated American* 5 (January 10, 1891): 263–70.

Shaw, Dennis. "The Battle of Wounded Knee: Myth versus Reality." Doctoral treatise, May 1981, University of Miami, Coral Gables, Florida.

Sheldon, Addison E. "After Wounded Knee—A Recollection." *Nebraska History* 22 (January–February 1941): 45.

———. "Ancient Indian Fireplaces in South Dakota Bad-Lands." *American Anthropologist*, new series 7 (January–March 1905): 44–48.

———. "Report on the Archives of the State of Nebraska." *Eleventh Report of the Public Archives Commission*, pp. 365–80. Washington, D.C.: American Historical Association, 1912.

Sheridan County Historical Society, comp. *Recollections of Sheridan County, Nebraska.* Rushville: Iron Man Industries, 1976.

Shockley, Philip M. "The Affair at Wounded Knee." *Quartermaster Review* 12 (January–February 1933): 39–44.

Shufeldt, Robert W. "Relics of Sitting Bull." *Great Divide* 10 (December 1893): 69.

Shunk, Harold W. (Mato Ska). "Reminiscing about the Dakota." *Kansas Quarterly* 3 (Fall 1971): 116–23.

The Sioux Nation and the United States: A Brief History of the Treaties of 1868, 1876, and 1889, between That Nation and the United States. Washington, D.C.: National Indian Defence Association, 1891.

Smith, Cornelius C. "The Last Indian War." In Carroll, *The Unpublished Papers of the Order of Indian Wars*, book 7, pp. 17–21.

Smith, Cornelius C., Jr. *Don't Settle for Second: Life and Times of Cornelius Smith.* San Rafael, Calif.: Presidio Press, 1977.

Smith, Oscaloosa M., W. H. Wassell, and Daniel S. Appleton. *History of the Twenty-Second United States Infantry, 1866–1922.* Governor's Island, N.Y.: Privately published, 1922.

Smith, Rex Alan. *Moon of Popping Trees.* New York: Reader's Digest Press, 1975.

Smith, Victor Grant. *The Champion Buffalo Hunter: The Frontier Memoirs of Yellowstone Vic Smith.* Ed. Jeanette Prodgers. Helena, Mont.: Twodot, 1997.

Smoak, Gregory E. *Ghost Dances and Identity: Prophetic Religion and American Indian Ethnogenesis in the Nineteenth Century.* Berkeley: University of California Press, 2006.

———. "The Mormons and the Ghost Dance of 1890." *South Dakota History* 16 (Fall 1986): 269–94.

Smythe, Donald. *Guerrilla Warrior: The Early Life of John J. Pershing.* New York: Charles Scribner's Sons, 1973.

———. "John J. Pershing: Frontier Cavalryman." *New Mexico Historical Review* 38 (July 1963): 220–43.

"Soddies to Satellites." In *Sheridan County Diamond Jubilee.* Rushville, Nebr.: Sheridan County Diamond Jubilee, 1960.

Spindler, Will H. *Tragedy Strikes at Wounded Knee*. Gordon, Nebr.: Gordon Journal Publishing Company, 1955.

Splete, Allen P., and Marilyn D. Splete. *Frederic Remington—Selected Letters*. New York: Abbeville Press, 1988.

Sprague, Donovin Arleigh. *Images of America: Cheyenne River Sioux, South Dakota*. Chicago: Arcadia Publishing, 2003.

———. *Images of America: Pine Ridge Reservation*. Chicago: Arcadia Publishing, 2004.

———. *Images of America: Rosebud Sioux*. Chicago: Arcadia Publishing, 2005.

———. *Images of America: Standing Rock Sioux*. Chicago: Arcadia Publishing, 2004.

Standing Bear, Luther. *My People the Sioux*. Ed. E. A. Brininstool. Boston: Houghton Mifflin Company, 1928.

Stands In Timber, John, and Margot Liberty. *Cheyenne Memories*. New Haven: Yale University Press, 1967.

Starita, Joe. *The Dull Knifes of Pine Ridge: A Lakota Odyssey*. New York: G. P. Putnam's Sons, 1995.

Stauffer, Helen Winter, ed. *Letters of Mari Sandoz*. Lincoln: University of Nebraska Press, 1992.

Steele, Mathew F. "The Death of Sitting Bull." In Carroll, *The Unpublished Papers of the Order of Indian Wars*, book 7, pp. 4–11.

Steinbach, Robert H. *A Long March: The Lives of Frank and Alice Baldwin*. Austin: University of Texas Press, 1989.

Steltenkamp, Michael F. *Black Elk: Holy Man of the Oglala*. Norman: University of Oklahoma Press, 1993.

———. *Nicholas Black Elk: Medicine Man, Missionary, Mystic*. Norman: University of Oklahoma Press, 2009.

Sugden, John. "Neolin." In Frederick E. Hoxie, ed., *Encyclopedia of North American Indians*, pp. 427–28. Boston: Houghton Mifflin Company, 1996.

Svingen, Orlan J. *The Northern Cheyenne Indian Reservation, 1877–1900*. Niwot: University Press of Colorado, 1993.

Sweeney, Marian Hopkins. "Indian Land Policy since 1887 with Special Reference to South Dakota." *South Dakota Historical Collections* 13 (1926): 250–83.

Sword, George. "The Story of the Ghost Dance." *Folklorist: Journal of the Chicago Folklore Society* 1 (July 1892): 28–31.

"Sword of General L. W. Colby." *Nebraska History* 14 (October–December 1933): 260–61.

Tallent, Annie D. *The Black Hills; or, Last Hunting Grounds of the Dakotahs*. St. Louis: Nixon-Jones Printing Company, 1899; reprint, Sioux Falls, S.Dak.: Brevet Press, 1974.

Tarbell, Wright. "History of the South Dakota National Guard." *South Dakota Historical Collections* 6 (1912): 363–490.

Tate, Michael L. *The Frontier Army in the Settlement of the West*. Norman: University of Oklahoma Press, 1999.

Taylor, Charles W. "The Surrender of Red Cloud." In Peter Cozzens (comp.), *Eyewitnesses to the Indian Wars, 1865–1890*, 4:611–14. 5 vols. Harrisburg, Penn.: Stackpole Books, 2001–2005.

Thompson, Erwin N. *Modoc War: Its Military History and Topography*. Sacramento: Argus Books, 1971.

Thrapp, Dan L. *The Conquest of Apacheria*. Norman: University of Oklahoma Press, 1967.

Thrupp, Sylvia, ed. *Millennial Dreams in Action: Essays in Comparative Study*. Comparative Studies in Society and History, Supplement 2. The Hague: Mouton and Company, 1962.

Tibbles, Thomas Henry. *Buckskin and Blanket Days: Memoirs of a Friend of the Indians*. Garden City, N.Y.: Doubleday and Company, 1957.

Torrey, Edwin C. *Early Days in Dakota*. Minneapolis: Farnham Printing and Stationery Company, n.d.

Traub, Peter. "The First Act of the Last Sioux Campaign." *Journal of the U.S. Cavalry Association* 15 (April 1905): 872–79.

———. "Sioux Campaign—Winter of 1890–'91." In John M. Carroll, comp., *The Papers of the Order of Indian Wars*, pp. 51–74. Fort Collins, Colo.: Old Army Press, 1975.

Trenholm, Virginia Cole. *The Arapahoes, Our People*. Norman: University of Oklahoma Press, 1970.

Trenholm, Virginia Cole, and Maurine Carley. *The Shoshonis: Sentinels of the Rockies*. Norman: University of Oklahoma Press, 1964.

"The Truth of the Wounded Knee Massacre." *American Indian Magazine* 5 (October–December 1917): 240–52.

Twenty-Second Annual Reunion of the Association of the Graduates of the United States Military Academy at West Point, New York, June 12, 1891. Saginaw, Mich.: Seemann and Peters, Printers and Binders, 1891.

Twenty-Third Annual Reunion of the Association of the Graduates of the United States Military Academy, at West Point, New York, June 9th, 1892. Saginaw, Mich.: Seemann and Peters, Printers and Binders, 1892.

Underhill, Ruth Murray. *Red Man's America: A History of Indians in the United States*. Chicago: University of Illinois Press, 1953.

Upton, Richard. *The Indian as a Soldier at Fort Custer, Montana, 1890–1895*. El Segundo, Calif.: Upton and Sons, 1983.

Utley, Robert M. "The Celebrated Peace Policy of General Grant." *North Dakota History* 20 (July 1953): 121–42.

———. *Frontier Regulars: The United States Army and the Indian, 1866–1890*. New York: Macmillan Company, 1973.

———. *Frontiersmen in Blue: The United States Army and the Indian, 1848–1865*. New York: Macmillan Company, 1967.

———. *Geronimo*. New Haven: Yale University Press, 2012.

———. *The Indian Frontier of the American West, 1846–1890*. Albuquerque: University of New Mexico Press, 1984.

———. *The Lance and the Shield: The Life and Times of Sitting Bull*. New York: Henry Holt, 1993.

———. *The Last Days of the Sioux Nation*. New Haven: Yale University Press, 1963.

———. "Nelson A. Miles." In Paul Andrew Hutton and Durwood Ball, eds., *Soldiers West: Biographies from the Military Frontier*, pp. 340–57. 2nd ed. Norman: University of Oklahoma Press, 2009.

———. "The Ordeal of Plenty Horses." *American Heritage: The Magazine of History* 26 (December 1974): 15–19, 82–86.

———. "Wounded Knee and Other Dark Images: The West of Dewey Horn Cloud." *American West: The Magazine of Western History* 16 (May–June 1979): 4–11.

Van Nuys, Laura Bower. *The Family Band from the Missouri to the Black Hills, 1881–1900*. Lincoln: University of Nebraska Press, 1961.

Vaughn, J. W. *The Reynolds Campaign on Powder River*. Norman: University of Oklahoma Press, 1961.

Vestal, Stanley, comp. *New Sources of Indian History, 1850–1890*. Norman: University of Oklahoma Press, 1934.

———. *Sitting Bull, Champion of the Sioux: A Biography*. Boston and New York: Houghton Mifflin Company, 1932.

———. *Warpath: The True Story of the Fighting Sioux Told in a Biography of Chief White Bull*. Boston: Houghton Mifflin Company, 1934.

Von Ostermann, Georg F. *The Last Sioux Indian War*. San Antonio: Palm Tree Press, 1942.

Wainwright, Robert P. Page. "The First Regiment of Cavalry." In Rodenbough and Haskin, *The Army of the United States*, pp. 153–72.

Walker, James R. *Lakota Belief and Ritual*. Ed. Raymond J. DeMallie and Elaine A. Jahner. Lincoln: University of Nebraska Press, 1980.

———. *Lakota Society*. Ed. Raymond J. DeMallie. Lincoln: University of Nebraska Press, 1982.

Wallace, Anthony F. C. *The Death and Rebirth of the Seneca*. New York: Alfred A. Knopf, 1969.

Warner, Ezra J., comp. *Generals in Blue: Lives of the Union Commanders*. Baton Rouge: Louisiana State University Press, 1964.

Warren, Louis S. *Buffalo Bill's America: William Cody and the Wild West Show*. New York: Alfred A. Knopf, 2005.

Washburn, Wilcomb E. *The Assault on Indian Tribalism: The General Allotment Law (Dawes Act) of 1887*. Philadelphia: J. B. Lippincott Company, 1975.

Watson, Elmo Scott. "The Last Indian War, 1890–91: A Study of Newspaper Jingoism." *Journalism Quarterly* 20 (September 1943): 205–19.

———. "Pine Ridge, 1890–1891." In Herbert O. Brayer, ed., *Denver Westerners 1945 Brand Book*, 1–6. Denver: Bradford-Robinson Printing Company, 1946.

Watson, Julia S. "A Sketch of George H. Harries, Reporter of Wounded Knee." *Westerners New York Posse Brand Book* 3, no. 4 (1956): 73, 75–76, 90.

Weist, Tom. *A History of the Cheyenne People*. Billings: Montana Council for Indian Education, 1977.

Wells, Philip F. "Ninety-Six Years among the Indians of the North West." *North Dakota History* 15 (October 1948): 265–312.

Welsh, Herbert. "The Meaning of the Dakota Outbreak." *Scribner's Magazine* 9 (April 1891): 429–52.

Weslager, C. A. *The Delaware Indians: A History*. New Brunswick, N.J.: Rutgers University Press, 1972.

West, Elliott. *The Contested Plains: Indians, Goldseekers, and the Rush to Colorado*. Lawrence: University of Kansas Press, 1998.

Wheeler, Homer W. *The Frontier Trail*. Los Angeles: Time-Mirror Press, 1923.

White, Richard. "The Winning of the West: The Expansion of the Western Sioux in the Eighteenth and Nineteenth Centuries." *Journal of American History* 65 (September 1978): 339–412.

White, Virgil D., comp. *Index to Pension Applications for Indian Wars Service between 1817 and 1898*. Waynesboro, Tenn.: National Historical Publishing Company, 1997.

"Why the Indians Fight." *Illustrated American* 5 (January 24, 1891): 391–93.

Wilhelm, Thomas. *A Military Dictionary and Gazetteer*. Rev. ed. Philadelphia: L. R. Hamersly and Company, 1881.

Wilkinson, William G. "The Death of Sitting Bull the Sioux Indian Chief, Grand River, S.D., Dec. 15, 1890." Don G. Rickey Papers. Variant in John M. Carroll, ed., *The Arrest and Killing of Sitting Bull: A Documentary*, pp. 53–65. Mattituck, N.Y.: Amereon House, 1986.

Williams, Roger L. *Military Register of Custer's Last Command*. Norman, Okla.: Arthur H. Clark Company, 2009.

Wilson, Dorothy Clarke. *Bright Eyes: The Story of Susette LaFlesche, an Omaha Woman*. New York: McGraw-Hill Book Company, 1974.

Wilson, Raymond. *Ohiyesa: Charles Eastman, Santee Sioux*. Urbana: University of Illinois Press, 1983.

Wilson, Richard H. "The Eighth Regiment of Infantry." In Rodenbough and Haskin, *The Army of the United States*, pp. 511–25.

Wilson, Thomas W. "The Attack on the Pine Ridge Indian Agency, S.D." *United Service*, new series 7 (June 1892): 562–68.

Wilson, Wesley C. "The U.S. Army and the Piegans: The Baker Massacre on the Marias, 1870." *North Dakota History* 32 (January 1965): 282–305.

Wiltsey, Norman B. "Death on the North Plains." *True West* 5 (May–June 1958): 24–36.

Woodruff, K. Brent. "The Episcopal Mission to the Dakotas." *South Dakota Historical Collections* 17 (1934): 553–603.

Wooster, Robert. *The Military and United States Indian Policy, 1865–1903*. New Haven: Yale University Press, 1988.

———. *Nelson A. Miles and the Twilight of the Frontier Army*. Lincoln: University of Nebraska Press, 1993.

Wounded Horse, Eugene (as told to Will Spindler). "Dewy Girl Was There." *Real West* 11 (July 1968): 20–21, 54.

"Wounded Knee Veterans." *Time* 31 (March 14, 1938): 15.

Wright, William M. "The Second Regiment of Infantry." In Rodenbough and Haskin, *The Army of the United States*, pp. 414–31.

Yost, Nellie Snyder, ed. *Boss Cowman: The Recollections of Ed Lemmon, 1857–1946*. Lincoln: University of Nebraska Press, 1969.

Zens, M. Serena. "The Educational Work of the Catholics among the Indians of South Dakota from the Beginning to 1935." *South Dakota Historical Collections* 20 (1940): 299–356.

SPECIAL REPORTS, COMMUNICATIONS, PRESENTATIONS, INTERVIEWS, CATALOGS, NEWSLETTERS

Bray, Kingsley M. E-mail to the author respecting Kicking Bird's background, December 10, 2012.

Descriptive Catalogue of War Material Manufactured by the Hotchkiss Ordnance Company, Limited. Washington, D.C.: undated, ca. 1891.

Fay, George E. comp. and ed. "Military Engagements between United States Troops and Plains Indians. Part IV: 1872–1890." *Occasional Publications in Anthropology*, Ethnology Series, No. 29. Greeley: Museum of Anthropology, University of Northern Colorado, 1973.

BIBLIOGRAPHY

Flandreau Santee Sioux Tribe Monthly Newsletter (March 2008).

Heritage Auction Catalog. Auction 681, November 10, 2007.

"Indemnity Bill for the Massacre of Chief Big Foot and His band, on December 29, 1890." Drafted by "the living Survivors of Cheyenne River and Pine Ridge Reservations," a process concluded at Wounded Knee, South Dakota, on June 22, 1935. Photocopy provided by Michael Her Many Horses.

Jensen, Richard E., and R. Eli Paul. National Register of Historic Places Registration Form for Wounded Knee National Historic Landmark, Wounded Knee, South Dakota, December 6, 1990.

Little Finger, Leonard. Interview, April 21, 2010, Lakota Circle Village, Oglala, South Dakota.

Lyon Curio Store, Clinton, Nebraska. 1930s catalog.

Mattes, Merrill J. *Special Site Report on Wounded Knee Battlefield, Pine Ridge Indian Reservation, South Dakota.* Omaha, Nebr.: National Park Service Midwest Regional Office, August 1965.

National Historic Landmark Summary Listing Assessment for Wounded Knee, 2010. National Park Service.

Paul, R. Eli. "'Relics' of Wounded Knee, and Appendix." Presentation before the Nebraska Academy of Science, Lincoln, April 10, 1992.

Proceedings of the Annual Meeting of the Order of Indian Wars of the United States Held Army and Navy Club, Washington, D.C., February 24, 1940. N.p., 1940.

Red Tomahawk, Francis. "Sitting Bull's Life Ends in Tragedy." Written on stationery of correspondent Robert B. McCaffree, *Scottsbluff Daily Star-Herald,* ca. 1935. Copy provided by Thomas R. Buecker.

NEWSPAPERS

Alliance Times-Herald (Nebraska). 1926.

American Weekly (Washington, D.C.). 1938.

Army and Navy Journal (New York). 1890, 1891, 1892, 1893.

Army and Navy Register (Washington, D.C.). 1890, 1891.

Aspen Weekly Times (Colorado). 1890.

Beatrice Daily Express (Nebraska). 1891.

Beatrice Daily Sun (Nebraska). 1891.

Beatrice Republican (Nebraska). 1891.

Billings Gazette (Montana). 1934.

Black Hills Chief (Rapid City, South Dakota). 1943.

Black Hills Daily Times (Rapid City, South Dakota). 1891.

Black Hills Journal (Rapid City, South Dakota). 1890.

Black Hills Weekly Times (Rapid City, South Dakota). 1890.

Boston Daily Globe (Massachusetts). 1890, 1904, 1908, 1981.

Boston Herald (Massachusetts). 1892.

Brooklyn Daily Eagle (New York). 1890.

Carbon County Journal (Wyoming). 1891.

Castle Rock Journal (Colorado). 1891.

Catholic Standard and Times (Philadelphia, Pennsylvania). 1913.

Chadron Advocate (Nebraska). 1889, 1890, 1891.

Chadron Citizen (Nebraska). 1891, 1893.
Chadron Democrat (Nebraska). 1889, 1890, 1891.
Chadron Journal (Nebraska). 1913.
Cheyenne Daily Leader (Wyoming). 1891.
Cheyenne Daily Sun (Wyoming). 1891.
Chicago Herald (Illinois). 1891.
Chicago Inter-Ocean (Illinois). 1890, 1891, 1900.
Chicago Tribune (Illinois). 1890.
Crandon Press Gazette (Wisconsin). 1955.
Daily Boomerang (Wyoming). 1891.
Daily Nebraskan (Lincoln). 1890.
Denver Field and Farm (Colorado). 1909.
Denver Post (Colorado). 1903, 1913, 1929.
Deseret News (Salt Lake City, Utah). 1890, 1891.
Deseret Weekly (Salt Lake City, Utah). 1890.
El Segundo Herald (California). 1928.
Fairbury Gazette (Nebraska). 1891.
Frank Leslie's Illustrated Newspaper (New York). 1890.
Fremont Clipper (Wyoming). 1891.
Fremont Weekly Herald (Nebraska). 1891.
Gage County Democrat (Nebraska). 1891
Gordon Journal (Nebraska). 1953.
The Graphic (London). 1890.
Gresham Gazette (Nebraska). 1926.
Harper's Weekly (New York). 1890, 1891, 1895, 1896.
Herington Times (Kansas). 1936.
Hot Springs Daily Star (South Dakota). 1890, 1891.
Hot Springs Weekly Star (South Dakota). 1890.
Indianapolis Sentinel (Indiana). 1890.
Indian Country Today (Rapid City, South Dakota). 1993, 1994.
The Indian Helper (Carlisle, Pennsylvania). 1890, 1891.
Indians at Work (Washington, D.C.). 1937, 1938.
Junction City Daily Union (Kansas). 1961.
Junction City Republican (Kansas). 1890, 1891.
Kansas City Star (Missouri). 1892, 1893.
Lakota Times (Rapid City, South Dakota). 1990, 1998.
Lincoln Daily Star (Nebraska). 1914.
Lincoln State Journal (Nebraska). 1891.
London Daily Telegraph. 1890.
Madison Daily Leader (South Dakota). 1938.
Middle Border Bulletin (Mitchell, South Dakota). 1944.
Minneapolis Tribune (Minnesota). 1890.
National Tribune (Washington, D.C.). 1893, 1934.
Nebraska City News. 1891.
Nebraska State Journal (Lincoln). 1890, 1891, 1941.
Newcastle News-Letter Journal (Wyoming). 1939.
New York Evening Post (New York). 1891.
New York Herald (New York). 1890.

New York Sun (New York). 1890.

New York Times (New York). 1889, 1890, 1891, 1893, 1894, 1897, 1940, 1955, 2007.

New York Tribune (New York). 1938.

New York Weekly Witness (New York). 1890.

New York World (New York). 1890, 1891.

Norfolk Daily News (Nebraska). 1891.

Northwest Nebraska News (Crawford). 1930.

Ogdensburg Advance (New York). 1890.

Omaha Bee (Nebraska). 1890, 1891.

Omaha World-Herald (Nebraska). 1890, 1891, 1898, 1923, 1999.

Philadelphia Inquirer (Pennsylvania). 1890.

Pierre Daily Capital Journal (South Dakota). 1941.

Pierre Daily Free Press (South Dakota). 1890.

Publisher's Auxiliary (Washington, D.C.). 1942.

Putnam County Gazette (Ohio). 1933.

Rapid City Daily Republican (South Dakota). 1937, 1938.

Rapid City Journal (South Dakota). 1913, 1914, 1938, 1940, 1950, 1952, 1955, 1969, 1970.

Rock County Leader (Nebraska). 1952.

Rocky Mountain News (Denver, Colorado). 1913, 1933.

Sheridan Enterprise (Wyoming). 1913.

Sioux City Journal (Iowa). 1891.

Sioux County Herald (Harrison, Nebraska). 1890.

Sioux County Journal (Harrison, Nebraska). 1891.

Sioux Falls Argus-Leader (South Dakota). 1891, 1906, 1937, 1955.

State-Line Herald (North Lemmon, North Dakota). 1911.

St. Louis Globe-Democrat (Missouri). 1890.

St. Louis Post-Dispatch (Missouri). 1891.

St. Paul Pioneer Press (Minnesota). 1890.

Stromsburg Headlight (Nebraska). 1891.

Sturgis Advertiser (South Dakota). 1891.

Sturgis Weekly Record (South Dakota). 1891.

Times-Star (Newport, Kentucky). 1891.

Valentine Republican (Nebraska). 1891.

Washington Evening Star (Washington, D.C.). 1890, 1891, 1939.

Washington Post (Washington, D.C.). 1891, 1893, 1906, 1909, 1917, 1925, 1937.

White Pine Cone (Colorado). 1891.

Winners of the West (St. Joseph, Missouri). 1930, 1935, 1939.

Woman's Home Weekly (Minneapolis, Minnesota). 1917.

Yankton Daily Press and Dakotaian (South Dakota). 1889.

HISTORICAL MAPS AND ATLASES

Bailey, G. E. "Map of Pine Ridge Agency, Showing Fortifications, Gen. Miles' Head-quarters, and Camps of Soldiers and Indians." Ca. 1891. Army War College, U.S. Army Military History Institute, Order of Indian Wars (OIW) Collection.

"Before the Battle." Sketched by correspondent Thomas H. Tibbles. *Omaha World-Herald*, January 6, 1891.

Collins, Charles D., Jr. *Atlas of the Sioux Wars* (maps 36 and 37). 2nd ed. Fort Leavenworth, Kansas: Combat Studies Institute Press.

Craft, Father Francis. "Battle Field [*sic*] of Wounded Knee, Showing the Position of Soldiers & Indians at the Moment the First Shot Was Fired." 1891. In Foley, *At Standing Rock and Wounded Knee*, p. 309.

"Map Furnished by Col. Forsythe [*sic*], 7th Cav, of Action of 29 Dec. 1890." Ca. 1891. National Archives, Record Group 77, War Department Map Collection, 30-South Dakota (also in NA Microfilm 983, Roll 1, following p. 820).

"Map of the Country Embraced in the Recent Campaign against the Hostile Sioux Indians of Dakota Showing the Different Positions of Troops from the Beginning to the Surrender in January 1891." 1891. National Archives, Record Group 77, War Department Map Collection, South Dakota 10 (also in *Report of the Secretary of War, 1891*, following p. 154).

"Map of Country Surrounding Pine Ridge Agency within a Radius of 200 Miles." Ca. 1890. Copy in Author's Collection.

"Map of a Portion of South Dakota, Showing the Country Adjacent to the Pine Ridge & Rosebud Indian Agencies." March 11, 1891. National Archives, Record Group 77. Records of the Office of the Chief of Engineers. Headquarters Map File, Q734-3.

"Map of Portions of the Departments of Dakota and the Platte, to Accompany Report of Brig. Gen. T. H. Ruger, U.S.A., October 19th 1891." In *Report of the Secretary of War, 1891*, following p. 188.

"Map of Sioux Indian Reservation Showing the Diminished Reservations and Ceded Lands in North Dakota and South Dakota" (1890). Department of the Interior, General Land Office. National Archives, Record Group 75, Central Map File, CA 276.

"Map of Standing Rock Reservation, Dak., Feby 10th 1890." James McLaughlin Papers, Microfilm Roll 34. South Dakota State Historical Society, Pierre.

"Map of That Part of the Field of Wounded Knee Where the Battle Opened and the First Shot Was Fired." By Father Francis M. Craft. *Catholic Standard and Times*, November 22, 1913.

Map of Wounded Knee Action by Private John W. Comfort, First Artillery, in letter to his brother, April 5, 1892. John W. Comfort Papers, Princeton University Library, Princeton, New Jersey.

"Map Showing Positions of Nebraska State Troops in Indian Campaigns of the Winter of 1890–91." Ca. 1893. Accompanying U.S. Congress, Senate, Committee on Military Affairs, *To Accompany S. 463, to Reimburse the State of Nebraska the Expenses Incurred by That State in Repelling a Threatened Invasion and Raid by the Sioux in 1890–'91*. S. Rept. 45, 53rd Cong., 1st sess., 1893.

"Pine Ridge Agency. Map Showing the Fortifications, General Miles' Headquarters, Government and Other Buildings, and Camps of Soldiers and Indians." 1891. *Chicago Inter-Ocean*, January 10, 1891.

"Rough Sketch of the Country Where the Fight between Indians and Indian Police Took Place on the Morning of Decr 15, 1890 [*sic*]." December 16, 1890. James McLaughlin Papers, Roll 35. South Dakota State Historical Society, Pierre.

Roy, Stanislaus. "Battle of Wounded Knee." Walter M. Camp Papers, Little Bighorn Battlefield National Monument.

"Scene of the Fight with Big Foot's Band, Dec. 29th 1890, Showing Position of Troops When First Shot Was Fired. From Sketches made by Lt. S. A. Cloman, Act'g Eng'r

Officer, Division of the Missouri." 1891. By Private James Hade, Sixth Cavalry. NA Microfilm 983, Roll 1, following p. 650. (This is the earliest version of the Hade map.)

"Scene of the Fight with Big Foot's Band . . ." 1891. Same general map, but includes topographic lines and wire fences. National Archives, Microfilm 983, Roll 1, following p. 650.

"Scene of the Fight with Big Foot's Band . . ." Ca. 1891. Same general map, but a later edition with more refined topography. National Archives, Record Group 94, AGO Misc. File, Envelope 207 #1, Box 19.

"Scene of the Fight with Big Foot's Band . . ." Ca. 1891. Same general map, but missing pronounced topographical definition. Private Hade's name omitted. Marked "C F McD" in lower left corner. National Archives, Record Group 77, War Department Map Collection, South Dakota 17.

"Scene of the Fight with Big Foot's Band . . ." Ca. 1891. Same general map, with minor illustrative changes, as published in *Report of the Secretary of War, 1891*, following p. 154.

Sketch Map A, Wounded Knee National Historic Landmark, Shannon County, South Dakota. 1990. (Contains overlay of modern intrusive highways.) Nebraska State Historical Society, Lincoln.

"Sketch of the Scene of the Mission Fight, December 30th 1890. Drawn under the Direction of Lieut. S. A. Cloman, Act'g Eng'r Officer Division of the Missouri." Ca. 1891. National Archives, Microfilm 983, Roll 1. (This map also appears in *Report of the Secretary of War, 1891*, following p. 154. A redrawn version appears in Carroll, ed., *To Set the Record Straight!*, following p. 178.)

South Dakota Atlas & Gazetteer. 3rd ed. Yarmouth, Maine: DeLorme, 2004.

Untitled map showing the country between Nebraska and the Cheyenne River Indian Reservation, with army posts and outposts indicated. Ca. 1891. National Archives, Record Group 75, Central Map File, CA 662.

Untitled sketch map of the Stronghold area. Ca. 1891. U.S. Army Military History Institute, Army War College, Guy V. Henry Collection, Box 1, "Wounded Knee" File.

Untitled topographic map, Army Map Service, October 1957. Badlands Bombing Range, Rapid City Air to Air Gunnery Range. Black Hills State University, Leland D. Case Library, E. Y. Berry Library-Learning Center, Special Collections, E. Y. Berry Collection.

"Wounded Knee Battlefield." Map compiled from one drawn by Second Lieutenant Thomas Q. Donaldson, Jr. In Mooney, "The Ghost-Dance Religion," following p. 868.

UNITED STATES GEOLOGICAL SURVEY MAPS

Cuny Table East Quadrangle, South Dakota–Shannon County. 7.5 Minute Series. U.S. Geological Survey, 1950, photo revised 1979.

Denby Quadrangle, South Dakota–Shannon County. 7.5 Minute Series. U.S. Geological Survey, 1967.

Manderson Quadrangle, South Dakota–Shannon County. 7.5 Minute Series. U.S. Geological Survey, 1967.

Manderson SW Quadrangle, South Dakota–Shannon County. 7.5 Minute Series. U.S. Geological Survey, 1967.

McIntosh, S. Dak.–N. Dak. 30 × 60 Minute Quadrangle. U.S. Geological Survey, 1980.

Miscol NE Quadrangle, South Dakota–Corson County. 7.5 Minute Series, U.S. Geological Survey, 1956.

Oglala Quadrangle, South Dakota–Shannon County. 7.5 Minute Series. U.S. Geological Survey, 1967.

Pine Ridge NE Quadrangle, South Dakota–Shannon County. 7.5 Minute Series. U.S. Geological Survey, 1967.

Pine Ridge Quadrangle, South Dakota–Shannon County. 7.5 Minute Series. U.S. Geological Survey, 1967.

Rockyford Quadrangle, South Dakota–Shannon County. 7.5 Minute Series, U.S. Geological Survey, 1951, photo revised 1979.

Rockyford SE Quadrangle, South Dakota–Shannon County. 7.5 Minute Series. U.S. Geological Survey, 1951.

Wounded Knee Quadrangle, South Dakota–Shannon County. 7.5 Minute Series. U.S. Geological Survey, 1967.

INTERNET RESOURCES

Alfred B. Welch Dakota Papers. http://www.welchdakotapapers.com.

Bray, Kingsley M., et al. http://www.americantribes.com/Lakota/BIO/Bigfoot-Mini conjou.htm.

Burnham, Philip. "The True Legend of Dewey Beard." *Indian Country Today*, posted online September 12, September 19, and September 26, 2005: www.legendsof america.com.

Find a Grave. http://www.findagrave.com/cgi-bin/fg.cgi.

Fuller, Ezra B. Letter from Pine Ridge Agency dated December 30, 1890 to unknown recipient. eBay auction, October 12, 2010, Item no. 250696000024.

Google Earth.

Green, Jerry. "The Medals of Wounded Knee," revised ed. http://www.dickshovel.com/ MedalsG.a.html.

National Congress of American Indians. Resolution to revoke Medals of Honor. http:// www.ncai.org/attachments/Resolution_fOSOgEonjTdXUoobgcGFhZGXS sjZtszItPfNyXQAQXAWisTSCWI_DEN-07-082_final.pdf.

National Register of Historic Places Registration Form, Wounded Knee National Historic Landmark. http://pdfhost.focus.nps.gov/docs/NHLS/Text/66000719.pdf.

Thomasson, William B. "Images of Wounded Knee (they speak for themselves)," November 8, 2007, to February 24, 2008. http://hoist.hrtc.net/~arabento/wounded knee.htm.

U.S. Naval Observatory Astronomical Applications Department. http://aa.usno.navy .mil/data/docs/RS_OneDay.html. eBay Auction #250969000024, October 12, 2010.

Index